BVR's Guide to Fair Value in Shareholder Dissent, Oppression, and Marital Dissolution

2009 Edition

Published by

BVR
What It's Worth

Business Valuation Resources, LLC
1000 SW Broadway, Suite 1200
Portland, OR 97205
(503) 291-7963 Fax (503) 291-7955 www.BVResources.com

BVR
What It's Worth

Copyright © 2009 by Business Valuation Resources, L.L.C. (BVR). All rights reserved. Printed in the United States of America.

No part of this publication may be reproduced, stored in a retrieval system or transmitted in any form or by any means, electronic, mechanical, photocopying, recording, scanning or otherwise, except as permitted under Sections 107 or 108 of the 1976 United States Copyright Act, without either the prior written permission of the Publisher or authorization through payment of the appropriate per copy fee to the Publisher. Requests for permission should be addressed to the Permissions Department, Business Valuation Resources, LLC, 1000 SW Broadway, Suite 1200, Portland, OR, 97205, (503) 291-7963, fax (503) 291-7955.

Information contained in this book has been obtained by Business Valuation Resources from sources believed to be reliable. However, neither Business Valuation Resources nor its authors guarantee the accuracy or completeness of any information published herein and neither Business Valuation Resources nor its authors shall be responsible for any errors, omissions, or damages arising out of use of this information. This work is published with the understanding that Business Valuation Resources and its authors are supplying information but are not attempting to render business valuation or other professional services. If such services are required, the assistance of an appropriate professional should be sought.

Managing Editor: Adam Manson
Guide Editor: Colin Murcray
Publisher: Doug Twitchell

Chair and CEO: David Foster
President: Lucretia Lyons
Sales: Linda Mendenhall
Customer Service Manager: Stephanie Crader
ISBN: 978-1-935081-03-6   1-935081-03-9

Dear Colleague,

Thank you for purchasing *BVR's Guide to Fair Value in Shareholder Dissent, Oppression, and Marital Dissolution*.

In shareholder oppression and dissent cases, the term "fair value" has been riddled with ambiguity. Because state statutes govern all corporate actions involving shareholder rights, fair value has become a legal term subject to court interpretation and application. Unfortunately, both the state statutes and the courts have broadly defined the term, so that its meaning can vary from state to state.

As a further complication, the current debate on the appropriateness of fair value in marital dissolution cases has gained more attention in the courts and also the business appraisal profession. Because of these new developments, it is now more important than ever for the practitioner to stay current on fair value trends and case law.

To combat the confusion in the courts, and to eliminate the practitioner's need for time consuming research, we have created this new *Guide*. The first portion is a collection of articles from leading valuation experts on statutory fair value in shareholder oppression, shareholder dissent, and marital dissolution cases. A comprehensive reference chart also lists the dissent and oppression statutes in all fifty states, and categorizes each according to how its case law typically addresses the application of discounts to fair value determinations.

The second portion of this *Guide* contains useful court case abstracts originally published in the *Business Valuation Update*™ (*BVU*) which pertain to fair value. This section begins with a summary table for quick reference, including the type of case (shareholder oppression, shareholder dissent, etc.), its name, date, the court and jurisdiction, and a brief statement about the case. The case abstracts provide on-point discussion of the court's decisions, and frequently include expert commentary by *BVU* editors as well as publisher emeritus Dr. Shannon Pratt. Moreover, as part of your purchase of this guide you have access to most of the full-text court opinions corresponding with the abstracts at BVLibrary.com.

Fair value is a complex and dynamic standard of value, requiring an up-to-date, comprehensive resource on the ever-changing case law, its definitions and determinations. Please use this BVR *Guide* as a tool to further your knowledge and to save yourself valuable time in your research.

We appreciate your business, and welcome your suggestions on how we can improve our service and all our valuation products.

–BVR Staff

Business Valuation Resources, LLC
1000 SW Broadway, Suite 1200
Portland, OR 97205
Phone: (503) 291-7963
Fax: (503) 291-7955
eMail: CustomerService@BVResources.com
Web: www.BVResources.com

Table of Contents

Chapter 1: Introduction

Introduction to BVR's Guide to Fair Value in Shareholder Dissent, Oppression, and Marital Dissolution 1-1
    By Shannon Pratt, CFA, FASA, MCBA, CM&AA

Chapter 2: Background on Fair Value

Fair Value Defined 2-1

Fair Value vs. Fair Market Value: Historical Perspective 2-2

Fair Value in Dissent and Oppression Chart by State 2-6

Current Business Corporation Law and What it Means for the Business Appraiser 2-23
    By John J. Stockdale Jr., Esq.

Recent Developments in Delaware Appraisal Cases 2-31
    By John E. Hempstead, ASA, CFA and J. Mark Penny, ASA

When Nothing Else Fits it Must be Fair Value 2-40
    By R. James Alerding, CPA/ABV, ASA, CVA and
    H. Edward Morris, Jr., ASA, CBA, BVAL, CPA/ABV

The World According to Delaware Chancery: A Vice Chancellor Offers Ten Tips to Appraisers 2-45

Fairness in Delaware Freezeout Transactions: How Two Discrepant Legal Standards Affect Valuations 2-49
    By Gilbert E. Matthews, CFA and Michelle Patterson, JD, PhD

Fair Value: A View from the Delaware Court of Chancery Bench 2-56
    By Shannon Pratt DBA, CFA, FASA, MCBA, CM&A, MCBC

Standards of Value: Theory and Applications 2-60
    BVR Telephone Conference Transcript October 24, 2006
    Speakers: Jay Fishman, Shannon Pratt, William Morrison

Chapter 3: Fair Value in Dissenting and Oppressed Shareholder Matters

Fair Value in Dissenting and Oppressed Shareholder Matters: How to Avoid Minefields 3-1
    By Jay Fishman, FASA, CBA

Judicial Valuation of Stock of a Delaware Corporation: The Legal Concept of "Fair Value" 3-39
    By Bruce L. Silverstein, Esq.

The Non-Delaware View of Fair Value in Shareholder Dissent and Oppression Cases 3-76
    By Noah Gordon, Esq.

Report of Donald J. Puglisi in the matter of Laurel Gonsalves, Petitioner, v. Straight Arrow Publishers, Inc., A Delaware Corporation Respondent 3-98

Shareholder Oppression & 'Fair Value': Of Discounts, Dates, and Dastardly Deeds in the Close Corporation 3-102
    By Douglas K. Moll, Esq.

The Fair Value of Cornfields in Delaware Appraisal Law 3-104
    By Lawrence A. Hamermesh, Esq. and Michael L. Wachter, Esq.

The Short and Puzzling Life of the 'Implicit Minority Discount' in Delaware Appraisal Law 3-105
    By Lawrence A. Hamermesh, Esq. and Michael L. Wachter, Esq.

Chapter 4: Valuing a Business on Fair Value

Valuing a Business (5th ed.) on Fair Value 4-1

Chapter 5: Fair Value in Marital Dissolution

The State of the Fair Value Standard in Divorce 5-1
    By John Stockdale Jr., Esq.

Fair Value in Marital Dissolution: Case Law 5-6
    By Noah Gordon, Esq.

Understanding Fair Value for Divorce 5-17
    By Lee D. Sanderson, CPA/ABV, CVA, MST

The New Business Valuation Standard for Divorce 5-21
    By Lee D. Sanderson, CPA, ABV, CVA, MST

Valuation of S Corporations for Purposes of Marital Dissolutions 5-25
    By R. James Alerding, CPA/ABV, ASA, CVA and
    H. Edward Morris, Jr., ASA, CBA, BVAL, CPA/ABV

Fair Value vs. Fair Market Value in Divorce Cases 5-28
    By Jerome W. Karsh, CPA

Fair Value as a Basis for Business Valuation in Divorce 5-35
    By Alan S. Zipp, Esq., CPA/ABV, CBA

Fair Value Versus Fair Market Value: Is There a Place for Fair Value in Marital Dissolution? 5-53
    By Robert Kleeman Jr. CPA/ABV, ASA, CVA

Chapter 6: Fair Value Under California Corporations Code Section 2000

Dissolution Actions Yield Less than Fair Market Enterprise Value (Appraising for "Fair Value" Under California Corporations Code Section 2000) 6-1
    By Arthur J. Shartsis, Esq.

Using California Corporations Code Section 2000 to Resolve 50-50 Shareholder Deadlocks in Privately Held Corporations 6-14
    By Arthur J. Shartsis, Esq.

Twists and Turns for Fair Value (and other Value) Definitions in California .6-25
    By Thomas E. Pastore, ASA, CFA, CPA

Chapter 7: Court Case Abstracts

CHAPTER 1
INTRODUCTION

Introduction to BVR's Guide to Fair Value in Shareholder Dissent, Oppression, and Marital Dissolution

By Shannon Pratt, CFA, FASA, MCBA, CM&AA[1]

Virtually every state has a dissenting stockholder statute, and now most states have minority oppression statutes. In almost all of these states, the statutory standard of value for stock is *fair value*.[2]

Appraisal actions under both dissent and oppression statutes are on the increase, and it is a fertile field for business appraisers. BVR's new *Guide* couldn't come at a more opportune time, and provides a great resource for BV appraisers and attorneys to use whenever their work involves fair value as a standard of value in dissenting stockholder actions, judicial appraisals, marital dissolutions, and more.

Throughout the *Guide*, there are many references to fair value as a standard in different contexts, such as dissenting stockholder actions, oppressed shareholder actions, and marital dissolutions. The appraiser or the attorney can gain many insights from these references when they are dealing with a fair value case in any of these contexts.

Also, interpretations of the fair value statute vary widely from state to state and with different circumstances. The appraiser or attorney can gain great insight into the thinking of courts in the different jurisdictions when dealing with a fair value case in that jurisdiction.

Dissenting stockholder actions

As many BV appraisers and attorneys know, dissenting stockholder suits usually arise as a result of a merger or a going private transaction, in which the company offers its shareholders either the stock in an acquiring company or cash. If stockholders are dissatisfied with the offer, then pursuant to the applicable statutory scheme, they can register their dissent and receive stockholder appraisal rights, which entitle them to a trial to determine the value of their stock.[3]

In my long business appraisal career, I have lost track of how many companies I have valued under these statutes, but I remember my first case. When the attorney for the plaintiffs showed me the facts, I intuitively thought that the offered price was low, at $3.75 per share. At trial, the expert who had priced the stock for the squeeze-out merger testified to a value of $3.75 per share, and I testified to a range of $9.00 to $11.00 per share. The court awarded the plaintiff $9.00 per share.

Why? The expert who testified to the $3.75 price had used the stock of a comparable company between the time the subject company had eliminated most of its outstanding stock through a

Chapter 1: Introduction

tender offer and the time he'd rendered his opinion that the $3.75 price was fair for the squeeze-out merger. Unfortunately, he had overlooked that the stock had a 2 for 1 stock split during the period. By his own methodology, correcting for that one error brought the value to $7.50 per share.

The state's statute had a provision, as do most all state dissenters' rights statutes, that the valuation should be the day before the action to which the stockholders dissented. Four months had elapsed between the rendering of the fairness opinion and the effective date of the merger, during which time stocks in the industry had risen 20%. Updating from the $7.50 at the time of the opinion to the date of the merger brought his value to $9.00. The lesson from that first case: Sometimes a well-organized rebuttal of the opposing expert's valuation conclusions carries the day.

The are two additional lessons to be learned from this experience. First, when doing any valuation or rendering a fairness opinion, always check every detail of your work. Second, when rendering a fairness opinion, always check to see whether it should be updated to the effective date of the action to which it pertains.

Delaware leads in dissent litigation

Delaware is the leading state in dissenting stockholder litigation. Many other states draw on Delaware case law for guidance, following either all or some portion of the holdings by the Delaware Court of Chancery or the Delaware Supreme Court. When I was retained to testify in a case of first impression under the State of Washington's dissenters' appraisal statute, I asked the attorney to request guidance from the judge. He said that he would follow Delaware law, so I prepared my report accordingly. The result: The court's opinion was within 3% of my value.

In this *Guide*, you will find the fair value precedent from the Delaware Courts to help in formulating and/or reviewing a valuation using the fair value standard as interpreted by the Delaware courts.

As these cases demonstrate, Delaware does not allow discounts for either lack of marketability or minority interest in statutory appraisal actions. In my own experience, two years after the State of Washington dissenting stockholder suit, I was retained to value the stock in the same company, this time for estate tax purposes, in connection with the shares of a large stockholder who had recently died. Although the company had done well in the intervening two years, my value for the estate was quite a bit lower, because the standard of value was fair market value, which allows discounts where appropriate. This illustrates the primary difference between the standards of fair value and fair market value in many states. Moreover, there is a trend toward more states adopting the position of no discounts in fair value for shareholder dissent/appraisal cases—as also illustrated by the current collection of state fair value cases in this Guide.

Until 1983, fair value calculations in Delaware used the "Delaware Block Method." This method used three "blocks," with varying weights accorded to each:

Introduction

1. **Investment value**, consisted of capitalizing some income variable such as earnings and/or dividends;

2. **Market value**, usually the subject stock's trading price (the more active the trading, the greater the weight); and

3. **Asset value**, the market value of the company's assets (less liabilities).

In 1983, the landmark *Weinberger v. UOP*[4] introduced the discounted cash flow method. In that case, the appellate court deemed acceptable any valuation method in general use in the financial community. Although on appeal, the plaintiff received only $1.00 per share more than the lower court had awarded using the Delaware Block Method, there were millions of shares outstanding, so the total difference was significant.

Today, although the Delaware Chancery Court accepts other methods, it favors the discounted cash flow method in fair value cases, and accords the previous trading price of the stock little or no weight. (Of course, the DCF must be based on what the company could do on its own, disregarding synergies with the acquiring company.)

The cases summarized in this *Guide* reflect this general trend. Commentators have credited the *Weinberger* case with leading to an increase in dissenting stockholder litigation, which currently encompasses many times the number of pre-1983 cases.

California leads in oppression actions

California is by far the leading state in oppressed stockholder and partnership actions. To bring an oppression case in California, the plaintiffs must own at least one-third of the stock or partnership, and must demonstrate either oppression or deadlock. The oppressed party is entitled to dissolution of the corporation or partnership. On the other side, the oppressing party can avoid dissolution by paying the oppressed party the fair value of his or her interest. The statute is confusing because it refers to "value in liquidation;" however, it also permits liquidation to be construed as the proceeds that would be received by selling the entire company as a going concern. Chapter 6 of this *Guide* has an in-depth article by Arthur Shartsis on appraising for fair value under California Corporations Code Section 2000.

There has been a marked increase in states enacting oppression statutes in recent years. Today most states have oppression statutes entitling oppressed owners to receive fair value for their interests. Most states also do not require a minimum ownership percentage to bring an appraisal action, only that the owners can show oppression.

Chapter 1: Introduction

Fairness opinions

Fair value is the statutory standard of value for dissenting stockholder suits in almost all states. However, as odd as it seems, there is no requirement for the renderer of the fairness opinion to take into consideration the value that may be concluded in a dissenting stockholder suit.

I believe that it is good practice to consider the value that may be concluded in a dissenting stockholder suit, and in rendering fairness opinions I always take this factor into consideration. To that end, this book has valuable guidance for the practitioner as to what states take what positions in dissenting stockholder suits.[5]

When either a public or private company is contemplating a transaction that affects minority stockholders, they often seek a "fairness opinion." The opinion routinely renders value as a range (such as $42 to $50 per share), and if the amount offered in the transaction falls within this range, the opinion states that "it is fair from a financial point of view."

Fairness opinions are normally rendered on behalf of a group of minority stockholders, usually selling stockholders. Therefore, if the price offered is above the range of value (which I have encountered several times), it is still fair to the stockholders for whom it is rendered. Usually, fairness opinions are commissioned by the independent members of the board of directors.

Occasionally, fairness opinions are requested by a Board of Directors on behalf of *buying* stockholders. It is my opinion that, if the buying company sought a fairness opinion, the incidence of overpaying would be much less.

Normally, the appraisal organization issuing the fairness opinion will make an in-person presentation to, at a minimum, the independent directors and perhaps to the full board. Business appraisers should insist on this step for the protection of their clients, who have a fiduciary obligation to their stockholders to understand the methodology used in arriving at the fairness conclusion. One time in my experience the fiduciaries were held not to have paid enough attention to the fairness opinion. Although the value was ultimately upheld, the fiduciaries were found liable for attorneys' fees, which were over $4 million!

Historically, fairness opinions on larger transactions have remained largely the province of Wall Street investment bankers, who typically charge $250,000 to over $500,000 for a fairness opinion on a transaction in which they are also receiving millions of dollars as an investment banking fee.

In December 2007, the NASD enacted changes to Rule 2290 to address this obvious conflict of interest. Rule 2290 requires independence in issuing fairness opinions—and it opens doors for more fairness opinions on larger transactions by independent business appraisers.

Introduction

What to do when the price offered is not within a range that we can opine to be fair? On a couple of occasions, I have indicated the price was marginally low, and the buyer increased it a dollar or two per share. On one occasion, I said the offered price was clearly below the range of fairness; the company wanted to sell, but the board rejected the offer. That buyer did not raise his offer, but fortunately, about six months later, the company received a higher offer that was within my range of a fair price. That is a classic example of how an independent fairness opinion protects stockholders against a lowball offer; and it is yet another example how understanding the fair value standard, as presented in this *Guide*, can help appraisers render independent valuation opinions in the growing field of rendering fairness opinions.

Statutory fair value: a moving target

As noted earlier, there is a trend among courts toward denying either discounts for lack of marketability or discount for a minority interest. Even among states with precedent on these matters, new cases may come along to override the existing law.

The second chapter of this *Guide* contains a chart[6] that provides a summary of dissent and oppression statutes in all 50 states and also groups the states' case law with respect to their typical treatment of discounts into several categories, including those which:

- Always deny both marketability and minority discounts;
- Always allow both marketability and minority discounts;
- Allow one discount but not the other;
- Decide discounts on a case by case basis;
- Have no precedent on one or both discounts.

Business appraisers and attorneys should keep up with the case law on statutory fair value standards, as these continue to be a "moving target" in states which have yet to address the issue, as well as those which continue to refine the precedent—often borrowing from other jurisdictions or relevant cases.

Increased opportunities for business appraisers

As the statutory standard of fair value continues to evolve, there will be many more opportunities for business appraisers in fair value and related matters, and I encourage business appraisers to pursue such opportunities—with the hope that you will find them as rewarding as I have. This *Guide* from BVR is a great resource to keep up with matters related to statutory fair value—or to begin working with the standard for the first time.

---

1. Shannon Pratt is Chairman and CEO of Shannon Pratt Valuations, Inc. (Portland, OR); shannon@shannonpratt.com. He is also Publisher Emeritus of *Business Valuation Update*™, a monthly newsletter available at www.bvresources.com.

Chapter 1: Introduction

2. See Shannon Pratt, Jay Fishman, and William Morrison, *Standards of Value: Theory and Applications* (John Wiley & Sons, Inc., 2007), for additional reading on dissent and oppression actions. (To order, go to www.bvresouces.com; (888) 287-8258).
3. State statutes vary as to what qualifies as a triggering event that gives rise to stockholder appraisal rights. They all require dissenting stockholders to file their dissent within some specified time to perfect their entitlement to appraisal rights; and all are quite strict about enforcing the deadlines.
4. *Weinberger v. UOP, Inc.,* 457 A.2d 701 (Del. 1983).
5. See *Fair Value in Dissent and Oppression Chart by State* in Chapter 2 for a summary in chart format.
6. See *Fair Value in Dissent and Oppression Chart by State* in Chapter 2.

Chapter 2
Background on Fair Value

Fair Value Defined[1]

> ...the value of the eligible holder's proportionate interest in the corporation, without any discount for minority status or, absent extraordinary circumstances, lack of marketability. Fair value should be determined using the customary valuation concepts and techniques generally employed in the relevant securities and financial markets for similar businesses in the context of the transaction giving rise to appraisal.[2]
>
> *–Principles of Corporate Governance, American Law Institute (1992)*

> The value of the shares immediately before the effectuation of the corporate action to which the shareholder objects using customary and current valuation concepts and techniques generally employed for similar businesses in the context of the transaction requiring appraisal, and without discounting for lack of marketability or minority status except, if appropriate, for amendments to the certificate of incorporation pursuant to section 13.02(a)(5).[3]
>
> *– Revised Model Business Corporation Act (RMBCA), American Bar Association (1999)*

Prior to 1999 RMBCA definition, the 1984 definition was:

> The value of the shares immediately before the effectuation of the corporate action to which the shareholder objects, excluding any appreciation or depreciations in anticipation of the corporate action unless exclusion would be inequitable.

It should be noted that the majority of states use the pre-1999 RMBCA definition. Some states use the 1999 version, a few use a hybrid of the 1999 and pre-1999 version, others use the pre-1999 version without the "unless exclusion would be inequitable" portion, while still others use the pre-1999 version with the "unless exclusion would be inequitable" phrase omitted but add in an additional portion that states that all relevant factors should be considered in determining value. For more information, see the "States that Adopted the RMBCA Definition of Fair Value" chart in Chapter 4, as well as the "Current Business Corporation Law and What it Means for the Business Appraiser" article in this Chapter.

---

1. Expanded definitions and their discussions by Jay Fishman can be found in Chapter 3.
2. Section 7.22(a) further observes that the ALI follows those jurisdictions that require "the appraisal court to value the firm as a whole, not specific shares, and to allocate that value proportionately, absent extraordinary circumstances."
3. According to the American Bar Association, Committee on Corporate Laws, "Revised Model Business Corporation Act" (1999), Section 13.02(a)(5) of the RMBCA states that "any other amendment to the articles of incorporation, merger, share exchange or disposition of assets to the extent provided by the articles of incorporation, bylaws or a resolution of the board of directors." The official comment to the 1999 RMBCA states that if the corporation grants appraisal rights voluntarily for certain transactions that do not affect the entire corporation, the court can use its discretion in applying discounts.

Fair Value vs. Fair Market Value: Historical Perspective

Fair Value versus Fair Market Value[1]

The two most widely used standards of value are fair market value and fair value. Before we discuss the definitions of these terms in valuation and law, we can look at their application on a purely linguistic level.

In plain language, fair value is a much broader concept than fair market value. Webster's *Thesaurus* gives these synonyms for the word *fair:* just, forthright, impartial, plain, upright, candid, sincere, straightforward, honest, lawful, clean, legitimate, honorable, temperate, reasonable, civil, uncorrupted, equitable, fair-minded.[2] Without the "market" modifier, fair value can be seen as a broad concept of a "value" that is "fair." Accordingly, the term *fair* gives a court wide latitude in reaching a judgment. The fair value of an asset could be its market value, its intrinsic value, or an investment value. Similarly, it could be a value in exchange, a value to the holder; it could represent a liquidation value or a going concern value.

The term *fair market value* is more limiting, by its use of the word *market*. Whether *market* applies to *fair* (as in fair market) or *value* (as in market value), we are limited to finding the value an asset would have in exchange, that is, on a market in the context of a real or hypothetical sale. Fair market value is the cornerstone for all other judicial concepts of value. Following a brief overview of common standards and premises of value in chapter one [of *Standards of Value: Theory and Applications*], we move first to a discussion of fair market value, as it sets the benchmark from which other standards of value are viewed.

Later, when we apply definitions set forth by the Internal Revenue Service, or the American Bar Association, or the Financial Accounting Standards Board (FASB), or any other professional or regulatory body providing guidance, we arrive at a set of assumptions that limit the scope of the valuation. As we will see, fair value is indeed subject to wider interpretation from a judicial perspective than fair market value.

Fair market value is well defined and established in legal, tax, and accounting settings, and fair value is defined in terms of financial reporting. However, there is no universal definition of fair value in the context of dissent and oppression cases. Perhaps the most relevant definition was laid out in the landmark 1950 shareholder dissent case *Tri-Continental Corp. v. Battye*,[3] where the court expressed the basic concept of fair value under the dissent statute as being "... *that the stockholder is entitled to be paid for that which has been taken from him, viz., his proportionate interest in a going concern.*"[4]

Fair Value vs. Fair Market Value: Historical Perspective

Interestingly, the definition of fair value in *Black's Law Dictionary* says "*see fair market value.*" Under the definition of fair market value, there is an example of a bankruptcy case.[5] In that case, the term *fair value* is used, as opposed to *fair market value*, as if the terms were interchangeable. This circular referencing makes the concepts of fair value and fair market value difficult to separate in a broad legal context; however, as we show through a review of case law, statutes, and commentary, the two concepts are regularly viewed as different.

We will explain how fair value differs from fair market value in its application in shareholder dissent and oppression. In divorce matters, we will look at a continuum over which businesses are valued and see how, under certain circumstances in certain jurisdictions, fair value is closely related to fair market value and, under others, it is not.

Historical Perspective

Today, the term *fair market value* is used often in the statutory context. For example, New Jersey's statutes use the term in 125 different sections of the code, from library material (§ 2A:43A-1) to farmland (§ 4:1C-31) to hazardous substances (§ 58:10-23.115). The term *fair value* is much less pervasive. Today, it is used mainly for financial reporting, shareholder oppression and dissent, and sometimes divorce matters. The historical development of fair market value, fair value, and the standard of value in divorce are briefly summarized next.

1800 to 1850

In searching case law, we begin to see references to standards of value in the early nineteenth century; however, the standards of value are not necessarily defined as such. One of the earliest references to fair market value is in a tariff case from 1832;[6] the term was set forth without further definition.

1850 to 1900

In the late nineteenth century, the emergence of the railroads allowed an expansion of commerce to a national scale and aided the development of national, multi-shareholder corporations. As tax law developed and business organizations progressed, there came a need for judicial and legislative involvement in corporate law. Majority rule emerged in corporations when the courts recognized the operational necessity of abandoning unanimous consent for corporate decisions. The courts began to look for a manner by which to value property for taxation and to find equitable solutions to the disagreements of shareholders that naturally grew out of this evolution.

The earliest references to fair value were found in cases involving contractual agreements between individuals regarding the ownership of stock, property, or other assets.[7] Like fair market value, the concept of fair value that emerged from these events remained undefined.

Chapter 2: Background on Fair Value

1900 to 1950

At the beginning of the twentieth century, the courts, the states, and other regulatory and advisory organizations began dealing more commonly with litigation involving business valuations. In the 1920s, the Commissioners for Uniform State Laws began developing a model code for businesses, but the Model Business Corporation Act of the American Bar Association (ABA) gained popularity and began to influence the state legislatures in the codification of dissenters' rights in their statutes. In 1933, the Illinois Business Corporation Act became the model statute for shareholder oppression, and in the early 1940s, California instituted a statutory buy-out provision where a corporation could elect to buy-out a shareholder who claimed to be oppressed, rather than going through dissolution litigation. Later that decade, the landmark case *Tri-Continental Corp. v. Battye*[8] introduced the concept that fair value should compensate a shareholder for that which had been taken.

In the 1920s, the definition of fair market value began to emerge through various case decisions. The concepts of willing buyer, willing seller, known and knowable, and the effect of compulsion on fair market value were discussed and established as elements to consider in determining fair market value. The first discount was applied for lack of control of a corporation at the behest of the IRS in *Cravens v. Welch*,[9] a California Tax Court case. A shareholder was looking to deduct taxable losses on the minority shares of a corporation, and while the shareholder desired to set a higher initial value of his shares, the IRS looked to lessen that value by applying a discount. Later the application of the minority discount (though benefiting the IRS in this case) would be applied commonly in estate and gift tax matters to the benefit of the shareholder.

1950 to 1975

Businesses began to change in the latter half of the twentieth century. The most valuable assets of a business were often no longer tangible assets, such as real property and equipment, but were intangible assets, such as patents, trademarks, trade names, and goodwill. Because of this, valuation theory itself had to evolve to cope with new sorts of assets, which required complex valuations. The need for judicial valuations grew because of the disputes that arose over the value of intangible assets.

In family law, equitable distribution and the concept of community property emerged in the 1970s and, along with the emergence of intangible value, created a new need for business valuations in the judicial context of divorce. In estate and gift tax matters, the definition of fair market value was codified and explained in Treasury Regulations as well as by IRS Revenue Rulings.

In stockholder matters, the states more broadly adopted dissent and oppression statutes. By the 1970s, the states widely implemented the fair value buy-out provision in dissolution statutes. Previously, the resolution to shareholder oppression was generally achieved by dissolving the existing corporation. Because of the availability of the fair value buy-out, oppressed shareholders were now better able to recover their investment upon filing suit as oppressed shareholders.

Fair Value vs. Fair Market Value: Historical Perspective

1975 to the Present

Despite codification, from 1975 to the present, the Tax Court continues to deal with fair market value issues including shareholder-level discounts, trapped in capital gains, and subsequent events. The family courts have struggled with the treatment of goodwill, the application of shareholder-level discounts and the weight accorded buy-sell agreements. Some of the most significant developments have occurred in shareholder oppression and dissent in the past 30 years. The courts had previously been hesitant to dissolve a company unless extremely harsh conduct was recognized, but with the institution of the fair value buy-out in many states, the courts in those states became more inclined to allow the minority shareholder to be compensated with a payment for the value of his or her stock. In the late 1970s, tests for oppression emerged in the form of cases establishing that a shareholder may be awarded his or her fair value if there is a breach of fiduciary duty, unfair or unreasonably burdensome conduct by the majority, or a breach of the minority shareholder's reasonable expectations. In the early 1980s, the Delaware decision *Weinberger v. UOP, Inc.*[10] established the notion that customary and current valuation techniques may be used in determining fair value in shareholder dissent cases instead of the rigid guidelines previously applied. Several iterations of the Revised Model Business Corporation Act published by the ABA and the *Principles of Corporate Governance* set forth by the American Law Institute (ALI) set suggested guidelines for determining fair value in these situations, and the states increasingly adopted these guidelines over this time period.

---

1. Jay Fishman, Shannon Pratt, and William Morrison, *Standards of Value: Theory and Applications*, John Wiley & Sons, Inc., 2006. Reprinted with permission of John Wiley & Sons, Inc. (To order, go to www.bvresouces.com; (888) 287-8258).
2. *Webster's New World Dictionary and Thesaurus* (New York: Simon & Schuster Macmillan, 1996), at 222.
3. 74 A.2d 71; 1950 Del. LEXIS 23; 31 Del. Ch. 523.
4. *Id.* at 3.
5. Bryan A. Gamer, *Black's Law Dictionary*, 8th ed. (St. Paul, MN, Thompson West, 2004), at 1587.
6. *United States v. Fourteen Packages of Pins*, 1832 U.S. Dist. LEXIS 5; 25 F. Cas. 1182; 1 Gilp 235.
7. *Montgomery v. Rose,* Court of Virginia, Special Court of Appeals 1855 Va. LEXIS 65; 1 Patton & H. 5, January, 1855. *The United States Rolling Stock Company v. The Atlantic and Great Western Railroad Company*, Court of Ohio, 34 Ohio St. 450; 1878 Ohio LEXIS 173, December 1878.
8. 74 A.2d 71, 72 (Del. 1950).
9. 10 F. Supp. 94 (D.C. Cal. 1935)
10. 457 A.2d 701, 713 (Del. 1983)

Fair Value in Dissent and Oppression Chart by State[1]

STATE	ALABAMA	ALASKA	ARIZONA
Valuation Term	Fair Value	Fair Value	Fair Value
Case Precedent in Allowing Discounts	Court's discretion		Court's discretion
Most Recent Case	*Offenbecher v. Baron Services*—2003: No discounts applied		*Pro Finish USA v. Johnson*—2003: No discounts applied
Definition of Valuation Term	§ 10-2B-13.01: Value of the shares immediately before the effectuation of the corporate action to which the dissenter objects, excluding any appreciation or depreciation in anticipation of the corporate action unless exclusion would be inequitable	§ 10.06.580: In fixing the fair value of the shares, the court shall consider the nature of the transaction giving rise to the right to dissent under AS 10.06.576, its effects on the corporation and its shareholders, the concepts and methods customary in the relevant securities and financial markets for determining the fair value of shares of a corporation engaging in a similar transaction under comparable circumstances, and other relevant factors.	§ 10-1301: Value of the shares immediately before the effectuation of the corporate action to which the dissenter objects, excluding any appreciation or depreciation in anticipation of the corporate action unless exclusion would be inequitable
Dissent/Appraisal Valuation Date	§ 10-2B-13.01: Immediately before the effectuation of the corporate action to which the dissenter objects	§ 10.06.580: The close of business on the day before the date on which the vote was taken approving the proposed corporate action	§ 10-1301: Immediately before the effectuation of the corporate action to which the dissenter objects
Dissolution by shareholder as a remedy for oppression or oppressive behavior?	Yes—§ 10-2B-14.30(2)(ii)	Yes*—§ 10.06.628 (4)	Yes—§ 10-1430 (B)(2)
Buy-out election in lieu of dissolution?	Yes—§ 10-2B-14.34	Yes—§ 10.06.630	Yes—§ 10-1434
Dissolution Valuation Date	§ 10-2B-14.34: The day before the date the petition was filed		§ 10-1434: The day before the date the petition was filed
Definition Following RMBCA	Yes—1984		Yes—1984

*"Oppression" not used as term in statute.

1. Shannon Pratt, Jay Fishman, and William Morrison, *Standards of Value: Theory and Applications* (John Wiley & Sons, Inc., 2006). Reprinted with permission of John Wiley & Sons, Inc.

Fair Value in Dissent and Oppression Chart by State

STATE	ARKANSAS	CALIFORNIA	COLORADO
Valuation Term	Fair Value	Dissent: Fair Market Value Dissolution: Fair Value	Fair Value
Case Precedent in Allowing Discounts		Court's discretion	Rejects discounts
Most Recent Case		*Mart v. Severson*—2002: No discounts applied. *Thompson v. Miller*—2003: Discounts applied.	*Pueblo Bancorporation v. Lindoe*—2003: No discounts
Definition of Valuation Term	§ 4-27-1301: Value of the shares immediately before the effectuation of the corporate action to which the dissenter objects, excluding any appreciation or depreciation in anticipation of the corporate action unless exclusion would be inequitable	§ 1300: The fair market value shall be determined excluding any appreciation or depreciation in consequence of the proposed action, but adjusted for any stock split, reverse stock split, or share dividend which becomes effective thereafter.	§ 7-113-101: Value of the shares immediately before the effectuation of the corporate action to which the dissenter objects, excluding any appreciation or depreciation in anticipation of the corporate action unless exclusion would be inequitable
Dissent/Appraisal Valuation Date	§ 4-27-1301: Immediately before the effectuation of the corporate action to which the dissenter objects	§ 1300: The day before the first announcement of the terms of the proposed reorganization	§ 7-113-101: Iimmediately before the effective date of corporate action
Dissolution by shareholder as a remedy for oppression or oppressive behavior?	Yes—§ 4-27-1430(2)(ii)	Yes*—§ 1800(b)(4)	Yes—§ 7-113-301-304
Buy-out election in lieu of dissolution?	No	Yes—§ 2000	No
Dissolution Valuation Date		*Trahan v. Trahan*—2002: Valuation date is the date the dissolution proceeding was initiated.	
Definition Following RMBCA	Yes—1984		Yes—1984

*"Oppression" not used as term in statute.

(*continues*)

Chapter 2: Background on Fair Value

STATE	CONNECTICUT	DELAWARE	FLORIDA
Valuation Term	Fair Value	Fair Value	Fair Value
Case Precedent in Allowing Discounts	Rejects discounts by statute	Rejects discounts by law, applies control premium	Rejects discounts by statute
Most Recent Case	Devivo v. Devivo—2001: Ext. Circ.: Discounts applied	Robert Michael Lane v. Cancer Treatment Centers of America, Inc.—2004: Control premium applied	Munshower v. Kolbenheyer—1999: Marketability discount allowed
Definition of Valuation Term	§ 33-855: Value of the shares immediately before the effectuation of the corporate action to which the shareholder objects using customary and current valuation concepts and techniques generally employed for similar businesses in the context of the transaction requiring appraisal, and without discounting for lack of marketability or minority status except, if appropriate, for amendments to the certificate of incorporation	§ 262: Value exclusive of any element of value arising from the accomplishment or expectation of the merger or consolidation, together with a fair rate of interest including all other relevant factors	§ 607.1301: Using customary and current valuation concepts and techniques generally employed for similar businesses in the context of the transaction requiring appraisal, excluding any appreciation or depreciation in anticipation of the corporate action unless exclusion would be inequitable to the corporation and its remaining shareholders. For a corporation with 10 or fewer shareholders, without discounting for lack of marketability or minority status.
Dissent/Appraisal Valuation Date	§ 33-855: Immediately before the effectuation of corporate action	§ 262: Date at the point before the effective date of the corporate action	§ 607.1301: Immediately before the effectuation of the corporate action to which the shareholder objects
Dissolution by shareholder as a remedy for oppression or oppressive behavior?	Yes—§ 33-896 (1)	No—§ 275: Majority of shareholders only	Yes*—§ 607.1430(3)(b)
Buy-out election in lieu of dissolution?	Yes—§ 33-900	No	Yes—§ 607.1436
Dissolution Valuation Date	§ 33-900: The day before the date on which the petition was filed or as of such other date as the court deems appropriate under the circumstances		§ 607.1436: The day before the date the petition was filed
Definition Following RMBCA	Yes—1999		Yes—1999

*"Oppression" not used as term in statute.

Fair Value in Dissent and Oppression Chart by State

STATE	GEORGIA	HAWAII	IDAHO
Valuation Term	Fair Value	Fair Value	Fair Value
Case Precedent in Allowing Discounts	Rejects discounts		Rejects discounts by statute
Most Recent Case	*Blitch v. People's Bank*—2000: No discounts applied		
Definition of Valuation Term	§ 14-2-1301: Value of the shares immediately before the effectuation of the corporate action to which the dissenter objects, excluding any appreciation or depreciation in anticipation of the corporate action	§ 414-341: Value of the shares immediately before the effectuation of the corporate action to which the dissenter objects, excluding any appreciation or depreciation in anticipation of the corporate action unless exclusion would be inequitable	§ 30-1-1301: Immediately before the effectuation of the corporate action to which the shareholder objects using customary and current valuation concepts and techniques generally employed for similar businesses in the context of the transaction requiring appraisal and without discounting for lack of marketability or minority status except for amendments to 30-1-1302(1)(e)
Dissent/Appraisal Valuation Date	§ 14-2-1301: Immediately before the effectuation of corporate action	§ 414-341: Immediately before the effectuation of corporate action	§ 30-1-1301: Immediately before the effectuation of the corporate action
Dissolution by shareholder as a remedy for oppression or oppressive behavior?	Yes*—§ 14-2-1430(2)(B)	Yes—§ 414-411(2)(B)	Yes—§ 30-1-1430(2)(b)
Buy-out election in lieu of dissolution?	Yes—under articles of a close corporation—§ 14-2-942	Yes—§ 414-415	Yes—§ 30-1-1434
Dissolution Valuation Date		§ 414-415: The day before the date the petition was filed	§ 30-1-1434: The day before the date the petition was filed
Definition Following RMBCA		Yes—1984	Yes—1999

*"Oppression" not used as term in statute.

(*continues*)

Chapter 2: Background on Fair Value

STATE	ILLINOIS	INDIANA	IOWA
Valuation Term	Fair Value	Fair Value	Fair Value
Case Precedent in Allowing Discounts	Court's Discretion	Rejects discounts	Rejects discounts by statute
Most Recent Case	*Jahn v. Kinderman*—2004: Discounts Not Applied	*Wenzel v. Hopper Galliher*—2002: No discounts applied	*Seig v. Kelly*—1997: Discounts not applied
Definition of Valuation Term	§ 805 ILCS 5/11.70: Value of the shares immediately before the effectuation of the corporate action to which the dissenter objects, excluding any appreciation or depreciation in anticipation of the corporate action unless exclusion would be inequitable	§ 23-1-44-3: Value of the shares immediately before the effectuation of the corporate action to which the dissenter objects, excluding any appreciation or depreciation in anticipation of the corporate action unless exclusion would be inequitable	§ 490.1301: Immediately before the effectuation of the corporate action to which the shareholder objects using customary and current valuation concepts and techniques generally employed for similar businesses in the context of the transaction requiring appraisal and without discounting for lack of marketability or minority status except for amendments to 490.1302(1)(e)
Dissent/Appraisal Valuation Date	§ 805 ILCS 5/11.70: Immediately before the consumation of the corporate action	§ 23-1-44-3: Immediately before the effectuation of the corporate action	§ 490.1301: Immediately before the effectuation of the corporate action to which the shareholder objects
Dissolution by shareholder as a remedy for oppression or oppressive behavior?	Yes—805 ILCS 5/12.55 : (2)	No—§ 23-1-47-1-4: Only in deadlock	Yes—§ 490.1430 (2)b
Buy-out election in lieu of dissolution?	Yes § 805 ILCS 5/12.55	No	Yes—§ 490.1434
Dissolution Valuation Date	§ 805 ILCS 5/12.55: Such date as the court finds equitable		§ 490.1434: The day before the date the petition was filed
Definition Following RMBCA	Yes—1984	Yes—1984	Yes—1999

*"Oppression" not used as term in statute.

Fair Value in Dissent and Oppression Chart by State

STATE	KANSAS	KENTUCKY	LOUISIANA
Valuation Term	Value	Fair Value	Fair Cash Value
Case Precedent in Allowing Discounts	Court's discretion	Generally allows discounts	Generally allows discounts
Most Recent Case	*Arnaud v. Stock Grower's Bank*—1999: No discounts applied	*Ford v. Courier-Journal Job Printing*—1982: Marketability discount allowed	*Shopf v. Marina Del Ray*—1989: Minority discount allowed
Definition of Valuation Term	§ 17-6712: The value of the stockholder's stock on the effective date of the merger or consolidation, exclusive of any element of value arising from the expectation or accomplishment of the merger or consolidation	§ 271B.13-010: Value of the shares immediately before the effectuation of the corporate action to which the dissenter objects, excluding any appreciation or depreciation in anticipation of the corporate action unless exclusion would be inequitable	§ 140.2: A value not less than the highest price paid per share by the acquiring person in the control share acquisition
Dissent/Appraisal Valuation Date	§ 17-6712: The effective date of the merger or consolidation	§ 271B.13-010: Immediately before the effectuation of corporate action	§ 134: If voted upon, the latter of the date prior to the date of the shareholders vote or the day 20 days prior to the consummation of the business combination, otherwise the date of the action
Dissolution by shareholder as a remedy for oppression or oppressive behavior?	No—§ 17-6804: Voluntary only; § 17-6812: Abuse, misuse, or non-use of corporate powers	Yes*—§ 271B.14-300 (2)(b)	No—§ 12:141-146: Voluntary, or deadlock, deadlock only if shareholders or corporation are suffering irreparable damage, or if the corporation has been guilty of ultra vires acts
Buy-out election in lieu of dissolution?	No	No	No
Dissolution Valuation Date			
Definition Following RMBCA		Yes—1984	

*"Oppression" not used as term in statute.

(*continues*)

Chapter 2: Background on Fair Value

STATE	MAINE	MARYLAND	MASSACHUSETTS
Valuation Term	Fair Value	Fair Value	Fair Value
Case Precedent in Allowing Discounts	Rejects discounts by statute		Rejects discounts
Most Recent Case	*In re the Valuation of Mcloon Oil Co.*—1989: No discounts applied		*BNE Massachusetts Corp. v. Sims*—1992: No discounts applied
Definition of Valuation Term	§ 1301: Immediately before the effectuation of the corporate action to which the shareholder objects using customary and current valuation concepts and techniques generally employed for similar businesses in the context of the transaction requiring appraisal and without discounting for lack of marketability or minority status	§ 3-202(b): On the date of stockholder vote, free of any appreciation or depreciation which directly or indirectly results from the transaction objected to or from its proposal	§ 13.01: Value of the shares immediately before the effectuation of the corporate action to which the dissenter objects, excluding any appreciation or depreciation in anticipation of the corporate action unless exclusion would be inequitable
Dissent/Appraisal Valuation Date	§ 1301: Immediately before the effectuation of the corporate action	§ 3-202(b)(1): On the day notice of a merger is given or the date of a stockholder vote for other transactions	§ 13.01: Day immediately before the effective date of the corporate action to which the shareholder demanding appraisal objects
Dissolution by shareholder as a remedy for oppression or oppressive behavior?	Yes—§ 1430 (2)B	Yes—§ 3-413(b)(2)	No—§ 14.30.34: Deadlock
Buy-out election in lieu of dissolution?	Yes—§ 1434	Yes—under articles of a close corporation—§ 4-603	No
Dissolution Valuation Date		§ 4-603: As of the close of business on the day on which the petition for dissolution was filed	
Definition Following RMBCA	Yes—1999		

*"Oppression" not used as term in statute.

Fair Value in Dissent and Oppression Chart by State

STATE	MICHIGAN	MINNESOTA	MISSISSIPPI
Valuation Term	Fair Value	Fair Value	Fair Value
Case Precedent in Allowing Discounts		Court's discretion	Rejects discounts by statute
Most Recent Case		*ACD v. Follet*—2000: Ext. Circ.: Marketability discount applied	*Missala Marine Services v. Jenny Kay Odom*—2003: Discounts allowed—dissolution/damage claim
Definition of Valuation Term	§ 450.1761: "Fair value," with respect to a dissenter's shares, means the value of the shares immediately before the effectuation of the corporate action to which the dissenter objects, excluding any appreciation or depreciation in anticipation of the corporate action unless exclusion would be inequitable.	302A.473: Value of the shares of a corporation immediately before the effective date of the corporate action	§ 79-4-13.01: Immediately before the effectuation of the corporate action to which the shareholder objects using customary and current valuation concepts and techniques generally employed for similar businesses in the context of the transaction requiring appraisal and without discounting for lack of marketability or minority status
Dissent/Appraisal Valuation Date	§ 450.1779: The latter of the day prior to the date of the vote and 20 days before the business combination, or the date of the business combination if there is no vote	§ 302A.473 (c): Value of the shares of a corporation immediately before the effective date of the corporate action	§ 79-4-13.01: Immediately before the effectuation of the corporate action to which the shareholder objects
Dissolution by shareholder as a remedy for oppression or oppressive behavior?	Yes—§ 450.1489	Yes*—§ 302A.751(b)(3)	Yes—§ 79-4-14.30(2)(ii)
Buy-out election in lieu of dissolution?	Yes—§ 450.1489(e)	Yes—§ 302A.751	Yes—§ 79-4-14.34
Dissolution Valuation Date		§ 302A.751: The date of the commencement of the action or as of another date found equitable by the court	§ 79-4-14.34: The day before the date the petition was filed
Definition Following RMBCA	Yes—1984	Yes—1984	Yes—1999

*"Oppression" not used as term in statute.

(continues)

Chapter 2: Background on Fair Value

STATE	MISSOURI	MONTANA	NEBRASKA
Valuation Term	Fair Value	Fair Value	Fair Value
Case Precedent in Allowing Discounts	Court's discretion	Rejects discounts	Rejects discounts
Most Recent Case	*King v. FTJ*—1988: Discounts applied	*Hansen v. 75 Ranch Co.*—1998: Discounts not applied	*Rigel v. Cutchall*—1998: No discounts applied
Definition of Valuation Term	§ 351.870: Value of the shares immediately before the effectuation of the corporate action to which the dissenter objects, excluding any appreciation or depreciation in anticipation of the corporate action unless exclusion would be inequitable	§ 35-1-826: Value of the shares immediately before the effectuation of the corporate action to which the dissenter objects, excluding any appreciation or depreciation in anticipation of the corporate action unless exclusion would be inequitable	§ 21-20,137: Value of the shares immediately before the effectuation of the corporate action to which the dissenter objects, excluding any appreciation or depreciation in anticipation of the corporate action unless exclusion would be inequitable
Dissent/Appraisal Valuation Date	§ 351.455(1): As of the day prior to the date on which the vote was taken	§ 35-1-826: Immediately before the effectuation of the corporate action to which the shareholder objects	§ 21-20,137: Immediately before the effectuation of the corporate action to which the shareholder objects
Dissolution by shareholder as a remedy for oppression or oppressive behavior?	Yes—§ 351.494(2)(b)	Yes—§ 35-1-938(2)(b)	Yes—§ 21-20,162(2)(a)(ii)
Buy-out election in lieu of dissolution?	Yes—under articles of a close corporation—§ 351.790	Yes—§ 35-1-939	Yes—§ 21-20,166
Dissolution Valuation Date			§ 21-20,166: The day before the date on which the petition was filed or as of such other date as the court deems appropriate under the circumstances
Definition Following RMBCA	Yes—1984	Yes—1984	Yes—1984

*"Oppression" not used as term in statute.

Fair Value in Dissent and Oppression Chart by State

STATE	NEVADA	NEW HAMPSHIRE	NEW JERSEY
Valuation Term	Fair Value	Fair Value	Fair Value
Case Precedent in Allowing Discounts	Court's discretion		Court's discretion
Most Recent Case	*Steiner v. Benninghoff*—1998: Discount applied, but only 25% weight given to that factor		*Wheaton*—1999: No discounts; *Balsamides*—1999: Marketability discount applied; *Casey v. Brennan*—2001: No discounts, control premium applied
Definition of Valuation Term	§ 92A.320: Value of the shares immediately before the effectuation of the corporate action to which the dissenter objects, excluding any appreciation or depreciation in anticipation of the corporate action unless exclusion would be inequitable	§ 293-A:13.01: Value of the shares immediately before the effectuation of the corporate action to which the dissenter objects, excluding any appreciation or depreciation in anticipation of the corporate action unless exclusion would be inequitable	§ 14A:11-3: As of the day prior to the day of the meeting of the shareholders at which the action was approved....excluding any appreciation or depreciation resulting from the proposed action
Dissent/Appraisal Valuation Date	§ 92A.320: Immediately before the effectuation of the corporate action	§ 293-A:13.01: Immediately before the effectuation of the corporate action to which the shareholder objects	§ 14A:11-3: The day of the meeting of shareholders when the action was approved or the day prior to which the board of directors authorized an action if no vote was needed
Dissolution by shareholder as a remedy for oppression or oppressive behavior?	No—In a Close Corporaiton, only if by provision of the articles of incorporation § 78-A160	Yes*—§ 293-A:14.30(b)(iii)	Yes—§ 14A:12-7(1)(c)
Buy-out election in lieu of dissolution?	No	Yes—§ 293-A:14.34	Yes -§ 14A:12-7
Dissolution Valuation Date		§ 293-A:14.34: The day before the date on which the petition was filed or as of such other date as the court deems appropriate under the circumstances	§ 14A:12-7: The date of the commencement of the action or such earlier or later date deemed equitable by the court, plus or minus any adjustments deemed equitable by the court if the action was brought in whole or in part under paragraph 14A: 12-7(i)(c)
Definition Following RMBCA	Yes—1984	Yes—1984	

*"Oppression" not used as term in statute.

(continues)

Chapter 2: Background on Fair Value

STATE	NEW MEXICO	NEW YORK	NORTH CAROLINA
Valuation Term	Fair Value	Fair Value	Fair Value
Case Precedent in Allowing Discounts	Court's discretion	Generally allows discounts (marketability only)	Court's discretion
Most Recent Case	*McCauley v. Tom McCauley & Sons*—1986: Discounts applied	*In re Brooklyn Home Dialysis Training*—2002: Marketability discount applied	*Tammy Garlock v. South Eastern Gas & Power*—2001: No Minority, Marketability, key man discount applied.
Definition of Valuation Term	§ 53-15-4: Value as of the day prior to the date on which the vote was taken approving the proposed corporate action, excluding any appreciation or depreciation in anticipation of the corporate action	§ 623(h)(4): Nature of the transaction giving rise to the shareholder's right to receive payment for shares and its effects on the corporation and its shareholders, the concepts and methods then customary in the relevant securities and financial markets for determining fair value of shares of a corporation engaging in a similar transaction under comparable circumstances and all over relevant factors	§ 55-13-01: Value of the shares immediately before the effectuation of the corporate action to which the dissenter objects, excluding any appreciation or depreciation in anticipation of the corporate action unless exclusion would be inequitable
Dissent/Appraisal Valuation Date	§ 53-15-4: The date prior to the day on which the vote was taken for the corporate action	§ 623: The close of business on the day prior to the shareholders' authorization date	§ 55-13-01: Immediately before the effectuation of the corporate action to which the shareholder objects
Dissolution by shareholder as a remedy for oppression or oppressive behavior?	Yes—§ 53-16-16(A)(1)(b)	Yes—§§ 1104-1118	Yes*—§ 55-14-30(2)(ii)
Buy-out election in lieu of dissolution?	No	Yes—§ 1118	Yes § 55-14-31: After dissolution has been okayed by court
Dissolution Valuation Date		*Re Dissolution of Public Relations Aids, Inc.*—1985: The day before the date the petition was filed	
Definition Following RMBCA			Yes—1984

*"Oppression" not used as term in statute.

Fair Value in Dissent and Oppression Chart by State

STATE	NORTH DAKOTA	OHIO	OKLAHOMA
Valuation Term	Fair Value	Fair Cash Value	Fair Value
Case Precedent in Allowing Discounts		Generally allows discounts	Rejects discounts
Most Recent Case		*English v. Atromik Int.*—2000: Discounts applied	*Woolf v. Universal Fidelity Life*—1992: No discounts applied
Definition of Valuation Term	§ 10-19.1-88: Fair value of the shares means the value of the shares the day immediately before the effective date of a corporate action.	§ 1701.85: The amount that a willing seller who is under no compulsion to sell would be willing to accept and that a willing buyer who is under no compulsion to purchase would be willing to pay, but in no event shall the fair cash value of a share exceed the amount specified in the demand of the particular shareholder.	§ 1091: Exclusive of any element of value arising from the accomplishment or expectation of the merger or consolidation…the court should take into account all relavent factors.
Dissent/Appraisal Valuation Date	§ 10-19.1-88: Day immediately before the effective date of a corporate action referred.	§ 1701.85: The day prior to that on which the shareholders' vote on the corporate transaction was taken	§ 1091: Effective date of the merger or consolidation
Dissolution by shareholder as a remedy for oppression or oppressive behavior?	Yes*—§ 10-19.1-115(b)(3)	No—§ 1701.91: Attorney general if corporation has acted unlawfully, voluntary dissolution; when it is established that it is beneficial to the shareholders that the corporation be judicially dissolved	No—§ 1906: Majority of shareholders
Buy-out election in lieu of dissolution?	No—§ 10-19.1-115: Only under court compulsion	No	No
Dissolution Valuation Date			
Definition Following RMBCA			

*"Oppression" not used as term in statute.

(continues)

Chapter 2: Background on Fair Value

STATE	OREGON	PENNSYLVANIA	RHODE ISLAND
Valuation Term	Fair Value	Fair Value	Fair Value
Case Precedent in Allowing Discounts	Rejects discounts		Rejects discounts
Most Recent Case	*Hayes v. Olmsted*—2001: No discounts applied		*Dilugio v. PAB*—2000: No discounts applied
Definition of Valuation Term	§ 60.551: Value of the shares immediately before the effectuation of the corporate action to which the dissenter objects, excluding any appreciation or depreciation in anticipation of the corporate action unless exclusion would be inequitable	§ 1572: The fair value of shares immediately before the effectuation of the corporate action to which the dissenter objects, taking into account all relevant factors, but excluding any appreciation or depreciation in anticipation of the corporate action	§ 7-1.2-1202: Value of the shares as of the day prior to the date on which the vote was taken approving the proposed corporate action, excluding any appreciation or depreciation in anticipation of the corporate action
Dissent/Appraisal Valuation Date	§ 60.551: Immediately before the effectuation of the corporate action to which the shareholder objects	§ 1572: Immediately before the effectuation of the corporate action to which the shareholder objects	§ 7-1.2-1202: As of the day prior to the date on which the vote was taken approving the proposed corporate action
Dissolution by shareholder as a remedy for oppression or oppressive behavior?	Yes—§ 60.952	Yes—§ 1981	Yes—§ 7-1.2-1314
Buy-out election in lieu of dissolution?	Yes—Close Corporation Provision Only—§ 60.952	No	Yes—§ 7-1.2-1315
Dissolution Valuation Date			§ 7-1.2-1315: The day on which the petition for dissolution was filed
Definition Following RMBCA	Yes—1984		

*"Oppression" not used as term in statute.

Fair Value in Dissent and Oppression Chart by State

STATE	SOUTH CAROLINA	SOUTH DAKOTA	TENNESSEE
Valuation Term	Fair Value	Fair Value	Fair Value
Case Precedent in Allowing Discounts	Rejects discounts	Rejects discounts by statute	
Most Recent Case	*Morrow v. Martschink*—1995: Discounts not applied	*First Western Bank of Wall v. Olsen*—2001: No discounts applied	
Definition of Valuation Term	§ 33-13-101: The value of shares immediately before the effectuation of the corporate action to which the dissenter objects, excluding any appreciation or depreciation in anticipation of the corporate action to which the dissenter objects. To be determined by generally accepted techniques in the financial community.	§ 47-1A-1301: Immediately before the effectuation of the corporate action to which the shareholder objects; using customary and current valuation concepts and techniques generally employed for similar businesses in the context of the transaction requiring appraisal; and without discounting for lack of marketability or minority status except, if appropriate, for amendments to the articles pursuant to subdivision (5) of § 47-1A-1302	§ 48-23-101: Value of the shares immediately before the effectuation of the corporate action to which the dissenter objects, excluding any appreciation or depreciation in anticipation of the corporate action
Dissent/Appraisal Valuation Date	§ 33-13-101: Immediately before the effectuation of the corporate action to which the dissenter objects	§ 47-1A-1301: Immediately before the effectuation of the corporate action to which the dissenter objects	§ 48-23-101: Immediately before the effectuation of the corporate action to which the dissenter objects
Dissolution by shareholder as a remedy for oppression or oppressive behavior?	Yes—§ 33-14-300(2)(ii)	Yes—§ 47-7-25-35	Yes—§ 48-24-301(2)(B)
Buy-out election in lieu of dissolution?	Yes—close corporation provision—§ 33-18-160	Yes—§ 47-1A-1434	No
Dissolution Valuation Date			
Definition Following RMBCA	Yes—1984	Yes—1999	Yes—1984

*"Oppression" not used as term in statute.

(continues)

Chapter 2: Background on Fair Value

STATE	TEXAS	UTAH	VERMONT
Valuation Term	Fair Value	Fair Value	Fair Value
Case Precedent in Allowing Discounts	Rejects minority discounts by statute	Court's discretion	Rejects discounts
Most Recent Case		*Hogle v. Zinetics*—2002: No discounts applied	*Waller v. American International Distribution*—1997: No discounts applied; *Trapp Family Lodge*—1999: Control Premium applied
Definition of Valuation Term	§ 10.362: The value of the ownership interest on the date preceding the date of the action excluding appreciation or depreciation in anticipation or as a result of the proposed action. (b) Consideration must be given to the value of the organization as a going concern without including in the computation of value any: (1) payment for a control premium or minority discount other than a discount attributable to the type of ownership interests held by the dissenting owner and, (2) limitation placed on the rights and preferences of those ownership interests.	§ 16-10a-1301: Value of the shares immediately before the effectuation of the corporate action to which the dissenter objects, excluding any appreciation or depreciation in anticipation of the corporate action	§ 13.01: Value of the shares immediately before the effectuation of the corporate action to which the dissenter objects, excluding any appreciation or depreciation in anticipation of the corporate action unless exclusion would be inequitable
Dissent/Appraisal Valuation Date		§ 16-10a-1301: Immediately before the effectuation of the corporate action to which the dissenter objects	§ 13.01: Immediately before the effectuation of the corporate action to which the dissenter objects
Dissolution by shareholder as a remedy for oppression or oppressive behavior?	No—§ 21.756: Shareholder may bring a derivative proceeding.	Yes—§ 16-10a-1430(2)(b)	Yes—§ 14.30(2)(B)
Buy-out election in lieu of dissolution?	No	Yes—§ 16-10a-1434	Yes—Close Corporation Provision—§ 20.15
Dissolution Valuation Date		§ 16-10a-1434: The day before the date the petition was filed	
Definition Following RMBCA	No	Yes—1984	Yes—1984

*"Oppression" not used as term in statute

Fair Value in Dissent and Oppression Chart by State

STATE	VIRGINIA	WASHINGTON	WASHINGTON D.C.
Valuation Term	Fair Value	Fair Value	Fair Value
Case Precedent in Allowing Discounts	Rejects discounts by statute	Rejects discounts	
Most Recent Case	*US Inspect v. McGreevy*—2000: No discounts applied	*Norton Co. v. Smyth*—2002: No discounts applied	
Definition of Valuation Term	§ 13.1-729: Value of the shares immediately before the effectuation of the corporate action to which the shareholder objects; using customary and current valuation concepts and techniques generally employed for similar businesses in the context of the transaction requiring appraisal; and without discounting for lack of marketability or minority status except, if appropriate, for amendments to the articles pursuant to subdivision A 5 of § 13.1-730	§ 23B.13.010: Value of the shares immediately before the effectuation of the corporate action to which the dissenter objects, excluding any appreciation or depreciation in anticipation of the corporate action unless exclusion would be inequitable	
Dissent/Appraisal Valuation Date	§ 13.1-729: Immediately before the effectuation of the corporate action to which the dissenter objects	§ 23B.13.010: Immediately before the effectuation of the corporate action to which the dissenter objects	§ 29-101.73: As of the day prior to the date on which the vote was taken approving the merger or consolidation
Dissolution by shareholder as a remedy for oppression or oppressive behavior?	Yes—§ 13.1-747(A)(1)(b)	Yes—§ 23B.14.300(2)(b)	No—§§ 29-101.88 and 101.90; By the court if due to "share abused their authority"
Buy-out election in lieu of dissolution?	Yes—§ 13.1-749.1	No	No
Dissolution Valuation Date			
Definition Following RMBCA	Yes—1999	Yes—1984	

*"Oppression" not used as term in statute.

(continues)

Chapter 2: Background on Fair Value

STATE	WEST VIRGINIA	WISCONSIN	WYOMING
Valuation Term	Fair Value	Fair Value	Fair Value
Case Precedent in Allowing Discounts	Rejects discounts by statute	Rejects discounts	
Most Recent Case		HMO v. SSM Health—1999: No discounts applied	
Definition of Valuation Term	§ 31D-13-1301: Immediately before the effectuation of the corporate action to which the shareholder objects using customary and current valuation concepts and techniques generally employed for similar businesses in the context of the transaction requiring appraisal and without discounting for lack of marketability or minority status except for amendments to § 31D-13-1302(5)(a)	§ 180.130: Value of the shares immediately before the effectuation of the corporate action to which the dissenter objects, excluding appreciation or depreciation in anticipation of the corporate action unless exclusion would be inequitable. With respect to a dissenter's shares in a business combination, means market value—the fair market value as determined in good faith by the board of directors of the resident domestic corporation	§ 17-16-1301: Value of the shares immediately before the effectuation of the corporate action to which the dissenter objects, excluding any appreciation or depreciation in anticipation of the corporate action unless exclusion would be inequitable
Dissent/Appraisal Valuation Date	§31D-13-1301: Immediately before the effectuation of the corporate action to which the shareholder objects	§ 180.1301: Immediately before the effectuation of the corporate action	§ 17-16-1301: Immediately before the effectuation of the corporate action to which the dissenter objects
Dissolution by shareholder as a remedy for oppression or oppressive behavior?	Yes—§ 31D-13-1301	Yes—§ 180.1430(2)(b)	Yes—§ 17-16-1430 (a)(ii)(B)
Buy-out election in lieu of dissolution?	Yes—§ 31D-14-1434.	Yes—close corporation provision—§180.1833	Yes—§ 17-16-1434
Dissolution Valuation Date	§ 31D-14-1434: The day before the date the petition was filed		§ 17-16-1434: The day before the date the petition was filed
Definition Following RMBCA	Yes—1999		Yes—1984

*"Oppression" not used as term in statute.

Current Business Corporation Law and What it Means for the Business Appraiser

By John J. Stockdale Jr., Esq.[1]

A business appraisal is an important document in corporate law situations. How the need arises, what the standard of value might be, and whether an appraisal is a requirement or simply a benefit is dependent upon each particular business law situation. In this article, we will discuss when the need for an appraisal may arise under a state's business corporation law.[2]

I. Dissenting Shareholder Actions

Historically speaking, it took a unanimous vote of all the shareholders to approve corporate action.[3] This provided the minority shareholder with the ability to block any corporate action that he or she found disagreeable.[4] In order to rectify this problem, which hindered the progress of industry and was disproportionate to the risk born by the minority shareholder, states began adopting business corporation laws that provided for the approval of the corporate action by a majority (or in some cases, supermajority) vote of the shareholders. In exchange for surrendering the ability to block the corporate action, the minority shareholder who disagreed with the corporate action was given the right to dissent from that action and receive the appraised value of his interest.[5]

The right to dissent from corporate action and receive the appraised value of the interest only applies to those actions specifically enumerated in the Model Business Corporation Act (MBCA or the Act). These "triggering events" include: the sale of all or substantially all of the assets of the business outside the normal course of business; a merger of the company where it is the target corporation; or a change to certain business forms.[6] Because a business corporation act is a creature of state law and the MBCA has gone through several revisions, the list of triggering events may change depending upon the jurisdiction. Moreover, appraisal rights are denied to shareholders of companies, whose stock is or could be traded over an active national exchange.[7] Once the right to dissent from a particular corporate action is triggered, the dissenter must take enumerated steps to perfect his or her right to appraisal.[8]

In assessing a proposed merger or sale, and whether it might be a "triggering event," a corporation's board of directors has a duty to make informed decisions in the best interest of the company.[9] In satisfying this duty, the board may rely on the opinions of outside accountants, appraisers, or investments bankers.[10] Depending on the size and sophistication of the business, the business's board of directors may engage an appraisal professional to issue a "fairness opinion."[11] However, there is no legal requirement under the MBCA that a fairness opinion be obtained in connection with the triggering action.[12]

Chapter 2: Background on Fair Value

The fairness opinion is a prophylactic measure designed to assist the board of directors in satisfying their fiduciary duty to make good faith, informed decisions on behalf of the company.[13] Generally speaking, a fairness opinion reviews a proposed transaction to determine whether it is "fair from a financial point of view"[14] and it is frequently expressed as a range of value. There is no fixed standard of value for use in fairness opinions; rather, it "usually discusses the price and terms of the deal in the context of comparable transactions, drawing attention to strategic considerations that might make a particular transaction worth more of less than others."[15] Thus, at least Sweeny sees the fairness opinion as a combination of market value plus synergies. This is very different from fair value.

While a fairness opinion need not, but may be disclosed to the shareholders in the notice of the corporate action, current revisions to the MBCA have increased the disclosure requirements.[16] In 2007, the current version of the MBCA was amended to require the business to send the annual financial statements, not older than 16 months from the date of notice, and the latest quarterly financial statements.[17] This revision is designed to permit the shareholders to make an informed decision in seeking fair value under the appraisal statute.[18]

Fair value is the standard of value used in appraisal proceedings.[19] The shareholder has the right to dissent from the corporate action and receive the fair value of their interest.[20] The MBCA definition of fair value has changed dramatically between revisions. The current version of the MBCA defines fair value as:

> (i) immediately before the effectuation of the corporate action to which the shareholder objects;
>
> (ii) using customary and current valuation concepts and techniques generally employed for similar businesses in the context of the transaction requiring appraisal; and
>
> (iii) without discounting for lack of marketability of minority status except, if appropriate, for amendments to the articles [of incorporation] pursuant to section 13.02(a)(5).[21]

The 1999 MBCA definition is not yet as widely accepted as the 1984 MBCA definition.[22]

The 1984 definition reads:

> The value of the shares immediately before the effectuation of the corporate action to which the dissenter objects, excluding any appreciation or depreciation in anticipation of the corporate action unless exclusion would be inequitable.

The 1984 definition created a lot of ambiguity as to the proper valuation approaches to use and discounts to apply. This ambiguity spawned much litigation, and case law interpreting the definition is not in short supply.[23] Generally speaking, courts have interpreted the 1984 definition to mean 'a pro rata share of the business on the day before the dissented to event, exclusive of appreciation or depreciation arising from the dissented to event and exclusive of discounts for lack of control (minority interest) and lack of marketability.' However, some courts had considered the "exception circumstances exception"[24] in determining whether a discount for lack of marketability should apply.[25]

In summary, the standard of value is often fair value in an appraisal action, which will arise when a shareholder dissents from certain enumerated, proposed corporate actions. Whether fair value is the appropriate standard is a question of state law, and not all states have adopted the MBCA in any of its incarnations.[26] Thus, prior to completing a valuation, appraisers must first confirm which standard of value the hiring attorney will apply, and whether any particular nuances of state law may impact your valuation conclusion.

II. Shareholder Oppression Cases

The concept of fair value has frequently been imported into the discussion of shareholder oppression actions. But just what is an oppression case? Loosely, an oppression case manifests itself when a party in control of the corporation takes action to obtain benefits incident to ownership that are denied to the non-controlling shareholders.[27] Under the MBCA, oppression is a subpart of chapter 13, which deals with dissolution of the corporation. The statute reads in pertinent part:

§14.30 Grounds for Judicial Dissolution

The [name or describe court of courts] may dissolve a corporation:

    (2)   in a proceeding by a shareholder if it is established that:

        (i)   the directors are deadlocked ...

        (ii)   the directors or those in control of the corporation have acted, are acting, or will act in a manner that is illegal, oppressive, or fraudulent;

        (iii)   the corporate assets are being misapplied or wasted;

        (iv)   the shareholders are deadlocked ....

Upon a showing under any prong of §14.30(2) the court will dissolve the corporation. The corporation or any shareholder(s) may elect to avoid the dissolution by purchasing the complaining shareholder's interest at fair value provided that the corporation's stock is not publicly traded.[28] The shareholders are then given a fixed amount of time to determine amongst themselves the fair value of the stock, and if they cannot agree, the court will determine the fair value of the stock.[29]

It is important to note here, that "fair value" is not defined in Chapter 14 of the MBCA nor is it defined in MBCA §2.02, which defines the terms used in the MBCA. Therefore, there is no guarantee that fair value for Chapter 14 purposes carries the same definition as it does for Chapter 13 purposes.[30] However, several courts decided that there was no material difference between fair value for each section.[31] Nevertheless, the court does account for the oppressive, fraudulent, or illegal acts in calculating the fair value of the oppressed shareholder's interest.[32]

While fraud and illegality are self-explanatory, "oppressive" as used in §14.30(2)(ii) is not further defined in Chapter 14 nor in the definitions section of MBCA. Thus, it is up to each jurisdiction to determine what constitutes oppressive shareholder or director conduct. For example, in New York the standard is the reasonable expectations test: Have the non-controlling shareholder's reasonable expectations in committing his capital to the business at the time the capital was committed been frustrated.[33] This can be compared with Michigan law, which considers conduct impacting shareholders as shareholders.[34] Most jurisdictions adopting a version of the MBCA have either by statute or case law manufactured their own individual definition of "oppressive."

Not all states have adopted an oppression statute. Several states circumvent this by placing shareholders in closely held companies[35] in a fiduciary duty to one another akin to that of partners in a partnership.[36] Breach of that duty provides the complaining shareholder with an equitable remedy. An equitable remedy is one that the judge thinks is fair under the circumstances and in light of the purpose of the statute. In determining whether there has been a breach and what the remedy may be, courts have considered the reasonable expectations test.[37] This may include a forced buy out of the complaining shareholder at fair value or disgorgement, among many others.

In analyzing what is oppressive behavior, many courts have found a corporate freeze-out, denial of employment, and reverse stock mergers to be oppressive. Because the definition of oppression and the remedy is state- and fact-specific, it is important for the appraiser to understand the standards when adjusting a fair value determination for the wrongful acts, if that standard is appropriate.

III. Breach of Director's Fiduciary Duty

In contrast to the fiduciary duty arising in certain states between shareholders in a close corporation,[38] directors, whether they are or are not shareholders of the corporation, have a fiduciary duty of loyalty to the corporation.[39] This duty generally requires directors to avoid transactions with the company in which they have a conflict-of-interest.[40] In an action for breach of the directors' fiduciary duty of loyalty, the conflicted directors bear the burden of proving that the transaction was "fair to the corporation."[41] If the court finds that the transaction was entirely fair, then the conflicted directors are not liable for money damages notwithstanding the conflict.[42]

In satisfying the directors' burden, they must show that the transaction was entirely fair to the corporation. The entire fairness test[43] is a two prong analysis consisting of procedural and substantive fairness.[44] Procedural fairness is also known as fair dealing. Under this prong, a court considers "how the transaction was timed, initiated, structured, negotiated, and approved."[45] The imperfection in the process must be of "sufficient gravity" for there to be a finding of unfair dealing.[46] Substantive fairness, also known as fair price, "focuses on the economic and financial considerations of the transaction, including all relevant factors such as assets, market value, earnings, future prospects, and any other elements that affect the intrinsic or inherent value of the company's stock."[47] Furthermore, "In a non-fraudulent transaction, ... 'price may be the preponderant consideration outweighing other features of ... [the contested transaction].'"[48] While the prongs of the entire fairness test are addressed individually, they are also viewed in the aggregate. "[A]n ultimate determination of entire fairness requires these components to be considered in a unitary, non-bifurcated way."[49]

Often a fair price analysis involves a valuation of the business or businesses at issue. For example, in a stock-for-stock merger, "the test of fairness is whether 'the minority holder[s] .... [received] the substantial equivalent in value of what [they] have before."[50] This contrasts with the test involving a cash-out merger, which is "whether the chosen appraiser actually came up with a fair exit price for the minority."[51] While these are only two examples, the appropriate test to be applied will depend upon the circumstances of a particular case and the relief sought by the parties.

At least one court has recently drawn the distinction between fairness and fair value. In analyzing whether there was a breach of fiduciary duty involving interested director, who also controlled the subject company, the Colorado Court of Appeals noted, "[T]his is not a dissenters' rights action. It involved the question of whether a transaction was fair, not the "fair value" of dissenters' shares, and therefore is not governed by ... [the appraisal statute]."[52] The line between fairness and fair value blurs when the claims are consolidated.

IV. The Hybrid Action

Delaware also recognizes a hybrid action where the minority dissents from corporate action under the appraisal statute and bring a breach of fiduciary duty of loyalty claim against the directors of the company in a consolidated action. In both claims, the minority shareholders seek a remedy based on the fair value of the stock.

The plaintiff must prove both claims. The breach of fiduciary claim is usually handled first.[53] In assessing the breach of fiduciary duty claim, the defendant-directors must prove the transaction was entirely fair in spite of their alleged breach.[54] Once that is determined, if procedural fairness has not been proven, the court then considers the fair value question.

In analyzing the fair value question, two differences are important. First, the court considers fair value without the wrongful act. Thus, the court will consider whether the merger consideration adequately accounted for the value of potential claims or wrongdoing.[55] A second aspect of the remedy is that the court will "endeavor to resolve doubts, at the margins, in favor of the ... of the minority shareholders who were involuntarily squeezed out."[56]

Chapter 2: Background on Fair Value

V. Conclusion

In this overview, we have endeavored to provide the reader with an overview of the business corporation law giving rise to an appraisal of the subject company. In the appraisal community, these scenarios are often collectively referred to as "shareholder disputes."[57] While there may have been some dispute between the shareholders leading to the filing of the claim, the nature of the claim dictates the available remedies. The appraiser is well advised to seek the input of the engaging attorney regarding the specific remedy sought, the standard of value used in the jurisdiction, and whether any particular circumstances or factors may need to be accounted for in the valuation.

---

1. John J. Stockdale, Jr., Esq. is an associate with Schafer and Weiner, PLLC (Bloomfield Hills, MI) where he practices bankruptcy, corporate, and transactional law. He has been following valuation and damage computation cases since 1995. John graduated summa cum laude from Cooley Law School and earned a bachelor's degree at The Citadel. John can be reached at 248.540.3340.

2. Because there are 50 states, each with its own business corporation law, an exhaustive review of the law on a state-by-state basis is beyond the scope of this article. Therefore, we will assume that the default law is the 1999 Model Business Corporation Act. Where a particular state is implicated, it will be discussed. In general, it is incumbent upon each appraiser to communicate with the engaging attorney to ascertain the particular state law and standard of value applicable to any engagement.

3. *Lawson Mardon Wheaton, Inc. v. Smith*, 734 A.2d 738, 745 (N.J. 1999); *Matthew G. Norton Co., v. Smyth*, 51 P.3d 159, 163 (Wash. App. Div. 1 2002) (citing *Voeller v. Neilston Warehouse Co.*, 311 U.S. 531, 536 n. 6 (1941)). The abstract of the *Lawson Mardon Wheaton, Inc. v. Smith* and *Matthew G. Norton Co., v. Smyth* cases are included in the court case abstract section of this *Guide*, and the full-text decision can be found at BVLibrary.com.

4. *Id., Smyth* at 163.

5. *Id., Smyth* at 163.

6. MBCA §13.02(a)(1-8) (1999).

7. §13.02(b)(1)(i-ii). Not all jurisdictions follow the MBCA on this point. *Gholl v. Emachines, Inc.*, No. Civ. A. 19444-NC, 2004 WL 2847865 (Del. Ch. Nov. 24, 2004) (Delaware); *Boettecher v. IMC Mortgage*, 871 So.2d 1047 (Fla. App. 2 Dist. 2004)(Florida); *Miller Bros. v. Lazy River*, 709 N.Y.S.2d 162 (N.Y.A.D. 1 Dept. 2000)(NY); But the market price is presumed to be the fair value. *Appelbaum v. Avaya*, 812 A.2d 880 (Del. 2002).

8. See MBCA, Chapter 13.B (1999) (The procedure for perfecting appraisal rights is well beyond the scope of this article and will not be discussed further).

9. §8.30(b-e).

10. §8.30(e).

11. *Smith v. Van Gorkom*.

12. See MBCA §13 (1999); Paul Sweeny, *Who Says It's A Fair Deal—Fairness Opinions in Securities Disclosures*, J. Acc. PP (August 1999) ("Fairness opinions almost never are required as a matter of law....").

13. *Id.*

14. James R. Hitchner et al., Financial Valuation: Applications and Models, 13 (2003) [hereinafter, *Financial Valuation*].

15. Sweeny, *supra* note 11.

16. *Cf.* Official Comment to §13.20, Committee on Corporate Laws, ABA Section of Business Law, "Changes in the Model Business Corporation Act—Amendments Relating to Chapters 8 and 13," 62 Bus. Law. 3, 1062 (2007) (citing In re Pure Resources Inc. Shareholder Litigtaion, 808 A.2d 421 (Del. Ch. 2002)).

17. Committee on Corporate Laws, ABA Section of Business Law, "Changes in the Model Business Corporation Act—Amendments Relating to Chapters 8 and 13, 62 Bus. Law. 3, 1062 (2007).

Current Business Corporation Law and What it Means for the Business Appraiser

18. *Id.*
19. MBCA §13.01(4) (1999).
20. §13.02(a).
21. §13.01(4); §13.02(a)(5) (providing that "any other amendment to the articles of incorporation, merger, share exchange or disposition of assets to the extent provided by the articles of incorporation, by law or a resolution of the board of directors" triggers a shareholder's appraisal rights).
22. The 1984 definition is still followed at least 27 states. *Pueblo Bancorporation v. Lindoe*, 63 P.3d 353, 364-65 (Colo. 2003))(noting that 27 states follow 1984 MBCA definition, 5 follow 1999 definition) ; Int'l Assoc. of Comm. Administrators, Report of the Study Committee on an Omnibus Business Organizations Code (May 3, 2006), http://www.iaca.org/downloads/BOS/EntityLaw/Omnibus_CommitteeReport_050306.pdf (26 states).
23. *Pueblo Bancorporation, supra* note 18, at 366 (citing cases from diverse jurisdictions). The abstract of *Pueblo Bancorporation v. Lindoe* is included in the court case abstract section of this *Guide*, and the full-text decision can be found at BVLibrary.com.
24. ALI, Principles of Corporate Governance, §7.22 (a) (1992): The fair value of shares ... should be the value of the eligible holder's proportionate interest in the corporation, without any discount for minority status or, absent extraordinary circumstances, lack of marketability.
25. *Advanced Communication Design, Inc. v. Follett*, 615 N.W.2d 285 (Minn. 2000); *Lawson Mardon Wheaton, supra* at note 2; *Wenzel v. Hooper*, 779 N.E.2d 30 (Ind. App. 2002); *Matthew G. Norton Co., supra*; comp. *Pueblo Bancorporation, supra* note 18. The abstract of *Advanced Communication Design, Inc. v. Follett* is included in the court case abstract section of this *Guide*, and the full-text decision can be found at BVLibrary.com.
26. Of particular note is California, which adopts a fair value in liquidation standard, *Trahan v Trahan*, 120 Cal. Rptr.2d 814 (Cal. App. 1 Dist. 2002), and New York. The abstract *Trahan v Trahan* is included in the court case abstract section of this *Guide*, and the full-text decision can be found at BVLibrary.com.
27. Control is different than majority shareholder. *Trifad Entertainment v. Anderson*, 36 P.3d 363 (Mont. 2001) (minority shareholder charged with oppressive behavior); Hollis v. Hills, 232 F.3d 460 (5th Cir. 2000) (50% shareholder in control); *Leech v. Leech*, 762 A.2d 718 (Pa. Super. 2000) (same).
28. MBCA §14.34(a).
29. §14.34(c-d).
30. The recent divorce case of *Erp v. Erp*, __ 2.d ___, 2008 WL 818822 (Fla. 2 DCA 2008), underscored this point. In *Erp*, the court declined to analogize divorcing owners to dissenting shareholder and deny the application of discounts for lack of marketability; rather, the court found that the proper analogy was to dissolution in the event of deadlock, which gives the trial court discretion to apply or deny the discount. *Id.* at *4.
31. *Lawson Mardon Wheaton, supra* note 2, at 748; *Advanced Communication Design, supra* note 21, at 290-291; *Prentiss v. Wesspur, Inc.*, No. 36321-2-I, 1997 WL 207971 at *4 (Wash App Div 1 Apr. 28, 1997) (holding that in a freeze out situation, the minority shareholder "was either a dissenting shareholder, or stood in the place of a dissenting shareholder, as that term is used in Washington's revised business corporations act.").
32. *Id.*
33. *Matter of Kemp & Beatley, Inc.*, 64 N.Y.2d 63, 72-73 (1984).
34. *Franchino v. Franchino*, 687 N.W.2d 620 (Mich. App. 2004) (rejecting the reasonable expectations text); M.C.L.A §450.1489 (West. 1993 & Supp. 2006) (the 2006 amendment to §450.1489 attempted to correct for *Franchino* by including employment and other benefits as distributions, but did not remove the shareholders or shareholders language. This modification has not been interpreted).
35. Also called close corporations.
36. *Advanced Communication Design, supra* note 21, at 293-294 (holding that control, majority, or equal shareholders in a close corporation have fiduciary duties to one another); Brodie v. Jordan, 857 N.E.2d 1076, 1076 (citing *Donahue v. Rodd Electrotype Co.* of New England, Inc., 328 N.E.2d 505 (Mass. 1975));
37. *Brodie, supra* note 31, at 1879-1080 (discussing cases from diverse jurisdictions).
38. See *infra* at Part II.

Chapter 2: Background on Fair Value

39. MBCA §8.30, §8.31 (1999).
40. §8.31((a)(2)(iii-v); §8.60-8.63.
41. §8.61(b)(3).
42. *Emerald Partners v. Berlin*, No. Civ. A. 9700, 2003WL21003437 at *21 (Del. Ch. April 28, 2000)
43. This is the test adopted in Delaware. A majority of jurisdictions test fairness in conflicted director and controlling shareholder transactions by asking "whether or not under all the circumstances the transaction carries the earmarks of an arm's length bargain." *Kim v. The Grover C. Coors Trust*, No. 04CA0583, 2007 Colo. App. LEXIS 394, *12 (Colo. App. Mar. 8, 2007) (citing *Pepper v. Liton*, 308 U.S. 295, 306-7 (1939)). The majority test considers several factors including (1) did the corporation receive full value in the transaction, (2) Was the transaction in the corporation's interest, (3) was the corporation able to finance the transaction, (4) did the corporate officers "siphon off corporate gain," and (5) was there full disclosure. *Id.*
44. *Weinberger v. UOP,*; *Emerald Partners*, supra note 37, at *22 ; *Delaware Open MRI Radiology Assoc. v. Kessler*, 898 A.2d 290, 299 (Del. Ch. 2006). The abstract of *Delaware Open MRI Radiology Assoc. v. Kessler* is included in the court case abstract section of this *Guide*, and the full-text decision can be found at BVLibrary.com.
45. *Emerald Partners, supra* note 37, at *22.
46. *Id.* at *39.
47. *Id.* at *22.
48. *Delaware Open MRI, supra* note 39, at 311.
49. *Emerald Partners, supra* note 37, at *38.
50. *Id.* at *29.
51. *Delaware Open MRI, supra* note 39, at 312.
52. *Kim, supra* note 38, at *30-31.
53. *Delaware Open MRI, supra* note 39, at 312; *but see Andaloro v. PRPF Worldwide, Inc.*, No. Civ. A. 20336, 2005WL2045640 (Del. Ch. Aug. 19, 2005). The abstract of *Andaloro v. PRPF Worldwide, Inc* is included in the court case abstract section of this *Guide*, and the full-text decision can be found at BVLibrary.com.
54. *See supra* at Part III.
55. *Delaware Open MRI, supra* note 39, at 312; *Andaloro, supra* note 48, at *8.
56. *Delaware Open MRI, supra* note 39, at 313; *Andaloro, supra* note 48, at *9 ("Because of the relationship between the appraisal and the equitable actions, I have, at the margins, in fact resolved doubts in favor of the ... [minority shareholders]. In other words, the valuation I set forth is more optimistic than is strictly justified and takes into account ... [particular circumstances of this case].).
57. *Financial Valuation* at 577-592.

Recent Developments in Delaware Appraisal Cases

By John E. Hempstead, ASA, CFA and J. Mark Penny, ASA[1]

Introduction

Delaware has long been America's preferred state of incorporation. More than 800,000 business entities have their corporate legal home in Delaware, including more than 50% of all U.S. publicly-traded companies and 60% of the Fortune 500. Businesses choose Delaware because it boasts modern and flexible corporate laws and a highly-respected court system to interpret the laws.

Among the duties of the Delaware Court of Chancery is determining the value of the stock of companies involved in dissenting shareholder actions. Because of the prominence of the Delaware courts and the nationwide influence of their valuation decisions, business appraisers and investment bankers follow their opinions with interest.

We have taken a look at the last three years of Delaware appraisal cases, and will try to identify some of the trends and tendencies we have observed, looking at these opinions from the point of view of a business appraiser.

Appraisal Actions—Fair Value

Appraisal actions arise when minority shareholders elect to dissent from a corporate action. A common example of a corporate action that can give rise to an appraisal action is a merger transaction in which a shareholder is forced to give up his stock for cash or for stock in an acquiring corporation. In such a case, if the shareholder believes that the merger price is unfair and has perfected his dissenters' appraisal rights, he is entitled have the fair value of his stock determined by a court, and to receive fair value for his shares.

Fair value, in Delaware, has been defined as the measure of "that which has been taken from [the shareholder], viz. his proportionate interest in a going concern."[2] The courts have also said that the determination of fair value "must include proof of value by any techniques or methods which are generally considered acceptable in the financial community."[3] The corporation subject to valuation is viewed as a going concern "based on the 'operative reality' of the company at the time of the merger."[4] This value must be reached regardless of the synergies obtained from the consummation of the merger,[5] and cannot include speculative elements of value arising from the merger's "accomplishment or expectation."[6] The value of the shares may not, however, reflect discounts for lack of marketability or illiquidity.[7]

Chapter 2: Background on Fair Value

General Observations

We have reviewed eight appraisal cases from the Delaware Chancery Court handed down over the past three years. From this review, we can make the following general observations regarding what these judges are thinking when they are reviewing and performing valuations.

- The discounted cash flow approach to valuation seems to be the gold standard of valuation methods. All but two of the cases employed it as the principal approach.

- There is a high level of sensitivity to the role of synergy in merger transactions, and an effort to insure that the dissenting shareholder is not unjustly enriched by the inclusion of synergy value in the fair value determination.

- There is a clear effort to distinguish between minority interest value and a minority shareholder's proportionate interest in the value of the company as a whole. The latter is deemed fair value for purposes of a dissenting shareholder appraisal.

- There is a high level of interest by the court in the provenance of financial projections used in preparing a discounted cash flow analysis. Courts generally hold in low esteem projections which have been prepared specifically for the purpose of performing a contested valuation. Considerably more credibility is accorded to projections performed for another purpose unrelated to the valuation, or performed before it was known that there would be a contested valuation. *Crescent/Mach I v. Dr. Pepper*[8] deals at some length with this issue.

- The court has great interest in the "operative reality" of a company under appraisal, seeking to be careful to include in the entity to be valued the benefits that its shareholders could have reasonably expected to enjoy, had the merger not occurred. This theme was developed at some length in *Delaware Open MRI v. Kessler*.[9]

- Like other business appraisers, the Chancery Court has had to deal with the special valuation issues surrounding Sub S corporations. *Delaware Open MRI Radiology v. Kessler*[10] provides an extensive insight into its thinking on these matters.

- The treatment of capital gains tax in the terminal value of a company is an issue in *In re United States Cellular*.[11]

We will now turn to each case and discuss it in further detail. Our approach is from the vantage point of a business appraiser who may be called upon to furnish an opinion of value in a dissenting shareholder case. Therefore we have focused on those issues which arise routinely in such valuations. The table at the end of this article summarizes a number of salient facts from each case.

Highfields Capital v. AXA Financial[12] involved the valuation of a life insurance company, The MONY Group Inc., which was acquired in a public takeover at $31 per share by AXA Financial, Inc.

Recent Developments in Delaware Appraisal Cases

The court gave a 75% weight in his appraisal to the negotiated market price of the transaction ($31 per share), adjusted for shared synergies in the transaction of $4.12 per share. The synergy adjustment was based on adjusted estimates made by AXA actuaries. The remaining 25% weight in the valuation was accorded to a "sum-of-the-parts" analysis of MONY. This analysis consisted of (1) an actuarial appraisal of the life insurance and annuity business, (2) a blended comparable company and comparable transactions approach to value the broker-dealer subsidiary, (3) a weighted discounted cash flow and comparable metric to value MONY's asset management business, and (4) a standard accounting approach to value MONY's corporate assets and liabilities.

The court gave the predominant weight in its analysis to the actual deal price, less synergies, because it had satisfied itself that the price had been arrived at in an arm's-length manner, was publicly known, and that there had been an opportunity available for a higher bid to emerge, if it were warranted.

The "sum-of-the-parts" analysis was also employed because the court believed it "is standard procedure in the financial community when valuing an insurance conglomerate ...where no directly comparable companies or transactions exist."[13]

The final value reached by the court was $24.97 per share.

Crescent/Mach I v. Dr. Pepper Bottling Co. of Texas[14] involved the appraisal of shares of Dr. Pepper Holdings, Inc. (Holdings), acquired in a merger on October 8, 1999. The merger consideration was $25 per share. Dissenting shareholders produced an expert who valued the shares at $48.69. The respondent's expert valued the shares at $25.10. Both experts used a discounted cash flow approach to value. The principal difference between the two analyses was that the petitioners' expert used a projected revenue growth rate of 4% per annum, while the respondents' expert used a growth rate of 3%. Both sets of projections had been prepared by the company. The court spent much time analyzing the motives behind the preparation of the two sets of projections, finally basing its analysis on the 3% growth model, and arriving at a valuation of $32.31 a share.

The company's public trading price was ignored as being based on too thin a market.

In Re PNB Holding Co[15] concerned an appraisal action seeking to determine the fair value of the stock of PNB Holding Company (PNB), a rural Illinois bank holding company. The merger took place at $41 per share. Petitioners' expert opined a value of $61 per share; respondents, $40 per share, "depressingly familiar parentheses...within whose capacious bounds I am to identify a single estimate of PNB's value,"[16] according to Vice Chancellor Strine.

Both experts used discounted cash flow, comparable companies, and comparable transactions. The court ended up discarding the comparable company and comparable transaction approaches of both experts on the grounds that none of the comparables were sufficiently similar to PNB.

Chapter 2: Background on Fair Value

The two experts used very similar cash flow projections. The differences in their conclusions stemmed from (i) different discount rates, and (ii) the assumption by the defendants' expert that he was to do a minority share valuation in which the only cash flow return to be included in the analysis was that which was actually paid out in dividends to the shareholders.

The court prepared its own cash flow projection. It used a discount rate that consisted of a risk-free rate of 4.3%, to which was added an equity premium of 7.0% (multiplied by a beta of .69) and a size premium of 3.6%. The CAPM approach was equally weighted with a Fama-French calculation to produce an equity discount rate of 12%.

For a terminal value, the court used a Gordon Growth formula with a 5% terminal growth rate. The analysis valued all of the cash flow that was available for dividends, after providing for regulatory capital requirements, producing a value of $52.34 per share.

Delaware Open MRI v. Kessler[17] arose out of a squeeze-out merger in which a 62.5% shareholder group of a chain of radiology centers bought out a 37.5% group at a price of $16,228.55 per share. The minority group pursued its appraisal rights. At the time of the merger, the company was operating two radiology centers in Delaware (numbers I and II). It had plans to open three more in Delaware within the next few months (numbers III, IV and V).

The majority group presented an expert who valued the stock at $17,038.67 per share. The minority group expert valued the stock at $66,074 per share. Both experts used a discounted cash flow approach to value. A major point of disagreement between the experts was whether or not to include the cash flows from planned centers III, IV and V in the analysis. The minority expert did so, the majority expert did not.

Delaware law requires that in an appraisal, the value of the company should include "elements of future value, including the nature of the enterprise, which are known or susceptible of proof as of the date of the merger and not the product of speculation."[18] After considering the status of the planning process for centers III, IV, and V, the court concluded that these expansion plans were part of the "operative reality" of Delaware Radiology as of the merger date, and therefore must be included in the value determination.

The other major valuation issue in this case was how to handle the fact that the company was an S corporation for federal tax purposes and therefore did not itself pay federal income taxes. Taxes are paid by the shareholders on the company's income, whether distributed or not. The majority appraiser applied a 40% tax to the company's income in developing his cash flow analysis, treating it as if it were a C corporation for tax purposes. The minority appraiser, by contrast, asserted the proposition that because Delaware Radiology was an S corporation and faced no corporate level income taxes, its earnings should not be tax affected.

The court believed that both approaches were off the mark. It felt that the majority approach was unfair because it in effect denied the minority the very real tax benefit that it would have had as shareholders of an S corporation. It saw no circumstances in which it would be likely that Delaware Radiology would convert to a C corporation.

The minority approach to the S corporation issue was equally flawed, in the eyes of the court. It pointed out that if an S corporation were sold to a C corporation, the buyer would pay no premium for the S status because such status would be of no value to a C corporation buyer.

To resolve the differences between the two approaches to dealing with the S corporation issue, the court devised a tax adjustment factor which fell between the extremes of a full 40% tax affecting of earnings, as advocated by the majority expert, and a zero tax rate, as advocated by the minority expert. The adjustment factor was a hypothetical tax rate of 29.4%, a rate which if applied as a corporate level tax to a company which paid out all of its earnings, would produce an after-tax return to shareholders equivalent to what they would receive from an otherwise identical S corporation.

One other appraisal note is of interest in this case. The court employed a build-up approach to develop equity rates of return, accepting an industry rate-of-return adjustment in lieu of beta. It also employed a 2% subjective specific company risk premium. The court employed differing weighted average costs of capital for the separate radiology centers, based on their individual risk and leverage profiles.

The concluded value by the court was $33,232.26 per share.

Henke v. Trilithic[19] involved the appraisal of a small manufacturing company for purposes of a dissenting shareholder action. The company was involved in a stock-for-stock merger transaction. Petitioner's expert valued the equity of the company at $6,494,526. Respondent's expert valued it at $222,425. (one-thirtieth of the petitioner's figure). The judge, Parsons, commenting on the "remarkably divergent valuations,"[20] conducted his own appraisal and concluded a value of $805,586.

Petitioner's expert used a DCF approach to arrive at his value. Respondent's expert performed a DCF but did not employ it in his valuation, relying instead on an acquisition transaction entered into by the company four years earlier as a comparable value data point.

The judge felt that the petitioner had used unreasonably rosy projections in his analysis, rendering it unacceptable. Respondent's past transaction data point was also rejected as stale, and given no weight.

The court adopted respondent's DCF as a reasonable starting point for his own analysis, in part, because the projections had been prepared for another purpose, the negotiation of the payment schedule of a loan. "The ... projections were presented to a state government agency; presumably, Trilithic did not present false or misleading information to such an agency."[21] With various modifications, and an equity discount rate of 24%, the court arrived at an equity value of $805,586.

Andaloro v. PFPC Worldwide[22] This case arose out of a transaction where PNC Financial Services Group, Inc. acquired a minority interest in a subsidiary, PEPC Worldwide, Inc., by merging it into

Chapter 2: Background on Fair Value

another subsidiary in a cash squeeze-out merger. The transaction price was $34.26 per share. Both experts used the DCF approach to valuation. Respondent's expert also employed a comparable company approach. Petitioners' expert's valuation was $60.76 per share. Respondent's was $21.35.

Both experts relied on the same set of projections, which had been prepared by management. They differed in how they carried out the "out year" projections, namely those for the period after 2007, which was the last year in the management projections. The respondent's expert used a "two stage" approach, which employed a single growth rate for all the years past the management projection period. Petitioners' expert used a "three stage" model, projecting one growth rate for the four years past the management projection period, and another, lower, rate thereafter. Both methods attempt to capture the future growth prospects of the firm, while recognizing that eventually, firms cannot grow at rates that materially exceed the growth rate of the economy. The judge selected a three stage model, using a growth rate of 8% for 2008 through 2010, and 5% in perpetuity thereafter.

The experts also disagreed on the appropriate discount rate to use to discount the cash flows. Both used the CAPM approach, but used different sources for beta. The court used a risk free rate of 4.7%, a risk premium of 7.0%, a beta of 1.2 and a size premium of .82 to come up with a cost of equity of 13.92%, which he rounded down to 13.5% (to be generous to the plaintiffs, he said). The court's value based on the DCF approach was $32.08 per share.

The court also felt that it was appropriate to give consideration to the comparable company approach to value. It did so by examining the market prices of six similar companies and calculating their ratio of market value of capital to EBITDA and EBIT. Before applying these ratios to the subject company, however, he made an adjustment to the equity price of the public comparables in order to "adjust minority trading multiples to account for the implied discount, in order to accurately arrive at a fair value of the entire entity."[23] He pointed out that the control premium adjustment should be applied only to the equity portion of the capitalization, as it is derived from equity premiums observed in third party merger transactions. The judge applied a 38% premium to his comparable company valuations. He admitted to making no synergy adjustments, conceding that he was being generous to the petitioners. His final value, based on EBITDA multiples, was $34.99. He then gave this value 25% weight and the DCF value 75%, to arrive at a final value of $32.81.

Finklestein v. Liberty Digital[24] This case arose out of a merger of Liberty Digital Inc. with a subsidiary of Liberty Media Corporation. Shareholders received one-quarter of a share of Liberty Media Class A stock for each share of Liberty Digital; an implied value of $3.31 per share of Liberty Digital. The parties had agreed on the value of all of the assets of Liberty Digital save one, an Access Agreement with AT&T. This was described as an "agreement to agree" with AT&T, for that company to carry a certain number of cable channels on its cable system.

Petitioner's expert presented a DCF analysis that placed a value of $2.2 billion on the Access Agreement ($9.52 per share). The court rejected his analysis as being excessively optimistic. "The problems with his DCF analysis are so pervasive and numerous that it is impossible to describe all of them."[25] Respondent's expert valued the Access Agreement contract by using a precedent transactions analysis which, basically, compared what Liberty Digital would have had to pay for access absent the agreement and would therefore save by having it. His analysis produced a value of $2.51 per share. The court made certain adjustments to the analysis of the respondent's expert, and arrived at a value of $134.55 million which, when added to the stipulated value of the other assets, produced a value of $2.74 per share (compared to transaction consideration of $3.31 per share).

In re United States Cellular[26] This case is a consolidation of two statutory appraisal actions. United States Cellular, on October 31, 2000, acquired two cellular operating companies, Janesville Cellular Telephone Company, Inc. (Janesville) and Sheboygan Cellular Telephone Company, Inc. (Sheboygan) by means of short-form mergers with a wholly-owned subsidiary, United States Cellular Operating Company (USCOC). Janesville shareholders received $43.85 per share and Sheboygan shareholders, $21.45 per share. Petitioners' expert used a discounted cash flow and comparable transaction approach to value both companies. He derived a fair value recommendation of $72.89 for Janesville and $41.39 for Sheboygan. Respondent's expert also employed a discounted cash flow and comparable transaction approach. His analysis yielded values of $45.11 for Janesville and $22.05 for Sheboygan.

Both experts prepared forecasts covering a ten-year period. Among the points of disagreement between the appraisers was the choice of the weighted average cost of capital (WAAC). The petitioners' expert used US Cellular's actual historical cost, arriving at a discount rate of 11.43%. Respondent's expert argued for using the cost of capital of a "theoretical buyer" rather than an actual buyer, producing a WAAC of 12%. The court found the surviving company's cost of debt to be the most informative, and calculated a WAAC of 11.82% by substituting USCOC's cost of debt in a calculation based on US Cellular's capital structure.

Another issue to be resolved between the experts was the terminal growth rate of the cash flow projection. Petitioners' expert opted for a terminal growth rate of 6%, which he said equaled the overall economic growth rate. Respondent's expert used a terminal multiple approach. He said that operating profit multiples for mature communications companies typically range from 8 to 12 times EBITDA. He used a multiple of 8, based on below-average growth prospects. He also deducted capital gains taxes from a hypothetical sale of the companies.

The court concluded that the 8 times multiple overstated the maturity of the companies, and selected a multiple of 10 times EBITDA. The court also rejected the adjustment for capital gains taxes, commenting as follows. "This adjustment does not accurately reflect the intrinsic value of the Companies. Such a capital gains tax would be paid to the government by the shareholders, not the Companies. Moreover, such a capital gains tax should not affect the value of the Companies as a going concern."[27]

The court performed an extensive review of the comparable transactions put forward by the parties, finally selecting about a half dozen. Using a price per capita metric, he calculated values

Chapter 2: Background on Fair Value

for both companies. Finally, expressing greater confidence in the DCF approach than the comparable transaction approach, the court assigned a 70% weight to the DCF approach and a 30% weight to the comparable approach, producing a value of $54.00 per share for Janesville and $30.13 for Sheboygan.

---

1. Mr. John E. Hempstead and J. Mark Penny are Managing Directors of Hempstead & Co. Inc., Haddonfield, NJ.
2. *Tri-ContinentalCorp. v. Battye*, Del. Supr. *31 Del.Ch. 523,* 74 A. 2d 71,72, Del. Supr. (1950)
3. *Weinberger v. UOP, Inc.*, 457 A. 2d 701, Del. Supr., (Del. 1983)
4. *M. G. Bancorp, Inc. v. Le Beau*, 737 A. 2d 513, 524, Del. Supr. (Del.1999)
5. *M. P. M. Enters., Inc. v. Gilbert*, 731 A. 2d 790, 797, Del. Supr (Del. 1999)
6. 8 *Del. C.* § 292(h).
7. *Bell v. Kirby Lumber Corp.*, 413 A. 2d 137, 147 (Del. 1980)
8. *Crescent/Mach I v. Dr. Pepper Bottling Co. of Texas, 2007 WL 1342263, Del. Ch. 2007*; Not reported in A. 2d;
9. *Delaware Open MRI v. Kessler*, 898 A.2d 290, Del. Ch. 2006
10. *Id.*
11. *In re United States Cellular*, 2005 WL 43994, Del. Ch. 2005; Not reported in A.2d
12. *Highfields Capital v. AXA Financial*, 939 A.2d 34, Del Ch. 2007
13. *Id.*
14. *Crescent/Mach I v. Dr. Pepper Bottling Co. of Texas*, 2007 WL 1342263 (Del. Ch. 2007); Not reported in A.2d.
15. *In Re PNB Holding Co.*, 2006 WL 2403999; 32 Del. J. Corp 654, Not reported in A.2d
16. *Id.*
17. *Delaware Open MRI v. Kessler*, 898 A.2d, 290, Del. Ch. 2006
18. *Weinberger*, 457 A.2nd at 713, Del. Supr, (Del. 1983)
19. *Henke v. Trilithic*, 2005 WL 2899667, Del. Ch., 2005
20. 2*Id.*
21. *Id.*
22. *Andaloro v. PFPC Worldwide*, 2005 WL 2045640, Del. Ch. 2005; Not reported in A.2d)
23. *Id.*
24. *Finklestein v. Liberty Digital*, (Del. Ch. April 25, 2005) – no citation available
25. *Id.*
26. *In re United States Cellular*, 2005 WL 43994, Del. Ch. 2005)
27. *Id.*

Recent Developments in Delaware Appraisal Cases

Table referenced on page 2-32

BVR ARTICLE ILLUSTRATION

CASE		VALUATION APPROACH		COST OF CAPITAL			TERMINAL ASSUMP		VALUES (PER SHARE)			
JUDGE	OPINION DATE	METHOD	WEIGHT	RATE	BASIS	METHOD	GRWTH RATE	MULTIPLE	TRANSACTION	PETITIONER	RESPONDENT	COURT
Highfields Capital v. AXA Financial Lamb	8/17/2007	Adjusted deal price "Sum of parts" approach	75% 25%	N/A N/A			N/A N/A		$31.00	$37-47	$21.00	$24.97
Crescent/Mach I v. Dr. Pepper Noble	5/2/2007	Discounted cash flow	100%	9.75%	WAAC	CAPM	3%		25.00	48.69	25.10	32.31
In re PNB Holding Co. Strine	8/18/2006	Discounted cash flow	100%	12%	EQ	CAPM(1)	5%		41.00	61.00	40.00	52.34
Delaware Open MRI Radiology v. Kessler Strine	4/26/2006	Discounted cash flow	100%	15.57-18.79%	WAAC	BUILD-UP	4%		16,228.55	66,074	17,038.67	33,232.26
Henke v. Trilithic Parsons	10/28/2005	Discounted cash flow	100%	24%	EQ	BUILD-UP	5%		N/A	2,164.84	74.14	217.02
Andaloro v. PFPC Worldwide Strine	8/19/2005	Discounted cash flow Comparables	75% 25%	13.50% N/A	EQ	CAPM	5% N/A		34.26	60.76	21.35	32.81
Finklestein v. Liberty Digital Strine	4/25/2005	Precedent transactions	100%	N/A			N/A		3.31	9.52	2.51	2.74
In re United States Cellular Parsons	1/6/2005											
Janesville		Discounted cash flow Comparables	70% 30%	11.82% N/A	WAAC	Acquirer's cost of capital	N/A	10X EBITDA	43.85	72.89	45.11	54.00
Sheboygan		Discounted cash flow Comparables	70% 30%	11.82% N/A	WAAC		N/A	10X EBITDA	21.45	41.39	22.05	30.13

N/A - NOT APPLICABLE
WAAC - WEIGHTED AVERAGE COST OF CAPITAL
EQ - EQUITY COST OF CAPITAL
(1) - EQUALLY WEIGHTED WITH FAMA-FRENCH METHOD

When Nothing Else Fits it Must be Fair Value

By R. James Alerding, CPA/ABV, ASA, CVA and
H. Edward Morris, Jr., ASA, CBA, BVAL, CPA/ABV

While reviewing a number of recent court cases, it became apparent to us the terms "fair value" and "fair market value" were often being used interchangeably, which creates confusion for everyone, including some valuation professionals. The courts haven't helped as they often mix and match the terms and underlying methodologies to support a given opinion. As a result, we decided to review the available information to gain a better understanding of what may be generating the confusion and what we as valuation professionals might do to provide some clarity. In essence, we would "peel the onion" and look at the issue layer by layer in the context of martial dissolution.

We began our analysis by approaching it as would most individuals interested in learning about a new topic: we went to the Internet and searched for the term "fair value" using Google. Our search returned 63,500,000 results, which included links to "fair value accounting" (we'll ignore these for the moment). With so many search results, we felt the place to begin was with the "definition" of the term, so we followed the links to the Merriam-Webster and Wikipedia online dictionaries. Following the link to the Merriam-Webster definition revealed that the result of the search was the definition of "fair market value," not "fair value," which it defined as:

> "a price at which buyers and sellers with a reasonable knowledge of pertinent facts and not acting under any compulsion are willing to do business."

Since this was admittedly "fair market value" and not "fair value," we then utilized the Wikipedia link which provided the following definition:

> Fair value, also called fair price (in a commonplace conflation of the two distinct concepts), is a concept used in finance and economics, defined as a rational and unbiased estimate of the potential market price of a good, service, or asset, taking into account such objective factors as:
>
> - acquisition/production/distribution costs, replacement costs, or costs of close substitutes
> - actual utility at a given level of development of social productive capability
> - supply vs. demand
>
> and subjective factors such as
>
> - risk characteristics
> - cost of capital
> - individually perceived utility

When Nothing Else Fits it Must be Fair Value

In accounting, fair value is used as an estimate of the market value of an asset (or liability) for which a market price cannot be determined (usually because there is no established market for the asset). Under GAAP (FAS 157), Fair Value is the amount at which the asset could be bought or sold in a current transaction between willing parties, or transferred to an equivalent party, other than in a liquidation sale. This is used for assets whose carrying value is based on mark-to-market valuations; for assets carried at historical cost, the fair value of the asset is not used. One example of where fair value is an issue is a College kitchen with a cost of $2 million which was built 5 years ago. If the owners wanted to put a fair value on the kitchen it would be of subjective nature because there is no active market for such items.

This introduced a new term we weren't familiar with—"fair price." Additionally, it introduced the layperson to the concept of "fair value" according to the accountants. The accountants didn't like some of the baggage associated with the term "fair market value," so they created their own definition as documented in Statement of Financial Accounting Standard 157, *Fair Value Measurements* as follows:

> The amount at which an asset (or liability) could be bought (or incurred) or sold (or settled) in a current transaction between willing parties, that is, other than in a forced or liquidation sale.

Based on this initial research, we began to understand why people were confused about the term "fair value" and decided to use our resources as valuation professionals to find out what the real definition was according to the intellectuals of the business valuation profession. Where else would such a search begin but with the writings of the godfather of business valuations, Dr. Shannon P. Pratt.

In Dr. Pratt's book, *Valuing a Business*,[1] he and his co-authors state the following:

> "To understand what the expression fair value means, you have to know the context of its use. For certain bookkeeping applications, fair value is defined in the relevant accounting literature. In business valuation, the term fair value is usually a legally created standard of value that applies to certain specific transactions.
>
> In most states, fair value is the statutory standard of value applicable in cases of dissenting stockholders' appraisal rights. It is also commonly used in valuations in state minority oppression cases, which have been on the rise.
>
> ...In states that have adopted the Uniform Business Corporation Act, the definition of fair value is as follows:
>
>> "Fair Value," with respect to a dissenter's shares, means the value of the shares immediately before the effectuation of the corporate action to which the dissenter objects,

Chapter 2: Background on Fair Value

> excluding any appreciation or depreciation in anticipation of the corporate action unless exclusion would be inequitable.[2]
>
> Even in states that have adopted this definition, there is no clearly recognized consensus about the interpretation of fair value in this context, but published precedents established in various state courts have not equated it directly to fair market value."

Although interesting, the above didn't add much clarity. As a result, we looked at another common reference—the *Business Valuation Body of Knowledge, Exam Review and Professional Reference,* which included the following:[3]

> Characteristics of fair value:
>
> - Only a little more that half of the states have precedential cases interpreting the fair value standard
>
> - Of those that have such precedential cases, certain issues, particularly applicability of discount for minority interest and lack of marketability vary widely
>
> - Some states (including Delaware) do not allow discounts for either minority interest or lack of marketability (Delaware tends to emphasis the value of a proportionate share of a going concern)
>
> - Some states either consistently apply or consistently reject discounts for marketability for minority interest
>
> - Some states have said that the treatment of minority and marketability discount is left to the discretion of the court to be determined on a case-by-case basis
>
> - Although the seller may not be assumed to be knowledgeable, the valuation will be based on the assumption that the seller or the seller's representative has reasonable knowledge

Dr. Pratt was the author of both of the above referenced books but we didn't see much clarity in those definitions for our purposes.

We then went to the resources available to us via the Business Valuation Resources ("BVR") website and its *Business Valuation Library*. There we found an article entitled "Fair Value versus Fair Market Value: A Detailed Overview for BV Experts," written by Jay Fishman, William Morrison and Shannon Pratt and published in the February 2009 edition of the *Deluxe Business Valuation Update*™ newsletter. This article begins with the definition of the term "fair value" and follows its evolution from the 1800s to the present. Unfortunately, the majority of article focuses on "fair market value" with some discussion of "fair value" but no clear definition. However, we found another book written by Fishman, Pratt and Morrison entitled *Standards of Value,* which defined fair value as:

> Fair Value is a legislative and judicial concept applied in shareholder dissent and oppression cases. It is determined on a state-by-state basis and is used by some states as the appropriate standard of value in determining the value of a business or business interest for marital dissolution cases. Generally, Fair Value is defined as fair market value without minority and marketability discounts and represents the cash price dissenting and oppressed shareholders will receive in exchange for their shares of stock.[4]

Another article in BVR's *Business Valuation Library* was "Fair Value in Marital Dissolution: Case Law" by Noah Gordon, which summarized court decisions in a variety of states. In the introductory paragraphs Mr. Gordon states:

> "Fair value cases can be identified by certain traits that they do, or do not, possess. For example, if a valuation takes a pro-rata portion of the enterprise value without lack of control or lack of marketability discounts, it can be inferred that the standard of value used is fair value. Similarly, if a case uses the concept of an unwilling buyer or unwilling seller, such use suggest that fair value is the standard of value being applied. A case that includes enterprise goodwill, or includes goodwill without necessarily distinguishing between personal and enterprise goodwill, and that rejects discounts, also suggests that the court is using a fair value standard."

Mr. Gordon goes on to highlight approximately 15 court decisions in various states supporting this variety of definitions.[5] This approach works backwards by identifying certain traits of fair value cases rather than a specific definition.

So what is the answer to the question "What is the definition of Fair Value?" The answer is "It depends!"

It is our observation that the term "fair value" is often bootstrapped by courts over to the arena of marital dissolution. Once there, it takes on the persona of the Hydra. It becomes the many headed monster that can mean whatever the court determines it to mean. Often, the marital courts simply adopt the fair market value term also and intermingle it with fair value. The lesson to be learned by all of this is that there really is no "standard of value" in marital dissolution. The courts may call it fair value or fair market value, but it is really whatever the courts want it to be. This is why, in our opinion, there are so many diverse opinions in the various marital courts and why there have evolved so many different heads of the Hydra in marital dissolution valuation cases. There is entity goodwill and personal goodwill; S Corp tax-affecting issues; discounting and no discounting, and other tangents. All of this in the name of fair value or fair market value.

To us fair value is a catch-all for anything that doesn't fit into the other standards of value[6] and may simply be "the value considered fair and equitable by the trier of the facts."

Chapter 2: Background on Fair Value

1. Pratt, Reilly, Schweihs, *Valuing a Business,* fourth edition, page 32
2. Oregon Revised Statutes, Section 60.551(4)
3. Pratt, *Business Valuation Body of Knowledge, Exam Review and Professional Reference,* page 30
4. Fishman, *Standards of Value,* 89
5. *BVR's Guide to Fair Value in Shareholder Dissent, Oppression and Marital Dissolution.* Mr. Gordon's article, "Fair Value in Marital Dissolution: Case Law," is available in this *Guide.*
6. Fair market value, Investment value, Intrinsic or Fundamental value per Pratt, Reilly, Schweihs, Valuing a Business, fourth edition, 28-32.

The World According to Delaware Chancery: A Vice Chancellor Offers Ten Tips to Appraisers[1]

At the recent AICPA National Business Valuation conference in Austin, an attendee was trying to get the attention of Dr. Shannon Pratt—when he turned and introduced her to Vice Chancellor Donald F. Parsons of the Delaware Chancery Court. "It was like meeting the equivalent of a U.S. Supreme Court Justice," she said. "I was overwhelmed."

Indeed, the Delaware Chancery is renowned among business appraisers and attorneys as the forum to which many states defer on corporate matters, as its five Vice Chancellors have been entrusted with the development of Delaware General Corporate Law since 1792. The Chancery Court hears no criminal or jury trials, but as a court of equity, is empowered to issue temporary injunctions and declaratory judgments—including those in judicial appraisal actions.

Judge is sole determiner of fair value

The history of Delaware appraisals began in 1943, according to Vice Chancellor Parsons, when a statute introduced judicial review into the appraisal process. Subsequent amendments have made the presiding judge the sole determiner of fair value—which is the standard in Delaware Chancery appraisal actions, Parsons reminded his AICPA audience, citing last year's *Finkelstein* case (see sidebar). "We value the firm as a going concern, specifically recognizing its market position and future prospects."

Appraisal actions "present huge challenges to the court," as they require familiarity with finance theory and valuation methodology. "None of us is a CPA or has been in private BV practice," he said. "But we are reasonably intelligent, diligent about our jobs and do our best to understand the law and the evidence in the case."

Neal Beaton, CPA/ABV, CFA, ASA (Grant Thornton LLP, Seattle), who participated in Parsons' session, cited his experience in the recent *Gesoff v. IIC Industries Inc.*, in which V.C. Lamb had a "total command of valuation theory," he said, including some esoteric valuation issues. (See the Sept. and Oct. 2006 *BVUs* for more on Gesoff and Beaton's expert insights.)

Beaton also brought up the very recent *In re Nellson Nutraceutical, Inc.*, where a federal bankruptcy court struck a valuation expert's DCF analysis under *Daubert*. "I ran that opinion by the other judges," Parsons said, and they agreed that a *Daubert* hearing is rare in any bench trial—and would be "fairly extreme" in the Delaware Chancery. But he alerted appraisers to the primary issue in *Nutraceutical*: The expert had apparently become so partisan, that his opinion became "worthless."

Chapter 2: Background on Fair Value

Top ten suggestions for presenting appraisals

Appearing in the Delaware Chancery Court can be "a little like Alice in Wonderland," Parsons said. To help business appraisers present valuation evidence with the greatest likelihood of success, he offered these "top ten" suggestions—which broadly apply to expert testimony in any judicial forum:

#10. *Be familiar with Delaware law and the judge's prior decisions.* "We don't look that frequently to the law in other states," Parsons said, "because very few have developed the statutory scheme we have—and fair value is always dependent on statute particulars."

Appraisers should know which valuation methods have met with the Court's prior approval; a new or less-favored method requires a well-prepared explanation. "I don't go into a case saying, 'I'll never use a company specific risk premium,'" Parsons said; it depends on the facts presented—and "persuasive reasoning" by the experts.

Beaton brought the point home by describing the cross-examination of an opposing expert in *Gesoff*. "Judge Lamb had a specific opinion on the use of management financials," Beaton said, "and he interrupted the witness at one point to caution: 'Make sure you know how I ruled before answering.'"

#9. *Prepare an effective report.* "Explain how the company makes money and tell a persuasive story concerning your valuation," Parsons said. Describe your approaches and methods; explain the inputs and assumptions; and determine an appropriate weight for each method. If a particular method is not appropriate, be prepared to explain. "Mistakes and last-minute changes undermine credibility."

The report should be in plain, understandable terms—"but feel free to use charts, graphs, and CDs with spreadsheets." Take advantage of your attorneys' resources, "but don't bury us with paper."

#8. *Critique opponent's report or prepare alternate valuation?* This is a tactical decision, and "sensitivity analysis is critical." In *Finkelstein*, for example, the Vice Chancellor (Strine) rejected one expert's report, but as the same expert had failed to critique the opposing report, the Court was left with "nothing to go on."

#7. *Post-valuation synergies.* May an appraiser consider post-merger information? "Normally—no," Parsons said. Section 262(h) of the Delaware statute excludes "any element of value [such as synergies] arising from the accomplishment or expectation of the merger." But appraisers may consider all facts that are "known or knowable" as of the date of the merger.

Parsons cited *Gholl v. eMachines, Inc.* (2004), where the company had completely changed its way of doing business eleven months before going private—and so there was only 11-months of real data. In reviewing several management projections, the Court (in an opinion by Parsons) selected a post-merger budget plan, which nevertheless was "primarily completed" by the merger date and contained facts "known or knowable" at the time.

#6. Reliability of projections. The *eMachines* case emphasizes the Court's preference for contemporaneous management projections, especially those prepared in the ordinary course. "You're not doing your job if you don't question the managers (and the attorneys) you're working with," Parsons said. Projections prepared when a fairness opinion or deal is in the offing are generally less reliable.

#5. Be prepared to justify a DCF. All inputs and aspects of a discounted cash flow analysis will come under scrutiny, including the discount rate and its inputs (WACC, cost of equity and debt) and the terminal value (growth in perpetuity model and exit multiples model). "Make sure that it all holds together."

#4. Implicit minority discount (IMD). When is it appropriate to factor in the IMD? A current working paper by U. Penn's Lawrence Hamermesh[2] calls the IMD a "doctrinal weed" in the soil of Delaware appraisal law:

[The basic premise] posits that, no matter how liquid and informed the financial markets may be, all publicly traded shares persistently and continuously trade in the market at a substantial discount relative to their proportionate share of the value of the corporation.

The academics fail to find "a single piece of financial or empirical scholarship" affirming the IMD. But the Delaware Chancery is still researching the issue. "I don't know how the debate will come out," Parsons said, "but I will take it seriously, listen and see who has the most persuasive argument."

#3. Check your 'reality-checks.' Market prices, control premiums, evidence of a "thorough and fair auction," etc.—in many cases, the Court has found these "reality" or reasonableness checks helpful.

#2. Don't forget interest. The Delaware Chancery often derives the compensatory interest rate from equal weightings of the "prudent investor rate" and the corporation's cost of debt. As the parties bear the burden of proof, appraisers should assist with this calculation, or—absent reliable evidence, the Court will use the statutory rate of 5%.

#1. Be skeptical and independent. V.C. Parsons once again cited *eMachines*, where the corporation's COO had tried to characterize the budget plan (eventually adopted by the Court) as a "hail Mary, triple reverse, flea-flicker with a pass to the quarterback in the end zone." Despite the company having produced the baseline budget in the ordinary course of business, during the trial, its appraiser had "jumped on the litigation team" and become an advocate instead of an independent analyst.

"The more you do that," Parsons warned, "the less likely you'll be able to persuade the Court—at least the Delaware Chancery." But the caution applies to most litigation settings, where appraisers who get "too cozy" with their own side risk losing their credibility.

Chapter 2: Background on Fair Value

World according to *Finkelstein*

In the recent case *Finklestein v. Liberty Digital*, (April, 2005), V.C. Strine provided this simple illustration of applying the fair value standard in Delaware Chancery actions:

In the real world, if a firm is worth $100, has 100 shares, and one stockholder owns 51 shares, and 49 other people each own one share, the 51 shares, as a bloc, could be worth $70 and the remaining shares worth $30. But in the world of [Delaware Chancery] appraisal, the 49 shares are worth $49.

"We realize this is not what the Tax Court does," Parsons noted, "but it is what the Delaware Chancery does."

---

1. *Business Valuation Update*, January 2007. Reprinted with permission from Business Valuation Resources
2. Hamermesh, Lawrence A. and Wachter, Michael L., "The Short and Puzzling Life of the 'Implicit Minority Discount' in Delaware Appraisal Law" (February 27, 2007). U of Penn, Inst for Law & Econ Research Paper No. 07-01. Visit BVLibrary.com for a copy of this article.

Fairness in Delaware Freezeout Transactions: How Two Discrepant Legal Standards Affect Valuations[1]

By *Gilbert E. Matthews, CFA and Michelle Patterson, JD, PhD*[2]

Delaware courts are currently applying two discrepant legal standards of fairness to freezeouts of minority shareholders. This article addresses their development and their impact on fairness opinions and valuations.

CONTRASTING STANDARDS OF FAIRNESS IN FREEZEOUTS

When control shareholders (controllers) take a company private by acquiring all the shares held by minority public shareholders, the transaction is described as a freezeout.[3] The two common formats for control shareholders of Delaware corporations to effectuate a freezeout are (a) the traditional one-step negotiated long-form merger (negotiated freezeouts) and (b) the newer two-step freezeout structured as a tender offer followed by a short-form merger (freezeout tender offers), which began being used in 2001.

Under current Delaware law, different standards of legal review for fairness are applied to these two forms even though their function – taking a company private – is the same.[4] Paradoxically, a controller who undertakes the traditional long-form freezeout and negotiates the merger terms with the target's independent directors is held to a higher standard of fairness than when the controller chooses to act unilaterally via a short-form freezeout tender offer.

The standard for the negotiated going-private transaction is a "strict scrutiny" review for "fairness" called "Entire Fairness." This review is both broad and exacting. The court looks at the fairness of the entire transaction by assessing not only whether minority shareholders were dealt with fairly – "fair dealing" – but also whether they received a "fair price" for being frozen out of their shareholdings. "Fair dealing" involves how the transaction was timed, initiated, structured, negotiated, disclosed and approved, and "fair price" includes all elements of value.[5]

Entire Fairness (fair dealing plus fair price) review is friendlier to minority shareholder plaintiffs than the "Business Judgment Rule" review which the Chancery Court has held to be the appropriate standard for the newer freezeout tender offers. The combined effect of two 2001 decisions, one by the Supreme Court in *Unocal Exploration*[6] and the other by the Court of Chancery in *Siliconix*,[7] was to make it possible for a control shareholder to avoid the negotiated freezeout's Entire Fairness standard by choosing the two-step freezeout tender offer. The Supreme Court has not yet ruled on whether controllers who use this new format get to avoid entire fairness scrutiny. The Supreme Court, in fact, "has never had an occasion to rule on the issue of what equitable standard of review applies in a tender offer freezeout."[8] Nevertheless, transaction planners and controllers, relying on the Court of Chancery's decisions, are increasingly availing themselves of this newer form of freezeout.

The Business Judgment Rule is considered "deferential" to corporate management because, under this standard, courts commonly defer to directors' and officers' judgment. When Business Judgment is applied, the freezeout is reviewed *only* in terms of "fair dealing," not "fair price." This narrower scope makes it difficult for plaintiffs to challenge the transaction. Thus, the Business Judgment review applied in the unilateral freezeout tender offer is friendlier to the controller. As a result, control shareholders are utilizing the freezeout tender offer format with increasing frequency in order to "freeze out" minority shareholders and achieve 100% ownership.

ENTIRE FAIRNESS IS THE SETTLED AND EXCLUSIVE STANDARD OF REVIEW FOR NEGOTIATED FREEZEOUTS

In 1994, the Delaware Supreme Court ruled in *Lynch*[9] that the stringent Entire Fairness test is the exclusive standard of review when a controller acquires the minority's shares through a negotiated freezeout, because it views these transactions as "presenting a risk of self-dealing by controllers."[10] Indeed, the Delaware Courts

> ... have long reviewed minority shareholder challenges to such pre-approved freeze outs under the exacting "entire fairness" standard [*footnote omitted*], reasoning that conflicts of interest faced by the controlled corporation's board of directors (who approve the transaction on the minority's behalf), along with the controlling shareholder's coercive capabilities, preclude application of the more deferential business judgment form of review.[11]

Moreover, in these freezeouts, the controller is often able to take the company private by voting its majority shares in favor of the merger without *any* vote by the minority.

Under Entire Fairness, there is an important shift in the ordinary litigation process that works to the advantage of the minority shareholder plaintiff. In most litigation, the plaintiffs bear the burden of proving their case. In contrast, with Entire Fairness, controller defendants have the burden of showing that their transactions were, in fact, fair. The law imposes this burden because the controller is seen as a conflicted, interested party. Nevertheless, there is a way for the controller to shift the burden back to the plaintiff. There is an "established equitable practice of allowing ratification by disinterested directors ... to insulate a self-dealing transaction from strict scrutiny for fairness [*footnote omitted*]."[12] If disinterested directors approve a corporate action, the courts usually allow the business action to be reviewed under the deferential Business Judgment Rule. However, because of the courts' concern regarding mergers by control parties, *even if* disinterested director approval is present, the review for fairness in negotiated freezeouts remains the broader Entire Fairness.

The courts, however, recognize under Entire Fairness the potentially minority-protective value of independent director and shareholder ratification, and afford the controller who provides for these in its transaction the benefit of being able to shift the burden of proof back to the plaintiff. The controller must show that its negotiated freezeout included *either* of two procedural safeguards:

(a) a special committee of independent directors of the subsidiary with the ability to block the transaction (independent committee approval) **or**

(b) a condition that an informed majority of the minority shareholders approve the transaction (majority of the minority approval).

Since a minority shareholder's challenge remains under the Entire Fairness standard, the Chancery Court must undertake a comprehensive and stringent review of price and dealing with no possibility for an early dismissal of the case. Thus, a defending controller cannot avail itself of the business judgment rule regardless of what procedurally fair steps it follows in its freezeout transaction.

FREEZEOUT TENDER OFFERS ARE SUBJECT TO BUSINESS JUDGMENT RULE REVIEW IF NONCOERCIVE AND IF DISCLOSURE IS ADEQUATE

Freezeout tender offers have become more popular since the Chancery Court ruled that they would be reviewed under the Business Judgment Rule rather than Entire Fairness unless the offer is coercive or material information is withheld (as discussed later). The Supreme Court in *Unocal Exploration* (2001) clarified the standard for review for short-form mergers, ruling that for short-form mergers, appraisal is the exclusive remedy available to a minority stockholder complaining of unfairness. The Court of Chancery ruled in *Siliconix* that the business judgment rule applied to a freezeout tender offer. The combined effect of *Unocal Exploration* and *Siliconix* was to enable a control shareholder to avoid the more exacting Entire Fairness standard applicable to a negotiated transaction by using the two-stage freeze-out process: a tender offer for enough outstanding shares to attain 90% ownership, followed by a short-form merger.

Neither Entire Fairness Nor the Business Judgment Rule Is Applicable to Short-Form Mergers—Minority Shareholders' Only Remedy is Appraisal

Delaware General Corporate Law §253 authorizes the corporate owner of 90% or more voting stock of a company to merge the subsidiary into itself without any requirement that the subsidiary's board of directors approve the merger (a "short-form merger").[13] *Unocal Exploration* held that Entire Fairness was not applicable to short-form mergers conducted under §253. The Supreme Court took note of the fact that a parent corporation and its directors are self-dealing fiduciaries who, under settled principles, would be required to establish Entire Fairness in a freezeout transaction, but said that §253, as written by the Legislature, does not hold them to do so. The court acknowledged that §253's merger procedure is inconsistent with customary notions of fair dealing.

Chapter 2: Background on Fair Value

In a short-form merger, there is no agreement of merger negotiated by two companies; there is only a unilateral act - a decision by the parent company that its 90% owned subsidiary shall no longer exist as a separate entity. The minority stockholders receive no advance notice of the merger; their directors do not consider or approve it; and there is no vote.[14]

Because minority shareholders are not entitled to an Entire Fairness judicial review, they are not entitled to the equitable remedies that an Entire Fairness review provides. The court held that "absent fraud or illegality, appraisal is the exclusive remedy available to a minority stockholder who objects to a short-form merger."[15]

Business Judgment Rule, Not Entire Fairness, Is the Standard for Noncoercive Freezeout Tender Offers

Also in 2001, a Chancery Court case provided the answer to the question of what the standard of judicial review for fairness would be if a controller combined a tender offer with a short-form merger to take a company private—the tender offer freezeout. Vice Chancellor Noble ruled that the control shareholder could acquire minority shares in a tender offer without the recommendation of the subsidiary's board of directors. He concluded that the controller had no duty to demonstrate Entire Fairness *unless* coercion or disclosure violations occurred, and that the appropriate standard of review was business judgment accompanied by the usual fiduciary duties imposed on controlling parties. However, Entire Fairness would be invoked if the offer were "coercive."

Vice Chancellor Strine subsequently defined "coercive" in *Pure Resources* (2002), ruling that a freezeout tender offer would be deemed coercive unless

(a) it was subject to a non-waivable condition that no shares would be accepted unless an informed majority of the minority tendered,
(b) the controller committed to a prompt short-form merger at the same price if it reached 90% ownership, and
(c) there were no threats of retribution if the offer was not accepted.[16]

Strine later made clear in *Cox* (2005) that a coercive tender offer could be subject to Entire Fairness if the controller did not conduct the transaction in conformity with a high level of fiduciary duty. He said that a noncoercive tender offer "requires the equivalent of an informed, uncoerced majority of the minority vote condition for a controller to avoid entire fairness review."[17]

Strine also ruled in *Pure* that (a) the target company should be allowed and enabled to set up an independent director committee, (b) the committee should review the controller's merger terms and make a recommendation, and (c) disclosure should include a summary of the substantive work performed by the financial advisor.[18] Strine's ruling has resulted in increased use of financial advisors in this form of freezeout.

IMPACT OF FAIRNESS STANDARDS ON VALUATIONS

When a controller proposes a going-private transaction, independent directors customarily retain financial advisors to value the minority shares and to render fairness opinions, thereby assisting the directors in carrying out their fiduciary duties. Delaware courts have recognized the value to independent directors and shareholders of fairness opinions and their underlying valuations. Indeed, the courts view the obtaining of these opinions as evidence of the directors' fulfillment of their obligations.

The financial advisor must consider the format of a Delaware freezeout that is being valued because the standard of fairness that will be applied affects the value of the minority shares. The remedy available to minority shareholders who believe that the price offered is inadequate also impacts fairness.

Fairness Opinions and Valuations in Negotiated Freezeouts

As discussed above, a negotiated freezeout is subject to Entire Fairness. The remedy for minority shareholders as a class is to receive "fair price," which the Supreme Court defined in *Weinberger* as "all relevant factors: assets, market value, earnings, future prospects, and any other elements that affect the intrinsic or inherent value of a company's stock."[19] This decision enabled the valuator to use forward-looking valuation methods in Delaware courts, and to use valuation approaches generally used by practitioners rather than the outmoded Delaware Block Method.

The valuation for a fairness opinion in a negotiated freezeout is similar to the analysis that a valuator undertakes for an arms'-length transaction with a third party with one exception. The exception is that the valuator should not apply a control premium to the minority shares because the controller already has control. The control premium to be excluded is an amount that a buyer would pay for an entire company in excess of its going-concern value as an independent business. The valuator should include a premium over market (the reciprocal of a minority discount) to the extent that it reflects the elimination of discounts for minority interest and lack of marketability.

Even if the procedures followed by the controller and the independent directors have succeeded in shifting the burden of proof to plaintiffs, the Court of Chancery will, in its Entire Fairness review, consider the fairness of the price. If there is a class action challenging fairness, all minority shareholders included in the class will receive the benefit of any award above the transaction price. In contrast, an award in an appraisal action is paid only to dissenting shareholders, not to the other minority shareholders.

Fairness Opinions and Valuations in Freezeout Tender Offers

A noncoercive freezeout tender offer consists of two steps: a tender offer for a majority of the minority shares and a short-form merger if the controller attains 90% ownership. Since the

Chapter 2: Background on Fair Value

Business Judgment Rule applies to the tender offer, minority shareholders cannot receive a court review of the fairness of the price. Each shareholder has the opportunity to decide whether to tender based on available information. *Pure* provides that the independent directors should (a) be given "both free rein and adequate time to react to the tender offer, by (at the very least) hiring their own advisors," (b) make a recommendation to minority shareholders, and (c) "disclos[e] adequate information for the minority to make an informed judgment."[20] For an informed recommendation, the directors who retain a financial advisor should ask for an opinion as to the fairness of the proposed transaction, and should disclose the advisor's recommendation and the basis for it, to the minority shareholders.

The exclusive remedy available to a minority shareholder who does not tender and objects to the price of the second-step short-form merger is appraisal. In a Delaware appraisal, a dissenting shareholder is entitled to receive a pro rata share of equity value of the company as a going concern, with no control premium and no discount for lack of marketability or minority interest. Certain factors that would otherwise be relevant to a fairness opinion, such as synergies, increases in value attributable to the transaction itself, reduction of excessive salaries, and eliminating corporate waste, may not be included in an appraisal valuation. In addition, liquidation value may not be used, even if liquidation value is higher than going concern value. Recent Delaware appraisal decisions have favored discounted cash flow, but have often also used guideline companies and guideline acquisitions, with adjustments to eliminate impermissible premiums and discounts.[21]

Independent directors, who fulfill their obligations as fiduciaries by hiring their own advisor, should ask their financial advisor for guidance as to the amount that minority shareholders might receive if they request appraisal. When the appraisal remedy is available, the value that a dissenting shareholder would receive in an appraisal represents a floor below which a proposed freezeout price is not fair. Since that appraisal value cannot be ascertained prior to litigation, the valuator should use appropriate valuation methods to determine the amount that might reasonably be awarded to a dissenting shareholder, and discuss the valuation with the independent directors. Disclosure of the financial advisor's valuation conclusions, and a description of inputs and methods used (with customary caveats), should be helpful to shareholders in deciding whether to tender or to seek appraisal.

Fairness Opinions When Tender Offer Might Not Achieve 90% Ownership

An issue not addressed in the recent Delaware decisions is the impact of a proposed freezeout tender offer on minority shareholders if the controller purchases a majority of the minority shares but does not reach the 90% ownership level required for a short-form merger. In that situation, non-tendering shareholders would then be left with a thinner market and with no assurance of being bought out. If the valuator believes that the proposed price is fair, the independent directors should be advised to consider negotiating for a 90% condition. The valuator's opinion should be qualified if the controller could complete the tender offer without attaining the 90% threshold. Depending on the valuator's conclusion, the fairness opinion could state that the transaction is fair, from a financial point of view,[22] to all minority shareholders only if the 90% level is reached, or that it is fair to shareholders who tender, with a negative opinion (or no opinion) expressed to non-tendering shareholders.

---

1. Originally published in Financial Valuation and Litigation Expert, FVLE Issue 8, August/September 2007, copyright 2007 Valuation Products and Services www.valuationproducts.com.
2. Gilbert E. Matthews serves as Senior Managing Director and Chairman of the Board with Sutter Securities Incorporated, a full-service investment banking firm headquartered in San Francisco. Michelle Patterson is a professor at San Francisco State University, a consultant with Sutter Securities, and a former associate with Gibson, Dunn & Crutcher, LLP.
3. "A freezeout is a transaction in which a controlling shareholder buys out the minority shareholders in a publicly traded corporation, for cash or the controller's stock. Freezeouts are also known, with some occasional loss of precision, as 'going private mergers,' 'squeezeouts,' 'parent-subsidiary mergers,' 'minority buyouts,' 'take outs,' or 'cash-out mergers.'" Guhan Subramanian, *Fixing Freezeouts*, 115 Yale L.J. 2 (2005), p. 5. Our article does not address third-party going-private transactions.
4. *See* William T. Allen, Jack B. Jacobs, and Leo E. Strine, Jr., *Function Over Form: A Reassessment of Standards of Review In Delaware Corporation Law*, Del. J. Corp. Law 859.
5. *Weinberger v. UOP*, 457 A.2d 701 (Del. 1983) at 711.
6. *Glassman v. Unocal Exploration Corp.*, 777 A.2d 242 (Del. 2001).
7. *In re Siliconix Incorporated Shareholder Litigation*, 2001 Del. Ch. LEXIS 83, 2001 WL 716787 (Del. Ch., June 19, 2001).
8. Faith Stevelman Kahn, *Freezeout Doctrine: Going Private at the Intersection of the Market and the Law*, Business Lawyer (forthcoming), pp. 24-5. http://papers.ssrn.com/sol3/papers.cfm?abstract_id=952331
9. *Kahn v. Lynch Communication Systems, Inc.*, 638 A.2d 1110 (Del. 1994).
10. Kahn, p. 24.
11. Peter V. Letsou & Steven M. Haas, *The Dilemma That Never Should Have Been: Minority Freeze Outs in Delaware*, Business Lawyer, Nov. 2005, p. 26.
12. Kahn, p. 23.
13. Del. Code Ann. tit. 8 §253.
14. *Unocal Exploration* at 247.
15. *Id.* at 248.
16. *In re Pure Resources, Inc. Shareholder Litigation*, 808 A.2d 421 (Del. Ch. 2002) at 445.
17. *In re Cox Communications, Inc. Shareholder Litigation*, 879 A.2d 604 (Del. Ch. 2005) at 607.
18. *Pure* at 445.
19. *Weinberger* at 711.
20. *Pure* at 445.
21. For a discussion of Delaware appraisals, see Gilbert E. Matthews, *A Review of Valuations in Delaware Appraisal Cases, 2004–2005*, Business Valuation Review, June 2006.
22. "Fairness, from a financial point of view," the customary language in fairness opinions, may equal or exceed the applicable legal standard for fairness.

Fair Value: A View from the Delaware Court of Chancery Bench[1]

By Shannon Pratt DBA, CFA, FASA, MCBA, CM&A, MCBC

Before his appointment as a Justice of the Delaware Supreme Court in 2003, Jack B. Jacobs served as Vice Chancellor of the Delaware Court of Chancery since October 1985, after having practiced corporate and business litigation in Wilmington, Delaware since 1968. He has written many widely quoted opinions on fair value in statutory appraisals and breach of fiduciary duty litigation over stock valuation. In this interview with Stacy Ison and myself, he provides guidance on the court's interpretation of fair value in statutory appraisals. He also discusses elements that may lead to amounts greater than a statutory appraisal value, which may arise in other actions, such as breach of fiduciary duty. He also offers some practical advice for both appraisers and attorneys. - Shannon Pratt

Dr. Shannon Pratt: As you know, precedents from the Chancery Court are widely referred to by other state courts, so your views of fair value will pique much national interest. As a starting point, it would be helpful to distinguish between "plain vanilla" statutory appraisal actions and appraisals that may arise in other legal actions.

Justice Jack Jacobs: We don't have a full range of developed law on all the differences and similarities between breach of fiduciary duty cases and statutory appraisal cases. But, generally, a breach of fiduciary duty case is like any other common law case, in the sense that a plaintiff must establish liability before becoming entitled to a remedy. So the plaintiff must establish that the directors did something wrong—that they violated some duty owed to the shareholders. And only after that do you reach the issue of what the remedy should be. In a Delaware statutory appraisal action, the petitioning stockholder does not have to establish that anyone is liable. Under the statute all one needs to show is that a merger (or other qualified corporate action) is structured in a way that triggers the right to an appraisal. Normally what triggers the right to an appraisal is a cash-out; or the issuance of stock of a company that has 2,000 shareholders or fewer; or that is not publicly traded. Once you establish that, the only issue is "fair value," which is a statutory concept that has been construed in many Delaware cases. It is now established that both types of actions may be filed in connection with the same merger.

SP: So how does the difference between a statutory appraisal case and a fiduciary duty case affect the appraisals and the action of the court?

JJ: The statutory appraisal case limits damages, on the upside, in that the value is fixed at one point in time, and is not supposed to include any synergies. There is no issue of burden of proof. If the court does not accept the valuation presented by one side or the other, it must perform independently its own valuation. In a breach of fiduciary duty case, the traditional burden of proof rules apply, whereby if the evidence on both sides is even (we say "in equipoise"), then the party that has the burden of proof loses. Another bright line difference is that in a fiduciary duty action, other measures of damages may be available, including damages calculated as of a date after the transaction. "Rescissory" damages would be an example.[2] Damages measured by that method would be available in a breach of fiduciary duty action, but not in a statutory appraisal case.

SP: So, if I understand correctly, "fair value" may be different depending on whether the proceeding is a statutory appraisal or a fiduciary duty case.

JJ: Actually, "fair value" is the measure of the recovery in an appraisal case. In a fiduciary case the measure of damages could be different.

SP: I think that this certainly helps to explain decisions that some people who are not familiar with this important distinction sometimes see as inconsistencies in positions taken by the court.

JJ: Apart from the distinctions I have already discussed, it is important to keep in mind that both my Court and the Delaware Supreme Court recognize that valuation cases are extremely fact-driven. Very few conclusions on valuation issues have universal applicability, though statements found in some opinions may have the appearance, and might be interpreted by some, as having sweeping generality.

SP: One of the big issues in fair value cases is control premiums and minority discounts. Some would interpret the Delaware opinions to say that you can't use guideline public companies because they have a built-in minority discount, and that you can't use mergers and acquisitions because they have a built-in synergistic premium, but you relied on the M&A method in *M.G. Bancorporation v. Le Beau*.[3]

JJ: Since that case is ongoing, I can't comment about it substantively, except to say that the corporation being valued in that case was a holding company. In that specific situation, a control premium may be applied to the value of each owned subsidiary to arrive at the holding company's "fair value."[4]

SP: I guess that also explains why, although both appraisers used a DCF method, that you did not feel obligated to reconcile their differences and reach your own conclusion.

JJ: Yes. In a statutory appraisal case, it is very likely that we would have done that. In a breach of fiduciary duty case, the traditional burden of proof rules may be used more freely as tools of decision.

SP: In that case and in *Rapid American*,[5] the court added a control premium to the derived fair value of the operating companies owned by a parent holding company, where the operating companies' values were based in part on minority stock trading prices.

JJ: Yes. When a holding company's business consists of holding stock in various operating companies, Delaware case precedent requires the court to add a control premium where the subsidiary's value is derived from stock market prices that represent "minority" trading values.

Chapter 2: Background on Fair Value

SP: People sometimes make the point that in today's highly priced stock market, many of those current minority prices are so high that they already meet or exceed the enterprise value of the entire company, and there isn't any room left for a control premium.

JJ: Well, to date nobody has made that argument in a case that has come before us. If someone does and can get some distinguished appraisal expert to testify to that effect, then that argument certainly would be considered. Whether or not it would be accepted is another question.

SP: That's good to know.

JJ: This is all very fact-intensive ... once we're capable of understanding the theory—which is a big "if."

SP: Other than statutes and case law, what sources do you consider for guidance?

JJ: Well, we have cited your book [*Valuing a Business*], and in some cases certain finance texts, but beyond that the valuation guidance we receive is often a matter of what the attorneys and appraisers present to us. And we do have some judicial training sessions.

SP: What guidelines can you give to limit a potential suit to a statutory appraisal case and avoid greater liability by failure to act within the scope of entire fairness?

JJ: Whenever there is a transaction involving a real or potential conflict, the Board should have totally independent directors, lawyers, and financial advisors. The control party should not be involved in selecting either the lawyers or the financial advisors. If the deal is fully negotiated with competent independent directors and advisors, it is much less likely that there will be an "entire fairness" problem.

Now let me ask you a question. What would you appraisers like to see from us?

SP: We would like to have questions posed to us from the bench, so that there is some dialogue. That helps to insure that we've fully communicated; and that we've had a chance to address whatever concerns you may have about our work.

JJ: I totally agree. I'm usually pretty active in asking questions from the bench, as are most of my colleagues, and I would encourage other judges to do so.

SP: The second thing we appraisers would like is to have you read and understand our reports before we get into court.

JJ: If you want us to read the expert's report ahead of time, have your attorney ask us to do so, and (absent some serious evidentiary problem), we will be glad to do it. [Unlike the Tax Court, where the report is the direct testimony], the report here is generally regarded as hearsay and admissible only after it is authenticated by the expert. That is why we usually hear the expert's direct testimony first.

A View from the Delaware Court of Chancery Bench

SP: Can you wrap up with a few suggestions on what you like to see from appraisal experts and their lawyers?

JJ: Explain simply and clearly why we should accept your valuation. Most judges do not have a finance background. Write a report that describes what the company is, what it owns, and how it uses those assets to generate revenues and profits. Then explain what valuation methods are appropriate for that company and why. You have to be fundamental and elementary with us. Assume that we are intelligent, but have a fifth grade education about this particular company and the valuation methods that are most appropriate for it.

SP: Thank you very much. You've given some very helpful insights. We'll look forward to keeping in touch.

---

1. *Business Valuation Update™*, September 1999. Reprinted with permission from Business Valuation Resources.
2. Rescissory damages "contemplate a return of the injured party to the position he occupied before he was induced by wrongful conduct to enter the transaction. When return of the specific property, right, etc. is not possible (*e.g.* in a stock fraud transaction, the stock is no longer available), the rescissory damages would be the monetary equivalent (*e.g.* value of stock)." *Black's Law Dictionary,* 6th Ed., 1994.
3. The abstract of *M.G. Bancorporation v. Le Beau* is included in the court case abstract section of this *Guide*, and the full-text decision can be found at BVLibrary.com.
4. The Court did accept the comparable acquisition method even though it had been typically rejected in Delaware appraisals due to its inclusion of a control premium. The court cited *Harris v. Rapid American* 603 A.2d 796 (Del. 1992) as support.
5. *Supra* note 7.

Standards of Value: Theory and Applications

BVR Telephone Conference Transcript October 24, 2006

Speakers: Jay Fishman, Shannon Pratt, William Morrison

Operator:	Ladies and gentlemen, this is your conference operator. Welcome to today's teleconference, *Standards of Value, Theory, and Applications*, with Ron Seigneur, Jay Fishman, William Morrison, and Shannon Pratt. Before we turn the call over to Ron Seigneur, the moderator, David Foster, BVR's Owner and President, would like to give you all a brief welcome and take the opportunity to introduce today's moderator. David, please go ahead.
David Foster:	Hello. I'd like to say welcome to everyone to another one of BVR's teleconferences, and particularly to thank Jay, William, Ron, and Shannon for participating. Obviously, the issue of standards of value has become even more critical these days with the recent court cases. Most of us were recently in Toronto last week where standards of value were talked about in almost all of the sessions at the American Society of Appraisers/Canadian Institute of Chartered Business Valuators (ASA/CICBV) Conference. And also importantly, Jay Fishman and William Morrison have a major book coming out from Wiley, which will be mentioned. Recently, that's coming out in a couple of weeks. So it's an important time to address this topic. The moderator today is Ron Seigneur. Ron and I share some past history in law firm management and an interest in rock-and-roll, so we have some common elements. But Ron's also a chronic volunteer. He's on the Steering Committee of the American Institute of Certified Public Accountants (AICPA) Conference in Austin later this fall. He's got his own book, the *Financial Valuation* book that's out from Wiley. He teaches for the National Association of Certified Valuation Analysts (NACVA). He's on the advisory panel for Ibbotson on their data. So we're lucky to have him involved, and I'll let him carry out the introductions with a huge thanks from everyone at BVR. So Ron, it's all yours. Thank you.
Ron Seigneur:	Thank you, David, I appreciate that. I'm very excited to be moderating today's call. I'd like to take a brief moment to introduce our three panelists. Jay Fishman is a Managing Director of Financial Research Associates and has been actively involved in the appraisal profession since 1974. He specializes

Standards of Value: Theory and Applications

in the valuations of business enterprises and their intangible assets, including patents, trademarks, customer lists, goodwill, and going concern.

We also have today Dr. Shannon Pratt. Dr. Pratt is the Chairman of Shannon Pratt Valuations and is the Founder of Business Valuation Resources. He was one of the founders of Willamette Management Associates and was a managing director of Willamette for over 35 years. He is also on the Board of Directors of Paulson Capital Corporation.

Our third panelist is William Morrison. He is the President of Morrison & Company, a forensic accounting firm located in --

Bill Morrison: Paramus.

Ron Seigneur: Paramus -- thank you, William -- New Jersey. He is a Certified Public Accountant (CPA) licensed in New Jersey and Florida with over 30 years experience as an investigator, forensic accountant, and business valuator.

I'd like to also mention that all three of these individuals, I think, as David had mentioned, are co-authors of a book that really is the foundation for today's call. That book is titled *Standards of Value, Theory, and Applications* that's being published by John Wiley & Sons, and I understand that book will be released very shortly, within the next week or so.

We're excited to have these three co-authors here, and with that said, I'm going to get started with some questions. And the first question I have I'm going to direct to Jay. I know this is part of a body of work that all three of you have been working on for quite some time and I'd like to have you talk a little bit about what attracted the three of you to this area and how you went about getting started.

Jay Fishman: Thanks, Ron -- thanks for the introduction. Like most of us, I'm a practitioner and I've been practicing for a long time, and over the years, these issues keep cropping up. But the person who really kind of set this in motion was Shannon because I remember him writing a monograph a number of years ago about common errors in business valuation. And what he said in the monograph was, "One of the most common errors is the failure of the expert to adhere to the proper standard of value." And I've seen that as well over the years where the words may say one thing but the underlying assumptions may be something else.

Then once I was appointed by a judge in Utah in an oppressed shareholder's case. And while he told me, and I knew that the standard of value was fair value,

Chapter 2: Background on Fair Value

the issue of discounts always comes up. And so I asked the Court for direction as to whether discounts at the shareholder level should be applied. And the response I got back from the Court was, "Well, what do you think?" And I think that's more a providence of the Court than it is of something for me.

And then lastly, I was involved in a long, bitter divorce case, where Roger Grabowski -- my friend, Roger Grabowski -- was on the other side. And there was actually a trial before the financial issues were decided in which the Court decided what the appropriate standard of value was and what the words meant, what the underpinnings meant. And frankly, that's the genesis of what you will hear Bill and Shannon talk about, about this continuum of value idea that we've come up with.

So over the years, we've looked and done research about this stuff and kind of that's how it got started.

Ron Seigneur: Great, excellent. Bill, tell me a bit about the historical underpinnings that your forthcoming book covers and why these points are relevant in today's environment. Especially, given that some of the discussion in the book reaches back several decades, and even in a couple of places I noted when I had an opportunity to review the book, it goes back even into the 1800s.

Bill Morrison: Ron, thanks again for your introduction and your kind words. With fair market value, we actually go back to 1832 with a tariff case, and that really begins the talk about the standards of value, which we now come to for estate and gift taxation.

But with fair value in oppression and dissenters' rights, that goes back to the late 1800s. And the important thing is what we see -- and so much of this was done by going through cases, and we read a tremendous number of cases and scouted out all the articles -- that what the courts are trying to do is come to some kind of equity. And what first happened was corporations were run strictly on a 100 percent vote. When you went to majority control, you had to have an exit strategy for someone who dissented from a major decision of the corporation. And we go all the way back to 1870 to see the first reference to fair value.

And as time went on and we got to oppression cases, we saw that the courts were trying to come up with a special form of value to do equity for people who were mistreated in some form in a corporation, and this we saw over time.

And of course, in divorce, with the equitable distribution statutes, we'll talk about how the different views of property came into play to form the cases and the decisions over time.

Standards of Value: Theory and Applications

So you really need to have a sense of where we've been historically to see where we are today.

Jay Fishman: There's another thing to be added. I think, first, the reason why we had such a historical perspective is that firstly, Bill and I were trained in liberal arts before this lifetime, and I was particularly trained as a historian. But the point that we try to make in going back that far is that while some of these definitions are rather concise and contain 10, 12, 14 words, you see the evolution of how those words were arrived at, and that the definition that we use today is not necessarily how it started out. You see that when we look at the Revised Model Business Corporation Act, and how each year, each time it was changed, what was added and why it was added. And you see the same thing, interestingly, in fair market value.

So the reason why we kind of did the historical perspective is to let people know that it's no accident that these words are what they are today, that they represent an evolution of a concept, and that they mean things, and have come about through the years as a result of situations.

Ron Seigneur: It'll be interesting to look back in 50 or 100 years at the definitions we're using today and see how they may have continued to evolve.

I'd like to direct a question to Dr. Pratt and it continues on the discussion that we're having. Failure to adhere to the proper standard of value is something that Jay's mentioned already. What's meant by that?

Shannon Pratt: Well, the standard of value is designated by statutes, by law. Fair market value is designated by the Federal law for all matters pertaining to gift or estate taxes or any Federal taxes. Fair value, in the context of dissent and oppression cases, is the standard of value in most states for dissent and oppression cases. And fair value, in another context, is the legally mandated standard of value for financial reporting. In divorces, you don't have any statutory standards of value so you have to read the case law.

Now I read a Delaware case. Now Delaware is a strictly fair value state. And one man, testifying before the Delaware Court, used fair market value instead of fair value. And the Court did not give any credence to his testimony.

I had another case, which was an arbitration. An industry expert came in and testified before me at great length, and he did a great discounted cash flow, did it very well, but he assumed that the companies were already merged. And the statute said, "without giving any credence or any credit to the outcome of the merger." So I couldn't use his testimony at all. I had to totally disregard his testimony.

So those are a couple of cases in which people did not adhere to the standard of value and their testimony was not worth anything.

Ron Seigneur: Jay, you've already talked about a similar situation with Roger Grabowski on the other side. And I'd ask you and Bill if you have any other examples you can think of in practice where you've seen situations of an appraiser doing solid work, like Shannon's just referred to, but relying on the wrong standard, and therefore, not having their opinions being given any weight.

Jay Fishman: Bill, shall I try this first?

Bill Morrison: Go ahead.

Jay Fishman: I think what we're trying to say, and by the way, we should say this, that we're approaching this topic, not as lawyers, but as valuation experts who are trying to find their way through this minefield called the "definition of value." And I first got involved in it because when I'm in a new jurisdiction or I'm doing a valuation in an area that I don't know about, I usually ask to read the cases. Because it's not that we want to be the lawyer, but at least if you read the cases, you can ask the client and the lawyers and whomever the right questions so that you can be guided.

So there are countless examples where people have used the words and then applied it in the way it wasn't intended. The classic one I hear is, "fair market value to the holder." We've had a couple of cases. Pennsylvania, when it comes to professional goodwill, is a very restrictive state, and you are required to distinguish between personal and enterprise goodwill. While New York, that's not necessarily true. And so when we work here in Pennsylvania, we've seen "fair market value to the holder," we've seen "value in exchange based on a going concern value."

The classic ones that we all kind of started with were the dissenters and oppressed shareholders' cases where experts got up and said, "Well, fair value and fair market value are the same. I never read the statute. I never read the cases. And therefore, I'm taking these entity-level discounts."

So those are a couple of examples that I've seen.

Bill Morrison: This is Bill. What I see is not so much that people use the wrong standard, but the judge will determine what they think is fair. So for instance, in

Standards of Value: Theory and Applications

New Jersey, we have a case, *Brown v. Brown*, where the articulated standard of value was fair market value. And the expert who used fair market was found to be less credible than the one who took no discounts. The Court then established the standard essentially based upon fair value and dissent and oppression cases. But the valuation expert really hadn't done anything wrong. The Court didn't think it was fair in this context to take discounts, especially the size that he'd taken. So I find it coming more from the courts, where the courts decide what they think is fair. And they will make a decision as to whether or not discounts apply, whether, as we'll talk about later, value to the holder of professional or personal goodwill will be included, and those sorts of things.

Shannon Pratt: This is Shannon. The interpretation by the court is far more prevalent in divorce than it is in tax or dissent or oppression or financial reporting.

Jay Fishman: Yeah, I think that's another point we're trying to make, which is, we've seen courts put labels on things like calling it "fair market value," but then attributing to it certain assumptions that we wouldn't commonly associate with fair market value. And I don't think this is a new problem, but it's a problem that we, as experts, need to be educated so we can ask the right questions.

Shannon Pratt: Well, most of the judges don't know what fair market value is in the context of appraisal literature.

Jay Fishman: Well, I wonder if that's not unintentional. There are a couple of quotes I'd like to read.

Jack Bogdanski, who probably has written more about fair market value than anything else, says, "Critics of the term 'fair market value' correctly point out that its application is highly uncertain, sometimes with little connection to objective reality."

And the classic one that we all look at is James C. Bonbright, in his *Valuation of Property*, where he says, "On the whole, the courts have preferred to keep the statutory language 'fair market value' while not taking its implications too seriously." And he wrote that in the 1930s.

So there is, as Bill said, a lot of leeway in terms of interpretation of what these words actually mean.

Ron Seigneur: Jay, I know your book goes in great depth in terms of reaching back, as Bill also mentioned, to go back and discuss kind of the foundation of those words and what they mean as they've evolved forward.

Chapter 2: Background on Fair Value

With that said, I'm going to move to another question and I'm going to direct this back to you, Jay. And I'm going to talk about kind of precisely what's meant by the term "standards of value," and talk a little bit about what the relationship is between what you call the "premises" and the "standard of value."

Jay Fishman: Well, everybody agrees that to do a credible appraisal, you have to identify the standard of value. And the term "standard of value" is actually relatively new. In the old days when we started, we used to call it the "definition of value." And the definition of value is what type of value are you looking for. And it kind of sets the framework from all else that follows.

But we have found, over the years, in our research, that above the standard of value is something we call the "valuation premise." And what we find is, again, on this continuum, it either falls on one end, which is "value in exchange," and on the other end, "value to the holder." And what we're going to talk about today is it isn't "all or nothing." Sometimes it depends where you are on that continuum in terms of how a particular state or purpose uses the standard of value.

So the way we kind of look at it at this point is fair market value would be considered "value in exchange," where investment value could be considered "value to the holder." And we kind of put "fair value" in the middle somewhere. And you'll hear, as we discuss this this afternoon -- or this morning -- the kind of *degrees* of where that premise falls relative to the definition of value.

We try to distinguish that from what we would call the "operational premises," which is, we all know either we value a business as a going concern or we value it upon liquidation. More than likely, we're valuing it as a going concern. And we wanted to call that an "operational premise" as opposed -- because you're assuming how the business is going to operate as compared to the kind of valuation premise framework that we use.

Ron Seigneur: Bill, let me, along the same thread, ask a question of you, and as Jay's just discussed, within the standard of value, there are additional premises and premises that are outside of the operational premises that Jay had just mentioned. Can you comment, additionally, on how these premises interrelate to the applicable standard of value?

Bill Morrison: Well, they're going to relate much more to how you do the valuation as opposed to the underlying premise of value in exchange or value to holder for the operational premises. And they're going to deal with the other issues you're going to have to address in doing a valuation.

Standards of Value: Theory and Applications

Ron Seigneur: Okay. Shannon, you deal with both the definition of various standards of value and also the application. What areas do you look at and why?

Shannon Pratt: Well, first, you have to look at the statutes, if there are any. There are clear-cut statutes on gift and estate tax matters for fair market value. There are less clear statutes but they're state by state in fair value for dissent and oppression cases. Most states say that it's as of the day before the event, without giving any credence to the outcome of the event itself, the consequences of the event. Most state statutes are silent on the question of whether you give discounts or not.

So you have to look at the case law for the interpretation. And many states, lately, have changed their posture in that regard. There's a trend toward fair value not allowing discounts of any kind, minority or marketability, but that's not universal. You have to look at the case law in each state. You also have to look at the case law in tax to derive the nuances that may be impounded in the case law. For example, the case law on subsequent events would seem to contradict the statutory law.

In divorce, there are no statutes on the definitions of value, so you have to look entirely to the case law in those cases. Now in the book, we have analyzed the 50 different states, both in dissent and oppression, and we've given references to the statutes in each state, and we've referenced how they interpret the statutes in those states. And then in each state, we've given the interpretations, as we see them, in divorce. But there are no statutes on standards of value in any state for divorce, so you have to look at the case law.

And then for fair value for financial reporting, there are Securities and Exchange Commission (SEC) Pronouncements, some of which are still being debated. The definition of fair value for financial reporting is still evolving, but it has recently come somewhat close to fair market value but without the nuances of the tax court. But there are no cases yet on fair value for financial reporting, so you can't look to cases. You have to look to SEC Pronouncements and Financial Accounting Standards Board (FASB) Pronouncements on that one.

Ron Seigneur: That's going to be definitely an interesting area to watch as it evolves forward, and I know there's recently been a FASB that's been released on Fair Value Measurements that I think will help fill in some of those gaps. I think that's Statement of Financial Accounting Standards Number 157, if I'm correct.

Jay Fishman: That's right.

Bill Morrison: Ron, this is --

Chapter 2: Background on Fair Value

Jay Fishman: When you said, "it fills in the gaps," was that your intent to make a pun there?

Ron Seigneur: Yeah, gaps with two As.

Bill Morrison: Ron, this is Bill. Just a point on the fair value in dissenters and oppression -- what happens there is that you have the case law, and then you have the American Law Institute's (ALI) Principles of Corporate Governance and the American Bar Association's Model Business Corporation Act and the various revisions. And you see the definitions changing there, and they've come out in 1969, 1984, and in 1999 for the Model Business Corporation Act. And ALI has a definition in 1992. And you see the state definitions changing -- as Shannon described, the case law changing. So there's been a consolidation and you can see it in the legal bodies and in the statutes where some of the state statutes now actually prohibit the use of discounts.

Shannon Pratt: Well, and Bill, another interesting thing is that even the states that haven't adopted the new definitions and their statutes have cases where the courts have adopted the ALI definitions, and they say, "no discounts." So it's not necessary for the state to have adopted the new definition in their statutes in order for the court to adopt it.

Ron Seigneur: I know I found, Bill, that the definitional discussion from these legal organizations that you just referenced quite enlightening when I was reviewing the book. I've been just vaguely aware of those, but I didn't realize the depth that they had been looking at these issues over the years.

I'd like to move a little bit to a different area, and this is back to Jay, and it has to do with estate and gift tax. It's an area we often find ourselves working, and we all know we normally use a fair market value standard, and I believe we're all familiar with that definition as it's promulgated by the U.S. Treasury. And I'd like to talk a little bit about kind of what else is important to know when working with this specific area of valuation.

Jay Fishman: Thanks, Ron. This is the standard of value that's most well known and most well used. There's a U.S. Tax Court case that was decided in 1998 where the judge indicated that approximately 243 sections of the Internal Revenue Service Code referenced fair market value estimates determining a tax liability on some 15 million tax returns.

We all know the definition that, "Fair market value is the price of which the property would change hands between a willing buyer and a willing seller, neither under compulsion to buy or sell, and both having reasonable knowledge of the relevant facts." And this has evolved over the years and it's changed in many ways.

There's a 1936 case where, as it applies to real estate, they use the term "highest and best use of the real estate." Now in Canada and the United Kingdom, they say, instead of "the price at which the property would change hands," it's the "highest price at which the property would change hands."

And I think the first thing to understand about FMV is it may not be a real concept. It's what the Canadians and the English call a "notional concept," because it assumes ground rules that may or may not be true in the marketplace.

So if you look at each one of the components, I think it's very interesting, even starting with the word "price." What fair market value means to us is that it requires a single point estimate of the cash or cash equivalent at the particular valuation date. So this is important in practice because, for example, let's say you had a comparable transaction in which an element of it was stock and the stock was not particularly liquid and it was not registered. It seems if you're going to put together that valuation multiple, you might have to reduce what was actually paid to its cash or cash equivalency.

The same thing when it has to do with earn-outs, and parenthetically, there's some great research that's been done by Nancy Fannon on the use of various market databases in which she points out that that's an issue that we all should look at, especially as it applies to earn-outs.

So then it says, "between a willing buyer and willing seller." Well, what is the definition of a willing buyer? Is it a group of buyers? Is it a pool of buyers? Is it one buyer? We used to think that fair market value does not entail synergies, and generally, I think that's been the way everyone in the valuation profession has looked at it. But there have been exceptions. I think the first thing is that the synergies that they're talking about are not *all* synergies but synergies that would be unavailable to all the buyers.

So as a result, there are a couple of cases. There's a case called *BTR Dunlop* where the tax court actually indicated that you should look at the pool of willing buyers, and there were six of them, each bringing a synergy to the table and that that was a relevant consideration. Now the fact pattern there is different.

I should add something. Jim Hitchner said something once that I thought was really interesting. He said, "You show me a position and I'll show you a U.S. Tax Court case that'll back it up."

Chapter 2: Background on Fair Value

So these things, as Bill has said, are so fact-sensitive.

In *BTR Dunlop*, which is a Section 482 case, there had been a sale and the sale involved the bidding of six particular synergistic buyers.

So what I'm saying is that you can break each one of these components down to look at that.

In *Mandelbaum*, the expert was criticized because he focused purely on what the willing buyer would do and not what the willing seller would do.

If you continue the definition, it says, "having reasonable knowledge of the relevant facts." And here's a great one. What does reasonable knowledge mean? People kind of believe that it's not totally informed. But again, referring to Bogdanski, he says, "Reasonable knowledge is a level of awareness that usually falls somewhere between perfect knowledge and complete ignorance," which I thought was amusing because it's somewhere in there and it doesn't necessarily mean "fully informed." And I could go on, but that issue of "fully informed" also impacts what was known or knowable at the valuation date.

I'll let Bill and Shannon kind of jump in a little bit, and then I can give you an interesting case in which known or knowable -- what we found is the courts go to great lengths to show things where known or knowable -- if the fact pattern fits the situation.

Ron Seigneur: This is Ron. I'd like to take just a moment to remind the listeners that if they have specific questions of the panelists, they can e-mail those to *tc-questions@bvresources.com -- tc-questions@bvresources.com*. We'll be devoting the last 30 to 40 minutes of our discussion today responding to those questions, and I know we have two or three that have come in already. So as we work through the program, we'll get back to those questions.

I'd like to -- yeah, go ahead.

Shannon Pratt: Later on in the call, the operator is going to open up the phone lines to live questions.

Ron Seigneur: Yeah, and we'll do that in about a half-hour and I'll turn it back to her to give instructions on that as well, Shannon. Thank you.

I'd like to turn, just because of our time constraints, to divorce matters so we make sure that we devote some attention there. And I'd like to direct

Standards of Value: Theory and Applications

this question to Bill to talk a little bit about the relationship between what we refer to as "marital property" and the "standard of value."

Bill Morrison: Thank you, Ron. Well, in divorce, it's very much, "that's the issue," and we'll talk a little bit later about how we developed the continuum of value and how the premises and standards of value fit in there. But we looked at all the statutes in all 50 states and in the District of Columbia. We only found two states which gave guidance as to how to value and what standard to use, and they were Louisiana, which said to use "fair market value," and Arkansas, which said to use "fair market value for securities."

But the issue we believe is -- "How does the state view value or property that's to be distributed?" And it really breaks down to -- "Does the state believe that property to be distributed in a divorce is only something that can be sold?" Hence, value in exchange or fair market value or some form of fair value? Or -- "Does the state view the ability to earn significant earnings that a professional, for instance, develops -- or you get when you have a license, is that viewed as value? And if it is, how is it calculated?" And then the controversy over personal efforts after the divorce (post-marital efforts), and personal attributes (the skill, the reputation, relationships) -- and that's really what's valued when you do a value to the holder or an investment value. It's personal -- often can't be sold.

So states come down very differently on that but we see a continuum. So it does very much, Ron, come back to -- "How does the state view property to be distributed?"

Ron Seigneur: Great, thanks, and I'm going to direct another question back to you, Bill, that follows along those same lines because I've done a lot of work in divorce and I've found that the valuation for divorce, often, the standard of value is ambiguous. Have you found that to be the case, and where are you most likely to find guidance concerning the standard of value for divorce purposes?

Bill Morrison: Well, as I just said, we looked at all the statutes in all 50 states and in the District of Columbia and found very little guidance. What you find is, as Shannon mentioned before -- you find the guidance in the case law. And the cases aren't always clear, but we found -- and again, we went through an enormous amount of cases -- and we found two states which gave you clear guidance in the statute, 12 altogether, including those two, that stated to use "fair market value." And then for the rest of the states, we had to look as to how they handled certain issues, and in doing that, we tried to place them into either value to the holder or value in exchange. Did they use a standard of investment value, fair value, or fair market value? And we can talk about these issues that we addressed.

Chapter 2: Background on Fair Value

Shannon Pratt: Some states are clearly fair market value in a walk-away sense. In other words, if the practitioner walked across the street and competed, what would the company be worth? That's Florida, Pennsylvania -- I think several other states like that. Some of the others are clearly investment value like California, Washington. And we sorted those out and tried to place them in various categories, and some we could place in certain categories clearly and others fell in between.

Ron Seigneur: Yeah, and I direct a question back to any of the three of you in terms of those states that are in between in terms of how you might go about resolving some of the differences in those specific states.

Jay Fishman: Well, I practice in a lot of states, and the first thing I do when I take a job is ask the lawyer to send me whatever the relevant cases there are so I can read them for myself and ask questions.

Again, it comes down to -- in divorce, divorce is probably the typical example where words are used and assumptions attached to those words are different.

And so we think that what you have to do is kind of define what you're doing and just say, "This is fair market value." But let's take that as an example. When we say "walk-away," there's a real issue that we used to talk about, which is, fair market value says, "a willing seller." The argument used to be, "Well, that a willing seller would cooperate with a willing buyer to get the highest price." If that meant that I had to stay on for three months, or six months, or some reasonable interregnum, then that's what it meant in order to achieve that goal. Well, some states look at it that way. They'll allow you an orderly transition. Other states, as Shannon pointed out, assume almost literally, you throw the keys at the buyer and you go across the street and set up shop. And there's a real question as to -- "Is that really what fair market value contemplated?" I think you need to read the cases to find where, on the continuum, your standard of value lies in a particular state.

But the biggest problem, as I said, is the courts constantly confusing a label of one thing with an attribute of another. There's a case in North Carolina called *Hamby* in which I know our colleague, George Hawkins, has written about this, and they talk about "fair market value as a going concern to the individual." Well, those are two different things to me, and I think they're two different things to most practicing valuers, yet you have to find your way in this continuum in order to come up with a proper appraisal.

Ron Seigneur: Bill, can you expand a little bit on this "continuum of value" that's associated with the "standards of value" for divorce?

Standards of Value: Theory and Applications

Bill Morrison: Well, I think the best way to look at it is -- Shannon just cited Florida and the walk-away standard. And there's a recent case in Florida called *Held*, which involved an insurance agency, and the Court found that even the covenant not to compete couldn't be included in the value. So Mr. Held was essentially allowed to walk across the street and compete with his old agency, and it was the value that remained. So that's at the one hand. You don't even have a covenant not to compete included.

If you then look at the language that California uses in the *Lopez* case, where they talk about all personal attributes (the skill, the reputation) that have been developed during the marriage, and that the practitioner has after the marriage, it's not fair that the practitioner can enjoy that and his spouse can't. So this is not anything that can be sold even, and it's at the other end of the continuum as are the license value cases in New York.

And then as we move across, you have situations -- and again, just to cite two cases -- if we go back to Florida, we have a case called *Thompson* where the fellow was a practitioner, a personal injury lawyer, and the Court found that his goodwill was personal to Mr. Thompson. And you compare that to New Jersey where, back in the 1983 when a lawyer was prohibited from transferring his practice, a gentleman by the name of Mr. Dugan's practice was valued, even though it couldn't be sold. And there was no distinction drawn between the personal goodwill and the enterprise goodwill.

So you see this continuum of valuing something that's totally personal to where we come over to where we don't even value something that clearly can be sold because there's some kind of effort involved in this interregnum period that Jay just described. And it's not always clear-cut in the different states.

Jay Fishman: Ron, to answer your question, given what Bill was talking about, is in this project, we ran into that issue. We had no statutory guidance except for Louisiana and Arkansas, and then we only found 10 states where they specifically mentioned the standard of value.

So what we decided to do was set up three criteria, and those three criteria were going to assist us in determining where, on this continuum, a particular state fell as to the appropriate standard and premises of value.

And the first one is what Bill just talked about. We looked at how a state treated personal versus enterprise goodwill. And the reason is if it's value to the holder, if you're in a value to the holder state where they talk about the age and health of the practitioner, it seemed to us that that would be more indicative of a value to the holder. And therefore, the issue of defining the difference between

Chapter 2: Background on Fair Value

personal and enterprise goodwill doesn't come up. In those states where they look at it as a value in exchange, those are the states in which the expert is often asked to differentiate between personal and enterprise goodwill.

Shannon Pratt: And I think Pennsylvania -- this is Shannon -- I think Pennsylvania case law has the clearest articulation of the difference between enterprise and personal goodwill.

Jay Fishman: So then the second criteria that we decided to look at is we looked at how a state viewed an entity-level discount -- I'm sorry -- a shareholder-level discount. Again, if it's value to the holder, it's pro rata share of the enterprise value, and therefore, discounts typically are not applied. If, on the other hand, it's value in exchange, then shareholder-level discounts are usually considered and, when appropriate, applied. And so that was the second kind of litmus test we used in determining whether we thought a state -- and again, I think we should say this -- it's not an "all or nothing," but a state that tended to favor the attributes of value in exchange versus value to the holder.

Shannon Pratt: Yeah, very few states are "all or nothing." Texas, Florida, Pennsylvania are "all or nothing" on the value in exchange, and Washington and California are "all or nothing" in terms of value to the holder. But very few states are "all or nothing."

Jay Fishman: A typical example of that, Ron, is your state where you have in Colorado -- I think it's called *Graff* -- the valuation of a State Farm Agency in which the Court determined that this agency had value and valued it and distributed some of it in the marital dissolution. While in Washington State, there's a case called *Ziegler* in which the same State -- not the same business -- but a State Farm Agency was -- it was requested that that be valued and distributed. And the Court said, "No, there is no value here." Now from an economic point of view, those two things didn't change because we crossed from Washington State into Colorado, but rather, it's how the Court viewed whether or not there was going to be a transaction.

The third criteria we used was how a state looked at the weight accorded a buy/sell agreement. Again, there are states -- Virginia is an example -- where they're talking about the value of the interest in the law practiced to the owner and did not apply the buy/sell agreement, which was in place and which had most of the attributes that, in a fair market value context, we all would consider at least useful if not definitive.

And so we looked at those situations to determine whether or not -- and as Shannon said, some states were clearer than others where they lined up kind of neatly, that is, all three kind of fell one way or another or were in the same place in the continuum. But unfortunately, other states would have no personal goodwill but would not consider shareholder-level discounts. And kind of we go over that in the cases that we looked at.

And I think the thread, as Bill talked about before, was sometimes it's just because the facts lead the courts to one direction. And they're not as concerned in following generally accepted appraisal principles as we have to be.

Ron Seigneur: A comment I'll make is -- Jay, you referred to the *Graff* case here in Colorado, and we have that plus two other cases, *Huff and Martin*, that make us look to what we refer to as a value to the owner standard here. And that seems to prevail in most all of the divorce actions that I've been involved in. But there still seems to be a notion that fair market value is appropriate, and I see some of my colleagues coming into Colorado courts and continuing to argue that as the proper standard. And maybe the question I have here is it seems like even though you have these case law precedents in each of the jurisdictions, you still have to be aware that in any particular court it's a court of equitable distribution, and you might find a particular judge that may not buy as strongly into the prevailing case law in some states. Any comments on that?

Bill Morrison: My thought -- and this is Bill -- is that it's going to very much depend upon the facts and circumstances. If you have a situation where clearly, a value to the holder, which is, if you're from Colorado and I'm from New Jersey, and we'll tend to go more towards the value to the holder concepts, if it's not fair, especially if you're in a state where it is a fair market value case and where they don't recognize personal goodwill, if you've got a situation where it would be very unfair not to do it, I could see a judge coming down that way. So I think the judge is going to look very much at the facts and circumstances.

Jay Fishman: But Ron, I think the point is that we, as valuation experts, are not the arbiters of what's fair. So when I'm in that situation, if the client will let you, I might show it both ways, and just say, "This is what it's worth without discounts and this is what it's worth if you apply the appropriate discounts," and let the court weave whatever solution it likes. But I don't want to be put in a position where I'm advocating that this is the appropriate standard of value. We heard that years ago when people went around the country arguing that there should be one divorce standard of value and that value was closest to value to the holder. Well, I wouldn't argue that if I was in Florida or Texas or Illinois or Pennsylvania and some of the other states that Shannon mentioned because they just don't buy it. Some of these decisions are a matter of public policy. And so in order to kind of get out of the line of fire, I would probably try to show it both ways, and say, "Listen, you guys argue it out."

Chapter 2: Background on Fair Value

Shannon Pratt: And this is Shannon. We've talked so far like most states are uniform in their interpretations, but not all states are uniform in their interpretations. In some states, various jurisdictions have their own individual interpretation and it depends on which jurisdiction you're in in the state.

Jay Fishman: Well, if your point that the interpretation of the standard of value can change not only from state to state, but within the state, Bill and I have found -- we also found it can change within the courthouse.

Ron Seigneur: Well, it's all under that umbrella of equitable distribution, as I've seen it.

I'd like to move us to another standards area for the sake of time, and I'm going to direct this question back to Shannon. And the question is -- most standards of value are viewed in comparison to fair market value as kind of the starting benchmark. In the context of dissent and oppression matters, what is the standard of value?

Shannon Pratt: Well, the standard of value in dissent and oppression matters is fair value in almost every state. But fair value is interpreted differently among different states. And as we said earlier, some states take minority discounts and not marketability discounts. Some states take marketability discounts and not minority discounts. Some states take both and some states take neither. Some states -- the case law says that the interpretation will be left up to the facts and circumstances of the individual case so have not made a pronouncement. So fair value is the standard of value that falls most in between the value to the holder and value in exchange. For example, we may go along the paths of fair market value to value the enterprise, but without taking any discounts, that's hardly value to the holder. So you have to look at the case law in order to decide which way it's going to jump.

Ron Seigneur: Excellent. Shannon, could you drill down a little further and talk a little bit about the differences between dissent, dissolution, and oppression matters?

Shannon Pratt: Well, dissent is more straightforward. When you dissent, you get your fair value and it's not normally related to the conduct of the dissenter. Now acceptance may occur when there was not fair dealing, because the Delaware courts have a different standard of fair dealing as opposed to fair price, and if there wasn't fair dealing that the company can be subject to additional penalties besides the fair value.

Now dissolution and oppression matters are different. They arise out of different issues and the conduct of the different parties may be taken into consideration by the courts.

Standards of Value: Theory and Applications

Jay Fishman: Yeah, I think in dissenter shareholders' matters, it's the shareholder dissents from a particular corporate action, usually a transaction. They don't prevent the transaction, but they get the fair value of their shares and they usually argue over what that consideration is.

In oppression or dissolution, most oppression situations fall under a dissolution statute except, as Shannon said, in Delaware. In oppression, it may not be that a transaction has occurred, but rather, the conduct of the majority has been so bad that I have been oppressed as a minority shareholder. That's why we teach people that states that have oppressed shareholder statutes, one could argue that the discount for lack of control would be less than a state that didn't because there are some protections that a minority shareholder has in those states.

In addition, the theory behind -- at least behind both of these statutes is those people that argue that you're entitled to your pro rata share of the enterprise make the argument, and there's a 1950 case that talks about this, that you should be given back what was taken away from you, and what was taken away from you was your proportionate share of the enterprise value.

So Shannon set up a really important distinction here between the two. But then they do cross over. When behavior's bad, that doesn't bode well for either the majority or those who started the dissent shareholder's action.

Shannon Pratt: Yeah, the behavior that Delaware courts don't like in dissenting stockholder suits is not having an independent fairness opinion in conjunction with a transaction. In other words, if one party stands on both sides of the transaction and is not an independent party, that makes this -- first of all, there should be independent directors, a minimum of three independent directors that are appointed to monitor the deal, and they should have their choice of an independent appraiser *and* an independent attorney. And when those conditions are not met, the Delaware courts at least, and some other courts, consider that there was not fair dealing. So in those cases, they may award damages over and above the value of the stock.

Jay Fishman: We have found that fair value actually can be interpreted differently from the dissent shareholder statute to the dissolution statute. That certainly is the case in California where they talk about liquidation value and also states like Ohio, which uses the term "actual cash value" or something like that -- "actual cash fair value." So it's very important to understand kind of the landscape.

And then the other thing that we found is that these law associations that Bill talked about, both the American Bar Association and the American

Chapter 2: Background on Fair Value

Law Institute, have started to add the term "equitable adjustments." And this is used by lots of lawyers to make the argument that discounts *are* appropriate in these cases even though the general trend has been the opposite. They try to differentiate their case from a typical case and make the argument that discounts are relevant. Bill can talk about one case that we know of called *Balsamides v. Perle* in which that was the issue. Bill?

Bill Morrison: Well, and I think one of the things is that we've got to remember that the oppression -- it's an oppression section to the dissolution statute. And so you can move to have a corporation dissolved, and in lieu of doing that, you can have a buy-out if you've been oppressed, but there are various reasons you can dissolve the corporation. And what can happen, though, is if there is no oppressive conduct, then you may not have fair value. You may have fair market value because fair value is a special standard that arises if someone is dissenting under the dissenters' statute or if someone has been oppressed in that section of the dissolution statute. So you can get a whole range of results.

And in New Jersey, they've used discounts -- in this case, a marketability discount -- because the oppressor was going to be bought out, and they felt that it would be unfair to have him bought out at the higher value after he had caused the problem, after he had been the oppressor. But had there been no oppression, the Court could have said it was fair market value or the Court could have said, "We're not going to give any buy-out because it's just dissention. We're going to leave everybody where they are."

So you can get a number of different results, including, under these equitable adjustment clauses, you can get essentially a damage claim. So you can get a tremendous range of results depending upon the equities and the legal issues, and your valuation is going to have to fall within what the court decides is appropriate.

Jay Fishman: People may be asking why we keep referring to Delaware. Well, Delaware is where, at least from a dissenter shareholder's point of view, the law is most well-developed. And in fact, in our research, we found that lots of states look to Delaware as kind of the model as to how the thing would work.

And the other point that I want to emphasize, that Bill made, is when oppression actions are brought, there are usually two parts to the trial. The first is, "Was, in fact, the minority oppressed? And then if so, how much are they entitled to?" I was involved in a very long, lengthy, expensive case where at the end of the day, the Court decided that I had the majority, that the majority did *not* oppress the minority and offered *no* relief, and kept them still as partners going forward, thereby, ensuring, I think, more litigation and more problems. But it's not a slum dunk all the time that you can get your liquidity just by bringing such an action.

Ron Seigneur: Those are great comments, Jay. I'd like to take a moment and have the operator come on and tell the listeners how they can either -- again, remind them on the e-mail address for their questions or the other avenue for asking a live question to the panelists.

Operator: If you have any questions that you would like answered, you can submit them at any time by e-mailing *tc-questions@bvresources.com*. Please include your name, location, and firm in your e-mail.

To ask your question by phone, you may press one key on your touch-tone telephone. This will place you into an electronic queue. If you hear your question answered, you may press one again to get out of the queue.

We would also like to remind you to please refer back to your registration e-mail after the conference and click on the link to fill out our post-conference survey. To receive CPE credit for today's call, you must fill out this short survey within the next five business days.

Again, if anyone would like to ask a question by phone, press the one key on your touch-tone phone.

Ron Seigneur: Thank you. I'm going to ask one more follow-up question on oppression and then we may move on to another area. Jay, I think you mentioned that there are states that have oppression states and some that do not, and I'm curious if you have any input on -- I think you addressed this a little bit, but the states without specific oppression statutes, where does one look for guidance on how to proceed in those venues?

Jay Fishman: Right. Well, as Shannon talked about, for example, Delaware does not have such a statute, and so, as a result, cases are brought under the dissolution statute or some other -- like a fair dealing kind of statute. In this regard, you have to look to the lawyer and ask that. One of the things we do in these kinds of cases is we ask for a copy of the complaint. And I must confess to you, we also ask for a copy of the complaint when relevant in divorce cases, but we just want to read them for our own information. But in this particular situation, you want to see what's being alleged and understand the context in which you're doing the valuation.

More and more, the issue of fair value revolves around a couple of things -- the issue of whether shareholder-level discounts are used; whether or not a control

Chapter 2: Background on Fair Value

premium is ever applied; how is the valuation date impacted; and the issue of -- most of the definitions use the term "before the effectuation of the subject action" -- so how does that impact? Meaning, in a dissenter's case, if we were bought by a particular buyer, and there were going to be benefits to that, how does that get factored into the valuation? Most states don't have you consider it.

And the other issue, by the way, involved in these kinds of cases is the weight associated with the asset-based or cost approach. There are many situations in which the business's going concern is worth less on a control basis than it would be upon liquidation. And there have been instances where people have tried to allege that the net asset value should be the preeminent method that you rely upon. And they really have not been able to sustain that position.

The other thing, I think, that's particularly interesting for those of us who do a lot of litigation is that in the dissenter and oppressed shareholder's action, the words that usually get used are "customary and current valuation techniques," and that comes really from a case in 1983 called *Weinberger v. UOP*. And it is the -- at least we see in Delaware -- it is the venue in which the discounted cash flow method is probably the most prevalent method and almost the method of choice with the comparable public company or comparable guideline transaction method as the kind of secondary method.

Shannon, didn't you find that to be the case as well?

Shannon Pratt: Yes, I did. In fact, one Delaware -- well, a number of Delaware cases say that the discounted cash flow method is currently the preferred method of choice in these matters before this Court.

Jay Fishman: Which is different, Bill, right, than what we see in a lot of divorce cases.

Bill Morrison: Absolutely. And in fact, there's a battle going on right now in one of our cases as to whether the DCF is appropriate. But Delaware likes to use it very much.

Jay Fishman: So what we're saying is, by reading the cases and kind of understanding how these things work, you begin to understand that. If you hadn't done a lot of work and walked into court and didn't use DCF in a dissenter's case, I think that could prove to be problematic.

Ron Seigneur: Just a side comment I'll make here on the evolution of using DCF models versus other models -- a lot of times, the argument is that the DCF is a forward-looking model, is too speculative. But yet, the same venues will allow you to use a capitalized earnings approach, which we know is nothing but a shortcut for a DCF model in the first place.

Standards of Value: Theory and Applications

Jay Fishman: Yeah, that's exactly correct.

Ron Seigneur: I'm going to ask a couple of questions that have come into us, and I find this first one interesting. This is from Peter O'Keefe. Pretty simple question -- "If a judge directs you to conduct a valuation under a standard of value that you believe is not applicable or appropriate, how would you handle that conflict?" So I take it that this is a situation where you're being asked to do the valuation at the direction from the bench and the judge has told you to do it but has directed you to use what you believe is an inappropriate standard of value for the particular assignment.

Shannon Pratt: Well, this is Shannon. I'll take the lead on that question. I would do as the court directs, but I would leave it to the attorney to argue that it's an inapplicable standard of value.

Bill Morrison: Ron, this Bill. I had that exact situation happen to me last year where a judge directed me in an oppression case where everybody had valued the business under fair value and took no discounts on both sides. He brought me in to reconcile the values, essentially, but said I should use fair market value. But he just wasn't thinking of it as we think of it as a term of art. So I would seek clarification. It could be something, as Jay's been saying, where they use a term that is totally incongruous to what they're doing, fair market value to the holder. So I think, depending upon the facts and circumstances, you may want to seek guidance from the court and say, as I do very often, "Fair value -- does that mean without discounts?" So you get everybody in agreement.

Ron Seigneur: That sounds like the best advice, is you definitely need to follow the judge's directive, but there's no reason why you can't seek additional guidance and clarification to help you to get over those hurdles.

I'm going to ask another question before we proceed into fair value. This one comes from Peter Vollers from Houston. And a little bit more difficult to set up but let me give it a go -- "We have a limited liability company (LLC) client group that has four members and that LLC client group owns eight private companies with different ownership percentages." So I'm taking that the four members in that client group have eight companies and they own those eight companies in different percentages. "One member owns a controlling interest in four of the eight companies and a minority interest in the other four companies. Client wishes to value individual companies for purposes of a tax-free consolidation and reorganization. Should these valuations be based on control/non-marketable or non-control/non-marketable basis?" So it's a matter of saying we've got kind of a different hybrid between these four -- I guess eight entities where there's controlling interest in some and non-controlling in others.

Chapter 2: Background on Fair Value

Anybody want to give that a go?

Jay Fishman: Well, I will. First of all, we're not giving legal advice. But one could look at it a couple of ways. I think if you're convinced that these are eight distinct business enterprises, then I think you could argue that you value each holding in each enterprise individually. And it's a kind of family attribution issue where you're not going to commingle and look at any kind of cross-ownership. You have all those family attribution cases -- *Bright, Propstra, Cidulka* -- and then you've got 93-12. So you make the argument that I'm looking at each one of these enterprises in a different -- in an independent way because I'm talking about no particular willing buyer and no particular willing seller and that I'm going to quarantine each one and value them individually. Now you have to make sure the facts are such that there isn't an interrelationship in some way from a business point of view to each one of these "A" entities.

Because the other way of looking at it is the situation in which one person owns voting and non-voting stock. Often in an estate tax way, the courts have looked it at as, "Well, that's one block. You're not going to sell the voting 'A' and not the non-voting 'B' individually."

But I think the issue would revolve, in my mind, around whether these were, in fact, eight distinct business enterprises.

Ron Seigneur: It sounds like they are. It sounds like we have one individual that has a controlling interest but it may be a different degree of control in each of those four entities, so I think that would also need to be taken into account.

Bill Morrison: Ron, this is Bill. But as a general comment, that valuation would fall under fair market value, and then the shareholder-level discounts would be taken if applicable, so that's really the analysis you'd go through, whereas, generally, in a fair value valuation, for dissent or oppression, you wouldn't be taking those discounts. But even though you're in the standard of fair market value where you can take the discounts, you'd have to go through the kind of analysis Jay is just describing. And the more complex your situation, the more you'd have to analyze to determine whether or nor you'd take a discount and the size of the discount.

Ron Seigneur: Let's turn our attention back to fair value for financial reporting purposes, and I'm going to have Jay lead this off and talk a little bit about how fair value for financial reporting differs from fair market value and, for that matter, fair value for statutory purposes.

Jay Fishman: Well, this is a particularly hot area right now because for a number of years, there's been an exposure draft out by the FASB. And this is really kind of based on how the FASB's viewed it as they are the arbiter of what's appropriate in terms of financial reporting. And then the SEC sits on top of that in terms of disclosure and things. So it's the FASB that's really dealt with these issues. And they made a decision awhile ago that rather than rely on cost, that the better measurement is fair value, which was some kind of market-based method.

And on September 15th of this year, they issued FASB 157, which is Statement of Financial Accounting Standards Number 157 on Fair Value Measurements, and that is a final standard. It is to be effective November 15, 2007. And people have seen this coming, and especially in connection with Business Combinations in FASB 141 and 142. And what the FASB says is that over 40 current accounting standards with generally accepted accounting principles require or permit entities to measure assets and liabilities at fair value. And the fair value measurement -- the fair value definition, as of the new standard, is, "Fair value is the price that would be received to sell an asset or pay to transfer a liability in an orderly transaction between market participants at the measurement date."

So it's pretty clear that we're talking about some type of value in exchange. Now these regulations are so new that people are still grappling with exactly the implementation.

They define each one of these terms. So you'll recall I used the term "orderly transaction." An orderly transaction has an entrance price and an exit price and it assumes exposure to the market for a period prior to the measurement date to allow for marketing activities that are usual and customary. They're not a forced or liquidation or distress sale. And here's an important thing -- they're considered from the perspective of a market participant that holds the asset or owes the liability, meaning an exit price.

And then they go through to define what a "market participant" is. And those of you who do this work know that there are three levels of measurement and the preference is always to look for an actual transaction price to determine the inputs. In terms of the fair value hierarchy, it prioritizes the inputs in terms of valuation technique, and gives the highest priority to quoted prices in active markets for identical assets or liabilities, and gives the lowest priority to unobservable inputs, meaning a lot of the income approach things that we use.

I think a couple of things are becoming apparent. The first is that they're looking for, as objective as possible, a standard to value these things. And I think, to a large extent, this came out of their Valuation of Financial Derivatives. And then secondly, they're looking to distance themselves as much as they can for the kind of subjective judgments that we normally make.

Chapter 2: Background on Fair Value

And so valuation people -- both auditors and people who use financial statements and those who assist the auditors in preparing them, doing valuation work -- have been grappling now with best practices to employ when coming up with these fair value inputs and valuations.

Recently, there are two things that are going on. The first is the International Valuation Standards Committee (IVSC), which is an international organization -- and their counterpart is the IASB, the International Accounting Standards Board -- is putting together standards on intangible assets. And secondly, the Appraisal Foundation has offered to step forward and has what they call a Best Practices for Financial Reporting Work Group (Steering Committee), a work group that's been put together in an effort to address issues where it comes to implementation of these definitions. And both of these groups are working. Bruce Bingham is the Chair of the IVSC task force and I am the Chair of the Appraisal Foundation task force.

So there's a lot of attention being paid to various implementation issues and best practice guidelines in this area.

Ron Seigneur: Jay, do you have any sense of when we might see some additional published guidance come out from either of those bodies?

Jay Fishman: Yeah. I think the IVSC is on a shorter turnaround than we are, and I would think that we're talking about perhaps the spring. We're going to be sending out a request for candidates and volunteers to put together a work group. We've picked three particular areas that we're dealing with. They deal with -- if you give me a second, I'll find a worksheet. That's my next conference call this afternoon. One of them is "Stratified Rates of Return." The other one is "Contributory Assets." And the third is some kind of implementation issue with regard to these types of intangible assets. And so people are going to see, both on the Foundation Web site and in other publications, a request for volunteers to participate in a work group to do this.

Our goal is to put together a document kind of similar to the In-Process Research and Development (R&D) document that will provide guidance for the implementation of some of these best practices.

Shannon Pratt: But Jay, if some of the participants on this call want to volunteer, how do they do that?

Jay Fishman: They should respond to the request. It's not on there yet, but the request that will be on the -- probably the best place is to go to the Appraisal

	Foundation Web site, *appraisalfoundation.com*, and there will be a posting on there asking for volunteers.
Ron Seigneur:	It's interesting from someone from the oil patch here in Colorado because I just recently gave a presentation on oil and gas accounting and reached back to some of the FASB's -- FASB 69 -- and I can't remember the other number -- that talked about kind of the fair value disclosures that have been required for years for oil and gas, the proven reserves. And I see a lot of this that we're talking about here being driven by the SEC trying to make the financial disclosures more meaningful for people to supplement the heretofore historical cost basis numbers that I think we're saying just doesn't work for the financial investment community.
Jay Fishman:	I found the three areas that we're looking at. One is "Contributory Assets." The second is "How Economic Rents on Contributory Assets Are Determined." And the third is the "Stratified Rates of Return for the Same Kind of Assets."
	So there isn't a lot of guidance. There's a lot of attention now in the 21st Century being paid to various, especially intangible assets, and it's becoming a global marketplace. So I know the IVSC is particularly interested in addressing that. And hopefully, we'll put together some best practices issues. The plan is to issue exposure drafts using kind of the infrastructure of the Appraisal Foundation and have hearings, et cetera, to try to make sure this is as widely vetted as possible.
Ron Seigneur:	A question I have as well, and I see this as a bullet that's in one of the slides that accompanies today's presentation -- it's under the "Other Issues -- Standards of Value in the International Context." And I know some of you, if not all of you, just came from the ASA Conference in Toronto, and if there's anything to comment on, please do with regard to anything else you see on kind of the international horizon for standards of value.
Shannon Pratt:	Well, the IVSC, the International Valuation Standards Committee, is being restructured, and it's on a fast track, as Jay said. It's expected to be restructured by this spring, and the restructuring is going to include a broader participation by other countries and broader participation on the part of various individuals, so it's going to become a broader group. And in 2005, they published the Seventh Edition -- this is the old -- the International Valuation Standards Committee is the oldest international committee around -- and in 2005, they published the Seventh Edition of the *International Valuation Standards*. And they expect to publish the Eighth Edition as early as next year, as 2007.

Chapter 2: Background on Fair Value

Jay Fishman: The other thing that came out of the session in Toronto, that our audience might find interesting, is that Congress passed House Resolution (HR) 4, which was a pension bill, a few weeks ago, and it contains guidelines for the valuation for gift purposes of non-cash charitable contributions. And the Treasury -- the IRS came out the middle of last week with some guidance because the law itself now requires these appraisals to be done by qualified appraisers using generally accepted appraisal standards. And so the implementation phase, which is supposed to end in January of 2007, the Treasury Department is going to determine whom a qualified appraiser is, and usually, it looks like someone with a designation from a recognized appraisal organization or someone who, by education and training, there's various requirements. And the big buzz that came out was in their implementation of what generally accepted appraisal standards are, the example they give is the Uniform Standards of Professional Appraisal Practice, which, by the way, the IVSC Business Enterprise Guidelines are very similar to. So we're having kind of a coming-together from a national/international point of view as to what appropriate standards and who defines -- and what the definition of qualified appraiser is.

Ron Seigneur: Jay, that notice --

Jay Fishman: There is no truth to the rumor that a qualified appraiser is anyone who has bought a book by Shannon Pratt.

Ron Seigneur: But it doesn't hurt. That notice -- I was just reviewing it the day before yesterday -- is IRS Notice 2006-96. And a couple of things I saw in there as well is these are interim guidance until regulations are produced, but it also specifies that a qualified appraiser is someone that regularly appraises the type of property that's the subject of the appraisal. And I think that's an interesting bit of verbiage as well because there are obviously issues of people that are qualified appraisers but they're not qualified to appraise a particular type of property --

Jay Fishman: That's a good point, Ron.

Ron Seigneur: For that purpose.

Jay Fishman: The other thing that came out was there was a person from the Internal Revenue Service who was talking about the increased enforcement of various regulations to the point where the Office of Professional Responsibility of the Internal Revenue Service is now empowered to implement disbarment proceedings for those appraisers who they found guilty of overstatement or understatement of valuation. So I think that's a topic probably for another teleconference for another day.

Standards of Value: Theory and Applications

Ron Seigneur: Overall, though, I think this is good news. I think it means we're going to have to pay more attention doing good work, but it also means that some of the dabblers on the fringes may be less inclined to issue their opinions for this particular purpose.

Jay, just to bring us back to fair value for a couple of minutes, you mentioned market inputs as being very relevant to the new fair value measurements, and could you tell us just a little bit more about kind of what you mean by market inputs?

Jay Fishman: Sure. Let me get back to where I was. Well, first of all, market participants are defined as those who are independent of the reporting entity, and are not related parties; those people who are knowledgeable, having reasonable understanding about the asset or liability and the transaction-based on all available information; able to transact -- remember, we learned this in economics -- it's not just wanting to buy but it's also having the ability to buy -- so those who are able to transact for the asset or liability; willing to transact.

The reporting entity itself need not identify specific market participants, rather, the reporting entity should identify characteristics that distinguish market participants generally, considering factors specific to the asset or liability, the principal market for the asset, and the market participants with whom the reporting entity would transact in that market.

In terms of inputs, it tells us the following. First of all, they suggest, not surprisingly, that there are three valuation methods -- market, income, and cost. One should pick the techniques that are appropriate in the circumstance for which the sufficient data is available. The technique should be consistently applied. And the change is appropriate if the change results in a measurement that is equally or more represented of fair value.

Then they have various levels of inputs. Level 1 inputs are quoted prices, unadjusted, in active markets for identical assets or liabilities that the reporting entity has the ability to access at the measurement date.

Level 2 inputs are inputs other than quoted prices included with Level 1 that are observable for the asset or liability either directly or indirectly. And Level 2 inputs should include quoted prices for similar assets or liabilities in active markets -- and it goes on with the whole list -- inputs other than quoted prices that are observable for the asset or liability. Remember, they're using words "observable," which means that it's not something that your judgment is based on but something that you're able to abstract directly from the marketplace that's contemporaneous.

Chapter 2: Background on Fair Value

	Level 3 are unobservable inputs for the asset or liability, that is, inputs that reflect the reporting entity's own assumptions about the assumptions market participants would use in pricing the asset or liability, including assumptions about the risk developed based on the best information available without undue cost or effort.
Shannon Pratt:	Can you tell the participants what you're referencing there?
Jay Fishman:	That was Level 3 participants. What's the question that you're asking, Shannon?
Shannon Pratt:	What's the document that you're referencing there?
Jay Fishman:	This is FASB 157.
Shannon Pratt:	All right.
Jay Fishman:	Okay, this is FASB 157. It seems, from what we've been hearing in our experience, that they are trying to differentiate fair value for financial reporting purposes from fair market value, that they do not want to be encumbered -- as our discussion talked about today, they do not want to be encumbered with all the nuances that we talked about -- and some of them we haven't -- that come with fair market value for tax and income tax purposes.

The other thing, it seems, in my observation, is that they're looking for -- I'm trying to put this -- they're looking for objective models that can be applied on a consistent basis. And some of the things that we're used to doing relative to that, in terms of judgments, clearly fall under Level 3 inputs.

It should be reminded that in the 141/142 work, that an assembled work force is not considered an identifiable intangible asset because of the FASB's belief of the judgmental nature of how the value is arrived at. I think that's some insight into how they're looking at it going forward. |
Ron Seigneur:	Jay, I find that comment fascinating when you say they're looking for objective models that can be applied on a consistent basis because it seems like that's what we're all looking for in most all of this work that we're doing.
Jay Fishman:	Exactly.
Ron Seigneur:	We've got about five minutes left and there are a couple of questions that have been submitted. I'd like to take an opportunity to get to those. And this question comes from Mason Packard from Concord, Massachusetts.

Standards of Value: Theory and Applications

And he actually had two questions and one was just to go back through the three levels that you just did, Jay, so that was very responsive.

This is another question from Mason and I'll read the question. "I have a question of values when appraising a Sub-S Corporation versus a C Corp, which, hopefully, is not too far from the core discussion today. Specifically, what standards of fair market value should be considered when looking at the enterprise with respect to possibly adjusting for tax effects? This seems to go to the continuum of intrinsic value to the 100 percent shareholder versus a perspective value to a new owner/buyer who will typically be a C Corp-oriented enterprise."

Jay Fishman: That clearly should be directed to Shannon.

Shannon Pratt: There was an entire issue in the *Business Valuation Review* that was dedicated to that question.

Jay Fishman: Well, I think a lot of terms are being mixed here. I guess the way we would look at it is, first of all, we probably wouldn't use the term "fair market value" and "intrinsic value" in the same sentence. I think the issue is -- how is fair market value applied relative to these pass-through entities? And there's been plenty written about this and there's been plenty of programs. I would suggest that perhaps there'd be reference to another teleconference and a transcript or something that was here because I know it's been discussed. I think, generally, when we're talking about 100 percent interest, there's an issue about identifying a willing pool and perhaps tax-impacting it. When we're talking about minority interests, which is the area that's well developed, there's a whole bunch of models -- Dan Van Vleet has come up with them -- Chris Treharne -- Roger Grabowski -- Chris Mercer -- and I would invite the caller to look at some of that data.

Ron Seigneur: I think that's a good point, that there's so much other guidance on that that they need to seek those answers out. But I also look at this, saying, gee, if you *are* looking at it from the context of what it's worth to the 100 percent shareholder, you're going to approach it much differently than saying if it's an outside buyer that is the premise, I guess.

Jay Fishman: Right.

Ron Seigneur: Let's see -- there's one more question here. Let's see if we can set this up. I think this might be a good way to kind of start wrapping things up. This question comes from Tom Larson. "Would there be any difference in the value arrived at for a professional practice in a divorce action between a fair

Chapter 2: Background on Fair Value

market value and a fair value report for a single-owner CPA firm with four other CPAs employed, and also with a caveat that state law in this particular situation is not conclusive as to the standard of value to be used?"

Shannon Pratt: This is Shannon. When the state law is not conclusive, most states tend to look at other states with similar statutes or similar case law.

Bill Morrson: Ron, is that in divorce or oppression?

Ron Seigneur: In a divorce action.

Bill Morrison: Well, this is Bill. I would think that comes to exactly where we started in looking at the three criteria of personal versus professional goodwill, shareholder-level discounts, and buy/sell agreements. And clearly, you'd look to what the trend is in that particular state. And fair value could be either, a value to the holder or a value in exchange, again, depending upon the individual state law. But with the smaller operations, especially sole proprietorships, where the states don't recognize personal goodwill, you're going to value the business very differently under value in exchange versus in a value to the holder context. With a bigger business, where enterprise value has taken over, there's not going to be a difference. And in fact, the personal goodwill is going to be much less to the individual. It's often going to be a much larger enterprise value.

Ron Seigneur: Well, again, that's one of the benefits of the treatise that you all have put together here because I think in this particular question, they can hopefully find some good guidance based upon the particular jurisdiction they're in as a good starting point.

I'd also like to make reference to a colleague, Nancy Fannon, who has just chimed in with a comment. And Nancy's one of the, I think, thought leaders on the tax-affecting issue that was part of that prior question. And her comment -- it's not a question -- is the IRS has overwhelming information that MOST buyers of private companies are NOT C Corporations. And I think that's just an important point to recognize, is that oftentimes when you're looking at these pass-through entities, you're saying, "Gee, a buyer -- that would be a C Corp that wouldn't qualify for the S status," and that *may* not be the case. And according to Nancy's comment, it likely isn't the case - just a good point to take into account.

Jay Fishman: I agree with that.

Ron Seigneur: We are about one minute past the time that we conclude for this call, so I think we could go on a bit further, but I think we ought to wrap things up.

And I would like to say a great thank you to our three panelists. I think this has been a very good discussion. It's very on point for a lot of the work that I do. And so I thank each of you for your time today and the input and the comments that you've made, as well as the work that you've all put in in producing standards of value that will be out very shortly.

And with that said, I think I would like to go ahead and turn this call back to our operator.

Jay Fishman: Thank you, Ron.

Operator: We would like to thank everyone for participating in today's teleconference. Please don't forget to refer back to your registration e-mail and click on the link to fill out the post-conference survey. To receive your CPE credit for today's call, you must fill out this short survey within the next five business days.

Please watch your e-mail or visit our *www.bvresources.com* Web site for information on upcoming conferences.

For updates on future telephone conferences, or to purchase past telephone conference CDs or transcripts, please e-mail *customerservice@bvresources.com*.

Chapter 3
Fair Value in Dissenting and Oppressed Shareholder Matters

Fair Value in Dissenting and Oppressed Shareholder Matters: How to Avoid Minefields[1]

By Jay Fishman, FASA, CBA[2]

Introduction

In this paper we will address theory and application of fair value in judicial matters regarding: 1) shareholders who dissent from a corporate action; and 2) those who avail themselves of the buy-out provision in dissolution statutes under situations of deadlock and oppression. As dissenters' and oppressed shareholder's rights have evolved in the courts, those who chose to use the term "fair value" did so to distinguish the concept from fair market value.

Because dissent and oppression matters deal with corporate actions, they are governed by statutes on a state-by-state basis. Fair value in this context is a legal term used in the vast majority of dissenter's rights and oppressed shareholders statutes, but only broadly defined. Accordingly, the term has been left to judicial interpretation.

There can be as many interpretations of fair value as there are states. In fact, in some instances, there are differing interpretations within a state. Because the interpretation of this standard of value is left to the courts, it is helpful to consider the different contexts in which the term is used.

Our analysis includes the development of dissenting shareholders' rights (sometimes called appraisal rights). We also address the development of a minority shareholder's right to petition for dissolution of a company, specifically in situations where oppression has occurred, and receive the fair value of his or her shares through a buy-out or a judicially directed dissolution of the corporation. We then examine the evolution of the standard and definition of fair value. To understand fair value as a standard of value in the context of dissenter's rights and oppression cases, we examine how various courts address current valuation concepts and techniques, especially the application of shareholder level discounts for lack of control and lack of marketability and the application of control premiums.

Dissenter's rights proceedings generally involve a minority shareholder who disagrees with the direction the board of directors is taking the company. A disagreement will generally involve a merger, sale of assets, or other major change to the nature of the investment, such that the shareholder is no longer involved in the company.

Oppression cases often include more egregious actions than do dissent cases. Oppressed shareholders are those who have been treated unfairly or prejudicially by the majority shareholders or the board of directors. Those cases often involve shareholder employees. Oppression cases can

Chapter 3: Dissenting and Oppressed Shareholder Matters

involve termination of dividends, compensation, or employment, or a siphoning of corporate assets for the benefit of the majority at the expense of the minority. In some states, shareholders may petition to dissolve the corporation in order to regain what was taken from them. The corporation may elect to buy their shares at fair value, or the courts may order the buy-out, if provided for by the individual state's statute.

Fair value is the standard of value used to determine the cash price dissenting and oppressed shareholders will receive in exchange for their shares of stock. Currently, this much-debated standard of value is widely understood to mean the proportionate value of the company as a whole. Today, this understanding is essentially correct in many jurisdictions, as the courts increasingly have interpreted fair value to be a pro-rata share of the entity-level value rather than the value of the individual minority shares themselves. While the general trend in many states is not to allow or to limit the use of minority and marketability discounts by statue or case law, some states still allow the discounts either by precedent, a court's discretion, or special circumstances.

In 1950, the Delaware Supreme Court defined fair value in *Tri-Continental Corp. v. Battye*[3] as the value which had been taken from the shareholder. To the present, the debate continues as to the nature of what has been taken and whether the value should relate to subject interest of the shareholder or a percentage of the company as a whole.

Two influential legal associations, the American Bar Association (ABA)[4] and the American Law Institute (ALI),[5] have each created their own definitions of fair value. By considering relevant case law from past decades, these organizations have influenced legislative and judicial understanding of fair value by publishing definitions in the Model Business Corporation Act (MBCA, from the ABA) and the *Principles of Corporate Governance* (from the ALI). The individual states' statutes have largely drawn from these institutions to establish their definitions of fair value, whose meanings are later reinterpreted by the courts in subsequent decisions. The nature of this process has led the states to interpret fair value in light of decisions in other jurisdictions as well as changes in valuation theory.

The fair value standard has been loosely defined in dissenter's rights statutes, which have been widely affected by the standards recommended by the MBCA.[6] However, the courts' decisions in dissent and oppression cases have had the most profound effect on defining fair value. The related case law, legal institutions, and statutes have all contributed to the development of the concept of fair value.

I. Fair value as defined by authorities and statutes

In order to address this standard of value for the purposes of shareholder dissent and oppression cases, let us address definitions offered by the American Bar Association's Model Business Corporation Act (MBCA). Statutes vary, but most draw inspiration from the MBCA or the later published Revised Model Business Corporation Act (RMBCA).

How to Avoid Minefields

The 1969 Model Business Corporation Act, the first in which the ABA explicitly defined fair value, contains the following definition:

> Such corporation shall pay to such shareholder, upon surrender of the certificate or certificates representing such shares, the fair value thereof as of the day prior to the date on which the vote was taken approving the proposed corporate action, excluding any appreciation or depreciation in anticipation of such corporate action.

In 1984, the ABA issued the Revised Model Business Corporation Act, which added the phrase: "unless exclusion would be inequitable". Accordingly, many states use the definition established by the 1984 RMBCA. The definition of fair value in this treatise reads:

> The value of the shares immediately before the effectuation of the corporate action to which the dissenter objects, excluding any appreciation or depreciation in anticipation of the corporate action unless exclusion would be inequitable.

The 1984 definition provides a guideline, however nonspecific, by which fair value should be determined. The company should be valued on the day before the corporate action occurs, and without any of the effects of the action unless their exclusion would be unfair. The passage does not give instructions on what method or valuation technique should be utilized to determine the fair value, nor does it define "inequitable." Twenty-one states[7] currently use this exact definition of fair value. In our view, the intentional ambiguity in this definition allows for wide interpretation of the assumptions that underlie this standard of value. Comments published by the ABA explain that this definition leaves the matter to the courts to determine "the details by which fair value is to be determined within the broad outlines of the definition."[8]

While insuring that the courts have wide discretion, the ambiguity can create confusion on the part of appraisers and appraisal users. Valuation professionals are well advised to discuss this with their attorney so as to come to an understanding of the specific interpretation relevant to the jurisdiction.

Although state statutes more often use the RMBCA's definition of fair value, six states have utilized the American Law Institute's concept of fair value in case law.[9] In the *Principles of Corporate Governance*, published in 1992, the ALI defined fair value as:

> ... the value of the eligible holder's proportionate interest in the corporation, without any discount for minority status or, absent extraordinary circumstances, lack of marketability. Fair value should be determined using the customary valuation concepts and techniques generally employed in the relevant securities and financial markets for similar businesses in the context of the transaction giving rise to appraisal.[10]

In 1999, following the development of substantial case law on dissent and oppression, as well as the publication of the *Principles of Corporate Governance*, the RMBCA was revised so that the definition of fair value reads:

Chapter 3: Dissenting and Oppressed Shareholder Matters

> The value of the shares immediately before the effectuation of the corporate action to which the shareholder objects using customary and current valuation concepts and techniques generally employed for similar businesses in the context of the transaction requiring appraisal, and without discounting for lack of marketability or minority status except, if appropriate, for amendments to the certificate of incorporation pursuant to section 13.02(a)(5).

Although still not outlining a specific method of calculating value, the 1999 RMBCA definition mirrors the ALI's *Principles of Corporate Governance,* in that it adds two important concepts to the framework: the use of customary and current valuation techniques, and the rejection of the use of marketability and minority discounts except, *"if appropriate, for amendments to the certificate of incorporation pursuant to section 13.02(a)(5)."* The dissenters' rights statutes of nine states[11] currently follow this definition.[12]

Other states have developed their own definitions of fair value or have used different standards of value in their statutes. For example, New Jersey has used fair value as its statutory standard since 1968.[13] In the dissolution statute, the explanation of fair value makes allowances for "equitable adjustments" in conjunction with oppression proceedings.

Ohio and Louisiana use "fair cash value" in their statute. Ohio uses the willing buyer/willing seller definition in its statute along with the term *fair cash value*. Decisions in Ohio involving closely held businesses have largely utilized significant discounts in valuing minority shares. Additionally, when the stock of a company is publicly traded, the Ohio court usually relies on that value as opposed to a hypothetical sale price for the entire corporation as indicated in *Armstrong v. Marathon Oil.*[14]

California uses a fair market value in dissent and the term *fair value in liquidation* in oppression. Its dissolution (oppression) statute states:

> The *fair value* shall be determined on the basis of the liquidation value as of the valuation date but taking into account the possibility, if any, of sale of the entire business *as a going concern in a liquidation.* [emphasis added]

California's dissent statute states:

> The *fair market value* shall be determined as of the day before the first announcement of the terms of the proposed reorganization or short-form merger, excluding any appreciation or depreciation in consequence of the proposed action, but adjusted for any stock split, reverse stock split, or share dividend which becomes effective thereafter.

The term *fair value in liquidation* as used in California's oppression statute is unique. Most states look to determine fair value in these circumstances under the assumption that the business will continue to operate as a going concern.

Dissenters' rights

I. Overview and History

In the early nineteenth century, common law[15] held that corporate decisions were to be made by consensus, meaning 100% shareholder approval was required. The prevailing perspective on business was that the investment made by the minority shareholder contractually connected the corporation to the shareholder, and the shareholder should not be required to comply with fundamental changes that he did not support. Therefore, any single shareholder could utilize his common law veto in order to prevent corporate action.[16]

This perspective could have a paralyzing effect on the decision-making process in a corporation. A minority shareholder could impulsively or arbitrarily threaten to reject a corporate action solely to collect a premium on an initial investment.[17] With the increasing need for flexibility caused by the industrial revolution, the country's growing infrastructure, and the birth and growth of the transcontinental railroads, corporations came to realize that consensus was not efficient for forward movement and growth.[18]

In 1892, the Illinois Supreme Court affirmed majority rule and the role of the minority shareholder in its decision in *Wheeler v. Pullman Iron & Steel Co.*[19] The court decided that the fundamental law of corporations should be that the majority should control policy. It revised the concept of the minority shareholder's investment, such that by investing in the corporation, the minority shareholder agrees to abide by the decisions sanctioned by the majority or the board of directors elected by the majority.[20]

Following the decision in *Wheeler*, the courts, recognizing the paralyzing effect of unanimity, became more sympathetic towards majority rule. Initially majority rule was in place only in cases of insolvency, but later it was considered controlling in mergers, asset sales, and so on, as long as the majority's decision was in the best interest of the corporation.[21] As a result, minority shareholders were left without the power to challenge such corporate decisions or the ability to exit the corporation if they disagreed with the actions of the majority. This in turn, led to the emergence of appraisal rights.

An 1875 Ohio case was early evidence of the emergence of fair value appraisal rights. In its decision, the Ohio Supreme Court stated:

> …our legislature has seen proper to provide that stockholders in a railroad corporation shall not be carried into a new or consolidated company against their consent. From this provision it is plain that a stockholder not only can not be compelled to become a member of the consolidated corporation, but the consolidation can not proceed until he is paid the *fair value* of his stock. It is impossible to force upon him the liabilities and responsibilities attaching to the new corporation; it is impossible to change the character of the enterprise in which he agreed to embark his money, until he has been paid the fair value of his investment.[22]

Chapter 3: Dissenting and Oppressed Shareholder Matters

Before the appearance of appraisal statutes, shareholders would sue for injunctive relief and to receive the value of their shares in cash. They would petition the courts to stop the corporation from pursuing a course of action until their desire to exit was satisfied. The courts would award a fair value in cash to shareholders, enabling them to escape the choice of either forced membership in a new corporation or pro-rata share in cash of the transaction's proceeds.[23] In order to protect the interest of minority shareholders, legislatures began to enact statutes with appraisal rights to allow the minority to dissent from a corporate transaction and receive a judicial determination of the fair value of their shares in the original corporation in cash.[24] The statutes also were enacted to prevent expensive and drawn-out injunction procedures and to allow corporations, during the dispute, to continue conducting business as usual.[25]

The U.S. Supreme Court clarified the purpose of dissenter's rights statutes in the 1941 case *Voeller v. Neilston Warehouse Co.*[26] In this case, Justice Black noted a Securities and Exchange Commission report describing the history and necessity of establishing majority rule and a remedy for minority shareholders:

> At common law, unanimous shareholder consent was a prerequisite to fundamental changes in the corporation. This made it possible for an arbitrary minority to establish a nuisance value for its shares by refusing to cooperate. To address this situation, legislatures authorized corporations to make changes by a majority vote. This, however, opened the door to victimization of the minority. To solve the dilemma, statutes permitting a dissenting minority to recover the appraised value of its shares were widely adopted.[27]

In 1927, the Uniform Business Corporation Act was introduced by the Commissioners for Uniform State Laws,[28] but it was adopted only by Louisiana, Washington, and Kentucky, likely because most states were not comfortable with the implied inflexibility of uniform laws and wanted to reserve their own legislative rights.[29] The ABA's Model Business Corporation Act (MBCA) gained much wider appeal and went on to provide a framework for state corporation statutes across the country.[30] Over the course of the first half of the twentieth century, nearly all states adopted an appraisal statute.[31]

II. Context of modern appraisal rights

Currently, the ABA and the ALI recognize various events that can trigger dissenter's rights. Each state has adopted different triggering events in its statutes, and these may have developed differently from those of the RMBCA and *Principles of Corporate Governance* because of the nature of the events that occurred in each state. Some common triggers are contained in the RMBCA, and include:

- Merger
- Share exchange
- Disposition of assets

- Amendment to the articles of incorporation that creates fractional shares
- Any other amendment to the articles from which shareholders may dissent
- Domestication from a foreign entity into a domestic entity
- Conversion of status to nonprofit
- Conversion to unincorporated entity

In most states, the process to dissent is as follows: a company's board of directors is required to give notice of an event from which dissenters may claim their rights. Before the vote, the dissenters give their notice to the board and demand payment of their shares. In doing so, the shareholders relinquish all rights, except to obtain payment of the fair value of their shares. The process and timetable of these events vary from state to state, but in most cases are strictly enforced. The process is referred to in most states as "perfecting dissenter's rights."

Certain states have statutory provisions whereby nonvoting stock is not eligible for appraisal rights. Twenty-five states follow the RMBCA and do not allow nonvoting stock to dissent. Three states explicitly allow nonvoting stock to dissent—Massachusetts, Kansas, and Utah. Delaware limits triggering events, but allows both voting and nonvoting stockholders to dissent.[32]

Oppression remedy

I. Development of oppression remedy

The oppression remedy emerged for similar reasons as did dissenter's rights. As the courts moved to majority rule, which based decisions on the best interests of the corporation rather than the shareholders, minority shareholders could be harmed or excluded without the intervention of the courts. Shareholders would have to bring suit for an injunction or to dissolve the corporation in order to recover their interest.

As with dissent, certain events trigger the right to call for judicial dissolution of a corporation.[33] Generally they fall under the categories of mismanagement, waste, fraud, or illegal acts by management and the board of directors. However, majority behavior does not necessarily have to be illegal or fraudulent to be unfair to a minority shareholder. Illinois was the first state to codify oppression as a trigger for dissolution in the 1933 Illinois Business Corporation Act. The ABA later modeled the MBCA's dissolution statute after Illinois's example.[34] The 1953 MBCA stated that a shareholder could call for dissolution if the acts of the directors or those in control of management are illegal, oppressive, or fraudulent.[35] Currently several states have oppression as grounds for dissolution; others do not.

Shareholder oppression occurs when the majority shareholders or the board of directors act in a manner that is detrimental to minority shareholders. Although oppression was once thought to encompass only illegal or fraudulent acts, the term has come to include conduct by the majority that breaches fiduciary duty, denies the minority shareholder his or her reasonable expectations in acquiring shares and entering into a shareholder agreement, or is burdensome, harsh, and wrongful to minority shareholder interests. Oppressive acts by the majority can be very damaging to a minority shareholder; for example, a majority decision may eliminate a minority shareholder's ability to receive dividends or other types of benefits from a corporation.

The shareholder oppression statutes are part of corporate dissolution statutes, which are the laws in place to provide guidelines for dissolving corporations. Many, if not most, states allow shareholder oppression as a triggering event for dissolution or a buyout of the claimant's shares.[36] Dissolution statutes vary much more widely than dissenter's rights statutes.

Events triggering dissenter's rights are fairly universal and deal with a decision by the majority to which a dissenting shareholder objects (merger, share exchange, amendment to the articles of incorporation, etc). Dissolution statutes exist to provide procedures by which businesses may wrap up their business affairs and end their existence. Although most states use a combination of similar triggering events, the statutes are generally unique to each state.

The RMBCA sanctions a buy-out of stock in lieu of dissolution as an alternative remedy under the dissolution statutes when a shareholder files for judicial dissolution. The buy-out option largely developed in the late 1970s to compensate minority shareholders for oppressive acts taken against them.

Most states allow for the minority shareholder to file for judicial dissolution; some do not, and leave the action to other channels.[37] Delaware, for instance, does not cite shareholder oppression in the dissolution statute. Instead, it leaves the decision of wrongdoing to the consideration of fairness under an appraisal proceeding.

The dissolution statutes vary based on the events that trigger dissolution in each state. Almost all states had adopted a statute for involuntary dissolution by 1965, and 12 states had oppression as grounds for dissolution.[38] Twenty-four states have provided oppression as a basis for dissolution since then.[39] Others do not specifically allow minority shareholders to file for dissolution citing oppression, but do provide shareholders the ability to dissolve the company citing acts that basically constitute oppression.[40] Many of the states that allow shareholder dissolution also have a buy-out provision written into their statutes. In other states, although no statutory buy-out option exists, case law recognizes the use of a buy-out at fair value as an equitable remedy. Several states also have a minimum-percentage share ownership requirement to file a judicial dissolution action.[41]

II. Alternative remedies

As long as dissolution was the primary remedy for oppressed minority shareholders, the courts were hesitant to find in favor of the minority shareholder.[42] Oppressive conduct had to be egregious—a waste of assets, or gross fraud or illegality. Dissolution was viewed as drastic.

An example of a court's failure to dissolve a corporation in a clearly oppressive situation is the case of *Kruger v. Gerth*,[43] a 1965 New York decision. In that case, a corporation was formed by investors to benefit shareholders by way of employment and salary. When one partner died, his wife maintained her husband's share of the corporation but was no longer permitted to benefit from the salary. The corporation refused to buy her out, and the court refused to dissolve the corporation.

Dissolution remained the statutory remedy until the states began to institute buy-out provisions for the shares of oppressed shareholders.[44] In 1941, California was the first to institute a buy-out provision; its statute[45] provided an option for a corporation to offer petitioning minority shareholders the fair cash value for their shares in lieu of dissolution.[46]

In the 1970s, the courts that adopted oppression as a trigger for dissolution began to explore alternative remedies to dissolution. Several judicial remedies for the oppressed shareholder emerged. The court could decide to:

- Require the company to liquidate and the proceeds be equitably distributed;

- Find no oppression and keep status quo; and
- Order a purchase of the shares and let the company continue.

A 1991 revision to the RMBCA introduced the statutory buy-out for shareholders filing for dissolution. The fair value buy-out as an alternative remedy was already in use in some states. It emerged in the late 1970s in cases like New York's *Topper v. Park Sheraton Pharmacy*,[47] a case that is discussed further in the context of oppression remedy.

III. Context of oppression remedy

Although dissent and oppression cases are often grouped together, their nature is very different. Oppression is generally more personal. It often involves the loss of employment, exclusion from a close corporation that the stockholder may have helped build, or a family fallout that results in the breaking up of a corporation. Dissent is generally less personal. Dissenter's rights proceedings usually involve shareholders with small interests in a corporation. They may not even include individuals who regularly participate in the business.

There are also similarities between dissent and oppression cases. The primary similarity is that they both use the fair value standard. Many courts understand the fair value definitions as expressed by the dissenter's rights statutes to carry over to the dissolution statutes. The ALI asserts that fair value can be viewed differently for oppression and dissent, but many courts view it otherwise. For example, in New Jersey's oppression case *Balsamides v. Protameen Chemicals*,[48] the Supreme Court of New Jersey agreed with Washington's Supreme Court in *Robblee v. Robblee*[49] that there is no reason to believe that fair value means something different in reference to dissenting shareholders than it does in the context of oppressed shareholders. In addition, many oppression and dissent cases cite each other for guidelines on how to deal with various elements of valuation.

Chapter 3: Dissenting and Oppressed Shareholder Matters

Both oppression and dissent were developed to protect minority shareholders from being excluded or abused by the majority. In states where the oppression remedy is unavailable, oppressed shareholders may claim dissenter's rights. For example, reverse stock splits are generally used to cash out minority shareholders by reducing the number of shares in a corporation such that certain members hold less than one share and are forced to sell it back to the corporation. The Northern District of Illinois Court decided in *Connector Service Corporation v. Briggs*[50] that the Delaware language governing reverse split cash-outs was similar to the language governing cash-out mergers and ordered the fair value of the stock to be determined using the same criteria as in a cash-out merger. This conclusion is consistent with the Delaware decision in *Metropolitan Life Insurance Co. v. Aramark Corp.*, which granted a quasi-appraisal remedy in a reverse split.[51]

IV. Recognizing oppression

As oppression became more widely recognized over the course of the twentieth century, the courts eventually had to find ways in which to identify whether oppression had actually occurred. Some viewed oppression as akin to fraudulent or illegal acts. The Illinois court's decision in *Central Standard Life Insurance v. Davis*[52] in 1957 applied the term *oppression* more broadly than fraudulent or illegal activity despite finding in favor of the corporation.

V. Reasonable expectations

A breach of reasonable expectations was established as a fundamental determination of oppression based on the 1980 New York case of *Topper v. Park Sheraton Pharmacy*.[53] In this case, the court found that the plaintiff's reasonable expectations were violated by an intentional freeze-out and ordered the buy-out of his shares.

Topper v. Park Sheraton Pharmacy

Three individuals, Topper, Goldstein, and Reingold, operated two pharmacies in prominent Manhattan hotels: the New York Sheraton and the New York Hilton. The shareholder agreements were executed in early 1979. The agreements provided no method for transfer or purchase of shares, nor did they specify terms of employment. Topper associated himself with the other two individuals in the two corporations (Center City Enterprise, Inc. and Park Sheraton Pharmacy, Inc.) with the expectation of being an active participant in the operations of the corporations. In order to participate, Topper ended a 25-year employment relationship with Continental Drug Corporation, and he and his family left their home in North Miami, Florida to move to New York to engage in the two corporations. Topper invested his life savings in the venture and executed personal guarantees of a lease extension and promissory notes for the purchase price of his stock interest.

The majority stockholders affirm that in February 1980, they discharged Topper as an employee, terminated his salary (after his salary had been raised from $30,000 to $75,000 in the first year), removed him as an officer and as a cosignatory on the corporate bank accounts, and changed the locks on the corporate offices to exclude him from entrance. The controlling shareholders claimed that the petitioner had suffered no harm, as his one-third interest remained intact. To date, the corporation had not paid dividends.

The court deemed that the actions of the majority constituted a freeze-out and were oppressive, as they violated Topper's reasonable expectations in joining the partnership. The court recognized that in a close corporation, the bargain of the participants is not necessarily reflected in the corporation's charter, by-laws, or other written agreement. In many small corporations, minority shareholders expect to participate in management and operations, and these expectations constitute the bargain of the parties by which subsequent conduct must be appraised.

The court also stated that the business corporation law determines that oppression of the "rights and interests" of minority shareholders in a close corporation is an abuse of corporate power. These rights are derived from the expectations of the parties underlying the formation of the corporation. The court awarded Topper the right to the fair market value[54] of his shares as of the day prior to the date of petition, as empowered by the business corporation law.

A shareholders' agreement can provide a basis by which the courts can determine the reasonable expectations of a shareholder.[55] An ABA report suggests that courts observe the provisions of a shareholder agreement unless the circumstances of the case suggest otherwise. The shareholder agreement may indicate a previously agreed upon value or method for determining fair value that can be used in the case of dissenter's rights or oppression cases.[56]

In the unreported Connecticut case of *Stone v. Health*,[57] the plaintiff sought to dissolve the corporation as tensions rose among the doctors in the corporation. The plaintiff claimed she was entitled to a fair value of $338,000 as her share, but the shareholders' agreement stated that she was entitled to the net book value of the assets she had contributed to the corporation, a little over $13,000. Since oppression was not found, the court determined that it was *not* inequitable or unfair under the circumstances to look to the stockholders' agreement for a determination of value.

This would seem to indicate that maintenance of and adherence to a shareholders' agreement provides a certain amount of clarity as to shareholder expectations, as long as a particularly egregious breach of the agreement has not occurred.[58]

VI. Breach of fiduciary duty

As one of the landmark cases offering relief to oppressed shareholders, the Massachusetts case of *Donahue v. Rodd Electrotype of New England*[59] established that a breach of fiduciary duty, the

Chapter 3: Dissenting and Oppressed Shareholder Matters

obligation owed to minority shareholders by the majority, may determine whether shareholder oppression has occurred.

Breaking down the components of fair value

One useful definition of fair value used by many states is the definition established by the 1984 RMBCA. The definition of fair value in this treatise reads:

> The value of the shares immediately before the effectuation of the corporate action to which the dissenter objects, excluding any appreciation or depreciation in anticipation of the corporate action unless exclusion would be inequitable.

I. Before the effectuation of the corporate action to which the shareholder objects

This portion of the definition suggests a time frame for the valuation. It instructs the court to set a valuation date immediately prior to the corporate action from which the shareholder dissents. Most states say that valuation should reflect the value on the day before the corporate action (occurred or was voted on) to which the shareholder dissents. This indicates that the shareholder should not suffer or benefit from the proceeds or effects of the transaction he or she dissented from, including benefits from synergies arising from the prospective transaction.

For example, in the case of *Pittsburgh Terminal Corporation v. the Baltimore and Ohio Railroad*,[60] minority shareholders in PTC objected to a merger that would effectively cash out their interest in the corporation. They argued that the consideration they received was considerably less than an outsider would bid for a controlling interest in the corporation. Upon review, the court found that the since the surviving shareholders had effective control before the merger, it would not be appropriate to place a premium on the share price in consideration of the merger.

In many cases the trial takes place long after the events occurred, and new information is available at the time of the trial. Events that are known and knowable as of the valuation date are generally to be considered in the appraisal. In the case of *Tri-Continental Corp. v. Battye*,[61] the court stated that in determining value, the appraiser and the courts must consider any facts that are known or that could be ascertained as of the date of the merger, as these are essential in determining value.

For example, in *Smith v. North Carolina Motor Speedway*,[62] while the dissenters focused on the growth and success of NASCAR in the three years after the acquisition, the defense claimed that subsequent success should not be relevant if not fully foreseeable at the date of the event., Apparently acknowledging that those subsequent events should not be considered, the jury awarded a price much closer to the defendant's value.[63]

In certain cases, future events are used to validate the calculation of value as of the valuation date and are used as a sanity test for the valuation. For example, in *Lane v. Cancer Treatment Ctrs. of America, Inc.,*[64] the court allowed postvaluation date discovery for a year after the action to test the value ascertained in a premerger discounted cash flow calculation.

In New Jersey's *Lawson Mardon Wheaton v. Smith,*[65] the lower court refused to consider a post-event acquisition price. After recognizing that Delaware has allowed the use of post-merger information in appraisal in order to better determine value at the time of merger,[66] the New Jersey Supreme Court allowed the consideration of post-event information. The dissenters claimed that the 1991 share price determined to be $41.50 was questionable because in 1996 an acquisition price of $63 per share was offered. The court reasoned that the value of $41.50 per share in 1991 (when the company was doing well) should be questioned in light of an actual sale in 1996 at $63 per share (when the company was doing poorly).

The ALI recommends that when determining what a buyer would pay, the court may include a share of any gain reasonably expected to result from the combination, unless special circumstances exist that would make it unreasonable. The ALI goes on to comment that the implications of the statutes that say "immediately before the effectuation of the corporate action" could result in unfairness. For instance, in a case where the majority intends to freeze out the minority party in order to collect a price of $80 per share for a stock that had previously traded no higher than $50, the ALI recommends that $80 should be determined as the fair value.[67]

II. Valuation date in oppression cases

If a corporation or its controlling shareholders are permitted by statute to elect to purchase the share of a minority shareholder who seeks involuntary dissolution on grounds of oppression, several valuation dates may apply. New York[68] uses the day before the date the petition was filed. Rhode Island[69] uses the date of filing. California[70] and New Jersey[71] suggest the date of filing, but leave the door open for the court to designate an alternative date if more equitable. For example, a court may use the date of the actual oppression if it believes that the minority will be adversely affected by changes in the company's value after the minority shareholder's role in management has unjustifiably ended.

III. Excluding any appreciation or depreciation in anticipation of the corporate action unless exclusion would be inequitable.

This portion of the definition requires valuing the company as if the corporate action did not take place, so as not to unfairly benefit either of the parties from the result of the action. However, this definition also suggests that post-merger information could be considered to the extent that it reflects appreciation unrelated to the merger.[72] Primarily, appreciation in value due to the normal course of business can be included, but the exclusion provision suggests that if the action was unfair or self-dealing by the majority, having enriched themselves at the expense of the dissenter, those acts may be considered in the determination of fair value. For example, if minority shareholders are excluded from a transaction, perhaps in a squeeze-out merger, and dissent from their exclusion, the courts may find that equitable relief would be to include the synergy from the transaction to provide compensation for the minority to account for actions of the majority. In addition, an often overlooked issue in valuation is that not all synergies should be disregarded. Only those synergies not available to a particular buyer may be indicative of investment value.

The ABA removed "excluding any appreciation or depreciation in anticipation of the corporate action unless exclusion would be inequitable" from the fair value definition in the 1999 RMBCA. The ABA's commentary on the removal indicates that the provisions have not been susceptible to significant judicial interpretation and that their exclusion would allow for the broadening of the concept of fair value. Instead of using these lines, the ABA follows the ALI in recommending the use of customary and current techniques to keep up with evolving economic concepts.[73]

IV. Customary and current valuation techniques

The ALI's *Principles of Corporate Governance* state that "[f]air value should be determined using the customary valuation concepts and techniques generally employed in the relevant securities and financial markets for similar businesses in the context of the transaction giving rights to the appraisal."[74]

In the notes to this section, the ALI discusses why using a customary valuation methods are necessary. It acknowledges that the main problem with valuation is definition and measurement. With respect to measurement, as corporations have different underlying assets, no universal technique of measurement can cover all industries. Therefore, it is necessary to allow flexibility in valuation so that the valuation professional and the courts can use their best judgment to find equitable outcomes.[75]

In 1983, the Delaware Supreme Court established the foundation for the use of current and customary valuation techniques used by the financial community in their decision in *Weinberger v. UOP, Inc.*[76] In this landmark decision regarding the determination of value in shareholder dissent cases, the court's opinion affirmed the concept that a company could be valued using alternative methods, rather than relying solely on the Delaware block method as the courts had in the past.

Weinberger did not entirely do away with the use of the Delaware block method; instead, it allowed the possibility for a widely accepted alternative valuation procedure to be used as well as industry-appropriate valuation techniques. The appropriate valuation method is not the same in every case. But it is likely that a court will use the most relevant evidence presented to it to determine value. As current and customary techniques evolve, so will the case law. Interestingly, the discounted cash flow method, a method often not accepted by some courts, is widely used in dissent cases. In fact, the court in *Grimes v. Vitalink Communications Corporation*[77] commented that the discounted cash flow method was increasingly the method of choice in valuations in the Delaware Chancery Court.

How to Avoid Minefields

The *Weinberger* court's directive that all methods typically used by the financial community be considered in these matters, resulted in courts permitting the use of a number of methodologies recognized by the financial community. Examples of several methods that have been utilized include:

- *Discounted cash flow* (DCF). *Weinberger v. UOP, Inc.* used the discounted cash flow method in its departure from the standard Delaware block method. The discounted cash flow (DCF) methodology is widely used in the determination of fair value, especially in Delaware. In the 1995 case of *Kleinwort Benson Limited v. Silgan*,[78] the Delaware court acknowledged DCF as a better way of determining the value of a corporation than a market-based approach. The court weighted DCF more heavily than the market approach, stating that the DCF method should have greater weight because it values the corporation as a going concern, rather than comparing it to other companies. In *Grimes v. Vitalink*,[79] the court referenced *Kleinwort Benson Limited v. Silgan* as evidence that the Court of Chancery increasingly uses DCF in its valuations.

- *Guideline methods.* These methods involve valuing a privately held company based on multiples generated from the market price of a guideline public company's traded shares (guideline public company method) or from guideline transactions involving both public and private companies (guideline transaction methods). Those values can vary greatly due to market conditions; and the courts often rely more heavily on other methods.

- *Excess earnings method.* Although not necessarily the preferred method of valuation, the excess earnings method has been employed in fair value cases. For example, in *Balsamides v. Protameen Chemicals, Inc.*,[80] the excess earnings method was used by the plaintiff's expert, claiming that the defendants would not provide the information needed to employ any other method.

- *Weighted methods.* In Nevada's *Steiner Corp. v. Benninghoff*,[81] the court weighted various methods in order to find a fair value of the stock. First, it looked to find enterprise value, weighting a DCF valuation 30% and what it called a mergers and acquisition method 70%. To find market value, the guideline company method was considered. Then enterprise value and market value were weighted 75% and 25% respectively. The Delaware Court of Chancery has also used weighting in some recent cases as well. In *Andoloro v. PFPC Worldwide, Inc.*,[82] the court weighted DCF at 75% and comparable companies at 25%. In *In re United States Cellular Operating Company*,[83] the weighting was 70% DCF and 30% comparable acquisitions. In *Montgomery Cellular Holding Co., Inc. v. Dobler*,[84] The court gave a 30% weight to DCF, 5% to comparable companies, and 65% to comparable acquisitions.

In many states, the appraisal remedy is primarily directed towards privately held corporations. Many states have a "market exception" built into their statutes. These states do not offer an appraisal remedy if the company has publicly traded shares.[85] The 1984 RMBCA did not include the market exception, but the 1999 revisions make appraisal rights unavailable if the

Chapter 3: Dissenting and Oppressed Shareholder Matters

shares are listed on the New York Stock Exchange or the American Stock Exchange, or are designated as a national market system security by the National Association of Securities Dealers. In addition, pursuant to these revisions, a shareholder in a private company with over 2,000 shareholders and with a market value over $20 million (exclusive of the value of such shares held by its subsidiaries, senior executives, directors, and beneficial shareholders owning more than 10% of such shares) is not entitled to dissenters' appraisal rights.[86]

Although in many states the market exception prevents publicly traded companies from being subject to appraisal remedy, the market approach to valuation can still be a useful tool in performing the valuation of a closely held corporation. For example, B*orruso v. Communications Telesystems International*,[87] the valuation expert used the guideline public company method, as there was insufficient information to adequately apply the DCF method or other income multiples (e.g. earnings before income, taxes, depreciation, and amortization [EBITDA]). The New Jersey courts recognized the importance of considering the market value in valuation in *Dermody v. Sticco*,[88] referring to the market price as a valuable corroborative tool.

A Federal Court, applying Delaware law, in *Connector Service Corporation v. Briggs*[89] noted that a multiple of EBITDA was a better method than DCF, because the EBITDA multiple was based on the multiples used by the subject company in two prior acquisitions.

It should be noted that merger and acquisition (M&A) market multiples may include the synergies. Appraisers usually avoid using any synergies that arise from the action to which the minority shareholder dissents, unless otherwise directed by legal counsel or the courts.

Discounts and premiums

A major issue in many fair value cases is whether discounts and/or premiums are applicable. If applicable, the issue becomes the *magnitude* of such discounts and/or premiums. The primary issues are shareholder-level discounts and applications of control premiums. The courts have debated whether minority shares should be valued by valuing the company on a pro-rata enterprise basis or by valuing the shares themselves with respect to their minority status. There are arguments for and against the application of discounts. Sometimes the use of discounts or their nonuse can result in the unfair enrichment of one of the parties.

The issue becomes the definition of what the minority shareholder has lost. If viewed as a pro-rata share of the enterprise value, discounts would likely not apply. If, however, valuation is viewed as what the investor could reasonably realize without the intervention of the courts, discounts would likely be applied.

In determining fair market value, typically, lack of control and marketability discounts are considered and when applicable, used. As on an open market, the buyer will consider the lack of control and liquidity before agreeing to purchase minority shares. One argument states that the nonuse of discounts unfairly enriches the minority shareholder. Minority shareholders would never get an undiscounted price on the open market, and they would have been aware of this when they purchased the minority shares in the first place.

Probably the most popular arguments against discounts involve the original purpose of the statute, as evidenced by the quote from Justice Black mentioned earlier. If the statutes were created to protect the shareholder from the controlling shareholders, a minority discount would be contrary to logic, as the majority shareholders would obviously benefit from a reduction in the amount they would have to pay the minority. With respect to marketability discounts, one could argue that the statute proposes that the judicial proceeding itself creates a market for the shares, and therefore no marketability discount can be taken at the shareholder level. Alternatively, if indeed the minority investor is losing a pro-rata proportion of the corporation in having to sell his or her shares, the application of discounts may be viewed as encouraging bad behavior by the majority, as they receive a premium for mistreating the minority.

I. Entity-level discounts

Entity-level discounts are those that apply to the company as a whole. Some maintain controlling shares command a discount for lack of marketability pointing to studies that show that private companies sold as a whole generally sell for a value less than their publicly traded equivalents.[90] As such, entity-level discounts should be deducted from the value indicated by the basic approach or approaches used to value the privately held business. Since they apply to the company as a whole, entity-level discounts should be deducted before considering shareholder-level discounts and premiums.[91]

The Delaware courts have historically understood the necessity of entity-level adjustments. In *Tri-Continental v. Battye*,[92] the company being valued was a closed-end investment company. Because of this structure, shareholders of the company had no right at any time to demand their proportionate share of the company's assets. For this reason and due to the company's various leverage requirements, the market value of the corporation as a whole was lower than its net asset value, and this was referred to as a discount. The important distinction, however, is that this discount was applied to the whole corporation, not just the shares of a minority shareholder.

Several entity-level discounts may be applied in a fair value determination. In addition to the consideration of an entity-level marketability discounts, when applicable, the valuator must be ready to defend the usage of a trapped-in capital gains discount, a portfolio (non-homogeneous assets) discount, a contingent liabilities discount, or a key man discount. In *Hodas v. Spectrum Tech., Inc.*,[93] a Delaware appraisal action, the court accepted the value determined by company's expert, concluding that the individual staying with the company was the key man. The expert applied a 20% key man discount, because the company could not be viewed as a going concern without the key man and would likely not continue at all if the key man left. The court rejected the 40% entity-level lack of marketability discount applied by the appraiser because of the lack of a readily available market.

Chapter 3: Dissenting and Oppressed Shareholder Matters

II. Control premiums

Although many believe that there is little support for adding a premium to values determined through the use of the guideline company method, there are instances in dissent and oppression cases for explicit consideration of such premiums. Accordingly, when ascertaining the value of a corporation for the purposes of an appraisal proceeding, a control premium may be applied, as the aim is generally to find the control value of the corporation as a whole or the value of the enterprise.

Rapid American v. Harris[94] is such an example. Since *Rapid American v. Harris* the Delaware Court of Chancery has consistently applied a control premium where the company was a controlled subsidiary.

Rapid American v. Harris

In 1974, Meshulam Riklis, chairman and CEO of Rapid American Corporation (Rapid), began purchasing Rapid's shares in the open market through his holdings in Kenton Corporation and American Financial Corporation (AFC). Rapid also began repurchasing large blocks of its own shares, effectively increasing Riklis's control.

In 1980, Rapid announced a merger with Kenton. On the eve of the merger, Kenton and AFC controlled 46.5% of Rapid's stock. After the merger, Rapid's shareholders would receive a compensation package worth $28 per share, including $25 principal in a 10% sinking fund subordinated debenture, $3 cash, and an additional $0.25, representing settlement consideration for pending derivative suits. Rapid employed an outside group, Standard Research Consultants, to review the fairness of the merger, and an examination concluded that the package was fair to Rapid's shareholders. The valuation technique used considered Rapid on a consolidated basis, based on an analysis of earnings and dividends. It figured each subsidiary's contribution to the parent's operating income for a set period of time.

Harris, a Rapid shareholder, retained Willamette Management Associates (WMA) to evaluate the merger. WMA reasoned that a segmented approach was appropriate because of the difficulty of finding a conglomerate comparable to Rapid, and evaluated each of Rapid's subsidiaries. The trial court ruled that WMA's segmented valuation was more reliable and ruled the fair value to be $51 per share. WMA examined the financial statements of the subsidiaries and the comparable companies to develop certain pricing multiples based on various factors. WMA included a control premium in the evaluation of each subsidiary. The Vice Chancellor rejected this, finding that the addition of a control premium violated Delaware law, which contravenes the proscription against weighing factors affecting shareholder-level valuation.

Rapid argued that WMA's valuation was incorrect on four counts:

1. The control premium
2. The valuation was based on a liquidation value of the subsidiaries
3. The valuation did not consider the value of the parent
4. WMA treated Rapid's debt at its market value rather than book value

With regard to the valuation at liquidation value, the court found no support for the valuation being similar to a liquidation approach, and WMA explicitly considered Rapid's subsidiaries as going concerns. In addition, the trial court explicitly considered parent-level financials and decided to exclude them.

Harris's cross-appeal claimed that the decision to exclude the control premium was a legal error, maintaining that WMA's valuation compared subsidiaries publicly traded equity value with the individual shares of similar corporations and that the market price of these corporations was discounted already, thereby giving Rapid a windfall at his expense. The appellate court reviewed the record and found that the trial court misinterpreted applicable legal precepts in omitting the control premium.

The appellate court acknowledged that a court is prohibited from adding a control premium at a shareholder level, reasoning that if the control premium arises out of the merger, it is not part of going concern value. In this case, however, the control premium represented a valid adjustment to the valuation at the company level against all assets. The share price that WMA arrived at was a price already at a discount from the control level, and therefore a premium would have to be employed to arrive at the value of a 100% ownership in the corporation.

The trial court's decision practically discounted Rapid's entire value, and the exclusion of the control premium effectively treated the whole corporation as a minority shareholder. The decision was remanded for recalculation of the value with any applicable control premium.

Along with *Rapid American v. Harris*, New Jersey's *Casey v. Brennan*[95] acknowledged the need for an entity-level control premium, in case an embedded or inherent minority discount may exist when valuing shares. In this case, the court rejected discounts and acknowledged the need for a control premium to reflect market realities and arrive at the value of the company as a whole, provided that anticipated future events are not included in that value.

When performing a valuation, it is important for a valuation professional to support the use or nonuse of a control premium through fact and valuation theory. Generally such premiums may be appropriate if a control buyer can extract more cash flow from the enterprise than the company's current owner. For example, when using control cash flows in a discounted cash flow valuation method, a control premium is not warranted. In the Delaware case of *In re Radiology Assocs., Inc.*,[96] no control premium was applied because the DCF method used control cash flows. The application of a control premium to a DCF valuation was expressly rejected in Delaware in *Lane v. Cancer Treatment Centers of America, Inc.*[97] and in *Montgomery Cellular Holding Co., Inc. v. Dobler*.[98]

Chapter 3: Dissenting and Oppressed Shareholder Matters

If the valuation professional uses a guideline public company method, the public multiples may result in a minority-marketable value. Therefore, a control premium may be necessary to derive the value of the enterprise. This was necessary in *Bomarko, Inc. v. International Telecharge, Inc*,[99] where the Court of Chancery supported the application of a control premium when the appraiser used the guideline public company method, which it found produced a minority value. The Court of Chancery has been quite consistent in applying a control premium to the results of the guideline public company method. In fact, in *Doft & Co. v. Travelocity.com, Inc.*,[100] the court added a control premium even though neither expert had done so.

III. Extraordinary circumstances

The ALI suggests that fair value should be the value of the eligible holder's pro-rata share of the enterprise value, without any discount for minority status or, absent extraordinary circumstances, lack of marketability. These so-called extraordinary circumstances require more than just a lack of a public market for shares. Instead, the court usually applies a discount only if merited by the circumstances of the case. The ALI offers the example of a dissenting shareholder withholding approval of a merger in an attempt to exploit the appraisal-triggering transaction in order to divert value to him- or herself at the expense of other shareholders. In that case, the court may make an adjustment.[101] *Devivo v. Devivo*,[102] a Connecticut case, found similar results as *Advanced Communication Design, Inc. v. Follet*[103] in Minnesota. The company would not be able to achieve the liquidity to compensate the departing shareholder, so the court applied a marketability discount in order to be fair to the parties involved.

Extraordinary circumstances are subject to de novo review. In *Lawson Mardon Wheaton v. Smith*,[104] the trial court held that an extraordinary circumstance existed because the dissenters exploited a fundamental corporate change, which triggered appraisal rights, that they had previously supported. However, the New Jersey Supreme Court did not find substantial evidence to consider this an extraordinary circumstance. The court stated that the dissenters wanted to sell their stock back to the corporation because they had no confidence in the new management. The court believed that these stockholders were only exercising their right to dissent. The court held that to find extraordinary circumstances in this case would be inconsistent with the purpose of the statute.

The treatment of discounts is largely addressed by each state individually. While some states have adopted the 1999 RMBCA definition of fair value, which prohibits discounts, other states either have unique definitions or adhere to the 1984 RMBCA definition and leave the decision on discounts to the judgment of the courts. However, the statutory definition and precedent set by case law are not set in stone. For example, Georgia's courts set the precedent in 1984 in *Atlantic States Construction v. Beavers*[105] to apply minority discounts but not marketability discounts. In 2000, however, this was overturned by *Blitch v. People's Bank*,[106] where the court rejected the application of minority or marketability discounts at the shareholder level.

How to Avoid Minefields

Although appraisal is a state law remedy, federal cases arise in multi-jurisdictional matters. They generally follow the law established in the states in their jurisdiction. Because dissent and oppression are based on state law, we would expect the federal courts to follow the most recent state court decisions in their jurisdictions. As a result, practitioners should seek legal guidance concerning the application of minority and marketability discounts in the applicable jurisdiction.

Equitable adjustments

I. Delaware's 'entire fairness'

Delaware does not have a shareholder oppression statute; instead, if a minority shareholder dissents, wrongful conduct by the majority is addressed under the expectation of "entire fairness" in determining the value of a corporation's shares. This requirement dictates to the Delaware courts whether adjustments or damage claims may be included along with the determination of fair value.

The standards of fair dealing and fair price require that value be determined by independent valuation showing fairness to minority shareholders. To comply with "entire fairness," a company must show consideration in the form of absolute and relative fairness. Absolute fairness addresses whether the consideration received by the shareholder was adequate relative to the value of the interest that was given up. Relative fairness addresses whether the consideration received was fair in comparison with what other stockholders received.[107]

There also must be procedural fairness, in terms of the independence of legal counsel, accountants, and appraisers from the influences of the controlling shareholders. The valuation also should be performed with competence and thoroughness. The board has fiduciary responsibility to the minority shareholders in making recommendations to the company.[108]

Complying with the standard of entire fairness can give proof to the court of the corporation's intention to show due care and consideration to the minority shareholders. A corporation can demonstrate that it is upholding its fiduciary duty by showing due care to shareholders and by doing so may avoid the burden of damages or fees for the mistreatment of the minority shareholder.

There are also consequences for a failure to adhere to these requirements. Lack of entire fairness implies that the directors violated the duty owed to the shareholders. If the shareholders establish that the board has violated the duty of fairness, then the measure of damages may go beyond the basic determination of fair value.[109] If, in a buyout, the court determines that minority shares have a fair value of $40 million and the corporation offered $10 million, the court may see fit to award the shareholder the $40 million plus damages for expenses and inconvenience. The next two cases, *Seagraves v. Urstadt Property Co, Inc.*[110] and *Bomarko, Inc. v. International Telecharge, Inc.*,[111] deal with decisions based on the corporation's entire fairness to minority shareholders.

Chapter 3: Dissenting and Oppressed Shareholder Matters

II. Consideration of wrongdoing

In states that have both dissenter's rights and oppression statutes, the definition of fair value is usually stated in connection with the dissenter's rights statute, unless the circumstance or the standard of value in oppression is different. As previously mentioned, California's dissolution statute contains an entirely unique definition of fair value, *fair value in liquidation*, while the state's dissenter's rights statutes use fair market value.

Although many cases consider fair value in dissent and oppression cases to be largely the same concept, the nature of the events leading to the valuation can have an effect on how the court determines what is fair. For example, New Jersey's dissolution statute offers equitable adjustments to fair value in cases of oppression. The text of the statute is:

> The purchase price of any shares so sold shall be their fair value as of the date of the commencement of the action or such earlier or later date deemed equitable by the court, plus or minus any adjustments deemed equitable by the court if the action was brought in whole or in part under paragraph 14A:12-7(1)(c).[112]

The official comment to the 1991 changes to the RMBCA leaves room for the court to consider the circumstances of the case in determining fair value:

> If the court finds that the value of a corporation has been diminished by the wrongful conduct of controlling shareholders, it would be appropriate to include as an element of fair value the petitioner's proportional claim for any corporate injury.[113]

The official comment to the 1999 changes to the RMBCA's definition of fair value asserts that although the new definition denies the application of discounts, fair value in dissenting shareholder matters should be seen as different from fair value in dissolution matters because of the differing circumstances of majority conduct in oppression and dissent cases.[114] The comment states:

> Section 14.34 (oppression) does not specify the components of 'Fair Value,' and the court may find it useful to consider valuation methods that would be relevant to a judicial appraisal of shares under section 13.30 (dissent). The two proceedings are not wholly analogous, however, and the court should consider all relevant facts and circumstances of the particular case in determining fair value. For example, liquidating value may be relevant in cases of deadlock but an inappropriate measure in other cases. If the court finds that the value of the corporation has been diminished by the wrongful conduct of controlling shareholders, it would be appropriate to include as an element of fair value the petitioner's proportional claim for any compensable corporate injury. In cases where there is dissension but no evidence of wrongful conduct, fair value should be determined with reference to what the petitioner would likely receive in a voluntary sale of shares to a third party, taking into account his minority status. If the parties have previously entered into a shareholders' agreement that

defines or provides a method for determining the fair value of shares to be sold, the court should look to such definition or method unless the court decides it would be unjust or inequitable to do so in light of the facts and circumstances of the particular case. The valuation date is set as the day before the filing of the petition under section 14.30, although the court may choose an earlier or later date if appropriate under the circumstances of the particular case.

Last, it appears that a well-written buy-sell agreement can be useful concerning the fair value buy-out of minority shareholders. The valuation professional should be cognizant of the provisions outlined in the buy-sell agreement as it pertains to a valuation. Such agreement may even permit the corporate activity that has caused the shareholder to dissent. In that case, the court may not look favorably on the dissenter, as he or she should have been aware of a buy-sell provision.

The comment suggests that in cases of appraisal pursuant to a dissent action, an individual should receive the undiscounted proportionate value of the company as a going concern. In an oppression action, there are many other considerations caused by the degree of oppression and misconduct by the majority. In the buy-out remedy, as evidenced by this passage, the company may elect to buy out the shareholder at fair value before a proceeding occurs, or the court can go on with the proceeding. This leaves four scenarios when oppression is alleged:

1. If the company elects the buy-out, fair value is to be paid.

2. If the company does not elect the buy-out option and the court finds that oppression has occurred, the company will ultimately pay fair value, plus any equitable adjustments the court requires.

3. If the court finds no oppression, the shareholder will likely not recover the fair value as a percentage of enterprise value, and the court may look to what the shareholder's share would bring on the open market, considering his or her minority status. This would imply the application of shareholder-level discounts.

4. If the court finds no oppression, there may be no buy-out and the shareholder may be compelled to remain with the corporation.

If there is a chance the corporation will be found to have committed acts of oppression, fraud, mismanagement, abuse; or if the corporation anticipates dissolution being the outcome of the court proceeding; or if the corporation wants to avoid the court proceeding altogether, it may elect to purchase the petitioner's shares at their fair value within the statutory time frame.[115] In this case, the dissolution proceeding will be put on hold (but not terminated) until an equitable settlement has been negotiated. One New York decision stated:

> Once the corporation has elected to buy the petitioning stockholders' shares at fair value, the issue of majority wrongdoing is superfluous.[116]

Chapter 3: Dissenting and Oppressed Shareholder Matters

Electing a buy-out may also help the corporation avoid the "equitable adjustments" the court might make in a case where wrongdoing is found, as well as other costs associated with a court proceeding. The unpublished Connecticut case *Johnson v. Johnson*[117] is particularly illuminating with respect to the treatment of fair value when wrongdoing is in question.

Johnson v. Johnson

A close family corporation, Johnson Corrugated Products Corporation involved siblings James, Cindy, and Randy Johnson and two unrelated board members. A suit was filed in 1999 by James and Cindy Johnson against their brother Randy for dissolution due to an alleged breach of fiduciary duty.

The corporation manufactured corrugated boxes. It was formed in 1964 by the litigants' father. Cindy and James each owned 7.8 shares, representing a 30.83% equity interest in the corporation. Cindy had been employed by the corporation for several years and took maternity leave in 1994. She tried to resume her employment in 1997, but Randy had blocked her return. Despite her absence, Cindy continued to be paid under a 1992 employment agreement. She believed that her stock ownership entitled her to employment, membership on the board of directors, and a share of the corporate profits.

James was employed at the corporation for 20 years, filling in as a handyman and floater where needed. After suffering a traumatic head injury, he felt that his father promised him he could always work at the company. He also believed that he was entitled to a position on the board of directors as a member of the Johnson family. He also continued to receive wages, although he no longer worked at the corporation.

Randy owned the remaining equity in the corporation, representing a majority share. He also functioned as the chief executive officer, majority shareholder, and chairman of the board of directors. He had substantial knowledge of the production process of the corporation.

Cindy and James asserted that Randy had acted in a manner that was illegal, oppressive, or fraudulent. The corporation elected to purchase the plaintiffs' stock with fair value to be ascertained by the court.

The experts came up with widely different figures, due to various factors, including the money to be saved by the installation of a new corrugator, the extent of excessive compensation, and depreciation.

With respect to the corrugator, minutes of a meeting suggested that the corrugator could save up to $700,000—the figure used by the plaintiffs' expert. Upon review of known and knowable details at the valuation date, the court concluded that this was wishful thinking on the part of the board of directors rather than fact and declared that no prudent investor would rely on that figure.

The excessive compensation was also a factor in the valuation. Although the compensation was not found to be tantamount to corporate waste, it did amount to more than a prudent investor would anticipate paying a competent non-owner CEO and financial officer. The compensation was set at $262,250 for valuation purposes rather than the $333,536 Randy was receiving.

The court went on to determine that the equity value of the corporation was between the values of the two experts. The court stated that the fair value of the plaintiffs' shares cannot be determined by a simple apportionment based on ownership percentage, because the statute allows for consideration of fraud, waste, and oppressive conduct as well as the minority status of shares being valued.

The court asserted that if no agreement on fair value could be reached, in a case of dissension where there is no evidence of wrongful conduct, fair value should be determined with reference to the value in a voluntary sale to a third party.

The plaintiffs argued that their apportioned value should be increased due to the defendant's oppressive and wasteful conduct, while the defendant argued that his apportionment should be increased due to the plaintiffs' minority status and the limited marketability of the minority shares.

The court was not persuaded by the defendant's marketability discount argument, as evidence suggested that the corporation enjoyed a niche in the market and the shares would be attractive to outside buyers. In addition, the court suggested that the appraiser should take the projected rate of return that a reasonable investor would require into consideration in assessing the risk factors flowing from the characteristics of the corporation. The court did find, however, that a 20% reduction in value due to minority status was acceptable.

In regard to additional compensation to the plaintiffs because of waste and oppression, the Superior Court of Connecticut looked to the RMBCA and concluded that if the value of the corporation had been diminished by the wrongful conduct of the controlling shareholders, a proportional claim for corporate injury could be assessed.

The plaintiffs claimed that the failure of the corporation to declare dividends was oppressive despite the fact that the corporation had never declared dividends; this was a company policy since the inception of the corporation. The plaintiffs also claimed that exclusion from the board of directors and employment was oppressive and that they should be compensated for Randy's excess compensation. The court found that these claims did not amount to oppression, considering the circumstances of this case, and that the equity value of the corporation already took into account the compensation when normalizing executive income. The court determined no further adjustments were necessary.

The finding of dissension without oppression caused the court to dissolve the corporation and ascertain fair value based on the third-party sale value—concluding that a minority discount was appropriate while a marketability discount was already accounted for in the projected rate of return. As no wrongdoing had occurred, the court did not find any adjustments necessary to the value of shares in favor of the plaintiffs.

The difference in fair value could be significant, based on the particular fact pattern and the statutes and case law of a specific state. Bearing in mind that Connecticut follows the 1999 RMBCA definition of fair value and thereby rejects discounts for dissent and oppression matters, it appears that the court could have decided the case in these ways:

- Found oppressive behavior, disallowed minority and marketability discounts, and adjusted the value for corporate waste; or

- Found dissension without oppression (which it did), and then considered minority and marketability discounts.

III. Discounts used as an 'equitable adjustment'

Equitable adjustments are one of the tools the courts can use to achieve what they believe to be an equitable result. The courts have used equitable adjustments in cases where they have perceived dishonorable, fraudulent, oppressive, or illegal behavior. An equitable adjustment may be the award of damages, expert fees, and attorney fees. In other circumstances, the courts may adjust a fair value determination by using discounts and premiums to raise or lower the value of the shares to achieve what is perceived to be an equitable result. In doing this, the court may or may not strictly adhere to all of the underlying assumptions that valuation professionals commonly associate with fair value.

By virtue of the definition of fair value in the New Jersey dissolution statute,[118] the New Jersey court can make equitable adjustments in the case of illegal, oppressive, or fraudulent conduct. For instance, the court may adjust the valuation date or make inclusions or exclusions of certain elements in the calculation of fair value. An example of this a New Jersey oppression case *Balsamides v. Protameen Chemicals*,[119] in which discounts were used to lessen the value of the shares in the corporation, because the oppressed shareholder would be remaining with the corporation. The very same day, a complementary decision was handed down in a dissent case, *Lawson Mardon Wheaton v. Smith*.[120] In both cases, the court considered the equities of the circumstances before making its decision.

Balsamides v. Protameen Chemicals, Inc.

Emanuel Balsamides and Leonard Perle went into business together over 25 years before the suit was filed. Balsamides had been a purchasing agent for Revlon and acted as the rainmaker for the corporation due to his many contacts. He was also responsible for advertising, marketing, and insurance. Perle, having a chemistry background, was responsible for the technical and administrative portion of the business. By mid-1995, gross sales exceeded $19 million, and each man had an annual income of between $1 and $1.5 million.

How to Avoid Minefields

In the late 1980s, each brought two sons into the business, expecting eventually to hand over management. Balsamides's sons worked in sales and received commissions, expense accounts, and company cars, as did other Protameen salesmen. Perle's sons started in administrative and office management positions. Perle believed his sons should receive the same compensation as Balsamides's sons, and hostilities ensued.

In the early 1990s, Perle's sons moved into sales. However, the feuding already had gone so far as to cause conditions at the company to deteriorate to the point where the families could no longer conduct business together. In June 1995, Balsamides sought relief as an oppressed minority shareholder. Perle answered by denying the allegations and seeking the sale of Protameen to a third party. The court directed Balsamides to cooperate.

Despite many claims and counterclaims being filed, all but the breach of fiduciary duty by Perle were dismissed. The court found that Balsamides was an oppressed shareholder and was entitled to buy out Perle in lieu of dissolution or sale. The court found both families at fault, but concluded that Perle conducted himself in a way that was harmful to the business of Protameen and his partner.

The fair value that was accepted by the trial court was that of Balsamides's expert, Thomas Hoberman, using an excess earnings method of valuation with a 35% marketability discount. Perle's expert, Robert Ott, valued the company using a combination of market and income approaches without any discount, because the court was creating a market for the shares by ordering the buy-out.

Ott's valuation was specifically rejected by the trial court, as it looked not to determine the value of Protameen in light of a buy-out but to determine the intrinsic value121 of the business, which does not change simply because the court directed a buy-out.

On appeal, the appellate court was concerned about the trial court's application of the 35% marketability discount in valuing Perle's stock. The appellate court stated that the shares were not being sold to the public, nor would they later be sold to the public. Therefore, any discount for marketability would be inappropriate as Balsamides would maintain 100% ownership. In addition, the court recognized that the IRS frowns on the excess earnings method of valuation, and Revenue Ruling 68-609 states that this method should be used to value intangible assets only if there is no better basis available.

Although Hoberman claimed that there was no better basis available, Ott claimed that he was able to use an income approach and verify his results with a market approach. The appellate court found that Hoberman was not given enough information to execute a valuation better than the excess earnings method allowed, and that this was due to Perle's noncooperation. Moreover, the only reason why Ott could calculate the income approach was because Perle provided him with more information than he provided Hoberman.

Chapter 3: Dissenting and Oppressed Shareholder Matters

There was also discussion of the 30% capitalization rate that Hoberman used. This rate was based on the lack of a full-time chemist, the projected decline in the market for the company's animal-and mineral-based chemicals over the coming years, the use of purchasing policies that placed priority on price over quality, the potential cancellation of a big contract, the reliance on six customers who account for 27% of sales, and the generation of nearly half the company's sales by Balsamides. The appellate court suggested that these items could be corrected with the corporation under Balsamides's management and should not contribute to such a high capitalization rate; however, the potential competition from Perle and his sons should be taken into consideration. Although the 30% was deemed high considering the factors offered by Hoberman, the existence of competition could merit the high rate if on remand the trial court decided to uphold its original acceptance of the 30% rate.

When the New Jersey Supreme Court reviewed the lower court's decision, it found that the appellate decision had not abused its discretion on most issues. However, in addressing the marketability discount, the Supreme Court pointed out the distinction between applying a discount at the corporate level versus the shareholder level and stated that the former may be appropriate if generally accepted in the financial community. It further cited the New Jersey dissolution statute, which directs the court to determine the fair value plus or minus any adjustments deemed equitable by the court. This statute gives the court substantial discretion to adjust the buy-out price.

Balsamides claimed that by not applying a discount, if he chose to sell the corporation at a later time, he would have to absorb the full reduction for the lack of marketability of a close corporation. The appellate court thought it would not be fair or equitable for the surviving shareholder to obtain the remaining interest at a discount, dismissing the idea that Balsamides would sell at a later time. Therefore, the market would be Balsamides himself, so no discount should be applied.

The New Jersey Supreme Court, however, called this an erroneous assumption, as there is a reality to the illiquidity of Protameen, and if the marketability discount is not applied at the buy-out, Balsamides would incur the full brunt of the illiquidity if and when he tried to sell the corporation at a later date. In addition, the Supreme Court stated that a consistent rule regarding the determination of fair value and the applicability of discounts should not be made, as the specific facts of the case may have an impact on the decision, and a marketability discount cannot be used unfairly to benefit the controlling or oppressing shareholder at the expense of the minority party.

Lawson Mardon Wheaton v. Smith

Twenty-six shareholders owning approximately 15% of the stock of a corporation dissented from a corporate restructuring, demanding fair value. The corporation offered $41.50 per share, calculated with a 25% marketability discount. The dissenters rejected the offer in April 1992, initiating the appraisal action. In the trial, the court upheld the 25% marketability discount, citing extraordinary circumstances. It believed that the dissenters had exploited a change that they themselves had championed and possibly prevented an initial public offering to the detriment of other shareholders. On appeal, the court found that a discount is generally inapplicable, but found that the record supported the conclusion that the actions constituted an extraordinary circumstance.

The New Jersey Supreme Court, however, did not agree. It did not consider the record to support a finding of extraordinary circumstances, noting that the appraisal statute is designed to provide a remedy to dissenting shareholders and should be liberally construed in their favor. The court believed that the record indicated that the dissenters wished to liquefy their assets because the corporation was now controlled by new management in whom they lacked confidence. The court denied that this was an extraordinary circumstance.

The court also recommended that the record be reopened in order to consider a later acquisition price, $63 per share in 1996. The company's financial statements disclosed that its fair value was greater in 1991 than 1996 and therefore may have had a bearing on the value of the corporation at the time of restructuring.

In its decision, the Supreme Court stated that the nature of the term fair value suggested that the courts must take fairness and equity into account in deciding whether to apply a discount to the value of the dissenting shares in an appraisal action, referencing the New Jersey oppression statute's support of equitable adjustments to fair value when the court deems it necessary. The court went on to conclude that there was no reason to believe that fair value should be viewed differently when addressing dissenter and oppressed shareholders.

The court stated that equitable considerations had led the majority of states to deny the application of discounts in appraisal actions and to award dissenting shareholders a proportional share of the fair market value of the corporation without discounts. It supported the argument that discounts penalize the minority for taking advantage of the protection afforded by the appraisal statute. However, the court left the issue open, stating that there may be situations where equity (and extraordinary circumstance) compels another result. The court also explained its same-day decision in Balsamides, applying the same principle of equity to apply a discount in favor of the oppressed shareholder.

Several cases do not support the consideration of improper conduct in the determination of value. In *Cede & Co. v. Technicolor, Inc.*,[122] the court stated that improper conduct should not be considered in an appraisal proceeding.

The appraiser needs to be aware that discounts may be considered by the court because of improper conduct, as in *Balsamides,* or where a damage claim for the loss of a job or other forms of wrongdoing can be brought in conjunction with the judicial appraisal. Accordingly, the appraiser should consult with counsel and obtain direction as to the applicability of discounts in connection with a claim of improper conduct.

Although sometimes employed as punishment, as in situations such as *Balsamides,* discounts are generally a poor calibration of what the actual recompense for damages should be. Some have suggested that there are more appropriate punishments for malfeasance, such as payment of court fees, the award of damages, or the use of injunctions.[123]

Even when a court's decision is not quite as clear as the 1999 decisions in New Jersey, a more favorable result for the dissenting or oppressed party generally will correlate to the court's view that some measure of mistreatment or prejudice by the corporation occurred. A more favorable result for the corporation will usually indicate that the court had the opposite view of what occurred.[124]

In *Weinberger v. UOP, Inc.,*[125] the court acknowledged the chancellor's empowerment to fashion any form of equitable and monetary relief that is appropriate, including monetary damages based on entire fairness, particularly in cases of fraud, misrepresentation, self-dealing, or deliberate waste. This might have been one of the reasons the court did not find that the Delaware block method was the sole method to be used in valuation.

In the Kansas case of *Arnaud v. Stockgrowers State Bank,*[126] the court held that minority and marketability discounts should not be applied when the fractional share resulted from a reverse stock split intended to eliminate a minority shareholder's interest in the corporation.

Based on an analysis of the official comments to the RMBCA, the ALI's *Principles of Corporate Governance,* and relevant case law, such as the decisions in *Johnson v. Johnson,*[127] *Lawson Mardon Wheaton v. Smith,*[128] and *Balsamides v. Protameen Chemicals,*[129] it appears as if fair value may be calculated in a different manner when oppression is proven as opposed to cases where there is only disagreement or dissension (not dissent) between shareholders.

IV. Damage claims

The loss of salary can be a significant issue in many oppression cases. Since a characteristic of a closely held business is that its shareholders are often its key employees, those shareholders have the expectation of income from employment (salary and benefits) as well as the benefits associated with ownership. In such a case, behavior by the majority to eliminate that job might be more damaging to the minority shareholder's interest than the elimination of the profits from the ownership. Here we are referring only to the salary that would be termed *replacement compensation* in the calculation of value. The profits in excess of replacement compensation, whether received as salary, perks, or dividends, are capitalized and included in the fair value of the owner's stock. In a damage claim, this amount may be mitigated by any compensation received as part of salary, whether similar to the position given up or not.

For example, consider a situation where a shareholder-employee of a corporation earned a salary of $200,000. A non-shareholder employee with a comparable position at a comparable company would earn a $125,000 salary. The termination of the shareholder employee causes him or her to lose the ability to receive $75,000 in salary. If the fair value of the shareholder's investment included compensation for the loss of a job, she would have to receive $75,000 per year in back pay from the time of termination to the time of the trial. In addition, that $75,000 may continue for a given or specified period of years after the date of trial, depending on the judgment of the court.[130]

The court in *Weinberger v. UOP, Inc.*[131] looked at the case of damages in fair value through the perspective of the statutory requirement of "all relevant factors." It stated: "When the trial court deems it appropriate, fair value also includes any damages, resulting from the taking, which the stockholders sustain as a class. If that was not the case, then the obligation to consider 'all relevant factors' in the valuation process would be eroded."[132]

Several cases have addressed the fact that minority shareholders often rely on their salary as the principal return on their investment.[133] The violation of the shareholder's expectation to continue employment in a close corporation may be sufficient to incur damages, back pay, or other adjustments to the value of his or her shares.[134]

The courts may find it difficult to calculate the value of damages. As in many cases, the fair value of shares is not sufficient to encompass all of the shareholder's loss. The courts may use discounts, or court fees, or other damage assessments, but it is difficult to ascertain the appropriate value and may largely become a judgment call for the court.[135] The New Jersey Superior Court, for instance, in *Musto v. Vidas*[136] suggested that after the petitioning shareholder's termination, the shareholder should continue to receive the same compensation as the defendants, as provided for in the initial shareholder agreement for a period of two years after the shareholder was frozen out.

In *Johnson v. Johnson,*[137] the court considered the issues of oppression and waste in determining compensation for the minority shareholders. It decided that the corporation's failure to declare dividends was not a sufficient condition to merit damages, especially because the company had not historically declared dividends. The court considered whether the level of compensation of the primary executive was oppressive and whether damages should be incurred for corporate waste. The court found that the level of compensation was not tantamount to waste, and although it might be more than a prudent investor would expect to pay, the court found no breach of reasonable expectations in this case and therefore no additional compensation was required.

Fair value and the minority shareholder

The bottom line in dissenting shareholder matters and when a shareholder petitions to dissolve a corporation alleging oppression is: What does the minority shareholder receive at the end of the day? In both types of cases, this is going to depend almost entirely on the circumstances of the case. With dissent, the outcome is more straightforward; a minority shareholder either can

Chapter 3: Dissenting and Oppressed Shareholder Matters

or cannot dissent based on a triggering event, and the court can look at the circumstances of the case to determine the fair value.

In oppression, the outcomes are a bit more complicated. If the shareholder files suit under the dissolution statute, two situations can occur:

1. The corporation could elect to buy out the petitioner's share at fair value. At that point, any decision regarding wrongdoing is suspended and the court's primary focus is to determine the fair value of the petitioner's shares.

2. The corporation can decide to gamble with a court proceeding, maintaining that its actions were not oppressive. If the court finds the corporation's actions to be oppressive or prejudicial, it will be required to pay the fair value plus any equitable adjustments the court deems necessary. This could include damages, court fees, or the application of discounts to benefit the oppressed shareholder. If oppression or wrongdoing is not found, however, the corporation will not be required to buy the shares, and the shareholder is likely to be forced either to remain a shareholder or to sell the shares at a value that would be received from a third party.

The chart below lays out the scenarios involved in filing for a dissolution action, and in states like Delaware, when entire fairness is an issue considered in an appraisal action.[138]

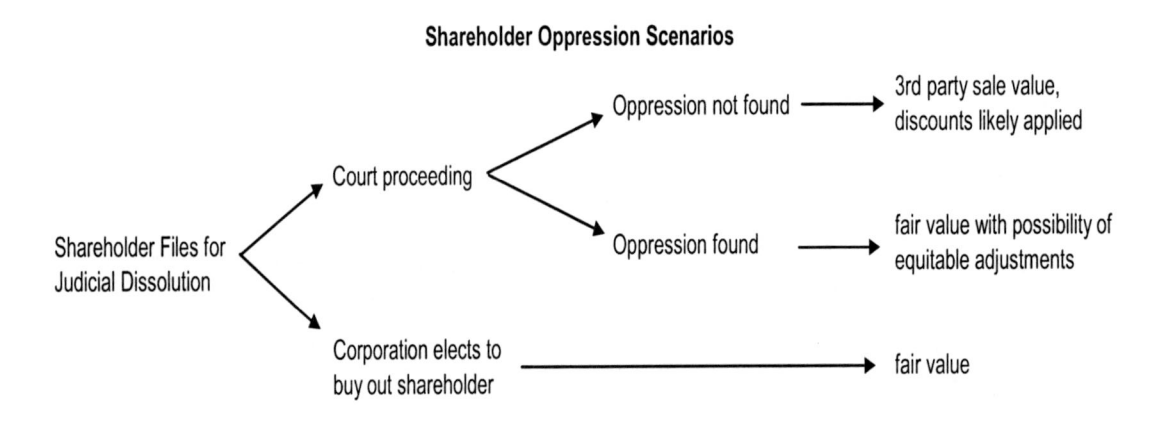

Shareholder Oppression Scenarios

Shareholder Files for Judicial Dissolution →
- Court proceeding →
  - Oppression not found → 3rd party sale value, discounts likely applied
  - Oppression found → fair value with possibility of equitable adjustments
- Corporation elects to buy out shareholder → fair value

If there is clear wrongdoing, self-dealing, or unfairness, in most states, it is likely that oppression will be found and the shareholder will receive the fair value of his or her shares based on case precedent. In those situations where there was egregious behavior on the part of the oppressor, the court may apply additional equitable adjustments. If shareholders bring a proceeding solely to cash out on an investment without any reasonable complaint, the court may decide that there is no oppression, and the shareholder will likely either receive a share price reflecting the third-party sale value or be compelled to remain as a shareholder.

Summary

This article has traced the history and development of fair value back through the nineteenth century when majority rule was instituted in place of unanimity. While fair market value evolved to mean the value arrived upon in a hypothetical transaction between willing participants, fair value was created for the purpose of shareholder dissent and oppression to protect a minority shareholder and to compensate the shareholder for that which has been taken.

The attempt to establish exactly what has been taken is the basis for the controversy over fair value. Based on loose guidelines set by the statutes, a valuation professional receives guidance on valuation date and certain elements to include and exclude from valuation. However, one still must determine exactly what one is valuing and the best methods and techniques to perform the valuation. These concepts have been shaped by legislatures, case law, the influence of the American Bar Association and the American Law Institute, and current valuation theory.

Although dissenters' and oppressed shareholders' rights developed throughout the twentieth century, they did not gain widespread usage until the decision in *Weinberger v. UOP, Inc.*[139] established the use of customary and current valuation techniques in valuing a business under these statutes. That decision, combined with the institution of the buy-out remedy and oppression doctrines, has significantly increased the popularity of cases determining fair value.

Each state has different definitions and treatments of fair value. As we have discussed, most states are now open to current and customary valuation techniques, but we can break the states down into roughly three groups based on the acceptance or rejection of discounts: those states that totally reject discounts, those that consider the facts and circumstances of the case, and those that accept discounts in most all situations.

Recently, the trend endorsed by the ABA and the ALI has directed that the value be set at a pro-rata share of the enterprise, without any shareholder-level discounts. Some states have adopted this treatment, while others are content with their own definitions of fair value. This trend, however, should not be seen to affect the need for entity-level adjustments made necessary by the cash flows used in valuation or the current circumstances of a given company. Once a value for the corporation as a whole is established by a proper valuation technique, the precedent-setting case law in each state may determine whether discounts are likely to be applied at the shareholder level.

Finally, and importantly, when a court reviews the facts and circumstances of a case, it attempts to compensate the parties involved equitably. This is the underlying basis for extraordinary circumstances, the award of damages, and any "adjustments" to value that would not normally be applied. Ultimately, a court may not be as concerned with strict adherence to the assumptions underlying fair value, and instead, may simply intend to find a means of fairly compensating the minority shareholder for that which as been taken.

Chapter 3: Dissenting and Oppressed Shareholder Matters

That having been said, the valuation professional should apply current and customary techniques that are generally accepted by the appraisal profession in determining value. Those techniques should be supported by reasonable facts and valuation theory. The final determination of value will be at the court's discretion based on the facts and circumstances of a given case.

---

1. Sections of this article include modified text from Shannon Pratt, Jay Fishman, and William Morrison. *Standards of Value: Theory and Applications*. John Wiley & Sons, Inc., 2006. Reprinted with permission of John Wiley & Sons, Inc. (To order, go to www.bvresources.com; (888) 287-8258).

2. Jay Fishman is a managing director of Financial Research Associates (www.finresearch.com), a regional business valuation and forensic accounting firm.

3. 74 A.2d 71, 72 (Del. 1950).

4. "The ABA provides law school accreditation, continuing legal education, information about the law, programs to assist lawyers and judges in their work, and initiatives to improve the legal system for the public." From the ABA's Web site at www.abanet.org. The MBCA is a model statute designed for use by state legislatures in revising and updating their corporation statutes, reflecting current views about business corporations. Robert W. Hamilton, "The Revised Model Business Corporation Act: Comment and Observation: Reflections of a Reporter," 63 *Texas Law Review*, 1455 (May 1985) at 1456.

5. The American Law Institute works to promote the clarification and simplification of the law and its better adaptation to social needs, to secure the better administration of justice, and to encourage and carry on scholarly and work." The institute drafts for consideration by its council and its membership and then publishes various restatements of the law, model codes, and other proposals for law reform. From the ALI's Web site at www.ALI.org. The basic purpose of the *Principles of Corporate Governance* was to "clarify the duties and obligations of corporate directors and officers and to provide guidelines for discharging those responsibilities in an efficient manner, with minimum risks of personal liability." American Law Institute, *Principles of Corporate Governance* (St. Paul, MN: American Law Institute Publishers, 1992), at President's Foreword, XXI.

6. Fair Value generally is undefined in dissolution statutes.

7. Alabama, Arizona, Arkansas, Colorado, Georgia, Hawaii, Indiana, Kentucky, Michigan, Minnesota, Missouri, Montana, Nebraska, Nevada, New Hampshire, North Carolina, Oregon, Pennsylvania South Carolina, Tennessee, Utah, Vermont, Virginia, Washington, Wyoming.

8. American Bar Association, A Report of the Committee of Corporate Laws, "Changes in the Revised Model Business Corporation Act—Amendments Pertaining to Close Corporations," *The Business Lawyer* 54 No. 209 (November 1998).

9. Colorado, Minnesota, New Jersey, Arizona, Connecticut, Utah.

10. American Law Institute, *Principles of Corporate Governance* (St. Paul, MN: American Law Institute Publishers, 1992), Section 7.22.

11. Connecticut, Florida, Idaho, Iowa, Maine, Mississippi, South Dakota, Virginia, West Virginia.

12. According to the American Bar Association, Committee on Corporate Laws, "Revised Model Business Corporation Act" (1999), Section 13.02(a)(5) of the RMBCA states that "any other amendment to the articles of incorporation, merger, share exchange or disposition of assets *to the extent provided by the articles of incorporation, bylaws or a resolution of the board of directors.*" [emphasis added] The official comment to the 1999 RMBCA states that if the corporation grants appraisal rights voluntarily for certain transactions that do not affect the entire corporation, the court can use its discretion in applying discounts.

13. *Balsamides v. Protameen Chemicals, Inc.*, 160 N.J. 352, 734 A.2d 721, 736 (N.J. 1999). The abstract of *Balsamides v. Protameen Chemicals, Inc.* is included in the court case abstract section of this *Guide*, and the full-text decision can be found at BVLibrary.com. The official comment to the 1999 RMBCA states that if the corporation grants appraisal rights voluntarily for certain transactions that do not affect the entire corporation, the court can use its discretion in applying discounts.

14. 513 NE.2d 776 (Ohio 1987).

15. Common law is a system of laws that had originated and developed in England based on court decisions and the doctrines implicit in those decisions, and on customs and uses rather than written law. http://www.answers.com/topic/common-law.

16. Michael Aiken, "A Minority Shareholder's Rights in Dissension—How Does Delaware Do It and What Can Louisiana Learn?" 50 *Loyola Law Review*, 231 (Spring 2004), at 235.

17. John D. Emory, "The Role of Discounts in Determining Fair Value Under Wisconsin's Dissenter's Rights Statutes: The Case for Discounts," 1155 *Wisconsin Law Review* (University of Wisconsin) (1995), at 1163.

18. Mary Siegel, "Back to the Future: Appraisal Rights in the Twenty-First Century," 32 *Harvard Journal of Legislation*, 79 (Winter 1995), at 87.

19. *Wheeler v. Pullman Iron & Steel Co.*, 143 Ill. 197, 207–08, 32 N.E. 420, 423 (1892): "Every one purchasing or subscribing for stock in a corporation impliedly agrees that he will be bound by the acts and proceedings done or sanctioned by a majority of the shareholders, or by the agents of the corporation [directors] duly chosen by such majority, within the scope of the powers conferred by the charter."

20. Charles W. Murdock, "The Evolution of Effective Remedies for Minority Shareholders and Its Impact upon Valuation of Minority Shares," 65 *Notre Dame Law Review*, No. 425 (1990), at 429.

21. Siegel, "Back to the Future."

22. *The Mansfield, Coldwater and Lake Michigan Railroad Company v. Stout*, 26 Ohio St. 241; 1875 Ohio LEXIS 397

23. Siegel, "Back to the Future," at 89.

24. Wertheimer, "Shareholders' Appraisal Remedy," at 619.

25. Siegel, "Back to the Future," at 87.

26. 311 U.S. 531, 535, 61 S. Ct. 376, 377, 85 L. Ed. 322, 326.

27. SEC Report on the Work of Protective and Reorganization Committees, Part VII, pp. 557, 590 (Washington DC: U.S. Government Print Office 1938).

28. The National Conference of Commissioners on Uniform state laws was formed in 1892 for the purpose of providing states with non-partisan, well-conceived, and well-drafted legislation that brings clarity and stability to critical areas of the law. http://www.nccusl.org/Update/.

29. Aiken, "A Minority Shareholder's Rights in Dissension," at 237.

30. Robert W. Hamilton, "The Revised Model Business Corporation Act: Comment and Observation: Reflections of a Reporter," 63 *Texas Law Review*,1455 (May 1985) at 1457.

31. Robert B. Thompson, "Exit, Liquidity, and Majority Rule: Appraisal's Role in Corporate Law," 84 *Georgetown Law Review*, 1 (November 1995), Appendix Table 2: New York 1890; Maine 1891; Kentucky 1893; New Jersey 1896; Delaware 1899; Connecticut and Pennsylvania 1901; Alabama, Massachusetts, Nevada, and Virginia 1903; Montana and New Mexico 1905; Ohio 1906; Tennessee 1907; Maryland 1908; Vermont 1915; Illinois and New Hampshire 1919; Rhode Island 1920; Arkansas, Florida, North Carolina, and South Carolina 1925; Minnesota and Oregon 1927; Louisiana 1928; Idaho and Indiana 1929; California, District of Columbia, and Michigan 1931; Washington 1933; Hawaii 1937; Georgia 1938; Arizona and Kansas 1939; Colorado and Nebraska 1941; Missouri 1943; Iowa, Oklahoma, Wisconsin, and Wyoming 1947; Mississippi 1954; South Dakota and Texas 1955; Alaska and North Dakota 1957; Utah 1961; West Virginia 1974.

32. *Id.* at n10, n241–242.

33. The case law and concepts we address in this chapter deal exclusively with oppression in *corporations* and focus mainly on close corporations. Partnerships are not subject to the same remedies because of the withdrawal rights available by statute in most states. For LLCs, case law is in its infancy because of the relative newness of the corporate form. For more information on the remedies to minority mistreatment in all three corporate forms, see Moll, Douglas. "Minority Oppression and the Limited Liability Company: Learning (or not) from Close Corporation History" University of Houston Public Law and Legal Theory Series 2006-A-01.

34. Murdock, "Evolution of Effective Remedies for Minority Shareholders," at 440.

35. Duke Law Review, "Oppression as a Statutory Ground for Corporate Dissolution," 128 *Duke Law Journal* (1965), at n2.

36. The only exception is Michigan, where an action citing oppression can be brought by the shareholder outside the dissolution statute, although dissolution (among others) may still be the remedy.

37. Delaware and Indiana allow shareholder dissolution only in the case of deadlock. Kansas and Louisiana allow shareholder dissolution in the case of deadlock, but only if irreparable damage is being done to the corporation or shareholders. Massachusetts requires that no less than 40% outstanding shareholders can file for dissolution, but only in cases of shareholder or management deadlock. Michigan allows shareholders to file if they cannot agree on management and corporation is not able to function properly. Nevada and Ohio allow shareholder dissolution only if petitioned by a majority. Oklahoma, Texas, and the District of Columbia do not allow shareholders to petition for dissolution.

Chapter 3: Dissenting and Oppressed Shareholder Matters

38. 3Alabama 1961; Alaska 1962; Illinois 1953; Iowa 1962; Missouri 1952; North Dakota 1960; Oregon 1961; Pennsylvania 1958; Texas 1956; Utah 1963; Virginia 1956; Wyoming 1963. 128 Duke Law Review, "Oppression as a Statutory Ground for Corporate Dissolution," at 134.
39. Arizona, Arkansas, Colorado, Connecticut, Hawaii, Idaho, Maine, Maryland, Michigan, Mississippi, Montana, Nebraska, New Hampshire, New Jersey, New Mexico, New York, Rhode Island, South Carolina, South Dakota, Tennessee, Vermont, Washington, West Virginia, Wisconsin.
40. California, Alaska, Florida, Georgia, Kentucky, Minnesota, North Carolina, North Dakota.
41. This information can be found in each state's statutes. As of the publication of this book, Alaska and California require 33 $^{1/3}$ share ownership to file a dissent action. New York and Georgia require a 20% share ownership.
42. 128 Duke Law Review, "Oppression as a Statutory Ground for Corporate Dissolution," at n2.
43. 16 N.Y.2d at 804, 210 N.E.2d at 356, 263 N.Y.S.2d at 2.
44. Murdock, "Evolution of Effective Remedies for Minority Shareholders," at 461.
45. 1941 Cal. Stat. 2058-59 (codified as amended at CAL. CORP. CODE § 2000 (West 1977 & Supp. 1989)).
46. Murdock, "Evolution of Effective Remedies for Minority Shareholders."
47. 107 Misc. 2d25; 433 N.Y.S. 2d 359 (N.Y. Sup. 1980)
48. *Balsamides v. Protameen Chemicals, Inc.,* 160 N.J. 352, 734 A.2d 721, 736 (N.J. 1999).
49. 68 Wash. App. 69, 841 P.2d 1289, 1294 (Wash. Ct. App. 1992).
50. No. 97 C 7088 U.S. Dist. Ct., 1998 Lexis 18864 (N.D. Ill. Oct. 30, 1998). The abstract of *Connector Service Corporation v. Briggs* is included in the court case abstract section of this *Guide*, and the full-text decision can be found at BVLibrary.com.
51. 1998 Lexis 70 (Del. Ch. 1998).
52. Ill.2d 566, 576, 1441 N.E.2d 45, 51 (1957).
53. 107 Misc. 2d 25, 34, 433. NYS2d 359, 365 (1980).
54. It should be noted that although the courts were empowered to award fair value by New York Statute Section 1118, the court seems to have used the term *fair market value* as a substitute. It is unclear whether that substitution was intentional
55. Ladd A. Hirsch, "Counseling the Small Business to be Litigation Savvy," speech presented at University of Houston Law Foundation, March 2003 (www.cdhlaw.com)
56. American Bar Association, A Report of the Committee of Corporate Laws, "Changes in the Revised Model Business Corporation Act—Amendments Pertaining to Close Corporations," *The Business Lawyer* 46, No. 297 (1991).
57. 2000 Conn. Super. LEXIS 2987
58. Hirsch, "Counseling the Small Business to be Litigation Savvy."
59. 367 Mass. 578; 328 N.E.2d 505, 1975.
60. 875 F.2d 549; 1989 U.S. App. LEXIS 6910 Applying Maryland Law.
61. 74 A.2d (Del. 1950).
62. No. 98-CVS-3766(NC Sup. Ct 2000). The abstract of *Smith v. North Carolina Motor Speedway* is included in the court case abstract section of this *Guide*.
63. Fishman, Pratt, and Griffith, "PPC's Guide to Business Valuation," at 1505.46.
64. No. CIV.A.12207, 1994 Del. Ch. LEXIS 67, at *10–11 (May 25, 1994).
65. 160 N.J. 383; 734 A.2d 738; 1999 N.J. LEXIS 835.
66. *Cede v. Technicolor, Inc.,* No. CIV.A.7129, 1990 Del. Ch. LEXIS 259 (Oct. 19, 1990), rev'd, 684 A.2d 289 (Del. 1996). The abstract of *Cede v. Technicolor, Inc.* is included in the court case abstract section of this *Guide*, and the full-text decision can be found at BVLibrary.com..
67. Id., at 315–322.
68. N.Y. Bus. Corp. Law Sec. 1118(b).
69. R.I. Gen. Laws Sec 7-1-90.1.

How to Avoid Minefields

70. California Corp. Code Sec.2000(f).
71. N.J. Stat. Ann Sec. 14A:12-7(8)(a)
72. Wertheimer, "Shareholders' Appraisal Remedy," at n432–437.
73. American Bar Association, Report of the Committee of Corporate Laws, "Changes in the Revised Model Business Corporation Act."
74. American Law Institute, *Principles of Corporate Governance*), at 315.
75. Id., at 318.
76. 457 A.2d 701; 1983 Del. LEXIS 371. The full-text decision of *Weinberger v. UOP, Inc.* can be found at BVLibrary.com.
77. 1997 Del. Ch. LEXIS 124. The abstract of *Grimes v. Vitalink Communications Corporation* is included in the court case abstract section of this *Guide*, and the full-text decision can be found at BVLibrary.com.
78. Del. Ch., C.A. No. 11107, 1995 Del. Ch. LEXIS 75, Chandler, V.C. (June 15, 1995).
79. 1997 Del. Ch. LEXIS 124.
80. 160 N.J. 352, 734 A.2d 721, 736 (N.J. 1999).
81. 5 F. Supp. 2d (D. Nev. 1998). The abstract of *Steiner Corp. v. Benninghoff* is included in the court case abstract section of this *Guide*, and the full-text decision can be found at BVLibrary.com.
82. 2005 WL 2045640 (Del. Ch. 2005).
83. 2005 WL 43994 (Del. Ch. 2004)
84. 2004 WL 2271592 (Del. Ch. 2004) and affirmed at 2005 WL 1936157 (Del. 2005). The abstract of *Montgomery Cellular Holding Co., Inc. v. Dobler* is included in the court case abstract section of this *Guide*, and the full-text decision can be found at BVLibrary.com.
85. Siegel, "Back to the Future," 79 at n79.
86. MBCA §13.02(b)(1) (1999).
87. C.A. No. 16316-NC, 1999 Lexis 197 (Del. Ch. Sept. 24, 1999). The abstract of B*orruso v. Communications Telesystems International* is included in the court case abstract section of this *Guide*, and the full-text decision can be found at BVLibrary.com.
88. 191 N.J. Super. 192, 199, 465 A.2d 948 (Ch. Div. 1983).
89. No. 97 C 7088 U.S. Dist. Ct., 1998 Lexis 18864 (N.D. Ill. Oct. 30, 1998).
90. Atulya Sarin, John Koeplin and Alan C. Shapiro, "The Private Company Discount." *Journal of Applied Corporate Finance*, Vol. 12, No. 4, Winter 2000.
91. David Laro and Shannon Pratt, *Business Valuation and Taxes,* at 266.
92. 74 A.2d 71, 72 (Del. 1950).
93. No. CIV.A.11265, 1992 Del. Ch. LEXIS 252, (Dec. 7, 1992).
94. 603 A.2d 796; 1992 Del. LEXIS 30.
95. 344 N.J. Super. 83; 780 A.2d 553; 2001 N.J. Super. LEXIS 331.
96. 611 A.2d 485, 498 (Del. Ch. 1991).
97. 2004 WL 1752847 (Del. Ch. 2004).
98. 2004 WL 2271592 (Del. Ch. 2004) and affirmed 2005 WL 1936157 (Del. 2005).
99. 794 a.2d 1161 (Del. Ch. 1999) and affirmed at 766 A.2d 437 (Del. 2000).
100. 2004 WL 1152338 (Del. Ch. 2004).
101. American Law Institute, *Principles of Corporate Governance*, at 325.
102. 2001 Conn. Super. LEXIS 1285. The abstract of *Devivo v. Devivo* is included in the court case abstract section of this *Guide*, and the full-text decision can be found at BVLibrary.com.
103. 615 N.W.2d 285 (Minn. 2000).
104. 160 N.J. 383, 397, 734 A.2d 738 (1999).

Chapter 3: Dissenting and Oppressed Shareholder Matters

105. 169 Ga. App. 584; 314 S.E.2d 245; 1984 Ga. App. LEXIS 1640.
106. 264 Ga. App. 453, 540 S.E. 2d 667 (2000). The abstract of *Blitch v. People's Bank* is included in the court case abstract section of this *Guide*, and the full-text decision can be found at BVLibrary.com.
107. Shannon P. Pratt, Robert Reilly, and Robert Schweihs, *Valuing a Business*, 4th ed. (New York: McGraw-Hill, (2000), at 792. (To order, go to www.bvresouces.com; (888) 287-8258).
108. *Id*. at 793
109. *Id*. at 794.
110. 21 Del. J. Corp. L. 1281 (Del. Ch. 1996).
111. 794 A.2d 1161 (Del. Ch. 1999) and affirmed at 766 A.2d 437 (Del. 2000).
112. N.J. Statute 14A:12-7-8(a).
113. *Id*.
114. American Bar Association, A Report of the Committee of Corporate Laws, "Changes in the Revised Model Business Corporation Act—Appraisal Rights," *The Business Lawyer* 54 (1998), at 209.
115. Douglass Moll, "Shareholder Oppression & Fair Value: of Discounts, Dates, and Dastardly Deeds in the Close Corporation," 54 *Duke Law Journal* 293 (2005), at 369.
116. *In Re Friedman*, 661 N.E.2d 972, 976 (NY 1985).
117. 2001 Conn. Super. LEXIS 2430 X07CV990060602S. The abstract of *Johnson v. Johnson* is included in the court case abstract section of this *Guide*, and the full-text decision can be found at BVLibrary.com.
118. N.J. statute 14(A):12-7(8)(a).
119. 160 N.J. 352; 734 A.2d 721; 1999 N.J. LEXIS 836.
120. *Lawson Mardon Wheaton Inc. v. Smith*, 160 N.J. 383; 734 A.2d 738; 1999 N.J. LEXIS 835.
121. It should be noted that although the language the court used is "intrinsic value," it appears that in this instance intrinsic value was used synonymously with fair value.
122. 684 A.2d 289, 298 (Del. 1996).
123. Moll, "Shareholder Oppression & 'Fair Value.'"
124. Wertheimer, "Shareholders' Appraisal Remedy."
125. 457 A.2d 701, 713 (Del. 1983).
126. 268 Kan. 163, 992 P.2d 216 (Kan.1999). The abstract of *Arnaud v. Stockgrowers State Bank* is included in the court case abstract section of this *Guide*, and the full-text decision can be found at BVLibrary.com.
127. 2001 Conn. Super. LEXIS 2430 X07CV990060602S.
128. *Lawson Mardon Wheaton Inc. v. Smith*, 160 N.J. 383; 734 A.2d 738; 1999 N.J. LEXIS 835.
129. 160 N.J. 352; 734 A.2d 721; 1999 N.J. LEXIS 836.
130. Moll, "Shareholder Oppression & 'Fair Value,'" at n180.
131. 457 A.2d 701, 713 (Del. 1983).
132. 457 A.2d 701; 1983 Del. LEXIS 371. The subsequent enactment of Delaware Code section 102 b(7) allows corporate charter provision to limit or eliminate the personal monetary liability of directors Del Code 102 b(7).
133. *Wilkes v. Springside Nursing Home, Inc.*, 353 N.E. 2d 657, 662 (Mass 1976); *Exadaktilos v. Cinnaminson Realty Co.*, 400 A.2d 554, 561 (N.J. Super. Ct. Law Div. 1979).
134. Mark A. Rothstein, et al. *Employment Law* §9.24 at 593 (1994).
135. Moll, "Shareholder Oppression & 'Fair Value,'" at n185.
136. 281 NJ Super. At 561.
137. 2001 Conn. Super. LEXIS 2430 X07CV990060602S.
138. The three scenarios in this chart are taken from the ABA's 2002 RMBCA, section 14.30 (1, 2, 3).
139. 457 A.2d 701, 713 (Del. 1983).

Judicial Valuation of Stock of a Delaware Corporation: The Legal Concept of "Fair Value"

By Bruce L. Silverstein, Esq.[1]

Under Delaware law, any determination of the "value" of the shares of stock of a corporation requires an appreciation of the specific factual context in which the determination is required. For example, the value of the shares in question may turn on a specific definition contained in a contract or other legal instrument. Alternatively, the value of the shares may depend upon the nature of a transaction involving the shares. The value also may turn on the nature of a particular cause of action asserted, or remedy sought, in a given case that gives rise to the need for the value to be determined.

As a general matter, Delaware law does not impose any specific concept of value in arm's-length transactions which involve no element of coercion or other breach of fiduciary duty (such as inadequate or misleading disclosure by a fiduciary). Thus, for example, parties to a stockholders' agreement typically are free to establish any definition of value upon which they are able to agree. By contrast, in cases where a stockholder's equity is eliminated without the stockholder's consent, Delaware law generally requires that the stockholder be paid the "fair value" of the shares. As discussed below, "fair value" in this context is a term of art under Delaware corporate law.

Because the determination of value is context-specific under Delaware law, liability for substantial damages may result from a corporate fiduciary's failure to appreciate the standard of "value" that applies in a given situation. By the same token, a stockholder's ability to appreciate this issue can help to avoid the loss of substantial value.

This paper provides an overview of the different ways in which the Delaware courts have adjudicated the "value" of stock in differing contexts. The main focus of this paper is upon the adjudication of "fair value" for purposes of a statutory "appraisal" proceeding – which is the context in which the Delaware courts have had the greatest opportunity to dilate on the question of valuation of stock. The paper does, however, address various other contexts in which the Delaware courts have been called upon to adjudicate the value of stock. The paper also addresses some of the more nuanced issues that are implicated when the valuation of stock is adjudicated.

I. "Fair Value" Defined

Under Delaware corporate law, the legal concept of "fair value" has its origins in the appraisal statute, currently codified as *Section 262* of the Delaware General Corporation Law (the "DGCL").[2] The Delaware Supreme Court has summarized the "fair value" standard, as follows:

Chapter 3: Dissenting and Oppressed Shareholder Matters

Fair value, in an appraisal context, measures "that which has been taken from [the shareholder], *viz.*, his proportionate interest in a going concern." In the appraisal process the corporation is valued "as an entity," not merely as a collection of assets, or by the sum of the market price of each share of its stock[.] Moreover, the corporation must be viewed as an on-going enterprise, occupying a particular market position in the light of future prospects.[3]

Stated somewhat differently:

[T]he company must be first valued as an operating entity by application of traditional value factors, weighted as required, but without regard to post-merger events or other possible business combinations. The dissenting shareholder's proportionate interest is determined only after the company as an entity has been valued.[4]

It is important to understand that the legal concept of "fair value" is not synonymous with the concept of the "fair *market* value." Although the terms often are used interchangeably outside of the context of Delaware corporate law, they are terms of art having materially different meanings as applied to the valuation of stock in Delaware corporations. As the Court of Chancery has observed:

The concept of fair value under Delaware law is not equivalent to the economic concept of fair market value. Rather, the concept of fair value for purposes of Delaware's appraisal statute is a largely judge-made creation, freighted with policy considerations.[5]

Under Delaware law (as in most jurisdictions, as well as in the "real world"), the term "fair market value" means "the price which would be agreed upon by a willing seller and a willing buyer under usual and ordinary circumstances, after consideration of all available uses and purposes, without any compulsion upon the seller to sell or upon the buyer to buy."[6] Consequently, where the shares of a publicly-owned corporation actively trade in a liquid market, it is generally recognized that the "fair market value" of the shares is best represented by the price at which the shares trade in that market.[7] Moreover, even in the case of shares that are not publicly traded, if a price is established by independently operating market forces, such as an active and competitive bidding process, the resulting price may be considered a reliable measurement of "fair market value."[8]

The material difference between the concepts of "fair market value" and "fair value," as they relate to the valuation of stock in Delaware corporations, has its origin in the Court of Chancery's 1934 decision in *Chicago Corp. v. Munds*.[9] In that case, certain stockholders dissented from a merger and sought a statutory appraisal of their shares. The "appraisers" (a non-judicial body that is no longer involved in statutory appraisal proceedings under Delaware law) thereafter determined the "fair value" of the dissenting stockholders' shares exclusively on the basis of the closing market price of the shares on the date of the merger.[10] In essence, the appraisers awarded the dissenting stockholders the "fair market value" of their shares. Rejecting the appraisers' approach as inconsistent with Delaware law, the Court of Chancery instructed that "'value' as used in [the appraisal statute] is not synonymous with market value."[11]

Judicial Valuation of Stock of a Delaware Corporation

The Court of Chancery derived its interpretation of the appraisal statute in *Chicago Corp.* both (i) by employing canons of statutory construction, and (ii) by considering the "purpose" of the statute. With respect to the latter aspect of the analysis, the Court of Chancery explained:

> At common law it was in the power of any single stockholder to prevent a merger. When the idea became generally accepted that, in the interest of adjusting corporate mechanisms to the requirements of business and commercial growth, mergers should be permitted in spite of the opposition of minorities, statutes were enacted in state after state which took from the individual stockholder the right theretofore existing to defeat the welding of his corporation with another. In compensation for the lost right a provision was written into the modern statutes giving the dissenting stockholder the option completely to retire from the enterprise and receive the value of his stock in money. Most of the statutes provide that what the unwilling stockholder who refuses to accept an interest in the consolidated enterprise shall be paid is the "value" of his stock....

> When a stockholder buys stock it is to be supposed that he buys into a corporation as a going concern. He does not buy on the theory that he is about to participate in a contemplated liquidation of the corporation's assets. He buys an aliquot share of a business, and he probably takes into account, or should at least take into account, not alone its present asset condition and earning power but as well its future prospects as a continuing enterprise. When a merger proposal is put through with which he chooses to dissociate himself, he is forced out of his investment and compelled to abandon his association with a business of which he was a part owner. As to him, the going concern is done. Others have decreed its cessation against his will. What he has been deprived of is his proportional share of an active enterprise which but for the compulsion of others he could continue to be associated with in the indefinite future. What he is deprived of is what he should be paid for....

> When it is said that the appraisal which the market puts upon the value of the stock of an active corporation as evidenced by its daily quotations, is an accurate, fair reflection of its intrinsic value, no more than a moment's reflection is needed to refute it. There are too many accidental circumstances entering into the making of market prices to admit them as sure and exclusive reflectors of fair value. The experience of recent years is enough to convince the most casual observer that the market in its appraisal of values must have been woefully wrong in its estimates at one time or another within the interval of a space of time so brief that fundamental conditions could not possibly have become so altered as to affect true worth. Markets are known to gyrate in a single day. The numerous causes that contribute to their nervous leaps from dejected melancholy to exhilarated enthusiasm and then back again from joy to grief, need not be reviewed. It would be most unfortunate indeed either for the consolidated corporation or for the objecting stockholder if, on the particular date named by the statute for the valuation of the dissenter's stock, viz., the date of the consolidation, the market should be in one of its extreme moods and the stock had to be paid for at the price fixed by the quotations of that day. Even when

conditions are normal and no economic forces are at work unduly to exalt or depress the financial hopes of man, market quotations are not safe to accept as unerring expressions of value. The relation of supply to demand on a given day as truly affects the market value of a stock as it does of a commodity; and temporary supply and demand are in turn affected by numerous circumstances which are wholly disconnected from considerations having to do with the stock's inherent worth.

I readily agree that for many purposes market values when they exist are accepted by the courts as the values to be taken for the admeasurement of damages. This is so in actions for the conversion of chattels, and may in some circumstances be equally so in actions for the conversion of shares of stock. The reason is that, generally in such cases the plaintiff can easily step into the market and replace presumably at the quoted prices the chattels or stock which the defendant converted. Paying him the market price puts him as a rule in position to restore what was taken from him.

But how can the payment to the holder of stock of its market value put him in the way of restoring his position as a continuing part owner of a going corporation, when a merger has destroyed its individual identity and wiped out of existence all the stock of the kind he owned? As there is none in existence, none is available to be bought. The only restoration that can be made to him is to substitute for the vanished stock its intrinsic worth, and if the market quotations are lower than what all the relevant facts that bear on value show it to have been worth, he should not be compensated according to the market's estimate.[12]

Sixteen years after the Court of Chancery first articulated the material difference between the concepts of "fair value" and "fair market value" in *Chicago Corp.*, the Delaware Supreme Court adopted the distinction in *Tri-Continental Corp. v. Battye*.[13] Today, it is well settled that the concept of "fair value" in Delaware law means "the value of the petitioners' shares on the assumption that they are entitled to a pro rata interest in the value of the firm when considered as a going concern, specifically recognizing its market position and future prospects."[14]

Notably, the Delaware courts have rejected the conceptualization that the "fair value" of a corporation's shares is the equivalent of the shares' pro rata value of the highest price that could be obtained in a sale of the company to a third-party purchaser.[15] In fact, the Delaware courts have held that Delaware law requires any "synergistic elements of value" arising from the completion of a merger or acquisition be eliminated from the calculation of "fair value".[16] Stated somewhat differently, "fair value" under Delaware law attempts to capture "the value of the company to the stockholder as a going concern, rather than its value to a third party as an acquisition."[17]

II. Adjudicating "Fair Value"

The overarching statutory principle guiding determinations of "fair value" under Delaware law is that the court "shall take into account all relevant factors."[18] The Delaware Supreme Court has construed this statutory principle to dictate that value may be proven "by any techniques or methods which are generally considered acceptable in the financial community and otherwise admissible in court."[19] As this rule suggests, the Delaware courts have adopted a flexible approach to valuation that recognizes that no one specific methodology necessarily provides an accurate measure of value in all factual contexts.[20] No matter the methodology relied upon, all relevant factors impacting value must be considered, which, among other things, may include "asset value, dividend record, earnings prospects and any additional factors that relate to financial stability or prospects for growth."[21] "In making the fair value determination, the court may look to the opinions advanced by the parties' experts, select one party's expert opinion as a framework, fashion its own framework or adopt, piecemeal, some portion of an expert's model methodology or mathematical calculations."[22] The court may not, however, engage in a "baseball arbitration" approach that adopts one party's valuation "hook, line, and sinker" solely on the grounds that the value proffered by one party is more reasonable than the value proffered by the other party.[23] Such an all-or-nothing approach has been found to be at odds with the nature of a valuation proceeding, in which the court is tasked with determining the fair value of the shares.[24]

Over the past two decades, the Delaware courts routinely have utilized one or more of three approaches or metrics to adjudicate "fair value": (i) the "market approach"; (ii) the "income approach"; and (iii) the "transaction approach."[25] Additionally, the Delaware courts have considered, but not relied exclusively upon, the "liquidation value" of a company in adjudicating its "fair value." As set out more fully below, there also are a number of special rules that have been developed by the Delaware courts, which serve as an overlay upon the standards employed in the financial community.

A. The Market Approach

The market approach also is commonly referred to as a "comparable," "comparative" or "guideline" [publicly traded] company approach. This approach provides an indication of value by applying observed market multiples of selected financial fundamentals of publicly traded companies perceived to be comparable to the subject company. As the Court of Chancery has explained:

> The comparable company valuation model involves: (1) identifying comparable publicly traded companies; (2) deriving appropriate valuation multiples from the comparable companies; (3) adjusting those multiples to account for the differences from the company being valued and the comparables; and (4) applying those multiples to the revenues, earnings, or other values for the company being valued.[26]

Despite the objectively verifiable nature of financial data underlying the market approach, the Delaware courts have recognized that the selection of the companies deemed to be comparable and the selection of the multiples upon which the valuation will be based injects significant subjectivity into the approach.[27] As a result, the Delaware courts have tended to condition their reliance on the market approach upon a showing that the "comparable companies" are, in fact, comparable to the company being valued,[28] and that the financial fundamentals

Chapter 3: Dissenting and Oppressed Shareholder Matters

used in the approach are, in fact, the fundamentals that are generally considered to be pertinent in the particular industry at issue.[29]

Within the market approach, no single industry multiple has garnered universal acceptance by the Delaware courts as the most reliable indicator of value.[30] Nonetheless, Delaware courts do often rely upon multiples of earnings before interest and taxes ("EBIT") or earnings before interest taxes, depreciation and amortization ("EBITDA").[31] Additionally, in appropriate cases, Delaware courts have relied upon multiples of book value and net earnings.[32] Delaware courts also have considered a multiple based on gross revenue as one of many multiples.[33]

The Delaware courts have utilized the market approach in a number of valuation cases – both as one factor among others in an integrated valuation analysis,[34] and as a check to gauge the reliability of a different valuation approach.[35] In one reported decision, Court of Chancery has even adjudicated the "fair value" of a subject company based exclusively upon the market approach.[36] By the same token, the Court of Chancery has declined to rely upon the market approach as even one factor among many where the court has determined that material dissimilarity between the subject company and the companies identified as "comparables" made a "meaningful comparison impossible."[37]

Additionally, as discussed more fully below (under the heading of "Discounts and Premia"), the Delaware courts have found that the market approach tends to include an embedded "minority discount" that must be eliminated in adjudicating "fair value." As such, the Delaware courts actually have employed a "modified" form of the market approach that varies from the manner in which this approach is "generally considered acceptable in the financial community."[38]

B. The Income Approach

The income approach provides an indication of "fair value" based upon the projected future income of the subject company.[39] The "discounted cash flow" (or "DCF") model is an example of the income approach. It has been described by the Delaware Supreme Court as follows:

> A DCF calculation takes into account cash flow, projected earnings, expenditures, taxes, and depreciation in determining the present value of a business. The appraiser first estimates the value of the firm's cash flow for a specific projection period, using contemporaneous management projections. Then, the value of the business attributed to cash flow from the post-projection period is estimated in order to arrive at a terminal value. Finally, the projected cash flow and the terminal value are discounted to present value to determine the business' "fair value."[40]

The Delaware courts frequently have employed the income approach "as at least one method of valuation."[41] Moreover, although "no method of valuation is preferable per se in Delaware,"[42] the Court of Chancery has observed that "Delaware courts tend to favor a DCF model over other available methodologies in an appraisal proceeding."[43]

Notwithstanding the expressed preference for employing the income approach in adjudicating "fair value," the Delaware courts have articulated reservations about using this approach where the evidence suggests that it is unreliable under the specific circumstances of a particular company.[44] As the Court of Chancery has explained:

> DCF is an acceptable methodology of valuing companies in an appraisal action. However, a DCF analysis is "only as good as the inputs to the model." Although "necessarily speculative in nature[, DCF inputs are] central to the reliability of the underlying methodology." "Delaware law clearly prefers valuations based on contemporaneously prepared management projections because management ordinarily has the best first-hand knowledge of a company's operations." Despite the inherent unreliability of post-merger, litigation-driven forecasts, this court has acknowledged the propriety of using DCF analysis based on such forecasts in the absence of viable alternatives.[45]

As with the market approach, there are cases in which the Delaware courts have relied exclusively upon the income approach in adjudicating the fair value of a subject company,[46] and there are cases where the Delaware courts have rejected the use of the income approach altogether.[47]

C. The Transaction Approach

The transaction approach also is commonly referred to as the "comparable transaction approach" and the "comparable acquisition approach." This approach "involves identifying similar transactions, quantifying those transactions through financial metrics, and then applying those metrics to the company at issue to ascertain a value."[48]

The Delaware courts have expressed mixed views regarding the appropriate use of the transaction approach in adjudicating "fair value."[49] This is because the Delaware courts have rejected the notion that the "fair value" of a corporation's shares is the equivalent of the shares' pro rata value of the highest price that could be obtained in a sale of the company to a third-party purchaser.[50] As the Court of Chancery has explained:

> In prior appraisal actions, this Court has rejected the use of a control premium derived from merger and acquisition data because the control premium incorporates post-merger value. [The valuation experts] testified that the premium over market price paid by an acquiror includes more than an adjustment for a minority discount. The acquiror may value the target corporation above its going concern value because of potential synergies or because the acquiror believes it will manage the target better. This portion of a control premium cannot be included in the appraisal value of a corporation because it reflects value arising from the accomplishment or expectation of the merger.[51]

Because the transaction approach provides an indication of the value that might be derived from the sale of the subject company, it is necessary to make an adjustment to the results of this approach in order to derive an indication of the subject company's "fair value." Specifically, it is necessary to adjust the results of the transaction approach to eliminate any element of "shared synergies" included in the comparable transactions.[52] In a sense, this is the "inverse" of the inherent minority discount the Delaware courts have found to be imbedded in the market approach.[53]

As is the case with the market approach (as well as the income approach), the Delaware courts have utilized the transaction approach in a number of valuation cases – both as one factor among others in an integrated valuation analysis,[54] and as a check to gauge the reliability of a different valuation approach.[55] There also are cases in which the Delaware courts have relied exclusively upon the transaction approach in adjudicating the fair value of a subject company,[56] and there are cases where the Delaware courts have rejected the use of the transaction approach altogether where the party (or expert) advocating its use has failed to establish an appropriate level of familiarity with the actual details of the transactions identified as "comparable" or has been unable to demonstrate that such a valuation is reliable and persuasive.[57] Moreover, "[e]ven in circumstances where the court accepted a comparable transactions analysis, the approach's ability to contribute to an appraisal of fair value has been recognized as limited by the similarity between the company the Court is valuing and the companies used for comparison."[58]

D. Liquidation Value

Liquidation value, which is also called net asset value, is determined on the basis of the market value of the corporation's assets (including any cash), less outstanding liabilities, debentures, and preferred stock.[59] Because liquidation value represents the theoretical value to which shareholders would be entitled if the corporation were to go out of business, it does not represent a value for the entity as a going concern.[60] Thus, the Delaware Supreme Court has instructed that "[l]iquidation value is one factor relevant to a fair value inquiry and an acceptable technique, with others, upon which the Court of Chancery can rely. Liquidation value cannot, however, be viewed as a substitute for, or interchangeable with, fair value."[61]

In *Cooper v. Pabst Brewing Corp.*, the Court of Chancery offered the following observation:

> Asset value has, under certain circumstances, been given substantial weight in the appraisal process, however. This has been particularly true in appraisals of natural resource companies because "the worth of a natural resource company lies in the value of its underlying assets[.]"[62]

III. Discounts & Premia

A. Discounts & Premia Cannot Be Considered at the "Stockholder Level"

When the legal concept of "fair value" is applicable, it is impermissible to consider "discounts" or "premia" at the "stockholder level."[63] Stated somewhat differently, in a "fair value" case, once the value of the corporation has been determined and "allocated" proportionately among all of the corporation's shares, it is impermissible to "adjust" the allocated value to account for external factors that might impact a specific stockholder's ability to sell the shares. To do so would, in essence, result in a "fair market value."

As the Court of Chancery has explained:

> [T]he purpose of a Delaware appraisal is to determine the fair value of 100% of the corporation, and to award to the dissenting stockholder his proportionate share of that fair value. The objective is not to value a specific minority stock interest in the corporation as such. That a stockholder might happen to own a significant block of stock will not, for that reason, entitle him to a premium above the appraised fair value of his shares. Similarly, that a dissenting stockholder may own a minority interest (which is the case in all appraisal proceedings) will not diminish his right to receive fair value by subjecting him to a penalty in the form of a "minority discount."[64]

On appeal, the Delaware Supreme Court similarly explained:

> The application of a discount to a minority shareholder is contrary to the requirement that the company be viewed as a "going concern." Cavalier's argument, that the only way Harnett would have received value for his 1.5% stock interest was to sell his stock, subject to market treatment of its minority status, misperceives the nature of the appraisal remedy. Where there is no objective market data available, the appraisal process is not intended to reconstruct a *pro forma* sale but to assume that the shareholder was willing to maintain his investment position, however slight, had the merger not occurred. Discounting individual share holdings injects into the appraisal process speculation on the various factors which may dictate the marketability of minority shareholdings. More important, to fail to accord to a minority shareholder the full proportionate value of his shares imposes a penalty for lack of control, and unfairly enriches the majority shareholders who may reap a windfall from the appraisal process by cashing out a dissenting shareholder, a clearly undesirable result.[65]

B. Discounts & Premia May Be Considered at the "Corporate Level"

Although consideration of discounts and premia is impermissible at the "stockholder level," it is permissible (indeed, necessary) to consider applicable discounts and premia that affect the value of the enterprise (i.e., at the "corporate level").[66] As the Court of Chancery explained in *Cavalier*:

> The [defendants] cite *Robbins and Company v. A. C. Israel Enterprises, Inc.*, Del. Ch., 1985 Del. Ch. LEXIS 498, C. A. No. 7919, Berger, V.C. (October 2, 1985) as authority for applying a minority discount. *Robbins* involved an appraisal of a closely held investment company whose principal asset was a portfolio of securities

in other corporations. There it was undisputed that the appropriate valuation method was an asset valuation, for which reason no "earnings" valuation was made. To determine the investment company's asset value, it was necessary to ascertain the fair market value of the component securities in its portfolio. The respondent corporation argued that to determine ultimate "fair value," a (so-called) "minority discount" must be applied to that fair market/net asset value figure. This Court agreed, because the portfolio's unadjusted net asset value represented a liquidation value that was not an appropriate measure of "fair value" under § 262. It was undisputed that the correct valuation measure was "going concern" value, and that the only method for determining going concern value was to discount the fair market values of the securities in the corporation's portfolio.

Thus, while *Robbins* did permit a so-called "minority discount," that discount (applied at the corporate, not at the shareholder, level) was required to arrive at an overall going concern value (fair value) for the corporation. *Robbins* does not hold that a corporation's fair value, once determined, must then be diminished to reflect that the petitioning stockholder owns only a minority interest.[67]

Where the corporation being valued is a holding company, Delaware courts have concluded that the fair value of the company includes a premium reflecting the value of the company's controlling ownership interest of its majority-owned or wholly-owned subsidiaries. As the Delaware Supreme Court has instructed, "any holding company's ownership of a controlling interest in a subsidiary at the time of the merger is an 'operative reality' and an independent element of value that must be taken into account in determining a fair value for the parent company's stock."[68] In an earlier decision, the Delaware Supreme Court similarly explained:

> [The subject company] was a parent company with a 100% ownership interest in three valuable subsidiaries. The trial court's decision to exclude the control premium at the corporate level practically discounted [the subject company]'s entire inherent value. The exclusion of a "control premium" artificially and unrealistically treated [the subject company] as a minority shareholder. Contrary to [the respondent]'s arguments, Delaware law *compels* the inclusion of a control premium under the unique facts of this case. [The subject company]'s 100% ownership interest in its subsidiaries was clearly a "relevant" valuation factor and the trial court's rejection of the "control premium" implicitly placed a disproportionate emphasis on pure market value.[69]

C. Specific Discounts

1. Minority Discounts

The Delaware courts have held that a minority discount may not be considered at the stockholder level when determining "fair value" both (i) in the context of a statutory appraisal proceeding,[70] and (ii) in the context of an "entire fairness" action.[71] By the same token, the Delaware courts have authorized the use of a minority discount for the purpose of determining the value of securities held by the corporation being valued.[72]

2. Marketability Discounts

The Delaware courts have held that a marketability discount may not be considered at the stockholder level when determining "fair value" in the context of a statutory appraisal proceeding.[73]

Although marketability discounts cannot be considered in connection with the determination of "fair value," the Court of Chancery has accepted the inclusion of a "small stock" premium for purposes of calculating the discount rate to be applied in a discounted cash flow analysis.[74] As the court has explained, "[a] small stock premium is appropriate to reflect that 'on average, smaller companies have higher rates of return than larger companies.'"[75] It has, however, been argued that inclusion of a "small stock" premium in a discounted cash flow analysis has "the same effect and rationale as marketability discounts," which are impermissible in a "fair value" determination.[76] Despite its general acceptance, the court may opt not to employ a small stock premium if its application is not supported by sufficient evidence.[77]

3. "Private Company" (or "Liquidity") Discounts

Two decisions of the Court of Chancery have rejected the application of a "private company" or "liquidity" discount (even at the "corporate level") to account for the fact that there was no public market for any of the subject corporation's shares. As the court explained in the more recent of the two decisions:

> In his analysis, [the respondent's expert] applied a final 20% discount, which is described in his report as a "Discount for Lack of Liquidity." His report states that this discount is "based on market observations" and "reflects the fact that [the subject company]'s common stock is not publicly traded." Respondent acknowledges that in *Cavalier Oil Corp. v. Harnett, Del. Supr., 564 A.2d 1137, 1144 (1989)*, the Supreme Court held that it is wrong to apply a discount "at the shareholder level" for a lack of marketability of shares. Nevertheless, Respondent argues that a discount "for lack of marketability that affects all shares equally is an appropriate corporate level discount," and claims that [its expert] "applied his liquidity discount to all the equity of [the subject company] because [it] was not a publicly traded company."
>
> To the extent Respondent is arguing for the application of a "corporate level" discount to reflect the fact that all shares of [the subject company] were worth less because there was no public market in which to sell them, I read *Cavalier Oil* as prohibiting such a discount. This is simply a liquidity discount applied at the "corporate level." Even if taken "at the corporate level" (in circumstances in which the effect on the fair value of

the shares is the same as a "shareholder level" discount) such a discount is, nevertheless, based on trading characteristics of the shares themselves, not any factor intrinsic to the corporation or its assets. It is therefore prohibited.[78]

In *Metropolitan Life Ins. Co.*, the court similarly rejected the application of a "private company" (or "illiquidity") discount for purposes of determining "fair value" in an action challenging a recapitalization that would have resulted in the elimination of the equity interests of the minority stockholders of a Delaware corporation that was not publicly-traded.[79] As in Borruso, the defendants in *Metropolitan Life Ins. Co.* had argued that the discount employed in that case was permissible, because it affected all shares of the corporation, and not only the shares being eliminated in the proposed restructuring. The court, however, in a bench ruling at the conclusion of a hearing on a motion for a preliminary injunction, initially found that the discount advocated by the defendants had been employed at the stockholder level, and not the company level. Accordingly, the court concluded that the discount was inconsistent with Delaware law in a case in which the concept of "fair value" applied.

The decisions in *Borruso* and *Metropolitan Life Ins. Co.* appear to be based upon the court's perception that a "private company" or "liquidity" discount is, in essence, a "marketability" discount applied to all shares.

4. Discounts Implicit in the Market Approach

More than twenty years ago, in a case that did not involve an issue of the determination of "fair value," the Delaware Supreme Court observed that "publicly-traded stock price is solely a measure of the value of a minority interest and, thus, market price reflects only the value of a single share." [80] In appraisal litigation, the Delaware Supreme Court's observation has led to a practice in which the Delaware courts have sought to eliminate the "implicit minority discount" perceived to be embedded in the market approach – typically by upwardly adjusting the indication of value derived by such an approach. As the Court of Chancery has explained:

> The comparable companies analysis generates an equity value that includes an inherent minority trading discount, because the method depends on comparisons to market multiples derived from trading information for minority blocks of the comparable companies. In a § 262 appraisal, the court must correct this minority trading discount by adding back a premium designed to offset it.[81]

Notably, despite the Delaware courts' general acceptance of the proposition that a market approach yields an indication of value that includes an embedded minority discount, the Delaware courts have not required any adjustment to the indication of value produced by a DCF analysis that uses market data (as opposed to transactional data) to estimate the terminal value or discount rate.[82] Moreover, the Court of Chancery recently questioned whether the Delaware courts' practice of upwardly adjusting the results of market approach to produce an indication of "fair value" is consistent with that of the financial community.[83] "Despite the court's pointed questioning at trial," however, the expert witnesses for both parties testified that it was their experience that a market approach does, in fact, tend to yield a minority discounted indication of value and that an adjustment is necessary to arrive at an enterprise value.[84]

5. Specific-Company Risk Premia

A specific-company risk premium is sometimes added to the discount rate in a discounted cash flow analysis in order to attempt to capture company-specific risk that is not already reflected in the measure of market risk or the small size premium.[85] The Court of Chancery has observed that it is "suspicious of expert valuations offered at trial that incorporate subjective measures of company-specific risk premia, as subjective measures may easily be employed as a means to smuggle improper risk assumptions into the discount rate so as to affect dramatically the expert's ultimate opinion on value." [86] As a result, the court will not apply such a premium unless it is supported by fact-based evidence at trial.[87]

6. Other Discounts

In a case where a corporation's value depends upon the corporation's ability to sell its assets (other than securities), the Delaware Supreme Court has sustained the consideration of "discounts" that would need to be accepted by the corporation in order to accomplish such a sale.[88] Such an approach is impermissible, however, where the value of the corporation does not depend upon its ability to sell its assets.[89]

D. "Control" Premia and "Synergy" Premia

There are cases in which the transaction triggering the need for a judicial determination of fair value involved an actual sale of the subject company to a third party. In such cases, "the Court of Chancery is free to consider the price actually derived from the sale of the company being valued, but only after the synergistic elements of value are excluded from that price."[90] Accordingly, a stockholder that opposes a proposed third-party acquisition should approach the decision to demand appraisal with caution, as there is a significant risk that a Delaware court will conclude that the "fair value" of the shares acquired in the merger is less than the actual price paid by the third-party acquiror.[91]

As previously noted, notwithstanding the Delaware courts' rejection of a control or synergy premia at the stockholder level, the Delaware courts have endorsed the inclusion of such premia when control exists at the "corporate level." Thus, where the corporation being valued is a holding company, Delaware courts have concluded that the fair value of the company includes a premium reflecting the value of the company's controlling ownership interest of its majority-owned or wholly-owned subsidiaries.[92]

Chapter 3: Dissenting and Oppressed Shareholder Matters

IV Pre-Merger Claims and Causes of Action

A. Valuing the Claims

The determination of "fair value" in a statutory appraisal proceeding includes consideration of the value, if any, of any claims or causes of action possessed by the corporation on the date of the merger giving rise to the appraisal proceeding.[93]

In cases where it is necessary to value pre-merger claims belonging to the corporation, the value of such claims is not determined by a "trial within a trial." Rather, "the value of the claims, if any, will be established through expert testimony in much the same manner that evidence typically is presented as to the value of other corporate assets."[94] Additionally, the court may conclude that it has "sufficient information, without the aid of expert testimony, upon which to base a reasonable estimate of the value of the claim."[95]

Delaware courts have taken two different approaches to valuing pre-merger claims for purposes of determining the value of the corporation possessing such claims. In Bomarko, the court valued the pre-merger claim by "multiplying (a) [the court's] assessment of the probability of success on the merits by (b) the likely amount of a favorable recovery, and subtracting from that result (c) the reasonable costs [the plaintiff] would have incurred in prosecuting the claim."[96] By contrast, in *Cavalier Oil Corp.* the Court determined the merits of the pre-merger claim of usurpation of a corporate opportunity in favor of the petitioner, and included in the court's valuation of the corporation the full value of the corporate opportunity that had been usurped, without employing any discount for (i) risk of loss, or (ii) the costs of obtaining a recovery on the underlying claim.[97]

B. Considering Pre-Merger Claims to "Adjust" Value

A pre-merger claim of excessive payments to corporate fiduciaries may be considered for the purpose of "adjusting" the corporation's projections of future income for valuation purposes. It is unclear, however, whether (i) such a claim would need to have been the subject of existing litigation at the time of the merger giving rise to the appraisal claim, or (ii) whether it would be sufficient that it is claimed in the appraisal action that the challenged payments were, in fact, actionable.[98]

In a case challenging the fairness of the allocation of merger consideration among different classes of stockholders, the Court of Chancery rejected the proposition that "the formal pendency of derivative proceedings pre-merger" is determinative of the question of whether viable derivative claims should have been considered by the board of directors in determining how to fairly apportion the merger consideration.[99] Instead, the court held that the directors' allocation determination was entitled to the protection afforded by the business judgment rule if the directors had evaluated "the derivative claims of which they had knowledge during the negotiation and merger processes."[100] The court elaborated that the directors would be deemed to have "knowledge" of derivative claims "when the directors become aware of facts sufficient to put a person of ordinary intelligence and prudence on inquiry which, if pursued, would lead to the discovery of injury."[101] The court rejected a more restrictive standard that required directors to consider derivative claims only if litigation actually had been initiated at the time the merger consideration was being allocated. The court reasoned that such a standard would exclude potentially viable claims and that the "inquiry notice standard places sufficient burden on the directors to value derivative claims that they have reason to be aware of, but does not require excessive action on the part of the directors to uncover claims."[102] Although the court's decision was made in the context of determining the appropriate legal standard against which the directors' conduct would be judged, the court's treatment of the issue comports with statutory appraisal precedent holding that "[i]n determining the fair value of a company a court should consider all relevant factors known or knowable at the time of the merger."[103]

V. When Is the Concept of "Fair Value" Implicated?

As a general matter, the concept of "fair value" is implicated (i) in statutory appraisal actions, (ii) in cases where a stockholder's equity is eliminated without the stockholder's consent, and (iii) in certain "self-dealing" circumstances giving rise to the test of "entire fairness." The specific circumstances in which the concept of "fair value" is implicated under Delaware corporate law are identified in greater detail below.

A. Statutory Appraisal Actions

The "fair value" standard is mandated by the appraisal statute.[104] Nonetheless, the Court of Chancery has observed that "[f]air value is, by now, a jurisprudential concept that draws more from judicial writings than from the appraisal statute itself."[105] Today, it is settled law that "[t]he dissenter in an appraisal action is entitled to receive a proportionate share of fair value in the going concern on the date of the merger."[106] Moreover, if a transaction gives rise to appraisal rights, it appears that the circumstances giving rise to the underlying transaction are irrelevant to the determination of whether the standard of "fair value" applies.

Despite the well developed body of decisional law appraising the fair value of common stock, only a few appraisal decisions involve shares of preferred stock. Indeed, in a recent appraisal action, the Court of Chancery observed that there was only one "reported *post-Weinberger* opinion involving an appraisal of preferred stock."[107] As the Court of Chancery explained:

> Unlike common stock, the value of preferred stock is determined solely from the contract rights conferred upon it in the certificate of designation. The only reported *post-Weinberger* opinion involving an appraisal of preferred stock, *In re Appraisal of Ford Holdings, Inc. Preferred Stock,* demonstrates the primacy of contract as the measure of the preferred's value. There, former-Chancellor Allen analyzed the rights conferred upon preferred shareholders by the certificate of designation because, "[t]o the extent it possesses

any special rights or powers and to the extent it is restricted or limited in any way, the relation between the holder of the preferred and the corporation is contractual." When determining the fair value of preferred stock, therefore, I must first look to the contract upon which the preferred stock's value is based. In other words, the valuation of preferred stock must be viewed through the defining lens of its certificate of designation, unless the certificate is ambiguous or conflicts with positive law. As former-Chancellor Allen recognized in *Ford Holdings,* statutory appraisal rights can be modified or relinquished by contract, but in the case of unclear or indirect drafting, this Court will not "cut stockholders off from a statutory right" to judicial appraisal of their preferred shares.[108]

Upon review of the certificate of designations of the preferred stock at issue, the Court of Chancery concluded that the certificate clearly and unambiguously fixed the valuation metric to be used in an appraisal proceeding and "that instrument provides all the 'fair value' to which [the preferred stockholders] are legally entitled in this appraisal proceeding."[109] Though the preferred stockholders had "vigorous[ly]" argued that traditional appraisal methodologies as used under § 262 should govern the fair value determination, the court rejected the attempt to "extract additional value for their shares through the appraisal process", noting that the certificate of designation created the stockholders' "sole right" to receive value in the event of a cash-out merger.[110]

B. Reverse Stock-Splits Involving Cash for Fractional Shares

Where a Delaware corporation effects a reverse stock split in which fractional shares will not be issued and equity interests of stockholders holding an insufficient number will be eliminated, *Section 155(2)* of the DGCL requires that the corporation "pay in cash the *fair value* of fractions of a share as of the time when those entitled to receive such fractions are determined."[111]

In *Applebaum v. Avaya,*[112] the Delaware Supreme Court held that fair value under Section 155 was not identical to the concept of fair value under *Section 262.*[113] Instead, the court instructed that a corporation "may satisfy the 'fair price' requirement of *Section 155(2)* by paying the stockholders an amount based on the average trading price of the corporation's stock."[114] In so holding, the Delaware Supreme Court rejected the argument that the "fair value" requirement of Section 155(b) of the DGCL imposes the same valuation analysis required by *Section 262* of the DGCL.[115]

Significantly, the Delaware Supreme Court's decision in *Applebaum* does not provide a statutory loop-hole that would permit a majority or controlling stockholder to avoid the "fair price" obligation of *Section 262* (and the common law developed to deal with freeze-out mergers) by eliminating minority stockholders through a reverse stock split, rather than through a merger transaction. In the case of a reverse stock split conducted to benefit a majority or controlling stockholder, a "fair value" analysis akin to that employed pursuant to *Section 262* of the DGCL may be required -- either as a matter of statutory law or pursuant to common law principles of fiduciary duty. As the Delaware Supreme Court explained:

Judicial Valuation of Stock of a Delaware Corporation

In both *Chalfin* [*v. Hart Holdings Co.*, C.A. No. 11611, 1990 Del. Ch. LEXIS 188 (Del. Ch. Nov. 20, 1990)] and [*Metropolitan Life Ins. Co. v.*] *Aramark* [*Corp.*, C.A. No. 16142, 1998 Del. Ch. LEXIS 70 (Feb. 5, 1998)], the Court of Chancery recognized that a transaction employing *Section 155* may warrant a searching inquiry of fair value if a controlling stockholder initiates the transaction. When a controlling stockholder presents a transaction that will free it from future dealings with the minority stockholders, opportunism becomes a concern. Any shortfall imposed on the minority stockholders will result in a transfer of value to the controlling stockholder. The discount in value could be imposed deliberately or could be the result of an information asymmetry where the controlling stockholder possesses material facts that are not known in the market. Thus, a *Section 155(2)* inquiry may resemble a *Section 262* valuation if the controlling stockholder will benefit from presenting a suspect measure of valuation, such as an out-dated trading price, or a wrongfully imposed private company discount.[116]

To appreciate the consistency of the Delaware Supreme Court's analysis, it is important to understand the factual backdrop for the reverse stock split at issue in *Applebaum*. In that case, (i) the corporation was a publicly traded company, with an active market for its shares, (ii) there was no majority or controlling stockholder, (iii) the reverse stock split was conducted for the purpose of reducing the corporation's costs by reducing the size of its stockholder base, and was not conducted in order to benefit any particular group of stockholders. As the Delaware Supreme Court explained:

> Although the Reverse/Forward Split will cash out smaller stockholders, the transaction will not allow the corporation to realize a gain at their expense. Unlike the more typical "freeze-out" context, the cashed-out Avaya stockholders may continue to share in the value of the enterprise. Avaya stockholders can avoid the effects of the proposed transaction either by purchasing a sufficient amount of stock to survive the initial Reverse Split or by simply using the payment provided under *Section 155(2)* to repurchase the same amount of Avaya stock that they held before the transaction.
>
> The Reverse/Forward Split merely forces the stockholders to choose affirmatively to remain in the corporation. Avaya will succeed in saving administrative costs only if the board has assumed correctly that the stockholders who received a small interest in the corporation through the Lucent spin off would prefer to receive payment, free of transaction costs, rather than continue with the corporation. The Transaction is not structured to prevent the cashed-out stockholders from maintaining their stakes in the company. A payment based on market price is appropriate because it will permit the stockholders to reinvest in Avaya, should they wish to do so.[117]

The facts in *Chalfin v. Hart Holdings Co.* – one of the two decisions approvingly discussed in *Applebaum* – supported a different outcome. In *Chalfin*, the proposed transaction involved a corporation whose shares were infrequently traded in a private market in which the corporation itself acted as the only buyer. In that setting, the Court of Chancery rejected the argument that

Chapter 3: Dissenting and Oppressed Shareholder Matters

the corporation had satisfied the "fair value" requirement of *Section 155(2)* of the DGCL by basing the payment to stockholders owning fractional shares on the pre-split market price of the stock. As the Court of Chancery explained:

> In essence, the defendants ask this court to rule as a matter of law that the defendants, by fixing the cash-out price for fractional shares on the basis of market price, met their statutory obligation to pay fair value for fractional shares. One may concede the possibility that market price may equate to fair value in a given case. However, that proposition is hardly axiomatic or universally valid. Indeed, the invalidity of the defendants' position is particularly apparent where, as here, the market price may have been depressed by the absence of any active trading and where the market price was set by the issuer company, acting as the primary (if not the sole) buyer.[118]

Notably, the Delaware Supreme Court's decision in *Applebaum* includes no mention of the prior decision in *Connector Service Corp. v. Briggs*,[119] which relied upon Delaware statutory appraisal case law to conclude that it was inappropriate to apply a minority discount in fixing the price for fractional shares resulting from a reverse stock split effected to eliminate minority stockholders. As the court in that case explained:

> The law governing reverse stock split cash-outs is found at *8 Del. C. § 155*. In the event of a cash-out the corporation "shall . . . pay in cash the fair value of fractions of a share as of the time when those entitled to receive such fractions are determined[.]" A number of decisions of Delaware courts have held that in a similar type of procedure, a cash-out merger, minority discounts are prohibited. *Cavalier Oil Corp. v. Harnett*, 564 A.2d 1137 (Del. S. Ct. 1989). However there is a separate statute, *8 Del. C. § 262*, that governs the rights of dissenting shareholders in cash-out mergers. Under this statute, a dissenting shareholder, who makes a statutory demand, is "entitled to an appraisal by the court [sic] of Chancery of the fair value of the stockholder's shares of stock[.]" The reason the Delaware courts have given in rejecting minority discounts in cash-out mergers is that the policy underlying a *§ 262* appraisal is to appraise "the corporation itself as distinguished from a specific fraction of its shares as they may exist in the hands of a particular shareholder." However, reverse stock split cash-outs are governed by *§ 155*. See *Edick v. Contran Corp.* 1986 Del. Ch. LEXIS 384, 1986 WL 3418 (Del. Ch. 1986). However, the holding of *Edick* is that a chancery court appraisal is not the exclusive remedy for a forced cash-out, and a minority shareholder may also pursue claims of fraud. The court assumed, for purposes of its decision, that previous court decisions affecting cash-out mergers applied with equal force to cash-out reverse stock splits. There are no cases directly on point, save *Metropolitan Life Ins. Co. v. Aramark Corp.*, 1998 Del. Ch. LEXIS 70, C.A. No. 16142 (Feb. 5, 1998), which was an oral bench ruling, not publishable, and of doubtful precedential value, specifically holding that minority discounts are not allowed in cash-out reverse stock splits.

The issue, therefore, is whether there is any difference between the two cash-out procedures that would justify a differing definition of "fair value." As already stated, the

Delaware courts have held in the § 262 appraisals cases, that the reason for not applying minority interest discounts is the state's policy to appraise the corporation rather than the individual's share of the corporation. However, § 262 does not specifically say this: it merely states that a minority shareholder is entitled "to an appraisal . . . of the fair value of the stockholder's shares of stock[.]" Although § 155 does not provide for a chancery court appraisal, this section uses language similar to § 262: a cashing-out corporation is to "pay in cash the fair value of fractions of a share[.]"

The court concludes that Delaware law does not allow for a minority discount for reverse stock split cash-outs. There are no Delaware cases allowing such a discount. The court cannot think of any reason why the Delaware courts would treat the two procedures differently and CSC does not suggest any. The purpose of the statutes is to protect a minority, dissenting shareholder from being unfairly cashed out against his will at an unfair price. It can be done against his will precisely because he is a minority shareholder and does not have the power to do anything about it. Since almost identical language is used in § 155 as is used in § 262, this court is hard pressed to find that there is another policy behind § 155. Accordingly, the court declines to assess the minority discount.[120]

Although the broad statutory construction of *Section 155(2)* advanced in *Connector Service* appears to have been overruled by the Delaware Supreme Court in *Applebaum*, the reasoning employed and the result reached in *Connector Service* seems to be in harmony with the decision in *Applebaum*. As distilled by the framework in *Applebaum*, the two constructs of "fair value" can be synthesized through an understanding of "the appropriate context for which a going-concern valuation may be necessary under *Section 155(2)*."[121] Specifically, if a reverse stock split does not implicate the type of self-dealing concerns involved in a freeze-out merger, "fair value" under *Section 155(2)* may be evaluated by looking to the market price of shares trading in an active and informed market. Alternatively, if the "context" of a reverse stock split raises the type of self-dealing concerns involved in a freeze-out merger, the "fair value" mandate of *Section 155(2)* may require a "going concern" valuation similar to that employed pursuant to *Section 262* of the DGCL. Additionally, where a reverse stock split treats a controlling or majority stockholder differently from the minority stockholders, the "fair price" prong of the "entire fairness" test will apply, in any event.[122]

C. Transactions Involving the Test of "Entire Fairness"

It is settled law that a "self-dealing" fiduciary must establish the "entire fairness" of a challenged transaction. Among other things, this standard of judicial review involves an inquiry into whether the consideration paid in the challenged transaction represented a "fair price."[123] According to the Delaware Supreme Court, the legal concept of "fair price" relates to "the economic and financial considerations of the proposed merger, including all relevant factors: assets, market value, earnings, future prospects, and any other elements that affect the intrinsic or inherent value of a company's stock."[124]

Although the issue is not entirely free from doubt, it is generally recognized that the legal concepts of "fair value" and "fair price" are synonymous as applied to the valuation of stock in Delaware corporations in cases involving cash-out mergers.[125] Outside the context of a statutory appraisal, however, a stockholder who successfully pursues a breach of fiduciary duty claim may not be limited to the "fair value" remedy.[126] As the Delaware Supreme Court has instructed, "[t]he Court of Chancery has greater discretion when fashioning an award of damages in an action for a breach of the duty of loyalty than it would when assessing fair value in an appraisal action."[127]

Outside the context of a cash-out merger, the determination of "fair price" of shares of a Delaware corporation may implicate the concept of "fair market price." For example, in a case in which a controlling stockholder of a Delaware corporation purchased a large block of shares of stock from the corporation he controlled, the Court of Chancery has held the determination of whether the fiduciary paid a "fair price" should be based upon a "market-driven" approach, and not on the basis of the "intrinsic value" of the shares.[128]

D. Other "Cash-Out" Transactions

The Court of Chancery has held that the concept of "fair value" applies whenever stockholders of a Delaware corporation are "cashed-out" of the corporation without their consent, without regard to whether the transaction takes the form of a merger, a reverse stock-split or a restructuring or recapitalization. As the Court has explained:

> The Supreme Court [has] said... that directors have a fiduciary duty to treat all stockholders fairly. What does that mean where minority stockholders are being cashed out by some means other than merger, where the statutes provide appraisal rights? I think it is agreed that under the doctrine of independent legal significance other methods of accomplishing the same result are permitted. But I believe that the fiduciary duty in this situation was to pay stockholders who are cashed out the fair value of their stock as that term is defined in the appraisal cases and in the breach of fiduciary duty cases in merger transactions. I cannot accept an argument that so long as directors are careful and try to get it right, the fact that they make a mistake on a matter of Delaware law will defeat a claim that a fair price was not paid to stockholders who are cashed out by some means other than a merger.[129]

E. Arm's-Length Mergers

As a general matter, Delaware courts will not review the "fairness" of the consideration in a stock-for-stock merger involving unaffiliated parties. Such a transaction might, however, implicate the "fair price" or "fair value" measure of damages if there were an adjudicated breach of fiduciary duty in connection with the merger.

Additionally, if the consummation of a merger will result in a transfer of control, it has been settled Delaware law since *Revlon, Inc. v. MacAndrews & Forbes Holdings, Inc.*[130] that "the directors must focus on one primary objective – to secure the transaction offering the best value reasonably available for all stockholders."[131] Moreover, where the merger consideration does not consist entirely of cash, "[w]hen assessing the value of non-cash consideration, a board should focus on its value as of the date it will be received by the stockholders."[132]

In a case in which control has been transferred in violation of the directors' fiduciary duty to seek to secure the transaction offering the best value reasonably available for all stockholders, it is arguable that the proper measure of damages would include consideration of a control premium at the stockholder level.[133]

In the pre-*Revlon* case of *Smith v. Van Gorkom*, the Delaware Supreme Court concluded that the director defendants had committed a breach of the fiduciary duty of care in approving a merger with an unaffiliated third-party.[134] At the conclusion of its decision, the Supreme Court offered the following instructions:

> On remand, the Court of Chancery shall conduct an evidentiary hearing to determine the fair value of the shares represented by the plaintiffs' class, based on the intrinsic value of Trans Union on [the date of the merger]. Such valuation shall be made in accordance with *Weinberger v. UOP, Inc.* . . . Thereafter, an award of damages may be entered to the extent that the fair value of Trans Union exceeds [the merger consideration].[135]

It is uncertain whether the Delaware Supreme Court would have offered the same instruction following *Revlon*. It also is uncertain whether the Delaware Supreme Court would have offered the same instruction if the merger in *Van Gorkom* had been a stock-for-stock merger.

F. Tender Offers

Delaware law does not impose any "fair price" obligation in connection with a voluntary, non-coercive tender offer that does not involve false or inadequate disclosures. As the Court of Chancery has explained:

> By its very nature and form, a tender offer is normally regarded as a voluntary transaction. Unlike a cash-out merger where public stockholders can be involuntarily eliminated from the enterprise, in a properly conducted tender offer the stockholder-offerees may freely choose whether or not to tender. That choice will normally depend upon each stockholder's individual investment objectives and his evaluation of the merits of the offer. Moreover, tender offers often afford shareholders a unique opportunity to sell their shares at a premium above market price. For those reasons, a tender offer that is voluntary (and that otherwise satisfies applicable legal requirements) will not be enjoined.[136]

Chapter 3: Dissenting and Oppressed Shareholder Matters

Although the Delaware Supreme Court has yet to squarely address the issue, the Court of Chancery repeatedly has concluded that the foregoing rule applies without regard to whether the party extending the tender offer is (i) a third-party, (ii) the corporation itself (i.e., a "self-tender"), or (iii) a controlling stockholder or other fiduciary as the first step of a two-step cash-out merger transaction.[137]

The Delaware Court of Chancery (and many commentators) have read the Delaware Supreme Court's decision in *Solomon v. Pathe Communications Corp.*[138] to provide appellate support for the rule that there is no "fair price" requirement in a tender offer extended by a majority or controlling stockholder that is to be followed by a cash-out merger.[139] A close reading of the Delaware Supreme Court's decision *Solomon*, however, reveals that it is far from clear that the decision provides the support identified by the Court of Chancery. Moreover, it is arguable that the Court of Chancery's decisions are inconsistent with the spirit of the Delaware Supreme Court's decision in *Kahn v. Lynch Communications Systems, Inc.*, which recognizes that there is "inherent coercion" present whenever a parent corporation desires to acquire the subsidiary's shares held by minority stockholders.[140]

In *Solomon*, the Delaware Supreme Court affirmed the dismissal of a complaint challenging a tender offer by a majority stockholder (not accompanied by a back-end merger), stating:

> In the case of totally voluntary tender offers, as here, courts do not impose any right of the shareholders to receive a particular price. . . . Delaware law recognizes that, as to allegedly voluntary tender offers (in contrast to cash-out mergers), the determinative factor as to voluntariness is whether coercion is present, or whether there is [sic] "materially false or misleading disclosures made to shareholders in connection with the offer." . . . A transaction may be considered involuntary, despite being voluntary in appearance and form, if one of these factors is present. . . . There is no well-plead allegation of any coercion or false or misleading disclosures in the present case, however.[141]

It is arguable that the foregoing ruling in *Solomon* has no application in cases involving tender offers by a controlling stockholder or other fiduciary as the first step of a two-step cash-out merger transaction. Among other things, the factual "context" of the parties' dispute in *Solomon* must be considered. As the Delaware Supreme Court explained in *Solomon*:

> The suit dismissed is a putative shareholder class action that challenge[d] the fairness of a tender offer made by Credit Lyonnais Banque Nederland N.V. ("CLBN") to purchase 5.9 million shares of the publicly traded common stock of Pathe Communications Corporation ("Pathe"). The tender offer was proposed in conjunction with CLBN's planned foreclosure on a security interest it held.[142]

Unlike the "context" of the tender offers in *In re Pure Resources, Inc. Shareholders Litigation, In re Aquila, Inc. Shareholders Litigation, In re Siliconix Inc. Shareholders Litigation,* and *In re Ocean Drilling & Exploration Co. Shareholders Litigation, Solomon* did not involve a two-step transaction designed to eliminate the equity interests of minority stockholders. Rather, the case involved a straight-forward tender offer designed to provide liquidity "for the 10% of Pathe stock that CLNB did not acquire in the foreclosure."[143] Of equal significance, the tender offer in *Solomon* was *requested* by a special committee of the board of directors of the subsidiary in a negotiation in which the special committee was threatening to cause the subsidiary to attempt to take legal action to prevent the parent from exercising its rights as a creditor of the subsidiary to foreclose on essentially all of the subsidiary's assets.[144] As such, there was no concern about "inherent coercion" (in the *Kahn v. Lynch*) sense, because the parent in *Solomon* did not desire to purchase the shares owned by the minority stockholder, but was *forced* to do so by the subsidiary's special committee in consideration of their agreement to forebear from taking legal action to interfere with the parent's foreclosure action.[145]

G. Stockholders' Agreements and Other Contracts

As a general matter, parties to a stockholders' agreement or other contract are free to establish any definition of value upon which they are able to agree.[146] As the Delaware Supreme Court has explained:

> The tools of good corporate practice are designed to give a purchasing minority stockholder the opportunity to bargain for protection before parting with consideration. It would do violence to normal corporate practice and our corporation law to fashion an ad hoc ruling which would result in a court-imposed stockholder buy-out for which the parties had not contracted.[147]

H. Cases Involving Claims of "Conversion" of Stock

"The traditional remedy for a conversion claim is to award the plaintiff the 'value of the property at the time of conversion, with interest.'"[148] In addition, where the value of converted stock fluctuates subsequent to the time of the conversion, it has been held that a plaintiff may recover "the highest value of the shares . . . from the time of their conversion up to a reasonable time after [the plaintiff] acquired knowledge of such conversion."[149]

Considering the case where shares of stock are converted, the Court of Chancery has observed:

> [T]he conversion remedy seem[s] at best duplicative of the appraisal option . . . at worst, the conversion remedy seem[s] inferior because it is not at all clear that the unique and largely petitioner-friendly "fair value" valuation rules that apply under 8 Del. C. § 262 would come into play in determining "fair market value" under the common law of conversion.[150]

In a case involving claims akin to conversion, the Delaware Supreme Court assumed, without deciding, that the determination of "value" would be "a 'fair value' price equivalent to that determined through appraisal."[151] In *Agranoff*, a self-dealing fiduciary wrongfully interfered with a Delaware corporation's right to repurchase shares of stock pursuant to a contractual right of first refusal. The remedy for such a breach was to require that the fiduciary transfer the shares to the corporation in exchange for the lesser of (i) the actual price paid for the shares by the fiduciary, or (ii) "the price for which he could have obtained it for the beneficiary."[152] In the peculiar facts of the *Agranoff* case, the disputed shares represented a "control block" when combined with other shares owned by the fiduciary. On the other hand, the shares represented only a marketable minority interest in the hands of the corporation. Although the Delaware Supreme Court assumed, without deciding, that the price to be paid by the corporation would be determined in the same manner as the "fair value" of the shares would be determined in a statutory appraisal proceeding, on remand the Court of Chancery concluded that "the judicial task at hand is to determine what price [the corporation] would have had to pay for a particular block of shares, a task that appropriately should consider block-specific value factors."[153] Stated differently, the Court of Chancery set the price to be paid on the basis of the "fair market value" of the shares.[154]

VII. Rescissory Damages

In an appropriate case, a stockholder may be able to recover "rescissory damages" (sometimes referred to as "recissory" damages), which is a measure of damages based on a valuation performed as of a date subsequent to the action giving rise to liability.[155] This aspect of the rescissory damage award is what makes this relief extraordinary – because damages are measured from the date of judgment, the risk that the stock might increase in value from the date of the transaction is shifted to defendants.[156] Although there is relatively little Delaware law on the subject of the calculation of rescissory damages, it is arguable that the determination of whether the concept of "fair value" or "fair market value" will supply the proper standard for calculating rescissory damages will depend upon the nature of the plaintiff's claim.

In a consolidated action involving both a statutory appraisal and claims for breach of fiduciary duty in connection with a merger, the Court may evaluate the entire fairness claims first and "may incorporate elements of rescissory damages into its determination of fair price if it considers such elements: (1) susceptible to proof; and (2) appropriate under the circumstances."[157] Where, however, the action involves exclusively a statutory appraisal, it appears to be the law that rescissory damages are not available. As the Delaware Supreme Court has instructed:

> [I]f the merger was timed to take advantage of a depressed market, or a low point in the company's cyclical earnings, or to precede an anticipated positive development, the appraised value may be adjusted to account for those factors. We recognize that these are the types of issues frequently raised in entire fairness claims, and we have held that claims for unfair dealing cannot be litigated in an appraisal. But our prior holdings simply explained that equitable claims may not be engrafted onto a statutory appraisal proceeding; stockholders may not receive rescissionary relief in an appraisal. Those decisions should not be read to restrict the elements of value that properly may be considered in an appraisal.[158]

Judicial Valuation of Stock of a Delaware Corporation

The foregoing instruction is consistent with earlier Delaware Supreme Court jurisprudence, in which the court observed that "a statutory appraisal proceeding under *Section 262* and a rescissory suit for fraud, misrepresentation, self-dealing and other actionable wrongs violative of 'entire fairness' to minority shareholders serve different purposes and are designed to provide different, and not interchangeable, remedies."[159] Moreover, it is well settled that the judicial objective of a statutory appraisal proceeding is to determine the fair value of the shares as of the effective date of the merger or consolidation giving rise to the appraisal proceeding.[160] Although this temporal qualification is not explicitly imposed by the current language of the appraisal statute, it was included in prior versions of the statute[161] and its current omission appears to be more the result of legislative oversight than an intentional determination to alter the date as of which the valuation is to be determined.[162]

---

1. Bruce L. Silverstein is a partner in Young Conaway Stargatt & Taylor, LLP in Wilmington, Delaware, and is the Chairman of the firm's Corporate Counseling and Litigation practice section. This paper is an updated and supplemented version of a paper previously authored by Mr. Silverstein. Substantial assistance in preparing this updated and supplemented version of the paper was provided by Kerrianne M. Fay, Esquire, an associate within the Corporate Counseling and Litigation practice section at Young Conaway Stargatt & Taylor, LLP.
2. Del. Code. Ann. tit. 8, § 262 (2007).
3. In re Shell Oil Co., 607 A.2d 1213, 1218 (Del. 1992) (alteration in original) (citations omitted).
4. Cavalier Oil Corp. v. Harnett, 564 A.2d 1137, 1144 (Del. 1989) (citation omitted).
5. Finkelstein v. Liberty Digital, Inc., C.A. No. 19598, 2005 Del. Ch. LEXIS 53, at *39 (Del. Ch. Apr. 25, 2005). See also Union Ill. 1995 Inv. Ltd. P'ship v. Union Fin. Group, Ltd., 847 A.2d 340, 356 (Del. Ch. 2003) ("Because the definition of fair value used in a [statutory appraisal] proceeding is not based on fair market value and involves policy considerations, such as the need to exclude synergies in order to value the entity as a going concern, the petitioners in an appraisal proceeding can be awarded a sum that deviates – upward or downward – from what an economist or investment banker or Warren Buffett would believe was the market value of the petitioners' shares.").
6. Poole v. N.V. Deli Maatschappij, 243 A.2d 67, 70 n.1 (Del. 1968). See also Steinhart v. Southwest Realty & Dev. Co., C.A. No. 583, 1981 Del. Ch. LEXIS 628, at *10 (Del. Ch. Dec. 28, 1981).
7. See, e.g., Applebaum v. Avaya, Inc., 812 A.2d 880, 889-90 (Del. 2002); Tansey v. Trade Show News Networks, Inc., C.A. No. 18796, 2001 Del. Ch. LEXIS 142, at *28 (Del. Ch. Nov. 27, 2001) ("To the extent that stock is traded on a recognized market, the court therefore can derive the [fair market] value from the trading price").
8. See Union Ill. 1995 Inv. Ltd., 847 A.2d at 356-59.
9. Chicago Corp. v. Munds, 172 A. 452 (Del. Ch. 1934).
10. See id. at 453.
11. Id. at 454.
12. Chicago Corp., 172 A. at 455-56.
13. Tri-Cont'l Corp. v. Battye, 74 A.2d 71, 72 (Del. 1950) ("We think the basic doctrine of valuation applied in Chicago Corporation v. Munds, supra, was formulated in accordance with proper principles and the better reasoned authorities."). Courts in a number of other jurisdictions have followed the lead of the Delaware courts in distinguishing between the concepts of "fair market value" and "fair value." See, e.g., Brown v. Arp and Hammond Hardware Co., 141 P.3d 673, 686 (Wyo. 2006) (rejecting interpretation of fair value as equivalent to fair market value); Matthew G. Norton Co. v. Smyth, 51 P.3d 159, 163 (Wash. Ct. App. 2002) ("It is clear, however, that our legislature's use of the term 'fair value' was not a slip of the pen – the legislature did not intend to say 'fair market value' instead.") (citation omitted); First W. Bank Wall v. Olsen, 621 N.W.2d 611, 617 (S.D. 2001) ("If the legislature intended dissenting shareholders to receive the fair market value of their shares, it would have so stated."); In re McLoon Oil Co., 565 A.2d 997, 1004-05 (Me. 1989) (explaining the difference between the "fair market value" of shares and the "fair value" to which stockholders

Chapter 3: Dissenting and Oppressed Shareholder Matters

are entitled when they are frozen out of a corporation); Robbins v. Beatty, 67 N.W.2d 12, 18 (Iowa 1954) (holding that the term "real value," as used in the appraisal statute, is not synonymous with "market value").

14. Finkelstein, 2005 Del. Ch. LEXIS 53, at *39 (citing In re Shell Oil Co., 607 A.2d at 1218 and Tri-Cont'l Corp., 74 A.2d at 72).

15. Bell v. Kirby Lumber Corp., 413 A.2d 137, 140-42 (Del. 1980). See also Highfields Capital, Ltd. v. AXA Fin., Inc., 939 A.2d 34, 42 (Del. Ch. 2007) (emphasizing that fair value is not the value of the corporation to a third-party); Dobler v. Montgomery Cellular Holding Co., C.A. No. 19211, 2004 Del. Ch. LEXIS 139, at *49 (Del. Ch. Sept. 30, 2004) (fair value is not "just the value of the company to one specific buyer"), aff'd, 880 A.2d 206 (Del. 2005); Union Ill. 1995 Inv. Ltd. P'ship, 847 A.2d at 356-57 (differentiating between fair value and value ascribed by third-party).

16. Courts in some other states have held that the concept of "fair value" encompasses a stockholder's proportionate share of the value of the entire company, based upon the highest price that could be obtained in a sale of the company to a third-party purchaser. See, e.g., Sarrouf v. New England Patriots Football Club, Inc., 492 N.E.2d 1122, 1125 (Mass. 1986) ("As a going concern, the value of an enterprise ... [in a statutory appraisal proceeding] is the price a knowledgeable buyer would pay for the entire corporation ...."); Cf. Northwest Inv. Corp. v. Wallace, 741 N.W.2d 782, 791 (Iowa 2007) (acknowledging deviation from Delaware law, but opting "to follow the position of jurisdictions who determine fair value based on 'what a willing buyer realistically would pay for the enterprise as a whole on the statutory valuation date'") (quoting BNE Mass. Corp. v. Sims, 588 N.E.2d 14, 19 (Mass. App. Ct. 1992). For example, the Maine Supreme Court has instructed, as follows:

17. In the statutory appraisal proceeding, the involuntary change of ownership caused by a merger requires as a matter of fairness that a dissenting shareholder be compensated for the loss of his proportionate interest in the business as an entity. The valuation focus under the appraisal statute is not the stock as a commodity, but rather the stock only as it represents a proportionate part of the enterprise as a whole. The question for the court becomes simple and direct: What is the best price a single buyer could reasonably be expected to pay for the firm as an entirety? The court then prorates that value for the whole firm equally among all shares of its common stock. The result is that all of those shares have the same fair value.

18. In re McLoon Oil Co., 565 A.2d at 1004.

19. Montgomery Cellular Holding Co. v. Dobler, 880 A.2d 206, 220 (Del. 2005). See also Highfields Capital, 939 A.2d at 59-62; Union Ill. 1995 Inv. Ltd., 847 A.2d at 356. It is arguable that this results from the statutory mandate that the Court must still subtract "any element of value arising from the accomplishment or expectation of the merger or consolidation" in adjudicating fair value. See Del. Code. Ann. tit. 8, § 262(h) (2007).

20. M.P.M. Enters. v. Gilbert, 731 A.2d 790, 795 (Del. 1999). See also In re Radiology Assoc., 611 A.2d 485, 494 (Del. Ch. 1991) (observing that "the appraisal process is not intended to reconstruct a pro forma sale but to assume that a shareholder was willing to maintain his investment position") (quoting Cavalier Oil Corp. v. Harnett, 564 A.2d 1137, 1145 (Del. 1989)).

21. Del. Code. Ann. tit. 8, § 262(h). The Delaware Supreme Court has observed that this statutory provision evinces "a legislative intent to fully compensate shareholders for whatever their loss may be, subject only to the narrow limitation that one can not take speculative effects of the merger into account." Weinberger v. UOP, Inc., 457 A.2d 701, 714 (Del. 1983).

22. Weinberger, 457 A.2d at 713.

23. See id. at 712-13 (concluding that prior case law that established precedent for exclusive reliance on "Delaware block" approach to valuation was "outmoded" and that it is time to "bring our law current on the subject").

24. Andaloro v. PFPC Worldwide, Inc., C.A. Nos. 20336 & 20289, 2005 Del. Ch. LEXIS 125, at *33-34 (Del. Ch. Aug. 19, 2005) (citing Universal City Studios, Inc. v. Francis I. DuPont & Co., 334 A.2d 216, 218 (Del. 1975)).

25. Andaloro, 2005 Del. Ch. LEXIS 125, at *34 (citation omitted). See also In re Nellson Nutraceutical, Inc., Ch. 11 Case No. 06-10072 (CSS), 2007 Bankr. LEXIS 99, at *63 (Bankr. D. Del. Jan. 18, 2007) ("When reviewing an expert opinion regarding the value of a corporation, courts frequently adjust or correct expert opinion analysis in reaching their final opinion on valuation.").

26. Gonsalves v. Straight Arrow Publishers, Inc., 701 A.2d 357, 361-62 (Del. 1997).

27. See id.

28. See Dobler, 2004 Del. Ch. LEXIS 139, at *34. See also In re Appraisal of Metromedia Int'l Group, C.A. No. 3351-CC, slip op. at 9-10 (Del. Ch. Apr. 16, 2009) ("Methods approved by this Court in determining fair value include the discounted cash flow valuation methodology, the comparable transactions approach, and the comparable company analysis.").

Judicial Valuation of Stock of a Delaware Corporation

29. Highfields Capital, 939 A.2d at 56 (quoting Dobler, 2004 Del. Ch. LEXIS 139, at *34). See also Doft & Co. v. Travelocity.com, Inc., C.A. No. 19734, 2004 Del. Ch. LEXIS 75, at *32 (Del. Ch. May 20, 2004 revised May 21, 2004) reconsideration granted on other grounds, 2004 Del. Ch. LEXIS 84 (Del. Ch. June 10, 2004); ONTI, Inc. v. Integra Bank, 751 A.2d 904, 915 (Del. Ch. 1999) (explaining that the market approach provides an indication of fair value based upon "first finding companies that are similar to the company under appraisal and then 'calculating the value of the company through the use of earnings and other multiples'") (quoting In re Radiology Assocs., 611 A.2d at 489).

30. See Cavalier Oil Corp. v. Harnett, C.A. No. 7959, 1988 Del. Ch. LEXIS 28, at *96, (Del. Ch. Feb. 22, 1988) (noting that the party's "portrayal of the comparable company approach as being more objective and scientific, and hence superior, appears vastly to understate the judgmental features of that method"), aff'd, 564 A.2d 1137 (Del. 1989).

31. See, e.g., Highfields Capital, 939 A.2d at 56-57 (concluding that lack of comparability made both expert's comparable company analyses unreliable); In re PNB Holding Co. S'holders Litig., Consol. C.A. No. 28-N, 2006 Del. Ch. LEXIS 158, at *96 & n.125 (Del. Ch. Aug. 18, 2006) (rejecting comparative approach where the experts "evidenced little familiarity with the actual details of their comparables"); ONTI, 751 A.2d at 915-16 (refusing to rely on comparative analysis when differences between subject company and comparables made "meaningful comparison impossible").

32. See, e.g., Highfields Capital, 939 A.2d at 57 (noting that expert's heavy reliance on price-to-earnings multiple contradicted with his assertions that "it was not an acceptable practice to derive stock values for an insurance company solely from earnings"); M.G. Bancorp. Inc. v. Le Beau, 737 A.2d 513, 522-23 (Del. 1999) (finding no error where Court of Chancery concluded that expert failed to establish that multiples relied upon provided a generally accepted technique for valuing a bank holding company).

33. Erik Lie and Heidi L. Lie, Multiples Used to Estimate Corporate Value, 58 Fin. Analysts J. 2, Mar./Apr. 2002 ("Although practitioners and academic researchers frequently use multiples to assess company values, there is no consensus as to which multiple performs best.").

34. See, e.g., Lane v. Cancer Treatment Ctrs. of Am., Inc., C.A. No. 12207-NC, 2004 Del. Ch. LEXIS 108, at *128 (Del. Ch. July 30, 2004) ("The most useful ratio in a comparative company's analysis frequently is the totally capital to EBITDA."); Doft, 2004 Del. Ch. LEXIS 75, at *42 (observing that both experts agreed that "EBITDA multiples are the preferred multiple to examine because they are closest to cash flow and are a better proxy for the firm's ongoing concern value"). But see LeBeau v. M.G. Bancorp., Inc., C.A. No. 13141, 1998 Del. Ch. LEXIS 9, at *29-30 (Del. Ch. Jan. 29, 1998) (rejecting valuation where expert failed to prove that multiples of EBITDA and EBIT are widely accepted in the financial community for valuing a bank or bank holding company), aff'd, 737 A.2d 513 (Del. 1999).

35. See, e.g., LeBeau, 1998 Del. Ch. LEXIS 9, at *28-29 (accepting that price-to-book value and price-to-earnings are the relevant ratios for valuing banks); Harris v. Rapid-Am. Corp., C.A. No. 6462, 1990 Del. Ch. LEXIS 166, at *24-51 (Del. Ch. Oct. 2, 1990) (applying multiples based on revenues, EBIT, EBITDA, and tangible book value of invested capital), aff'd in part and rev'd in part, 603 A.2d 796 (Del. 1992).

36. See, e.g., Gray v. Cytokine Pharmasciences, Inc., C.A. No. 17451, 2002 Del. Ch. LEXIS 48 (Del. Ch. Apr. 25, 2002) (finding that comparable company analysis based partly on revenue multiple was reliable indicator of going concern value); Agranoff v. Miller, 791 A.2d 880, 893 (Del. Ch. 2001) (weighing equally multiples based on revenues, EBIT, and EBITDA). Though any valuation approach is susceptible to distortions if improperly utilized, the reliance upon multiples of gross revenue have been singled out as being particularly susceptible to abuse. Indeed, one respected commentator has warned that "[w]hen gross revenue multipliers are used for valuation without the user completely understanding the limitations that apply to each case, the result can be an extremely misleading estimate of value." Shannon P. Pratt, Valuing Small Businesses and Professional Practices 230 (2d ed. 1993).

37. See, e.g., Dobler, 2004 Del. Ch. LEXIS 139, at *65-67; Gray, 2002 Del. Ch. LEXIS 48, at *35-37; Agranoff, 791 A.2d at 890-95; Bomarko, Inc. v. Int'l Telecharge, Inc., 794 A.2d 1161 (Del. Ch. 1999), aff'd, 766 A.2d 437 (Del. 2000); Borruso v. Commc'ns Telesystems Int'l., 753 A.2d 451 (Del. Ch. 1999); Kleinwort Benson Ltd. v. Silgan Corp., C.A. No. 11107, 1995 Del. Ch. LEXIS 75 (Del. Ch. June 15, 1995); Hodas v. Spectrum Tech., Inc., C.A. No. 11265, 1992 Del. Ch. LEXIS 252, at *4-6 (Del. Ch. Dec. 7, 1992); Rapid-Am. Corp., 1990 Del. Ch. LEXIS 166, aff'd in part and rev'd in part, 603 A.2d 796.

38. See, e.g., Crescent/Mach I P'ship v. Turner, C.A. Nos. 17455-VCN & 17711-VCN, 2007 Del. Ch. LEXIS 63, at *56 n.101 (Del. Ch. May 2, 2007) (using DCF to calculate the fair value of the shares, but noting that an EBITDA multiple provided a useful comparison resulting in an outcome not inconsistent with the DCF analysis).

39. See Borruso, 753 A.2d at 455 & n.5 (employing comparable company valuation when no other method could appropriately be relied upon). See also Doft, 2004 Del. Ch. LEXIS 75, at *32 ("The court . . . may use a comparable company valuation on a stand-alone basis in an appraisal action when it is the only reliable method of valuation offered by the parties.").

Chapter 3: Dissenting and Oppressed Shareholder Matters

40. Crescent/Mach I P'ship, 2007 Del. Ch. LEXIS 63, at *53 (Del. Ch. May 2, 2007) ("a good industry comparison is crucial if a multiplier methodology is employed, but the Respondent has not established that appropriate comparables are available"), modified by, 2008 Del. Ch. LEXIS 68 (Del. Ch. June 4, 2008). See also Highfields Capital, 939 A.2d at 56; ONTI, 751 A.2d at 916; In re PNB Holding Co., 2006 Del. Ch. LEXIS 158, at *96 & n.125 (concluding that comparable company approach could not be relied upon by the Court where the experts failed to establish that it was a suitable methodology and that the comparables selected provided a sound basis on which to value the company); In re Radiology Assoc., 611 A.2d at 490 (noting that differences from comparable companies in terms of "product mix, revenues, profit margins, revenue and earnings growth rates, assets and geographic markets combine to make any comparison with Radiology meaningless"). Notably, one study reports that certain companies with a high intangible value, such as high technology companies, "dotcom" companies, or those having high research and development expenses, are not well-suited to valuations based on multipliers at all. See Malcolm Baker & Richard S. Ruback, Estimating Industry Multiples (Div. of Res. of the Harvard Graduate Sch. of Bus. Admin., Working Paper, 1999), available at http://www.people.hbs.edu/mbaker/cv/papers/EstimatingIndustry.pdf.

41. See Highfields Capital, 939 A.2d at 57 n.72 ("Although Delaware courts now seem to accept that the application of this valuation metric requires such an adjustment, the debate in the legal and financial community continues."); see also Andaloro, 2005 Del. Ch. LEXIS 125, at *31 ("The elimination of minority discounts . . . represents a deviation from the fair market value of minority shares as a real world matter in order to give the minority a pro rata share of the entire firm's value – their proportionate share of the company valued as a going concern."); Agranoff, 791 A.2d at 893 n.28 (observing that "[s]ome commentators claim that this technique . . . has become accepted solely because of the need to adapt financial valuation methods to legal rules forbidding the valuation of minority shares qua minority shares, and that it is not used in the non-legal context") (citing John C. Coates, IV, "Fair Value" As An Avoidable Rule of Corporate Law: Minority Discounts in Conflict Transactions, 147 U. Pa. L. Rev. 1251, 1286 n.118 (1999)).

42. See e.g., Neal v. Alabama By-Prods. Corp., C.A. No. 8282, 1990 Del. Ch. LEXIS 127, at *20 (Del. Ch. Aug. 1, 1990), aff'd, 588 A.2d 255 (Del. 1991).

43. Crescent/Mach I P'ship v. Dr Pepper Bottling Co., 962 A.2d 205, 207 (Del. 2008).

44. ONTI, 751 A.2d at 916. See also Crescent/Mach I P'ship, 2007 Del. Ch. LEXIS 63, at *33-58; In re PNB Holding Co., 2006 Del. Ch. LEXIS 158, at *98-117; Gesoff v. IIC Indus., Inc., 902 A.2d 1130, 155 & n.138 (Del. Ch. 2006); Andaloro, 2005 Del. Ch. LEXIS 125, at *35-62; Dobler, 2004 Del. Ch. LEXIS 139, at *67-72; Gray, 2002 Del. Ch. LEXIS 48, at *31-35; M.P.M. Enters. v. Gilbert, 731 A.2d 790, 793-95 (Del. 1999); Hintmann v. Fred Weber, Inc., C.A. No. 12839, 1998 Del. Ch. LEXIS 26 (Del. Ch. Feb. 17, 1998); Kleinwort Benson Ltd, 1995 Del. Ch. LEXIS 75; Hodas, 1992 Del. Ch. LEXIS 252, at *6-7; In re Radiology Assocs., 611 A.2d 485; Alabama By-Prods. Corp., 1990 Del. Ch. LEXIS 127.

45. ONTI, 751 A.2d at 916. But see Crescent/Mach I P'ship, 2008 Del. Ch. LEXIS 68, at *19 n.46 ("a fair value determination, even if principally driven by the results of a DCF analysis, should be informed by other applicable valuation methodologies"), rev'd on other grounds, 962 A.2d 205 (Del. 2008).

46. Highfields Capital, 939 A.2d at 52. See also Crescent/Mach I P'ship, 2007 Del. Ch. LEXIS 63, at *33 ("Although it is appropriate to consider all accepted methodologies, the Court tends to favor the discounted cash flow method"); Andaloro, 2005 Del. Ch. LEXIS 125, at *78 (observing that "a DCF valuation is the best technique for valuing an entity when the necessary information regarding the inputs is available"); Cede & Co. v. JRC Acquisition Corp., C.A. No. 18648-NC, 2004 Del. Ch. LEXIS 12, at *6 (Del. Ch. Feb. 10, 2004) ("In recent years, the DCF valuation methodology has featured prominently in this Court because it 'is the approach that merits the greatest confidence' within the financial community.") (quoting Ryan v. Tad's Enters., Inc., 709 A.2d 675, 702 (Del. Ch. 1996)); Grimes v. Vitalink Commc'ns Corp., C.A. No. 12334, 1997 Del. Ch. LEXIS 124, at *3 (Del. Ch. Aug. 26, 1997) (describing the discounted cash flow approach as "increasingly the model of choice for valuations in this Court").

47. See, e.g., Highfields Capital, 939 A.2d at 54 (concluding that court would not rely on "a pure DCF methodology" because the trial evidence showed that "industry experts and executives do not consider a DCF a particularly important framework for valuing a company whose primary business is selling life insurance").

48. Dobler, 2004 Del. Ch. LEXIS 139, at *67-68 (footnotes and citations omitted). See also Crescent/Mach I P'ship, 2008 Del. Ch. LEXIS 68, at *16-17 ("The most complicated, substantive facets of any DCF analysis are determining the appropriate model and the proper inputs for use in that model.").

49. See, e.g., Crescent/Mach I P'ship, 2008 Del. Ch. LEXIS 68, at *19 n.46 (relying exclusively on DCF valuation where company's unique market position made other valuation methodologies not particularly helpful, but remarking that DCF fair value calculation was not "inconsistent" with other indicators of value); In re PNB Holding Co., 2006 Del. Ch.

LEXIS 158, at *95-96 (relying exclusively upon the income approach after concluding that the other proffered approaches were not supported by a reliable evidentiary record, and observing that "focusing exclusively upon a DCF analysis is consistent with the heavy emphasis the experts themselves have given to this method"); In re Emerging Commc'ns, Inc. S'holders Litig., C.A. No. 16415, 2004 Del. Ch. LEXIS 70 (Del. Ch. May 3, 2004) (relying exclusively upon DCF to adjudicate the "fair value" of the subject company). Accord Andaloro, 2005 Del. Ch. LEXIS 125, at *35 ("The DCF method is frequently used in this court and, I, like many others, prefer to give it great, and sometimes even exclusive, weight when it may be used responsibly.").

50. See, e.g., Doft & Co. v. Travelocity.com, C.A. No. 19734, 2004 Del. Ch. LEXIS 75, at *17-32 (concluding that lack of reliability of fundamental inputs makes "a DCF analysis of marginal utility as a valuation technique in this case"), reconsideration granted on other grounds, 2004 Del. Ch. LEXIS 84 (Del. Ch. June 10, 2004); M.G. Bancorp. Inc. v. Le Beau, 737 A.2d 513 (Del. 1999) (affirming Court of Chancery's adjudication of "fair value" that did not include a DCF analysis or other use of the "income approach").

51. Highfields Capital, 939 A.2d at 54. See also U.S. Cellular Operating Co., C.A. No. 18696-NC, 2005 Del. Ch. LEXIS 1, at *69 (Del. Ch. Jan. 6, 2005); Dobler, 2004 Del. Ch. LEXIS 139, at *34.

52. Compare Prescott Group Small Cap, L.P. v. Coleman Co., C.A. No. 17802, 2004 Del. Ch. LEXIS 131, at *92-105 (Del. Ch. Sept. 8, 2004) (rejecting the contention that the transaction approach was an impermissible measure of going concern value because "[c]ontrol value – the value derived from a sale of the company as a whole without any discounts for minority status or premia for synergies – is not a prescribed measure of going concern value") with Harris v. Rapid-Am. Corp., C.A. No. 6462, 1990 Del. Ch. LEXIS 166, at *20 (Del. Ch. Oct. 2, 1990) (rejecting transaction approach because it "necessarily incorporates control premiums and liquidation values that produce inflated values that do not accurately reflect the going concern value of the company at issue"), aff'd in part and rev'd in part, 603 A.2d 796 (Del. 1992).

53. See, e.g., Bell v. Kirby Lumber Corp., 413 A.2d 137, 140-42 (Del. 1980); Highfields Capital, 939 A.2d at 42; Dobler, 2004 Del. Ch. LEXIS 139, at *49; Union Ill. 1995 Inv. Ltd. P'ship v. Union Fin. Group, Ltd., 847 A.2d 340, 356-57 (Del. Ch. 2003).

54. Kleinwort Benson Ltd., 1995 Del. Ch. LEXIS 75, at *9-10 (citations omitted). See also Onti, 751 A.2d at 913 (explaining that the Court will "not specifically consider studies of control premiums paid in merger transactions because those reflect expected future profits after the merger (i.e., synergy values)").

55. See, e.g., Coleman Co., 2004 Del. Ch. LEXIS 131, at *92-98 & n.141 (explaining that any synergistic elements of value specific to a particular buyer captured by transaction approach must be excluded from a going concern valuation). See also Kleinwort Benson Ltd., 1995 Del. Ch. LEXIS 75, at *12-13 (concluding that transaction analysis was not helpful in valuing corporation as a going concern because the "merger and acquisition data undoubtedly contains post-merger value, such as synergies with the acquiror, that must be excluded from appraisal value").

56. See Agranoff v. Miller, 791 A.2d 880, 897 n.43 (Del. Ch. 2001) (citing John C. Coates, IV, "Fair Value" As An Avoidable Rule of Corporate Law: Minority Discounts in Conflict Transactions, 147 U. Pa. L. Rev. 1251, 1272 n.69 (1999)). See also Highfields Capital, 939 A.2d at 47-57 (warning that where the market has knowledge of a potential merger or acquisition, the addition of a premium under the market approach to negate an embedded minority discount would result in an inflated value because the market would have priced speculative elements of value).

57. Unfortunately, it may difficult, if not impossible, to determine whether the price paid in comparable transactions included a sharing of expected synergies resulting from the transaction. Even more difficult, if not impossible, is determining the value of such shared synergies. Agranoff, 791 A.2d at 897 ("As a practical matter . . . it is impossible to make precise determinations about what motivated an acquiror to pay a premium."). See also Hintmann, 1998 Del. Ch. LEXIS 26, at * 31 n.52 (noting that determination of amount to discount control premium to eliminate post-merger synergies was necessarily "arbitrary and subjective" but finding that it was appropriate nonetheless).

58. See, e.g., Highfields Capital, 939 A.2d 34 (employing combined shared synergies and sum-of-the-parts analysis, of which transaction approach was a component, to value an insurance conglomerate); In re U.S. Cellular Operating Co., 2005 Del. Ch. LEXIS 1, at *77 (awarding fair value measured as 70% of DCF calculation and 30% comparable transaction analysis).

59. See, e.g., Union Ill. 1995 Inv. Ltd., 847 A.2d at 353-56 (expert used comparable transactions approach to check reasonableness of DCF calculation).

60. See, e.g., Gentile v. SinglePoint Fin., Inc., C.A. No. 18677-NC, 2003 Del. Ch. LEXIS 21 (Del. Ch. Mar. 5, 2003) (adjudicating fair value based solely on comparable transaction analysis because emerging technology company could not be reliably valued under other methodologies); M.G. Bancorp. Inc. v. Le Beau, 737 A.2d 513 (Del. 1999) (affirming Court of Chancery's adjudication of "fair value" based exclusively upon the transaction approach).

Chapter 3: Dissenting and Oppressed Shareholder Matters

61. See, e.g., Highfields Capital, 939 A.2d at 57-62 (finding that both experts failed to demonstrate that their comparable transactions analyses formed a legitimate basis from which to derive fair value); In re PNB Holding Co. S'holders Litig., 2006 Del. Ch. LEXIS 158, at *96 & n.125 (declining to apply the comparable company or comparable transaction analyses relied upon by the experts because the valuations were not sufficiently supported by the record and the experts' testimony indicated a lack of familiarity with comparables); Taylor v. Am. Specialty Realty, C.A. No. 19239, 2003 Del. Ch. LEXIS 75, at *31-36 (Del. Ch. July 25, 2003) (rejecting transaction approach where experts did not provide sufficient information to allow the Court to assess the reliability of the approach).

62. In re U.S. Cellular Operating Co., 2005 Del. Ch. LEXIS 1, at *69 (citations omitted).

63. See, e.g., Bell v. Kirby Lumber Corp., 413 A.2d 137, 140-42 (Del. 1980); Tri-Continental Corp. v. Battye, 74 A.2d 71, 74 (Del. 1950).

64. Id.

65. In re Shell Oil Co., 607 A.2d 1213, 1221 (Del. 1992) (citation omitted). See also Ng v. Heng Sang Realty Corp., C.A. No. 18462, 2004 Del. Ch. LEXIS 69, at *23-28 (Del. Ch. Apr. 22, 2004, revised May 18, 2004) (approving of expert's use of "net asset value" where it was "at most a minor component, and certainly not the sole basis, for valuing [the subject company] as a going concern"), aff'd, 867 A.2d 901 (Del. 2005); Kahn v. Household Acquisition Corp., C.A. No. 6293, 1988 Del. Ch. LEXIS 64, at *41 (Del. Ch. May 6, 1988) ("It is settled law that asset value, being a liquidation value, cannot be used as the sole measure of fair value.").

66. Cooper v. Pabst Brewing Corp., C.A. No. 7244, 1993 Del. Ch. LEXIS 91, at *16 (Del. Ch. June 8, 1993) (citing Alabama By-Prods. Corp., 1990 Del. Ch. LEXIS 127, at *19; Kirby Lumber Corp., 413 A.2d 137 (40% weight given to asset value in appraisal of timber company); In re Shell Oil Co., C.A. No. 8080, 1990 Del. Ch. LEXIS 199 (Del. Ch. Dec. 11, 1990) (valuation of production operations of energy company based on asset value), aff'd sub nom, 607 A.2d 1213 (Del. 1992)).

67. See, e.g., Paskill Corp. v. Alcoma Corp., 747 A.2d 549, 557 (Del. 2000) ("[A]fter the entire corporation has been valued as a going concern by applying an appraisal methodology that passes judicial muster, there can be no discounting at the shareholder level."); Salomon Bros. Inc. v. Interstate Bakeries Corp., C.A. No. 10,054, 1992 Del. Ch. LEXIS 100, at *16 (Del. Ch. May 1, 1992) ("The number of shares owned by the dissenting stockholder is not to be considered in the valuation process either by application of a discount or a control premium adjustment at the stockholder level."); Harris v. Rapid-Am. Corp., C.A. No. 6462, 1990 Del. Ch. LEXIS 166, at *20 (Del. Ch. Oct. 2, 1990) ("Respondents have done exactly what Delaware law forbids, i.e., applied a discount at the shareholder level."), aff'd in part and rev'd in part, 603 A.2d 796 (Del. 1992).

68. Cavalier Oil Corp. v. Harnett, C.A. Nos. 7959, 1988 Del. Ch. LEXIS 28, at *28 (Del. Ch. Feb. 22, 1988), aff'd, 564 A.2d 1137 (Del. 1989). See also id. at *30 (observing that "under § 262 the thing being valued is the entire corporation as a going concern, not individualized configurations of its shares").

69. Cavalier Oil Corp., 564 A.2d at 1145.

70. See, e.g., Rapid-Am. Corp. v. Harris, 603 A.2d 796, 806-07 (Del. 1992); Poole v. N.V. Deli Maatschappij, 243 A.2d 67, 70-72 (Del. 1968) (holding that the determination of the "fair value" of the corporation requires consideration of the "fair market value" of the corporation's assets).

71. Cavalier Oil Corp., 1988 Del. Ch. LEXIS 28, at *25-29 (citing Robbins & Co., 1985 Del. Ch. LEXIS 498, at *25-26).

72. M.G. Bancorp, Inc. v. Le Beau, 737 A.2d 513, 525 (Del. 1999).

73. Rapid-Am. Corp., 603 A.2d at 806-07 (footnote omitted). See also Paskill Corp., 747 A.2d at 556 ("[A] corporate level comparative acquisition approach to valuing a company, which include[s] a control premium for a majority interest in a subsidiary, [is] a relevant and reliable methodology to use in an appraisal proceeding to determine the fair market value of shares in a holding company."); M.G. Bancorp., Inc., 737 A.2d at 525 ("Because [the subject company] held a controlling interest in its two subsidiaries, it was necessary to determine the value of those controlling interests in order to ascertain the value of [the subject company], as a whole, as a going concern on the Merger date."); Dobler, 2004 Del. Ch. LEXIS 139, at *48-49 (quoting Paskill); Agranoff, 791 A.2d at 898-99 n.45 ("The case law requires that a § 262 valuation of an entity value wholly-owned subsidiaries on a basis that includes a control premium recognizing the possibility that the subsidiaries could be sold."); Hintmann v. Weber, Inc., C.A. No. 12839, 1998 Del. Ch. LEXIS 26, at *29 (Del. Ch. Feb. 17, 1998) ("[A] control premium may be added not only when a third party acquires a majority interest in a corporation, but also as a means of making the valuation of a company more realistic.").

74. See, e.g., Cavalier Oil Corp., 564 A.2d at 1144; Tansey v. Trade Show News Networks, Inc., C.A. No. 18796, 2001 Del. Ch. LEXIS 142, at *26 n.32 (Del. Ch. Nov. 27, 2001) ("[I]n a statutory appraisal, the court may not apply a minority discount to determine the value of a minority block of shares."); Agranoff, 791 A.2d at 888-89; In re Vision Hardware

Group, 669 A.2d 671, 677 (Del. Ch. 1995) ("Delaware courts will attempt to value the whole enterprise as a going concern, and will afford dissenting shareholders their pro-rata portion free of any 'minority discount.'") (citation omitted); In re Shell Oil Co., 1990 Del. Ch. LEXIS 199, at *13, aff'd, 607 A.2d 1213 (Del. 1992).

75. See, e.g., Nebel v. Southwest Bancorp., Inc., C.A. No. 13618, 1999 Del. Ch. LEXIS 30 (Del. Ch. Mar. 9, 1999) (fiduciary duty action challenging cash-out merger); Metropolitan Life Ins. Co. v. Aramark Corp., C.A. No. 16142, 1998 Del. Ch. LEXIS 70 (Del. Ch. Feb. 5, 1998) (fiduciary duty action challenging recapitalization that would result in "cash-out" of minority stockholders).

76. See, e.g., Cavalier Oil Corp., 564 A.2d at 1144; Tri-Cont'l Corp., 74 A.2d at 72. See also Tansey, 2001 Del. Ch. LEXIS 142, at *27 n.32 ("In the real world, fair market value will take into account the fact that a person is selling a minority block of shares in a company with a controlling stockholder."); See also Metropolitan Life Ins. Co., 1998 Del. Ch. LEXIS 70, at *7 ("There may be situations where a discount is proper when it affects the value of the assets of the company, but I do not believe it is proper when it affects the stock of the company.").

77. See, e.g., Cavalier Oil Corp., 564 A.2d 1137; Highfields Capital, 939 A.2d at 42 (observing that "the value of a petitioner's shares may not reflect discounts for lack of marketability or illiquidity"); Hodas v. Spectrum Tech., Inc., C.A. No. 11,265, 1992 Del. Ch. LEXIS 252, at *14 (Del. Ch. Dec. 7, 1992); In re Shell Oil Co., 1990 Del. Ch. LEXIS 199, at *13.

78. See Onti, Inc. v. Integra Bank, 751 A.2d 904, 920 (Del. Ch. 1999). See also Gesoff v. IIC Indus., Inc., 902 A.2d 1130, 1161 (Del. Ch. 2006); Del. Open MRI Radiology Assocs. v. Kessler, 898 A.2d 290, 338-40 (Del. Ch. 2006); Hintmann, 1998 Del. Ch. LEXIS 26, at *14-15.

79. Hintmann, 1998 Del. Ch. LEXIS 26, at *14-15 & n.23 (quoting Shannon P. Pratt, et al., Valuing A Business 171 (3d ed. 1996)). See also Gesoff, 902 A.2d at 1159 ("The small size premium, although somewhat controversial, is a generally accepted premise of both financial analyses and of this court's valuation opinions.") (citing Onti, 751 A.2d at 920).

80. John C. Coates, IV, "Fair Value" As An Avoidable Rule of Corporate Law: Minority Discounts in Conflict Transactions, 147 U. Pa. L. Rev. 1251, 1272 n.69 (1999).

81. Gesoff, 902 A.2d at 1160-61 (finding no justification to apply small stock premium for business operating in a developing foreign market).

82. Borruso v. Commc'ns Telesys. Int'l,, 753 A.2d 451, 459-60 (Del. Ch. 1999).

83. Metropolitan Life Ins. Co., 1998 Del. Ch. LEXIS 70, at *5-7.

84. Smith v. Van Gorkom, 488 A.2d 858, 876 (Del. 1985).

85. Agranoff, 791 A.2d at 892-93 (footnote omitted). See also M.G. Bancorp., Inc. v. LeBeau, 737 A.2d 513, 523 (Del. 1999) (affirming Court of Chancery's rejection of "capital market approach" that valued subject company on the basis of comparable publicly traded companies, but failed to adjust the indicated value to eliminate the "minority discount" inherent in the indicated value); Andaloro v. PFPC Worldwide, Inc., C.A. No. 20336 & 20289, 2005 Del. Ch. LEXIS 125, at *65 (Del. Ch. Aug. 15, 2005) ("To honor the Supreme Court's teaching that plaintiffs should receive their pro rata share of the entity as a going concern, this court's decisions adjust minority trading multiples to account for the implied discount, in order to accurately arrive at a fair value of the entire entity."); Prescott Group Small Cap, L.P. v. Coleman Co., C.A. No. 17802, 2004 Del. Ch. LEXIS 131, at *84-85 (Del. Ch. Sept. 8, 2004) (describing comparable company method as flawed where the expert did not add offsetting control premium to negate inherent minority discount); Lane, 2004 Del. Ch. LEXIS 108, at *129 ("To determine the "intrinsic worth of a corporation on a going concern basis, a premium must be added to adjust for the minority discount.") (citations omitted); Doft & Co. v. Travelocity.com, C.A. No. 19734, 2004 Del. Ch. LEXIS 75, at *45-46 (Del. Ch. May 20, 2004 revised May 21, 2004); Bomarko, Inc., v. Int'l Telecharge, Inc. 794 A.2d 1161, 1186 (Del. Ch. 1999); Borruso, 753 A.2d at 457-58; Kleinwort Benson Ltd v. Silgan Corp., C.A. No. 11107, 1995 Del. Ch. LEXIS 75, at *7-9 (Del. Ch. June 15, 1995). But see Salomon Bros. Inc. v. Interstate Bakeries Corp., C.A. No. 10054, 1992 Del. Ch. LEXIS 100, at *14-15 (Del. Ch. May 1, 1992) (rejecting the portion of an expert's valuation that compensated for an implied minority discount, and commenting that there was a "real question" of whether such an adjustment was "recognized and accepted in the financial community").

86. See, e.g., In re Toys "R" Us, Inc. S'holder Litig., 877 A.2d 975, 1013 (Del. Ch. 2005) ("It is not my understanding that a DCF valuation . . . embeds a minority discount. Rather, that value is a value of the entity itself."); Lane v. Cancer Treatment Ctrs. of Am., Inc., C.A. No. 12207-NC, 2004 Del. Ch. LEXIS 108, at *118 (Del. Ch. July 30, 2004).

87. See Highfields Capital, Ltd. v. AXA Fin., Inc., 939 A.2d 34, 57 n.72 (Del. Ch. 2007). Accord Salomon Bros. Inc., 1992 Del. Ch. LEXIS 100, at *14-15 (questioning whether such an adjustment was "recognized and accepted in the financial community"). See also Lawrence A. Hamermesh & Michael L. Wachter, The Short and Puzzling Life of the "Implicit Minority Discount["] in Delaware Appraisal Law, 156 U. Pa. L. Rev. 1, 47-52 (2007) (describing the adjustment for the

Chapter 3: Dissenting and Oppressed Shareholder Matters

implied minority discount as a "remarkable divergence" from Delaware valuation case law that is otherwise consistent with modern finance theories).

88. Highfields Capital, 939 A.2d at 57 n.72.

89. Gesoff, 902 A.2d at 1157-59.

90. In re Loral Space & Commc'ns Consol. Litig., C.A. Nos. 2808-VCS, 3022-VCS, 2008 Del. Ch. LEXIS 136, at *83 (Del. Ch. Sept. 19, 2008) (quoting Gesoff, 902 A.2d 1158).

91. Id. (criticizing DCF valuation that "included a subjective 5% company specific risk premium, which was made ... without any basis in academic theory or market returns").

92. See, e.g., Poole v. N.V. Deli Maatschappij, 243 A.2d 67 (Del. 1968).

93. See Paskill Corp. v. Alcoma Corp., 747 A.2d 549 (Del. 2000) (holding that the Court of Chancery (i) erred by valuing company on liquidation basis that included reduction for hypothetical tax liabilities when no sale of its assets was contemplated, and (ii) properly excluded hypothetical transaction costs that would be incurred in such a sale). See also Cavalier Oil Corp., 1988 Del. Ch. LEXIS 28, at *39 (finding "legally untenable under § 262" a party's argument that "fair value" should be determined by reference to the after-tax price that the subject company would realize in a sale of its assets).

94. Montgomery Cellular Holding Co. v. Dobler, 880 A.2d 206, 220 (Del. 2005) (citation omitted). See also Highfields Capital, 939 A.2d at 59 (observing that "a court may derive fair value in a Delaware appraisal action if the sale of the company in question resulted from an arm's-length bargaining process where no structural impediments existed that might prevent a topping bid," but that "[t]he court must ... exclude synergistic elements from the sale price to arrive at a fair value"); Union Ill. 1995 Inv. Ltd. P'ship v. Union Fin. Group, Ltd., 847 A.2d 340, 356 (Del. Ch. 2003) ("[T]his court "must endeavor to exclude from any appraisal award the amount of any value that the selling company's shareholders would receive because a buyer intends to operate the subject company, not as a stand-alone going concern, but as a part of a larger enterprise, from which synergistic gains can be extracted."). Accord Andaloro, 2005 Del. Ch. LEXIS 125, at *52 n.55 ("What has to be factored out is any value that might be attributable to synergies that the selling entity might generate when combined with the buying company, regardless of whether a share of such synergies are typically paid to the seller to induce the sales transaction."); Coleman Co., 2004 Del. Ch. LEXIS 131, at *95 ("In determining 'going concern' value, the central inquiry is: what would the asset command in the market, if synergistic elements of value are excluded?").

95. See, e.g., Highfields Capital, 939 A.2d at 60-62 (shared synergies found to constitute approximately 13.29% of merger consideration); Union Ill. 1995 Inv. Ltd., 847 A.2d at 343, 364 (shared synergies found to constitute approximately 7.02% of merger consideration); Cooper v. Pabst Brewing Co., C.A. No. 7244, 1993 Del. Ch. LEXIS 91, at *6, *23, *31 (Del. Ch. June 8, 1993) (awarding the petitioners $27 per share, where the merger consideration, which was established through a competitive bidding process, consisted of $32 per share). See also Berger v. Pubco Corp., 2008 Del. Ch. LEXIS 63, at *19-20 (Del. Ch. May 30, 2008) ("this quasi-appraisal action should be structured to replicate a modicum of the risk that would inhere if this were an actual appraisal action, i.e., the risk that the Court will appraise [Pubco] at less than [$ 20] per share and the dissenting stockholders will receive less than the merger consideration.") (citing Gilliland v. Motorola, Inc. 873 A.2d 305 (Del. Ch. 2005)).

96. See, supra, notes 66-69 and accompanying text.

97. See, e.g., Cavalier Oil Corp., 564 A.2d at 1142-45 (affirming Court of Chancery's determination in a statutory appraisal proceeding that the value of the subject company as of the date of the merger included the value of a pre-merger claim for usurpation of a corporate opportunity); Delaware Open MRI Radiology Assoc. v. Kessler, 898 A.2d 290, 312-13 (Del. Ch. 2006) ("in appraising [the subject company], it is relevant to consider the value of the claims belonging to the entity, as they are an asset of the firm that is part of its value"); Onti, Inc. v. Integra Bank, 751 A.2d 904, 917 n.55 (Del. Ch. 1999) (noting that claims of excessive fees may be valued in appraisal action); Bomarko v. Int'l Telecharge, Inc., C.A. No. 13052, 1994 Del. Ch. LEXIS 51, at *7 (Del. Ch. May 16, 1994) ("breach of fiduciary duty claims that do not arise from the merger are corporate assets that may be included in the determination of fair value"); In re Radiology Assocs., Inc., C.A. No. 9001, 1990 Del. Ch. LEXIS 58, at *41 (Del. Ch. May 16, 1990) ("Those claims ... that are derivative in nature and precluded for lack of standing, may be considered in the appraisal phase of this litigation."); Porter v. Texas Commerce Bancshares, Inc., C.A. No. 9114, 1989 Del. Ch. LEXIS 130, at *18 (Del. Ch. Oct. 12, 1989) ("If the company has substantial and valuable derivative claims, they, like any asset of the company, may be valued in an appraisal."); accord Turner v. Bernstein, 776 A.2d 530, 546 n.38 (Del. Ch. June 6, 2000) (noting that pre-merger claims may be valued in connection with "fair price" determination in a statutory appraisal action, and suggesting that such claims also can be valued in a post-merger action for breach of fiduciary duty).

98. Bomarko, 1994 Del. Ch. LEXIS 51, at *8.

99. Bomarko, 794 A.2d at 1189.

100. See id.

101. Cavalier Oil Corp., 1988 Del. Ch. LEXIS 28, at *36-40.

102. Compare Gonsalves v. Straight Arrow Publishers, Inc., 701 A.2d 357, 363 (Del. 1997) (affirming Court of Chancery's evidentiary ruling that precluded an appraisal petitioner from arguing for a valuation based on an adjustment to management's compensation "in the absence of a derivative claim attacking excessive compensation"), aff'd in part, rev'd in part 1999 Del. LEXIS 7 (Del. Jan. 5, 1999), with Montgomery Cellular Holding Co., 880 A.2d at 224-25 (affirming Court of Chancery's adjustment of subject company's financial statements to eliminate from the DCF valuation certain pre-merger "management fees" paid to the parent corporation, which were found to be "essentially a pretext, unrelated to the actual furnishing of management services, that [the parent company] used to justify upstreaming money").

103. Oliver v. Boston Univ., C.A. No. 16570-NC, 2006 Del. Ch. LEXIS 75, at *87 n.190 (Del. Ch. Apr. 14, 2006).

104. Id. at *83-86.

105. Id. at *86 (citations omitted).

106. Id. at *86-87.

107. In re U.S. Cellular Operating Co., C.A. No. 18696-NC, 2005 Del. Ch. LEXIS 1, at *62 (Del. Ch. Jan. 6, 2005) (citing Weinberger, 457 A.2d at 713).

108. Del. Code. Ann. tit. 8, § 262(h) (2007).

109. Del. Open MRI Radiology Assocs., 898 A.2d at 310.

110. Paskill Corp., 747 A.2d at 554. See also Cavalier Oil Corp., 564 A.2d at 1144 ("the objective of a section 262 appraisal is 'to value the corporation itself, as distinguished from a specific fraction of its shares as they may exist in the hands of a particular shareholder'") (quoting Court of Chancery opinion at 1998 Del. Ch. LEXIS 28, at *27 (Del. Ch. Feb. 22, 1088)) (emphasis in original).

111. In re Appraisal of Metromedia Int'l Group, C.A. No. 3351-CC, 2009 Del. Ch. LEXIS 60, at *14 (Del. Ch. Apr. 16, 2009) (citing In re Appraisal of Ford Holdings, Inc. Preferred, 698 A.2d 973 (Del. Ch. 1997)). Although there are other decisions where the appraisal petitioner had owned preferred stock, the litigants in those cases treated the preferred stock the same as common stock for valuation purposes, and the Court did not, sua sponte, reject that approach.

112. Id. at *14-15 (footnotes omitted).

113. Id. at *21-22 n.25.

114. Id. at *21-22 n.25, 34.

115. Del. Code. Ann. tit. 8, § 155 (2007).

116. Applebaum v. Avaya, Inc., 812 A.2d 880 (Del. 2002).

117. See id. at 892.

118. Id. at 889..

119. See id. at 891.

120. Id. at 891 (footnotes and citations omitted).

121. Applebaum, 812 A.2d at 892.

122. Chalfin, 1990 Del. Ch. LEXIS 188, at *8 n.3

123. No. 97 C 7088, 1998 U.S. Dist. LEXIS 18864 (N.D. Ill. Oct. 30, 1998).

124. Id. at *17-20 (footnote omitted).

125. Applebaum, 812 A.2d at 891.

126. See, e.g., J. L. Schiffman & Co. v. Standard Indus., Inc., C.A. No. 11267, 1993 Del. Ch. LEXIS 143, at *6 (Del. Ch. July 15, 1993) (suggesting that the need to pay a "fair price" for shares eliminated in a reverse stock split exists, as a matter of fiduciary obligation, where the reverse stock split is accomplished to benefit a controlling stockholder).

127. See, e.g., Weinberger, 457 A.2d at 711.

128. Id.

Chapter 3: Dissenting and Oppressed Shareholder Matters

129. See, e.g., Poole, 243 A.2d at 69 (noting the affirmance of a Court of Chancery decision, which held that the measure of damage in a class action challenging a cash-out merger would be the difference, if any, between the consideration paid in the challenged merger and "the actual or true value of the stock . . . determined by considering the various factors of value . . . deemed relevant in a stock evaluation problem arising under . . . § 262"); Gesoff, 902 A.2d at 1153 n.127 ("in general, the techniques used to determine the fairness of price in a non-appraisal stockholder's suit are the same as those used in appraisal proceedings"); Del. Open MRI Radiology Assocs., 898 A.2d at 344 (concluding that petitioners had prevailed on their fiduciary duty claim because the merger was unfair, but noting that, "[t]he remedy for that claim, however, is identical to my appraisal award"); In re PNB Holding Co., 2006 Del. Ch. LEXIS 158, at *84-85 ("[T]o measure whether the Merger price was unfair, the court must conduct the same essential inquiry as in an appraisal, albeit with more leeway to consider fairness as a range and to consider the remedial objectives of equity."); Andaloro, 2005 Del. Ch. LEXIS 125, at *30, *32 (explaining in a "combined appraisal and equitable action," the appraisal value serves as "a proxy for the damages that would be awarded to any of the plaintiffs if they succeed in their equitable action" because the difference between the fair value of the stock as determined by the appraisal process and the amount of the merger consideration received "will usually be determinative of the damages question in an equitable action for breach of fiduciary duty, absent a basis to award rescissory damages or some other non-typical form of relief"); In re Emerging Commc'ns, 2004 Del. Ch. LEXIS 70, at *37-38 ("Because the plaintiffs' class action damages claim is identical (dollar-wise) to their statutory appraisal claim, the fiduciary "fair price," and statutory "fair value," contentions converge and are addressed in connection with the statutory appraisal claim."); Rabkin v. Hunt, C.A. No. 7547, 1990 Del. Ch. LEXIS 50, at *12 n.4 (Del. Ch. Apr. 17, 1990) ("It seems unmistakably clear from Weinberger that the determination of fair price in an entire fairness proceeding is the same as the determination of fair price in an appraisal proceeding."), aff'd, 586 A.2d 1202 (Del. 1990). See also Strassburger v. Earley, 752 A.2d 557, 579 (Del. Ch. 2000) ("where a merger is found to have been effected at an unfairly low price, the shareholders are normally entitled to out-of-pocket (i.e., compensatory) money damages equal to the 'fair' or 'intrinsic' value of their stock at the time of the merger, less the price per share that they actually received"); Nebel v. Southwest Bancorp., Inc., C.A. No. 13618, 1999 Del. Ch. LEXIS 30, at *27-28 (Del. Ch. Mar. 9, 1999) (holding that proper measure of damages in "entire fairness" action challenging cash-out merger is the difference between the merger consideration and the "fair value" determined in companion appraisal action).

130. See Weinberger, 457 A.2d at 714 (stating that appraisal remedy may not be adequate in cases involving fraud, misrepresentation, self-dealing, etc); Lynch v. Vickers Energy Corp., 429 A.2d 497 (Del. 1981) (finding that Court of Chancery erred by limiting recovery for breach of fiduciary duty to the appraisal formula of damages).

131. Bomarko, Inc., 766 A.2d at 441.

132. See Kahn v. Tremont Corp., C.A. No. 12339, 1997 Del. Ch. LEXIS 150, at *15 (Del. Ch. Oct. 27, 1997). But see In re Loral Space & Commc'ns Consol. Litig., C.A. Nos. 2808-VCS, 3022-VCS, 2008 Del. Ch. LEXIS 136, at *95-125 (Del. Ch. Sept. 19, 2008) (adopting a balanced approach that weighted equally a comparable transaction analysis and the fair market value because the "market trading price [wa]s not an entirely reliable estimate of value" to remedy a breach of the duty of loyalty involving an interested transaction with a large stockholder that possessed positive, non-public information about the company's future prospects).

133. Metropolitan Life Ins. Co., 1998 Del. Ch. LEXIS 70, at *5-6. Accord Agranoff, 791 A.2d at 888-89 ("if a majority stockholder wishes to involuntarily squeeze-out the minority, it must share the value of the enterprise with the minority on a pro rata basis").

134. Courts in other jurisdictions have reached a similar conclusion. See, e.g., Woolf v. Universal Fid. Life Ins. Co., 849 P.2d 1093, 1095 (Okla. Ct. App. 1992) (holding that the same valuation standard applies where stockholders dissent from a major change in the Certificate of Incorporation as where the dissent is from a cash-out merger). Accord Prentiss v. Wesspur, Inc., No. 36321-2-I, 1997 Wash. App. LEXIS 637, at *10-12 (Wash. Ct. App. Apr. 28, 1997) (explaining that a different standard of valuation applies where the cash out is nonconsensual than where it is between a willing seller and willing buyer); In re McLoon Oil Co., 565 A.2d at 1004-05 (explaining the difference between the "fair market value" of shares and the "fair value" to which stockholders are entitled when they are frozen out of a corporation, and holding that "[a]ny rule of law that gave the shareholders less than their proportionate share of the whole firm's fair value would produce a transfer of wealth from the minority shareholders to the shareholders in control").

135. 506 A.2d 173 (Del. 1986).

136. McMullin v. Beran, 765 A.2d 910, 918 (Del. 2000).

137. Paramount Commc'ns v. QVC Network, Inc., 637 A.2d 34, 45 n.14 (Del. 1994). Cf. MacLane Gas Co. Ltd. P'ship v. Enserch Corp., C.A. No. 10760, 1992 Del. Ch. LEXIS 260, at *32-33 (Del. Ch. Dec. 9, 1992) (in assessing whether shares of stock exchanged for holdings of minority unitholders in a self-dealing exchange offer by majority unitholder

Judicial Valuation of Stock of a Delaware Corporation

represented a "fair price," the Court, applying Texas law, concluded that the shares must be valued on the basis of their market value, as opposed to their "intrinsic" or "fair" value, because the minority unitholders were not entitled to appraisal of the stock received and had no means of liquidating the shares for anything more than their current market value), aff'd without opinion, 633 A.2d 369 (Del. 1993).

138. See, e.g., In re Netsmart Tech., Inc. S'holders Litig., 924 A.2d 171, 208 n.118 (Del. Ch. 2007) ("As a theoretical matter, the damages inquiry of a Revlon case is relatively easy to frame – the difference between what the stockholders received in the deal tainted by Revlon violations and what they would have received had the directors complied with their Revlon duties.").

139. Smith v. Van Gorkom, 488 A.2d 858, 876 (Del. 1985).

140. Id. at 893.

141. Eisenberg v. Chicago Milwaukee Corp., 537 A.2d 1051, 1056 (Del. Ch. 1987) (citations omitted).

142. See generally In re Pure Res, Inc. S'holders Litig., 808 A.2d 421 (Del. Ch. 2002); see also Pfeffer v. Redstone, C.A. No. 2317-VCL, 2008 Del. Ch. LEXIS 12, at *20-22 & n.25 (Del. Ch. Feb. 1, 2008) (noting that there is no duty to offer a fair price when a non-coercive tender offer is made either by a controlling stockholder or by the corporation); In re The Limited Inc. S'holders Litig., Consol. C.A. No. 17148-NC, 2002 Del. Ch. LEXIS 28, at *35 (Del. Ch. March 27, 2002) (holding that Court will "not evaluate the wisdom of the bargain or the adequacy of the consideration" in a self-tender offer); In re Aquila, Inc. S'holders Litig., 805 A.2d 184, 190 (Del. Ch. 2002) ("Delaware law does not impose a duty of entire fairness on controlling stockholders making a non-coercive tender or exchange offer to acquire shares directly from the minority holders."); In re Siliconix Inc. S'holders Litig., C.A. No. 18700, 2001 Del. Ch. LEXIS 83, at *22 (Del. Ch. June 19, 2001) ("as a general principle, our law holds that a controlling shareholder extending an offer for minority-held shares in the controlled corporation is under no obligation, absent evidence that material information about the offer has been withheld or misrepresented or that the offer is coercive in some significant way, to offer any particular price for the minority-held stock") (quoting In re Ocean Drilling & Exploration Co. S'holders Litig., Consol. C.A. No. 11898, 1991 Del. Ch. LEXIS 82, at *9-10 (Del. Ch. Apr. 30, 1991)); Weiss v. Samsonite Corp., 741 A.2d 366, 371 (Del. Ch. 1999) ("The Board decisions under challenge here--to leverage the company and then distribute a substantial amount of cash to shareholders via a self-tender--are business decisions that are entitled to business judgment rule protection."), aff'd, 746 A.2d 277 (Del. 1999); Abajian v. Kennedy, C.A. No. 11425, 1992 Del. Ch. LEXIS 6, at *24 n.5 (Del. Ch. Jan. 17, 1992) ("I see the self-tender as a voluntary transaction; an offer slightly above the market that shareholders could take or leave as they thought most prudent. In that circumstance, the corporation had no obligation to extend an offer at only a fair price (i.e., a price that after trial would be judicially held to have been fair."); In re Ocean Drilling, 1991 Del. Ch. LEXIS 82, at *9-10 (Del. Ch. Apr. 30, 1991) (instructing that the controlling stockholder "was under no duty to offer any particular price, or a 'fair' price, to the minority shareholders . . . unless actual coercion or disclosure violations are shown"). But see Feldman v. Cutaia, C.A. 1656-N, 2006 Del. Ch. LEXIS 70 (Del. Ch. Apr. 5, 2006) (refusing to dismiss complaint where allegations of self-dealing relating to tender offer by corporation suggested entire fairness standard would apply because directors stood to receive a financial benefit not shared equally with the stockholders), subsequently dismissed on other grounds, 2007 Del. Ch. LEXIS 111 (Del. Ch. Aug. 1, 2007) (dismissing amended complaint because plaintiffs had no standing to bring derivative claims following cash out merger); Lewis v. Fuqua Indus., C.A. No. 6534, 1982 Del. Ch. LEXIS 575, at *7 (Del. Ch. Feb. 16, 1982) (rejecting the argument that the test of entire fairness would apply in the context of a tender offer by a majority stockholder because, among other things, "the defendants have assured the Court that no freeze out plan is now contemplated"); Joseph v. Shell Oil Co., 482 A.2d 335, 340 (Del. 1984) (observing, in the context of a tender offer by a majority stockholder that was to be followed by a cash-out merger, that "[i]t is elementary that defendants, because they stand on both sides of the transaction, are under a fiduciary duty to the minority stockholders of [the subsidiary]," and that "therefore, the burden of persuasion would fall upon the defendants [at trial]").

143. 672 A.2d 35 (Del. 1996).

144. See, e.g., In re Pure Res., Inc., 808 A.2d at 444-46; In re Aquila, Inc., 2002 Del. Ch. LEXIS 5, at *14; In re Siliconix Inc., 2001 Del. Ch. LEXIS 83, at *23; In re Ocean Drilling, 1991 Del. Ch. LEXIS 82, at *9-10.

145. Kahn v. Lynch Comm'cn Sys., 638 A.2d 1110, 1116 (Del. 1994).

146. Solomon, 672 A.2d at 39-40 (citing Lynch v. Vickers Energy Corp., 351 A. 2d 570, 576 (Del. Ch. 1976), rev'd on other grounds, 383 A.2d 278 (Del. 1977); Weinberger, 457 A.2d at 703; Eisenberg v. Chicago Milwaukee Corp., 537 A.2d 1051, 1056 (Del. Ch. 1987).

147. Id. at 37.

148. Solomon v. Pathe Commc'ns Corp., C.A. No. 12563, 1995 Del. Ch. LEXIS 46 (Del. Ch. Apr. 21, 1995).

149. See Solomon, 672 A.2d at 37.

Chapter 3: Dissenting and Oppressed Shareholder Matters

150. Additionally, it is noteworthy that the decision in Solomon was authored by Justice Hartnett, who also decided Joseph v. Shell Oil Co., 482 A.2d 335 (Del. Ch. 1984) and Lewis v. Fuqua Indus., C.A. No. 6534, 1982 Del. Ch. LEXIS 575 (Del. Ch. Feb. 16, 1982) – both of which arguably suggest that the "entire fairness" standard applies in the context of a tender offer by a majority stockholder, and neither of which is cited, much less discussed, in the opinion in Solomon. Thus, it is questionable whether Solomon would have swept these decisions aside without so much as mentioning the fact that it was doing so.

151. See, e.g., Nixon v. Blackwell, 626 A.2d 1366, 1380 (Del. 1993) ("a stockholder intending to buy into a minority position in a Delaware corporation may enter into definitive stockholder agreements, and such agreements may provide for elaborate earnings tests, buy-out provisions, voting trusts, or other voting agreements").

152. Id.

153. Tansey v. Trade Show News Networks, Inc., C.A. No. 18796, 2001 Del. Ch. LEXIS 142, at *25-26 (Del. Ch. Nov. 27, 2001) (quoting Wyndham, Inc. v. Wilmington Trust Co., 59 A.2d 456, 459 (Del. Super. 1948)).

154. Id. at *26 n.31 (quoting DuPont v. Del. Trust Co., 364 A.2d 157, 161 (Del. Ch. 1975)).

155. Id. at *26.

156. Miller v. Agranoff, 750 A.2d 530 (Del. 2000).

157. Id. at *26.

158. Agranoff, 791 A.2d at 889.

159. See id. at 890.

160. See, e.g., Lynch v. Vickers Energy Corp., 429 A.2d 497 (Del. 1981) (awarding rescissory damages calculated from the date of judgment to account for the incremental value enjoyed by the majority shareholder as a result of acquiring the stock of minority shareholders through a breach of fiduciary duty).

161. See, e.g., Strassburger v. Earley, 752 A.2d 557, 579 (Del. Ch. 2000).

162. Int'l Telecharge, Inc. v. Bomarko, Inc., 794 A.2d 1161, 1177 (Del. Ch. 1999), aff'd, 766 A.2d 437 (Del. 2000).

163. Glassman v. Unocal Exploration Corp., 777 A.2d 242, 248 (Del. 2001) (footnote omitted). In Brown v. Brown, 141 P.3d 673 (Wyo. 2006), the Court observed that "[t]he Weinberger decision by the Delaware Supreme Court is notable ... for allowing recissory damages in an appraisal proceeding." Id. at 682 n.18 (citing Robert B. Heglar, Note: Rejecting the Minority Discount, 1989 Duke L. J. 258, 265 (1989)). Weinberger, however, involved a challenge to the entire fairness of a merger and the Delaware Supreme Court explicitly noted that the "plaintiff has not sought an appraisal." Weinberger, 457 A.2d 701, 714 (1983). Thus, it would appear that the Court was mistaken in Brown.

164. Cede & Co. v. Technicolor, Inc., 542 A.2d 1182, 1186 (Del. 1988) (citing Weinberger, 457 A.2d 701, 711). See also id. at 1187 ("[I]n a section 262 appraisal action the only litigable issue is the determination of the value of the appraisal petitioners' shares on the date of the merger ... and the only relief available is a judgment against the surviving corporation for the fair value of the dissenters' shares.").

165. See, e.g., Montgomery Cellular Holding Co. v. Dobler, 880 A.2d 206, 222 (Del. 2005) ("Delaware law requires that in an appraisal action, a corporation must be valued as a going concern based on the operative reality of the company as of the time of the merger.") (quoting M.G. Bancorp. Inc. v. Le Beau, 737 A.2d 513, 525 (Del. 1999)); Finkelstein v. Liberty Digital, Inc., C.A. No. 19598, 2005 Del. Ch. LEXIS 53, at * 39 (Del. Ch. Apr. 25, 2005) (describing the Court of Chancery's task in a statutory appraisal as "the familiar one of determining the fair value of the petitioners' shares on the date of the merger").

166. The "original" version of the appraisal statute that currently appears at Section 262 of the DGCL was adopted in 1899. That statute consisted of a single paragraph, and it expressly directed that the dissenting stockholder was entitled to "the value of the stock at the date of consolidation." See 21 Del. Laws ch. 273, § 56. See also Chicago Corp. v. Munds, 172 A. 452 (Del. Ch. 1934) (observing that the dissenting stockholder was entitled to receive the value of the shares "on the particular date named by the statute for the valuation of the dissenter's stock, viz., the date of the consolidation"). The appraisal statute was amended a number of times between 1899 and 1976, and all such amendments retained the explicit statutory directive that the dissenting stockholder be paid the value of the shares as of the effective date of the merger or consolidation giving rise to appraisal proceeding. Prior to the 1976 amendment to Section 262 of the DGCL, the statute provided, in pertinent part, as follows: "If any such stockholder shall ... demand in writing ... payment of the value of his stock, the surviving or resulting corporation shall ... pay to him the value of his stock on the effective

date of the merger or consolidation, exclusive of any element of value arising from the expectation or accomplishment of the merger or consolidation." 8 Del. Code. Ann. tit. 8, § 262(b) (1974) (emphasis added).

167. A 1976 amendment to Section 262 of the DGCL omitted the explicit statutory directive that the dissenting stockholder be paid the value of the shares as of the effective date of the merger or consolidation giving rise to appraisal proceeding. That amendment effected a number of changes to the statute, including the substitution of a valuation by the Court of Chancery in place of a valuation performed by an "appraiser." See 60 Del. Laws ch. 371, §§ 3-12. According to the official Synopsis to the 1976 amendments, the changes that year were "designed to effect the procedural means by which a minority stockholder is able to obtain an appraisal" and there was "no intent to modify or affect the substantive law which is determinative of the right to an appraisal or the substantive law used to value shares of stock subject to an appraisal." See Synopsis to H.B. 916, 128th Gen. Assembly, 2nd Sess. Since 1976, various provisions of Section 262 of the DGCL have included references to the effective date of merger or consolidation for various purposes, but there has not been an express provision directing that the valuation be as of the date of the merger or consolidation giving rise to the appraisal proceeding. Accordingly, there is no legislative history that would suggest that the statute's current silence respecting the date as of which the valuation is to be made was intended to effect a change in the historical provision that the valuation be made as of the effective date of the merger or consolidation giving rise to the appraisal proceeding. Moreover, it is notable that the statute expressly directs that interest is to be calculated "from the effective date of the merger through the date of payment of the judgment." Del. Code. Ann. tit. 8, § 262(h) (2007). This provides implicit support for the statutory intent to have the judicial valuation determination made as of the effective date of the merger giving rise to the appraisal proceeding.

The Non-Delaware View of Fair Value in Shareholder Dissent and Oppression Cases

By Noah Gordon, Esq.[1]

Delaware's Court of Chancery and Supreme Court are recognized as the leading judicial authorities on corporate law, and many states follow Delaware's lead in adjudicating corporate law disputes. One area of corporate law in which Delaware courts have issued more opinions than any other courts is in the realm of dissenting stockholder actions, also known as appraisal actions.[2] Although Delaware tends to be at the forefront in setting corporate law precedent, when it comes to stockholder oppression cases for judicial dissolution, for example, California has the most case law,[3] and Delaware's approach is unique.

Although most states apply a fair value standard of value in dissenting stockholder and minority oppression actions, the statutory definition of "fair value" may differ from one state to the next, and the parameters of judicially created "fair value" in both appraisal and oppression cases may similarly differ among the states. Even if the same statutory definition of fair value is used, such definitions are sufficiently loose to endow the courts with broad discretion and leeway, so that different jurisdictions may develop different approaches to fair value using the same statutory definition. Although the different jurisdictions may differ in their view of fair value, one thing that is common to all shareholder dissent and oppression cases is that the meaning given to "fair value" will significantly impact all parties involved in the litigation.[4]

Thus, while it is critical to review Delaware case law to understand how fair value is applied in shareholder dissent actions in the great majority of states, it is likewise instructive to consider the viewpoints of other states that apply a fair value standard of value in such actions but depart from the Delaware approach in doing so. It is also instructive to see how fair value is handled in oppression cases, where the concept of fair value may or may not be the same as that used in appraisal actions.

To obtain this non-Delaware perspective of fair value, this article reviews select case law from states that apply a fair value standard of value to shareholder dissent and oppression cases, but that do not strictly follow Delaware precedent or principles in doing so. The article examines the difference between Delaware's and other states' conceptualization of fair value; the case law in dissenting shareholder cases; and the case law in minority shareholder oppression-judicial dissolution cases.

THE "FAIR VALUE" NOTION

In *Bell v. Kirby Lumber Corp.*,[5] the Delaware Supreme Court affirmed the Chancery Court's rejection of a fair value construct based on an "arm's length" standard, since such a standard "presupposes an acquisition value based upon the very fact that the company will not continue

The Non-Delaware View of Fair Value in Shareholder Dissent and Oppression Cases

in business on the same basis that existed immediately prior to the merger. It introduces another element, namely the value another would place upon it as a price for merger as opposed to the corporation's independent value as a going concern." In other words, Delaware's notion of fair value attempts to ascertain "the value of the company to the stockholder as a going concern, rather than its value to a third party as an acquisition."[6] Accordingly, Delaware requires that synergies that might occur as the result of a merger, acquisition, or similar transaction be disregarded in calculating fair value (since such synergies represent value to an acquiror).[7]

A few jurisdictions, contrary to Delaware, however, conceptualize fair value as the shareholder's pro rata share of the highest price a willing and knowledgeable third-party purchaser would pay for the company in an arm's length transaction. This construct emphasizes value based on value to an acquiror.

For example, in *Sarrouf v. New England Patriots Football Club, Inc.*,[8] the Massachusetts Supreme Judicial Court said that in an appraisal action "As a going concern, the value of an enterprise . . . . is the price a knowledgeable buyer would pay for the entire corporation . . . ." In that case, the entity being valued was the New England Patriots football corporation, and the court indicated that its fair value included what a purchaser would pay for the National Football League (NFL) franchise, the stadium lease, various contracts, goodwill, and other assets and liabilities.

In a subsequent case out of Massachusetts, *BNE Mass. Corp. v. Sims*,[9] that state's Appeals Court likewise said that "The task assigned to the court by [the appraisal statute] is not to reconstruct an 'intrinsic value' of each share of the enterprise but, rather, to determine what a willing buyer realistically would pay for the enterprise as a whole on the statutory valuation date." Thus, in that case, the appellate court reversed and remanded the trial court's determination of fair value where the trial court furnished no explanation for its implicitly assigning equal weight to values based respectively on actual trading price, on per share earnings, and on per share book equity, and where one of the trial court's own subsidiary findings had foreclosed the use of trade prices as a "principal index."

Similarly, in *In re McLoon Oil Co.*,[10] the Maine Supreme Court said:

> In the statutory appraisal proceeding, the involuntary change of ownership caused by a merger requires as a matter of fairness that a dissenting shareholder be compensated for the loss of his proportionate interest in the business as an entity. The valuation focus under the appraisal statute is not the stock as a commodity, but rather the stock only as it represents a proportionate part of the enterprise as a whole. The question for the court becomes simple and direct: What is the best price a single buyer could reasonably be expected to pay for the firm as an entirety? The court then prorates that value for the whole firm equally among all shares of its common stock. The result is that all of those shares have the same fair value.

More recently, in determining whether a control premium may be added to value under the 1999 RMBCA dissenters' rights definition of fair value, the Iowa Supreme Court in *Northwest*

Chapter 3: Dissenting and Oppressed Shareholder Matters

Inv. Corp. v. Wallace,[11] expressly rejected adopting the Delaware concept of fair value and instead relied on the "arm's length" standard where fair value is determined by what a willing buyer realistically would pay for the enterprise as a whole on the statutory valuation date. After reciting the Delaware concept of fair value, the court said, "While this position may be the law in Delaware, we choose to follow the position of jurisdictions who determine fair value based on 'what a willing buyer realistically would pay for the enterprise as a whole on the statutory valuation date.'" (citing *BNE Mass. Corp. v. Sims*). Accordingly, the court explained that it would be appropriate to add a control premium because "buyers are willing to pay a large premium when purchasing an entire financial institution as opposed to a minority interest. The minority shareholders are entitled to the proportionate share of the control premium [the entity] likely would obtain if the corporation were for sale."

Ohio uses "fair cash value" as the standard of value in dissenters' rights cases. That term is defined as:

> The fair cash value of a share ... is the amount that a willing seller who is under no compulsion to sell would be willing to accept and that a willing buyer who is under no compulsion to purchase would be willing to pay, but in no event shall the fair cash value of a share exceed the amount specified in the demand of the particular shareholder. In computing fair cash value, any appreciation or depreciation in market value resulting from the proposal submitted to the directors or to the shareholders shall be excluded.[12]

While this standard might be viewed as a variant of fair value, since it uses a willing buyer element and also incorporates the concept of fairness, it is arguable that this is closer to a fair market value standard given that it uses a willing seller-willing buyer test. Ohio courts have taken the view that fair cash value is not fair value. Thus, in *English v. Atromick Int'l Inc.*,[13] the Ohio Court of Appeals emphasized that "[t]he concept of 'fair value' is far different from the 'fair cash value' concept," and, based on this distinction, rejected precedent from jurisdictions using a "fair value" standard that held that discounts are inappropriate in determining the value of a dissenting stockholder's shares. The court accordingly permitted the application of both discounts for lack of control and for lack of marketability.

Louisiana also uses what it terms a "fair cash value" standard in control share acquisitions, but unlike Ohio, it defines "fair cash value" as "a value not less than the highest price paid per share by the acquiring person in the control share acquisition."[14] This definition seems to be more akin to the "arm's length" standard of fair value, discussed above, that is used in states such as Massachusetts. Similarly, in partnership withdrawal buyouts, Louisiana uses what it calls a fair market value standard, which, however, seems in fact to be a fair value standard in those situations where a minority interest is bought by the remaining partners: the value is a pro rata share of the value of the entire enterprise, with no application of control or marketability discounts.[15]

California uses a fair market value standard in appraisal actions and fair value *in liquidation* in oppression cases.

The Non-Delaware View of Fair Value in Shareholder Dissent and Oppression Cases

The appraisal statute sates:

> The fair market value shall be determined as of the day before the first announcement of the terms of the proposed reorganization or short-form merger, excluding any appreciation or depreciation in consequence of the proposed action, but adjusted for any stock split, reverse stock split, or share dividend which becomes effective thereafter.[16]

The dissolution statute states:

> The fair value shall be determined on the basis of the liquidation value as of the valuation date but taking into account the possibility, if any, of sale of the entire business as a going concern in a liquidation.[17]

Although the definition in the California dissenters' rights statute uses the term "fair market value," the inherent assumptions appear very close to the definition of fair value found in those states that follow the 1984 MBCA. Fair value on the basis of liquidation, as defined in the oppression statute, should be calculated as the liquidation value net of the cost of liquidation,[18] time value of money, losses associated with liquidation, and expense to operate during liquidation. From there, the difference between the liquidation and sale price of the company as a going concern should be determined and the probability of sale should be taken into account. In fact, a dual valuation is prepared.[19] Liquidation value is unique to California's oppression statute, in that most states look to determine only a going concern value. Thus, for example, in the California dissolution case of *Trahan v. Trahan*,[20] the court affirmed the appraisal of "fair value" of the corporation's shares as the value upon piecemeal sale of the assets, without taking account of uncompleted contracts (which potentially would have been quite profitable upon completion), where it was uncontested that the company could not be sold in liquidation as a going concern. Delaware, on the other hand, has expressly held that although liquidation value is a relevant factor in determining fair value, such liquidation value cannot be viewed as a substitute for, or interchangeable with, fair value.[21] In New Jersey, which, like Delaware, views going concern value as acceptable to determine the fair value of a dissenting shareholder's interest, where a sale transaction price is deemed to be fair value, and going concern value is merely used to corroborate that the sales price is an arm's length price, the court must provide its basis for accepting the sale transaction price over the going concern value.[22]

DISSENTING SHAREHOLDER ACTIONS

The "Fair Market Value" to "Fair Value" Continuum

Delaware takes the position that "fair value" does not equate with "fair market value." In *Tri-Continental Corp. v. Battye*, 74 A.2d 71, 72 (Del. 1950), the Delaware Supreme Court defined fair value by saying, "The basic concept of value under the appraisal statute is that the stockholder is entitled to be paid for that which has been taken from him, viz., his proportionate interest in a going concern. By value of the stockholder's proportionate interest in the corporate enterprise is meant the true or intrinsic value of his stock which has been taken by the merger." Most commentators agree that this oft-quoted definition of value differentiates "fair value" from "fair market value." The Delaware Court of Chancery subsequently confirmed this position: "The concept of fair value under Delaware law is not equivalent to the economic concept of fair market value."[23] While most courts follow Delaware's lead in this area, accepting that there is a distinction between these two definitions, and that they are not synonymous, not all do.

For example, the court (Wisconsin) in *Pohl v. Milsco Manufacturing Co.,*[24] attributed the same meaning to the terms "fair value" and "fair market value," saying:

> In cases where a ready market for shares exists, courts have used the term fair market value. Where no market exists, another valuation method is employed to determine the fair value of shares. Essentially, these values are the same, only determining fair value without the aid of a market place causes the court to adopt and recognize other methods of evaluation which are most equitable under the facts.

This echoes the view held by some commentators that "'fair value' is merely a judicial fiction, an imaginary market created for the benefit of minority shareholders to reach the best approximation of a 'fair market value.'"[25]

Other courts have indicated that use of a fair market value analysis may inform the fair value standard of value where such an analysis is a "relevant factor," and that although the market value may be accorded little or no weight by a factfinder, the fair market value analysis may not be excluded and must be permitted at trial.[26] The Eleventh Circuit, while acknowledging that "fair value" and "fair market value" are not synonymous, has also indicated that they are not "mutually exclusive," so that when "potentially distorting corporate actions" such as a merger or sale or not at issue, fair market value may serve as an estimate of fair value.[27] Additionally, some older cases have held that the market approach is dispositive in determining fair value.[28]

Discounts

A key characteristic of Delaware fair value cases is that "shareholder level" discounts for lack of marketability and lack of control are disallowed. Other courts determining fair value in appraisal actions have permitted, or would permit, such discounts, depending on the particular circumstances of the case.

The New Jersey Supreme Court in *Lawson Mardon Wheaton v. Smith,*[29] although rejecting the trial court's ruling that an extraordinary circumstance existed where the dissenters exploited a change that they had previously supported, nonetheless indicated that whereas marketability discounts generally should not be applied when determining the "fair value" of dissenters' shares in a statutory appraisal action, there are special situations where equity compels another result. The court added that "[t]hose situations are best resolved by resort to the 'extraordinary circumstances' exception in 2 ALI Principles, 7.22(a)." The American Law Institute (ALI) explicitly confirms the interpretation of fair value as the proportionate share of the value of 100% of the equity, by entitling a dissenting shareholder to a "proportionate interest in the corporation, without any discount for minority status or, absent extraordinary circumstances, lack of marketability."

In *Matthew G. Norton Co v. Smyth*, the Washington Court of Appeals ruled that a discount for lack of marketability was appropriate at the entity level, but rejected a "bright-line rule" that such a discount is never available at the shareholder level. The court indicated that shareholder-level discounts may be available where warranted by extraordinary circumstances. Accordingly, the court held that the trial court's decision would be affirmed to the extent that it was intended to declare that, absent extraordinary circumstances, no such discount can be applied at the shareholder level.[30]

Other jurisdictions leave the matter of discounts to the courts' discretion. An example is a 1997 Colorado decision:

> [O]ur review of the out-of-state cases cited by WCM reveals a majority rule that a marketability discount is not required as a matter of law but, rather, may be employed by a fact finder, depending upon the particular facts and circumstances. See *Perlman v. Permonite Manufacturing Co.*, 568 F. Supp. 222 (D. Ind. 1983) (applying Indiana law); *Columbia Management Co. v. Wyss*, supra; *Independence Tube Corp. v. Levine*, 179 Ill. App. 3d 911, 129 Ill. Dec. 162, 535 N.E.2d 927 (1988); *Ford v. Courier-Journal Job Printing Co.*, 639 S.W.2d 553 (Ky. App. 1982); *Atlantic States Construction, Inc. v. Beavers*, 169 Ga. App. 584, 314 S.E.2d 245 (1984); *King v. F.T.J., Inc.*, 765 S.W.2d 301 (Mo. App. 1988); contra *In re Dissolution of Gift Pax, Inc.*, 123 Misc. 2d 830, 475 N.Y.S.2d 324 (1984); *Raskin v. Walter Karl, Inc.*, 129 A.D.2d 642, 514 N.Y.S.2d 120 (1987).[31]

Illinois case law also leaves the question of applicability of both lack of control and lack of marketability discounts to the court's discretion:

> With respect to the Bank's argument that the minority and illiquidity discounts were arbitrary and lacked foundation, we find that the trial court acted within its discretion to apply such discounts even though not required to do so....[32]

In a 1997 Illinois dissenting shareholder case decision, after citing case law supporting consideration of a minority interest and a marketability factor, the appellate court decided that "[a]pplying such discounts is left to the trial court's discretion."[33] It should be noted, however, that since these cases were handed down, Illinois modified its dissenters' rights statute to provide that fair value is determined without discounting for lack of control, and, absent extraordinary circumstances, lack of marketability.[34] This change will inevitably reduce the courts' discretion in this area.

Similarly, the federal district court in *Swope v. Siegel-Robert, Inc.*,[35] interpreting and applying Missouri law, emphasized that its determination was discretionary:

Although both parties in their thorough briefs argue at various junctures that this case or that policy mandates that the Court apply or decline to apply discounts, the principle which emerges most strongly and clearly from King [*King v. F.T.J., Inc.*, 765 S.W.2d 301, 303) (Mo. App. 1989)] is that such a decision is discretionary. The Court's discussion of Missouri case law, as well as that of other states, must, therefore, proceed with the understanding that no law or policy requiring or forbidding the application of discounts may hold sway with the Court, which is required by its interpretation of Missouri law to rest its decision on its own discretion, after considering every relevant fact and circumstance.

However, on appeal, the Eight Circuit reversed as to the trial court's application of a discount for lack of control, and affirmed the trial court's refusal to apply a discount for lack of marketability—reaching its conclusion by relying heavily on Delaware precedent. In fact, the court noted the "compelling logic of the current trend toward disallowing" minority and marketability discounts in dissenting shareholders fair value appraisals, and concluded that the Missouri Supreme Court would follow this trend if presented directly with this issue.[36]

In Oregon, a marketability discount will be applied in a dissenters' case, but a lack of control discount will not.[37] In *Columbia Management Co. v. Wyss*, the minority shareholder elected to exercise his statutory dissenter's rights and the corporation valued his stock at slightly over $ 1,000,000. The corporation filed an action asking the court to determine the fair value of the stock. Business valuation professionals valued the corporation, adjusted for the shareholder's holdings, and applied lack of control and lack of marketability discounts. This value was accepted by the trial court but the Oregon Court of Appeals modified the judgment. The court held that applying a marketability discount was appropriate because the potential volatility in the corporation's value was a risk that anyone holding the shareholder's stock would have to accept and that risk would make the shares unmarketable if the price were simply their proportionate share of the enterprise value. The court said, "there are no hard and fast rules for determining the fair value of dissenters' shares ... . [However, m]arket value is certainly one approach to fair value, and a marketability discount would take that approach into consideration." However, the court held that applying a discount for lack of control was inappropriate because it would provide a windfall for the majority.[38]

Control Premiums

The Delaware courts have accepted the application of an ownership control premium in determining fair value under two delimited circumstances. The first is when the base valued is a publicly traded equivalent value derived by the guideline publicly traded company method, and the second is when valuing a controlling ownership position in a subsidiary company. The justification for adding the control premium is that a control premium may be necessary to adjust value of the corporation's shares, not merely the minority or majority shares.

For example, in *Rapid American Corp. v. Harris*,[39] the Delaware Court of Chancery valued Rapid American Corp.'s subsidiaries by the guideline publicly traded company method. The Delaware

The Non-Delaware View of Fair Value in Shareholder Dissent and Oppression Cases

Supreme Court affirmed the application of an ownership control premium, explaining that, "The exclusion of a control premium artificially and unrealistically treated Rapid as a minority shareholder." In *Hintmann v. Fred Weber*,[40] the court valued the subsidiaries on the basis of a simple average of the guideline publicly traded company method and the DCF method. Finding the case analogous to *Rapid American*, the court added a 20% ownership control premium to the resulting indicated values of the subsidiaries. The court has even added a control premium sua sponte where it believed that "The equity valuation produced in a comparable company analysis does not accurately reflect the intrinsic worth of a corporation on a going concern basis. Therefore, the Court, in appraising the fair value of the equity, 'must correct this minority trading discount by adding back a premium designed to correct it.'"[41] However, the Delaware courts have rejected a control premium where control cash flows are used as part of a discounted cash flow analysis,[42] and have expressly rejected the application of a control premium to a DCF valuation.[43]

While other jurisdictions have followed Delaware's reasoning in granting entity-level control premiums in certain situations,[44] others have not. As discussed earlier, the court in *Northwest Inv. Corp. v. Wallace*,[45] while accepting a control premium, reasoned that it was appropriate to do so not because a guideline publicly traded company method base value was involved, or because what was being valued was a controlling ownership position in a subsidiary company (although the case did involve the valuation of a bank holding company), but because the minority shareholders were entitled to a proportionate share of the control premium the selling entity likely would obtain if the corporation were sold.

In *New Mexico Banquest Investors Corp. v. The Peters Corp.*,[46] the trial court rejected the addition as a matter of law of a control premium to a base value determined by the guideline publicly traded company method. In that case, the minority shareholders argued that a 40% control premium was required to increase the total business value of the company arrived at under the guideline publicly traded company method. They cited to other jurisdictions, including Delaware, that, they contended, recognize "that when a publicly traded companies [method] is used in determining fair value . . . there is an inherent minority trading discount" because "the [valuation] method depends on comparisons to market multiples derived from trading information for minority blocks of comparable companies." They argued, therefore, that in reaching a fair value, an expert or district court must, as a matter of law, correct for the minority trading discount by adding back a control premium. The court, however, said, "[s]uch a premium is not consistent with the total value of a publicly traded corporation[,]" and "[the expert] failed to present credible evidence as to the basis for such a price premium."

On appeal, the New Mexico Court of Appeals affirmed. The court noted that the addition of a control premium, for reasons other than that the sale is of an actual control block of shares, may unreasonably burden the buyers or the buying corporation and may call into question the responsibility of the directors to the corporation's other shareholders in buying the shares for more than they are worth. The court said, [w]hile courts have dealt in a variety of ways with the allegations that a minority discount is built into the guideline publicly traded market methodology, there is by no means any consensus on the issue." (Citing John C. Coates, IV, "'Fair

Chapter 3: Dissenting and Oppressed Shareholder Matters

Value' as an Avoidable Rule of Corporate Law: Minority Discounts in Conflict Transactions," *147 U. Pa. L. Rev. 1251*, June 1999, at 1287). The court also quoted commentators who have argued that "… the addition of a control premium is inconsistent with settled corporation law and good policy that there is no basis for the assumption that market prices routinely build in a minority discount. In other words, the courts have gone too far in an effort to guard against minority discounts and have infringed on the legitimate rights of majority stockholders to enjoy the recognized perquisites of control."[47] Ultimately, the court espoused a case-by-case approach, giving deference to the fact finder in upholding or denying adjustments to fair value for a control premium or a minority discount. Finding that the trial court decision was supported by the evidence, and that the trial court correctly found that the minority shareholders' expert did not present evidence to support the addition of a control premium, the court ruled that the trial court had not erred in denying the control premium.

Subsequent Events

Delaware courts dealing with discovery issues in appraisal proceedings have permitted the use of post-merger information that may be probative of a corporation's value at the time of the merger. For example, in *Lane v. Cancer Treatment Centers of America, Inc.*,[48] the court allowed post valuation date discovery for a year after the action to test the value ascertained in a pre-merger discounted cash flow calculation. (The Delaware courts permit such an approach in breach of fiduciary actions as well.[49])

Other courts may not permit consideration of post-merger information. For example, in *Smith v. North Carolina Motor Speedway*,[50] the dissenters presented evidence of the growth and success of NASCAR, of which the company was a part, in the three years after the acquisition. The defendants, however, claimed that subsequent success should not be considered relevant if not fully foreseeable at the date of the event. The jury awarded a price much closer to the defendant's value, thus indicating that subsequent events should not be considered.[51]

In *East Park Ltd. Partnership v. Larkin*,[52] the Maryland court faced the interesting question of whether limited partners are entitled to appraisal rights comparable to those enjoyed by dissenting corporate shareholders, i.e., would they be entitled to receive the fair value of their partnership shares upon withdrawal. While the court determined that they are, since both withdrawing partners and dissenting shareholders are exercising a statutory right to withdraw from an entity and the entity is absorbing the withdrawing individuals' interests, the core issue was whether it was appropriate to apply discounts for lack of control or lack of marketability in arriving at "fair value." As to this issue, the court ruled that, ordinarily, discounts should not be applied since no open market transaction takes place when a partner withdraws from a limited partnership.

On appeal, the general partner argued that the trial court had erred in barring his testimony about post-valuation date events relating to the partnership's real estate venture, including the partnership's failure to realign a nearby street, the notification by the anchor tenant of its

The Non-Delaware View of Fair Value in Shareholder Dissent and Oppression Cases

intention to vacate the property, and the decline in rental rates. The appellate court rejected this argument, finding that the subsequent events were irrelevant given that Maryland's statute clearly stated that fair value is to be determined "as of the date of withdrawal." The court further noted that "Expert opinions as to valuation are not always correct; they are merely reasonable predictions based on certain assumptions. That those predictions may one day be proved wrong does not mean that they were unreasonable at the time there were made."

In *MS Holdings, LLC v. Malone*,[53] the company, a limited liability corporation (LLC), wished to form a new subsidiary to pursue a new venture, which required member approval. In addition, members were given the option to dissent. Malone, one of the members, voted against the new venture and pursued dissenters' rights in connection with the LLC's action, seeking fair value for his interest.

The company tendered $27,000 to Malone for his interest, even though its analysis indicated that its value was zero. Malone, however, demanded close to $2.7 million and the company brought suit for judicial appraisal and attorneys' fees. A court-appointed appraiser concluded that Malone's interest was nominal if the value excluded any future business prospects. If he considered the prospects for the future, the most optimistic estimate of value would be in the $100,000 to $150,000 range. The appraiser also asked for a ruling from the court on whether the projected future performance of the subsidiary should be taken into account. The court ruled that Malone could not simultaneously dissent from the company's future business but also seek to benefit from any projected income that it might produce. Accordingly, the appraiser's report excluded projected future income and concluded that Malone's interest was worth only $10,000 as of the valuation date. Malone did not file any exceptions to the appraiser's report, and the court ordered him to pay the company $17,000—the difference between the $27,000 he had already received and the $10,000 appraised value of his interest—in addition to around $63,000 in attorneys' fees and costs.

On appeal, Malone argued that the trial court had erred in excluding projected income. In support of his position, he cited the well-known Delaware Supreme Court case *Weinberger v. UOP*,[54] which permits the consideration in appraisal proceedings of plans in place but not yet executed on the valuation date. The Tennessee Court of Appeals, however, noted that the estimate of future performance should not be used to determine value where the evidence is entirely speculative. In this case, the court found that the vehicle through which the LLC hoped to increase its earnings had not even been created on the valuation date nor had the contracts and licensing agreements which the LLC hoped would turn out to be profitable, been finalized. The court remarked that although the company's remaining equity owners hoped that their action would result in future profits, "as of the valuation date any future profits were just that, hope." Finding no justification for the Malone's demand, the court affirmed.

The outcomes in *East Park Ltd. Partnership v. Larkin* and *MS Holdings, LLC v. Malone* may not constitute a strict departure from the Delaware approach, since some Delaware decisions have held that it is inappropriate in the appraisal process to use speculative evidence of future performance or information acquired after the event giving rise to the appraisal proceeding. For example, the Delaware Court of Chancery in *Gonsalves v. Straight Arrow Publishers, Inc.*,[55] ruled that hindsight was an "inappropriate" means of determining whether earnings in the year preceding the merger were sustainable.

OPPRESSION ACTIONS

Unlike many other states, Delaware does not statutorily provide oppressed minority shareholders with a dissolution remedy, and only in the case of deadlock may shareholders file for the involuntary dissolution of the corporation (only Kansas and Oklahoma follow suit in this regard). In addition, the Delaware Supreme Court has rejected the judicial creation of special rules to protect minority shareholders of closely held corporations,[56] in part as a matter of public policy, since actions for oppression generally run counter to the doctrine of independent legal significance, given that the majority shareholder has not violated any specific provision in the state's corporations statute. Instead, the Delaware courts have left the question of minority oppression for review under an exacting "entire fairness" standard of judicial review, one component of which is "fair dealing" and another component of which is a determination of "fair price," which is akin to a determination of "fair value" in an appraisal action.[57] In certain circumstances, the effective remedy for oppression is the appraisal remedy itself. However, if controlling shareholders or directors have failed the entire fairness test, damages may go beyond the appraisal remedy. Conceptually, this is because the courts will treat the claims independently, as though there were an appraisal action and, in addition, a separate breach of fiduciary duty action.[58] Delaware's approach in the minority oppression area is unique, and there is little uniformity in the approaches taken by the other states; "[a] true legislative and judicial patchwork has emerged."[59]

Discounts

Although there is little uniformity in the remedy for minority oppression, as with the appraisal remedy, there are key issues involved in the determination of fair value for oppressed minority shareholders. One of the most significant issues is whether discounts may be applied at the shareholder level, which Delaware does not permit.

A Minnesota case, for example, did not take the Delaware approach in *Advanced Communication Design, Inc. v. Follett*,[60] where a minority shareholder in a closely held corporation sought dissolution as a counterclaim to the company's suit against him for breach of fiduciary duty. The Minnesota Supreme Court reviewed the state's dissenters' rights statute and noted that it was designed to produce a fair and equitable result, and that allowing a marketability discount could enable the corporation to reap the benefits of oppression. At the same time, the court chose not to apply a bright line rule barring marketability discounts in all cases as that may not be equitable from case to case. The court noted that the exclusion of a marketability discount in this case yielded a valuation that was in excess of the company's operating cash flow, net income, or net worth. The court employed a marketability discount to yield a more equitable value at which the minority shareholder could be bought out. This was viewed as an extraordinary circumstance, as recognized by the ALI in its definition of fair value. In another Minnesota case, *Helfman v. Johnson*,[61] (discussed below in greater detail), a discount for enumerated factors other than lack of control or lack of marketability was permitted.

Similarly, *Devivo v. Devivo*,[62] a Connecticut case, relying on *Advanced Communication,* found extraordinary circumstances where the company would not be able to achieve the liquidity to compensate the departing shareholder, so the court applied a marketability discount in order to be fair to the parties involved. Specifically, the fair value of the company was 1.6 times the company's net worth, more than 2.7 times its operating cash flow, and 7 times its net income for that year; this warranted application of a 35% lack of marketability discount.

In another Connecticut oppression case, *Johnson v. Johnson*,[63] the Connecticut court, finding that the alleged oppressive conduct (failure to declare dividends and to nominate the plaintiffs to the board) did not constitute oppression, assessed a 20% lack of control discount. The Court indicated that the decision was within its discretion, and that assessing the discount was in accord with "sound business judgment."

It should be noted, however, that around the time these cases were handed down, Connecticut adopted the American Bar Association's 1999 Revised Model Business Corporation Act (RMBCA), which provides that fair value is determined without discounting for lack of control or lack of marketability.[64] This change most likely will impact Connecticut's case law regarding the applicability of discounts in the determination of shareholder fair value in oppression cases, since the courts typically look to the fair value definition in the state's appraisal statute for guidance in determining fair value in oppression cases—notwithstanding the ALI's position that fair value can be viewed differently for oppression and dissent cases. In fact, some courts have expressly indicated that they believe that the meaning of fair value is the same in both the shareholder dissent and shareholder oppression contexts.[65]

In *Balsamides v. Protameen Chemicals*,[66] a 50% shareholder claimed oppression and brought a dissolution action pursuant to New Jersey's oppression statute, which permits the consideration of equitable adjustments in case of illegal, fraudulent, or oppressive conduct. The trial court rejected the idea of dissolving the corporation, concluding that it was worth significantly more as a going concern. It concluded that a buy-out by the plaintiff shareholder presented the greatest possibilities of resolving the matter quickly and of maximizing the benefit to both parties. It reached this conclusion based on its belief that the defendant was more at fault; that the company's dynamic growth primarily resulted from the plaintiff's skill and connections; and that most customers viewed the plaintiff as the face of the company. Accordingly, the trial court ordered the defendant shareholder to sell his interest in the company to the plaintiff shareholder, and, in determining the fair value of the shares, accepted the plaintiff's expert's use of the excess earnings method, which resulted in a 35% lack of marketability discount. On appeal, the New Jersey Appellate Division reversed as to the discount, finding that such a discount was inappropriate because there was no sale of the defendant's stock to the public, nor was the plaintiff buying an interest that might result in the later sale of that interest to the public. On further appeal, the New Jersey Supreme Court reversed, concluding that the lack of marketability discount was appropriate in this particular case. The court reasoned that the discount would ensure that the oppressing defendant shareholder was not unjustly enriched by the undiscounted value of his shares since disallowing the discount would force the oppressed plaintiff shareholder to incur the effects of the diminished value if he were ultimately to sell the company to an outside investor.

It is noteworthy that the same day that it decided *Balsamides,* the New Jersey Supreme Court also decided *Lawson Mardon Wheaton v. Smith,* discussed above, where the court rejected the application of shareholder-level discounts in a dissenters' rights action.

As in dissenters' rights actions in Illinois, the courts of that state take the position in oppression cases that the issue of lack of control and lack of marketability discounts should be decided on a case-by-case basis depending on the facts and circumstances of the particular case. This approach was used by the court in *Jahn v. Kinderman,*[67] which said, "We believe that Illinois law firmly establishes that [shareholder-level discounts] [are] a matter for the trial court's discretion." (In that case, noting the preponderant view that such discounts are not to be applied in determining fair value, the court rejected the application of discounts.)

The New Mexico courts have "vast discretion" in deciding whether to apply discounts in arriving at fair value. In *McCauley v Tom McCauley & Son, Inc.*[68] the trial court applied a 25% lack of control discount in a closely held family corporation where it found that the minority shareholder had been frozen out of corporate management and profit sharing. On appeal, the plaintiff minority shareholder argued that had the court ordered liquidation, as she claimed it was required to do, she would have received her proportionate share of the corporation's assets. The appellate court noted that the trial court was not bound to simply order dissolution, but could choose from a variety of available remedies "including utilization of its 'reservoir of equitable powers.'"

New York courts have also permitted discounts in the determination of fair value and have ruled that market value comprises one component of fair value.[69]

Massachusetts courts have failed to adopt a bright-line rule against discounts and determine the issue on a case-by-case basis. In *Keating v. Keating,*[70] the 49% minority shareholder in a family-owned close corporation brought suit against the majority shareholder, his father, for breach of fiduciary duty on the grounds that by discharging him, his father froze him out of his stock ownership. The court found that a freeze-out had occurred and ordered a buyout. In determining the value to which the son was entitled, the court said, "The Court must decide whether it is appropriate to compute damages on the basis of the stock's *fair value* or its discounted *fair market value.*" The court also noted, "Where freezeout conduct is of an exacerbated nature without mitigating factors, then the remedy should include a punitive aspect. Conduct which intentionally inflicts injury on a blameless fiduciary is an example of conduct that warrants no marketability discount. On the other hand, the absence of a *mens rea* may well warrant consideration of

The Non-Delaware View of Fair Value in Shareholder Dissent and Oppression Cases

mitigation and the award of compensatory damages which more approximates fair market value damages." The court held that the father's decision to discharge the son "was a highly emotional one without an analysis of the repercussions" and, thus, found discounts appropriate since there were no exacerbating factors. Significantly, the court considered the conduct of the parties when determining whether to apply a discount.

Similarly, in the New York case, *In the Matter of Markman,*[71] a 50% shareholder in each of three closely held corporations petitioned for judicial dissolution, alleging wrongdoing, including that the manager/director had paid himself excessive compensation, purchased his wife a life insurance policy, and rented a luxury car for their personal use. In response, the nonpetitioning shareholders invoked their statutory right to purchase the petitioner's shares and avoid liquidation.

The parties submitted the issue of the fair value of the petitioner's shares in two corporations to a special referee, but only the nonpetitioners offered expert valuation evidence. The referee relied on this evidence, accepting an income/investment value method to capitalize the excess earnings via a cash flow analysis for the first company, and accepting a comparable sales approach for the second company. Although the petitioner had not challenged either valuation or obtain additional expert appraisals, on appeal, the petitioner claimed that the referee had failed to adjust either valuation for the alleged misdeeds by the corporate director/manager.

The trial court agreed, concluding that the referee had erred in valuing the shares of the first corporation without considering petitioner's allegations of misappropriation of corporate funds. The court reasoned that those allegations were relevant to the proper valuation of petitioner's shares if any alleged misconduct adversely impacted the corporation's value. In fact, the court said that the issue of misappropriation was "intertwined with the determination of 'fair value' of [a] petitioner's shares." If proven, the alleged misappropriation of corporate funds would have had a detrimental effect on the corporation's value under the investment value method. Specifically, net income would have to be adjusted by eliminating excess compensation and the unauthorized purchase of personal life insurance and rental of a luxury car. As for the valuation of the second corporation, the court ruled that the referee had erred in refusing to adjust the stock valuation by adding the corporation's excess cash. Accordingly, the court remanded the case to the referee.

In the federal case *Hall v. Glenn's Ferry Grazing Assoc.,*[72] which interpreted Idaho law, the court permitted a minority discount. Hall was a minority shareholder in Glenns Ferry Grazing Association (GFGA). The purpose of GFGA was to "engage in the business of providing . . . lands for grazing and recreational purposes." Dissension developed between Hall and the other shareholders, and Hall brought suit in federal district court for dissolution of GFGA based on oppression.

To arrive at a fair value of GFGA, Hall's expert used the adjusted net tangible asset method, subtracting tangible liabilities from tangible assets, and then adjusting for market value. The expert also used comparable sales of land. GFGA's expert calculated a minority discount of 8.74%, which the court accepted and applied. Hall objected to the discount. The court, however, referenced a comment to the appraisal statute, which states in pertinent part that "[i]n cases where there is dissension but no evidence of wrongful conduct, 'fair value' should be determined with reference to what [Hall] would likely receive in a voluntary sale of shares to a third party, taking into account his minority status." The court found dissension but no wrongful conduct, and, accordingly concluded that fair value should be determined by taking into account a minority discount.

Perhaps one of the first decisions to permit a discount for built-in capital gains under the fair value standard is the New York Supreme Court (trial court) decision in *Murphy v. U.S. Dredging Corp.*[73] In this case, the company held property with $11.6 million in capital gains taxes that had been deferred. After minority shareholders brought suit to dissolve the company, and the company agreed to purchase their shares at fair value, a key issue was how to handle the built-in capital gains.

The company's expert deducted 100% of the $11.6 million deferred capital gains tax to arrive at a company value of approximately $15 million, to which he applied a 15% discount for lack of marketability to arrive at a value of $12.8 million. The minority owners' expert deducted approximately $3.4 million in gains tax representing present value, assuming liquidation in 19 years, to arrive at a company value of $24.8 million. He applied no discount for lack of marketability.

The New York trial court agreed that liquidation was not imminent, but also found persuasive the minority owners' position that such liquidation would occur in the future after a lengthy holding period. Accordingly, it concluded that while a willing buyer would not expect to deduct the entire gains tax, some deduction for this tax was appropriate. The court reasoned that:

> ...under these circumstances with the [built-in gains] representing such a large portion of corporate assets it appears that a willing purchaser would expect to deduct the present value of the [built-in gains] tax along with a percentage for lack of marketability.

Therefore, the court deducted the $3.4 million present value of the gains tax liability and applied a 15% discount for lack of marketability to arrive at a net asset valuation of the company of approximately $18 million.

Valuation Approaches

In determining fair value, Delaware requires the consideration of "all relevant factors" and permits all current and customary valuation techniques,[74] including the asset approach, market approach, and income approach (also known as investment value approach). However, the Delaware Court of Chancery has expressed a preference for the discounted cash flow (DCF) method (an income approach method) because it values the corporation as a going concern, rather than comparing it to other companies.[75] Although Delaware prefers the DCF method, this method, which depends on reliable projections, will not be permitted where there are no reliable projections or the data supporting the DCF is weak. Additionally, the type of business may lead to a different approach to valuation. For example, in *Highfields Capital, Ltd. v. AXA Financial, Inc.*,[76] the case involved an insurance company. In that case, the Delaware Court of

The Non-Delaware View of Fair Value in Shareholder Dissent and Oppression Cases

Chancery held that a combined sum-of-the-parts and shared synergies analysis was more appropriate than a DCF analysis for an insurance company.

Departing from Delaware's preference for the DCF method, New Jersey has permitted the excess earnings method to determine fair value. In *Balsamides v. Protameen Chemicals, Inc.*,[77] an oppression case, the excess earnings method was used by the plaintiff's expert, and accepted by the New Jersey Supreme Court, because the defendants would not provide the information needed to employ any other method. The court indicated that although the excess earnings method is not preferred, it is acceptable.

In *Helfman v. Johnson*,[78] the appraisal expert for the minority shareholder in an oppression case used the income approach to arrive at a value for the company of $1.85 million, whereas the opposing expert used an adjusted assets method to reach a value of $11,000. The trial court found that the valuation by the minority shareholder's expert was "overly optimistic," based largely on past performance, and that the valuation by the majority's expert was "unrealistically low," because it did not value the business as a going concern. Finding neither approach persuasive, the court arrived at fair value by bridging the values reached by the opposing experts through the use of a 24.6% discount related to specific circumstances—1) the lack of a non-compete agreement; 2) the lack of employment contracts binding employees; and 3) a declining market at the valuation date—rather than to lack of control or lack of marketability. The Minnesota Court of Appeals affirmed, finding that the evidence supported the discount and the trial court's methodology.

California's Notion of Fair Value in Oppression-Dissolution Cases

As indicated earlier, California's minority oppression dissolution statute, California Corporations Code § 2000, which must be invoked by the majority shareholder(s) seeking to avoid dissolution, provides that a complaining minority shareholder who seeks dissolution of the corporation is entitled to "fair value." However, unlike "fair value" in most states, fair value in California is "determined on the basis of the liquidation value as of the valuation date but taking into account the possibility, if any, of sale of the entire business as a going concern in a liquidation."[79]

As in Delaware, "fair value" in California does not mean "fair market value." Not only did the California legislature not use the term "fair market value" (which it used in the state's appraisal statute), but the elements of "fair value" provided in § 2000 do not include some of the elements typically found in a "fair market value" standard, such as a willing buyer and seller. Instead, the seller (the majority) is unwilling and is under a compulsion to sell. For example, in *Ronald v. 4-C's Packaging Inc.*,[80] the court rejected a valuation that assumed that "fair value" in § 2000 is the equivalent of "fair market value" and accordingly the court rejected an appraisal that relied solely on a price-earnings ratio analysis.

Notwithstanding that a "fair value" determination, and not a "fair market value" determination, is the goal, § 2000 can require a valuation exercise that is conducted in connection with a

Chapter 3: Dissenting and Oppressed Shareholder Matters

fair market value analysis: a determination of value based on a hypothetical willing buyer and hypothetical willing seller. That is because there is inherent in § 2000 a dual valuation concept. The first value to be determined is the piecemeal liquidation value of the company's assets. The second is the company's going concern value in liquidation, if a going concern in liquidation sale is possible, which means that an appraiser must evaluate the possibility that a buyer can be found for the company before its assets are liquidated piecemeal.[81] Because the going concern in liquidation value must be determined where such a going concern sale is possible:

> [S]ection 2000 necessarily requires that the appraisers contemplate a hypothetical sale scenario: *a sale of the entire corporation, in a liquidation setting, on the valuation date.* Further, since the corporation will almost always be closely held, "there will be no actual market value or any actual cash sales by which the market value could be determined. Therefore, the value to be determined must necessarily be a constructed or hypothetical market value at which the hypothetical willing seller would sell and the hypothetical willing buyer would purchase." (Citing 2 Marsh et al. Cal. Corporation Law, (4th ed. 2001 supp.) § 21.08[C], pp. 21-45.)[82]

Thus, in *Mart v. Severson*,[83] the California Court of Appeals held that the appraisers applied § 2000 properly by assuming that a hypothetical willing seller of the corporation would execute a covenant not to compete with the corporation after the sale, and reversed the trial court's decision that rejected the appraisers' fair value determination because it found that determination was premised upon the execution of an effective covenant not to compete by the parties and no such covenant had been or could be executed in the case. In that case, the court also indicated that the appraisers should assume that the parties to the hypothetical sale would negotiate the other requisite terms to the hypothetical sale agreement, which presumably could include employment agreements, warranties, representations, indemnities, and other terms that might not be given in reality. It can thus be seen that, unlike the notion of fair value in Delaware, the notion of fair value in California can encompass fictitious covenants and terms—which tend to increase the value being determined—as part of a hypothetical willing buyer and willing seller transaction.

One of the factors that must be accounted for in a § 2000 fair value determination is pending derivative litigation. Thus, in *Cotton v. Expo Power Systems, Inc.*,[84] the court held that it was inappropriate to affirm a valuation that did not account for such litigation and to defer the buyout date until after the resolution of a related derivative action. In that case, Cotton, a 33% minority shareholder in Expo Power Systems, Inc. (Expo) brought two actions against the company's majority owners for their alleged breach of fiduciary duties. In one action, Cotton sought statutory dissolution of the company. In the other, he brought shareholder derivative claims, accusing the majority shareholders of diverting Expo's assets for their own use. While the derivative action was still pending, the majority shareholders invoked their § 2000 rights to purchase Cotton's interest.

Because the parties could not agree on value, the trial court appointed three independent appraisers to value Expo. The appraisers indicated in their valuation report and responses to interrogatories that they did not attempt to value Cotton's derivative claims and did not take

The Non-Delaware View of Fair Value in Shareholder Dissent and Oppression Cases

those claims into account in determining the fair value of his shares. Rather, they recommended that the purchase of the shares be conditioned on Expo's assignment of the derivative claims to Cotton. The appraisers took this position because they believed that they could not extend their authority to a "quasi-judicial" evaluation of the shareholder suit, and because they did not want to burden the parties with the cost of valuing claims that the court would eventually resolve. In particular, they opined "that no reasonable buyer would increase whatever amount he would otherwise pay for the business to obtain the benefits of the disputed claims. ...If anything, a reasonable buyer might place a relatively high valuation on the expense and burden of litigation as well as the risk of loss. ...Accordingly, in the real world, a potential buyer might reduce whatever amount he would otherwise pay." They valued Expo at $100,000, and the trial court adopted this value, concluding that it could not determine the impact, if any, of the pending derivative action. For this reason, it deferred the majority's purchase of the Cotton's shares until after the parties completed the litigation, and noted that if either side disputed Expo's fair value at that time, they could file a motion for adjustment.

On appeal by the majority shareholders, the California Court of Appeals reversed and remanded, ruling that deferring the majority shareholder's repurchase until after resolution of the derivative action did not comply with the statutory appraisal scheme, which "mandates" determination of the company's fair value as of the date a dissolution suit begins. Because the appraisal did not take into account the effect of the derivative action, the court held it was incomplete as a matter of law. The court also ruled that conditioning the buyout on the company's assignment of the litigation would be contrary to shareholder derivative law, which requires that a plaintiff shareholder maintain continuous ownership throughout the proceedings; if such ownership ceases, the plaintiff lacks standing and any financial interest in a recovery that inures to the company's benefit.

Summary

This article has highlighted some of the key differences between the Delaware approach to determining fair value in dissenting stockholder and oppressed minority shareholder action, and the approach taken by other jurisdictions. The non-Delaware approach in most instances is clearly the minority viewpoint. In dissenters' rights cases, the national trend is to follow Delaware's lead, by disallowing shareholder-level discounts, by permitting entity-level control premiums, and by allowing the use of post-merger information that may be probative of a corporation's value at the time of the merger. All states permit the use of current and customary valuation techniques, including the asset approach, market approach, and income approach. While Delaware favors the discounted cash flow method as a general rule, others state permit less favored approaches, such as the excess earnings approach. Many of these principles have carried over to judicial dissolution-minority oppression cases, but in that area the law among the states is still a patchwork, and some states, like California, have a unique paradigm for determining fair value in this context. While it is almost universally recognized that the meaning of "fair value" is not the same as "fair market value," a small number of exceptions to this principle exist in cases with

Chapter 3: Dissenting and Oppressed Shareholder Matters

unique facts and circumstances, and, on rare occasion, fair value may be determined through a hypothetical willing seller-hypothetical willing buyer analysis.

Because dissenters' rights actions and shareholder oppression-judicial dissolution actions are becoming more common, and the definition of fair value is continuing to evolve, it is important that valuation professionals and attorneys keep up with case law precedent not only from the state in which suit is brought, but also from other precedent-setting jurisdictions such as Delaware, as to the parameters of fair value—many of which were discussed in this article.

---

1. Noah J. Gordon serves as Legal Counsel for Shannon Pratt Valuations, Inc. Mr. Gordon is a regular contributor to valuation and legal publications. This article was written for the first version of this Guide and was updated by the author in 2009.
2. Shannon P. Pratt with Alina V. Niculita, *Valuing a Business: The Analysis and Appraisal of Closely Held Companies*, 5th ed. (New York: McGraw-Hill, 2008), p. 916.
3. Ibid. See also Arthur Shartsis' and Tom Pastore's contributions to this *Guide*.
4. For a general discussion of the fair value standard in shareholder dissent and oppression cases, see Jay E. Fishman, Shannon P. Pratt and William J. Morrison, *Standards of Value: Theory and Applications* (New York: John Wiley & Sons, 2007).
5. *Bell v. Kirby Lumber Corp.*, 413 A.2d 137 (Del. 1980).
6. *M.P.M. Enters. v. Gilbert*, 731 A.2d 790, 795 (Del. 1999).
7. See, e.g., *Montgomery Cellular Holding Co. v. Dobler*, 880 A.2d 206 (Del. 2005).
8. *Sarrouf v. New England Patriots Football Club, Inc.*, 492 N.E.2d 1122 (Mass. 1986).
9. *BNE Mass. Corp. v. Sims*, 588 N.E.2d 14 (Mass. App. Ct. 1992).
10. *In re McLoon Oil Co.*, 565 A.2d 997, 1004 (Me. 1989).
11. *Northwest Inv. Corp. v. Wallace*, 741 N.W.2d 782 (Iowa 2007).
12. Ohio Rev. Code Ann. § 1701.85.
13. *English v. Atromick Int'l Inc.*, 2000 Ohio App. LEXIS 3580 (Ohio Ct. App. 2000).
14. La. R.S. § 12:140.2(C).
15. See, e.g., *Cannon v. Bertrand*, 2 So. 3d 393, 2009 La. LEXIS 11 (La. 2009) (the Louisiana Supreme Court held that it was error to apply minority discounts to the value of a partnership where the withdrawing minority shareholder's interest was being bought out by the remaining partners who intended to continue the business, reasoning that while "[m]inority and other discounts, such as for lack of marketability, may have a place in our law...such discounts must be used sparingly, and only when the facts support their use," and adding that when the remaining partners are the buyers of a withdrawing partner's share, the market value of the underlying partnership assets is the most equitable manner to value the shares at issue.)
16. Cal. Corp. Code § 1300(a).
17. Cal. Corp. Code § 2000(a).
18. Continued cost of operation unit liquidation is completed; Legal fees incident to negotiations and required liquidation notices and filings; Brokerage fees paid on sale of real estate and other significant assets; fees paid to auctioneers and others who assist in liquidating assets; Corporate income taxes that may arise from the disposition of assets; Accounting and other professional fees incident to the winding up of business; Legal fees incurred in resolving any outstanding contingent liabilities or other disputes; Cost of administer the liquidating trust which is often employed to marshal the sums to be distribution to stockholders; Reserve for contingencies; Employee termination costs; Payment of debts; Resolution of long term obligation, such as leases.
19. Arthur J. Shartsis,, "Dissolution Actions Yield Less than Fair Market Enterprise Value (Appraising for 'Fair Value' under California Corporations Code Section 2000)," in Chapter 6 of this *Guide*.
20. *Trahan v. Trahan*, 99 Cal. App. 4th 62, 2002 Cal. App. LEXIS 4216 (Cal. Ct. App. 2002).

The Non-Delaware View of Fair Value in Shareholder Dissent and Oppression Cases

21. *In re Shell Oil Co.*, 607 A.2d 1213 (Del. 1992).
22. *Holiday Medical Center, Inc. v. Weisman*, 2008 WL 2677504 (N.J. App. Div. 2008) (unpublished). In this case, where liquidation value was higher than going concern value—but less than the price at which the company sold—the court rejected the contention that as a matter of law the appropriate standard for determining fair value was "highest and best use."
23. *Finkelstein v. Liberty Digital, Inc.*, 2005 Del. Ch. LEXIS 53 (Del. Ct. Ch. 2005).
24. *Pohl v. Milsco Mfg. Co.*, No. 89-CV-02091, slip op. (Wis. Cir. Ct., Milwaukee County Jul. 12, 1991).
25. Robert A. Rabbat, "Application of Share-Price Discounts and Their Role in Dictating Corporate Behavior: Encouraging Elected Buy-Outs Through Discount Application," 43 Willamette L. Rev. 107, 123 (Winter 2007).
26. *Bair v. Purcell*, 2008 U.S. Dist. LEXIS 6518 (M.D. Pa. 2008).
27. *Cox Enterprises, Inc. v. News-Journal Corp.*, 2007 U.S. App. LEXIS 29533 (11th Cir. 2007).
28. See, e.g., *Gallois v. West End Chem. Co.*, 8 Cal. Rptr. 596, 600-01 (Cal. Dist. Ct. App. 1960); *In re Paterson & Hudson River R. Co.*, 94 A.2d 657, 660 (N.J. 1953); *Armstrong v. Marathon Oil Co.*, 513 N.E.2d 776, 787-90 (Ohio 1987); cf. *Oakridge Energy, Inc. v. Clifton*, 937 P.2d 130, 132-35 (Utah 1997) (holding that the trial court erred in relying exclusively on market value, but that the error was harmless in this instance); Jones v. Healy, 55 N.Y.S.2d 349, 359-60 (N.Y. Sup. Ct. 1945) (holding that market value was entitled to "particular weight," but it was not the only measure employed), aff'd mem., 62 N.Y.S.2d 605 (N.Y. App. Div. 1946).
29. *Lawson Mardon Wheaton v. Smith*, 315 N.J. Super. 32, 716 A.2d 550 (1999).
30. *Matthew G. Norton Co v. Smyth*, 51 P.3d 159, 112 Wash. App. 865 (Wash. Ct. App. 2002).
31. *WCM Industries v. Trustees of the Harold G. Wilson 1985 Revocable Trust*, 948 P.2d 36 (Colo. Ct. App. 1997).
32. *Stanton v. Republic Bank of South Chicago*, 581 N.E.2d 678 (Ill. 1991); see also *Swope v. Siegel-Robert, Inc.*, 74 F. Supp. 2d 876 (E.D. Mo. 1999).
33. *Weigel Broadcasting Co. v. Smith*, 682 N.E.2d 745 (Ill. Ct. App. 1997).
34. Ill. Compiled Statutes Ch. 805, §5/11.70(j)(i) (2008).
35. *Swope v. Siegel-Robert, Inc.*, 74 F. Supp. 2d 846, aff'd in part and rev'd in part, 243 F.3d 486, 492 (8th Cir. 2001).
36. *Swope v. Siegel-Robert, Inc.*, 243 F.3d 486, 2001 U.S. App. LEXIS 2760 (8th Cir. 2001).
37. *Columbia Management Co. v. Wyss*, 94 Ore. App. 195, 765 P.2d 207 (Ore. Ct. App. 1988).
38. But see, *Hayes v. Olmsted & Associates, Inc.*, 173 Or. App. 259, 21 P.3d 178 (Or. App. Ct. 2001), where the Oregon court rejected the application of both the lack of control and lack of marketability discounts in a shareholder oppression case.
39. *Rapid American Corporation v. Harris*, 1992 Del. Ch. LEXIS 252 (Del. Ct. Ch. 1992), aff'd, 603 A.2d 796 (Del. 1992).
40. *Hintmann v. Fred Weber, Inc.*, 1998 Del. Ch. LEXIS 26 (Del. Ct. Ch. 1998).
41. See *Doft & Co. v. Travelocity.com, Inc*, 2004 Del. Ch. LEXIS 75 (Del. Ct. Ch. 2004).
42. See, e.g., *In re Radiology Associates, Inc.*, 611 A.2d 485 (Del. Ct. Ch. 1991).
43. *Lane v. Cancer Treatment Centers of America, Inc.*, 2004 Del. Ch. LEXIS 108 (Del. Ct. Ch. 2004); *Montgomery Cellular Holding Co., Inc. v. Dobler*, 880 A.2d 206, 2005 Del. LEXIS 295 (Del. 2005).
44. See, e.g., *In re Valuation of Common Stock of Penobscot Shoe Company*, 2003 Me. Super. LEXIS 140 (Me. Super. Ct. 2003). (in a dissenters' rights action involving a small, closely held business, the Maine Superior Court permitted a control premium adjustment, concluding that the control premium could properly be used as an upward adjustment of the value of the subject company's shares when compared to similar companies in the industry); *Casey v. Brennan*, 780 A.2d 553 (N.J. App. Div. 2001) (entity level control premium required where an embedded minority discount existed and the premium was necessary to reflect market realities and arrive at the value of the company as a whole).
45. *Northwest Inv. Corp. v. Wallace*, 741 N.W.2d 782 (Iowa 2007).
46. *New Mexico Banquest Investors Corp. v. The Peters Corp.*, 159 P.3d 1117 (N.M. Ct. App. 2007).
47. Richard A. Booth, "Minority Discounts and Control Premiums in Appraisal Proceedings," *57 Bus. Law. 127,* November 2001, at 128.
48. *Lane v. Cancer Treatment Centers of America, Inc.*, 1994 Del. Ch. LEXIS 67 (Del. Ct. Ch. 1994). See also *Ross v. Proco Management, Inc.*, 1983 Del. Ch. LEXIS 494 (Del. Ct. Ch. 1983) (permitting discovery of post-merger events that

Chapter 3: Dissenting and Oppressed Shareholder Matters

are "reasonably calculated to lead to admissible evidence"); *Kaye v. Pantone, Inc.*, 1981 Del. Ch. LEXIS 607 (Del. Ct. Ch. 1981) (permitting discovery limited to time periods "reasonably related to the date of the merger" and stating that "three years after the merger should be an adequate time period").

49. See, e.g., *Onti, Inc. v. Integra Bank*, 1996 Del. Ch. LEXIS 52 (Del. Ct. Ch. 1996) (discovery of post-merger information permitted in breach of fiduciary action).
50. *Smith v. North Carolina Motor Speedway*, No. 98-CVS-3766 (N.C. Super. Ct. 2000).
51. Jay E. Fishman, Shannon P. Pratt, J. Clifford Griffith and James R. Hitchner, *PPC's Guide to Business Valuation*, 18th ed., Thompson PPC, 2008, at 1505.144.
52. *East Park Ltd. Partnership v. Larkin*, 893 A.2d 1219 (Md. Ct. App. 2006).
53. *MS Holdings, LLC v. Malone*, 2008 WL 1700156, 2008 Tenn. App. LEXIS 225 (Tenn. Ct. App. 2008),
54. *Weinberger v. UOP*, 457 A.2d 701 (Del. 1983).
55. *Gonsalves v. Straight Arrow Publishers, Inc.*, 1996 Del. Ch. LEXIS 144 (Del. Ct. Ch. 1996).
56. *Nixon v. Blackwell*, 626 A.2d 1366 (Del. 1993).
57. *Gesoff v. IIC Indus. Inc.*, 902 A.2d 1130, 1153 n.127 (Del. 2006) ("[I]n general, the techniques used to determine he fairness of price in a non-appraisal stockholder's suit are the same as those used in appraisal proceedings.").
58. See, e.g., *In re Emerging Communications, Inc. Shareholders Litigation*, 2004 Del. Ch. LEXIS 70 (Del. Ct. Ch. 2004).
59. John H. Matheson and R. Kevin Maler, "A Simple Statutory Solution to Minority Oppression in the Closely Held Business," 91 Minn. L. Rev. 657, February 2007, p. 661.
60. *Advanced Communication Design, Inc. v. Follett*, 615 N.W.2d 285, 292 (Minn. 2000).
61. *Helfman v. Johnson*, 2009 Minn. App. Unpub. LEXIS 212 (Minn. Ct. App. 2009).
62. *Devivo v. Devivo*, 2001 Conn. Super. LEXIS 1285 (Conn. Super. Ct. 2001).
63. *Johnson v. Johnson*, 2001 Conn. Super. LEXIS 2430 (Conn. Super. Ct. 2001).
64. Conn. Gen. Stat. §33-855(4) (2008).
65. See, e.g., *Balsamides v. Protameen Chemicals*, 160 N.J. 352, 734 A.2d 721, 1999 N.J. LEXIS 836 (N.J. 1999); *Robblee v. Robblee*, 68 Wash. App. 69, 841 P.2d 1289, 1294 (Wash. Ct. App. 1992).
66. *Balsamides v. Protameen Chemicals*, 160 N.J. 352, 734 A.2d 721, 1999 N.J. LEXIS 836 (N.J. 1999).
67. *Jahn v. Kinderman*, 2004 Ill. App. LEXIS 628, (Ill. Ct. App. 2004).
68. *McCauley v Tom McCauley & Son, Inc.* 104 N.M. 523, 724 P.2d 232 (N.M. Ct. App. 1986).
69. See, e.g., *In re Joy Wholesale Sundries, Inc.*, 508 N.Y.S.2d 594, 595-96 (N.Y. App. Div. 1986) (upholding lack of marketability discount); *Blake v. Blake Agency, Inc.*, 486 N.Y.S.2d 341, 349 (N.Y. App. Div. 1985) (discussing various components used to determine fair value and ruling that a lack of marketability discount is appropriate, but a lack of control discount is not, since the corporation would receive a windfall for electing to purchase the minority shareholder's stock if such a discount were applied); *In re Fleischer*, 486 N.Y.S.2d 272, 274-75 (N.Y. App. Div. 1985) (noting market value comprises one component of fair value).
70. *Keating v. Keating*, 17 Mass. L. Rep. 241, 2003 Mass. Super. LEXIS 472 (Mass. Super. Ct. 2003).
71. *In the Matter of Markman*, 2006 N.Y. Slip. Op. 26528, 14 Misc. 3d 910, 831 N.Y.S.2d 656, 2006 N.Y. Misc.. LEXIS 3969 (N.Y. Sup. Ct. 2006).
72. *Hall v. Glenn's Ferry Grazing Assoc.*, 2006 U.S. Dist. LEXIS 68051 (D. Idaho 2006).
73. *Murphy v. U.S. Dredging Corp.* 2008 NY Slip Op 31535 (N.Y. Sup. Ct. 2008).
74. *Weinberger v. UOP, Inc.*, 457 A.2d 701 (Del. 1983).
75. See, e.g., *Grimes v. Vitalink*, 1997 Del. Ch. LEXIS 124 (Del. Ct. Ch. 1997); *Gholl v. eMachines, Inc.*, 2004 Del. Ch. LEXIS 171 (Del. Ct. Ch. 2004); *Andaloro v. PFPC Worldwide, Inc.*, 2005 Del. Ch. LEXIS 125 (Del. Ct. Ch. 2005); *In re United State Cellular Operating Co.*, 2005 Del. Ch. LEXIS 1 (Del. Ct. Ch. 2005); *In re PNB Holding Co.*, 2006 Del. Ch. LEXIS 158 (Del. Ct. Ch. 2006).
76. *Highfields Capital, Ltd. v. AXA Financial, Inc.*,
77. *Balsamides v. Protameen Chemicals*, 160 N.J. 352, 734 A.2d 721, 1999 N.J. LEXIS 836 (N.J. 1999).

The Non-Delaware View of Fair Value in Shareholder Dissent and Oppression Cases

78. *Helfman v. Johnson*, 2009 Minn. App. Unpub. LEXIS 212 (Minn. Ct. App. 2009).
79. Cal. Corp. Code § 2000(a).
80. *Ronald v. 4-C's Packaging Inc.*, 168 Cal. App. 3d 290, 214 Cal. Rptr. 225 (Cal. Ct. App. 1985).
81. For a detailed discussion of Cal. Corp. Code § 2000's dual valuation requirement, see Arthur J. Shartsis, "Dissolution Actions Yield Less than Fair Market Enterprise Value (Appraising for 'Fair Value' under California Corporations Code Section 2000)," in Chapter 6 of this *Guide*.
82. *Mart v. Severson*, 95 Cal. App. 4th 521, 115 Cal. Rptr. 2d 717, 2002 Cal. App. LEXIS 791 (Cal. Ct. App. 2002).
83. Ibid.
84. *Cotton v. Expo Power Systems, Inc.*, 2009 Cal. App. LEXIS 158 (Cal. Ct. App. 2009)..

Report of Donald J. Puglisi in the matter of Laurel Gonsalves, Petitioner, v. Straight Arrow Publishers, Inc., A Delaware Corporation Respondent

*The following text is the introduction to a report from Donald Puglisi, Managing Director of Puglisi & Associates. Donald was working as the Delaware Court of Chancery's expert in this dissenting shareholder case. He was constrained by the previous experts' reports and findings, as well as the court's previous rulings, and sought to determine the correct methodology that should be used in this case. To view the entire report, as well as other complimentary online content available as part of your purchase of this Guide, please refer to the "Report of the Court's Expert" file available at BVLibrary.com.

I. INTRODUCTION

A. Overview of the Current Assignment

I have been retained to examine certain financial issues in the matter of *Laurel Gonsalves, Petitioner, v. Straight Arrow Publishers, Inc., a Delaware CoMoration, Respondent*, Civil Action No. 8474, in the Court of Chancery of the State of Delaware in and for New Castle County (Action). The Action involves, at least in part, events that took place in 1986. Petitioner Gonsalves was the owner of 2,000 shares of common stock of Straight Arrow Publishers, Inc. (SAP). Straight Arrow Publishers Holding Company was merged with and into SAP (Merger) on January 8, 1986 (Merger Date). In the Merger, each share of SAP common stock was either converted into the right to receive $100 cash or canceled. Gonsalves dissented from the Merger and undertook this Action to have the Court of Chancery determine the fair value of her shares, as of January 8, 1986 (Valuation Date), pursuant to Section 262 of the Delaware General Corporation Law.

The Court of Chancery has made two attempts to determine the fair value of Gonsalves' shares in SAP. The first attempt resulted in the Court of Chancery's December 5, 1996 Memorandum Opinion in this matter. That decision was appealed to the Supreme Court of the State of Delaware (Supreme Court). In an October 21, 1997 decision, the Supreme Court reversed, in part, the Court of Chancery's judgment and remanded the case to the Court of Chancery for further consideration that was to be consistent with the Supreme Court's decision.

The Court of Chancery's second attempt to determine the fair value of Gonsalves' SAP shares is summarized in a March 26, 1998 Memorandum Opinion After Remand and an April 20, 1998 Order. That decision, like the first, was appealed to the Supreme Court. In its January 5, 1999 Order, the Supreme Court affirmed in part and reversed in part the Court of Chancery's 1998 judgment.

Laurel Gonsalves, Petitioner, v. Straight Arrow Publishers, Inc.

Following the Supreme Court's January 1999 Order, the Court of Chancery, in an Order dated May 11, 1999, appointed me to serve as its Neutral Expert to present my expert opinions concerning the Open Issues that the Court of Chancery identified in its March 30, 1999 letter to counsel to the parties in this Action. Those issues are stated below.

B. Issues to be Addressed

Based on my understanding of the record in this Action, many, if not most, of the issues pertaining to the determination of the fair value of SAP's common stock on the Valuation Date have already been decided. However, four issues, three of which relate directly to a determination of fair value of the SAP common stock at the Valuation Date and the fourth of which relates to the rate of interest that should be paid Gonsalves for her foregone use of that fair value due her since the Valuation Date, remain open (Open Issues). Those Open Issues are the primary subjects of the analyses and conclusions that are discussed in this report.[1] Those issues, as set forth in the Court of Chancery's March 30, 1999 letter to counsel in this matter and that are more fully described and discussed below, are:

1. The treatment of deferred subscription income (DSI) in determining the proper measure of SAP's financial performance;

2. The capitalization rate used to bring the measure of financial performance to a measure of the value of SAP as an operating entity;

3. Excess cash that may not be needed for the operation of the company but which may accrue to the benefit of the providers of capital to the company; and

4. The appropriate rate and form of pre-judgment interest.

C. Summary of Opinions to be Rendered

Based on my review of the record that has been presented to me in this Action, I have concluded the followed with regard to the Open Issues:

1. The treatment of DSI as suggested by Gonsalves lacks a sound financial basis and should be rejected.

2. The capitalization rate that should be multiplied times SAP's weighted average five-year historical earnings before interest and taxes is 11.00.

3. SAP's proposed excess cash adjustment is incorrect both in the context of the valuation methodology advocated by SAP and adopted by the Court of Chancery and as a

Chapter 3: Dissenting and Oppressed Shareholder Matters

purely financial matter. From a strictly methodological perspective, SAP's cash and cash equivalents must be added to Enterprise Value less the effective amount of outstanding interest bearing debt to determine the value of SAP's common stock. From a financial perspective, SAP did not have a cash and cash equivalents deficiency, which would be the equivalent of an additional non-common stock claim on SAP's Enterprise Value. Absent such a deficiency, subtracting an additional amount from SAP's Enterprise Value in deriving the value of SAP's common stock is not warranted.

4. The appropriate rate of pre-judgment interest in this matter is a simple average of SAP's cost of borrowing and Gonsalves' opportunity cost. SAP's cost of borrowing, as derived from SAP's actual loan arrangements, should be measured as the prime rate of interest less .25%, compounded monthly to produce an annual percentage rate (APR). Gonsalves' opportunity cost should equal the return that she would have expected to have earned had she continued to own her shares of SAP common stock. Based on extant finance theory and practice, that return equals the return expected on a common stock whose systematic risk is equivalent to that of SAP. Given SAP's estimated beta, i.e., measure of systematic risk, of 1.0 versus the S&P 500 stock index, that return in this instance happens to equal the rate of return on the S&P 500 stock index. That return is expressed on a per annum basis. The annual APRs should be compounded annually to determine Gonsalves' cumulative rate of interest. Suggested alternatives to mv recommended rate and form of interest are presented in the body of this report.

In addition to the above, I have concluded that the fair value per share of SAP common stock on the Valuation Date was 5287.86 and that the fair value of Gonsalves 2,000 shares of SAP common stock was 5575,726.04 on the Valuation Date. The bases for my conclusions are discussed in detail below.

---

1. In pursuing this assignment, I found it necessary to also examine other issues that were, in my view, inextricably linked to the Open Issues. In this report. I have tried to make clear which of my opinions may stray somewhat from the Open Issues so that the Court of Chancery may give each of my opinions and their quantitative implications for the fair value of SAP common stock the weight the Court feels is appropriate.

The following is a presentation of abstracts from papers that have been recently cited by the courts in fair value decisions. To view the entire paper, as well as other complimentary online content available as part of your purchase of this Guide, please refer to BVLibrary.com.

Shareholder Oppression & 'Fair Value': Of Discounts, Dates, and Dastardly Deeds in the Close Corporation

By Douglas K. Moll, Esq.[1]

*Below is an abstract of this paper. To view the entire paper, as well as other complimentary online content available as part of your purchase of this Guide, please refer to BVLibrary.com.

Abstract

The task of measuring value is a task of great importance in corporate law. Indeed, the need to determine the fair value of close corporation stock has arisen frequently in recent years. This frequency has coincided with the rise of the shareholder oppression doctrine - a doctrine that seeks to safeguard the close corporation minority investor from the improper exercise of majority control. Over the past few decades, a number of jurisdictions have authorized, either by statute or judicial decision, a buyout of an oppressed close corporation investor's stock at the fair value of the shares. When a minority investor establishes shareholder oppression, in other words, the question of fair value often takes center stage, as the remedy for oppression typically involves a court-ordered buyout of the minority's holdings at a judicially-determined fair value. For shareholders seeking to exit an oppressive situation, therefore, fair value is a concept of considerable significance.

But what does fair value mean? The question affects the lives of countless close corporation investors. Two conflicting approaches to the meaning of fair value have developed. The first approach equates fair value with fair market value. Under this position, a court values an oppressed minority's shares by considering what a hypothetical purchaser would pay for them. Because minority shares, by definition, lack control, a hypothetical purchaser is likely to pay less for minority shares than it would for shares that possess control (the minority discount). Moreover, because close corporation shares lack a ready market and are, as a consequence, difficult to liquidate, a hypothetical purchaser is likely to pay less for close corporation shares than it would for readily-traded public corporation shares (the marketability discount). Under the fair market value interpretation of fair value, therefore, minority and marketability discounts are appropriate. The second approach to the meaning of fair value defines fair value simply as a pro rata share of the company's overall value. Under this enterprise value approach, further discounting for the shares' lack of control and lack of liquidity is inappropriate. Because the combined effect of minority and marketability discounts can reduce the value of a pro rata stake in a company by 50% or more, the propriety of discounts and the related debate over the meaning of fair value are issues of critical importance to close corporation investors.

Just as oppressed investors are affected by the meaning of fair value in a buyout proceeding, so too are they affected by the choice of the valuation date. As mentioned, the remedy for shareholder oppression typically involves a buyout of the aggrieved investor's holdings at the fair value of the shares, but fair value as of when? The date of the oppressive conduct? The date of the filing of the oppression lawsuit? The date of trial? The date of judgment? In the age of Enron and internet ventures, it hardly needs to be said that a company's value can change dramatically in a relatively short period of time. Given how quickly a company's fortunes can change, the question of when to measure fair value is a critical inquiry in and of itself, as the choice of date can have a significant impact on the ultimate fair value conclusion. This article grapples with the difficult valuation issues surrounding discounts and dates in the shareholder oppression context. The article methodically builds a case against discounts by using both conventional and novel arguments to support an enterprise value approach to fair value. In the course of constructing that case, the article challenges some of the traditional arguments that courts and commentators have routinely relied on (and still rely on) to reject discounts. By analyzing the shortcomings of those arguments, the article addresses the weaknesses of the case against discounts as well as the strengths. In addition, by discussing the importance of the valuation date and various factors that should affect its designation, this article adds to the fair value literature.

---

1. Douglas K. Moll, Esq.: Beirne, Maynard & Parsons, L.L.P. Law Center Professor of Law, University of Houston Law Center. B.S. 1991, University of Virginia; J.D. 1994, Harvard Law School. This article was originally printed in the *Duke Law Journal* (November 2004) and has been reprinted with the author's permission.

The Fair Value of Cornfields in Delaware Appraisal Law

By Lawrence A. Hamermesh, Esq. and Michael L. Wachter, Esq.[1]

* Below is an abstract of this paper. To view the entire paper, as well as other complimentary online content available as part of your purchase of this Guide, please refer to BVLibrary.com.

Abstract

The Delaware Supreme Court's opinions in Weinberger and Technicolor have left a troublesome uncertainty in defining the proper approach to the valuation of corporate shares. That uncertainty—increasingly important as going private mergers become more frequent—can be resolved by a blend of financial and doctrinal analysis. The primary problem—the potential opportunism by controlling shareholders in timing going private mergers—can be addressed by a more complete understanding of corporate finance. The definition of fair value must include not only the present value of the firm's existing assets, but also the future opportunities to reinvest free cash flow, including reinvestment opportunities identified, even if not yet developed, before the merger. This issue has been incompletely articulated by the courts. On the other hand, value created by the merger that can only be achieved by means of the merger itself—such as reduced costs of public company compliance—should not be included in determining fair value. We also show that except in the case of acquisitions by third parties (where actual sale value, minus synergies, is a useful measure of fair value), hypothetical third party sale value does not and should not ordinarily be taken as a measure of fair value.

---

1. Lawrence Hamermesh: Widener University School of Law. Michael Wachter: William B. Johnson Professor of Law and Economics; Co-Director, Institute for Law and Economics, University of Pennsylvania Law School. This article was originally printed in *The Journal of Corporate Law* (Fall 2005) by The University of Iowa College of Law and has been reprinted with the authors' permission.

The Short and Puzzling Life of the 'Implicit Minority Discount' in Delaware Appraisal Law

By Lawrence A. Hamermesh, Esq. and Michael L. Wachter, Esq.[1]

* *Below is an abstract of this paper. To view the entire paper, as well as other complimentary online content available as part of your purchase of this Guide, please refer to BVLibrary.com.*

Abstract

The implicit minority discount, or IMD, is a fairly new concept in Delaware appraisal law. A review of the case law discussing the concept, however, reveals that it has emerged haphazardly and has not been fully tested against principles that are generally accepted in the financial community. While control share blocks are valued at a premium because of the particular rights and opportunities associated with control, these are elements of value that cannot fairly be viewed as belonging either to the corporation or its shareholders. In corporations with widely dispersed share holdings, the firm is subject to agency costs that must be taken into consideration in determining going concern value. A control block-oriented valuation that fails to deduct such costs does not represent the going concern value of the firm. As a matter of generally accepted financial theory, on the other hand, share prices in liquid and informed markets do generally represent that going concern value, with attendant agency costs factored or priced in. There is no evidence that such prices systematically and continuously err on the low side, requiring upward adjustment based on an implicit minority discount.

Given the lack of serious support for the IMD in finance literature, this article suggests that the Delaware courts may be relying on the IMD as a means to avoid imposing upon squeezed-out minority shareholders the costs of fiduciary misconduct by the controller. Where either past or estimated future earnings or cash flows are found to be depressed as a result of fiduciary misconduct, however, or where such earnings or cash flows fail to include elements of value that belong to the corporation being valued, the appropriate way to address the corresponding reduction in the determination of fair value is by adjusting those subject company earnings or cash flows upward.

This approach to the problem of controller opportunism is more direct, more comprehensive in its application, and more in keeping with prevailing financial principles, than the implicit minority discount that the Delaware courts have applied in the limited context of comparable company analysis. The Delaware courts can therefore comfortably dispense with resort to the financially unsupported concept that liquid and informed share markets systematically understate going concern value.

---

1. Lawrence Hamermesh: Widener University School of Law. Michael Wachter: William B. Johnson Professor of Law and Economics; Co-Director, Institute for Law and Economics, University of Pennsylvania Law School. Reprinted with permission.

Chapter 4
Valuing a Business on Fair Value

Valuing a Business (5th ed.) on Fair Value[1]

Fair Value under State Statutes

To understand what the expression *fair value* means, you have to know the context of its use. For certain bookkeeping applications, fair value is defined in the relevant accounting literature. In business valuation, the term *fair value* is usually a legally created standard of value that applies to certain specific transactions.

In most states, fair value is the statutory standard of value applicable in cases of dissenting stockholders' appraisal rights. It is also commonly used in valuations in state minority oppression cases, which have been on the rise. In these states, if a corporation merges, sells out, or takes certain other major actions, and the owner of a minority interest believes that he or she is being forced to receive less than adequate consideration for his or her stock, the owner has the right to have his or her shares appraised and to receive fair value in cash. In states that have adopted the Uniform Business Corporation Act, the definition of fair value is as follows:

> "Fair value," with respect to a dissenter's shares, means the value of the shares immediately before the effectuation of the corporate action to which the dissenter objects, excluding any appreciation or depreciation in anticipation of the corporate action unless exclusion would be inequitable.[2]

Even in states that have adopted this definition, there is no clearly recognized consensus about the interpretation of fair value in this context, but published precedents established in various state courts have not equated it directly to fair market value. When a situation arises of actual or potential stockholder dissent or dissolution action, it is necessary to carefully research the legal precedents applicable to each case. The appraiser should solicit the view of counsel as to the interpretation of fair value and, in most cases, should not assume that there is a definition that is clear and concise.

The term *fair value* is also found in the dissolution statutes of those states in which minority stockholders can trigger a corporate dissolution under certain circumstances (e.g., California Code Section 2000). Even within the same state, however, a study of case law precedents does not necessarily lead one to the same definition of fair value under a dissolution statute as under that state's dissenting stockholder statute.

Several countries undergoing privatization have adopted the term *fair value* to apply to certain transactions, often involving specific classes of buyers, such as employees. Such statutes vary widely in their definitions of fair value.

Chapter 4: Valuing a Business on Fair Value

Examples of Matching the Purpose of the Valuation with the Standard of Value	
Purpose of Valuation	**Applicable Standard of Value**
Gift, estate, and inheritance taxes and charitable contributions	Fair market value.
Purchase or sale	Generally fair market value, but in many instances investment value, reflecting unique circumstances or motivations of a particular buyer or seller.
Marital dissolution	No statutory standards of value. Courts have wide discretion to achieve equitable distribution. Requires careful study of relevant case law.
Buy-sell agreements	Parties can do anything they want. Very important that all parties to the agreement understand the valuation implications of the wording in the agreement.
Dissenting stockholder actions	Fair value in almost all states. Consider relevant statute and case law to determine how interpreted in the particular state.
Minority oppression action	Generally, fair value in those states that address it at all. Not always interpreted the same as fair value for dissenting stockholder actions.
Employee stock ownership plans (ESOPs)	Fair market value.
Ad valorem (property) tax	Generally, fair market value with varied nuances of interpretation. In many states, intangible portion of value excluded by statute.
Going private	Fair value in most states; governed by state statutes.
Corporate or partnership dissolution	Fair value under minority oppression statutes.
Antitrust cases	Damages based on federal case law precedent; varies from circuit to circuit.
Other damage cases	Mostly governed by state statute and case law precedent; varies by type of case from state to state.
Financial reporting	Fair value, as defined by FASB.

Standard of Value

Fair value is a statutorily mandated standard of value. In the United States, it is applicable in almost all states to dissenting stockholder actions and, in the states that have corporate and partnership dissolution statutes, to such dissolutions. It is interpreted by judicial precedent in each state. As a generality, in most states it is a broader standard that incorporates market value along with values indicated by income and asset approaches. Therefore, we would say that a guideline publicly traded company method usually would be a part of the analysis when fair value is the standard.

Valuing a Business (5th ed.) on Fair Value

Dissenting Stockholder and Minority Oppression Actions

The incidence of adjudicated actions brought by minority stockholders increased dramatically from 1995 through 2005. All indications are that this trend will continue.

These actions brought by minority shareholders generally fall into one of two categories:

1. Dissenting stockholder actions.

2. Minority oppression actions. Either may be accompanied by claims of breach of fiduciary duty.

Dissenting Stockholder Actions

All states and the District of Columbia have dissenting stockholder statutes. These statutes essentially provide that if a company effects an extraordinary corporate action—typically identified in the statutes—stockholders may dissent from the action and be paid the *fair value* of their shares.

The "triggering events" allowing a dissent action vary somewhat from state to state. They apply in all states if a stockholder is forced to give up his or her stock, such as a cash-out merger (sometimes called a "squeeze-out") or a merger where the stockholders would receive stock in the acquiring corporation. In many states, dissenters' rights are triggered by the sale of major corporate assets, as defined in the respective states' statutes.

Most states require that if a minority stockholder wishes to dissent from a corporate action, the decision must be registered in writing at or within a few days following the stockholder meeting at which the action is approved by the majority of stockholders. This process often is referred to as *perfecting dissenters' appraisal rights*. The courts are virtually unanimous in prohibiting dissenters' appraisal rights unless they have been perfected within the time specified in the statute and pursuant to the procedures specified therein. In addition, there typically are other procedural "hoops" that a stockholder must jump through.

In virtually all states, the statutory standard of value is *fair value*. The Revised Model Business Corporation Act (RMBCA), which many of the states have adopted, defines fair value as:

> The value of the shares immediately before the effectuation of the corporate action to which the dissenter objects, excluding any appreciation or depreciation in anticipation of the corporate action unless exclusion would be inequitable.[3]

None of the state statutes gives any further definition to the standard of fair value. According to the official comment of the Model Business Corporation Act, the definition of fair value leaves to the parties (and, ultimately, to the courts) the details by which fair value is to be determined within the broad outlines of the definition. Thus, case law precedent provides guidance as to how each state interprets the standard of fair value. The interpretations vary greatly, as discussed in the next chapter, but virtually no state specifically equates *fair value* with *fair market value*. In some cases, the ultimate value standard that is applied is fair market value but this is a consequence of following the fair value guidance rather than the other way around. Many states have no precedential case law on fair value, in which case they look at decisions from other states for guidance.

In 1999, following the development of substantial case law on dissent and oppression cases, the RMBCA was revised so that the definition of fair value reads:

> The value of the shares immediately before the effectuation of the corporate action to which the shareholder objects using customary and current valuation concepts and techniques generally employed for similar businesses in the context of the transaction requiring appraisal, and without discounting for lack of marketability or minority status except, if appropriate, for amendments to the certificate of incorporation pursuant to section 13.02(a)(5).[4]

Although still not outlining a specific method of calculating value, the 1999 RMBCA definition adds two important concepts to the framework: (1) the use of customary and current valuation techniques, and (2) the rejection of the use of marketability and minority discounts except, "if appropriate, for amendments to the certificate of incorporation pursuant to section 13.02(a)(5)."

Very few states have incorporated this revision into their statues. However, some judicial decisions, even in states that have not incorporated the revision in their statutes, reference the revised version in rejecting minority and marketability discounts.

Interpretation of the Fair Value Standard in Dissent Cases
'That which Has Been Taken'

A typical interpretation of the philosophy of fair value in a dissenting stockholder situation is the following:

> Fair value, in an appraisal context measures "that which has been taken from [the shareholder], viz., his proportionate interest in a going concern." *Tri-Continental Corp. v. Battze*, Del. Supr. 74 A.2d 71, 72 (1950).[5]

The Delaware Block Method

Prior to 1983, dissenting stockholder cases primarily utilized the "Delaware block method." This method develops values in each of three categories:

Valuing a Business (5th ed.) on Fair Value

1. Investment value.
2. Market value.
3. Asset value.

Mathematical weightings are then assigned to the indications of value from each of the three categories (although the weight to one, or even two in extreme cases, could be zero), and the resulting weighted average is the concluded value.

Delaware Block Method—Sample Valuation Conclusion		Indicated Value per Share	Weight	Weighted Value
Investment value				
	Capitalization of earnings	$10.00	0.40	$4.00
	Capitalization of dividends	$6.00	0.10	$0.60
Market value		$12.00	0.25	$3.00
Asset value		$15.00	0.25	$3.75
Weighted value per share				$11.35

The definitions of *investment value* and *market value* in the context of the Delaware block method are different from those discussed in the three basic approaches to value.

Investment value in the context of the Delaware block method means value based on expected earnings and/or dividends. It is akin to the value based on the income approach in the three basic approaches to value. It may be arrived at by discounted cash flow (DCF), capitalization of earnings, or capitalization of dividends. In this sense, it mixes the traditional income approach and market approach in that it may derive capitalization rates either by traditional income approach methods or by traditional market approach methods.

Market value, on the other hand, has historically been based on prior transactions in the subject company's securities. This contrasts with the traditional appraisal concept of *market value*, where market value uses multiples of both income statement and balance sheet parameters based on comparable transactions.

A summary of a valuation conclusion under the Delaware block method would typically appear in the form presented in the Exhibit above.

Should Consider All Relevant Factors

A landmark case in 1983 decided that the traditional factors considered under the Delaware Block Rule alone were not necessarily sufficient; instead, "all relevant factors" should be considered. In that particular case, the court specifically made the point that projections of future earnings were available and should be considered. The court also made the point that a determination of *fair value* "must include proof of value by any techniques or methods which are generally considered acceptable in the financial community."[6]

The interpretation of fair value is a subject of continued debate and is difficult to generalize. Most states, however, have embraced the notion that "all relevant factors should be considered." Note that the Delaware block method factors are not abandoned by *Weinberger*; the case just states that all relevant factors must be considered. Both historically and currently, courts have treated *investment value* (defined in this context as value based on earning capacity) as the most important of the three categories of value.

Requirement for Entire Fairness

There are many subtleties to the application of fair value for corporate law purposes. For example, some states consider concepts of "entire fairness." There are two major aspects of entire fairness:

1. Fair consideration.
2. Procedural fairness.

Fair Consideration

The notion of fair consideration within the context of entire fairness also encompasses two criteria:

1. Absolute fairness.
2. Relative fairness.

Absolute fairness generally addresses whether the consideration received was adequate relative to the value of the interest that was given up.

Relative fairness means whether the consideration received was fair in comparison with what other stockholders received. For example, are the controlling stockholders receiving some consideration that actually should be shared with all stockholders (e.g., an "employment agreement" for which no services are required and which contributes nothing to the buying company)?

Procedural Fairness

Within the concept of procedural fairness, there generally are two broad criteria:

1. Independence.
2. Competence and thoroughness.

Independence refers both to parties affiliated with the company and also to outside legal and financial advisers.

If there are potentially conflicted board members, some companies appoint a committee of outside directors with authority to retain independent legal counsel and independent financial advisers, and to negotiate on an arm's-length basis. They have the fiduciary responsibility to protect the interests of all the stockholders, especially those not a part of the control group.

Independence with respect to outside advisers means retaining legal counsel and financial advisers who are independent of the control parties. Generally speaking, this means professional advisers who do not have a direct or indirect financial interest in the company or the parties to the dispute.

Competence and thoroughness similarly applies to parties affiliated with the company and also to their outside advisers.

It is not expected that board members themselves be expert in either legal matters or in financial valuation or deal structuring. It is, however, expected that they use prudent diligence and care in evaluating the qualifications of the expert that they choose to retain. It is also expected that they exert the time and effort necessary to understand and evaluate the recommendations of the outside experts in exercising their fiduciary responsibility to make recommendations in reliance on those experts. The experts merely provide advice. It is the directors who have the fiduciary responsibility to recommend action based on that advice.[7]

Consequences of Lack of Entire Fairness

Lack of entire fairness implies that the directors violated some duty owed to the shareholders. If the plaintiffs establish such liability, then the measure of damages may go beyond simply fair value as contemplated in the dissenters' rights statutes.

As explained by former Vice Chancellor Jack Jacobs of the Delaware Court of Chancery (currently a justice of the Delaware Supreme Court):

> The statutory appraisal case limits damages, on the upside, in that the value is fixed at one point in time, and is not supposed to include any synergies. There is no issue of burden of proof. If the court does not accept the valuation presented by one side or the other, it must perform independently its own valuation.

In a breach of fiduciary duty case, the traditional burden of proof rules apply, whereby if the evidence on both sides is even (we say "in equipoise") then the party that has the burden of proof loses.

Chapter 4: Valuing a Business on Fair Value

Another bright line difference is that in a fiduciary duty action, other measures of damages may be available, including damages calculated as of a date after the transaction. "Rescissory" damages would be an example. Damages measured by that method would be available in a breach of fiduciary duty action, but not in a statutory appraisal case.[8]

Minority Interest Dissolution Actions

An increasing number of states have been enacting "judicial dissolution statutes." These generally allow minority shareholders to sue for dissolution of the corporation or partnership if they can demonstrate minority oppression or a deadlock on decision making. As can be seen in the Exhibit below, a majority of states now have such statutes.

Dissolution Statutes
Has Judicial Dissolution Statute
Alabama, Alaska, Arizona, Arkansas, California, Colorado, Connecticut, District of Columbia, Florida, Georgia, Hawaii, Idaho, Illinois, Indiana, Iowa, Kentucky, Louisiana, Maine, Maryland, Massachusetts, Michigan, Minnesota, Mississippi, Missouri, Montana, Nebraska, New Hampshire, New Jersey, New Mexico, New York, North Carolina, North Dakota, Ohio, Oregon, Pennsylvania, Rhode Island, South Carolina, South Dakota, Tennessee, Texas, Utah, Vermont, Virginia, Washington, West Virginia, Wisconsin, Wyoming
No Judicial Dissolution Statute
Delaware, Kansas, Nevada, Oklahoma, Guam, Northern Mariana Islands, Puerto Rico, Virgin Islands
Adapted from: Jay Fishman, Shannon Pratt, and William Morrison. *Standards of Value: Theory and Applications*. Hoboken, N.J. John Wiley & Sons, 2006.

The triggering events vary from state to state. In some states, the minority bringing suit must constitute some minimum percentage of the ownership, while other states have no minimum percentage requirement.

In California, the leading state in minority dissolution actions, if stockholders owning 33.33% or more of a company's stock can demonstrate minority oppression, their remedy is a dissolution of the corporation. The majority stockholders can prevent such a dissolution by paying, in cash, the fair value pursuant to California Corporations Code Section 2000.[9] The following is the process involved:

1. Minority stockholders sue for dissolution.
2. The court determines whether conditions warranting the dissolution have occurred.
3. If so, and parties cannot agree on a price to buy out the minority stockholders, majority stockholders move to stay the dissolution pending valuation to determine how much the minority stockholders would receive if liquidation proceeded.

4. Court appoints three appraisers. Parties can agree upon, and seek court confirmation in an appointee process, or can allow the court to select the appraisers. Unless otherwise agreed by the parties, the conclusion of the appraisers is advisory to the court rather than binding.
5. The court adopts a value.
6. The court enters a decree "which shall provide in the alternative for winding up and dissolution of the corporation unless payment is made for the shares within the time specified by the decree."
7. The majority stockholders may elect to pay the amount in cash prior to the deadline.
8. If the majority stockholders decline to pay, the company is liquidated and all shareholders receive a proportionate share of the resulting cash proceeds.[10]

Interpretation of the Fair Value Standard in Dissolution Cases

Courts in different states vary from one to another (and sometimes from one case to the next in the same state) in their interpretation of fair value for dissolution cases, and may not interpret this standard in the same manner as for dissenting stockholder cases.

California has what might seem at first reading an internally contradictory definition of fair value in the context of its dissolution statutes:

> The fair value shall be determined on the basis of the liquidation value as of the valuation date but taking into account the possibility, if any, of sale of the entire business as a going concern in a liquidation.

While the above may seem abstruse at first blush, the evolution of case law makes it clear. The value may be based on a liquidation of assets and/or selling all or parts of the operations as a going concern if that would produce higher net proceeds.

In any case, as with fair value in the context of dissent cases, the definition of fair value in dissolution cases is missing some of the elements of the traditional definition of fair market value. As California corporate attorney Art Shartsis points out, many of the assumptions underlying fair market value are not present:

- There is no willing seller. In the dissolution the seller is involuntarily disposing of the assets.
- The seller is under compulsion to sell.
- The involuntary seller under compulsion does not have the luxury of waiting for a top offer; the sale must be completed under the adverse conditions of a corporate dissolution conducted in accordance with California law.
- Implicitly, the buyer is aware of the seller's weakened position.[11]

Chapter 4: Valuing a Business on Fair Value

Summary

Stockholder disputes that are resolved under the statutory standard of fair value typically fall clearly into one of two distinct categories:

1. Dissenting stockholder actions.

2. Minority owner dissolution actions.

Actions under both types of statutes have been on the increase in recent years. All states have dissenting stockholder statutes. The standard of value is usually fair value.

A majority of states now have "judicial dissolution statutes" which allow minority shareholders demonstrating oppression to sue for dissolution of the entity. To prevent dissolution, the controlling owners can pay the oppressed minority owners the fair value of their shares.

For both types of actions, the respective states' court case precedents interpret the standard of fair value. Some states do not have precedential case law on fair value, in which instance they tend to look at case precedents from other states. In almost any case, the strict definition of fair value differs from the traditional definition of fair market value, although, in some cases, the outcome is the same.

Dissenting Stockholder and Minority Oppression Court Cases

Delaware has by far the most judicial precedent in the realm of dissenting stockholder actions. Many states have none at all or none that may have addressed certain specific issues. When states lack their own precedent, they often look to other states' precedents.[12] Delaware tends to be the leader, but states also look particularly at decisions in other states that have statutes worded the same or similarly to their own.[13]

In the realm of stockholder oppression cases for judicial dissolution, California has by far the most precedential case law. As noted in the previous chapter, Delaware is one of the states that does not have a judicial dissolution statute.

A primary purpose of appraisal statutes is to protect minority shareholders and, to this end, courts generally give weight to the highest realistic price that a willing, able, and fully informed buyer would pay for the corporation as an entity.

Readers Must Interpret Cases Carefully

A study of the relevant case law is an essential prerequisite to estimation of fair value for either a dissenting stockholder action or a suit for dissolution in any jurisdiction. After having done

one's best, however, rarely will the reader have clear-cut guidance as to the court's likely posture on every possible valuation issue.

The facts and circumstances of cases vary significantly from one to another. Thus, while prior cases should be studied for guidance, one must be very careful in interpreting them as a bright line of final authority.

Former Vice Chancellor Jack Jacobs of the Delaware Court of Chancery, now a Justice on the Delaware Supreme Court, clearly sounds this warning:

> Both my Court and the Delaware Supreme Court recognize that valuation cases are *extremely* fact-driven. Very few conclusions on valuation issues have universal applicability, though statements found in some opinions may have the appearance, and might be interpreted by some, as having sweeping generality.[14]

A case in point is a decision by the Supreme Court of Kansas on a dissenting stockholder suit arising out of a reverse stock split forcing a cash-out of minority stockholders. The Westlaw head-notes make the sweeping statement, without qualification, that "minority and marketability discounts are not appropriate when the purchaser of the stock is either the majority shareholder or the corporation itself." It would seem misleading to accept this broad interpretation, since the question put to the Kansas Supreme Court was limited to a forced cash-out, not to all events that could trigger a dissenting stockholder action.

The question put to the Kansas Supreme Court was:

> Is it proper for a corporation to determine the "fair value" of a fractional share pursuant to K.S.A. § 17-6405 by applying minority and marketability discounts when the fractional share resulted from a reverse stock split intended to eliminate the minority shareholder's interest in the corporation?[15]

The court concluded as follows:

> In answering the certified question before us, we hold that minority and marketability discounts should not be applied when the fractional share resulted from a reverse stock split intended to eliminate a minority shareholder's interest in the corporation.[16]

The sweeping generality of the Westlaw head-notes combined with the actual very specific applicability prompted the following comment:

> I think that it is important to recognize that this decision's applicability is limited to the narrow circumstances of the question put to the court.... There are many other actions where dissenters' rights are triggered even though the stockholders are not forced to be pushed out, a fact set which would seem to be very distinguishable from this case.[17]

Chapter 4: Valuing a Business on Fair Value

Fair Value Is Not Fair Market Value

In most states, the standard of value for dissenting stockholder suits and for minority oppression suits is fair value.[18] Some states apply the fair value standard to withdrawing limited partners, comparing them to dissenting stockholders.[19] Several states statutes indicate that either "fair cash value" or simply "value" is the appropriate standard. The majority of states have adopted the fair value definition found in the Revised Model Business Corporation Act (RMBCA), promulgated by the American Bar Association. The RMBCA was revised in 1999.

Until 1999, the RMBCA definition was:

> The value of the shares immediately before the effectuation of the corporate action to which the shareholder objects, excluding any appreciation or depreciations in anticipation of the corporate action unless exclusion would be inequitable.

In 1999, the definition changed to:

> "Fair value" means the value of the corporation's shares determined:
>
> I. immediately before the effectuation of the corporate action to which the shareholder objects;
>
> II. using customary and current valuation concepts and techniques generally employed for similar businesses in the context of the transaction requiring appraisal; and
>
> III. without discounting for lack of marketability or minority status except, if appropriate, for amendments to the articles....

The majority of states use the pre-1999 definition, and only a handful have adopted the 1999 version. A minority of states use the pre-1999 definition without the "unless exclusion would be inequitable" phrase, and some states omit this phrase but, in addition, add a clause that states that all relevant factors should be considered in determining value. Florida uses a hybrid of the pre-1999 and 1999 definitions,[20] as does Illinois. The Exhibit below groups the states by the definition they have adopted. However, even some states that have not adopted the 1999 revisions in their statutes have adopted the language in their case law by reference. While the various states interpret fair value quite differently from one another, and sometimes differently under differing facts and circumstances, they do *not* strictly equate fair value with fair market value.

This point is illustrated well by a New York court's rejection of an expert's valuation report based on fair market value in a dissenting stockholder case. The court stated:

> Because the petitioner's expert …in its valuation report (on title page) and on 15 occasions refers to its valuation to be based on Fair Market Value, and the Business Corporation Law only uses the term Fair Value … the Court considers it a threshold question as to whether Fair Value and Fair Market Value are synonymous.

> The Standard upon which [the company's expert's] valuation was based was Market Value.... the statutory standard is much broader....The Court may give *no weight* [emphasis supplied] to market value if the facts of the case so require.[21]

The court ultimately did reject the report based on the standard of fair market value (concluding $52 per share) and awarded the dissenters $99 per share.

In *Le Beau v. M.G. Bancorporation, Inc.*, the investment banker had issued a fairness opinion on a squeeze-out merger based on fair market value rather than on fair value. The Delaware Court of Chancery stated that this was "legally flawed" as evidence regarding fair value.[22]

In *Pueblo Bancorporation v. Lindoe, Inc.*,[23] the Colorado Supreme Court, after an extensive review of the law in other jurisdictions, said, "We are convinced that 'fair value' does not mean 'fair market value.'" The New Jersey Supreme Court has expressed a similar sentiment,[24] as have the majority of other courts.[25]

In another Colorado case—but not a dissenters' rights case—involving a minority shareholder's challenge of a transaction as "unfair," in response to the shareholder's contention that no discounts should be allowed, the court admonished that "this case is not a dissenters' rights action....It involves the question of whether a transaction was fair, not the 'fair value' of dissenters' shares." Accordingly, the court held it was proper to discount the stock value by 15 to 20% for lack of marketability.[26] The case demonstrates the importance not only of being clear as to which standard of value is being applied, but also what kind of case is involved.

Chapter 4: Valuing a Business on Fair Value

States that Adopted the RMBCA Definition of Fair Value	
State	**Applicable State Statute**
Pre-1999 Definition of Fair Value	
Alabama	Ala. Code §10-2B-13.01(4) (Michie 2006)
Arizona	Ariz. Rev. Stat. Ann §10-1301(4) (2006)
Arkansas	Ark. Code Ann. §4-27-1301(3) (2006)
Colorado	Colo. Rev. §7-113-101(4) (2006)
Hawaii	Haw. Rev. Stat. §414-341 (2006)
Indiana	Burns Ind. Code §23-1-44-3 (2006)
Kentucky	Ky. Rev. Stat. Ann. §271 B.13-010(3) (Michie 2006)
Massachusetts	Ann. Laws of Mass. GL Ch. 156D §13.01 (2006)
Michigan	Mich. Comp. Laws Serv. §450.1761(d) (2006)
Missouri	Mo. Ann. Stat. §351.870 (2006)
Montana	Mont. Code. Ann. §35-1-826(4) (2006)
Nebraska	Neb. Rev. Stat. §21-20,137(4) (2006)
Nevada	Nev. Rev. Stat. §92A.320 (2006)
New Hampshire	N.H. Rev. Stat. Ann. §293-A:13.01(3) (2006)
North Carolina	N.C. Gen. Stat. §55-13-01(3) (2006)
Oregon	Or. Rev. Stat. §60.551(4) (2006)
South Carolina	S.C. Code Ann. §33-13-101(3) (2005)
Vermont	Vt. Stat. Ann. Tit. 11A, §13.01(3) (2006)
Washington	Wash. Rev. Code §23B.13.010(3) (2006)
Wisconsin	Wis. Stat. §180.1301 (2006)
Wyoming	Wyo. Stat. § 17-16-1301 (a) (iv) (2006)
Pre-1999 Definition of Fair Value Without "Exclusion" Phrase	
Georgia	Ga. Stat. Ann. §14-2-1301(5) (2006)
New Mexico	N.M. Stat. Ann. §53-15-4(A) (Michie 2007)
Rhode Island	R.I. Gen. Laws §7-1.2-1202(a) (2006)
Tennessee	Tenn. Code Ann §48-23-101(4) (2006)
Utah	Utah Code Ann. §16-10a-1301(4) (2006)

Valuing a Business (5th ed.) on Fair Value

States that Adopted the RMBCA Definition of Fair Value (continued)

Pre-1999 Definition of Fair Value With "Relevant Factors" Phrase and Without "Exclusion" Phrase

Delaware	Del. Code Ann. Tit. 8, §262(h) (2006)
Oklahoma	Okla. Stat. Ann. Tit. 18, §1091(H) (2006)
Pennsylvania	15 Pa.C.S. §1572 (2006)

1999 Definition of Fair Value

Connecticut	Conn. Gen. Stat. §33-855(4) (2006)
Idaho	Idaho Code §30-1-1301 (2006)
Iowa	Iowa Code §490.1301(4) (2005)
Maine	13-C Maine Rev. Stat. §1301(4) (2006)
Mississippi	Miss. Code Ann. §79-4-13.01(4) (2006)
South Dakota	S.D. Codified Laws §47-1A-1301 (2006)
Virginia	Va. Code Ann §13.1-729 (Michie 2006)
West Virginia	W. Va. Code §31D-13-1301 (4) (2006)

Hybrid Definition of Fair Value

Florida[a]	Fla. Stat. §607.1301(4) (2006)
Florida[b]	Ill. Compiled Statutes Ch. 805, §5/11.70(j) (i) (2006)

Note:

[a] The Florida Statute incorporates the first two clauses of the 1999 definition, but then adds the last clause of the pre-1999 definition and a clause limiting the definition to a corporation with 10 or fewer shareholders. Florida also uses this definition for appraisal rights of limited liability company members [Fla. Stat §608.4351 (2006)].

[b] Before the pre-1999 definition, the Illinois Statute adds the following: "the proportionate interest of the shareholder in the corporation, without discount for minority status or, absent extraordinary circumstance, lack of marketability."

Copyright © 2008 Thomson Tax & Accounting. All Rights Reserved. For subscription information, call (800) 323-8724 or visit ppc.thomson.com

Discounts and Premiums

A major issue in many fair value cases is whether or not discounts and/or premiums are applicable. If so, there is always the issue of the magnitudes of such discounts and/or premiums.

The primary issues are lack of control (i.e., minority ownership interest) discounts, ownership control premiums, and discounts for lack of marketability. The published opinions that have addressed these issues vary considerably from state to state:

Chapter 4: Valuing a Business on Fair Value

1. Some do not allow either lack of control or lack of marketability discounts.[27]

2. Some allow both lack of control and lack of marketability discounts.

3. Some allow discounts for lack of control but not for lack of marketability.

4. Some allow discounts for lack of marketability but not for lack of control.

5. Several states have taken the position that discounts for lack of control and lack of marketability must be decided in each case on the basis of the facts and circumstances of that case.

6. Some states have applied ownership control premiums under certain specific circumstances.

Lack of Control Discounts Rejected

In its case of first impression on the issue of a lack of control discount in a dissenting stockholder suit, the Wisconsin Court of Appeals rejected the 30% minority interest (i.e., lack of control) discount that had been applied by the trial court. The court reviewed cases from several states (including Delaware, New York, and Oklahoma) and concluded that lack of control discounts should not be applied. The court agreed with the rationale that was stated in *Cavalier Oil Corp. v. Harnett*:

> Discounting individual shareholdings injects into the appraisal process speculation on the various factors which may dictate the marketability of minority shareholdings. More important, to fail to accord to a minority shareholder the full proportionate value of his shares imposes a penalty for lack of control, and unfairly enriches the majority shareholders who may reap a windfall from the appraisal process by cashing out a dissenting shareholder, a clearly undesirable result.[28]

Because of this "clearly undesirable result," the Wisconsin Court of Appeals held that lack of control discounts are inappropriate in dissenters' rights cases as a matter of law, and it remanded to the lower court to award SSM the pro rata share of HMO-W's net assets without a lack of control discount.[29] The Wisconsin Supreme Court affirmed.

In Pueblo Bancorporation v. Lindoe, Inc.,[30] the Colorado Court of Appeals rejected lack of control discounts, saying:

> [I]n determining the "fair value" of a dissenter's shares in a closely held corporation, the trial court must first determine the value of the corporation and the pro rata value of each outstanding share of common or equity participating stock. In the case of a going concern, no minority discount is to be applied...."[31]

Numerous other courts have come to the same conclusion,[32] and some federal Courts of Appeals have adopted this line of reasoning and have rejected lack of control discounts in determining fair value in appraisal actions.[33]

In *Brown v. Arp and Hammond Hardware Co.*,[34] the Wyoming Supreme Court, finding that the clear majority of courts have held that minority discounts do not apply when determining fair value in the appraisal context, ruled that it would join the majority and not permit such discounts.

A 1999 Montana Supreme Court decision demonstrates the need to always research the latest decisions. The Montana Supreme Court reversed itself! In a 1999 dissenting stockholder case,[35] the Supreme Court disallowed a lack of control discount, overruling its own decision to allow a lack of control discount in a 1996 shareholder oppression suit.[36]

Lack of Control Discounts Accepted

Although the majority trend is to reject lack of control discounts, some courts have accepted such discounts. For example, in *Johnson v. Johnson*,[37] a stockholder oppression case, the Connecticut court, finding that the alleged conduct (failure to declare dividends) did not constitute oppression, assessed a 20% lack of control discount. The Court indicated that the decision was within its discretion, and that assessing the discount was in accord with "sound business judgment."

In *Hall v. Glenn's Ferry Grazing Assoc.*,[38] an oppression case, the court referenced a comment to the appraisal statute, which stated in pertinent part that "[i]n cases where there is dissension but no evidence of wrongful conduct, fair value should be determined with reference to what [the minority shareholder] would likely receive in a voluntary sale of shares to a third party, taking into account his minority status." The court found dissension but no wrongful conduct and, accordingly concluded that fair value should be determined by taking into account a minority discount.

Ownership Control Premium Accepted

The Delaware Court of Chancery has accepted the application of an ownership control premium under two specific circumstances:

1. When the base valued is a publicly traded equivalent value derived by the guideline publicly traded company method.

2. When valuing a controlling ownership position in a subsidiary company.

Otherwise, premiums may not be applied at the shareholder level. The Delaware cases permitting premiums for subsidiaries lead to the anomaly that, whereas a business conducted through a subsidiary is entitled to a premium, an identical business conducted through a division is not.[39]

Chapter 4: Valuing a Business on Fair Value

The most common control premium applied is one that is essentially the inverse of the discount for lack of control, which some courts believe is inherent in a comparable company analysis because that method depends on comparisons to market multiples derived from trading information for minority blocks of comparable companies. For example, in *Doft & Co. v. Travelocity.com, Inc.*,[40] the Court, on its own, without prompting by the parties, added a 30% control premium, saying that "The equity valuation produced in a comparable company analysis does not accurately reflect the intrinsic worth of a corporation on a going concern basis. Therefore, the Court, in appraising the fair value of the equity, 'must correct this minority trading discount by adding back a premium designed to correct it.'"

In *Agranoff v. Miller*,[41] the Delaware Chancery Court explained that the determination of such a control premium is necessarily imprecise because to determine what the implicit minority discount in a comparable companies analysis is, one is forced to look at the prices paid for control blocks. Such prices are frequently paid in connection with a merger or other fundamental transaction. The Court found that this source of data is therefore problematic, because the premiums arguably reflect value that is not related to the value of the acquired companies as going concerns under their preexisting business plans, such as synergistic values attributable to transactionally specific factors. The Court acknowledged that it is impossible to make precise determinations about what motivated an acquirer to pay a control premium. In this case, the Court decided that the adjustment should be 30%.

In *In re Valuation of Common Stock of Penobscot Shoe Company*,[42] a dissenters' rights action involving a small, closely held business, the Court permitted a control premium adjustment, concluding that the control premium could properly be used as an upward adjustment of the value of the subject company's shares when compared to similar companies in the industry.

In *Bomarko, Inc. v. International Telecharge, Inc.*,[43] the Delaware Chancery Court permitted the addition of a control premium as part of a comparative public company analysis.

In *Borruso v. Communications Telesystems International*,[44] the Court relied on the guideline publicly traded company method. Both experts agreed that an ownership control premium should be applied, but disagreed as to the stage of the analysis at which it should be applied. The dissenters' expert applied a premium to the market value of invested capital (MVIC) to revenue pricing multiples to reflect the control issue. The company's expert applied the control premium to the guideline publicly traded company analysis result. The court accepted the latter procedure, noting that the dissenters' expert's procedure had the effect of altering the methodology itself.

Two cases in which the Delaware Court of Chancery placed an ownership control premium on the indicated values of wholly owned subsidiaries are *Rapid American Corporation v. Harris*[45] and *Hintmann v. Fred Weber, Inc.*[46] In *Rapid American*, the court valued the subsidiaries by the guideline publicly traded company method. The Delaware Supreme Court concluded that an ownership control premium was appropriate, explaining, "The exclusion of a control premium artificially and unrealistically treated Rapid as a minority shareholder."

Valuing a Business (5th ed.) on Fair Value

In *Hintmann v. Fred Weber*, the Court valued the subsidiaries on the basis of a simple average of the guideline publicly traded company method and the DCF method. Saying that the case was analogous to *Rapid American*, the Court then added a 20% ownership control premium to the resulting indicated values of the subsidiaries. However, a commentator on the decision, investment banker Gil Matthews, criticized the decision as distinguishable from *Rapid American* in that the subsidiary values were based partly on the DCF method:

> DCF value should represent the full value of the future cash flows of the business. Excluding synergies, a company cannot be worth a premium over the value of its future cash flows. Thus, it is improper and illogical to add a control premium to a DCF valuation.[47]

In another case, the Delaware Court of Chancery implicitly allowed an ownership control premium by accepting the guideline merged and acquired company method (see *Le Beau v. M.G. Bancorporation* referenced earlier).

Lack of Marketability Discounts Rejected

The Delaware Court of Chancery is one venue that has regularly rejected discounts for lack of marketability. For example, in *Borruso v. Telesystems International*,[48] the Court rejected the company's expert's "discount for lack of liquidity," citing *Cavalier Oil*[49] and saying that it was essentially a discount for lack of marketability which is inappropriate in a fair value determination.

In *Ex parte Baron Services, Inc.*,[50] a shareholder oppression case, the Alabama Supreme Court rejected the application of an entity-level marketability discount because the company's expert did not rely on publicly traded companies and did not use the guideline public companies approach. The Court also rejected a shareholder-level marketability discount because it found that any "cost of capital" difference between the subject company and public companies was accounted for in the discount and capitalization rates used in the valuation.

In *Pro Finish USA Ltd. v. Johnson*,[51] in a case of first impression in Arizona, the Court denied the application of a lack of marketability discount, concluding that the focus should be upon the value of the company as a whole, and prorated equally, rather than discounting the dissenting shareholders' pro rata share of the sale price. Similarly, the Supreme Court of Colorado, in *Pueblo Bancorporation v. Lindoe, Inc.*,[52] rejected the application of lack of marketability discounts. In determining the proper interpretation of fair value in a dissenters' rights case, the Court held that it is the shareholders' proportionate ownership interest in the corporation's value, without discounting for lack of marketability. The Court stated that this (majority) view is consistent with the underlying purpose of appraisal rights statutes and the national trend against both lack of control and lack of marketability discounts in dissenters' rights cases.[53]

Iowa courts have not issued a definitive opinion on discounts for lack of marketability. In *Sieg v. Kelly*,[54] the trial court disallowed the lack of marketability discount and the case was appealed.

Chapter 4: Valuing a Business on Fair Value

The Supreme Court of Iowa noted: "Iowa was clear at the time Sieg made its valuation that a....discount is not permitted." It noted, however, that some jurisdictions allow lack of marketability discounts and other do not. In the final analysis, it found no error in rejecting the lack of marketability discount, but did not issue a generalized pronouncement on the issue.

In the New Jersey dissenting stockholder case of *Wheaton v. Smith*,[55] the Supreme Court overturned the trial court's acceptance of a discount for lack of marketability, which had been affirmed by the New Jersey Appellate Division.

Relying on 2 ALI, *Principles of Corporate Governance: Analysis and Recommendations*, ∂7.22(a), the trial court concluded that the application of a lack of marketability discount was appropriate because of "extraordinary circumstances" that were present. The New Jersey Supreme Court explained as follows:

> Such circumstances require more than the absence of a trading market in shares; rather, the court should apply this exception only when it finds that the dissenting shareholder has held out in order to exploit the transaction giving rise to appraisal so as to divert value to itself that could not be made available proportionately to other shareholders.

On the same day, the New Jersey Supreme Court accepted a lack of marketability discount in the minority oppression case of *Balsamides v. Protameen Chemicals*, discussed in the next section.

Lack of Marketability Discounts Accepted

In *Matthew G. Norton Co v. Smyth*,[56] the Washington Court of Appeals ruled, in a case of first impression in that state, that a discount for lack of marketability was appropriate at the entity level, and rejected a "bright-line rule" that such a discount is never available at the shareholder level. However, the Court also held that the trial court's decision would be affirmed to the extent that the trial court's order was intended to declare that, absent extraordinary circumstances, no such discount can be applied at the shareholder level.

Similarly, in *Advanced Communication Design, Inc. v. Follett*,[57] an oppressed shareholder case, the Minnesota Supreme Court, noting that the value assigned by the trial court must be "fair and equitable to all parties," rejected a bright-line rule denying the application of a marketability discount in all cases. According to the Court, establishing a bright-line rule foreclosing consideration of discount would be inconsistent with the legislative policy of flexibility and fairness to all parties and could hamper the Courts' ability to take into account circumstances that might lead to an unfair wealth transfer. Such a transfer of wealth would constitute an example of "extraordinary circumstances," as where the exercise of a minority shareholder's appraisal rights in a financially strained corporation with illiquid assets would yield a price far greater than the price that would actually be paid for the shares in a market transaction. Finding such extraordinary circumstances in the case at bar, the Court directed that the discount should be somewhere between 35 and 55%.

Valuing a Business (5th ed.) on Fair Value

In *Devivo v. Devivo*,[58] a Connecticut court relied on the decision in *Advanced Communication* when it found "extraordinary circumstances"—the fair value of the company was 1.6 times the company's net worth, more than 2.7 times its operating cash flow, and 7 times its net income for that year—that warranted application of a 35% lack of marketability discount.

In a New Jersey minority oppression case, *Balsamides v. Protameen Chemicals, Inc.*,[59] the trial court accepted a 35% discount for lack of marketability. The New Jersey Superior Court, Appellate Division, reversed, and, on appeal, the New Jersey Supreme Court upheld the lack of marketability discount. The New Jersey Supreme Court explained as follows:

> The position of the Appellate Division ignores the reality that Balsamides is buying a company that will remain illiquid because it is not publicly traded and public information about it is not widely disseminated. Protameen will continue to have a small base of available purchasers. If it is resold in the future, Balsamides will receive a lower purchase price because of the company's closely-held nature.
>
> If Perle and Balsamides sold Protameen together, the price they received would reflect Protameen's illiquidity. They would split the price and also share that determent. Similarly, if Balsamides pays Perle a discounted price, Perle suffers half of the lack-of-marketability markdown now; and Balsamides suffers the other half when he eventually sells his closely-held business. Conversely, if Perle is not required to sell his shares at a price that reflects Protameen's lack of marketability, Balsamides will suffer the full effect of Protameen's lack of marketability at the time he sells. Accordingly, we find that Balsamides should not bear the brunt of Protameen's illiquidity merely because he is the designated buyer.

On the same day, the New Jersey Supreme Court rejected a lack of marketability discount in the dissenting stockholder case of *Wheaton v. Smith*, discussed in the previous section.

It is not unheard of to apply some particular discount to the results of one or more valuation methods but not to the results of one or more other methods. For example, as seen in an earlier case reference, the court applied a 25% discount for lack of marketability to the results of the guideline publicly traded company method, but no discount to the results of the DCF method or the guideline merged and acquired company method.

Lack of Combinatorial Value Discount Rejected

In *Dobler v. Montgomery Cellular Holding Company, Inc.*,[60] the Court rejected a discount for lack of combinatorial value. The case involved a telecommunications holding company. The expert for the company argued that cellular companies are significantly more valuable in specific combinations, and, since the subject company was a stand alone cellular company, it had a lack of combinatorial value as part of a network. Accordingly, the expert proposed discounting the company's value by 48%. The Court disagreed with this argument, reasoning that the company was already in

Chapter 4: Valuing a Business on Fair Value

combination with other cellular companies owned by the company's parent. In addition, the Court found that the expert was intending to deprive the minority shareholders of existing value through the discount for lack of combinatorial value. The Delaware Supreme Court agreed,[61] indicating that the expert incorrectly attempted to value the company on a stand-alone basis, as if it were not a going concern that had contractual relationships with other cellular providers. However, those relationships represented value to which the minority shareholders were entitled.

Discounts for Trapped-In Capital Gains

In *Matthew G. Norton Co. v. Smyth*,[62] the valuation consultant for the company recognized built-in capital gains in its final valuation. The Washington trial court held that, as a matter of law, a corporation may not use trapped-in capital gains in determining the fair value of a dissenter's shares. The Washington Court of Appeals, however, rejected a bright-line rule in this regard. The Court ruled that, while discounts for built-in capital gains are not generally appropriate in dissenters' rights appraisal cases where no liquidation of the corporation is contemplated, such discounts might be appropriate, at the corporate level, if the business of the company is such that appreciated property is scheduled to be sold in the foreseeable future, in the normal course of business.

The Court, therefore, remanded, with instructions that if the company wished the trial court to consider the tax implications of built-in capital gains, it would need to provide the trial court with a reasonable explanation of why such built-in gains should be considered in light of the fact that it had converted to Subchapter S status, thereby avoiding the double taxation problems of C corporations, and would need to show the Court by substantial evidence and appropriate briefing that the dissenting shareholders were not already taxed for their fair share of the gain on any such appreciated assets by virtue of the corporation's redemption of their appreciated shares for "fair value." The Court discussed the 10-year rule, based on changes to the tax code in the Tax Reform Act of 1986 by which future taxation of appreciated assets became a virtual certainty unless a C corporation was to convert to an S corporation and hold the property for 10 years, by which means it could, indeed, avoid recognizing the gain on the property.[63]

In *Brown v. Arp and Hammond Hardware Co*,[64] the Wyoming Supreme Court ruled that under the state's appraisal statute, based on the pre-1999 version of the Model Business Corporation Act (MBCA), absent clear evidence that the company was undergoing liquidation, a discount for trapped-in capital gains would violate the purpose of the statute: to compensate dissenting shareholders for the "fair value" of their shares in a going concern.

Discounts Left to Court's Discretion

Opinions in a minority of states have rejected the notion that there should be a sweeping policy that lack of control discounts, ownership control premiums, and/or lack of marketability discounts should be either accepted or rejected in all fair value cases.

Instead they have taken the position that the issue of lack of control and lack of marketability discounts should be decided on a case-by-case basis depending on the facts and circumstances of the particular case.

Illinois, for example, is in the camp of leaving lack of control and lack of marketability discounts to the courts' discretion. In *Wigel Broadcasting v. Smith*,[65] a reverse split squeeze-out, the company's independent expert concluded $115 per share, reflecting a combination discount for lack of control and lack of marketability of 50%. The Dissenter's expert was at $78.14 per share. The Appellate Court of Illinois concluded $126 per share. The appellate court cited case law supporting discounts for lack of control and lack of marketability and concluded, "Applying such discounts is left to the trial court's discretion."

In *Jahn v. Kinderman*,[66] involving a freeze-out of minority members in a closely held corporation, the Illinois Court of Appeals reiterated that whether to apply such discounts is within the Court's discretion, but also noted the preponderant view that such discounts are not to be applied in determining fair value. The Court upheld the lower court's discretionary decision not to apply a discount for lack of marketability. This discretionary approach has come under increasing attack.[67]

Summary of Dissenting Stockholder and Minority Oppression Court Cases

By selected examples, this section has demonstrated the great diversity of positions taken by courts in interpreting the standard of fair value in dissenting stockholder and minority oppression cases. One conclusion that is obvious is that virtually no court specifically equates "fair value" with "fair market value."

It also seems apparent that both the valuation analyst and/or the attorney need to read relevant judicial precedent with great care. In particular, analysts should be careful about attributing broad applicability to seemingly sweeping statements. Facts and circumstances vary greatly from one case to another, and courts will consider these variations in deciding whether a principle articulated in one case is applicable to the instant case at bar.

Another important point in estimating fair value is whether or not there was procedural fairness in the entire transaction. If controlling owners acted unfairly toward noncontrolling stockholders (or vice versa), there may, in some jurisdictions, be considerable elements of damages incurred beyond just the basic appraisal under dissenters' stockholder rights.

Generally speaking, the elements of market value, investment value, and asset value should all be considered, although the final conclusion may be based on only one or two of these elements. The most important element in most cases is *investment value*, followed by market value and asset value. Investment value in this context means value based on production of income, as opposed to value to a particular owner or investor, as the standard of investment value is defined in other appraisal contexts.

Chapter 4: Valuing a Business on Fair Value

Accepted valuation methods vary greatly, depending on the type of company, the facts and circumstances of each case, the relative quality of evidence available for different valuation methods, and the preferences of the court. Courts sometimes weight two or more methods and other times ultimately depend on the results of a single method.

The courts' postures toward discounts and premiums is highly variable, both from jurisdiction to jurisdiction and, in many jurisdictions, depending on the distinguishable facts and circumstances from one case to another within a jurisdiction.

Many states have no precedential case law in the area of dissenting stockholder suits and/or minority oppression suits. Others have some case law, but most have not addressed all the various issues that may arise. In the face of lack of their own precedential case law, courts usually look to precedential case law from other states. Thus, although dissent and oppression valuation cases are nominally state-specific, it is important for valuation analysts and attorneys working in this area to have a broad familiarity with the various precedents of many states. This section has not attempted to provide a comprehensive treatise, but has provided examples to illustrate variations of courts' positions on issues commonly encountered.

Marital Dissolution

Although no state expressly uses the term "fair value" as the standard of value to be used in a divorce proceeding, a few states have essentially used that standard. These states typically reference shareholder dissent and oppression cases, which overwhelmingly use a fair value standard. Under the fair value standard, the court exercises a great deal of discretion in delimiting the standard's parameters, and, ordinarily, discounts are disallowed. In addition, in shareholder cases, fair value is often regarded as the pro-rata share of an enterprise's value. Similarly, in the divorce setting, a court evaluating discounts may see the application of discounts as an unfair advantage to the party that will continue to enjoy the benefits of the asset. In this respect, divorce and shareholder oppression cases are similar in that they can both be viewed in terms of the reasonable expectations of those entering into a partnership or contract (business or marital).

For example, in *Brown v. Brown*,[68] a New Jersey trial court used the language of fair value and referred to New Jersey shareholder dissent and oppression cases to determine the standard of value to be used in the case. As another New Jersey court indicated in *Piscopo v. Piscopo*,[69] since both shareholder oppression and marital dissolution cases are actions brought in a court of equity, it would be unreasonable to treat value one way in one type of case, and another in another type of case; equity requires that the court find a value that is fair.

Bobrow v. Bobrow[70] concluded value as the pro-rata share of the enterprise value, despite a buy-sell agreement that specified that the husband's interest in the accounting firm Ernst & Young was only what was in his capital account. Such an approach is similar to the way value would be treated under a fair value standard in a dissenting or oppressed shareholders' case.

Valuing a Business (5th ed.) on Fair Value

Occasionally, courts will use a hybrid standard that involves fair value and investment value, which is discussed in the next section. Although the Louisiana case of *Ellington v. Ellington*,[71] referenced investment value concepts in the continuing benefits of ownership and employment, the predominant language of the case involved fair value constructs. In that case, the wife's expert used an excess earnings method and came to a value of $668,000, whereas the husband's expert determined that the fair market value of liabilities outweighed assets by approximately $55,000, and therefore the company had negative value. The court rejected both experts' testimonies, as they both used a fair market value standard, which the court ruled was inappropriate because neither party was a willing seller. Based on its own approach, the court came to a value of $293,000. The appellate court approved this decision on the fair value logic that the husband would retain ownership, current management would continue, and the husband would continue to benefit from his ownership.

In other instances, some cases are considered either as using an investment standard of value or a fair value standard of value. For example, in *Neuman v. Neuman*,[72] the dispute was over the value of the husband's minority interest in a trucking business. The trial court accepted the wife's valuation, which applied no discounts on the argument that the husband had no plans to sell his stock. The Wyoming Supreme Court affirmed,[73] creating a difference between the value of a business to a willing buyer and the value of a business for divorce purposes. On one hand, this could be considered an investment value case because value was measured by the value to the husband of his retained interest. On the other hand, this could be considered a fair value case because the husband was receiving his pro-rata share of the company's value.

In *Howell v. Howell*,[74] the court recognized personal goodwill and excluded discounts on the grounds that "intrinsic" value should be determined based on the husband's staying with his law firm. Thus, this can be categorized as an investment value case, where the value is measured by the value to the owner, or as a fair value case, because value is calculated as a percentage of the enterprise value.

---

1. Shannon Pratt with Alina Niculita, *Valuing a Business*, 5th ed. (McGraw-Hill 2008). Reproduced with permission from The McGraw-Hill Companies. (To order, go to www.bvresouces.com; (888) 287-8258).
2. Oregon Revised Statutes, Section.60.551(4).
3. Model Business Corporation Act, Section 13.01(3) (1998).
4. Model Business Corporation Act, 1999 revision.
5. *In Matter of Shell Oil Co.*, 607 A.2d 12B (Del. Supr. 1992).
6. *Weinzbeger v. UOP, Inc.*, 457 A.2d 701 (Del. 1983).
7. In *Smith v. Van Gorkom*, 488 A.2d 858 (1985), the Delaware Supreme Court pierced the business judgment rule and imposed individual liability on independent (even eminent) outside directors of Trans Union Corporation because the court thought they had not been careful enough, and had not inquired enough, before deciding to accept and recommend to Trans Union's shareholders a cash-out merger at a per-share price that was less than the "intrinsic value" of the shares. At no time did the board engage either a formal valuation of the stock or a fairness opinion. The court also indicated that "[a] substantial premium may provide one reason to recommend a merger, but in the absence of other sound valuation information, the fact of a premium alone does not provide an adequate basis upon which to assess the fairness of an offering price.... Using market price as a basis for concluding that the premium adequately reflected the true value of the Company was a clearly faulty, indeed fallacious, premise." The business judgment rule is a common law rule used by courts to minimize the number of shareholder complaints that undergo

Chapter 4: Valuing a Business on Fair Value

judicial review by protecting a corporate board decision from substantive review (e.g., under a "fairness" or "reasonableness" test) if four conditions are met. First, the board must make a decision. A decision not to act meets this requirement. Second, the board must have engaged in a process to become adequately informed of all material information reasonably available to make its decision. Third, the board must have made its decision in good faith. Fourth, disinterested directors of the board must have made the decision. In *Van Gorkom*, the Delaware Supreme Court essentially indicated that it was serious about the "informed" element of the business judgment rule. At the time, the decision shocked the legal, corporate, and insurance communities by demonstrating that directors could be found liable for monetary damages if not sufficiently informed when making a board decision. The decision closely linked the duty of care with being sufficiently informed, and is credited with the practice of corporate boards of obtaining a fairness opinion before recommending a merger. Because the board and management are often familiar with the business and in a better position than outsiders to gather relevant information, there is no absolute requirement for a fairness opinion, but such an opinion will be given weight by a court assessing the fairness of a merger, as will the approval of the terms of the merger by disinterested directors. Soon after *Van Gorkom* was decided, the Delaware legislature added Delaware General Corporation Law Code Section 102(b)(7), a statutory provision that largely protects directors from monetary liability for any actions arising from a breach of their duty of care if the corporation's shareholders incorporate into the certificate of incorporation a provision exculpating directors from such liability. Most Delaware corporations have incorporated such exculpatory provisions into their certificates of incorporation. Notwithstanding the enactment of § 102(b)(7), directors still have a duty of care to be informed. Moreover, the exculpatory provision only relates to money damages against the director personally, and does not preclude injunctive relief. Also, by invoking the exculpatory clause, directors can place the burden of proof on themselves where breaches of fiduciary duties in addition to the duty of care are asserted, thus placing themselves at a procedural disadvantage in judicial proceedings. In the final analysis, it is very important for directors to be informed when making decisions, for legal as well as practical reasons.

8. Shannon P. Pratt, "Fair Value: A View from the Delaware Court of Chancery" (interview with Jack B. Jacobs). For a copy of this article, see Chapter 2 of this Guide.

9. For more information on fair value pursuant to California Corporations Code Section 2000, as well as a flow chart, see Chapter 6.

10. Arthur J. Shartsis, "Dissolution Actions Yield Less Than Fair Market Enterprise Value." For a copy of this article, see Chapter 6.

11. Ibid., pp. 5–6.

12. See, e.g., *Casey v. Amboy Bancorporation*, No. A-0715-04T3 (N.J. Supr. App. Div. Aug. 8, 2006).

13. Because statutes of several states undergo revision every year, it is impractical to publish even summaries of all of them in a book such as this. Many state government web pages provide their state statutes on-line or they are available at law libraries.

14. Shannon P. Pratt, "Fair Value: A View from the Delaware Court of Chancery" (interview with Jack B. Jacobs). For a copy of this article, see Chapter 2 of this Guide.

15. *Katherine B. Arnaud, et al. v. Stockgrowers State Bank of Ashland, Kansas, et al.*, 992 P.2d 216, 1999 Kan. LEXIS 645 1999 WL 1000415 (Kan. Nov. 5, 1999).

16. Ibid.

17. Shannon P. Pratt, "Kansas Supreme Court Disallows Discounts in Reverse Split Forced Cashout," *Judges & Lawyers Business Valuation Update*, December 1999, p. 6.

18. For a comprehensive discussion of fair value in shareholder dissent and oppression cases, see Jay E. Fishman, Shannon P. Pratt, and William J. Morrison, *Standards of Value: Theory and Applications* (Hoboken, NJ: John Wiley & Sons, 2007).

19. See *East Park Ltd. Partnership v. Larkin*, 2006 Md. App. LEXIS 32 (Md. Ct. App. 2006).

20. In *Boettcher v. IMC Mortgage Co.*, 871 So. 2d 1047, 2004 Fla. App. LEXIS 6582; (Fla. App. May 12, 2004), the Florida Court of Appeals ruled that "'Fair value,' with respect to a dissenter's shares, means the value of the shares as of the close of business on the day prior to the shareholders' authorization date, excluding any appreciation or depreciation in anticipation of the corporate action unless exclusion would be inequitable."

21. *Matter of Slant/Fin. Corp. v. The Chicago Corp.*, (N.Y. Sup. Ct. Oct. 5, 1995), aff'd 236 A.D.2d 547, 654 N.Y.S.2d 627 (N.Y. App. Div. Feb. 18, 1997).

22. *Le Beau v. M.G. Bancorporation, Inc.*, 1998 Del. Ch. LEXIS 9, 1998 WL 44993 (Del. Ch. Jan. 29, 1998).

23. *Pueblo Bancorporation v. Lindoe, Inc.*, 63 P.3d 353, 2003 Colo. LEXIS 53 (Colo. Jan. 21, 2003).

24. In *Lawson Mardon Wheaton, Inc. v. Smith*, 160 N.J. 383, 734 A.2d 738 (N.J. 1999), the Court concurred with the intermediate appellate court, which said, "Fair Value carries with it the statutory purposes that shareholders be fairly

compensated, which may or may not equate with the market's judgment about the stock's value. This is particularly appropriate in the close corporation setting where there is no ready market for the shares and consequently no Fair Market Value." 716 A.2d 550, 558 (N.J. Super. App. Div. Aug. 26, 1998).

25. See, e.g., *Swope v. Seigel-Robert, Inc.*, 243 F.3d 486, 2001 U.S. App. LEXIS 2760 (8th Cir. 2001); *Wenzel v. Hopper & Galliher, P.C.*, 779 N.E.2d 30, (Ind. Ct. App. 2002); *First W. Bank Wall v. Olsen*, 2001 SD 16, 621 N.W.2d 611, (S.D. 2001); *Matthew G. Norton Co. v. Smyth*, 112 Wn. App. 865, 51 P.3d 159, (Wash. Ct. App. 2002); *HMO-W, Inc. v. SSM Health Care Sys.*, 2000 WI 46, 234 Wis. 2d 707, 611 N.W.2d 250 (Wis. 2000).

26. *Kim v. The Grover C. Coors Trust*, 2007 Colo. App. LEXIS 394 (Colo. App. March 8, 2007).

27. In the Maryland case, *East Park Ltd. Partnership v. Larkin*, 2006 Md. App. LEXIS 32 (Md. Ct. App. 2006), the court, in determining whether discounts should be applied to determining fair value of withdrawing limited partner interests, noted that the majority of states that have considered the issue in the dissenting shareholder context have concluded that discounts do not apply to a fair value analysis. The court also ruled, however, that as with dissenting shareholder cases, the method used in determining the fair value of shares is specific to each case.

28. *Cavalier Oil Corp. v Harnett*, 564 A.2d 1137 (Del. 1989).

29. *HMO-W v. SSM Health Care System*, 598 N.W.2d 577, 1999 WL 395650 (Wis. App. June 17, 1999), *aff'd*, 611 N.W.2d 250, 2000 Wisc. LEXIS 313 (W.SC. 2000).

30. *Pueblo Bancorporation v. Lindoe, Inc.*, 37 P.3d 492, 2001 Colo. App. LEXSI 1330 (Colo. App. August 16, 2001).

31. *Pueblo Bancorporation v. Lindoe, Inc.*, 63 P.3d 353, 2003 Colo. LEXIS 53 (Colo. 2003).

32. *Blitch v. Peoples Bank*, 246 Ga. App. 453, 540 S.E.2d 667 (Ga. Ct. App. 2000); *Security State Bank v. Ziegeldorf*, 554 N.W.2d 884 (Iowa 1996); *Arnaud v. Stockgrowers State Bank*, 268 Kan. 163, 992 P.2d 216 (Kansas 1999); *In re Valuation of Common Stock of McLoon Oil Co.*, 565 A.2d 997 (Maine 1989); *Rigel Corp. v. Cutchall*, 245 Neb. 118, 511 N.W.2d 519 (Neb. 1994); *Cooke v. Fresh Express Foods Corp.*, 169 Ore. App. 101, 7 P.3d 717, 2000 Ore. App. LEXIS 1128 (Ore. Ct. App. July 12, 2000). *First Western Bank Wall v. Olsen*, 2001 SD 16, 621 N.W.2d 611 (South Dakota 2001); *In re Stock of Trapp Family Lodge, Inc.*, 169 Vt. 82, 725 A.2d 927 (Vt. 1999); see also Barry M.Wertheimer, "The Shareholders' Appraisal Remedy and How Courts Determine Fair Value," *47 Duke L.J. 613*, February 1998, p. 635 (noting the unavailability of minority discounts in the majority of courts).

33. *Swope v. Seigel-Robert, Inc.*, 243 F.3d 486, 2001 U.S. App. LEXIS 2760 (8th Cir. 2001).

34. *Brown v. Arp and Hammond Hardware Co.*, 141 p. 3d 673, 2006 Wyo. LEXIS 115 (Wyo. 2006).

35. *Hansen v. 75 Ranch Company*, 957 P.2d 32, 1998 WL 180831 (Mont. Apr. 9, 1998).

36. *McCann Ranch, Inc. v. Sharon Quigley-McCann*, 276 Mont. 205, 208, 915 P.2d 239, 241 (1996).

37. *Johnson v. Johnson*, 30 Conn. L. Rptr. 260, 2001 Conn. Super. LEXIS 2430 (Conn. Super. Ct. Aug. 15, 2001).

38. *Hall v. Glenn's Ferry Grazing Assoc.*, 2006 U.S. Dist. LEXIS 68051 (D. Idaho 2006).

39. Gilbert E. Matthews, "A Review of Valuations in Delaware Appraisal Cases, 2004-2005," *Business Valuation Review*, Vol. 25, No. 2 (Summer 2006).

40. *Doft & Co. v. Travelocity.com, Inc*, 2004 Del. Ch. LEXIS 75 (Del. Ch. May 20, 2004).

41. *Agranoff v. Miller*, 2001 Del. Ch. LEXIS 71 (Del. Ch. May 15, 2001).

42. *In re Valuation of Common Stock of Penobscot Shoe Company*, 2003 Me. Super. LEXIS 140 (Me. Super. May 30, 2003).

43. *Bomarko, Inc. v. International Telecharge, Inc.*, 794 A.2d 1161, 1999 Del. Ch. LEXIS 211 (Del Ch. Nov. 4, 1999), *aff'd*, 766 A.2d 437 (Del. 2000).

44. *Carl Borruso and William Lee v. Communications Telesystems International*.

45. *Rapid American Corporation v. Harris*, 603 A.2d 796 (Del. 1992).

46. *Hintmann v. Fred Weber, Inc.*, 1998 Del. Ch. LEXIS 26 (Del. Ch. 1998).

47. Gilbert E. Matthews, "Delaware Court Adds Control Premiums to Subsidiary Value," *Business Valuation Update*, May 1998, p. 10.

48. *Carl Borruso and William Lee v. Communications Telesystems International*.

49. *Cavalier Oil Corp. v. Harnett*.

Chapter 4: Valuing a Business on Fair Value

50. *Ex parte Baron Services, Inc.*, 874 So. 2d 545 (Ala. April 4, 2003).
51. *Pro Finish USA Ltd. v. Johnson*, 63 P.3d 288, 204 Ariz. 257 (Ariz. App. Feb. 6, 2003).
52. *Pueblo Bancorporation v. Lindoe, Inc.*, 63 P.3d 353, 2003 Colo. LEXIS 53 (Colo. 2003).
53. See, e.g., James H. Eggart, "Replacing the Sword with a Scalpel: The Case for a Bright-Line Rule Disallowing the Application of Lack of Marketability Discounts in Shareholder Oppression Cases," *44 Ariz. L. Rev. 213* (Spring 2002), urging the adoption of a bright-line rule denying discounts in all dissenters' rights cases. The article emphasizes the inappropriateness of allowing discretion in the application of discounts and explains why a bright-line rule disallowing the application of lack of marketability discounts in all cases would be superior to a discretionary approach, or even one that permits discounts in "extraordinary circumstances." Oregon is an example of a state that disallows both lack of marketability and lack of control discounts. See, e.g., *Cooke v. Fresh Express Foods Corp.*, 169 Ore. App. 101, 7 P.3d 717, 2000 Ore. App. LEXIS 1128 (Ore. Ct. App. July 12, 2000).
54. *Sieg Company v. Kelly*, 568 N.W.2d 794, 1997 Iowa Sup. LEXIS 243, 1997 WL 575996 (Iowa Sept. 17, 1997).
55. *Lawson Mardon Wheaton, Inc. v. Smith, et al.*, 160 N.J. 383, 734 A.2d 738, 1999 WL 492634 (N.J. July 14, 1999).
56. *Matthew G. Norton Co v. Smyth*, 51 P.3d 159, 112 Wash. App. 865 (Wash. App. Aug. 5, 2002).
57. *Advanced Communication Design, Inc. v. Follett*, 615 N.W.2d 285 (Minn. Aug. 3, 2000).
58. *Devivo v. Devivo*, 30 Conn. L. Rptr. 52, 2001 Conn. Super. LEXIS 1285 (Conn. Super. Ct. May 7, 2001).
59. *Emanuel Balsamides, et al. v. Protameen Chemicals, Inc., et al.*
60. *Dobler v. Montgomery Cellular Holding Company, Inc.*, 2004 Del. Ch. LEXIS 139 (Del. Ch. Sept. 30, 2004).
61. *Montgomery Cellular Holding Co. v. Dobler*, 880 A.2d 206, 2005 Del. LEXIS 295 (Del. Aug. 1, 2005).
62. *Matthew G. Norton Co. v. Smyth*, 112 Wn. App. 865, 51 P.3d 159, (Wash. Ct. App. 2002).
63. See generally 26 U.S.C. §§ 1374, 1374(d)(7) (1988). If a corporation is eligible for a subchapter S election, therefore, a technique does exist for avoiding recognition of gain.
64. *Brown v. Arp and Hammond Hardware Co.*, 2006 Wyo, LEXIS 115 (Wyo. 2006).
65. *Weigel Broadcasting Company v. Smith, et al.*, 682 N.E.2d 745 (Ill. App. July 24, 1997).
66. *Jahn v. Kinderman*, 351 Ill. App. 3d 15, 814 N.E.2d 116, 2004 Ill. App. LEXIS 865 (Ill. App. July 26, 2004).
67. See, e.g., Charles W. Murdoch, "Squeeze-outs, Freeze-outs, and Discounts: Why Is Illinois in the Minority in Protecting Shareholder Interests?" *35 Loy. U. Chi. L.J. 737* (Spring, 2004).
68. *Brown v. Brown*, 348 N.J. Super. 466, 792 A.2d 463, 2002 N.J. Super. LEXIS 105 (N.J. App. Div. 2002).
69. *Piscopo v. Piscopo*, 232 N.J. Super. 559, 557 A.2d 1040 (N.J. Super. 1989).
70. *Bobrow v. Bobrow*, No. 29D01-0003-DR-166 (Ind. Super. Sept. 2002).
71. *Ellington v. Ellington*, 842 So. 2d 1160 (La. Ct. App. 2003).
72. *Neuman v. Neuman*, 842 P.2d 575 (Wyo. 1992).
73. *Neuman v. Neuman*, 842 P.2d 575 (Wyo. 1992).
74. *Howell v. Howell*, 46 Va. Cir. 339; 1998 Va. Cir. LEXIS 256 (Va. Cir. Sept. 4, 1998), *aff'd*, 31 Va. App. 332, 523 S.E.2d 514 (2000).

Chapter 5
Fair Value in Marital Dissolution

The State of the Fair Value Standard in Divorce

By John Stockdale Jr., Esq.[1]

Many states' courts apply the fair market value standard when appraising the value of closely held businesses in divorce cases.[2] These courts generally define fair market value by reference to tax guidance: the price a willing buyer and a willing seller would agree upon when neither is under any compulsion and both are knowledgeable of the business.[3]

However, the argument for replacing fair market value with fair value as the standard of value in divorce cases has grown increasingly prevalent in recent years. Most statutory schemes define fair value as the pro rata share of the business as a going concern without reference to discounts for lack of marketability or for minority interests (lack of control).[4] Courts' reactions to requests to adopt the fair value standard have been mixed.

This article will first address the rationale for applying fair value rather than fair market value in the divorce context. The second part will discuss several landmark cases that considered the issue in depth, and the final section will distill several general rules from these cases.

Analogy to dissenters' rights

As early as 1989, attorneys for the non-business owning spouse began arguing that fair market value is not the appropriate standard of value in divorce. They claim that denying the non-operating spouse a pro rata share of a marital business inequitably enriches the operating spouse and denies the non-operating spouse the fruits of his or her contributions to growing the business during the marriage. By analogy, the proponents of fair value point to the dissenting shareholders' rights and remedies under the applicable state business corporation act.

The analogy is largely based on the Delaware Supreme Court's landmark decision in *Cavalier Oil Corp v. Harnett*,[5] which reviewed a case originally decided by the Delaware Chancery Court that denied discounts for lack of marketability and lack of control in calculating fair value in dissenting shareholder actions. The application of discounts at the shareholder level was contrary to the fair value mandate to value the business as a going concern, the higher court held, and cited three reasons:

1. fair value does not assume a hypothetical sale of the minority's interest, but assumes that the minority will maintain his or her investment in the business;
2. applying discounts at the shareholder level injects speculation into the appraisal process; and
3. discounts penalize dissenting shareholders for enforcing their rights while providing majority shareholders a windfall by cashing out the minority at a discounted price.

The Delaware Supreme Court found this result "undesirable."

Chapter 5: Fair Value in Marital Dissolution

Applying fair value analogy to divorce

Only a handful of state courts have addressed the issue of fair value as the standard of value in divorce in a meaningful way. As discussed below, these states include North Dakota, New Jersey, Florida, and Washington. By contrast, courts in states such as Arkansas have refused to entertain the notion as contrary to established law.[6]

1. North Dakota. The North Dakota Supreme Court first considered whether fair value was the appropriate standard of value in the divorce context in *Kaiser v. Kaiser*,[7] which assessed a wife's 9.2% interest in a family-owned oil business. The husband argued that no discount for minority interest should apply because the wife's family owned the stock and had no plans to sell the stock to unrelated, unknown buyers. The wife's expert claimed that a minority discount ranging from 25% to 40% was appropriate. The lower court applied an 11.3% minority discount and no discount for lack of marketability.

On appeal, the Supreme Court affirmed the application of a reduced discount, explaining that North Dakota's business corporation act provided sufficient protection to the wife under the dissenters' rights statutes. Further, the court reasoned that the wife's family owned all the remaining stock in the subject business and was not contemplating sale to unrelated third parties.

The same court revisited the issue in *Fisher v. Fisher*.[8] In this case, the husband started the business but transferred ownership and control to the wife, to take advantage of minority-owned business contracts. Both parties owned stock in the business (the husband a minority interest), but shortly after filing for divorce the wife demoted the husband and removed him from the board of directors. The trial court valued the parties combined 88% interest at $9,094.74 per share and reallocated the interests 51% to the husband and 37% to the wife, based on the husband's proposal and desire to maintain control in the firm. To balance the unequal split of stock, the court ordered the husband to pay $2,365,070.34 in cash to the wife within 90 days after entry of judgment.

The wife appealed to the state Supreme Court. She argued that because of the husband's post-divorce oppression, she would have to sell her interest or petition for dissolution of the business. Further, if she sold her interest she would realize much less than the value the trial court accorded to the stock, because it did not apply a minority interest discount.

The Supreme Court disagreed, finding that the trial court had properly valued the stock without reference to a marketability discount. Moreover, a minority business interest might be worth less to a potential purchaser, but this was not sufficient reason to discount her minority shares in the marital dissolution proceedings when the wife's corporate rights provided adequate remedies. For example, the wife could petition for dissolution of the business, the court noted, or enforce her dissenters' rights and obtain the stock's fair value. It further reasoned that in assessing fair value, other courts (including the Delaware Supreme Court in *Cavalier Oil Corp.*) have declined to discount minority stock interests because the discount was too speculative; the discount penalized the dissenter by denying the dissenter his or her pro rata share of the value; and it enriched the majority shareholders by allowing them to repurchase the dissenter's stock at a discounted price. By applying the fair value analogy from corporate cases, the *Fisher* court thus affirmed the denial of the minority interest discount in divorce.[9]

2. New Jersey. In *Brown v. Brown*,[10] the husband received a 47.5% gifted interest in a closely held wholesale florist. (His brother held the remaining interest.) The husband was actively involved in the business during the marriage while the wife was otherwise employed. At trial, the parties' experts took divergent views regarding discounts: The wife's expert did not apply any discounts while the husband's expert applied a 25% discount for lack of marketability and 15% minority interest discount. The trial court adopted the wife's position and declined to apply the discounts.

The appellate division affirmed. For purposes of equitable distribution, it was not appropriate to apply discounts to the husband's interest in the business. The court considered the then-recent New Jersey Supreme Court cases that denied, absent a showing of wrongful conduct by the dissenter or oppressed shareholder, discounts for lack of marketability and minority interest in dissenting and oppressed shareholder cases.[11] These cases effectively adopted the *Cavalier Oil Corp.* rationale: the discounts were speculative; application contravened the purposes of the dissenters' rights and oppression statutes; and discounts would provide the majority shareholders with a windfall.

The court reasoned that the application of discounts in the equitable distribution context resulted in similar unfairness. The husband and his brother were the only shareholders; they did not contemplate a sale and they would continue to operate the business in the same manner for the foreseeable future. The dissenters' rights and oppression statutes also protected the husband, allowing him access to fair value. In the absence of extraordinary circumstances, the court concluded that there was no reason to allow one spouse to minimize the marital estate at the expense of the other spouse.

3. Washington. In *Baltrusis v. Baltrusis*,[12] the husband and the wife held individual minority interests in a bank holding company owned by the wife's family. At trial, only the wife introduced valuation testimony, which included a 33% marketability discount in determining the fair market value of the stock. The trial court generally adopted the wife's valuation but declined to apply the lack of marketability discount.

The Washington Court of Appeals affirmed the denial of the discount. The court stated that the husband was akin to a dissenting shareholder, because he was an "unwilling seller with no bargaining power." He was under a court-ordered compulsion to sell, the only market was his ex-wife's family, and his ex-wife was in a position to fully enjoy the benefits of ownership. Since a marketability discount was inappropriate in the dissenters' rights context, the court reasoned that it was inappropriate in this context as well.

4. Florida. More recently, in *Erp v. Erp*[13] the parties owned equal shares in the majority interest in a recreational vehicle dealership. (Their children owned the remaining interests). Both parties vied for control over the dealership and presented valuation experts at trial. In awarding the majority interest to the husband (and an equalization payment to the wife), the trial court rejected a minority discount but applied a marketability discount. The wife appealed. Citing the analogy of dissenting shareholder cases, she argued that a marketability discount was never appropriate where one spouse was purchasing the stock of the other.

The appellate court rejected the wife's analogy. Her position did not resemble a dissenting shareholder, since the wife was not the victim of oppressive behavior and was not avoiding a fundamental change in the corporation. Instead, the court found that her position was more akin to a shareholder seeking dissolution of the business for corporate deadlock under Florida's business corporation act. Because Florida gave courts the discretion to apply marketability discounts in the dissolution of a business scenario, divorce courts should have the same discretion. Further, the best way to address the application of the discount is through expert witness testimony.

Argument for application of fair value

Several general rules emerge from these cases. First, when the spouses hold stock in a closely held business—particularly one that is majority-owned and controlled by one of their families—discounts for lack of marketability and lack of control (minority interest) may not be appropriate under the analogy of the divorce to dissenters' and oppressed shareholders cases. The "outside" spouse is akin to the oppressed/dissenting shareholder, subject to a forced sale of his or her interest to the "inside" spouse, who would receive a windfall by acquiring the stock at a discount. At the same time, the inside spouse enjoys recourse to the corporate appraisal statutes, which require application of the fair value standard should post-divorce, intra-family dealings go awry.

The facts in *Erp* and *Fisher* illustrate a corollary rule: When both spouses are actively involved and own shares in the business, a discount for lack of marketability and lack of control may be appropriate as within the discretion of the court. This situation positions the parties more like deadlocked shareholders who petition the court for dissolution of the business.

While these rules may be distilled in a general way from these cases, they by no means apply beyond the jurisdictions that have adopted them. Legal authorities and commentators need to develop broader support regarding the application of fair value principles to martial dissolution statutes and equitable distribution schemes. Given equity's emphasis on fairness to the parties and consistency of outcomes, state legislatures and courts are urged to apply fair value principles to the disposition of business interests in divorce.

This article is an excerpt from the Fair Value in Marital Dissolution chapter of BVR's recently-updated *Guide*, entitled *BVR's Guide to Fair Value in Shareholder Dissent, Oppression, and Marital Dissolution*. For more information on this *Guide*, visit www.BVResources.com/Publications.

The State of the Fair Value Standard in Divorce

1. John J. Stockdale, Jr., Esq. is an associate with Schafer and Weiner, PLLC (Bloomfield Hills, MI) where he practices bankruptcy, corporate, and transactional law. He has been following valuation and damage computation cases since 1995. John graduated summa cum laude from Cooley law School and earned a bachelor's degree at The Citadel. John can be reached at 248.540.3340.
2. *See generally* Jay E. Fishman, Shannon P. Pratt, William J. Morrison, *Standards of Value* (2007).
3. *See generally* I.R.S. Rev. Rul. 59-60.
4. Model Business Corporation Act §13.02 (1999).
5. 564 A.2d 1137 (Del. 1989).
6. *Layman v. Layman*, 780 S.W.2d 560, 562 (Ark. 1989) (rejecting fair value over dissent); *Crismon v. Crismon*, 34 S.W.2d 763, 765 (Ark. App. 2000) (same).
7. 555 N.W.2d 585 (N.D. 1996).
8. 568 N.W.2d 728 (N.D. 1997).
9. However, the court reversed the lower court's decision awarding shares to both parties. "[A] corporate remedy should be implemented concurrently with this divorce to avoid multiplying litigation and to achieve judicial economy. If [the parties] cannot get along as husband and wife, the courts cannot expect them to get along as business associates."
10. *Brown v. Brown*, 792 A.2d 463, 470 (N.J. Super. A.D. 2002).
11. *Balsamides v. Protameen Chemicals, Inc.*, 734 A.2d 721 (N.J. 1999); *Lawson Marden Wheaton, Inc. v. Smith*, 734 A.2d 738 (N.J. 1999); and *Casey v. Brennan*, 780 A.2d 553 (N.J. 2002).
12. 113 Wash. App. 1037 (2002)(unpublished).
13. *Erp v. Erp*, 976 So.2d 1234 (Fla. 2008).

Fair Value in Marital Dissolution: Case Law

By Noah Gordon, Esq.[1]

In marital dissolution cases, the standard of value applied varies from state to state. In the great majority of cases, the case law of the state, rather than its statutes, must be analyzed to understand the standard of value used and the contours of that standard. Although "fair value" may be inferred as the applicable standard of value, the parameters of the "fair value" standard often vary among the states, and may even vary within a single state. This is because the standard is largely a product of the court's discretion. In some situations, however, the standard of value is determined by the parties' stipulation, rather than by reliance on case law.[2] Differences arise primarily with regard to the applicability of discounts, the valuation of intangible assets such as goodwill, the willingness of the parties to the transaction, buy-sell agreements, and other related factors. Ultimately, the facts and assumptions of each case determine how the court will apply the "fair value" standard.

Fair value cases can be identified by certain traits that they do, or do not, possess. For example, if a valuation takes a pro-rata portion of the enterprise value without lack of control or lack of marketability discounts, it can be inferred that the standard of value used is fair value. Similarly, if a case uses the concept of an unwilling buyer or unwilling seller, such use suggests that fair value is the standard of value being applied. A case that includes enterprise goodwill, or includes goodwill without necessarily distinguishing between personal and enterprise goodwill, and that rejects discounts, also suggests that the court is using a fair value standard. On rare occasion, the court even expressly indicates it is determining "fair value."[3]

Where the court emphasizes the fairness of property distribution, rather than merely equal distribution, that, too, can be an indicator of fair value. For example, if the value of a business indicated in a buy-sell agreement is accepted or rejected because doing so would be fair (or unfair) to one or both of the parties, because the value indicated in the agreement is unrealistic, the standard of value may be considered fair value. Finally, some cases have indicated that because marital dissolution and shareholder dissent and oppression cases are actions brought in equity, it would be unreasonable to treat the standard of value in these differently.

Pro-Rata Portion of Enterprise Value, No Discounts

One case that illustrates the fair value standard is *Bobrow v. Bobrow*,[4] where the court awarded the wife a share of the value of the husband's partnership interest in the accounting firm Ernst & Young (E&Y) based on his pro rata share of the value of the enterprise. In that case, one of the issues was the value of E&Y's enterprise goodwill. Although there was a partnership agreement limiting an owner's interest to the value of the capital account, thereby excluding goodwill, the husband conceded that the agreement only applied to a transaction of his partnership interest (resignation, retirement, or death). Based on prior precedent, the court recognized that the assets of

E&Y were not personal to the partner, but belonged to the institution of which each partner had a share. These institutional assets—all of which were transferable to an outside purchaser—included such intangible assets as E&Y's trade name; the entity's favorable business reputation and name recognition; methods and tools for conducting its business; and its relationships with suppliers. Accordingly, the court included the value of enterprise goodwill in valuing E&Y and awarded the wife a portion of the husband's interest based on his pro rata share of E&Y's value.

Similarly in *Howell v. Howell*,[5] the court also calculated the value of the distributable marital business asset as a percentage of enterprise value. In that case, the husband, an attorney with the law firm of Hunton & Williams, contended that the firm's partnership agreement defined the value of the partnership interest upon termination or death by entitling the partner to receive only the balance of his capital account and his share of the net income through the date of withdrawal. As in *Bobrow*, the husband maintained that the agreement fixed the value of his partnership interest for equitable distribution purposes, and, accordingly precluded consideration of whether his interest had goodwill. The trial court rejected this argument and instead ruled that the husband's partnership interest had goodwill because the law firm's agreement made no provision for goodwill and did not control on this issue. The trial court carefully distinguished between personal and enterprise goodwill and selected a value that was solely attributable to the husband being a partner in the firm. As such, the goodwill represented the premium due to the husband's association with the firm and the economic advantage he enjoyed by virtue of being a partner in that firm, but did not include any value attributable to him personally, and it did not rely upon any earnings due to the husband's own expertise, reputation, experience, skill, knowledge, or personality.

The court also rejected a 40% discount for lack of marketability and a 30% discount for lack of control "because no transfer of the partnership interest was foreseeable and no one in the firm, nor any group within it, exercised majority control." On appeal, the Virginia Court of Appeals affirmed, finding that "The large discount for lack of marketability was inappropriate, as the highest and best use for the defendant's share is to remain with Hunton & Williams." The appellate court thus used the concept of highest and best use to determine that the highest value that could be realized was that which would be realized through the husband's continuing to own an interest in the firm, rather than on a sale of that interest. The court accordingly affirmed the exclusion of personal goodwill and discounts, and the inclusion of enterprise goodwill, on the basis of the husband's staying with the firm. This case can also be characterized as using an investment value or intrinsic value standard of value on this basis, since investment or intrinsic value is the value to a particular owner—in this case, the husband qua law firm partner.

Another Virginia case, which, like *Howell*, can be considered an intrinsic value case as well as a fair value case on the basis that it awarded the pro-rata share of the business without permitting discounts, is *Owens v. Owens*.[6] In *Owens*, in the year that the parties were married, the husband and his brother formed a closely held corporation, and each was a 50% shareholder. In valuing the corporation, the husband's expert applied a 33% lack of control discount (as well as a discount for trapped-in capital gains tax), contending that because the husband's interest was less than 51%, it should be considered a minority interest. The expert stated that the size of the discount was dependent on the "amount of control that the person has over the corporation." Because the corporation had two 50% owners, the expert opined that a one-third discount for lack of control was appropriate. The wife's expert, on the other hand, did not apply such a discount. The trial court ultimately adopted the husband's expert's valuation method and lower-range value, but without adjusting the value for any discounts. It rejected the expert's discounts and reductions because those decrements did not reflect the intrinsic value of the business to the husband, but the value to a third party purchaser—and the evidence clearly showed that no sale was imminent or planned.

On appeal, the husband argued that the lower court erred as a matter of law when it failed to apply a minority interest discount when valuing a 50% interest in a closely held company. The Virginia Court of Appeals disagreed, saying that "husband's position as a 50% owner does not necessarily mandate the use of a minority discount." It then considered the shareholders' actual operating history and the legal remedies available to a minority shareholder. It concluded that, "In this case, given the absence of any suggestion of actual oppression relating to husband's alleged minority status coupled with the availability of judicial remedies for the most egregious forms of potential oppression, we reject husband's assertion that his position as an equal co-owner should entitle him as a matter of law to a minority discount for equitable distribution purposes." Citing *Howell*, the court further noted that although a discount may be necessary in circumstances where a sale is probable, no evidence showed that a sale of all or some part of the husband's interest would be required. Thus, the court affirmed the trial court's decision denying the discount.

In *Neuman v. Neuman*,[7] the dispute was over the value of the husband's minority interest in a closely held family trucking business. The husband's expert applied a 35% discount for lack of marketability, but the trial court accepted the wife's valuation, which used a capitalization of earnings approach and applied no discounts, on the basis that the husband had no plans to sell his stock. The Wyoming Supreme Court affirmed, citing an article by Alan Zipp,[8] (see Mr. Zipp's contribution in this chapter) which argued that there is a difference between the value of a business to a willing buyer and the value of a business for divorce purposes, primarily because there is no willing buyer in a divorce and the business will not be sold. In addition, a willing buyer is contemplating future profitability and earnings in the future when making a valuation decision while, in the divorce case, the post-divorce earnings are considered property outside the scope of the rules for distribution of marital property. The legal concept of marital property recognizes the business value as it exists at the date of divorce or separation, and income to be earned after the divorce is not part of that marital property. Accordingly, the court found that the capitalization of earnings approach to the valuation of stock in such cases was supported by the Zipp article. This case can be considered a fair value case because the husband received his pro-rata share of the company's value.

In *Bertuca v. Bertuca*,[9] the Tennessee Court of Appeals observed that "fair market value is typically not a reasonable method for valuing a closely held corporation, because the stock is rarely traded and there is no 'market.'" Although other Tennessee courts have used a fair market value standard of value to value businesses in other marital dissolution cases,[10] and even though the

Fair Value in Marital Dissolution: Case Law

trial court in this case was attempting to determine "fair market value," the appellate court determined that fair market value was inappropriate in valuing a partnership that owned seven McDonald's franchises, and instead used a fair value standard of value.

In this case, the husband and his father were the partnership's only two partners. The husband owned a 90% interest, but both the father and son had equal management rights, including any decision to sell. The partnership had a buy-sell agreement that set a purchase price at book value and that, in the alternative, provided for liquidation.

The partnership had purchased the franchises a year before the divorce. To finance a part of his 90% share, the husband borrowed $124,200 from his father—a debt that remained outstanding at the divorce. The father, who owned and operated other McDonalds through a separate entity, provided management services at no charge so that his son's partnership could gain a foothold in the franchise business. The McDonald's Corporation owned the underlying real estate and rented it to the partnership, and the partnership was prohibited from selling any franchise without McDonald's' consent. The partnership was also obligated to rebuild one of the franchises in its entirety, at an estimated cost of $950,000.

The husband's valuation expert, who specialized in McDonald's franchises, opined that as of the valuation date, the partnership's seven franchises were worth no more than the purchase price paid the year before. To reach this conclusion, he first calculated the gross value of each franchise by using a multiple of free cash flow—which he testified was standard practice for valuing a McDonald's franchise. Cash flow was determined from each operation's net income during the prior twelve months and reducing it by interest expense, depreciation, amortization, and general/administrative expense. Multiplying this by a factor of five (4.5 to 5 was the standard for McDonald's, he said), he reached the gross value. He added current assets and deducted current liabilities to arrive at a total net value for the seven stores of approximately $485,000. Given the partnership's obligation to rebuild one restaurant and the husband's obligation to repay his father's loan, the expert said the marital interest in the partnership actually had a negative value.

The wife's expert used a capitalization of earnings method and a 12% capitalization rate, and initially valued the partnership at just over $3.078 million, excluding debt. Applying cash flow figures supplied by the husband's expert and the same general/administrative expense—adjusted downward for what he believed to be unnecessary expenses and excess profits—the wife's expert reached a final value for the husband's 90% interest of $1.671 million. The husband presented a rebuttal expert who also specialized in valuing McDonald's franchises. This expert criticized the wife's expert for using a 12% capitalization rate to reach a cash flow multiple of 8.33—higher than she'd seen for any sale of a McDonalds. The preferred method according to her was a discounted cash flow method (DCF). Her DCF projected the income of each restaurant over seven years discounted by a 20% discount rate. Although her DCF indicated that the seven franchises had not appreciated beyond the purchase price, the partnership had $493,000 in equity. After applying a 20% discount for lack of marketability and deducting the loan to his father, she valued the husband's 90% interest at $231,000.

Chapter 5: Fair Value in Marital Dissolution

Based on the three expert reports, the trial court valued the fast food partnership at $1 million, and the husband's interest at $900,000. The husband appealed, claiming the valuation was contrary to the evidence and failed to account for the buy-sell value and a marketability discount.

The Tennessee Court of Appeals found that a number of factors complicated the partnership valuation, in particular the recent acquisition of the franchises, their limited earnings history, and the need to entirely rebuild one of them. The partnership earnings were also skewed by the father's contribution of management services for free. In addition, there were problems with each of the primary experts. The husband's expert applied excess depreciation and amortization. The wife's expert failed to consider the cost of the rebuild. The rebuttal expert's valuation conclusion was wholly dependent on the "appropriateness of the methods and assumptions" she used.

The court also noted that the trial court based its opinion upon the "fair market value" of the partnership. However, in the appellate court's view, the primary value of the partnership was the income it produced, so that the preferred method of valuation would be to determine its earnings value using a capitalization of income approach. Adjusting for interest expense on the rebuild and excess depreciation, the court reached normalized cash flow of $442,978. It used the 12% capitalization rate from the wife's expert to reach a value of nearly $3.7 million. After adjustments for cash on hand and liabilities—including the obligation to rebuild—the court determined a value of $1.033 million. Because this value approximated the trial court's conclusion, its findings were left undisturbed.

As to discounting the partnership's value for lack of marketability, the court said, "Since our determination as to value is based upon the earnings value of the partnership, that value would not be impacted by the lack of marketability of [the husband's] interest unless it appeared from the record that his needs or situation were such that a sale of his interest would be necessary or desirable....Thus the value of the business is not affected by the lack of marketability and discounting the value for nonmarketability in such a situation would be improper." Similarly, the court concluded that the buy-sell agreement did not affect the ultimate value conclusion because a sale was not planned or imminent. In sum, the husband's pro rata share of the partnership was distributed as a marital asset.

Spouse Are Not Willing Buyers or Sellers

Ellington v. Ellington,[11] which rejected a fair market value standard of value on the basis that neither the husband nor the wife was a willing seller, predominantly used fair value constructs. In that case, the wife's expert used an excess earnings method and came to a value of $668,000, whereas the husband's expert determined that the fair market value of liabilities outweighed assets by approximately $55,000, and therefore the company had negative value. The court rejected both experts' use of a fair market value standard, which the court ruled was inappropriate because neither party was a willing seller. Based on its own approach, the court came to a value of $293,000. The appellate court approved this decision on the fair value logic that the husband would retain ownership, current management would continue, and the husband would

Fair Value in Marital Dissolution: Case Law

continue to benefit from his ownership. Incidentally, such logic also supports an investment value (also called intrinsic value) standard of value.

Goodwill Included, No Discounts

As indicated in *Bobrow* and *Howell*, above, the fair value standard can be inferred where the court includes enterprise goodwill, even where no sale is imminent, contemplated, or even possible, but declines to take any shareholder-level discounts. In *Bobrow*, the enterprise goodwill was comprised of specified intangible assets, including the firm's trade name, favorable business reputation and name recognition, the methods and tools for conducting its business, and its relationships with suppliers. In *Howell*, the enterprise goodwill was defined not in terms of specific assets, but rather in terms of the economic "premium" or benefit the entity conferred on anyone associated with it, and was distinguished from the efforts of its personnel. The courts in both cases included enterprise goodwill, regardless of how that was defined, and the courts rejected the application of shareholder-level discounts.

Use of Shareholder Oppression and Dissent "Fair Value"

Some courts deciding marital dissolution cases have expressly referred to the fair value standard found in shareholder oppression and dissent cases. An excellent example is *Brown v. Brown*,[12] where the court, in the second sentence of its opinion, indicated that it was looking to corporate law principles found in shareholder oppression and dissent cases to determine that, in the absence of extraordinary circumstances, neither marketability nor minority discounts apply to the valuation of a spouse's interest in a closely-held corporation for purposes of equitable distribution. The rationale of cases such as *Brown*, therefore, is that a spouse who owns a fractional interest in an enterprise must be compensated for what has been taken—either the pro rata share of the going concern, or what the owner would have reasonably expected to receive from continuing involvement with the enterprise. Applying discounts to the spouse's share where the spouse retains the interest would unfairly reduce the value of the marital estate.

In *Brown*, the husband owned 47.5% of a florist supply company and was a company officer. He had a reported W-2 income of $75,000, 1099 income of $75,000, and interest income of $7,131. The trial court had accepted the wife's expert's valuation of the husband's interest in the company at $561,925, excluding any discount for marketability or lack of control. The wife's expert had valued the business as a whole as of the date of complaint, and then took a percentage to establish the husband's proportionate interest. The expert assumed that the full value of that interest should be included in equitable distribution. The husband's expert valued the same interest, but applied a 25% discount for lack of marketability and a 15% discount for lack of control—which the trial court had rejected.

On appeal, the husband challenged the amount of the equitable distribution award related to his business interest. The New Jersey Appellate Division found no previous decisions in New Jersey addressing the applicability of discounts for the purposes of equitable distribution. After reviewing the assumptions and elements of both valuations, the court was more persuaded by the testimony of the wife's expert. The court reasoned that since the corporation in question was a close corporation, any liquidity issues were not of consequence as there was no intention to sell the business. The court referred to the fair value determinations made in *Balsamides v. Protameen Chemicals, Inc.*[13] (an oppression case) and *Lawson Mardon Wheaton, Inc. v. Smith*[14] (a dissenter's rights case), which had adopted the position of the American Law Institute (ALI) as set forth at 2 ALI *Principles of Corporate Governance* § 7.22(a) and comment e thereto. The ALI's rationale for the fair value, no-discount rule, is that neither the dissenting (minority) shareholder, nor the oppressive (majority) shareholder, nor a veto-wielding (50%) shareholder, can be allowed to exploit the very situation that triggered the right to an appraisal, thereby capturing more than a proportionate share of the corporation's value and depriving other shareholders of their fair share. Applying this principle, the court said, "The distinction between fair value and fair market value appears to us equally applicable in the valuation of one spouse's interest in [the] family's closely-held corporation for purposes of equitable distribution." The court emphasized that "fair value" is not the same as, or short-hand for, "fair market value." Instead, fair value carries with it the statutory purpose that shareholders be fairly compensated, which may or may not equate with the market's judgment about the stock's value. The court opined that this is particularly appropriate in the close corporation setting where there is no ready market for the company's shares and consequently no fair market value. The court also stated that "We see no reason to reward the spouse who holds title to the shares by allowing him to retain the value of the entire bloc at a bargain 'price,' that is, crediting the non-owner spouse with less than the owner's proportionate share of full value when determining equitable distribution of the marital assets. Here, allowing the marketability or minority discounts would unfairly minimize the marital estate...."

Finding no reason to apply a different approach to equitable distribution in marital dissolution cases, finding no extraordinary circumstances warranting any discounts, and finding that the divorce would not trigger a sale of the husband's shares, the court held that the application of discounts was inappropriate in this case.

The Vermont Supreme Court in *Drumheller v Drumheller*,[15] in upholding the trial court's decision to disallow minority discounts where the husband continued to receive full income from his partnership based on full valuation, cited the proposition in *Brown* that minority discounts should be applied only in exceptional circumstances and where it would be inequitable not to do so. In this case, the husband held a 10% interest in a company in which he was the CEO, and he also was a one-third partner in a real estate partnership that owned the company's land and building. The trial court had permitted small minority and liquidity discounts when valuing the company itself, but disallowed minority discounts to the husband's 33% interest in the partnership because there was no evidence that a sale of his interest was "in any way possible," especially since he controlled the partnership's only tenant as its CEO. On appeal, the Vermont Supreme court agreed that denying the discounts was within the trial court's discretion since, based on the *Brown* reasoning, it would be unfair to the wife to have discounted the value of the husband's interest in the partnership.

Fair Value in Marital Dissolution: Case Law

In *Fisher v. Fisher*,[16] the North Dakota Supreme Court rejected a wife's contention that the value of her minority interest in a family business owned with her husband should be discounted from a proportionate fraction of the corporation's agreed value, thereby increasing the share of other assets required to equalize her share of the marital estate. The court held that the wife would be adequately protected by her statutory right to receive "fair value" for her shares.

In this case, the husband and the wife agreed on the per share value of the stock—but that seems about all they agreed on. Although they both wanted control of the company, neither was willing to work with the other. Accordingly, the trial court split the stock between the parties, awarding the husband 51% and the wife 37%. The wife appealed, claiming that the stock either should have been distributed to the husband, or that her share should have been discounted to account for her minority position in the company and her cash settlement increased.

On appeal, the wife argued that the husband would have exclusive use of her only income-producing asset, and that because she would not have an effective voice in the corporate activities or a share in the corporate income, her remedies would be either to sell the stock at a discount to account for her minority position or to seek an involuntary dissolution of the corporation. The North Dakota Supreme Court disagreed, observing that the wife could also petition the court to force either the husband or the company to repurchase her shares at their "fair value." The court found that the wife's corporate remedies were adequate to protect her minority interest. It said, "the purpose of the corporate dissolution remedy intends no discount should be applied simply because the interest to be valued represents a minority interest in the corporation....The statutes suggest that a minority shareholder who brings an action for the involuntary dissolution of a corporation should not, by virtue of the controlling shareholders invocation of the buy-out remedy, receive less than he would have received had the dissolution been allowed to proceed. ... to fail to accord to a minority shareholder the full proportionate value of his shares imposes a penalty for lack of control, and unfairly enriches the majority shareholders who may reap a windfall from the appraisal process by cashing out a dissenting shareholder." This seemed particularly true to the court where, as here, the affected shareholders agreed to the total value of the corporation. Thus, the court affirmed the trial court's refusal to apply a minority discount to the wife's stock.

The court in *Piscopo v. Piscopo*,[17] a "celebrity goodwill" marital dissolution case involving the comedian Joe Piscopo, also took the position that it would be unreasonable to treat value one way in the context of one court where one could sue for damage to their name, and another way in a family court. The trial court said, "The court cannot countenance the anomaly that would result if one branch of Chancery vigorously protected plaintiff's person and business from another's 'unjust enrichment by the theft of [his] goodwill,' while another branch deprived a spouse from sharing in very same protectible interest." The rationale of this case supports the similar rationale used in *Brown v. Brown*, discussed above, for using a fair value standard borrowed from shareholder dissent cases in a marital dissolution action.

In this case, the court's valuation expert valued Piscopo's production business, through which Piscopo received his income, as a professional corporation, taking into account Piscopo's goodwill. The expert arrived at Piscopo's celebrity goodwill by taking 25% of Piscopo's average gross earnings over a three year period. The trial court held that Piscopo's celebrity goodwill was a marital asset, and the appellate court affirmed. Notably, no discounts were taken, and goodwill was included as a marital asset—traits of a case applying a fair value standard of value.

Other courts, however, reject the reasoning that it would anomalous to treat value differently in the marital dissolution context and in the shareholder dissent and oppression context. For example, the court in *In re Marriage of Thornhill*,[18] involving the husband's 70.5% interest in an oil and gas business found that the conditions applicable to shareholder appraisal actions do not apply to marital dissolution cases. The court observed that the state's divorce statutes did not contain the "fair value" language of the state's business corporation statutes, and also concluded that in marital dissolution, courts should retain the discretion whether to apply marketability discounts. The court expressly declined to adopt the reasoning of *Brown v. Brown,* finding—as have many other jurisdictions—that such a discount in privately held companies reflects "the fact that shares of stock in such corporations are less marketable than publicly traded stock, a factor that an ordinary buyer would take into consideration in deciding what to pay for the shares." The court reasoned that the failure to apply a marketability discount to an equitable division of marital property under Colorado law could unfairly penalize a party for ownership of shares that could not be readily sold or liquidated. Accordingly, the court also rejected the wife's contention that, based on the Colorado Supreme Court's holding in *Pueblo Bancorporation v. Lindoe, Inc.*[19] which precluded marketability discounts when determining the fair value of a dissenting corporate shareholder's interest pursuant to the state dissenters' rights statutes, no marketability discounts should apply as a matter of law to the value of the husband's business. (In fact, the *Pueblo Bancorporation* court had ruled that "fair value" does not mean "fair market value," and the court in *Thornhill* relied on this as support for treating value differently in these two different contexts.)

Buy-Sell Agreement Value Rejected as Controlling

Whether a buy-sell agreement was controlling as to the value of an insurance benefits brokerage firm was the key valuation issue in *In the Matter of Overbey*.[20] The husband and wife owned a one-third interest in the firm, but the husband was one of the firm members. The membership was subject to a buy-sell agreement that provided that certain events, including divorce, would trigger the agreement and require the member to sell his interest to the other members for the greater of 1.5 times the annual commissions of the company, on an accrual basis, or $1.25 million. In anticipation of the divorce and effectuation of the buy-sell agreement, the spouses jointly hired a business appraiser to value the firm.

The appraiser determined that the buy-sell agreement's formula placed the value of the firm at around $13.7 million, but opined that such a value was excessive relative to the firm's current cash flows. Although the appraiser's market approach yielded a similarly inflated value for the firm ($13.5 million), his income approach yielded a value of around $3.4 million, which he believed was the most accurate and represented the company's *"fair value."* [Emphasis in original.] At trial, the court adopted this valuation over a valuation prepared by the wife's expert, who stated that the firm should be valued at $22 million pursuant to the formula contained in the buy-sell agreement. In reaching its conclusion, the trial court concluded, among other things, that the buy-sell formula was inapplicable because it was artificially inflated.

On appeal, the wife contended that the trial court had erred by not using the buy-sell agreement's valuation formula or, alternatively, by not accepting the expert's market approach value. The Washington Court of Appeals disagreed with her assessment, finding that the buy-sell agreement was not a binding separation contract, and that while the formula contained therein was relevant, it was not determinative of the firm's value. The court noted that the trial court had discretion to rely on the appraiser's opinion, especially since it was supported by ample evidence and the appraiser's substantial experience and competence in valuing buy-sell agreements. The court also indicated that the valuation of closely-held companies presents particularly difficult questions. It said, "[b]ecause interests in such companies are rarely offered for sale, it is difficult to determine the value of such companies based on their fair market value." Accordingly, it affirmed the lower court's valuation—on a fair value basis.

In *Scott v. Scott*,[21] a Virginia case that cited to *Howell* (discussed above), the trial court also rejected the buy-sell provisions of a shareholder/employment agreement as controlling as to the firm's value. The husband, an accountant, was effectively a one-third owner of a CPA firm that, although registered as a corporation, operated like a partnership. Under the "shareholder" agreement, a departing shareholder was entitled to receive the increase in accounts receivable and work in process from the time he acquired his stock to the time he left the company multiplied by his ownership interest in the company. Given the firm's accrued debts since the agreement had been entered, all of the shareholders (and even the wife's expert) agreed that the husband would receive "no money under the employment agreement." The trial court, however, did not use this "zero" value under the buy-sell provisions in valuing the firm, and, accepting the wife's expert's valuation, concluded that the husband's portion of the firm was worth $145,200.

On appeal, the husband argued, inter alia, that the trial court had erred in ignoring the zero value of his interest under the terms of the shareholder agreement's buyout provisions. As for the probability that the husband would not receive anything for his shares if he left, the appellate court referenced prior decisions that suggested this is too speculative a consideration to overcome the deference owed to the finder of fact because there was no evidence that the husband actually planned to leave the firm. In fact, the court noted, the husband's testimony was that he planned to stay because of a non-competition contract that he had signed. The court then stated that "[t]he reason for rejecting the value set by buyout provisions is that they do not necessarily represent the intrinsic worth of the stock to the parties." Accordingly, because there was no evidence that the husband planned to leave the company, the court held that the trial court did not err in accepting the wife's expert's figure instead of what the husband might have received for his shares if he had left the company. Like the *Howell* case, this case can also be considered an intrinsic, or investment, standard of value case.

Chapter 5: Fair Value in Marital Dissolution

1. Noah J. Gordon serves as the Legal Counsel for Shannon Pratt Valuations, Inc. Mr. Gordon is a regular contributor to valuation and legal publications. This article was written for the first version of this Guide and was updated by the author in 2009.

2. For example, in *Grelier v. Grelier*, 2008 Ala. Civ. App. LEXIS 769 (Ala. Civ. App. 2008), the stipulated standard of value was fair market value. Accordingly, the trial court reversed a special master's decision not to apply discounts and applied a combined 40% discount for lack of control and for lack of marketability. On appeal, the Alabama Court of Civil Appeals, while acknowledging that the question whether fair market value or fair value applied in marital dissolution cases was a question of first impression in Alabama, held that it did not need to reach the question because the parties had agreed to apply the fair market value standard. Accordingly, the appellate court rejected the wife's contention that, as a general matter, discounts were inappropriate when valuing business interests in the divorce context.

3. See, e.g., *In the Matter of Overbey*, 2007 Wash App. LEXIS 1651 (Wash. Ct. App. 2007).

4. *Bobrow v. Bobrow*, State of Indiana, Hamilton Superior Court Cause No. 29D01-0003-DR-166.

5. *Howell v. Howell*, 1998 WL 972312 (Va. Cir. Ct. Sept. 4, 1998), *aff'd* 523 S.E.2d 514 (Va. Ct. App. 2000).

6. *Owens v. Owens*, 2003 Va. App. LEXIS 639 (Va. Ct. App. 2003).

7. *Neuman v. Neuman*, 842 P.2d 575 (Wyo. 1992).

8. Alan S. Zipp, "Divorce Valuation of Business Interests: A Capitalization of Earnings Approach," XXIII *Fam. L. Q.* 89 (1989).

9. *Bertuca v. Bertuca*, 2007 Tenn. App. LEXIS 690 (Tenn. Ct. App. 2007).

10. See, e.g., *Alsup v. Alsup*, 1996 Tenn. App. LEXIS 425 (Tenn. Ct. App. 1996).

11. *Ellington v. Ellington*, 842 So. 2d 1160 (La. Ct. App. 2003).

12. *Brown v. Brown*, 348 N.J. Super. 466; 792 A.2d 463, 2002 N.J. Super. LEXIS 105 (N.J. App. Div. 2002).

13. *Balsamides v. Protameen Chemicals, Inc.*, 160 N.J. 352, 368, 734 A.2d 721 (N.J. 1999).

14. *Lawson Mardon Wheaton, Inc. v. Smith*, 160 N.J. 383, 397, 734 A.2d 738 (N.J. 1999).

15. *Drumheller v. Drumheller*, 2009 VT 23, 2009 Vt. LEXIS 27 (Vt. 2009).

16. *Fisher v. Fisher*, 1997 N.D. 176, 568 N.W.2d 728, 1997 N.D. LEXIS 195 (N.D. 1997).

17. *Piscopo v. Piscopo*, 231 N.J. Super 576 (N.J. Super. 1988), *aff'd*, 232 N.J. Super. 559; 557 A.2d 1040 (N.J. App. Div. 1989).

18. *In re Marriage of Thornhill*, 200 P.3d 1083, 2008 WL 3877223, 2008 Colo. App. LEXIS (Colo. Ct. App. 2008).

19. *Pueblo Bancorporation v. Lindoe, Inc.*, 63 P.3d 353 (Colo. 2003).

20. *In the Matter of Overbey*, 2007 Wash App. LEXIS 1651 (Wash. Ct. App. 2007).

21. *Scott v. Scott,* , 2007 Va. App. LEXIS 454 (Va. Ct. App. 2007).

Understanding Fair Value for Divorce

By Lee D. Sanderson, CPA/ABV, CVA, MST[1]

Changing to fair value for divorce

The standard of value used for business valuation in divorce cases has historically been *fair market value*. This standard of value has been defined as "the price property would change hands between a willing buyer and a willing seller…" In practical terms, it is the price a business, or a business interest, could be sold for in an arm's-length transaction.

The *fair value* of a business interest is different from its fair market value. Fair value is not intended to represent the price that interest could be sold for in an arm's-length transaction. It is a term most commonly used for shareholder disputes to compensate shareholders involuntarily deprived of their property. Accordingly, fair value is not based on the concept of a willing buyer and a willing seller; an essential element to all fair market value appraisals.

In recent years, many states have made a departure from the traditional fair market value standard used in divorce cases and adopted a standard that they refer to as fair value. Unfortunately, the courts have not established a clear and consistent definition of fair value as it relates to marital dissolution resulting in a great deal of speculation in this area. Many believe that the appropriate standard for divorce should be fair value as it has been used in dissenting shareholder disputes while others maintain that fair market value is still the most appropriate standard.

The purpose of this article is to highlight the effect of applying fair value in the unique context of divorce litigation. The decision regarding the appropriate standard to use for divorce in each state belongs to the courts. Our role as appraisers and experts is to educate the judges and attorneys on these matters so they can strive to achieve results that are truly equitable for the divorcing parties.

Effect of a change to fair value on divorce cases

There needs to be more uniformity in the standard of value used for business valuation in divorce cases. Perhaps that standard will ultimately become fair value or some variation of it for divorce. However, I am not convinced that a strict application of the fair value standard, used in shareholder disputes, creates a result that is necessarily "fair" because of the unique purpose of valuation in a divorce case.

In a recent presentation I made to the Academy of Matrimonial Lawyers, I discussed the shift away from fair market value to fair value and the potential implications for divorce cases. In the absence of a clear definition, there is a great deal of potential for misunderstanding and abuse that could result in unfair consequences for divorcing parties. Some of the potential implications to consider are as follows:

Chapter 5: Fair Value in Marital Dissolution

1. A business interest will be valued significantly higher using fair value than that the asset could possibly be sold for. This creates an unfair result for the business owner spouse.

2. When the concept of a willing buyer and a willing seller in a market transaction is removed from the equation, the discounts for lack of marketability and the minority interest discounts are typically not used. This contributes to the significantly higher value.

3. In addition to the removal of discounts, a shift away from fair market value may also affect the normalizing adjustments made to the financial statements. Many of the typical adjustments appraisers make are to adjust expenses to reflect market levels. If the premise of an arm's-length sale is removed, wouldn't it follow that market level expense adjustments would no longer apply?

4. Fair value for business appraisal results in an inconsistent application of valuation standards with all other assets being valued at fair market value for property division. Accordingly, the business interest would be the only asset valued using a different standard preventing an "apples to apples" comparison of assets.

5. If fair value as it relates to shareholder disputes becomes the new standard for divorce, there would likely be a significant financial advantage to the business owner of selling the business prior to a divorce. If this is the case, it is a clear indication that an inequitable result has been achieved.

Understanding the divorce process

Understanding the purpose and context of a valuation is essential to a fair value engagement. Divorce cases have some unique elements to them that must be considered.

In a divorce case, the assets of a marital estate are divided between the parties with the goal being to achieve an "equitable division of assets". To achieve this, the attorneys compile a list of all assets owned by the divorcing parties with values assigned for those assets.

The assets of the marital estate include all cash, investments, real estate, business interests, other tangible assets and some intangible assets. These assets are all typically listed at fair market value in order to compare any division of property on an "apples to apples" basis. In many cases, it is common for assets to be converted to a "cash equivalent" basis in order to remove the potential effect of taxes from built-in gains.

The percentage that each spouse receives of the total marital estate is decided between the lawyers or the court based on the unique circumstances of each case. The goal is to achieve a division of property that is equitable to the parties. In many cases, the value assigned to a business interest is the most contested asset of a marital estate. Accordingly, the standard of value for business valuation used can have a significant impact on the ultimate division of properties for the parties.

Understanding Fair Value for Divorce

It is very important to understand that business valuation for divorce does not exist in a vacuum. It is one piece of the puzzle and its value will likely be offset against other assets valued at fair market value. The ultimate value is likely to be negotiated between the parties during settlement discussions and other offsetting factors such as other assets and support payments will be considered.

The need for change

If fair market value has been the historical standard, and all other assets are valued according to this standard, then why has there been a need for change with respect to business valuations for divorce? One reason may be that the use of discounts has been unfortunately abused by some business appraisers and lawyers in divorce cases.

I have witnessed many cases where appraisers have prepared reports taking excessive discounts and therefore undervaluing the business asset for divorce purposes. I recently experienced a case where an appraiser, when valuing a business with $1,000,000 of annual cash flow, applied a 100% discount for lack of marketability for divorce purposes.

A review of cases nationally reveal that the courts have been disallowing discounts perhaps in an effort to prevent such abuse and ensure that a business interest is not undervalued. However, in doing so, they may have unintentionally created a problem of overvaluation and an inequitable result to the business owner spouse.

If fair value for divorce will become a newly defined standard, care must be taken to understand the divorce process and to achieve a result that is truly fair for each of the divorcing parties. I would suggest that the solution is not a complete elimination of discounts, but rather a more accurate, ethical and independent application of them.

Fair Value Considerations

When performing a business valuation for divorce using a fair value standard, the following items should be considered and discussed with the attorney:

1. Has fair value been adopted as the appropriate divorce standard of value (for business valuation) in the state you are practicing in?

2. Has fair value been defined by the courts where you practice in the context of divorce?

3. If fair value has not been adopted, is there case law that establishes a departure from fair market value? If so, a complete understanding of such case law is essential to the engagement.

Chapter 5: Fair Value in Marital Dissolution

4. If valuation discounts have been disallowed by the courts of your home state, were they disallowed as a matter of valuation theory or were they disallowed in a fact specific case in order to prevent some abuse and undervaluation?

5. The attorney may want to understand the actual difference in value obtained using fair market value versus fair value to assist with settlement negotiations.

6. In cases where each spouse was a stockholder and employee of the business in question, will one spouse be divested of his/her stock interest as a result of the divorce? This situation may have unique differences compared to a situation where only one of the spouses owns and works in the business.

7. Will the application of a fair value standard result in an overstatement of value and an inequitable result for the divorcing parties? If so, it may affect the percentages used for property division or a support calculation.

8. Has the income of the business owner spouse been normalized appropriately and has it been accounted for in a manner to avoid any "double dip" issue with support payments? Although fair value appraisals are not entirely bound by market data, the compensation level used for the valuation and for support purposes must be synchronized in order to obtain a fair result.

Conclusion

A review of cases nationally indicates a trend by the courts to move towards adopting fair value as the appropriate standard for divorce. It is our role as appraisers and experts to continue making judges and attorneys aware of the differences between fair market value versus fair value so that they can strive to achieve an equitable result for the divorcing parties. Toward that end, we must apply the existing standards of our state while being in a position to inform the judges and attorneys as to how those existing standards are affecting business value in the unique context of property division for divorce.

---

1. Lee D. Sanderson, CPA/ABV, CVA, MST, is a business appraiser in Framingham, MA, specializing in business valuation and forensic accounting for divorce cases.

The New Business Valuation Standard for Divorce[1]

By Lee D. Sanderson, CPA, ABV, CVA, MST[2]

The standards for valuing a business for the purpose of equitably dividing assets in divorce cases have been ruled upon in Massachusetts, and that ruling will likely have implications for divorce valuations nationwide. This is the first Supreme Court ruling of its kind with detailed guidance on the debate over "tax-affecting" for S corporations and discount issues specific to divorce valuations. The conclusions provide appraisers nationwide with guidance on these important issues.

In *Bernier v. Bernier*, SJC-09836 (Sept 14, 2007), the Massachusetts Supreme Judicial Court considered the question of whether it is proper to discount the value of an S corporation by tax-affecting income at the rate applicable for C corporations. The court also considered whether the trial court judge erred in discounting the fair market value of the S corporation by applying key man and marketability discounts, which are widely used by appraisers when calculating fair market value. Many businesses will now be assigned a higher value for divorce purposes as a result of this opinion.

The following summarizes the outcome of the opinion and the new standards:

1. The court's opinion represents a departure from the use of fair market value in divorce cases.

2. The court ruled that tax-affecting is necessary when valuing S corporations.

3. When tax-affecting S corporations, it is not appropriate to use an average 35% corporate tax rate.

4. Key man discounts are not appropriate in cases where the owner does not intend to sell the business and the owner is not critical to the financial success of the business.

5. Discounts for lack of marketability are not appropriate in cases where the owner does not intend to sell the business

Here is how these standards will play out in many cases: Use of a lower tax rate for tax-affecting will result in a higher after-tax earnings stream for the business. A higher after-tax earnings stream results in a higher value to the business. Key man and marketability discounts are reductions taken in a valuation calculation under the income approach to arrive at fair market value. Eliminating these discounts results in a higher value in the valuation calculation. The combination of these two factors can result in a significantly higher value.

Chapter 5: Fair Value in Marital Dissolution

Example of *Bernier* impact

Table 1 illustrates this potential impact. Example A represents a hypothetical valuation calculation similar to the facts of the *Bernier* case. It includes a 35% tax rate, a key man discount, and a marketability discount. The calculated value is $2,080,000.

Example B in Table 1 takes the same calculation but modifies it in accordance with *Bernier*. A lower tax rate is used for tax-affecting and both discounts have been removed. The recalculated value then becomes $3,060,000—a difference of 47%.

Table 1	Example A	Example B
Earnings before Federal Taxes	1,000,000	1,000,000
Federal Taxes	(350,000)	(235,000)
After Tax Earnings	650,000	765,000
Sample Capitalization Rate	0.25	0.25
Calculated Value before Discounts	2,600,000	3,060,000
Less Key Man Discount 10%	(260,000)	
Less Marketability Discount 10%	(260,000)	
Calculated Value	2,080,000	3,060,000
Increase in Value		980,000
Percentage Increase in Value		47%

FMV vs. Investment Value

There are several standards of value used by professional appraisers, including fair market value (FMV), investment value, and fair value. Business valuations for divorce in Massachusetts have historically been prepared according to the FMV standard. Revenue Ruling 59-60 defines FMV as "the price at which the property would change hands between a willing buyer and a willing seller, neither being under any compulsion to buy or sell, and both having relevant knowledge of relevant facts." FMV in this context is essentially the price someone would pay for a business in the open market.

The *Bernier* opinion departs from this widely accepted standard. Despite references to FMV, the court's position was more reflective of what appraisers call investment value, emphasizing that "the judge must take particular care to treat the parties not as arm's length hypothetical buyers and sellers in an open market but as fiduciaries entitled to equitable distribution of their marital assets." An investment value approach is used to calculate the value of a business to a particular investor rather than to buyers in the open market. Some states have adopted a similar standard called fair value, which is also applied to shareholder disputes. If the new standard is going to be a departure from FMV, it will have a significant impact on future valuations.

Tax-affecting issue

In the *Bernier* case, the long running debate over tax-affecting played out in opposite positions. One expert treating the S corporation as if it were a C corporation and applying an average 35% corporate tax rate. The opposing expert did not tax-affect at all, taking the position that S corporations don't pay any corporate-level tax. The court agreed that tax-affecting is necessary for S corporations, but disagreed with the application of C corporation tax rates. It stated, "Careful financial analysis tells us that applying the C corporation rate of taxation severely undervalues the fair market value of the S corporation." The court concluded that the metric employed in the *Del. Open MRI Radiology v. Kessler* case, 898 A.2d, 327 (Del. Ct. Ch.2006), provides a fairer mechanism for accounting for the tax consequences. The Delaware court determined that a 29.4% rate was appropriate. This rate was determined by creating a fictional percentage to represent federal corporate tax at the entity level, and dividend tax at the shareholder level, to arrive at the same equivalent figure that would be left in the pockets of an S corporation shareholder.

I would like to comment that the calculations used to arrive at the 29.4% figure (in the Delaware case) assumed that the shareholder paid income tax at the highest individual tax rate in effect at that time (2001), which was close to 40%. The highest individual tax rate for 2006 was only 35%, which means that the calculation requires adjustment before being applied to current valuations. Also, it would seem that business owners who are not in the highest individual tax bracket would need to apply a modified percentage as well, while still utilizing the same metric.

Table 2 illustrates the court's calculation of an appropriate rate to tax-affect an S corporation. The table demonstrates the different results using 40 versus 35%.

Table 2: Tax Affecting Calculations
Application of Bernier Case Methodology

	Calculation A		Calculation B	
	S Corp 40% Indiv Tax Rate	Bernier Tax Rate Calculation	S Corp 35% Indiv Tax Rate	Bernier Tax Rate Calculation
Earnings	100.0	100.0	100.0	100.0
Less tax	(40.0)	(29.4)	(35.0)	(23.5)
Net of tax	60.0	70.6	65.0	76.5
Less Dividend Tax	0	(10.6)	0	(11.5)
Net of all taxes	60	60	65	65
Tax Rate	40.0%	29.4%	35.0%	23.5%

Calculation A shows how a "Bernier tax rate" of 29.4% was calculated in the methodology described in the Bernier case (based on 40% individual income tax rate).

Calculation B applies the same methodology, but assumes a 35% individual tax rate rather than a 40% rate, resulting in a "Bernier tax rate" of 23.5%—which represents a 20% difference (29.4 minus 23.5, divided by 29.4).

Chapter 5: Fair Value in Marital Dissolution

Disallowing discounts

In *Bernier*, the trial court accepted the husband's expert, who took a key man discount on the premise that the husband's expertise was critical to the success of the enterprise. He also took a discount for marketability to adjust for a lack of liquidity in the ownership interest. Both of these discounts are widely used by business appraisers.

The Supreme Judicial Court disagreed with the decision to accept both discounts. The court stated that "given the husband's uncontradicted testimony that he would maintain total control of the business, i.e., not sell it, it is beyond reason to conclude that the business's value should be reduced to account for the loss of a man who is the whole show." Using a similar rationale, the court also concluded that the discount for marketability was also inappropriate, since the husband did not plan to sell the business.

Applying *Bernier*

The *Bernier* decision will affect many cases, but there are certain situations where it may not have an impact. Certainly the opinion on tax-affecting for S corporations will impact all future S corporation valuations, but you should take caution in calculating the tax rate based on current rates for the specific business owner.

The court's opinion regarding key man discounts seems to indicate that these discounts may still be allowable, but that they will apply in fewer circumstances. It seems clear that discounts for lack of marketability will not be allowed when the owner testifies that the intention is not to sell the business. However, this raises the question as to how the result would differ if the owner testified to the possibility of a sale. In a fair market value analysis based on the open market, the owner's intention would not be considered. Under the standard employed in the *Bernier* case, it is now a contributing factor.

There are other aspects of a business valuation that may be affected by *Bernier*, including certain normalizing adjustments to adjust expenses to market level, the application of the market approach in cases where no sale is contemplated, distinctions between enterprise and personal goodwill when no sale is contemplated, and others. Certainly, more guidance will be needed from the courts to address these important issues.

---

1. *The Value Examiner*, November/December 2007. Reprinted with Permission.
2. Lee D. Sanderson, CPA/ABV, CVA, MST, is a business appraiser in Framingham, MA, specializing in business valuation and forensic accounting for divorce cases.

Valuation of S Corporations for Purposes of Marital Dissolutions

By R. James Alerding, CPA/ABV, ASA, CVA and
H. Edward Morris, Jr., ASA, CBA, BVAL, CPA/ABV

Marital dissolutions are not only emotionally difficult but financially difficult. Dissolutions that involve businesses can create long periods of disagreements. Each state differs in their handling of dividing assets in marital dissolutions. This article will look at one state's approach (Massachusetts) and its Supreme Court's recent decision that could impact the valuation of a business or business interest for the purpose of marital dissolution in other states.

The three standards of value often used in marital dissolution cases are fair market value, fair value, and investment value. The following are definitions for each standard of value:

> Fair market value is defined by the American Society of Appraisers as: The price, expressed in terms of cash equivalents, at which property would change hands between a hypothetical willing and able buyer and a hypothetical willing and able seller, acting at arm's length in an open and unrestricted market, when neither is under compulsion to buy or sell and when both have reasonable knowledge of the relevant facts.[1]

> Fair value[2] is a legislative and judicial concept applied in shareholder dissent and oppression cases. It is determined on a state-by-state basis and is used by some states as the appropriate standard of value in determining the value of a business or business interest for marital dissolution cases. Generally, the fair value is defined as fair market value without minority and marketability discounts and represents the cash price dissenting and oppressed shareholders will receive in exchange for their shares of stock.[3]

> *Investment value* means the value of an asset or business to a specific or prospective owner.[4]

Generally, most state courts have recognized that there isn't a willing seller in cases involving shareholder dissent and oppression, which is a critical element in the definition of fair market value. Therefore, the courts are generally seeking an "equitable" resolution as they want to avoid rewarding controlling shareholders for their bad behavior.

In the case of *Bernier v. Bernier (449 Mass. 774, 873 N.E.2d 216)*, decided on appeal by the Supreme Judicial Court of Massachusetts on September 14, 2007 the Massachusetts Supreme Court has in essence expanded the use of the fair value standard of value from dissent and oppressed shareholder litigation to marital dissolution cases by promulgating a valuation methodology consistent with the concept of fair value.

Chapter 5: Fair Value in Marital Dissolution

The central issues for the appeal of the lower court's decision were:

1) Whether or not to tax-affect the earnings of two S corporations in the determination of the value of two S Corporations for marital dissolution purposes; and

2) Whether or not it was appropriate to apply key man and marketability discounts in determining the value of two S Corporations for marital dissolution purposes.

On the surface it would appear the Massachusetts Supreme Court rejected the concept of tax-affecting the earnings of an S corporation but a careful reading of this opinion indicates just the opposite. The facts of the case and the court's rational follow.

The husband's valuation expert (Horvitz) arrived at a value for 100% of the two entities of $7.85 million while the wife's valuation expert (Leicester) arrived at a value of $16.391 million for 100% of the two entities. Both Horvitz and Leicester agreed that the income approach was best for valuing the S corps but differed on whether to tax-affect the earnings in arriving at the value of the business. Horvitz applied a 35% average tax rate to the S corporations' earnings and further reduced the value 10% for a key man discount (being the husband) and 10% marketability discount. On the other hand, Leicester did not tax affect the S corporations' earnings nor did he take any key man or marketability discount. The trial court adopted Horvitz's value and methodology citing the *Gross* case and the IRS valuation guide as authority supporting Horvitz's methodology.

The appellate court decided that the trial court judge had erred in invoking the *Gross* case to support her conclusions, as not only did the *Gross* case not support tax-affecting, the interests valued were minority interests being valued for gifting purposes not marital dissolution. Additionally, the court ruled the judge "improperly relied on the IRS valuation guide as authority to justify the tax affecting advocated by Horvitz" when the guide clear states that "Under no circumstances should the contents be used or cited as authority for setting or sustaining a technical position" and the IRS itself in the *Gross* case put for the position of not tax affecting S corporation's earnings for valuation purposes. For this case the court emphasized "that the valuation of the supermarkets [S corporations] was undertaken pursuant to....for purposes of equitable distribution in a divorce matter."

The court continued by admonishing the judge "to look past the all-or-nothing approach of the parties' experts and pay particular attention to the facts of this case over more abstract considerations."

In a detail discussion of the issue of tax-affecting or not tax-affecting the earnings of S corporations and reference to a number of court cases dealing with this issue, the court placed great weight what it referred to as the *Kessler* case which is better known as *Delaware Open MRI Radiology Associates, P.A. v. Kessler, et al.*, 2006 Del. Ch. LEXIS 84 (April 26, 2006). In essence, the court's position rejected the "all-or-nothing" approach in favor of the approach used in the *Kessler* decision which used an effective tax rate of 29.4% to tax effect the S corporation earnings. This effective 29.4% tax rate represented the Delaware court's calculation of the C corporation tax rate necessary to put same amount of money in pocket of the shareholder as would be in the pocket of the shareholder if it were an S corporation.

The court stated "We conclude that the metric employed by the Kessler court provides a fairer mechanism for the accounting for the tax consequences of the transfer of ownership of the supermarkets from one spouse to the other in the circumstances of record. On remand on the issue of valuation, the judge is to employ the tax affecting approach adopted in Kessler."

The Court also addressed the issue of discounts ruling the key man discount was not appropriate "given the husband's uncontradicted testimony that he would maintain total ownership and control of the supermarkets, it is beyond reason to conclude that the business's value should be reduced to account for loss of the man who is 'the whole show.'" They did note the difference between this situation and the situation where the key person had died which could justify a key man discount.

The court also rejected the concept of a marketability discount "in light of the husband's testimony negating any possibility of sale."

Therefore, the court has effectively said, the value of the business for marital dissolution purposes it fair value which is often described as fair market value without minority or marketability discounts.

So while the court rejected the use of a 35% C corporation tax rate for tax affecting the earning of a S corporation, it instructed the lower court on remand to follow the methodology used in the *Kessler* case which did tax-affect S corporation earnings using a blended rate of 29.4%. The court also rejected key man and marketability discounts effectively arriving at a fair value for the two S corporations rather than fair market value.

It is likely this case, along with the *Kessler* case, will continue to influence marital dissolution cases not only in Massachusetts but also in other states as the positions taken and supporting rational were intended to arrive at an "equitable" value in marital dissolution cases. It will be interesting to see if other states follow the lead of the Massachusetts Supreme Court and effectively adopt fair value as the standard of value for marital dissolution cases.

---

1. American Society of Appraisers Business Valuation Standards, Definitions
2. Fair value, in the context of financial reporting, is defined by the FASB as: The amount at which an asset (or liability) could be bought (or incurred) or sold (or settled) in a current transaction between willing parties, that is, other than in a forced or liquidation sale.
3. Jay E. Fishman, Shannon P. Pratt, and William J. Morrison, *Standards of Value: Theory and Applications* (Hoboken, NJ: John Wiley & Sons, 2007), pg 89.
4. *Ibid*, 24.

Fair Value vs. Fair Market Value in Divorce Cases[1]

By Jerome W. Karsh, CPA

> *The valuation of a business is an art –not a science. A representation as to value that is painted in abstract colors and looks only to the past creates an unrealistic print, whereas an expert who paints the canvas with an objective brush, based on an honest analysis of the economic benefits that currently exist, as well as ones that are anticipated in the future, is a realist.*
>
> *—Jerome Karsh*

HYPOTHESIS:

There is probably little if any disagreement, in modern times at least –depending on whether the jurisdiction follows the common law or is a community property state –that the underlying philosophy intended to dictate the findings in most divorce actions is to arrive at an equitable or equal division of the marital property –and that the measure of that division is monetary.

The first cited definition of the word *standard* found in *Webster's College Dictionary* is: "something considered by an authority or by general consent as a basis of comparison." The word *value*, as defined in the same dictionary, is: "the worth of something in terms of some medium of exchange." In the context of business valuations in family law the question often arises as to: (1) whether there is a uniform standard of defining value, and (2) the validity of the value that any standard produces.

An over-used metaphor states that: "value, like beauty, lies in the eyes of the beholder." Of course, the same can be said about anything that defines personal worth to any individual. Thus, it seems self-evident that the measurement of an equitable or equal distribution is entirely a function of the standard of value(s) that is applied and how the "trier of the facts" interprets that standard for the given circumstances.

Though state statutes have not defined it as such, in the majority of divorce cases involving business valuations, *fair market value* historically has been the standard of value that has been applied; and since its introduction in 1959, much of the valuation philosophy as well as the definition of fair market value are referenced to that which is found in Revenue Ruling 59-60:

> .02 Section 20.2031-1(b) of the Estate Tax Regulations (section 81.10 of the Estate Tax Regulations (section 86.19 of Gift Tax Regulations 108) define fair market value, in effect, as the price at which the property would change hands between a willing buyer and a willing seller when the former is not under any compulsion to buy and the latter is not under any compulsion to sell, both parties having reasonable knowledge of relevant facts.

Fair Value vs. Fair Market Value in Divorce Cases

For whatever reason, the authors of the revenue ruling chose not to acknowledge that the "buyer" and the "seller" are hypothetical in the definition but rather to express it basically as an addendum:

> Court decisions frequently state in addition that the hypothetical buyer and seller are assumed to be able, as well as willing to trade and to be well informed about the property and concerning the market for such property.

Over the years the area of business valuation has grown from a part-time endeavor to a full-time profession. Whereas at the time that Revenue Ruling 59-50 was issued, little literature was available, today there is a plethora of material. The authority of the contents, for the most part, is from "experts" that became recognized as such either through their affiliation with an association, through published writing, or because they have been qualified in a court of law as having the necessary knowledge to testify on the subject. Currently at least four organizations now offer certification in business valuations; however, at an academic level, one cannot major or receive an undergraduate or advanced degree in this newly developed discipline. Despite the efforts of some to bring more uniformity to the process, the area of business valuations realistically cannot be confined by such constraints. Even Revenue Ruling 59-60, by its own caveat, does not provide a method for arriving at a value but, rather, only presents issues to consider in pursuit of hypothetical value:

> .01 A determination of fair market value, being a question of fact, will depend upon the circumstances in each case. No formula can be devised that will be generally applicable to the multitude of different valuation issues arising in estate and gift tax cases. Often, an appraiser will find wide differences of opinion as to the fair market value of a particular stock. In resolving such differences, he should maintain a reasonable attitude in recognition of the fact that valuation is not an exact science. A sound valuation will be based upon all the relevant facts, but the elements of common sense, informed judgment, and reasonableness must enter into the process of weight those facts and determining their aggregate significance.

Conceptually, if economic value is defined as: the future anticipated benefit to be received measured in current dollars; other than the ability to provide a computed number, what justification can be made for expressing an opinion of value if it is an erroneous monetary amount that could or would be realized in an arms-length transaction –where a seller desires to transact for the most he or she can attain and the buyer wishes to transact for the least– with perceived equity to both? If indeed an equal or equitable division is truly the desired goal, what rationale can be presented to support a "finding of fact" that is knowingly based on a supposition that ignores such reality?

The problem with fair market value

Through his writings (and lecturing), the most prominent pioneer in the evolution of this endeavor (and probably the most often quoted) is Dr. Shannon Pratt. Dr. Pratt's first book,

Chapter 5: Fair Value in Marital Dissolution

published by Dow Jones-Irwin in 1981, became the foundation of much of the literature that has followed. Certainly the valuation concepts expressed in the book have been expanded over time –some by Dr. Pratt himself– and some have taken on new characteristics because of court decisions; however, the underlying valuation philosophy has pretty much remained the same. The question is: does that philosophy provide the information needed to fulfill the goals intended for either an equal or equitable division of property in divorce actions?

Over the past forty plus years the art of business valuation, and the philosophies involved, has experienced its greatest development and with this growth came the need for distinguishing between fair market value and values that violated its basic concepts. Probably to most, the term fair market value is associated with the amount that something is sold for. As an example, even today, if a couple during the pendency of their divorce sells their home, in all probability, even to the court, the selling price will be considered the "fair market value". This, perhaps, is the major dilemma when dealing with the definition itself: the perception that fair market value is not a hypothetical value but, rather, the actual amount that something would sell for.

Under most case law, the seller and the buyer must remain "hypothetical," which rules out strategic and synergistic buyers. It is unlikely that, if a person wishes to sell something, he or she would not want to achieve the highest price possible and it is only logical that they would attempt to find a buyer who would pay such an amount. A few tax court cases as well as an IRS training manual have expressed this viewpoint; but unfortunately, this philosophy leads to the perception to many that the government is only seeking the highest value in order to achieve a higher tax.

> "It is also implicit that the buyer and seller would aim to maximize profit and/or minimize cost in the setting of a hypothetical sale." See *Estate of Watts v. Commissioner*, F. 2d 483, 486 (11th Cir. 1987), *affg*. T.C. Memo.

In 2001 the IRS published new proposed valuation standards Business Valuation Guidelines: Section 2.3.6.3 of the Guidelines states that:

> "other levels of value considerations, such as the impact of strategic or synergistic contributions to value". If such considerations are used then there is a violation of the definition of fair market value.

In reference to fair market value there is no question that the arrived at value, as necessitated by the circumstances, will be hypothetical in nature and that the buyer and seller are imaginary "non-entities" defined only to be not under compulsion and that they are willing and able to transact. Before examining the consequences of utilizing unidentified buyers and sellers it is essential to first look to the arena and context that relates to the revenue ruling rather than to family law matters. Citing from the ruling itself:

> The purpose of this Revenue ruling is to outline and review in general the approach, methods and factors to be considered in valuing shares of the capital stock of closely held

corporations for *estate tax and gift purposes* [emphasis added]. The methods discussed herein will apply likewise to the valuation of corporate stocks on which market quotations are either unavailable or are of such scarcity that they do not reflect the fair market value.

Here, another supposition must be made, that the doctrines set forth in the document apply to all forms of business entities (and perhaps all property in general) and not just the "shares of capital stock of closely held corporations."

There is also no doubt that Revenue Ruling 59-60 is an excellent treatise which sets forth fundamental principles to consider when valuing closely held corporations for tax related purposes even though its application is highly individualistic and subjective. The question is: does fair market value change for an intended purpose? Logically, except for words with multiple meanings, if a definition, by definition, is definite, then it can only change in the context in which it is used. For purposes here, the contexts are Tax Court and Divorce Court.

Every student of the law knows that the foundation of our jurisprudence system is taken from English common law. From that genesis came two distinct courts: (1) Courts of Law; and, (2) Courts of Equity (sometimes referred to as chancery courts). The distinction between "legal" and "equitable" relief is an important aspect of our American legal system. Historically, areas of the law that deal with disputes between persons when neither of them has done anything against the law, but there is a conflict between their rights or claims, have been matters for a chancery court. The other matters, basically dealing with the legal principles established from common law and laws enacted by government and from case law, have been "heard" in Courts of Law.

Today, all federal courts and most state courts have combined the two courts, offering a plaintiff the ability to receive both legal and equitable relief from the same proceeding. Yet, it would stretch reality to say that the judicial discretion that prevails in a divorce court is available in a tax court. If a classification can be made in this regard, a divorce court is a court of equity whereas the tax court is a court of law.

Why does this become important? Ever since its introduction, Revenue Ruling 59-60 has defined the standards and the fundamental concerns to be utilized when valuing a business for tax-related purposes. Because of the ruling's conceptual recognition by the federal court, it has also been became the criterion utilized in most of the valuations of divorcing couples –cited time and time again by experts not only in defining fair market value but as the basis for substantiating the method(s) they used in formulating their opinions. Further, because the requirements and restrictions imposed by the federal courts induced the need for greater sophistication in the valuation of closely held businesses (as well as other property i.e., real estate), on the surface at least, the standards that are defined by the Federal Tax Court cases should provide more credibility in arriving at a "fair market value" –no matter the purpose of the determination. The reality here is that not only can an argument be made that the standards of value are not the same; the standards of law that are applied are also different. In legal matters addressed by a tax court there is little, if any discretion with regard to "the letter of the law." Additionally, the rules of evidence in federal court (being

Chapter 5: Fair Value in Marital Dissolution

a court of law) are stricter and more closely adhered to than those found in a family law resolution. Such definition is non-existent in divorce matters with each case being unique and a court's determination dependent on the totality of the issues presented. Also, almost all of the cases that are heard in Tax Court deal with "material dollars" as the cost of trying an action in federal court would negate bringing a small dollar case to trial. On the other hand divorce cases, even with negligible value, must be presented in some form to a designated legal authority.

Our courts have always been perceived as issuing their rulings based on the evidence that has been presented in a particular case. If that ruling is based on evidence that disregards actual reality, a valid conclusion would probably only be achieved by mere chance. Fair market value presents such a scenario. Fair market value is a theoretical number that is being offered as representative of the amount that a business or property would sell for based on constraints that would not exist if the property actually were to be sold. By definition it must ignore the attributes that may be lost with the departure of the identifiable owner as well as the attributes that may exist from a specific buyer.

Minority and marketability discounts

There is probably no better example of some of the contradictions and shortcomings of fair market value than to look at the resultant fair market values of minority ownership. There is little doubt that the ownership of most closely held businesses that have multiple owners consist of either family members and/or persons who have more than a casual relationship. By definition, these relationships must be ignored; yet, under such circumstances, it is difficult to define a market that exists outside of the other owners. An inquiry of estate attorneys and their disposition of the minority ownership of deceased persons would easily substantiate this premise. Further, only by giving definition to a purchaser could a real value be approximated: a range that would go from zero, if the current owners have no desire to purchase, to a premium, where the selling of the interest would create a majority ownership.

Fair value

Another standard of value that is finding favor in divorce actions is "fair value".

Under generally accepted accounting principles, as stated in the Statement of Financial Accounting Standards, the definition of fair value for financial reporting purposes is: fair value (of an asset or liability) is the amount at which that asset or liability could be bought (or incurred) or sold (or settled) in a current transaction between willing parties, that is, in other than a forced or liquidation sale. FASB, Statement of Financial Accounting Standards No. 141, Business Combinations (June 2001).

Fair Value vs. Fair Market Value in Divorce Cases

In an earlier FASB, fair value was defined as: "the value determined by bona fide bargain between well-informed buyers and sellers, usually over a period of time: the price at which an [asset] can be bought or sold in an arm's length transaction between unrelated parties: value in a sale between a willing buyer and a willing seller, other than a forced or liquidation sale: an estimate of such value in the absence of sales or quotations." Statement of Federal Financial Accounting Standards No. 11: Amendments to Accounting for Property, Plant, and Equipment (July 1999).

Fair value, however, when used in legal proceedings has taken on an entirely different meaning. In this context, fair value is an invention of state legislative bodies and has been implemented to compensate dissenting or oppressed minority shareholders. Recently, however, some experts and some courts have utilized the concept in valuing minority shares of divorcing couples. Whereas fair market value involves a willing buyer and a willing seller, fair value involves a transaction in which the dissenter is forced to sell his interest for less than what he or she perceives the value to be.

> The price that fairly compensates an owner involuntarily deprived of the benefit of his or her ownership interest when neither a willing buyer nor willing seller exists.

Because fair value is a legally created "standard" that applies to given situations as defined in various state statues, there is no definition of the term as such but rather a point in time as to when the value should be determined. In states that have adopted the Uniform Business Corporation Act, fair value, regarding dissenter's shares is defined as:

> The value of the shares immediately before the effectuation of the corporate action to which the dissenter objects, excluding any appreciation or depreciation in anticipation of the corporate action unless exclusion would be inequitable.

As a generality the court cases articulate that the appraisal shall preclude any discount for minority interest–and possibly discounts for marketability–because the utilization of such discounts: (1) would value minority shares below majority shares resulting in unequal treatment of the same class of shares; (2) would undermine the goal of dissenters' rights statutes which are intended to prevent minority shareholders from being forced to sell at unfairly low values; and (3) may encourage oppressive conduct by the majority.

Though there is great validity for precluding such discounts in dissenting and oppressed minority shareholder suits, it is difficult to understand the rationale of denying their existence in divorce actions. Simple logic would indicate that by not considering a discount one party is being penalized while the other party is benefiting from a value that in all likelihood will never be realized or could possibly be attained on the valuation date. Further, based on the reason such value is in existence, the use of such in a divorce action seems to introduce an element of fault where none should exist.

Conclusion

With or without a defined standard of value the fact remains, that absent an arms length sale, the true "cash market value" of an interest in a closely held business is an unknown amount, and its valuation, based on a hypothetical sale as of a specific date can only be an approximation.

> Valuations, moreover, represent approximations. "The valuation process is an 'inexact science' requiring reasonable practical, and rational approximation based upon all information before the court." *Kraft, Inc. v. United States*, 30 Fed. CL. 739, 765 (1994).

> It (business valuations) is an inexact science at best, capable of resolution only by "Solomon-like" pronouncements. *Ketteman Trust v. Commissioner*, 86 T.C. 91, 98 (1986).

If the opening hypothesis in this article is correct then it is only logical that the "approximate" valuation(s), in order to have validity, should rely on the reality that exists rather than a theoretical number in a phantom environment.

The parties in estate tax cases often play a "valuation game" and advocate high and low values to provide the finder of facts with limits within which the parties may be satisfied with the final decision. Because of that phenomenon, we may expect that estates will report the lowest possible value, and that the Commissioner will determine the highest possible value. Those very dynamics may raise suspicion about the parties; positions on estate tax valuation issues…T.C. Memo. 2001-258.

Divorce is not a game –it is a tragic event in a family's life. It involves real people. Intellectual honesty should preclude a philosophy that allows for a high and low parameter without any intention of trying to reach the real monetary worth of a business interest.

> …the underlying philosophy intended to dictate the findings in most divorce actions is to arrive at an equitable or equal division of the marital property –and that the measure of that division is monetary.

---

1. Originally published in the *American Journal of Family Law*, Volume 20, Number 2, Summer 2006. Reprinted with permission.

Fair Value as a Basis for Business Valuation in Divorce[1]

By Alan S. Zipp, Esq., CPA/ABV, CBA

Few people doubt there should be a uniform standard of business value for divorce. After all, divorce is an equitable proceeding, and it is hardly equitable to value the same business differently depending on where its owner lives. Equitable distribution is the underlying premise of divorce in nearly all states. For example:

- In Maryland, "It is the policy of this State that when a marriage is dissolved the property interests of the spouses should be adjusted fairly and equitably."[2]

- In New York, "The equitable distribution law was enacted in recognition of the fact that marriage is, among other things, an economic partnership and, upon its dissolution, property accumulated during the marriage should be distributed in a manner which reflects the individual needs and circumstances of the parties."[3]

- In Pennsylvania, the Divorce Code is intended to "effectuate economic justice between the parties ... and insure a fair and just determination of their property rights."[4]

Just as all income, estate, and gift tax valuations apply a uniform standard of fair market value, divorce valuations of business interests should also apply a uniform standard of value. A uniform standard would eliminate one of the most common areas of dispute in divorce litigation involving family business interests, namely, the appropriate application of business valuation theory.

Clearly it would be better if all states valued closely held businesses in divorce cases using the same standard of value. That would go a long way toward emphasizing the "equitable" in equitable distribution. But, is it possible to achieve uniformity among the states? And, if it is possible, what should be the standard of value applicable to business valuations in divorce?

Is a uniform business valuation standard for divorce possible?

In theory, the answer is yes; it is possible to apply a uniform standard of business valuation to divorce cases throughout the nation. After all, a uniform standard of business value has been adopted nationwide for all income, estate, and gift tax matters. But that standard took decades to adopt uniformly. Further, it was through a single federal agency, the Internal Revenue Service, and its rulings and regulations, together with numerous court decisions evolving over a long period of time, to achieve the uniformity of the "fair market value" standard.

Chapter 5: Fair Value in Marital Dissolution

Even with the uniform definition of fair market value there remain numerous subjective judgments resulting in constant disputes over the value of a business for income, estate, or gift tax purposes. This suggests that even if a uniform standard of business value for divorce is adopted, disputes will continue about business value for divorce purposes. So then, what is the point of creating a uniform standard of divorce value if it will not eliminate disputes over value in divorce cases?

Eliminate disputes over valuation theory

A uniform standard of divorce value will eliminate arguments over the appropriate definition of business value to use in divorce cases. The ensuing disputes will then focus on the substantive issues of the particular case such as the application of appraiser judgment, as in income, estate, and gift tax litigation matters. That is why a uniform standard of divorce value is a good idea. It will eliminate controversy over business valuation theory and focus attention to the substantive issues of the case. The premise of value in divorce should be uniformly measured as the intrinsic value to the marital community.

Divorce value is intrinsic value to the parties

Virginia and California illustrate the view of measuring intrinsic value to the parties rather than the price a hypothetical third party willing buyer might pay:

- "Trial courts valuing marital property for the purpose of making a monetary award must determine from the evidence that value which represents the property's intrinsic worth to the parties upon dissolution of the marriage."[5]
- "Intrinsic value is a very subjective concept that looks to the worth of the property to the parties."[6]
- "The value of community goodwill is not necessarily the specified amount of money that a willing buyer would pay for such goodwill. In view of the exigencies that are ordinarily attendant in a marriage dissolution, the amount obtainable in the marketplace might well be less than the true value of the goodwill."[7]
- "The goal of any appraisal of a business or professional practice in a family law proceeding is to establish the value of the interest to the spouse retaining it." "Marital Value is the investment value of the business interest to a defined investor."[8]

How to achieve a uniform standard?

Just as in the case of income, estate, and gift tax matters, a single concerted effort is needed to lead the way. While there is no federal agency with regulation-writing power available to act as the catalyst in the drive toward uniformity in divorce valuation standards, there is the business appraisal profession itself, which can create standards and make recommendations for their adoption nationwide. Those proposed standards can serve as a recommendation to the state legislatures and to the divorce courts for the adoption of uniform business valuation standards for divorce.

Over time, state legislatures and divorce courts will begin adopting the uniform standards for divorce cases and eventually uniformity will be achieved. Of course, state laws governing divorce will always determine the outcome of the case; but unless contrary rules are legislated with regard to the applicable standard of value, the industry-adopted standard can be applied throughout the nation by professional business appraisers. In this manner the business appraisal industry itself can become the catalyst for the creation and adoption of a uniform standard for business value in divorce cases.

The business appraisal profession includes several national organizations with substantial influence, including the American Institute of Certified Public Accountants, the American Society of Appraisers, the Institute of Business Appraisers, and the National Association of Certified Valuation Analysts. If these professional organizations support the use of a uniform standard of business value applicable in divorce cases, it would seem only a matter of time before divorce courts throughout the country apply the uniform standard in their cases.

What should be the premise of the divorce value standard?

The theory of equitable distribution is that marriage is a partnership whose assets should be fairly and equitably distributed when the partnership breaks up.

Consequently, the appropriate standard of divorce value should be based on generally accepted valuation principles applicable to disputes between partners and shareholders when they break up their business relationships. This premise of value is based on "fair value" and not "fair market value."

In fair value appraisals, value is measured from the perspective of the current owners.

In fair market value appraisals, value is measured from the perspective of an outside third party willing buyer.

Fair value is not the same as fair market value

"Fair value" is not the same as, or short-hand for, "fair market value." Fair value carries with it the statutory purpose that shareholders be fairly compensated, which may or may not equate with the market's judgment about the stock's value. This is particularly appropriate in the closely held corporation setting where there is no ready market for the shares and, consequently, no fair market value.

- "Fair value in minority stock appraisal cases is not equivalent to fair market value. Dissenting shareholders, by nature, do not replicate the willing and ready buyers of the open market. Rather, they are unwilling sellers with no bargaining power. ... Because fair market value is irrelevant to the determination of fair value, market forces, such as the availability of buyers for the stock, do not affect the ultimate assessment of fair value in an appraisal proceeding."[9]

- "Fair value is not synonymous with fair market value. ... There is no inflexible test for determining fair value and an assessment of fair value requires consideration of proof of value by any techniques or methods which are generally acceptable in the financial community and otherwise admissible in court."[10]

When appraising shares of a closely held corporation, fair value cannot be fairly equated with the company's fair market value. Closely held corporations by their nature have less value to outsiders, but at the same time their value may be even greater to other shareholders who want to keep the business in the form of a closely held corporation.

Divorce Value is Similar to Fair Value

Disputes among shareholders and disputes between a husband and wife have many similarities. In both cases, one party will purchase the interest of the other at a price which is intended to be fair to both sides. Consequently, it is appropriate to apply the equitable principles of fair value to divorce appraisals, as was done in New Jersey:

> The distinction between fair value and fair market value appears to us equally applicable in the valuation of one spouse's interest in the family's closely held corporation for purposes of equitable distribution.[11]

As in fair value, the premise of value for divorce should be based on value to the marital community and not value to a hypothetical willing buyer. This assumes the business will not be sold and the present owner will continue operations after the divorce. Colorado looks to the intentions of the parties as to whether the business will be sold or continued in operation by one of the parties:

> The Court is rejecting the $42,442 evaluation which is based upon the partnership agreement. The reason the Court is rejecting this figure is because all the evidence before the Court is that [the husband] has every intention of staying with [the law firm] and would not be withdrawing as of this date and thus be entitled to receive only his portion of the accounts receivable pursuant to the partnership agreement. To accept the $42,000 figure ignores all the present facts and intentions of the parties.[12]

Virginia considers the intentions of the parties and held that since the husband intended to continue as a partner in the business that a discount for lack of marketability was inappropriate as no sale was contemplated:

Fair Value as a Basis for Business Valuation in Divorce

The large discount for lack of marketability was inappropriate, as the highest and best use for the defendant's share is to remain with [his law partnership].[13]

Marketability is not relevant to shareholder or divorcing parties

The fair value concept is inherently inconsistent with discounting value to reflect limited marketability. The lack of marketability of a closely held business reflects its lack of liquidity, or its limited ability to be readily converted into cash. Discounts for minority ownership interest reflect nothing more than a further limited market for the sale of a non-controlling interest in such a business. But liquidity is of little consequence in a divorce case where there is no evidence of a contemplated sale of all or part of the business, forced or otherwise:

> Minority discounts have little validity when the purchaser is someone who is already in control of the corporation.[14]

Wyoming and Rhode Island have declined to apply a marketability discount in a divorce valuation because the husband was not going to sell his interest in the business:

- The 35% minority discount for the lack of marketability the husband's expert proposed was not applicable in this instance, since it was a divorce case, and the husband was not going to sell his shares of stock.[15]

- The minority and marketability discounts should not be applied when a corporation is purchasing the stock from its minority shareholders.[16]

The concept of fair value requires that the business be valued as a going concern and not as if it were to be sold or liquidated. The fair value of a minority interest is its pro rata share of the enterprise value as a going concern. Discounts for a lack of liquidity, whether marketability or minority, conflict with the underlying premise of value as a going concern and penalize the minority by presuming a sale. Delaware has long held this view:

> The application of any type of discount is contrary to the requirement that the company be valued as a going concern, and to fail to accord to a minority shareholder the full proportionate value of his shares imposes a penalty for lack of control, and unfairly enriches the majority shareholders who may reap a windfall from the appraisal process by cashing out a dissenting shareholder, a clearly undesirable result.[17]

Oregon declined to apply marketability discounts in divorce because the husband did not contemplate a sale of his interest in the business:

> We conclude that a marketability discount is not appropriate here. Husband testified that he did not contemplate a sale and that, although he did not know whether he was

Chapter 5: Fair Value in Marital Dissolution

restricted from selling to outside parties, if he sold his interest in the family farms, he would likely sell it only to other family members...There was no evidence that husband would be forced to sell his interest to his family at a discount rate or that if the family sold an entire farm that it would have to sell at a discount rate. We hold that the trial court erred in applying a discount to the value of the farm interests.[18]

Publicly traded shares should be valued at market price

In cases where the business is publicly traded and a ready and active market exists for its shares, the appropriate standard of value is the market price for the shares. Clearly a marketable security is appropriately valued by reference to its market price. On the other hand, a closely held business without a ready and active market for its shares cannot be valued with reference to market price. Hence, such business is appropriately valued using the divorce value standard.

Delaware totally eliminates market value from consideration in fair value appraisals where there is no active market for the stock. Fair value becomes intrinsic value to the owners without regard to discounts for marketability or liquidity:

> In cases where there was no free and active market for the stock in question, market value has been eliminated totally as an element of appraised value.[19]

California restricts fair market value to marketable assets. A closely held business is not readily marketable so another standard of value is applicable in California:

> In our view, the fair market value of a marketable asset in marital dissolution cases is the highest price on the date of valuation that would be agreed to by a seller, being willing to sell but under no obligation or urgent necessity to do so, and a buyer, being ready, willing and able to buy, but under no particular necessity for so doing. We restrict the use of this definition to marketable assets because some marital assets are not marketable, but nonetheless may have to be valued.[20]

Colorado articulated specific reasons for disallowing minority discounts in fair value appraisals. These reasons are equally applicable to divorce appraisals where no sale of the interest is contemplated and the business will continue as a going concern in the hands of the present owners:

> In appraising a going concern, the minority discount should not, as a matter of law, be applied. The application of a minority discount: (1) deprives minority shareholders of their proportionate interest in a going concern; (2) values minority shares below majority shares, resulting in unequal treatment of the same class of shares; (3) undermines the primary goal of the dissenters' rights statute, i.e., preventing minority shareholders from being forced to sell at unfairly low values while allowing the majority to proceed as it desires; and (4) encourages oppressive conduct by the majority.[21]

Fair Value as a Basis for Business Valuation in Divorce

Divorce value and fair value are remarkably similar in purpose

Disputes among shareholders of closely held corporations have existed for centuries. Historically, major corporate transactions could only be approved by unanimous shareholder consent. Until the early 1900's the only remedy available in a shareholder deadlock situation was the forced liquidation of the company.

State legislatures created fair value for shareholder equity

Early in the twentieth century, state legislatures changed the requirements for shareholder approval of major corporate transactions by allowing majority rather than unanimous shareholder approval. In exchange for the loss of the minority owners' veto power over the majority, the state legislatures created appraisal rights to protect minority shareholders from being deprived of their ownership interests by majority shareholders. Early in the 1900's appraisal statutes came into the law of all the states.

Under these appraisal statutes, dissenting shareholders are entitled to be paid the "fair value" of their proportionate ownership interest in the corporation.

In appraisal rights litigation, a minority shareholder gives up his ownership in the corporation in exchange for the payment of the fair value of that ownership interest.

State legislatures created marital rights for equitable purposes

To resolve marital disputes, the state legislatures created marital property statutes and the right of equitable distribution. Under these statutes, each spouse is entitled to receive an equitable interest in all marital property. Business interests acquired during the marriage are generally considered marital property subject to valuation and equitable distribution.

In divorce litigation, one party gives up his or her marital rights in the closely held business in exchange for money or property of equal value.

The similarities between divorcing parties and dissenting shareholders are remarkable. In both situations:

- The minority owner has an interest in the business but lacks the power of control.
- The controlling party wants the minority owner to relinquish all claims of ownership.
- There is no active or ready market in which to sell the minority owner's interest.
- The controlling party will continue to operate the business after the minority owner has sold his interest.

Chapter 5: Fair Value in Marital Dissolution

- The minority owner is not a willing seller but rather is involuntarily disposing of his interest in the company because of the dispute.
- The minority owner is under a compulsion to sell pursuant to the litigation.
- The sale of the minority owner's interest is not based on a price determined after negotiation with a willing buyer.
- The minority owner is in a very weak bargaining position and the controlling owner if fully aware of that fact.
- The law provides for an equitable valuation remedy for both the dissenting shareholder and the divorcing spouse.

The big difference between the dissenting shareholder and the divorcing spouse is that no uniform divorce standard of value exists, while there is one for the dissenting shareholder.

Dissenting shareholders have the uniform fair value standard

For dissenting shareholder litigation, the uniform standard is "fair value". All states have adopted the "fair value" standard in their statutes with regard to dissenting shareholder litigation. Because of the similarities between shareholder disputes and divorce litigation, it is appropriate for the states to apply their fair value standards to divorce valuations of business interests.

How the fair value standard became uniform

Since the beginning of the twentieth century the rules governing the standard of fair value in shareholder cases have evolved, crystallized, and are now relatively uniform throughout the country. But that did not happen at one time, and it did not happen by itself. The American Law Institute (ALI) was a critical catalyst in achieving uniformity in the fair value standard.

The American Law Institute was organized in 1923 to deal with certain defects in American law, namely, its uncertainty and its complexity. The Institute's charter states its purpose as "to promote the clarification and simplification of the law." For more than fifty years the Institute has collaborated with the National Conference of Commissioners on Uniform State Laws. Projects of the Institute have resulted in the development of model statutory formulations including the Model Business Corporation Act and the Principles of Corporate Governance. Current projects of the Institute include studies of the Law of Family Dissolution.

Many State legislatures have adopted the specific language of the ALI Model Business Corporation Act while others have used its principles and language as a guide in writing their own statutes. At the present time, all states have appraisal rights statutes for the purpose of appraising the value of closely held businesses to determine the value of an owner's interest for sale to the corporation.

Fair Value as a Basis for Business Valuation in Divorce

An appraisal proceeding is a limited statutory remedy. Its legislative purpose is to provide equitable relief for shareholders dissenting from the actions of the majority. The equitable relief affords the dissenting minority shareholders the right to a judicial determination of the fair value of their shareholdings. The statute provides that the shareholder is entitled to be paid his proportionate interest in the corporation:

> The objective of a fair value determination is to ascertain the actual worth of that which the dissenter loses because of his unwillingness to go along with the controlling stockholders.[22]

Model Business Corporation Act

The ALI's Model Business Corporation Act established the valuation principles of fair value and created a uniform standard of value for use by states throughout the nation. In some respects the standard promulgated by the ALI was broadly worded and did not address important valuation issues, such as the application of discounts for the lack of liquidity or the lack of control by the interest being valued. Over the years numerous courts around the country have decided these issues and have come to the same conclusion that neither discount is generally appropriate in a fair value appraisal.

Discounts for marketability or minority are not appropriate

The common finding of the courts has been that the valuation is not related to the specific shares of a specific shareholder, but rather, the value is a proportional part of the value of the entire corporation as a going concern:

- The objective of the appraisal is to value the corporation itself, as distinguished from a specific fraction of its shares as that may exist in the hands of a particular shareholder. Under the statute the dissenting shareholder is entitled to his proportionate interest in the overall fair value of the corporation, appraised as a going concern.[23]
- The notion of a nonmarketability discount, like a minority discount, rests upon the invalid premise that what is being valued are specific shares in the hands of a particular dissenting stockholder. Under the statute the thing being valued is the entire corporation as a going concern, not individualized configurations of its shares. For that reason, efforts to discount going concern value for reasons of nonmarketability have been rejected under Delaware case law.[24]
- The unstated premise of the minority discount concept is that the function of an appraisal is to value specific shares in the hands of a specific stockholder. If that were so, then the size of a dissenter's stock holdings would be an important consideration. That premise runs counter to the statutory policy underlying the dissenters' rights statute.[25]

Chapter 5: Fair Value in Marital Dissolution

Fair value measures pro rata value of the enterprise

The fair value standard measures the pro rata share of the enterprise without subjecting the minority to a penalty by diminishing its right to receive the fair value of its ownership interest. This is the fundamental distinction from the fair market value standard which measures value to a willing buyer of a specific minority interest.

The objective of a fair value determination is to ascertain the actual worth of that which the dissenter loses because of his unwillingness to go along with the controlling shareholders:

> The real objective is to ascertain the actual worth of that which the dissenter loses.[26]

Principles of corporate governance

Over the years many courts have looked for guidance to the ALI Principles of Corporate Governance which provides that "the fair value of shares should be the value of the eligible holder's proportionate interest in the corporation, without any discount for minority status or, absent extraordinary circumstances, lack of marketability."[27] As a result, most courts have adopted that view in fair value appraisals:

- We are persuaded by the ALI position and those cases holding that the marketability discount should not be imposed in dissenters' rights actions except in extraordinary circumstances. Accordingly, we hold that in determining the fair value of a dissenters' shares in a closely held corporation, the trial court must first determine the value of the corporation and the pro rata value of each outstanding share of common or equity participating stock. In the case of a going concern, no minority discount is to be applied; and, except under extraordinary circumstances, no marketability discount is to be applied.[28]

- "The stockholder is entitled to be paid for that which has been taken from him, viz., his proportionate interest in a going concern. By value of the stockholder's proportionate interest in the corporate enterprise is meant the true or intrinsic value of his stock." [29]

Model Business Corporation Act explicitly excludes discounts

In 1999, the Model Business Corporation Act was amended to State categorically that fair value excludes discounts for lack of marketability or minority ownership.

Principles of the fair value standard

Under the Model Business Corporation Act, fair value means:

Fair Value as a Basis for Business Valuation in Divorce

- The value of the corporation's shares determined using customary and current valuation concepts and techniques generally employed for similar businesses; and,

- Without discounting for lack of marketability or for minority status.[30]

The Official Comment to the Model Act explains:

> Subsection (iii) of the definition of fair value establishes that valuation discounts for lack of marketability or minority status are inappropriate in most appraisal actions, both because most transactions that trigger appraisal rights affect the corporation as a whole and because such discounts give the majority the opportunity to take advantage of minority shareholders who have been forced against their will to accept the appraisal-triggering transaction. Subsection (ii), in conjunction with the lead-in language to the definition, is also designed to adopt the more modern view that appraisal should generally award a shareholder his or her proportional interest in the corporation after valuing the corporation as a whole, rather than the value of the shareholder's shares when valued alone.[31]

Principles of equitable valuation

Numerous courts have reviewed equitable valuation issues in both dissenting shareholder and divorce cases and provided specific guidance in the application of these equitable valuation principles. The following case decisions illustrate some of the underlying fundamental equitable theories of business valuation. From these and related cases, a standard of value for divorce can be developed and proposed for acceptance by the professional business appraisal industry.

Stock is worth same to both the transferee and the transferor

Montana eloquently explains that a hypothetical buyer might pay less than pro rata value for a minority interest because the buyer gains no right to control or manage the corporation. On the other hand, an existing owner or the corporation itself as the buyer would suffer no loss in its existing right to control or manage the corporation. Consequently, there is no basis for such a buyer to pay less than pro rata value for a minority interest.

> Applying a discount is inappropriate when the shareholder is selling her shares to a majority shareholder or to the corporation. The sale differs from a sale to a third party and, thus, different interests must be recognized. When selling to a third party, the value of the shares is either the same as or less than it was in the hands of the transferor because the third party gains no right to control or manage the corporation. However, a sale to a majority shareholder or to the corporation simply consolidates or increases the interest of those already in control. Therefore, requiring the application of a minority discount

when selling to an 'insider' would result in a windfall to the transferee. This is particularly true since the transferring shareholder would expect that the shares would have at least the same value in her hands as in the hands of the transferee.[32]

New Jersey similarly believes a discount for a sale to an existing owner is not justified, as no change in control results; and in a marital case, it would unfairly reduce the value of the business interest to the marital community:

> We see no reason to reward the spouse who holds title to the shares by allowing him to retain the value in the entire bloc at a bargain "price," that is, crediting the non-owner spouse with less than the owner's proportionate share of full value when determining equitable distribution of the marital assets. Here, allowing the marketability or minority discounts would unfairly minimize the marital estate to Ellen's detriment and is inconsistent with the concept of equitable distribution. While there is no ready market for the shares and consequently no fair market value of Florist, James's shares in the going concern have value to him and to his co-owners that does not depend upon a theoretical sale to an outsider and has not changed as a result of the divorce complaint or judgment.[33]

Likewise, in Delaware, "A determination of fair value does not involve an inquiry into claims of wrongdoing."[34]

Unequal treatment is inherently unfair

Missouri and Kansas recognize that discounts are inherently unfair to the party selling her shares in fair value shareholder dispute cases. This notion is equally applicable in divorce:

- "To allow a discount would discourage investments in corporations by persons who would acquire a minority interest because it would enable the majority shareholders to seize the minority shareholders' interest in the corporation to the extent a minority or marketability discount is allowed. Investments should be encouraged, not discouraged."[35]

- "The appraisal statute provides an equitable remedy, compensating minority shareholders for their lack of control and ensuring that they retain the same proportionate value of their stock regardless of undesired changes dictated by majority vote."[36]

Minority owners should not be unfairly penalized

- "Based on our review of the history and policies behind dissenters' rights and appraisal statutes, we found most persuasive those cases holding that marketability discounts generally should not be applied in determining the fair value of a dissenting shareholder's stock in an appraisal action. Of course, there may be situations where equity compels another result."[37]

- "The size of the holding being valued and the number of restrictions attached to the stock are factors in determining an appropriate lack of marketability discount. Both of these factors may affect the value of particular shares, but have no impact on the value of the company as a going concern."[38]

- "The dissenting shareholder's proportionate interest is determined only after the company as an entity has been valued. In that determination the trial court is not required to apply further weighing factors at the shareholder level, such as discounts to minority shares for asserted lack of marketability."[39]

Proposed divorce value standard

Based on the equitable principles applied in making business appraisals in both dissenting shareholder and divorce litigation cases, an equitable divorce value standard can be developed. This standard can be used by the professional business appraisal industry and recommended for adoption by state legislatures and divorce courts throughout the nation.

The following proposed divorce value standard contains the fundamental equitable principles of valuation identified in major cases throughout the country and can serve as the appropriate definition of business value for divorce appraisals:

DIVORCE STANDARD OF BUSINESS VALUE

Preamble

Unless state statute or case law provides otherwise, and unless the business interest is expected to be sold or is readily marketable on an established exchange, the goal or purpose of any appraisal of a business or professional practice in a family law proceeding is to establish the intrinsic value of the interest to the parties upon dissolution of the marriage. This standard of value shall be referred to as "Divorce Value."

Standard of Value

The intrinsic value of the business interest shall be measured in terms of its value to the marital community and not in terms of its value to a willing buyer, and shall be determined by an independent, unbiased, and qualified business appraiser who shall apply the following standards:

1. The value of the business interest shall be determined using customary and current valuation concepts and techniques generally employed for similar businesses.

Chapter 5: Fair Value in Marital Dissolution

2. The business interest shall be valued at its intrinsic worth to the marital community and not at its value to an outside willing buyer.
3. The business shall be valued as a going concern.
4. If the interest being appraised is less than the entire business the value of the interest shall be determined as considered appropriate by the appraiser either as:
   (a) A pro rata share of the enterprise value; or
   (b) The present value of the expected future benefits from the interest.
5. Absent extraordinary circumstances, the value of the interest being appraised shall be determined without discounting for lack of marketability or for minority status.

Official Comment:

Divorce Value is based on the premise that marriage is, among other things, an economic partnership between the parties. The value of a business interest therefore, should be measured for divorce purposes in a manner similar to its measurement as if the parties were not getting divorced. The value should be based on the economic benefits of ownership which are expected to be realized by the parties over the life cycle of the business.

It is the court's duty, and not the appraiser's, to determine the marital interest each party has in the business. However, the court needs the independent and unbiased appraised value of the business interest in order to apply state marital property laws in making an appropriate equitable distribution decision in a manner which reflects the individual needs and circumstances of the parties.

Intrinsic value is a very subjective concept that looks to the worth of the property to the parties rather that measuring value as if it were to be sold to an unrelated third party. Where there is no evidence of an anticipated sale of the business interest it is improper to measure value to a hypothetical willing buyer when in fact the business will be continued under its present ownership by either the husband or the wife.

Divorce Value is not equivalent to fair market value. Divorcing parties, by nature, do not replicate the willing and ready buyers and sellers of the open market. Rather, they are unwilling buyers and sellers with no bargaining power. Because fair market value is irrelevant to the determination of Divorce Value, market forces, such as the availability of buyers for the business interest, do not affect the ultimate assessment of value in a divorce appraisal.

There is no inflexible test for determining Divorce Value and an assessment of Divorce Value requires consideration of proof of value by any techniques or methods which are generally acceptable in the professional appraisal community and otherwise admissible in court.

The premise of value for divorce is based on value to the marital community and not value to a hypothetical willing buyer. This assumes the business will not be sold and the present owner

Fair Value as a Basis for Business Valuation in Divorce

will continue operations after the divorce. However, this assumption must be based on all the present facts and intentions of the parties.

Minority discounts have no validity when the purchaser is already the owner of the business interest. Likewise, discounts for lack of marketability are irrelevant when the business owner has no intention of selling the business interest. The application of any type of liquidity discount is contrary to the requirement that the business be valued as a going concern as it suggests a value based on the sale of the business interest to an outside buyer. Such discounts undermine the primary goal of equitable distribution, i.e., to adjust fairly and equitably the economic interests of the parties upon dissolution of the marriage.

In cases of closely held businesses where there is no free and active market for the business interest in question, market value is eliminated totally as an element of Divorce Value. While there is no ready market for the shares and consequently no fair market value, the owner's interest in the going concern has value to him that does not depend upon a theoretical sale to an outsider and the value of that interest has not changed as a result of the divorce complaint or judgment.

The objective of a Divorce Value determination is to ascertain the actual worth of the business interest to the marital community so that a court can make an equitable distribution based upon the State's marital property principles applicable to the unique facts and circumstances of the parties before the court.

As the marital community is considered a single unity between the husband and the wife, applying any form of liquidity discount is inappropriate when the business owner is deemed to be selling the interest to himself. In such a deemed sale there will be no change in position or control with regard to the business nor will its value be any more or less than it was immediately before the deemed transfer. Consequently, absent extraordinary circumstances, Divorce Value identifies the same value to the current owner immediately before, as well as after, the divorce. An example of an extraordinary circumstance justifying a discount would apply where both spouses actively work in the business and after the divorce one of them would be leaving the business. In appropriate circumstances a discount may be justified where the value of the business can be expected to decline due to the loss of a key manager as a result of the divorce.

In divorce valuations a business interest is appropriately valued in terms of its intrinsic worth to the parties. The methods of valuation should take into consideration the parties themselves and the different situations in which they exist. The business interest may have no established market value, and neither party may contemplate selling it; indeed, sale may be restricted or forbidden. When the parties do not contemplate sale and one of the two is going to enjoy the benefits of the property with no likelihood of leaving the business, a restrictive agreement will have little bearing on the value to the parties.

Generally, one party will continue to enjoy the benefits of the business while the other must relinquish all future benefits. Under marital property rules the intrinsic value of the business must be

Chapter 5: Fair Value in Marital Dissolution

translated into a monetary amount for equitable distribution purposes. Intrinsic value is measured in relation to the parties and depends on the facts of the case. Intrinsic value, like investment value and fair value, can be determined by generally accepted business valuation methods.

The value of unique property, such as a family business, is properly measured from the unique perspective of its value to the marital community in which it exists. The same business viewed from the perspective of a hypothetical willing buyer in contrast to its current owner can easily reflect two distinctly different values. For divorce purposes the appropriate perspective of value is the marital community and not an outside willing buyer.

Minority Interest May Be Valued Using Discounted Future Benefits

The application of generally accepted business valuation methods to a minority ownership interest may determine that a direct valuation method is the most appropriate approach to valuation for a particular divorce case. This method is in contrast to the appraisal of the enterprise and the subsequent determination of the minority interest value.

For example, where the parties own a small fractional interest in a large partnership, the appraisal of the entire business may be impractical. In such case a direct valuation of the economic benefits that a minority ownership interest is expected to realize over the life of the investment may be appropriate.

Conclusion

Marital property rules direct the trial court to value all property of the parties, but those rules rarely define the term, "value," for equitable distribution purposes. State statutes rarely set the standard of value, that is, the measure of property's worth for equitable distribution. "Value" is a mercurial term; the term has numerous, distinct meanings. The various meanings are not interchangeable. The meaning of the term, "value," depends on what is being valued, who is interested, and why it is being valued. A piece of property may have different values for different purposes. The purpose for which it is being valued determines which definition, which standard of value, is proper. Purpose determines the standard of value, which in turn determines the appropriate methods of valuation.

In divorce valuations a business interest is appropriately valued in terms of its intrinsic worth to the parties. The methods of valuation should take into consideration the parties themselves and the different situations in which they exist. The business interest may have no established market value, and neither party may contemplate selling it; indeed, sale may be restricted or forbidden. When the parties do not contemplate sale and one of the two is going to enjoy the benefits of the property with no likelihood of leaving the business, a restrictive agreement will have little bearing on the value to the parties.

Fair Value as a Basis for Business Valuation in Divorce

Generally, one party will continue to enjoy the benefits of the business while the other must relinquish all future benefits. Under marital property rules the intrinsic value of the business must be translated into a monetary amount for equitable distribution purposes. Intrinsic value is measured in relation to the parties and depends on the facts of the case. Intrinsic value, like investment value and fair value, can be determined by generally accepted business valuation methods.

Divorce is a unique transaction of life. It involves unique people with unique facts and circumstances. These special characteristics are considered differently in each case by the divorce court. An equitable distribution under one set of facts may be wholly inappropriate in another case with slightly different facts. Divorce courts can vary dramatically, from state to state, and even within the same state, in making property divisions, support awards, and divorce rulings.

Consequently, the value of unique property, such as a family business, should be measured from the unique perspective of its value to the marital community in which it exists. It is generally known that value varies, depending on the perspective from which it is measured. The same business viewed from the perspective of a hypothetical willing buyer in contrast to its current owner can easily reflect two distinctly different values. The question is not which value is right, but rather, the question is which is the appropriate standard of value for the purpose of the measurement.

Divorce courts strive to make equitable decisions based on the unique facts of each case. In every case, the court seeks an appropriate solution to the specific problems of the parties. Why then, should the value of unique property be treated any differently from the unique problems facing the divorcing couple? Why should the family business be valued with reference to a hypothetical sale which is neither contemplated nor realistically expected any more than an award of alimony be made without regard to the facts and circumstances of the parties?

The answer to the question, should there be a uniform standard of value for divorce, is a resounding yes. In fact, the absence of such a uniform standard continues the perception that divorce is not the fair and equitable process State legislatures want it to be. It should be only a matter of time before the appraisal industry develops a uniform standard of business value applicable to divorce appraisals and encourages its use by divorce courts throughout the country. That is the way to achieve uniformity in divorce valuations of business interests. The divorce value standard proposed in this paper can serve as a model for consideration by the business appraisal industry.

A uniform business valuation standard for divorce is not only possible, it is necessary.

---

1. The author regularly presents and updates this material, most recently at the NACVA Conference in Columbia, Maryland on October 6, 2006.
2. Ch. 794, 1978 Md. Laws 2304, 2305 (from the Maryland Marital Property Act's preamble).
3. *Litman v. Litman*, 463 N.E.2d 34 (N.Y. 1984).
4. 23 Pa.C.S.A. sec 3102(a)(5).3.
5. *Bosserman v. Bosserman*, 384 S.E.2d 104, (Va.App. 1989).

Chapter 5: Fair Value in Marital Dissolution

6. *Howell v. Howell*, 523 S.E.2d 514 (Va.App. 2000).
7. *In re Marriage of Foster*, 42 Cal. App. 3d 577 (Cal. 1974).
8. Rule 1.28 of the San Diego County Superior Court Rules, Division III, Family Law.
9. *Swope v. Siegel-Roberts, Inc.*, 243 F.3d 486 (8th Cir. 2001). The abstract of *Swope v. Siegel-Roberts, Inc.* is included in the court case abstract section of this *Guide*, and the full-text decision can be found at BVLibrary.com.
10. *Lawson Mardon Wheaton, Inc. v. Smith*, 160 N.J. 383 (N.J. 1999).
11. *Brown v. Brown*, 792 A.2d 463 (N.J. 2002). The abstract of *Brown v. Brown* is included in the court case abstract section of this *Guide*, and the full-text decision can be found at BVLibrary.com.
12. *In re Marriage of Huff*, 834 P.2d 244 (Colo. 1992).
13. *Howell v. Howell*, 1998 WL 972312 (Va. Cir. Ct. Sept. 4, 1998), aff'd 523 S.E.2d 514 (Va. App. 2000).
14. *Brown v. Allied Corrugated Box Co.*, 91 Cal. App. 3d 477, 486 (Cal. 1979).
15. *Neuman v. Neuman*, 842 P.2d 575 (Wyo. 1992).
16. *Charland v. Country View Golf Club, Inc.*, 588 A.2d 609, 612 (R.I. 1991).
17. *Cavalier Oil Corp. v. Harnett*, 564 A.2d 1137 (Del. 1989).
18. *In re Marriage of Batt*, 945 P.2d 517 (Or. 1997).
19. *Francis I. DuPont & Co. v. Universal Studios, Inc.*, Del. Ch., 312 A.2d 344 (Del 1973)
20. *In re Marriage of Cream*, 13 Cal. App. 4th 81, 89, 16 Cal. Rptr. 2d 575 (1993).
21. *M Life Insurance Co. v. Sapers & Wallack Insurance Agency, Inc.*, 40 P.3d 6 (Colo. App. 2001).
22. *Sieg v. Kelly*, 568 N.W.2d 794 (Iowa 1997).
23. *Weinberger v. UOP, Inc.*, 457 A.2d 701 (Del. 1983).
24. *Robins & Co. v. A.C. Israel Enterprises*, Del. Ch., C.A. No. 7919 (Del. 1985).
25. *Cavalier Oil Corp. v. Harnett*, 564 A.2d 1137 (Del. 1989).
26. *Warren v. The Baltimore Transit Company*, 154 A.2d 796 (Md. 1959).
27. ALI *Principles of Corporate Governance*, ¶7.22 (1994).
28. *Pueblo Bank Corporation v. Lindoe, Inc.*, 37 P.3d 492 (Colo. App. 2001).
29. *Tri-Continental Corp. v. Battye*, 74 A.2d 71 (Del. 1950).
30. ALI Model Business Corporation Act, 13.01, as amended in 1999
31. 54 Bus. Law. 256-257.
32. *Hansen v. 75 Ranch Co.*, 957 P.2d 32, 41 (Mt. 1998). The abstract of *Hansen v. 75 Ranch Co.* is included in the court case abstract section of this *Guide*, and the full-text decision can be found at BVLibrary.com.
33. *Brown v. Brown*, 792 A.2d 463 (N.J. Super. Ct. App. Div. 2002).
34. *Cede & Co., v. Technicolor, Inc.*, 542 A.2d 1182 (Del. 1988).
35. *Arnaund v. Stockgrowers State Bank of Ashland*, 992 P.2d 216 (Kan. 1999).
36. *Dreiseszun v. FLM Indus. Inc.*, 577 S.W.2d 902 (Mo. 1979).
37. *Balsamides v. Protameen Chemicals, Inc.*, 160 N.J. 352 (N.J. 1999).
38. *Hodas v. Spectrum Technology*, Del. Ch. No. 11,265 (Del. 1992).
39. *Rapid-American Corp., v. Harris*, 603 A.2d 796, (Del. 1992).

Fair Value Versus Fair Market Value: Is There a Place for Fair Value in Marital Dissolution?[1]

By Robert Kleeman Jr. CPA/ABV, ASA, CVA[2]

Previously, the concept of "fair value" has been limited strictly to shareholder oppression or shareholder rights matters. State law - including family statutes - typically does not define fair value, other than in the dissenters' rights statutes. Recently, however, family law practitioners have attempted to value business interests for marital purposes using the fair value standard.

What is the fundamental difference?

The standard of value drives the ultimate valuation of any asset. Currently, the most widely used standard is fair market value, which is required for any tax or other federally mandated valuations and is widely accepted as the standard for marital dissolutions. Fair value is a creation of state legislatures and was designed to be applied to shareholder oppression actions. The definition and application of the fair value standard varies widely from state-to-state.

The most basic difference between the valuation of an ownership interest under the fair market value standards and valuation under the fair value standard is the consideration and application of discounts or premiums relating to majority, minority, and marketability. Under most fair value standards, minority and marketability discounts are either limited or not applicable. So why the move from the widely accepted and understood fair market value standard to the less frequently used fair value standard? Quite simply, in most instances, the fair value of a minority, non-marketable ownership interest is higher than the fair market value of the same ownership interest.

Guidance from the courts

The movement to create a "divorce value" or "fair value" for marital proceedings has slowly moved across the country from the east coast to the west. *Brown v. Brown*[3] was probably the most clear statement from a court regarding the use of fair value in a family law context. I have argued both at the trial court level, as well as in writings and presentations that the use of "fair value" or a newly defined "divorce value" presents a distortion of the value of an asset that is part of the marital estate.

The Colorado Supreme Court rendered a decision on the concept of fair value in a dissenters' rights matter in *Pueblo Bancorporation v. Lindoe, Inc.*[4] This decision provides guidance on the difference between fair value and fair market value.[5] Close examination of this case points out the difficulties that arise with the use of fair value in determining the value of a business interest.

The sole issue in the case was whether the dissenting shareholders' shares should be discounted for lack of marketability. The parties agreed on the value of the shares prior to the application of discounts. The court explained that the dissenting shareholder rights statutes provide detailed procedures that ultimately result in the filing of an action to determine the appropriate value of the dissenting shareholders' shares.

In the ruling, the court concluded that "the meaning of fair value is ambiguous. It is a term that does not have a commonly accepted meaning in ordinary usage, much less in the business community." Their comment was footnoted to the testimony of Leslie Patten—one of the experts in the case—who stated that "fair value has no common meaning." In his view, the term is "judicially ambiguous," a legal standard of value, not a "recognized business valuation standard of value."[6]

The court went on to state that fair value must have a "definitive meaning" and that prior Colorado appellate courts had not provided a consistent interpretation of fair value, particularly on the issue of discounts. The court also pointed out that the legislature chose the term fair value for dissenting shareholders for a reason, and that it must therefore mean something different than fair market value. If the legislature had wanted to provide for dissenting shareholders to receive fair market value for their shares, "it knew how to provide it: the phrase has been used many times in a wide variety of statutes."

The court further commented that in the 60-year history of Colorado's dissenters' rights statute, the measure of compensation has changed from 'value" to 'fair value," but the legislature has never required that dissenters be paid fair market value for their shares. With the *Pueblo* case, the Colorado Supreme Court made a clear distinction between fair value and fair market value in the dissenters' rights arena.

The argument for fair value in divorce matters

Those advocating the creation of a new valuation standard for divorce choose to follow the fair value standard and argue that the breakup of a marriage is similar to a shareholder objecting to a corporate transaction, being oppressed, or being forced out by the majority. On the surface, this seems to be a compelling argument, but when viewed in an economic light, the shareholder analogy is not really accurate.

Unlike a shareholder dispute, the breakup of a marriage normally does not impact the day-to-day operations of the business. In fact, most of the fair value proponents make that very argument, that is, that the corporation operates the same on the day after the divorce as it did the day before. That is precisely why a fair value standard should not apply. The entity is not fundamentally changing the way it does business. No one is objecting to a business transaction. No shareholder is being oppressed or squeezed out.

Fair Value Versus Fair Market Value

Fair value standard unfair to propertied spouse

What is the justification for applying a seldom-used standard versus one that has been in place for over 50 years? Why should we apply a valuation standard that will yield a higher value conclusion than what the owner can achieve without as a shareholder oppression action? Judge Courlis raised that very issue as a concern in her dissent, namely, that one of the parties would reap a windfall, rather than the value that reflects an arm's-length transaction, taking into consideration the investment's illiquidity.

Fair value proponents also argue that the non-propertied spouse is not a "willing seller," and therefore the fair market value standard cannot apply by definition. This is another specious argument. The reality is that the ownership is not being sold, but the fair market value standard assumes a universe of willing buyers and sellers a one of the foundations for the methodology. The fair value proponents further argue that there will be no sale, and therefore any marketability or minority interest is fictitious and/or remote. But an imminent sale is not necessary for a valuation. For gift and estate tax purposes, this hypothetical exercise is conducted every day, with no expectation of a sale, and in fact, the fair market value standard is required for all tax valuations.

Last, the proponents imply that a fair value standard is fairer to the non-propertied spouse, No empirical evidence suggest that the creation of a new standard will be any fairer than the proper application of existing standards and methodologies. The corollary is whether fair value is also fair to the propertied spouse. The fair value proponents do not address this issue. Why? Because it is inherently unfair to the propertied spouse.

The unintended consequences of a new standard for divorce

Let us assume, for the sake of argument, that for divorce purposes and only divorce purposes that a new standard of value should be adopted, and that the appropriate standard of value is fair value. What dichotomies does this create? How do we reconcile the conflicting outcomes? If we had to complete a valuation the day before the divorce, or the day after divorce, for tax purposes or other federally mandated purpose, the most likely required standard of value would be fair market value. If, on the day of the divorce, we had to apply a "fair value" or "divorce value" standard, it is most likely that this value would be higher than the fair market value requirements. Is it appropriate for one spouse to compensate the other using a value that cannot be achieved in an arm's-length transaction?

Should we apply this same fair value standard to any publicly traded stock held by the parties? The general consensus in the business valuation community is that, by definition, publicly traded stock is valued on a minority, marketable basis. Since the fair value standard would allow no minority discount, must we then increase the value of the public stock holdings to remove the implicit minority discount? If not, what is the rational for treating closely held investments differently from publicly held investments?

Chapter 5: Fair Value in Marital Dissolution

Alan Zipp, Esq., CPA/ABV, CBA, a leading proponent of the creation of a new standard of valuation for divorce, has admitted that the larger the closely held entity, the less appropriate is fair value, as opposed to fair market value.[7] What increment of size triggers that distinction, and how do we measure it? Is the size differential based on revenues, profits, or market capitalization? Why can we apply fair market value standards to any size valuation, but fair value will cease to be relevant when an entity reaches a certain size? Is this a standard only for small divorces? What is a small marital action?

The argument for fair market value

Fair market value has been used for more than 50 years. Every major business valuations professional association, the federal government, and most states agree on the definition of fair market value. In the *Pueblo Bancorporation* decision, the court noted that a number of Colorado statutes use the term fair market value. Fair value is used only in the dissenting shareholders' rights statues. Myriad judicial decisions discuss fair market value in detail, as well as address the issue of discounts and premiums for marketability and minority/control. Fair market value can be applied to any business of any size. Many generally accepted methodologies can be followed to determine the fair market value of a business interest.

Despite all the collective years of practitioners' and courts' experience in applying and refining fair market value, the ultimate conclusion of value remains subjective. The experience, judgment, and reasonableness of the valuation professional all impact the ultimate conclusion. Two very competent analysts can reach different conclusions on the same engagement. However, competent valuation professionals can describe the difference in their methodologies or assumptions and can reconcile (or at least compare) the different conclusions.

What would be gained by creating a new fair value standard? Would any of those potential differences be eliminated? Some might argue yes, that the discounts for minority and/or lack of marketability would no longer be part of the calculation. That is naïve. A fundamental theory of business valuation says that the rate of return required by an investor is directly impacted by the perceived risks of the investment. Removing any discounts for the risk of illiquidity, or of being in the minority does not change that theory. If the risk involved with being a minority owner, or holding non-marketable stock is not recognized as a separate and distinct item (such as a discount for minority or marketability), then the investor will recognize that risk somewhere else, perhaps in the capitalization rate.

We cannot legislate an increase in the value of an interest in a closely held business simply by saying that minority and marketability discounts cannot be applied.

As Judge Courlis stated in the *Pueblo Bancorporation* decision, investors are going to account for the illiquidity of the stock when they buy minority shares in a close corporation. If this is the reality of the marketplace, doesn't it seem logical that the fair market value standard should apply to dissolution of marriage matters?

Fair Value Versus Fair Market Value

The real issue is competent valuation conclusions

The argument most widely advanced by fair value proponents is that using fair market value and allowing discounts for minority or marketability undervalues the ownership interest in the divorce context and engenders additional argument over the appropriate size, if any, of those discounts. The fair value proponents' undervaluation argument considers only the viewpoint of the spouse who will not be retaining the business interest.

If the rationale of *Pueblo Bancorporation* is applied to marital litigation, no minority or marketability discounts can be taken from the pro-rata value of the entity. Doubtless, under this application, the fair value of a business interest will never be less than the fair market value of the same interest and will almost always be substantially greater. If the only concern of the fair value proponents is undervaluation of business interests in marital litigation, their proposal does not solve the problem.

It is not so much the standard of value that under or overvalues an ownership interest, but the competence and independence of the valuation professional. Applying inappropriate and unsupportable discounts, for example, has far greater impact on the value conclusion than any other item. There is no "normal" discount for marketability or minority. The appropriate discount is determined by careful analysis of the subject entity.

While it is true that a fair value standard eliminating these discounts conveniently makes that issue disappear, it does nothing to demonstrate that the ultimate valuation conclusion is appropriate. It appears that using fair value is a way of "dumbing down" the valuation process. We might remove difficult issues, but that doesn't make the process better. In fact, we even complicate matters if we need to quantify the real risk in another way.

Conclusion and what should appraisers do

Either the legislature or judiciary should clearly state that fair market value is the appropriate standard of value for marital dissolution matters. Today, we have guidance from a recent Colorado case, which I believe to be the first family law matter to directly address this issue. In August of 2008, the Colorado Court of Appeals handed down a decision in the marital dissolution matter of *Thornhill v. Thornhill*.[8] In their opinion, the Court of Appeals specifically stated that the "fair value" language that was the basis of the *Pueblo Bancorporation* litigation is not contained in the dissolution statutes of the State of Colorado. The Court of Appeals also declined to adopt the holdings of *Brown v. Brown* regarding using the shareholder statutes as part of marital litigation. The Court went on to state, "We are instead persuaded by the decisions of numerous other jurisdictions that have concluded marketability discounts may be applied in valuing shares in closely held corporations in dissolution proceedings. Such a discount would be applied to reflect the fact that shares of stock in such corporations are less marketable than publicly traded stock, a factor that an ordinary buyer would take into consideration in deciding what to pay for the shares."[9]

Chapter 5: Fair Value in Marital Dissolution

Furthermore, expert witnesses need to apply the fair market value standard consistently. Valuation conclusions must meet the minimum requirement of expert testimony. Valuation reports and/or testimony should demonstrate reasonable, well thought out, and supported assumptions; appropriate financial statement adjustments; and proper determinations of the appropriate capitalization rates.

In addition, the valuation professional owes the court a cogent discussion of any discounts taken for minority and or marketability and why those discounts are appropriate for the case at hand. It is the responsibility of the valuation professional to provide independent expert opinion to the court, and not to become an advocate for a specific side in the litigation. Over the last 15 years or more, the business valuation profession has changed dramatically, becoming more sophisticated and relying more on empirical data.

With an agreed standard of value and a common use of the business valuation body of knowledge, business valuators still might not agree on the value of a specific business interest. However, they can reconcile their differences and explain them to all of the parties, as well as to the judge.

---

1. Originally published in the *Business Valuation Update*™ and updated by the author in January 2009. Reprinted with permission from Business Valuation Resources.
2. Robert E. Kleeman is Managing Director of OnPointe Financial Valuation Group, LLC. His practice concentration includes business valuation and litigation support. In addition to be being a well-known speaker, he co-authored *The Handbook for Divorce Valuations* and has written several business valuation articles.
3. *Brown v. Brown*, 792 A.2d 463 (N.J. Super. Ct. App. Div. 2002)
4. *Pueblo Bancorporation v. Lindoe, Inc.*, 2003 Colo. LEXIS 53 (Colo. Jan. 21, 2003) (en banc).
5. The decision covers only dissenters' rights but is used here to illustrate the difference that could arise in a marital litigation context.
6. See footnote 4 to the decision.
7. See Alan Zipp's article "Fair Value as a Basis for Business Valuation in Divorce" in Chapter 5 of this Guide.
8. *Thornhill v. Thornhill*, Colorado Court of Appeals No. 07CA1654 (Mesa County District Court No. 05 DR 1025) Announced August 21, 2008.
9. Page 10, & 11, of the Thornhill decision.

Chapter 6
Fair Value Under California Corporations Code Section 2000

Dissolution Actions Yield Less than Fair Market Enterprise Value (Appraising for "Fair Value" Under California Corporations Code Section 2000)

By Arthur J. Shartsis, Esq.[1]

> While virtually all states have dissenters' rights appraisal statutes, only a few states have "dissolution statutes," addressing a minority stockholder's right to receive "fair value" in instances of minority oppression. California has had such a statute, with some amendments, for over twenty years. Minority oppression litigation is growing, and many other states' courts may look to California for precedent in similar cases of first impression. Here California attorney Art Shartsis summarizes his views on appraisal of a company under California Corporations Code Section 2000.
>
> – *Shannon Pratt*

"The fair value shall be determined on the basis of the liquidation value as of the valuation date but taking into account the possibility, if any, of sale of the entire business as a going concern in a liquidation." Section 2000(a)

Introduction

California Corporations Code Section 2000 provides majority shareholders with a manner for determining "fair value" in order to buy the shares of a complaining minority shareholder who seeks dissolution of a corporation. Aside from the single sentence in Section 2000(a) quoted above, "[l]ittle help, if any, is provided by the statutory procedure which governs the appraisal process in a dissolution proceeding of a closely held corporation."[2]

The few cases interpreting Section 2000 also fail to provide complete guidance regarding how to determine "fair value" as required by the statute. None of the court decisions address directly the issue that Section 2000 is part of the statutory scheme applicable to corporate dissolution, intended to give the complaining shareholder the full benefit of a corporate dissolution, but nothing more. Rather, the cases provide a patchwork of insights, only some of which are consistent with the basic purpose of Section 2000.

This situation has led to both confusion and inconsistent valuation methodology among those responsible for appraising "fair value" under Section 2000. As Harold Marsh[3] has observed:

Chapter 6: Fair Value Under California Corporations Code Section 2000

> A number of CPAs appointed as appraisers under Section 2000 of the GCL have simply refused to follow the statutory language and instead have determined a "fair market value" for the shares being appraised, although one court stated that this was impermissible under the language of Section 2000. [Citing *Ronald v. 4-C's Electronic Packaging, Inc.*, 168 Cal. App. 3d 290, 214 Cal. Rptr. 225 (1985).] The courts have had a difficult time applying the valuation standard specified in Section 2000 . . . [4]

This article will address the "fair value" appraisal of a business that is subject to a dissolution proceeding by a minority shareholder.

The Purpose of Section 2000

The central valuation provision of Section 2000(a) mandates as follows: "The fair value shall be determined on the basis of the liquidation value as of the valuation date but taking into account the possibility, if any, of sale of the entire business as a going concern in a liquidation." "Fair value" is distinctly different from the traditional appraiser's determination of "fair market value." The reasons for this difference are found in the code provision itself.

In order to understand why "fair market value" or the traditional "going concern" value of a company is not the same as "fair value" as used in Section 2000, it is important to focus on what a Section 2000 proceeding is and how it comes about. Section 2000 is part of Chapter 20 of the General Corporation Law which provides "General Provisions Relating to Dissolution." A Section 2000 proceeding arises because a minority shareholder has brought a lawsuit to dissolve the corporation.[5] If the dissenting shareholder is successful with that lawsuit, the corporation is dissolved. Upon dissolution, the corporation is liquidated in accordance with California law and the shareholders receive whatever proceeds are left after the entire liquidation process has been paid for and completed.

Section 2000 was created for majority shareholders to "avoid the dissolution of the corporation and appointment of any receiver" by having a court-supervised appraisal determine how much the minority shareholder would have received if the dissolution proceeding had been taken to its final conclusion of liquidating the corporation and distributing the proceeds. It is not the majority shareholder who takes the initiative to force out or buy out the minority shareholder. Rather, it is the minority shareholder who seeks to dissolve the corporation in accordance with California law. Section 2000 merely provides a way to give the minority shareholder the benefit that was sought by the dissolution action while at the same time giving the majority the option to preserve the existence of the corporation. Thus, as reported by Marsh, it was the intention of the drafting committees who authored Section 2000 "that the moving parties [the minority shareholder] should not be entitled to more than the liquidation value of the shares, i.e., what they would receive if their objective [liquidation of the Company] is obtained."[6] Citing Marsh, the court in *Brown v. Allied Corrugated Box Co.*.[7] observed that the object of the appraisal proceeding is "to award plaintiffs what they would have received had their involuntary dissolution action been allowed to proceed to a successful conclusion."

Dissolution Actions Yield Less than Fair Market Enterprise Value

An important concept of Section 2000 is the fact that even though Section 2000 has been invoked by the majority shareholder to avoid the liquidation of a company in a dissolution proceeding, liquidation may still occur for all parties involved. This is how the Section 2000 process works. (1) The minority shareholder sues for dissolution.[8] (2) If the parties cannot agree upon a value of the minority share, the majority shareholder moves to stay the dissolution proceeding to obtain a valuation to determine how much the minority shareholder would have received if liquidation of the Company were actually completed.[9] (3) The court appoints three appraisers[10] to determine the "fair value" (as defined in Section 2000(a)) of the shares owned by the minority shareholder.[11] (4) The court adopts an appraised value of what the minority shareholder would have received at the end of the liquidation process.[12] (5) The "court shall enter a decree which shall provide in the alternative for winding up and dissolution of the corporation unless payment is made for the shares within the times specified by the decree."[13] (6) If the majority shareholder elects to pay the appraised amount, that amount is paid in cash prior to the deadline set up by the court.[14] (7) If the majority shareholder elects not to pay the minority shareholder the appraised amount, the company is actually liquidated and all shareholders receive a proportional share of whatever the resulting cash proceeds are.[15]

Since the minority shareholder has sought dissolution, the minority shareholder is entitled to receive that amount that would have been available for the minority shareholder following the completion of the dissolution proceeding. In this way the minority shareholder receives the full benefit of the dissolution proceeding that the minority shareholder has commenced.

"Fair Value" vs. "Fair Market Value"

A concept of "fair value" and not "fair market value" must be used in a Section 2000 proceeding. It is obvious that the legislature intended "fair value" to be something other than "fair market value," or it would have used the phrase more common to conventional appraisal practices.[16] Perhaps the easiest way to understand the difference between the "fair value" definition of Section 2000 and "fair market value" is to look at Revenue Ruling 59-60, which is the traditional basis of going concern valuations. Revenue Ruling 59-60 defines "fair market value"

> as the price at which the property would change hands between a willing buyer and a willing seller when the former is not under any compulsion to buy and the latter is not under any compulsion to sell, both parties having reasonable knowledge of relevant facts.

A number of critical elements found in Revenue Ruling 59-60 are not present in a Section 2000 proceeding. First, a willing seller is not involved. In a corporate dissolution, the seller is involuntarily disposing of the assets or the company. Second, the seller is under a "compulsion" to sell, specifically because of the pendency of the dissolution proceeding; this is entirely opposite from the provisions of Revenue Ruling 59-60 that contemplate that the seller "is not under any compulsion to sell." Third, the involuntary seller under a compulsion to sell pursuant to Section 2000 does not have the luxury of waiting for a top offer; the sale must be completed under the adverse conditions of a corporate dissolution conducted in accordance with California law. Fourth, implicitly, the buyer is aware of the seller's weakened position specifically because the sale of assets or sale of the business is occurring in a dissolution proceeding.[17]

Dissolution Valuation

There are two ways to dispose of a company in a dissolution. One is by simply liquidating the assets in a piecemeal fashion. The other is the possibility that after the dissolution proceeding has been commenced the seller will be able to find a party that will buy the entire business before the business has to be liquidated in the dissolution proceeding.[18] These two methods of sale provide the dual valuation concept of Section 2000(a) that "the fair value shall be determined on the basis of the liquidation value as of the valuation date, the taking into account the possibility, if any, of the sale of the entire business as a going concern in a liquidation."[19]

The dual valuation concept of Section 2000(a) means that it is necessary to consider two values in order to arrive at the "fair value" to be paid to the minority shareholder pursuant to Section 2000. The first value to be determined under Section 2000 is the straight "liquidation value" of the assets as of the valuation date. The law mandates that this "liquidation value" is the "basis" of a Section 2000 proceeding.[20] Such a piecemeal liquidation would be conducted in accordance with California law and therefore any valuation must properly adjust for the depressive effect of a forced liquidation sale of a company's assets in a dissolution proceeding. The second value to be considered relates to the "possibility" that the "entire business as a going concern" could be sold "in a liquidation." This means that the appraisal should evaluate the possibility of whether a buyer for the whole business could be found after the dissolution proceeding commenced, but before the separate assets are liquidated.

If the appraisers determine that there is no realistic possibility that the "entire business as a going concern" could be sold in liquidation, then such an alternative value would not have to be developed and the appraisers should determine only the piecemeal liquidation value of the assets.[21] On the other hand, if the appraisers determine that there is a realistic possibility that "the entire business as a going concern" could be sold in a liquidation proceeding, then the appraisers must determine what such a forced sale might yield. The statute, however, does not suggest that the mere possibility of a sale of a going concern in a liquidation leads to the conclusion that a going concern value should be the final value in the Section 2000 proceeding. Rather, there has to be a realistic prospect that the sale for cash of the entire business can be made in a time frame consistent with a dissolution proceeding, as required by Section 2000. Thus, it would be unreasonable to consider the possibility of a sale of the entire business if such purchaser could not be found and the sale could not be closed on a timely basis. Finally, the statute is clear that this "possibility" of "sale of the entire business as a going concern in a liquidation" should be taken "into account." The statute does not mandate that this value be used.

While appraisers routinely assume in "fair market value" valuations that there is always a willing buyer for a business, that may not, in fact, be the case. Many types of businesses are routinely

Dissolution Actions Yield Less than Fair Market Enterprise Value

bought and sold; in such case the appraisers could properly assume a very high probability of sale. However, some unique or specialized businesses may not be easy to sell, or may not have many or any likely buyers. This reality must be reflected in a Section 2000 valuation.

In sum, the piecemeal liquidation value forms the benchmark for determining "fair value." Taking into account the realistic possibility, if any, that a sale of the entire business as a going concern could occur may increase the "fair value" above such piecemeal liquidation value, but the possibility of such sale has to be discounted by the probability that such sale will not occur. The conditions and costs of conducting such a sale in a liquidation must also be considered, as discussed below.

The formula for determination of "fair value" under Section 2000 therefore is as follows:

$$\text{Fair Value} = \text{Piecemeal Liquidation Value} + \text{Incremental value based on the percentage of possibility, if any, of the sale for cash of the entire business as a going concern in a liquidation}$$

Section 2000 Dissolution Conditions

Section 2000, properly applied, takes into account certain conditions that affect the amount that can be realized by the shareholders in a corporate dissolution. These conditions are necessary to yield to the minority shareholder exactly what would have been received if the company actually had been liquidated or the entire business had been sold as a going concern in a liquidation proceeding. In effect, the appraisers must treat the company as if it is going through an actual dissolution proceeding.[22]

A. Conditions for Both Piecemeal Liquidation of Assets or Forced Sale

The following conditions that arise in a corporate dissolution apply both to the piecemeal liquidation of assets and the forced sale of the entire business as a going concern.

1. Public Announcement that the Company is in a Dissolution Proceeding

The minority shareholder instituting the suit should be in the same position as if the dissolution sought by that shareholder had actually occurred. California law provides:

> (c) When an involuntary proceeding for winding up has commenced, the corporation shall cease to carry on business except to the extent necessary for the beneficial winding up thereof and except during such period as the board may deem necessary to preserve the corporation's goodwill or going-concern value pending a sale of its business or assets, or both, in whole or in part. The directors shall cause written notice of

Chapter 6: Fair Value Under California Corporations Code Section 2000

the commencement of the proceeding for involuntary winding up to be given by mail to all shareholders and to all known creditors and claimants whose addresses appear on the records of the corporation, . . . [23]

It is therefore clear that for the purposes of determining fair value under Section 2000, the appraisal must consider the negative impact of such public notice on both the piecemeal liquidation value and the possible sale of the company as a going concern in a dissolution proceeding. A number of adverse conditions must be anticipated upon such public notice. For example:

a. Key personnel may leave once it becomes obvious that the company is in liquidation.

b. Commercial relationships may not be renewed or continued.

c. Payment of loan obligations may be accelerated.

d. Sales are likely to be lost to competitors.

e. Accounts receivable collection becomes more difficult.

f. Suppliers lower credit limits, require advance payment, impose C.O.D. terms, or otherwise reduce their credit exposure.

g. Unions, customers, suppliers or anyone else who had been willing to yield a current benefit in anticipation of a future outcome, become less flexible and more interested in extracting the most value in the present time frame.

h. Financial statements might reflect lower net worth and earnings because the company would no longer be assumed to be a "going concern". As a result, banks and other credit grantors would lower or eliminate available credits.

Generally speaking, the business is at a competitive and cash flow disadvantage once its pending liquidation is made known, as required by law.

2. Cost of Piecemeal Liquidation or Forced Sale of the Company

Section 2000 allows the minority shareholder to receive in cash what would be received if the action to dissolve the corporation succeeded. Therefore, it is necessary to take into account costs that would be incurred in liquidating the assets and achieving the required cash liquidity. Such costs include auction fees, sales commissions, sales taxes, legal fees, accounting fees and other expenses that would result from the liquidation. As dealt with below, there are certain different costs applicable to the piecemeal sale of assets and the forced sale of the entire business.

3. Time Value of Money

A piecemeal liquidation can take from several months to several years to complete, rather than being completed all at once. Assuming that all the assets can be sold, some of the proceeds can be withheld for years in a liquidating trust to reserve for claims that may arise from acts that either took place while the Company was in existence or arose as part of the liquidation. Given the time value of money, the net proceeds which are to be distributed to the shareholders at the end of this period are worth less than the same amount of cash in hand today.

The same considerations apply to a forced sale of the entire business as a going concern in a dissolution proceeding. Even though the sale itself is conducted on an urgent basis, some time will pass before the transaction is completed and the cash is received, undetermined claims are resolved and can be paid, and the surplus is distributed to the shareholders.

The amounts which would be derived over time in a liquidation or a sale of the entire business must therefore be discounted to present value, since the minority shareholder in a Section 2000 proceeding will receive cash at the time of the stock repurchase if the company is not actually dissolved.

B. Conditions for Piecemeal Liquidation of Assets -- Costs of Liquidation

Because costs would be incurred in a piecemeal liquidation of assets, those costs must be deducted to determine what the shareholders would actually receive after the liquidation is completed. Costs incurred in liquidating individual assets may include, but are not limited to:

1. Continued cost of operation until liquidation is completed.

2. Legal fees incident to negotiations and required liquidation notices and filings.

3. Brokerage fees paid on sale of real estate and other significant assets.

4. Fees paid auctioneers and others who assist in liquidating assets.

5. Corporate income taxes that may arise from the disposition of assets.

6. Accounting and other professional fees incident to the winding up of business.

7. Legal fees incurred in resolving any outstanding contingent liabilities or other disputes.

8. Costs of administering the liquidating trust which is often employed to marshal the sums to be distributed to stockholders.

9. Reserve for contingencies.

10. Employee termination costs.

11. Payment of debts.

12. Resolution of long term obligations, such as leases.

B. Conditions for Forced Sale of the Entire Business in the Course of a Dissolution Proceeding

1. Sale of the "Entire Business"

After determining the "liquidation value" as the basis for the valuation, Section 2000(a) explicitly requires the appraisers to take into account the possibility "of the sale of the entire business as a going concern in a liquidation." The appraisers must therefore determine the likelihood that a single purchaser would purchase the "entire business" for cash as constituted as of the appraisal date. Presumably in an actual liquidation some combination of a sale of assets and a sale of an operating portion of the business might occur; however, such a combination is specifically not contemplated by Section 2000.

2. Hypothetical Assumptions

The actual sale of a business ordinarily requires certain agreements and representations on the part of a motivated seller. Accordingly, *Mart v. Severson*, supra, requires that the "appraisers should always assume a hypothetical seller's covenant not to compete just as they should assume that the parties to the hypothetical sale will negotiate the other requisite terms to a sales agreement."[24] Presumably this extends to seller's warranties, agreements to assist in transition to new management, and the like. *Mart* indicates that the standard for such hypothetical assumptions is "the reasonable person's conduct."[25]

3. Time Restraints on the Forced Sale.

A going concern that is up for sale in the ordinary course of business has the opportunity to await the optimum time for sale, without the time pressures and other adversities created by an involuntary dissolution. As discussed above, this is one of the crucial differences between Revenue Ruling 59-60 and Section 2000. If the dissolution sought by minority shareholder proceeded through liquidation, any possible transaction involving sale of the entire business would proceed under pressure to be concluded promptly. A receiver may be appointed. Because the intent of Section 2000 is to keep the moving party in the same position as if the forced sale had actually occurred, it is reasonable to assume that the forced sale would take place immediately since the operation would be under the dissolution constraints described above. Such an immediate sale under liquidation conditions would limit the company's ability to optimize its sale price.

4. Cash Proceeds Required

As pointed out by Marsh, Section 2000, ". . . contemplates the purchase for cash only . . ."[26] This concept eliminates from consideration the sale of the Company in exchange for stock, debt or other non-cash consideration. This cash requirement sharply limits the population of potential purchasers for any business. Public companies often use stock when acquiring a business in order to conserve cash, preserve availability of net operating losses for tax purposes, or to achieve "pooling of interest" treatment for financial reporting purposes. Installment purchase cannot be considered. Also eliminated are leveraged buy-outs and other transactions requiring the seller to accept debt as consideration. Further, the appraisal cannot consider any agreements which have significant contingencies in the purchase price determination. Such transactions typically provide for the seller to receive additional compensation if certain post acquisition date targets are achieved. Long-term payouts based on non-competition agreements would obviously be precluded. Eliminating all these possible acquirers from consideration has a dampening effect on the valuation. The appraisal is restricted to considering only those buyers who are willing and able to pay a fixed price in cash at the time of purchase.

5. Lack of Marketability Discount

Whether by forced sale or otherwise, it is well established that an ownership interest in a closely held corporation must be discounted from its initially calculated value to reflect its lack of marketability. This is separate from a minority share discount, which is not appropriate in a Section 2000 proceeding because all minority and majority interests would be paid off proportionately in a completed dissolution.[27] If shares of the same corporation were publicly traded, a shareholder could sell his shares on the open market and realize cash. However, it is usually much more difficult to find a willing buyer for an entire closely held business than to trade stock in an available market.

6. Cost of Sale of Entire Business as a Going Concern in a Dissolution Proceeding

Sale of the entire business as a going concern in a dissolution proceeding may require the employment of an investment banker or other merger/acquisition specialist in order to maximize the yield. Such transactions can require the preparation of an Offering Memorandum or other such documents, with their attendant legal, accounting and printing costs. Attorneys and accountants must also be engaged to protect the sellers' interests. Such costs must be included in the valuation to determine what a shareholder of the selling company would ultimately receive.

Section 2000 Decision Flow Chart

The following flow chart summarizes the steps necessary to give the minority shareholder the full benefit of the dissolution that has been sought. For illustration purposes, this chart makes

Chapter 6: Fair Value Under California Corporations Code Section 2000

Section 2000 Decision Flowchart

Piecemeal Liquidation Value

Sale as a Going Concern in a Liquidation

1. Determine the net realizable value available from liquidation of the Company's assets subject to settlement of liabilities and commitments.

   ← If No —

5. Is there a "possibility, if any, of sale of the entire business as a going concern in a liquidation" subject to all Section 2000 conditions?

   If Yes ↓

6. If there is some "possibility, if any, of sale," estimate the value of the Company if sold as a going concern in liquidation. Apply two methods:

   a. Discounted Cash Flow   b. Multiple of Earnings

2. Reduce by the costs associated with such liquidation including corporate taxes, brokerage, legal and other fees.

7. Reduce by factors reflecting:
   - all cash sale
   - sale of "entire business" required
   - impact of rapid forced sale
   - lack of marketability discount

3. Reduce by a time value of money factor to reflect the impairment of the value of the net proceeds due to delay in receiving proceeds in a dissolution proceeding.

8. Reduce by estimate of brokerage fees and other costs of arranging the sale.

9. Reduce by a time value of money factor to reflect the impairment of the value of the net proceeds due to delay in receiving proceeds in a dissolution proceeding.

4. Calculate Piecemeal Liquidation Value.

10. Determine value based on Discounted Cash Flow analysis.

10. Determine value based on Multiple of Earnings analysis.

11. Compare values developed by both analyses and determine the value of the Company based on a sale as a going concern in a liquidation

12. Compare Values

(No comparison is necessary if there is no "possibility, if any, of sale of the entire business as a going concern in a liquidation.")

Dissolution Actions Yield Less than Fair Market Enterprise Value

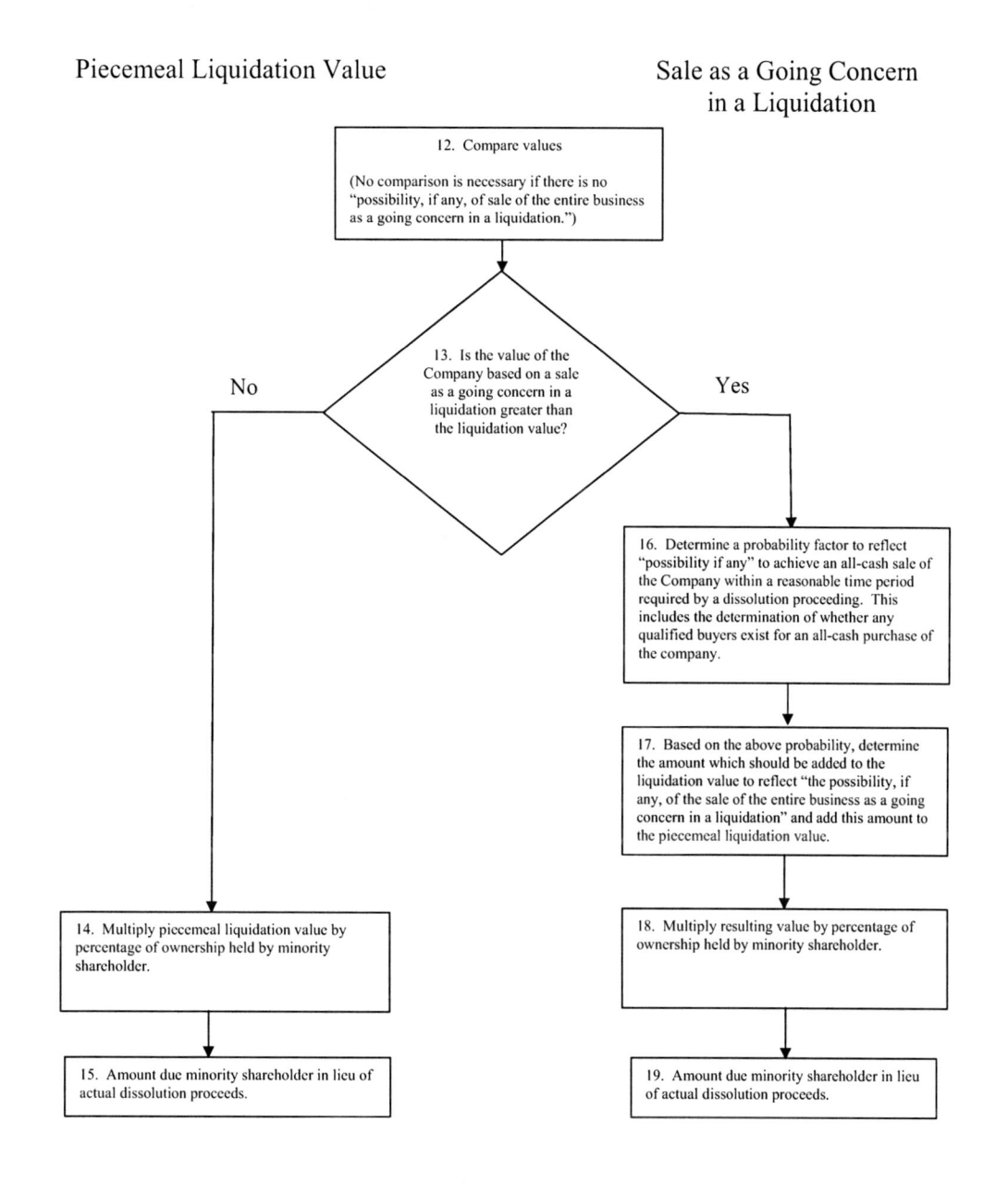

Piecemeal Liquidation Value

Sale as a Going Concern in a Liquidation

12. Compare values

(No comparison is necessary if there is no "possibility, if any, of sale of the entire business as a going concern in a liquidation.")

13. Is the value of the Company based on a sale as a going concern in a liquidation greater than the liquidation value?

No →

Yes →

16. Determine a probability factor to reflect "possibility if any" to achieve an all-cash sale of the Company within a reasonable time period required by a dissolution proceeding. This includes the determination of whether any qualified buyers exist for an all-cash purchase of the company.

17. Based on the above probability, determine the amount which should be added to the liquidation value to reflect "the possibility, if any, of the sale of the entire business as a going concern in a liquidation" and add this amount to the piecemeal liquidation value.

14. Multiply piecemeal liquidation value by percentage of ownership held by minority shareholder.

18. Multiply resulting value by percentage of ownership held by minority shareholder.

15. Amount due minority shareholder in lieu of actual dissolution proceeds.

19. Amount due minority shareholder in lieu of actual dissolution proceeds.

the assumption that with regard to the sale of the business in a liquidation the appraisal might apply two of the conventional valuation methods, discounted cash flow and multiple of earnings. It may be that the appraisers determine that other valuation methods should be used; if so, steps 6a and b and step 10 would be different depending upon the method chosen.

Conclusion

A Section 2000 proceeding will yield to the moving minority shareholder less than fair market value of the shares. This must logically follow from the fact that the value to be determined is that of shares of a company liquidated or sold as a going concern in dissolution proceeding, not shares of a company sold as a going concern without any compulsion to sell under any financial arrangement acceptable to the seller. When the court in *Brown v. Allied Corrugated Box Co.* correctly held that a minority share discount did not apply in a Section 2000 proceeding, the court did not intend that the complaining minority shareholder receive an amount that would be higher than traditional fair market value by removing the discount.

It must be kept in mind that the basis of Section 2000 is dissolution. Section 2000 is not a theoretical division of the business. It is not an exercise of dissenting shareholders rights pursuant to Cal. Corp. Section 1300, et seq., and not a forced buy-out of a minority shareholder. While appraisal of stock in such other circumstances might yield something closer to fair market value, Section 2000 should not. Section 2000 appraisers must adhere to the fundamental statutory concept that they are trying to ascertain in good faith what the resulting proceeds would be for a minority shareholder if the company actually went through a complete dissolution proceeding pursuant to California law.

---

1. The author is a partner at Shartsis Friese LLP, a San Francisco law firm, at SFLAW.com. This article was originally printed in the *Business Valuation Update*™ and was updated by the author in 2009. Reprinted with permission.
2. *Ronald v. 4-C's Electronic Packaging, Inc.*, 168 Cal. App. 3d 290, 297 (1985).
3. Harold Marsh, one of the leading commentators on California Corporations law, served as the draftsman of the new General Corporation Law for the Assembly Select Committee on Revision of the Corporations Code and the State Bar Committee on Corporations, which drafted the basic revisions to the current version of Section 2000 that provides the "fair value" provision.
4. H. Marsh & R. Finkle, Marsh's California Corporation law, Section 2A.14 at 118.56 (3d Ed. 1990).
5. Section 2000(a).
6. H. Marsh & R. Finkle, Marsh's California Corporation Law, Section 21.20 at 1782 (3d ed. 1990).
7. *Brown v. Allied Corrugated Box Co.* (1971) 91 Cal. App. 3d 477, 489.
8. Section 2000(a).
9. Section 2000(b).
10. The parties can agree upon, and seek, court confirmation of an appointment process, or can allow the court to select the appraisers.
11. Section 2000(c).
12. Section 2000(c).

Dissolution Actions Yield Less than Fair Market Enterprise Value

13. Section 2000(c). Note: The trial court's decree is "not automatically stayed pending appeal." *Veyna v. Orange County Nursery, Inc.*, 170 Cal. App. 4th 146, 155 (2009). The purchasing party must apply first to the superior court "regarding the manner and time within which the purchasing party must post the money, security, or combination thereof, to guaranty the purchase of the shares." *Id.* at 157, 158.

14. Section 2000(d).

15. Section 2000(e).

16. *Ronald v. 4-C's Electronic Packaging, Inc.*, 168 Cal. App. 3d 290, 294 (1985) rejected the methodology of the majority appraisers where "they expressly assumed that 'fair value' is equivalent to fair market value." Ronald cited with favor the Marsh view "that the moving parties [plaintiffs] should not be entitled to more than the liquidation value of the shares, i.e., what they would receive if their objective is obtained." Citing Marsh Cal. Corporation Law (2d ed. 1981) §20.22, p. 638.

17. Shannon Pratt's Valuing a Business, 3rd Edition, discusses at page 24 the "fair market valuation" definition of the American Society of Appraisers, which "comports to that found in the U.S. Tax Code and in Revenue Ruling 59-60." On the same page he also discusses the Appraisal Foundation definition of "market value." These three definitions are basically the same, with some minor differences. None of these three "fair market value" definitions apply to a Section 2000 proceeding because they assume the seller either to be under no compulsion to sell, or to be "typically motivated," neither of which conditions is present in a Section 2000 proceeding. The Appraisal Foundation also explicitly acknowledges that "a reasonable time is allowed for exposure in the open market," also a condition not present in a forced sale under Section 2000. At page 27 Pratt discusses "fair value" as it generally applies to dissenting shareholders' appraisal rights. Pratt readily acknowledges that "various state courts certainly have not equated [fair value] to fair market value." At page 28 Pratt goes on to acknowledge that fair value under a dissolution statute like Section 2000 is, in turn, different than "fair value" under a dissenting shareholder statute.

18. *Mart v. Severson*, 95 Cal. App. 4th 521, 533 (2002).

19. The appraisers must consider everything that could have a material effect on valuation. For example, appraisers must determine and consider the value of "derivative or direct claims on behalf of or against" the company. *Cotton v. Expo Power Systems, Inc.*, 170 Cal. App. 4th 1371, 1379 (2009).

20. Section 2000(a).

21. In *Brown v. Allied Corrugated Box Co.*, 91 Cal. App. 3d 477, 490 (1979), the majority of appraisers in fact determined that the situation of the particular business "made a going concern liquidation unlikely." The minority "reached the opposite conclusion." The court reserved to itself the resolution of this factual dispute, noting that neither approach was "invalid per se." *Id.* at 489. Similarly, in *Trahan v. Trahan*, 99 Cal. App. 4th 62, 78 (2002), the appraisers determined that the corporation could not be sold as a going concern in a liquidation.

22. Consistent with taking into account the full cost of dissolution in the appraisal, the majority appraisers in *Brown*, supra, adjusted their appraisal by establishing a liquidation value and then "subtracting therefrom the cost of liquidating the corporation's assets and winding up its business...." *Brown* at 483. It is unclear from the opinion what specific costs were included.

23. California Corporations Code Section 1805(c).

24. 95 Cal. App. 4th at 534.

25. *Id.*

26. H. Marsh & R. Finkle, Marsh's California Corporation Law, § 21.20, at 1782 (3d ed. 1990).

27. In *Brown v. Allied Corrugated Box Co.*, 91 Cal. App. 3d 477, 486, the court correctly reasoned that a minority share discount should not apply since a dissolution would result in a distribution of "the exact same amount per share." *Brown* implicitly confirms that "fair market value" is the wrong standard since a minority share discount is an element in the "fair market value" of a minority ownership. *Brown*'s holding underscores the concept that the valuation is of the entire business subject to sale in a dissolution proceeding.

Using California Corporations Code Section 2000 to Resolve 50-50 Shareholder Deadlocks in Privately Held Corporations[1]

By Arthur J. Shartsis, Esq.[2]

Introduction

All too frequently, in the absence of applicable buy-sell or other shareholder agreements, serious problems arise when two owners, each owning half of a private corporation, develop irreconcilable differences either personally or about the business. Often a breakup of the ownership becomes the objective of one of the equal shareholders, who either wants to sell out or force out the other shareholder. The principal factor that often motivates these business divorces, and also makes them more complicated, is that one owner may play a much more significant role than the other in the conduct of the business. Although California has a variety of laws dealing with deadlocked boards of directors, shareholder rights, and buy-outs in lieu of dissolution, the strategies in representing 50-50 shareholders are both subtle and complex, and implicate a whole range of laws and regulations, including corporate governance, fiduciary duty, valuation, and merger and acquisition law and practices.

This article will discuss strategies that can accomplish the separation of the ownership interests of 50-50 shareholders, with a focus on companies in which there is unequal participation in the business by the two shareholders. Some of the most effective strategies are complicated and sophisticated, and if managed poorly can expose parties to significant liability or losses. Because of this complexity, and because of the variety of interests and relationships involved in such 50-50 situations, there is no conventional approach to resolving such deadlocks.

Circumstances leading to dissolution

Fifty-fifty ownership can result from any number of business or personal circumstances, including an initial agreement between co-founders, accumulated ownership of interests, or inheritance. When the participation in or contributions to the business by the equal owners become too disparate, friction can result. This friction can reinforce the disparate contributions by causing the more active owner to take steps to minimize the involvement of the co-owner. As a result, resentment can develop for both owners: the more active owner may resent receiving only half of the profits while working harder and bringing more value to the business, while the less active owner may feel undervalued or pushed out and believe that his or her reduced influence in business affairs is adversely affecting the company.

Using California Corporations Code Section 2000

Both owners can also feel under-compensated. The more active owner may expect and demand higher compensation for his or her contribution, and believe that the other owner deserves less or no compensation. The less active owner, who can or does control half of the board, may be unwilling to agree to higher compensation for the other owner or lower compensation for him or herself. The less active owner may also believe that the more active owner is taking excessive benefits and using company money for personal expenses. The less active owner may come to view the other owner as being abusive, violating corporate obligations to treat shareholders fairly, or otherwise taking improper advantage. Resentment can build for both parties.

In some circumstances, a less active owner may be satisfied with the other owner doing more of the work but nonetheless being obligated to share equally in all profits beyond whatever employment compensation is being paid. Further resentment may develop for the more active owner who perceives his or her contribution as the principal value in the business, which cannot fully be adjusted by any differential in employment compensation. In those cases, the more active owner may believe that the entire value of the business rests on him or her and that the other 50% shareholder is not fairly entitled to 50% of the profits. The less active owner may not view the other owner's contribution as being that significant, and believe that independent management could do a better job, possibly at a lower cost, so that both shareholders would simply receive equal dividends. The more active owner rarely agrees to step down.

These and other personal dynamics may lead to an impasse between equal owners if the board of directors is correspondingly equally divided. The superior court is empowered to deal with such an impasse by the appointment of a "provisional director."[3] Although court appointment of a provisional director will enable a majority vote on items that come before the board, it may not satisfy the sensibilities of the more active owner, who is constrained by having to answer to a provisional director who is in a position to control the board when the two owners cannot agree. Moreover, this judicially imposed tie-breaking vote is usually not healthy for the continued operation of the company. Unless the owners can resolve their differences, inevitably some other solution is required.

Impasse on basic business issues, differences in participation, personal resentment, compensation disputes, and the different perceptions of the equal owners can all lead to the desire by one or both of the owners to disengage from the company, to sell out to or buy out the other owner, or to sell the company to a third party. Differences are very likely to arise regarding what duties each shareholder owes the other in a sale situation, and who gets what and at what value. Not infrequently, the more active owner wants to buy out the other owner, but is unwilling to meet the requested price. The more active owner may also feel that equal division of sale proceeds obtained from a third party buyer is indefensible based on different past contributions; the other owner is not likely to agree to any unequal division.

Chapter 6: Fair Value Under California Corporations Code Section 2000

Strategies and remedies of the two owners

Absent a buy-sell or other contractual arrangement, if the parties cannot reach agreement for one to buy the shares of the other, or to sell the company to a third party, there are limited statutory mechanisms that may lead to one party selling to the other. Either shareholder can attempt to sell his or her 50% interest to a third party (generally an unlikely possibility and an unattractive buying opportunity under the circumstances); attempt to induce the other owner to purchase his or her 50% interest at an appraised value; or compel a liquidation sale of the whole company. However, neither shareholder can compel the other to sell out by appraisal.[4] Each 50% shareholder has the same available remedies, but the value and use of each remedy differs for each of them.

Less active owner's strategic choices

The less active owner may elect simply to continue to receive half of the profits while the other owner does more than half of the work. As a 50% shareholder who can or does control half of the board of directors, the less active owner is potentially in a position to control the salary and benefits of the more active owner, and to exert influence over a court-appointed provisional director to limit such compensation. In addition, the less active owner may also receive some salary for historic reasons, or as a result of providing services. As a party who controls half of the board, the less active owner may be in a position to extract a salary, whether earned or not.

However, if the less active owner wants a more active role but cannot get it, disagrees with business decisions, believes that the other owner is abusing his or her position, or otherwise wants to terminate the relationship, he or she may take steps that will result in being bought out by the more active owner, being bought out by a third party, or receiving half of the liquidation value of the company. The most direct resolution is a negotiated purchase by the other owner, if possible. While the less active owner cannot require the other owner to buy his or her shares, legal steps are available to enhance that possibility.

Any 50% shareholder has a statutory right to wind up and dissolve the corporation, which, one way or another, will result in money being paid to the party moving for dissolution, assuming that the company has any value.[5] If the less active owner seeks a dissolution of the corporation as a matter of right, this sets into motion a number of possible outcomes. If no action is taken by the other shareholder, winding up and dissolution will result in the sale of the company as a going concern or the liquidation of the company in the form of a piecemeal sale of the assets, depending on the condition of the company. The winding up and dissolution will be conducted either by the board of directors (Corp C § 1903) or the superior court (Corp C §1904). The equal shareholders will divide the proceeds of sale equally.

If the 50% shareholder not moving for dissolution under Corp C §1900 wishes to avoid the winding up and dissolution of the company, that party may invoke Corp C §2000. Under §2000, the superior court oversees a valuation of the corporation to enable the shareholder not seeking dissolution to purchase at an appraised value the shares of the shareholder seeking dissolution. This valuation in lieu of liquidation is designed to yield, as nearly as possible, a value that would reflect what the shareholder moving for dissolution would obtain in the event the corporation were actually dissolved. The valuation is based on what Corp C §2000 calls the "fair value" of the company, and not on a traditional "fair market value" appraisal (as "fair market value" is defined in Rev Rul 59-60, 1959-1 Cum Bull 237).[6] In general, "fair value" will be somewhat less than fair market value, because a sale in dissolution necessarily has some distress aspects that are not present with a willing buyer and willing seller acting with full knowledge and without compulsion to buy or sell in connection with an ongoing business.

After the Corp C §2000 valuation is completed, the shareholder not seeking dissolution (i.e., the co-owner who has invoked §2000) may or may not elect to buy out the shareholder seeking dissolution at the appraised "fair value." The party who invokes §2000 but declines to purchase at the "fair value" will be liable for the expenses, including attorney fees, incurred in the §2000 proceeding by the party moving for dissolution.[7] If the shareholder who invoked §2000 declines to buy out the shareholder seeking dissolution, the corporation's assets must be sold.

The less active owner can thus either accept the status quo of co-ownership, negotiate a sale if possible, or move to wind up and dissolve the company and be bought out for 50% of appraised "fair value" or whatever is received in a winding up and dissolution. No law prohibits either shareholder from buying the business as a going concern or buying assets of the company following a rejected §2000 appraisal, or following the exercise of Corp C §1900 if §2000 is not invoked.

Active owner's strategic choices

The more active owner has the same options as the less active owner, but different considerations. If the more active owner is unable to negotiate an acceptable resolution of differences or a buyout with the other owner, the more active owner's only mechanism for changing the status quo is to invoke Corp C §1900 to wind up and dissolve the corporation.

Should the more active owner elect to dissolve the company, he or she gives the other owner the opportunity to purchase the corporation in a §2000 proceeding. Thus, the owner who is more involved in the operation of the business must risk losing the business in order to obtain a business divorce.

Once the more active owner initiates dissolution, the other owner may elect to buy the company in order to operate it or to resell it. Should the less active owner have a strategy of buying the company and then immediately reselling or "flipping" the ownership, or just bringing in new owners, there will be problems attracting such buyers for the reasons described below.

The different relationships the two owners have to the business substantially effects whether or not the less active owner will exercise the right to buy the company at a §2000 appraised

Chapter 6: Fair Value Under California Corporations Code Section 2000

fair value if the more active owner elects to wind up and dissolve the corporation. First, the less active owner may have different personal objectives and interests, which may not include running the business. Second, the less active owner may no longer have (or may never have had) the skill, experience, or knowledge to run the business. Third, the less active owner may be unwilling to risk buying out the other owner, even at an appraised fair value, without the confidence that he or she can successfully run the business.

In evaluating a purchase of the company, the less active owner must also consider a number of important negative factors that are controlled by the other owner. Because of the nature of the Corp C §2000 sale, the more active owner has no obligation to provide the sorts of warranties, representations, and agreements not to compete that would be given in an ordinary voluntary sale of a going concern. Perhaps the most critical factor in the less active owner's decision to buy is the right (absent some prior agreement) of the more active owner immediately to compete directly with the old business once it is sold to the less active owner. The more active owner is under no legal obligation to remain in management or to perform the traditional functions of a selling owner in assisting in the transition to the new ownership. Thus, the less active owner, who may be less familiar with the business, will be assuming significant risks in buying out the more active owner through a §2000 proceeding. The reverse is probably not true for an active owner who buys through a §2000 process, because he or she is fully familiar with the business, is already running it, and may not be concerned about any serious competition from the less active selling owner.

The artificial nature of the Corp C §2000 valuation process also compounds the less active owner's problems. California courts have held that the court-appointed appraisers must assume for purposes of valuation that the selling shareholder will enter into a noncompetition agreement, even if it is not actually required or agreed to.[8] Although this fiction will cause the company to be valued at a higher amount than it would be if the absence of a noncompetition agreement is assumed, the fact is that on sale by the more active shareholder to the other shareholder, there will be no noncompetition agreement unless compensation for such an agreement is negotiated.

Mart v. Severson also indicates that the appraisers should assume that the parties to the hypothetical sale will negotiate the other requisite terms to a sale agreement.[9] These "requisite terms" referenced in Mart presumably include warranties, representations, and employment agreements, all of which may not in fact be given. However, because the appraisers apparently must assume these "requisite terms" of the sale, the valuation price presumably will be increased.

Thus, when the less active owner is the buyer, the true value of the business when sold in liquidation after a §2000 valuation may be less than the appraised "fair value," which must be based on the assumption of a fictitious covenant not to compete and other beneficial sale terms. When the more active owner is the buyer, under §2000 these fictitious value concepts do not have the same impact, because the business will retain the value provided by the more active owner. Because of this fiction, the less active shareholder may be overpaying at "fair value." The court in *Mart* suggests that even though these fictitious benefits are properly assumed in the "fair value" appraisal, if the potential seller really wants to sell at fair value, the seller will negotiate such terms.[10] However, if the potential seller is the more active owner, such a negotiation may be rejected for personal or strategic reasons.

The more active owner who has given the other owner the Corp C §2000 purchase opportunity has every incentive to persuade the appointed appraisers to set the highest "fair value" in a §2000 appraisal, so that he or she can receive the highest price possible from the less active owner, or discourage the less active owner from buying the company. A number of strategies can be used potentially to increase or decrease the "fair value," although the details of these strategies are beyond the scope of this article. Given these considerations, the more active owner may risk moving to dissolve the company, since the chance of the less active co-owner actually buying the business is relatively small. Thus, the more active owner's best strategy for gaining sole ownership and control of the company may be to dissolve it. Before such a bold decision is made, however, the more active owner should realistically evaluate whether the less active owner might buy the company to operate it or sell it to a third party, all in light of the strategies discussed below.

Active owner's purchase advantage in a dissolution sale

If the more active owner invokes the dissolution procedures of Corp C §1900 and the business is not bought by the other owner based on the Corp C §2000 "fair market" appraisal, or if §2000 is never invoked, the more-active owner is in a position to buy the company at a liquidation sale. A sale must occur because Corp C §1900 mandates that the company must be wound up and dissolved if not purchased at the appraised "fair value" by a party invoking §2000.

Once a company is in dissolution, Corp C § 1903 requires the board of directors to conduct the company's business for the purpose of winding up its affairs. Thus, the board is obligated either to sell the assets of the corporation piecemeal or sell the corporation as a going concern. It would violate the letter and spirit of the dissolution provisions simply to continue to operate the corporation without moving toward some form of sale. If the directors fail to move the dissolution forward, any shareholder holding over 5% of the stock can move to invoke court control over the process.[11]

Moreover, once voluntary dissolution has begun, certain actions are required that have a negative effect on the continued conduct of business.[12]

Although the Corp C §2000 valuation creates a hypothetical sale value that basically assumes normal motivation by the owners to sell the company, the self-interest of the more active owner who intends to buy the company in liquidation at the lowest possible price may induce different conduct during the sale process than assumed by §2000. For example, in a normal sale, the owners ordinarily will agree to some period of noncompetition. Selling owners ordinarily also will agree to cooperate in the transition to the new owners, which may include some period of continued employment by the selling owners. A buyer ordinarily requires and obtains extensive warranties, representations, and indemnities from a seller. While the §2000 valuation may assume some or all of these factors, the actual sale may not include any of them, making the company less attractive to possible third party buyers.

Chapter 6: Fair Value Under California Corporations Code Section 2000

If the more active owner wants to buy the company in liquidation, he or she can drive down the purchase price of the company by making it unattractive to potential competing buyers. To achieve this, the active owner can legally refuse to agree not to compete, to assist in transition, or to provide any warranties, representations, or indemnities. Moreover, a potential third party buyer will be most interested in obtaining these types of concessions from the more active owner, who knows the most about the business that is being sold, and who will be a competitive threat to any new owner. Such concessions from the less active owner may be viewed as being of less value.

The less active owner may not be in a position to provide valuable assistance to a new owner, meaningful warranties, representations, or indemnities, or a noncompetition agreement that has significant value. Accordingly, the price of the company in a liquidation sale will be substantially reduced if the more active owner is interested in purchasing the company and decides not to promote or support the sale.

Finally, Corp C §2000(a) mandates that the corporation be valued for a cash sale only. This is consistent with the statutory scheme that applies to liquidation, which ultimately can only result in a cash sale unless a majority of the shareholders agree to accept some other form of consideration, such as the stock of an acquiring company.[13] As a result, if the more active shareholder wishes to acquire the company, he or she must be prepared to pay cash in a §2000 or §1900 sale unless the selling shareholder will accept other consideration. At the same time, the cash requirement further reduces the marketability of the company, because a purchase by a third party using stock, debt, or some form of earn-out over time, is not available if either shareholder refuses to agree to those terms and requires all cash. Refusal to accept consideration other than cash is another strategic option that may possibly further reduce the number of available buyers and therefore presumably reduce the price.

The net result of these factors is that if the more active shareholder wants to buy the company, that shareholder legally may take, or refuse to take, certain actions that will make the company unattractive to most buyers (other than himself or herself), except at a highly reduced price. By depressing the price, the more active shareholder may enhance his or her own bargain purchase opportunity, because the board of directors must still favor the highest price, no matter how low it is. At the same time, the less active owner may recognize that the ability of the active owner to drive the price down in an open market sale means that it would be better to accept some negotiated buyout than to run the risk that the company will sell (to a third party or the other owner) for a fraction of the value that could be achieved in a sale by motivated owners. Finally, the more active owner must be careful to avoid certain significant legal risks while attempting to gain the pricing advantage.

Risks and complications of a bargain purchase by active owner

If the more active owner invokes Corp C §1900 for dissolution of the corporation with the goal of ultimately being the purchaser, potential conflicts arise if the more active owner remains on the board of directors or as the chief executive of the company if and when it is offered for sale. Because a more active owner interested in buying has no assurance that he or she will be the high bidder, this potential buyer faces a dilemma. On the one hand, the buyer always wants the lowest price. On the other hand, if the more active owner is not the low bidder and the company is sold to a third party, the desired price is the highest possible price. These two positions cannot be reconciled. If the more active shareholder wants to assure the highest price, he or she should act like a motivated seller. The highest price can generally be achieved only with a full array of the "requisite terms,"[14] including noncompetition agreements, employment agreements, warranties, representations, and indemnities. The more active owner may demand from the less active owner separate compensation for providing these "requisite terms," and in this way attempt to obtain differential compensation to re-fleet earlier contributions. Agreeing to this special compensation may actually be in the interest of the less active owner if the result is a higher net sale amount going to the less active owner. A demand by the more active owner for special compensation for providing "requisite terms," if rejected, may make it impossible to obtain maximum value. However, legally depressing the price to obtain a bargain purchase calls for an entirely different strategy.

The board of directors is obligated to the shareholders generally to obtain the maximum sale price for the corporation. As a potential buyer, the more active owner acting as a director may be confronted with conflicting positions regarding how the company should conduct itself to maximize the sale price. These conflicting positions arise notwithstanding the active owner's strategic and legal refusal to provide noncompetition and employment agreements or warranties, representations, or indemnities that would enhance the sale price. Inevitably, if it has not occurred already, a tie-breaking director will be selected by the two owners or by the court to serve on the liquidating board. The active owner's position as an active buyer will cause the power of governance to shift to the tie-breaking director.

While trying to be a buyer at a low price, the more active owner, who is also managing the business, must act with extraordinary care to avoid a successful claim by the less active owner for breach of fiduciary duty. It is important to note that no case in California has held that one 50% shareholder has a fiduciary duty to the other 50% shareholder based solely on such share ownership. Nor does a fiduciary duty arise "in the course of arm's-length buyout negotiations between two equal shareholders of a corporate enterprise," even when one shareholder relies on the other to "paint the truest picture possible of where the company is right now."[15] Thus, the active shareholder assumes a fiduciary duty to all shareholders only as a result of being a director or officer of the company.

Because the more active owner is more responsible for the continued operation and success of the company, it is difficult for that person to remove him or herself completely from management of the company during the sale process. This is particularly true if the active owner hopes eventually to own 100% of a business that has continued to flourish during the sale period, which can become quite extended. It is difficult for a business to continue to operate at its normal profitable level while going through an adversarial sale process. The longer the process takes, the greater the potential damage to the business. Thus, careful decisions must be made regarding what matters should be voted on by the board. This also presents complications in

Chapter 6: Fair Value Under California Corporations Code Section 2000

the selling process, where the active owner may also be a bidder. Difficult decisions also must be made about how and to what extent the chief executive or director who is also a competing buyer should participate in the process.

The business may be sold in a number of ways, including sale of the assets, or sale of some or all of the business as a going concern through negotiation, auction, or a brokered sale. Brokerage may be conducted by a business broker or investment banker. A variety of sale strategies are available.

If the majority of the board elects a competitive sale through brokerage, any shareholder as a potential buyer stands to be excluded from participating in the preparation of the sale materials or in the selling process. Because both shareholders are potential buyers, regardless of any nonbinding declaration of noninterest in purchase they may make, the burden of overseeing the preparation of sale materials and the sale may fall on the independent director or any special consultant that the board may retain. That consultant may be the broker or investment banker, or may also be a separate party.

If the active shareholder is a potential buyer, his or her nonparticipation in preparing sale materials may negatively affect the quality of those materials. The active shareholder as the most senior corporate executive normally would actively assist in the sale, providing key information and leading presentations to possible buyers. This traditional executive role must somehow be reconciled with also being a potential buyer. The active shareholder must be careful, however, not to act in some way, as an officer or director, that can be construed to undermine the sale process, or claims of breach of fiduciary duty may arise.

In particular, following the notice of voluntary dissolution under Corp C §1900, the more active shareholder who is an officer or a director will be in a vulnerable position regarding any corporate activity he or she undertakes. In what may be a very contentious environment—especially if the more active owner takes legally permitted actions that may depress the sale price—the less active shareholder may scrutinize the other shareholder's corporate activities to find grounds for a breach of fiduciary duty claim in order to obtain some leverage in the process. Under these circumstances, the more active shareholder will be well served to assure that any significant corporate actions are reviewed and approved by a majority of the board. This may be a frustrating process when one of the initial reasons for the dissolution is disagreement about the conduct and direction of the business. In the most extreme circumstances, the more active shareholder should consider resigning as an officer or director in order to be an aggressive purchaser without fiduciary duty exposure. However, resignation will limit his or her influence over the sale process and diminish control over the continuing conduct of the business.

Assuming that the board of directors is seeking to fulfill its obligation to maximize shareholder value by maximizing the sale price, the more active shareholder as an officer or director may be excluded from most or all of the selling process, except as a potential buyer. The board must also decide whether it will negotiate with interested bidding parties, including the more active shareholder, following an initial bidding round. The sale process and the extent of participation in that process by the more active shareholder have serious implications for the ultimate outcome of the sale. Whatever procedure the board selects may influence whether third parties seriously enter the bidding process. This all may be complicated further if the less active shareholder wants to maximize value or simply deprive the other shareholder of ultimate ownership regardless of the cost.

Possibility of a negotiated sale between the shareholders during the selling process

The difficult situation described above may cause the equal shareholders to negotiate a sale between them, taking into account some or all of the following possible values and factors present: (1) the fair market value of the company; (2) the highly depressive affect on the sale price caused by the legal noncooperation of the more active owner; (3) the risk to the more active owner of a claim for breach of fiduciary duty; (4) the risk to the more active owner of losing the purchase to another buyer; (5) the generally negative effect on the company's operations of the forced sale process and management dislocation; and (6) a contentious board situation with a court appointed tie-breaking director. Consideration of all of these factors, taken together, may enable the disputing parties to establish a realistic value for the company under the circumstances.

Conclusion

Unless sometime during the sale process the parties negotiate a mutual resolution of ownership, the separation of interests of equal 50-percent shareholders through dissolution and sale is fraught with risk and complication for both sides. The more active shareholder stands either to purchase at a bargain, or to sell at less than full value. The less active shareholder is unlikely ever to obtain the kind of fair market value available in a sale by motivated owners. A comprehensive understanding of corporate and fiduciary law, as well as valuation, is essential to guiding an owner successfully through this process and optimizing that owner's outcome.

---

1. This material is reproduced from *California Business Law Reporter* (v. 27, 5. March 2006) copyright 2006, by the Regents of the University of California. Reproduced with permission of Continuing Education of the Bar – California. (For information about CEB publications, telephone toll free 1-800-CEB-3444 or visit CEB.com).
2. The author is a partner at Shartsis Friese LLP, a San Francisco law firm, at SFLAW.com.
3. See California Corporations Code Section (hereafter referred to as "Corp C §") 308.
4. See § 1900, 2000, and 2001.
5. See Corp C §1900.
6. For a discussion of the considerations that go into determining a "fair value" valuation under California Corporations Code Section 2000, see Shartsis, *Dissolution Actions Yield Less than Fair Market Enterprise Value (Appraising for "Fair Value" Under California Corporations Code Section 2000)*, in Chapter 6 of this *Guide*.
7. Corp C §2000(b)–(c).

Chapter 6: Fair Value Under California Corporations Code Section 2000

8. *Mart v. Severson* (2002) 95 CA4th 521, 115 CR2d 717; *Brown v Allied Corrugated Box Co.* (1979) 91 CA3d 477, 154 CR 170.

9. 95 CA4th at 534. See also *Abrams v. Abrams-Rubaloff & Assocs.* (1980) 114 CA3d 240, 249, 170 CR 656 ("the appraisers are not only entitled, but are required, to consider the manner in which the parties to such a hypothetical sale are most likely to maximize their return").

10. 95 CA4th at 535.

11. Corp C § 1904.

12. See, e.g., Corp C § 1903(c) (requiring notice to creditors of liquidation, and that the corporation cease carrying on business except to the extent necessary to wind up).

13. Corp C §§152, 1001, 2001.

14. *Mart v. Severson* (2002) 95 CA4th 521, 534, 115 CR2d 717.

15. *Persson v. Smart Inventions, Inc.* (2005) 125 CA4th 1141, 1162, 23 CR3d 335.

Twists and Turns for Fair Value (and other Value) Definitions in California

By Thomas E. Pastore, ASA, CFA, CPA[1]

There are some unique aspects to definitions of value for use in shareholder disputes and marital dissolution in the Golden State. This article will present the various definitions and then provide a brief case example of how significantly different values for the same company may result from the use of disparate value definitions.

Corporate Dissolution Matters

For dissenting shareholder lawsuits, many states have adopted the definition of *fair value* from the Uniform Business Corporation Act which is:

> "Fair value," with respect to a dissenter's shares, means the value of the shares immediately before the effectuation of the corporate action to which the dissenter objects, excluding any appreciation or depreciation in anticipation of the corporate action unless exclusion would be inequitable.

This is fairly (no pun intended) vague compared to the more precise definition for fair market value promulgated by the U.S. Treasury and U.S. Department of Labor for estate tax and Employee Stock Option Plan (ESOP) appraisals.[2]

For corporate dissolution actions in California, Section 2000 of the California Corporation Code for the General Provisions Relating to Dissolution defines fair value more precisely than the Uniform Business Corporation Act as:

> The fair value shall be determined on the basis of the liquidation value as of the valuation date but taking into account the possibility, if any, of sale of the entire business as a going concern in a liquidation. The parties agree it would be possible to sell the entire business as a going concern.

In these dissolution matters discounts for lack of control are typically not considered. The California Appellate Court stated in *Brown v. Allied Corrugated Box Co., 91 Call.App.3d 477 [Civ. No. 54318 Second Dist., Div. Three. Apr. 3, 1979]*:

> It has been noted, however, that the rule justifying the devaluation of minority shares in closely held corporations for their lack of control has little validity when the shares are to be purchased by someone who is already in control of the corporation. In such

a situation, it can hardly be said that the shares are worth less to the purchaser because they are non-controlling.

As a result of the above, business appraisers also do not generally apply a discount for lack of marketability, or only apply one based on the Lehman formula (5-4-3-2-1% of first through fifth and beyond $1 million increments of business sales price) or business brokers fees (7 to 10% of business sales price).

The liquidation aspect in the definition is particularly challenging in its application as the appraiser must also take into account *the possibility of the sale of the entire business as a going concern in liquidation*. All of the Section 2000 dissolution matters I have been involved with were for businesses which were going concerns. An illustration of how I and other appraisers on the same engagement have applied this unique part of the definition is presented later in this article.

Marital Dissolution Matters

The appropriate definition of value for marital dissolution matters can be an even more challenging issue since the definitions can vary on a county by county basis. To illustrate, I will provide definitions used generally in many counties and then specifically in San Diego county.

Historically, the standard of value was fair market value defined in California Code of Civil Procedure Section 1263.320 as:

> The highest price [emphasis added] on the date of valuation that would be agreed to by a seller willing to sell but under no particular or urgent necessity for doing so and a buyer that is ready, willing, and able to buy but under no particular necessity for doing so-and each party is dealing with the other with full knowledge of all the uses and purposes for which the property is reasonably adaptable and available.

Over the years, however, family law cases appear to have moved away from strict adherence to this definition, which is derived from California eminent domain law. Specifically, the courts have stated that appraisal methodology is not restricted to market value.

In re Marriage of Hewitson, the court did create a name –investment value- for the intangible and undefined interest in a business. In *Hewitson*, the court recognized the following possible methods of determining the investment value of closely held shares in an engineering company: 1) capitalization of earnings, 2) capitalization of dividends, and 3) book value or net asset value. The decision criticizes the capitalization of dividends method in a footnote. Additionally, the court did not define "investment value" except to say the method must take into account the factors set forth in the U.S. Treasury Department IRS Revenue Ruling 59-60.

Twists and Turns for Fair Value (and other Value) Definitions in California

In contrast, San Diego County has a very specific detailed description of investment value. San Diego Superior Court Rule 5.12.8, Appraisal of Closely Held Business Interests, requires the following:

A. *Standard of Value for Business appraisal – The standard of value is marital value which means the investment value of the business interest to a hypothetical, objective investor, considering the following factors:*

1. *Since there will be no change of ownership, there will be no reduction in value to reflect the risk inherent in a transfer of the business interest.*

2. *Pursuant to Family Code section 771, in establishing sustainable earnings, separate property earnings attributable to the operating spouse's efforts after the date of separation will not be considered.*

3. *There will be no reduction in value for capital gain or other taxes associated with sale.*

4. *A business may have marital value even though it is not saleable.*

5. *The business interest being valued may include assets and liabilities which would not be included in sale, such as cash, accounts receivable, accounts payable and non-operating assets and/or liabilities.*

In A.1. above, it appears that key person risks should not be taken into account. Also, like corporate dissolution matters, appraisers will generally not apply discounts for lack of control and marketability in marital dissolution cases. In particular, in regards to A. 3. above, capital gains taxes on appreciated assets cannot be deducted to determine value in San Diego County.[3]

If you use the "highest price" fair market value definition under California Code of Civil Procedure Section 1263.320, it would appear to yield a value that could be significantly different, i.e., higher than that obtained in the fair value "going concern" liquidation basis for shareholder dissolution matters. A similar result would seem to be the case using San Diego County's investment value definition. Taking into account the history of value definitions and their application in California and San Diego County in particular, it appears that values for marital dissolution appraisals should be higher than those for corporate dissolution matters. The next section presents a case example.

Valuations of DissoLute, Inc.[4]

DissoLute, Inc. is a privately held California Subchapter S Corporation which provides web-based information technology services to businesses in Southern California. The following provides a summary of the company's historical revenues and earnings before interest taxes depreciation and amortization (EBITDA).

Chapter 6: Fair Value Under California Corporations Code Section 2000

Year	2003	2004	2005	2006	2007
Revenues	$20,500,000	$21,000,000	$22,000,000	$24,000,000	$25,000,000
EBITDA	$3,500,000	$4,000,000	$4,500,000	$5,000,000	$5,200,000

We will assume a valuation of a 100% equity interest in DissoLute under two different engagements: (1) a shareholder dissolution matter; and (2) a marital dissolution matter. The date of value, December 31, 2007, is the same for each valuation. Furthermore, for ease of comparison of the resulting valuation conclusions, we will only use one method: EBITDA multiplier guideline private company market approach.

After researching the various transaction databases for appropriate guideline companies, we select 10 companies with the following range of EBITDA multiples:

Minimum	Lower Quartile	Median	Upper Quartile	Maximum
3x	4x	6x	7x	8x

Taking into account the risk/reward profile of DissoLute, economic and industry conditions, and the company's financial profile compared to the guideline companies, would normally result in our selecting the median EBITDA multiple of 6x to determine the fair market value in an estate tax matter. This multiple would be applied to DissoLute's latest adjusted twelve month EBITDA of $5,000,000 resulting in a value of $30,000,000. The adjusted EBITDA is the 2007 EBIDTA of $5,200,000 reduced by $200,000 to reflect the additional compensation of a qualified executive needed to replace the founder/president of the company, i.e. an adjustment for key person risk.

First, let's consider how the valuation could turn out under a shareholder dissolution matter. Our analysis establishes that DissoLute is expected to continue as a going concern. The fair value definition establishes that we must consider the sale as a going concern in liquidation. Business appraisers actively involved in shareholder dissolution cases usually interpret this to mean a relatively quick sale of the company that would occur in a shorter time span than would normally be the case if a financial intermediary were hired to find potential qualified buyers and get the highest reasonable price for the company. Given the sales limitation time under a liquidation, our analysis indicates that a 5x multiple would be appropriate, i.e., a multiple between the median and lower quartile range of the guideline companies. This results in a value of $25,000,000.

Now, let's consider DissoLute's valuation in a marital dissolution in San Diego County. Under the investment value standard, we must assume there will be no change of ownership and therefore there will be no reduction in value to reflect the risk inherent in a transfer of the business interest. Accordingly, we will not reduce EBITDA by $200,000 to reflect key person risk. Applying the 6x median guideline companies multiple to actual 2007 EBITDA of $5,200,000 results in a value of $31,200,000.

Twists and Turns for Fair Value (and other Value) Definitions in California

From the above, we can observe that DissoLute's value is about 25% greater in marital dissolution compared to shareholder dissolution. Besides informing us that divorce is a better alternative than shareholder litigation (at least from a purely financial perspective), there are a few other factors for business appraisers to consider in performing shareholder and marital dissolution valuations:

1. Keep abreast of appropriate statutes and case law dealing with the definitions and unique requirements for shareholder and marital dissolution matters.

2. Search for examples of the prevailing valuation expert witness' work in actual court cases as well as in authoritative textbooks.

3. Do not consider 1 and 2 to require absolute rigid adherence to a particular valuation approach or method. Exercise your own independent analysis and judgment for the specifics of the company you are valuing and your particular case. Also, consult with your client's attorney at the outset of the case to discuss the particular valuation definition and how it could affect the company's value.

---

1. Mr. Pastore is Chief Executive Officer and co-founder of Sanli Pastore & Hill, Inc. He has been involved in financial consulting for more than 20 years, specializing in investment and financial analysis, litigation consulting and public accounting. Extensive experience encompasses valuing numerous businesses in a wide range of industries including retail, services, manufacturing and holding companies. He has served as an expert witness in federal and state courts for business litigation cases in California, Texas, Arizona and Nebraska. Mr. Pastore can be reached via e-mail at tpastore@sphvalue.com or via phone at (310) 571-3400 ext 234.

2. The fair market value definition is: *The price at which the property would change hands between a willing buyer and a willing seller when the former is not under any compulsion to buy and the latter is not under any compulsion to sell, both parties having reasonable knowledge of the relevant facts.*

3. While not a direct topic of this article, this treatment of capital gains taxes is in direct contrast to recent estate tax case law. On November 15, 2007, the U.S. Court of Appeals for the Eleventh Circuit (the Court) decided *Estate of Frazier Jelke III v. Commissioner of the IRS* (Case No. 05-15549, Docket No. 3512-03; PDF, 53 pages) regarding the value, for federal estate tax purposes, of a 6.44% business interest burdened by a built-in capital gains tax at the holder's death. The following was the Court's decision as to the treatment of the built-in capital gains tax:

   Under a de novo review, as a matter of law, we vacate the judgment of the Tax Court and remand with instructions that it recalculate the net asset value of [the company] on the date of Jelke's death, and his 6.44% interest therein, using a dollar-for-dollar reduction of the entire $51 million built-in capital gains tax liability of [the company], under the arbitrary assumption that [the company] is liquidated on the date of death and all assets sold.

   As stated in the above excerpt, the Court found that built-in capital gains taxes should be treated as a direct dollar-for-dollar reduction in the determination of a company's value.

4. The following is a hypothetical case example. For actual valuation engagements, the selection of company earnings, valuation multiples and other variables depends on the facts and circumstances of each particular valuation assignment and can differ substantially from those shown in this article's case example.

Chapter 7
Court Case Abstracts

The abstracts in this section are arranged into tables by case type, then sorted first by state/jurisdiction, and then by case name. The index at the end of this Guide lists the abstracts by case name. To view the full text court opinions, as well as other complimentary online content available as part of your purchase of this Guide, please refer to BVLibrary.com.

Breach of Fiduciary Duty

Breach of Fiduciary Duty

Case Name	Date	Court	State/Jurisdiction	Comments	Page
Lawton v. Nyman	04/29/03	Court of Appeal	1st Circuit Federal	Fair value damages potentially include strategic premium.	171
Thompson, et al. v. Miller Jr., et al	09/30/03	Court of Appeals	California	Lack of marketability discount permitted when valuing stock in breach of fiduciary duty case.	174
Kim v. The Grover C. Coors Trust	03/08/07	Court of Appeals	Colorado	Fair value is not the standard of value in this shareholder dispute and serves as a good reminder that standard of value should be among the first, if not foremost, point of discussion between analysts and attorneys after initiating a valuation engagement.	246
Crescent/Mach I Partnership v. Turner	05/02/07	Court of Chancery	Delaware	The Court reviews 10 critical DCF assumptions in this fair value conclusion.	230
Crescent/Mach I Partnership v. Turner (Critique)	05/02/07	Court of Chancery	Delaware	Gilbert Matthews critique of *Crescent/Mach I Partnership v. Turner*	235
Kahn v. Tremont Corporation (I)	03/21/96	Court of Chancery	Delaware	Court indicates that the relatively small discount from market was not unfair to the buyer.	3
Kahn v. Tremont Corporation (II)	06/10/97	Supreme Court	Delaware	Court finds financial and legal advisors not independent, therefore the case was reversed and remanded for a new fairness determination.	21
Le Beau v. M.G. Bancorporation/ Nebel v. Southwest Bancorp, Inc.	04/30/99 03/09/99	Supreme Court and Court of Chancery	Delaware	No independent committee leads to "unfair dealing." Control premium upheld.	64
Ansin et al. v. River Oaks Furniture,Inc., et al.	2/3/1997	US Court of Appeals	First District	Anticipated IPO considered in determining fair value.	14
Small v. Sussman and Day Surgicenters, Inc.	06/01/99	Court of Appeals	Illinois	Court concludes that derivative causes of action should be considered when determining fair value.	222
Demoulas v. Demoulas	12/22/98	Supreme Judicial Court	Massachusetts	It was determined that "fair value" rather than "fair market value" was appropriate in the circumstances of this case.	50
Kortum v. Johnson	08/28/08	Supreme Court	North Dakota	The buy-sell agreement did not relieve the shareholders of their statutory duties.	263

Case Summary by Type

Business Dissolution

Business Dissolution

Case Name	Date	Court	State/Jurisdiction	Comments	Page
Cotton v. Expo Power Systems, Inc.	02/09/09	Court of Appeals	California	Statutory fair value must account for pending shareholder derivative suit.	277
Khatkar v. Dhillon	01/28/09	Court of Appeals	California	Court determines that statutorily defined standard for fair value in judicial dissolution is liquidation value.	270
Mart v. Severson	01/23/02	Court of Appeals	California	Section 2000 fair value assumes a hypothetical seller's covenant not to compete.	138
Trahan v. Trahan	06/07/02	Court of Appeals	California	Uncompleted contracts not included in fair value, defined as liquidation value.	146
Devivo v. Devivo	05/07/01	Superior Court	Connecticut	The Court found that minority and marketability discounts were not appropriate absent extraordinary circumstances, then found such circumstances in this case to warrant a 35% marketability discount.	111
Fierro v. Templeton	09/24/03	Court of Appeals	Florida	Issue is whether the shareholder who elects to purchase the shares of the shareholder who filed the dissolution action can, after a buy-out value has been determined, elect to have the corporation dissolved instead.	173
G&G Fashion Design, Inc. v. Enrique Garcia	02/11/04	Court of Appeals	Florida	The Court of Appeals upheld the Trial Court's valuation, stating that calculating "fair value" was a fact-specific determination that must take into account market value, net asset value, investment value, and other factors.	178
Cannon v. Bertrand	01/21/09	Supreme Court	Louisiana	When a partner lawfully withdraws from a limited liability partnership and the remaining partners elect to purchase the withdrawing partner's interest and continue the partnership, a minority interest discount is not warranted because it is inequitable.	272
Helfman v. Johnson	02/24/09	Court of Appeals	Minnesota	After review, the Appellate Court found that the discount applied by the Trial Court was not related to minority or marketability discounts.	278

BVR's Guide to Fair Value in Shareholder Dissent, Oppression, and Marital Dissolution   7-A

Chapter 7: Court Case Abstracts

Business Dissolution

Case Name	Date	Court	State/Jurisdiction	Comments	Page
Detter v. Miracle Hills Animal Hospital, P.C.	04/06/04	Supreme Court	Nebraska	Expert goodwill not included in valuation to avoid dissolution.	181
Torres v. Schripps, Inc.	07/09/01	Superior Court, Appellate Division	New Jersey	Fair value determination remanded due to lack of evidence. The parties failed to present sufficient expert testimony, which requires the trial court to "seek assistance from other sources to aid [its] decision of fair value."	119
Collision Depot Inc. v. Zigman	05/20/02	Supreme Court, Appellate Division	New York	Valuation within the range presented at trial is affirmed.	146
Murphy v. U.S. Dredging Corp.	05/19/08	Supreme Court	New York	Fair value award deducts present value of built-in gains tax.	267
Vetco, Inc., In re; Wolk v. Kornberg	03/04/02	Supreme Court, Appellate Division	New York	The Court concluded that the appropriate percentage for the illiquidity discount was 25% when determining fair value in this case.	143
Garlock, et al. v. Southeastern Gas & Power, Inc. and Hilliard	11/14/01	Superior Court	North Carolina	The Court considered key man factors in this fair value determination.	133
Anjoorian v. Kilberg	12/04/03	Supreme Court	Rhode Island	Although the opinion refers to fair market value, the Rhode Island dissolution statute says that the shareholder's shares will be purchased at fair value. Further, the Rhode Island Supreme Court has, on more than one occasion, held that no discounts apply to a determination of the fair value of a shareholder's shares.	175
DiLuglio v. Providence Auto Body	06/30/00	Supreme Court	Rhode Island	No marketability discount applied because purchaser (majority shareholder) was known.	92
Marsh v. Billington Farms, LLC	08/02/07	Superior Court	Rhode Island	Fair value of real estate company must include marketplace cost and risks.	248

Case Summary by Type

Marital Dissolution

Case Name	Date	Court	State/Jurisdiction	Comments	Page
Grelier v. Grelier	12/19/08	Civil Court of Appeals	Alabama	After seeking fair market value at Trial Court, wife cannot assert on appeal that the Court should have applied the fair value standard.	271
Crismon v. Crismon	12/13/00	Court of Appeals	Arkansas	The Court stated: "The concept of fair value in the context of a dissenting stockholder facing a corporate merger seems more applicable to the situation in this case."	99
Marriage of Thornhill, In re	08/21/08	Court of Appeals	Colorado	The Court declined to adopt *Brown v. Brown* and held that marketability discounts were appropriate.	265
Erp v. Erp	11/28/07	Court of Appeals	Florida	The wife analogized the divorce context to that of an oppressed and/or dissenting shareholder case, stating the DLOM should not be applied. The Court found it more akin to a shareholder seeking dissolution, which gives Florida Courts the discretion to apply marketability discounts	226
Marriage of Becker, In re	11/29/07	Court of Appeals	Iowa	The Court originally referenced *Wallace*, a dissenting shareholder case, but omitted the citation in this decision. This makes it unclear what the Court implying regarding the application of statutory fair value to divorce cases	223
Bernier v. Bernier	09/14/07	Supreme Court	Massachusetts	The Court likened the fiduciary considerations that constrain the equitable property division in divorce cases to those that constrained the minority/majority shareholders in the *Delaware Open MRI Radiology* case.	224
Brown v. Brown	02/28/02	Superior Court, Appellate Division	New Jersey	Appellate Court expressly held that the ALI Principal of Corporate Governance, which states that discounts are not to be applied absent extraordinary circumstances, is applicable in marital dissolution cases.	140
Fisher v. Fisher	09/08/97	Supreme Court	North Dakota	By applying the fair value analogy from corporate cases, the *Fisher* court thus affirmed the denial of the minority interest discount in divorce.	256

Chapter 7: Court Case Abstracts

Marital Dissolution

Case Name	Date	Court	State / Jurisdiction	Comments	Page
Anderson v. Anderson	09/05/06	Court of Appeals	Tennessee	CPA calculates fair value, then applies a marketability discount which the court rejects.	220
Boyd v. Boyd	01/03/02	Court of Appeals	Texas	The husband claimed that the trial court erred in determining the value of his stock options. The Appellate Court affirmed the Trial Court's decision on finding the fair value of the husband's stock options.	137
Drumheller v. Drumheller	03/06/09	Supreme Court	Vermont	Divorce Court favors "minimal use" of discounts.	274
Baltrusis v. Baltrusis	09/16/02	Court of Appeals	Washington	Appellate Court affirms valuation because husband's situation is similar to a dissenting shareholder's, thus requiring a determination of fair value and rendering marketability irrelevant.	156
Overbey, In the Matter of	06/18/07	Court of Appeals	Washington	Appellate Court affirmed the Lower Court's valuation—on a fair value basis.	228

Shareholder Dissent

Case Name	Date	Court	State / Jurisdiction	Comments	Page
Zatz, et al. v. U.S.A., et al	07/09/98	Court of Appeals	2nd Circuit	Court rejects valuation based on infirm offer to purchase.	41
Berens v. Ludwig (II)	02/17/98	United States Court of Appeals	7th Circuit Federal	Court examines the issue of "excess capital."	30
Swope v. Siegel-Robert, Inc. (II)	02/26/01	United States Court of Appeals	8th Circuit Federal	After the Trial Court applied a minority discount, but not a marketability discount, the Eight Circuit modified judgment to eliminate minority discount based on what it believed Missouri Supreme Court would do.	104

Case Summary by Type

Shareholder Dissent

Case Name	Date	Court	State / Jurisdiction	Comments	Page
Pacific Telecom, Inc. v. Gabelli Funds, Inc.	12/30/98	Court of Appeals	9th Circuit Federal	The Ninth Circuit reversed the district court's fair value appraisal and stated that third party sale value must be considered.	52
Cox Enterprises, Inc. v. News-Journal Corp.	12/21/07	United States Court of Appeals	11th Circuit Federal	The Court states that fair market value may serve as an estimate of fair value when the effects of an impending sale or merger, or other "distorting" corporate action, are not at issue.	258
Offenbecher v. Baron Services, Inc. (I)	05/18/01	Court of Civil Appeals	Alabama	The Trial Court had applied a 50% marketability discount, which was originally uphold by the Court of Civil Appeals. After an application for rehearing, the Court of Civil Appeals found that applying a discount to fair value was error as a matter of law. The Supreme Court affirmed the Court of Civil Appeals' rejection of a discount.	114
Offenbecher v. Baron Services, Inc. (II)	05/10/02	Court of Civil Appeals	Alabama		144
Offenbecher v. Baron Services, Inc. (III)	04/04/03	Supreme Court	Alabama		169
Pro Finish USA, Ltd. v. Johnson	02/06/03	Court of Appeals	Arizona	Court of Appeals upheld the refusal to apply discounts, noting that the trend in the law is to focus on the value of the firms as a whole.	167
M Life Ins. Co. v. Sapers & Wallack Ins. Agency, Inc.	02/01/01	Court of Appeals	Colorado	Appellate Court found that application of a marketability discount must be determined on a case-by-case basis. Trial court erred in rejecting discount as a matter of law.	102
Pueblo Bancorporation v. Lindoe, Inc. (I)	08/16/01	Court of Appeals	Colorado	Supreme Court affirms court of appeals; no marketability discounts in dissenters' rights cases as a matter of law, but left open the issue of whether an extraordinary circumstances exception is available under Colorado law.	127
Pueblo Bancorporation v. Lindoe, Inc. (II)	01/21/03	Supreme Court	Colorado		164
WCM Industries, Inc. v. Trustees of Wilson Trust	04/03/97	Court of Appeals	Colorado	Court of Appeals found that a marketability discount should be determined on a case-by-case basis.	17
Allenson v. Midway Airlines Corp.	07/06/01	Court of Chancery	Delaware	Concessions under merger agreement not elements of fair value.	117
Andaloro v. PFPC Worldwide, Inc.	08/19/05	Court of Chancery	Delaware	Delaware looks to DCF in determining fair value.	198

BVR's Guide to Fair Value in Shareholder Dissent, Oppression, and Marital Dissolution

Chapter 7: Court Case Abstracts

Shareholder Dissent

Case Name	Date	Court	State / Jurisdiction	Comments	Page
Applebaum v. Avaya, Inc., et al.	11/20/02	Supreme Court	Delaware	The Court affirmed the lower court's definition of fair value as market value for Sec. 155 purposes.	157
Borruso v. Communications Telesystems International	09/24/99	Court of Chancery	Delaware	Discount "for lack of liquidity" same as marketability discount, inappropriate in fair value determination.	79
Cede & Co. v. Technicolor, Inc.	05/04/05	Supreme Court	Delaware	The Supreme Court found that the Chancery Court erred by not using a law-of-the-case discount rate in finding fair value.	193
Delaware Open MRI Radiology Associates, P.A. v. Kessler	04/26/06	Court of Chancery	Delaware	The Court shows favor for S-Corp tax affecting in this fair value case.	203
Delaware Open MRI Radiology Associates, P.A. v. Kessler (Discussion)	04/26/06	Court of Chancery	Delaware	Delaware Open MRI Radiology experts discuss the case.	207
Emerging Communications, Inc., In re	05/03/04	Court of Chancery	Delaware	The court shows preference for DCF and accepts small stock premium in fair value calculation. Court goes on to state that market price is not indicative of fair value.	186
Finkelstein, et al. v. Liberty Digital, Inc.	04/25/05	Court of Chancery	Delaware	Court finds DCF method inappropriate for valuation of contract with uncertain future rights.	190
Gilbert v. M.P.M Enterprises, Inc.	10/09/97	Court of Chancery	Delaware	Court uses DCF to determine fair value of dissenter's shares.	27
Gonsalves v. Straight Arrow Publishers, Inc. (I)	11/27/96	Court of Chancery	Delaware	The Court of Chancery relies on one expert's methods in determining Rolling Stone's fair value. Supreme Court finds error in Court of Chancery's pretrial decision. The Court of Chancery's decision is reversed and remanded for a new valuation hearing. Without more information, the Court of Chancery states that they are unable to determine if a minority interest discount is appropriate.	11
Gonsalves v. Straight Arrow Publishers, Inc. (II)	10/21/97	Supreme Court	Delaware		29
Gonsalves v. Straight Arrow Publishers, Inc. (III)	03/26/98	Court of Chancery	Delaware		34
Gonsalves v. Straight Arrow Publishers, Inc. (IV)	09/10/02	Court of Chancery	Delaware		154

7-F   BVR's Guide to Fair Value in Shareholder Dissent, Oppression, and Marital Dissolution

Case Summary by Type

Shareholder Dissent

Case Name	Date	Court	State / Jurisdiction	Comments	Page
Grimes v. Vitalink Communications Corporation	08/26/97	Court of Chancery	Delaware	Delaware Chancery Court endorses DCF model in determining fair value.	23
Henke v. Trilithic, Inc.	10/28/05	Court of Chancery	Delaware	Delaware sees DCF approach as best for appraisal action.	200
Highfields Capital, Ltd. v. AXA Financial, Inc.	08/17/07	Court of Chancery	Delaware	Axa's "sum of the parts" analysis also proves reliable in this fair value conclusion.	241
Hintmann v. Fred Weber, Inc.	02/17/98	Court of Chancery	Delaware	The Court favors CAPM, doesn't support company specific risk, and places a control premium on a firm's subsidiaries	32
Hodas v. Spectrum Technology, Inc.	12/07/92	Court of Chancery	Delaware	Court determines fair value in an appraisal proceeding may not include any shareholder-level discount for lack of marketability.	284
Le Beau v. M.G. Bancorporation	04/30/99	Supreme Court	Delaware	Court accepts comparable acquisition method and deems control premium appropriate.	60
M.P.M. Enterprises, Inc. v. Gilbert	06/25/99	Supreme Court	Delaware	Merger terms and unconsummated prior offers not relevant to fair value determination.	72
Montgomery Cellular Holding Co., Inc., et al. v. Dobler, et al.	08/01/05	Supreme Court	Delaware	Supreme Court upholds decision of no control premium and reduces weight attributable to the comparable transaction method to account for synergies.	195
Paskill Corp. v. Alcoma Corp. (I)	06/16/99	Court of Chancery	Delaware	Investment company fair value includes capital gains tax discount, but no sales expense adjustment.	67
Paskill Corp. v. Alcoma Corp. (II)	03/07/00	Supreme Court	Delaware	The Court finds that net asset value not fair value and instructed in that it may be appropriate, on remand, for the Court of Chancery to consider a discount.	84
Ryan v. Tad's Enterprises, Inc.	04/24/96	Court of Chancery	Delaware	Court shows preference for DCF in finding fair value and does not apply discounts.	6

Chapter 7: Court Case Abstracts

Shareholder Dissent

Case Name	Date	Court	State / Jurisdiction	Comments	Page
Union Illinois 1995 Investment Ltd. Partnership, The v. Union Financial Group Ltd.	01/05/04	Court of Chancery	Delaware	Arm's-length merger price less synergies equals fair value.	176
PNB Holding Co., In re	08/18/06	Court of Chancery	Delaware	The Delaware Court of Chancery shows strong preference for the "traditional" method of DCF.	216
Boettcher, et al. v. IMC Mortgage Company	05/02/04	Court of Appeals	Florida	Trading price on the valuation date is not the fair value of public stock.	185
Blitch v. The Peoples Bank	10/23/00	Court of Appeals	Georgia	Court of appeals reversed trial court, holding that minority and marketability discounts should not be used to determine fair value of dissenting shareholder.	98
Croxton v. MSC Holding, Inc.	07/09/97	Court of Appeals	Georgia	The issue in this case is whether shareholder waived his right to receive an individual, independent contractual amount for his shares when he demanded fair value for his stock.	22
Hall v. Glenn's Ferry Grazing Assoc.	09/21/06	District Court	Idaho	Court applies minority discount in fair value determination.	221
Berens v. Ludwig (I)	02/13/97	United States District Court	Illinois	Court cites Delaware law, but applies its own interpretation.	15
Connector Service Corp. v. Briggs	10/30/98	United States District Court	Illinois	In this case, the Court disallows discounts in determining fair value of a reverse stock split cash-out.	46
Weigel Broadcasting Co. v. Smith	12/12/96	Appellate Court	Illinois	Trial Court found corporation's expert, who included discounts, more credible and valued stock near his value. Court of appeals upheld, finding application of discounts was matter of trial court discretion.	13
Settles v. Leslie	11/06/98	Court of Appeals	Indiana	Judicial appraisal exclusive remedy for Indiana shareholders.	47
Trietsch v. Circle Design Group	06/19/07	Court of Appeals	Indiana	Lack of fair value appraisal leaves minority shareholder with assessment of discounts.	252

Case Summary by Type

Shareholder Dissent

Case Name	Date	Court	State / Jurisdiction	Comments	Page
Carter Crookham v. Peter Riley, et al.	09/23/98	Supreme Court	Iowa	Damages amounting to fair value awarded for attorney's negligent handling of dissenter's appraisal action.	44
Ely, Inc. v. Wiley	12/23/98	Supreme Court	Iowa	Compulsion sale not evidence of fair value.	51
Northwest Investment Corp. v. Wallace	07/13/07	Supreme Court	Iowa	A control premium, if supported by the evidence, is deemed appropriate.	250
Sieg Co. v. Kelly	09/17/97	Supreme Court	Iowa	Supreme Court did not address trial court's rejection of marketability discount because corporation did not appeal this issue, but found corporation had good faith legal and factual basis for applying marketability discount in initial offer.	24
Arnaud v. Stockgrowers State Bank	11/05/99	Supreme Court	Kansas	Minority and marketability discounts are inappropriate when purchaser of stock is either majority shareholder or corporation itself.	83
Pink v. Cambridge Acquisition, Inc	04/09/99	Court of Appeals	Maryland	Judicial appraisal time barred where wrong corporation named.	59
Rainforest Cafe, Inc. v. State of Wisconsin Investment Board, et al.	04/13/04	Court of Appeals	Minnesota	The Court rejects the experts' opinion and uses tendered price as fair value. Also states that book value was not a good indicator of fair value.	183
Richton Bank & Trust Co. v. Bowen	10/31/01	Supreme Court	Mississippi	Statutory definition of fair value in Mississippi had been amended to disallow discounts after Trial Court's decision.	131
Swope v. Siegel-Robert, Inc. (I)	06/23/99	United States District Court	Missouri	Trial Court exercised its discretion per Missouri Court of Appeals case and applied a minority discount but no marketability discount. The Eight Circuit would later modify judgment to eliminate minority discount based on what it believed Missouri Supreme Court would do.	69
Hansen v. 75 Ranch Company (I)	04/09/98	Supreme Court	Montana	Montana Supreme Court finds dissenters owed fair value for shares and disallows discounts.	36
Hansen v. 75 Ranch Company (II)	02/01/99	District Court	Montana	The Court rejects the income approach in favor of the asset approach for determining fair value, and disallows discounts.	55

Chapter 7: Court Case Abstracts

Shareholder Dissent

Case Name	Date	Court	State / Jurisdiction	Comments	Page
Steiner Corp. v. Benninghoff	05/26/98	United States District Court	Nevada	Fair value under Nevada law is pre-merger market value, discounted for illiquidity.	37
Casey v. Amboy Bancorporation	8/8/2006	Superior Court, Appellate Division	New Jersey	The Court affirmed the trial court's deduction of synergies from fair value.	212
Gagliano v. Brenna (I)	08/01/01	Superior Court, Appellate Division	New Jersey	This case involved a fairness opinion that applied both minority and marketability discounts, but the proxy statement failed to disclose the discounting. Court of appeals held that fair value does not include minority and marketability discounts.	121
Gagliano v. Brenna (II)	07/16/02	Supreme Court	New Jersey	The Supreme Court affirms the appellate division holding that minority and marketability discounts should not be applied.	149
Holiday Medical Center, Inc. v. Weisman	07/10/08	Superior Court	New Jersey	The Court rejects that statutory fair value should be based on a "highest and best use" analysis.	261
Lawson Mardon Wheaton, Inc. v. Smith (I)	08/26/98	Superior Court, Appellate Division	New Jersey	"Extraordinary circumstances" provide for 25% marketability discount.	42
Lawson Mardon Wheaton, Inc. v. Smith (II)	07/14/99	Supreme Court	New Jersey	Supreme court rejected trial court's finding of "extraordinary circumstances" warranting application of a marketability discount.	75
Grace v. Rosenstock	10/29/98	United States District Court	New York	Appraisal action exclusive remedy for dissenters.	45
Slant/Fin. Corp. v. The Chicago Corp	10/05/95	Supreme Court (trial court NY only)	New York	Court rejects marketability and minority discounts.	1
Smith v. North Carolina Motor Speedway	04/26/00	Superior Court	North Carolina	Jury awards dissenters greater than merger price.	87
English v. Artromick International, Inc.	08/10/00	Court of Appeals	Ohio	The concept of "fair value" is far different from the "fair cash value" concept.	96
G.I. Joe's, Inc. v. Nizam	07/31/02	Court of Appeals	Oregon	Fair value affected by existence of stock options.	149

Case Summary by Type

Shareholder Dissent

Case Name	Date	Court	State / Jurisdiction	Comments	Page
First Western Bank Wall v. Olsen	01/31/01	Supreme Court	South Dakota	Appellate Court held that fair value is the minority shareholder's proportionate share of the corporation as a whole, so that no minority or marketability discounts should be applied.	101
MS Holdings, LLC v. Malone	04/14/08	Court of Appeals	Tennessee	The dissenting shareholder interest does not include the value of future income as the future performance here is too speculative.	257
Hogle v. Zinetics Med., Inc.	12/13/02	Supreme Court	Utah	Supreme Court held marketability discount inappropriate in determining fair value.	161
Oakridge Energy, Inc. v. Clifton	04/18/97	Supreme Court	Utah	Determines that Trial Court erred in using stock market price as fair value, but err is harmless as per share value under asset approach is less.	19
In re 75,629 Shares of Common Stock of Trapp Family Lodge, Inc.	01/15/99	Supreme Court	Vermont	The Supreme Court upheld the use of the control premium determining the fair value of the stock because it was supported by the testimony of both experts.	53
Matthew G. Norton Co v. Smyth	08/05/02	Court of Appeals	Washington	No DLOM absent extraordinary circumstances; bright-line rule prohibiting built-in gains discount rejected.	151
Prentiss et al. v. Wesspur, Inc. et al.	04/28/97	Court of Appeals	Washington	Frozen shares lack discounts in this dissenting shareholder action.	21
HMO-W v. SSM Health Care System (II)	06/07/00	Supreme Court	Wisconsin	Wisconsin Supreme Court rules no minority discount in fair value determination.	88
HMO-W, Inc. v. SSM Health Care System (I)	06/17/99	Court of Appeals	Wisconsin	Wisconsin Court refuses to apply minority discount in dissenting shareholder case.	68
Brown v. Arp and Hammond Hardware Co.	08/29/06	Supreme Court	Wyoming	After the District Court applied a minority discount in this fair value case, the Supreme Court reverses their decision.	218

Chapter 7: Court Case Abstracts

Shareholder Oppression

Shareholder Oppression

Case Name	Date	Court	State / Jurisdiction	Comments	Page
Cox Enterprises, Inc. v. News-Journal Corp.	12/21/07	United States Court of Appeals	11th Circuit	The 11th Circuit Court of Appeals acknowledged that "fair value" and "fair market value" are not synonymous; neither are they "mutually exclusive."	258
Johnson v. Johnson	08/15/01	Superior Court	Connecticut	Fair value includes 20% minority discount where no oppressive conduct found.	123
Jahn v. Kinderman	06/07/04	Court of Appeals	Illinois	The Trial Court noted a trend against rejecting discounts in fair value cases. The court of appeals affirmed because it said this was a matter for the discretion of the trial court and there was no abuse.	190
G & N Aircraft, Inc. and Paul Goldsmith v. Erich Boehm	11/30/98	Court of Appeals	Indiana	Punitive damages allowed and minority interest discount rejected when majority oppression is evidenced.	48
Kaplan v. First Hartford Corp.	03/20/09	District Court	Maine	The Court arrived at fair value primarily from trades of the company's stock, corrected for the minority and marketability discounts.	280
Advanced Communication Design, Inc. v. Follett (I)	11/02/99	Court of Appeals	Minnesota	Although generally marketability and minority discounts would not be applicable, a marketability discount was applied due to "extraordinary circumstances" in this case.	82
Advanced Communication Design, Inc. v. Follett (II)	08/03/00	Supreme Court	Minnesota		94
Advanced Communication Design, Inc. v. Follett (III)	05/29/01	Court of Appeals	Minnesota		116
Billigmeier v. Concorde Marketing, Inc.	12/04/01	Court of Appeals	Minnesota	The Court of Appeals noted that when a buyout is ordered under the Minnesota Business Corporations Act, fair value means "the pro rata share of the value of the corporation as a going concern."	135

Case Summary by Type

Shareholder Oppression

Case Name	Date	Court	State / Jurisdiction	Comments	Page
McCann Ranch, Inc. v. Sharon Quigley-McCann	04/18/96	Supreme Court	Montana	Court upholds 25% minority discount.	5
Trifad Entertainment, Inc. v. Brad Anderson, et al.	11/15/01	Supreme Court	Montana	Fair value may be awarded to controlling shareholder when minority shareholder is the oppressing party.	134
Balsamides v. Perle (I)	06/17/98	Superior Court, Appellate Division	New Jersey	Chancery court ordered oppressor shareholder to sell his stock to oppressed shareholder at price that includes marketability discount. Appellate division reversed.	40
Balsamides v. Protameen Chemicals, Inc. (II)	07/14/99	Supreme Court, Appellate Division	New Jersey	Supreme Court reversed appellate division, finding application of marketability discount was appropriate on these facts.	77
Penepent Corp., In re	05/01/01	Court of Appeals	New York	Minority and marketability discounts, plus discount for pending litigation, rejected in case involving four brothers with 25% interest each.	109
Cooke v. Fresh Express Foods	07/12/00	Court of Appeals	Oregon	No discount should be applied where court orders majority shareholder to buy out oppressed minority shareholder.	93
Hayes v. Olmsted & Assoc.	03/28/01	Court of Appeals	Oregon	Fair value in Oregon shareholder oppression case is undiscounted pro rata share of going concern value.	107
Tifft v. Stevens	03/11/99	Court of Appeals	Oregon	The Trial Court's order compelling the majority to buy out Tifft's stock at appraised fair value, excluding any minority or marketability discounts, was affirmed.	57
McDuffie v. O'Neal	08/12/96	Court of Appeals	South Carolina	Court of Appeals accepts averaging of 2 experts' values, but does not necessarily recommend it.	9
Edler v. Edler	12/27/07	Court of Appeals	Wisconsin	The Court likens oppression to dissent situations and rejects marketability and minority discounts.	255

Withdrawing Partner

Case Name	Date	Court	State/Jurisdiction	Comments	Page
Winn v. Winn Enterprises	10/10/07	Court of Appeals	Arkansas	The Court finds this situation analogous to that of dissenting shareholders and refuses to apply discounts for lack of marketability or lack of control.	254
Wenzel v. Hopper & Galliher, P.C.	11/22/02	Court of Appeals	Indiana	In case of first impression, court held no marketability discount absent extraordinary circumstances (none presented in the case at bar).	158
East Park Ltd. Partnership v. Larkin, et al.	03/06/06	Court of Appeals	Maryland	This case concerns whether DLOM applies to a fair value assessment of limited partnership interests in a partnership dissolution case; the court looked to analogous corporate dissolution cases to determine that no marketability discounts apply.	201
Conti v. Christoff	10/02/01	Court of Appeals	Ohio	The Court of Appeals found that the Trial Court did not abuse its discretion in looking to fair cash value for guidance in defining fair value.	129
Spivey v. Page	02/24/04	Court of Appeals	Tennessee	Balance sheet dated two months after shareholder withdrawal not evidence of fair value on date of withdrawal.	180

Slant/Fin. Corp. v. The Chicago Corp

Citation: Mecklenberg County Case No. 98-CVS-3766
Court: Naussau County
State/Jurisdiction: New York
Date of decision: October 5, 1995
Judge: Molloy

The company, a manufacturer of heating and air conditioning equipment, did a cash-out merger effected on July 13, 1993, at $52 per share, based on an independent appraisal conducted by Jeffrey Green of Ernst & Young. Dissenters exercised their rights to an appraisal of the "fair value" of their stock as of the close of business on the day before the merger.

Dissenters claim the standard of value used by Ernst & Young was contrary to the statute, and that the price paid was justified by an analysis based on unreasonable forecasts and inappropriate comparable companies. Dissenters relied on the expert report of John E. Hempstead of Hempstead and Co. who appraised the stock at $130 per share.

Standard of Value

The Court stated:

> Because the petitioner's expert, Ernst & Young, in its valuation report (on title page) and on fifteen occasions refers to its valuation to be based on Fair Market Value, and the Business Corporation Law only uses the term Fair Value... the Court considers it a threshold question as to whether Fair Value and Fair Market Value are synonymous...

The Court finds:

> The Standard upon which Ernst & Young's valuation was based was Market Value ... the statutory standard is much broader ... The Court may give no weight [emphasis supplied] to market value if the facts of the case so require.

Marketability and Minority Discounts

The Ernst & Young value reflected a 10% discount for the stock's illiquidity (not traded actively) and a 20% discount for minority interest.

The Court finds:

> To arrive at Fair Value, the 10% illiquidity discount and the 20% discount for minority interest are rejected. To do otherwise would in a closely held corporation induce those

in control to do exactly what Slant/Fin is doing and receive a premium as in this case of 30%. The Court concludes that such discounts can only result in an unfair and not a fair valuation.

Discounted Cash Flow Method

The Court stated "The underpinning of the value put on the stock by Ernst & Young... was a pessimism regarding the past performance and the future of the company."

The Court finds:

> ...no validity in the petitioner's expert's presentation because Ernst & Young used financial forecasts and projections provided to it by the petitioners... The Court did not accept the Discounted Cash Flow Method because the necessary projections were rigged at the outset by information provided by the petitioner and relied upon by the expert Mr. Green...

> Ernst & Young was not independent in its evaluation and was unduly controlled and influenced by the petitioner to arrive at a low figure.

Market Approach

With respect to prior transactions:

> Court rejects, before valuation date, market transaction approach because stockholders were captive to decision of major stockholders/officers/directors and there existed little or no market and consequently the respondents could accept the tender figure or litigate.

With respect to comparables:

> ...the Court rejects both parties' suggested comparables and finds that among all suggested there is none that is similar enough to have probative value.

Impact of Merger on Value

Most state dissenter appraisal rights statutes expressly exclude from fair value "appreciation or depreciation directly or indirectly induced by the corporate action or its proposal." New York had such a statute, but in 1982 amended it by deleting the foregoing phrase and including a phrase "all other relevant factors."

In the SCM case, the Court stated (referring to the statute revision) "the Legislature was not encouraging the abandonment of the three basic methods of valuation... Rather, it intended Courts to supplement these approaches by also considering elements of future value arising from the accomplishment or expectation of the merger and not the product of speculation." In the SCM case, the Court reflected the value of a tax benefit to SCM resulting from the merger.

In Slant/Fin. the Court:

> ...rejects consideration of any value regarding conversion to a subchapter "S" corporation because while the company may consider converting to a subchapter S corporation after the merger, as of the valuation date, July 12, 1993, it is not eligible and the Court will not speculate into the future that the company will become eligible and the tax code will not change. Therefore, the Court will not as urged by the respondents add value to the stock because of such possible conversion.

Conclusion

In conclusion, the Court finds:

> ...the officers/directors despite being fiduciaries used every mechanism available to them to advance their personal goals and interests to the prejudice of the minority stockholders and that their acts constituted over reaching.

The Court added back substantial charitable contributions in determining an earnings level to capitalize and considered value of intangibles, patents, undervalued real estate and a foreign subsidiary.

In the final analysis:

> The result of all the above convinces the Court that the proper figure to arrive at fair value is $99.00 per share as of July 12, 1993.

Kahn v. Tremont Corporation (I)

Citation: 1996 Del. Ch. LEXIS 40
Court: Court of Chancery
State/Jurisdiction: Delaware
Date of decision: March 21, 1996
Judge: Allen

Kahn challenges as unfair to Tremont a December 3, 1991 transaction in which that corporation purchased a block of 7.8 million shares of common stock of NL Industries, Inc. (representing 15% of NL's outstanding shares) from defendant Valhi, Inc. The price was $11.75 per share, or $91.65 million in cash. It was approximately a 7% discount from the price of the publicly traded shares at the time the purchase was approved.

Chapter 7: Court Case Abstracts

The transaction was all in the family, so to speak. It is alleged in the complaint that defendant, Harold Simmons, effectively controlled all three of these related companies through his control of Contran Corporation.

The core allegations are:
- The price was too high
- The investment was inappropriate
- The process was not fair

In this abstract we address only the issues of the process and the price.

Judge Allen concluded that the process was fair. The following were the highlights of the process:
- The board appointed a special committee of disinterested directors with authority to veto the transaction
- The special committee hired special counsel and an independent fairness opinion (Continental Partners, a subsidiary of Continental Bank), who were provided with and directed to evaluate management's 5 year projections
- There was active negotiation of the transaction's price and terms

Judge Allen defined a "fair price" as "a price that is within a range that reasonable men and women with access to relevant information might accept." He further elaborated, "between the lowest plainly unfair' price and the highest clearly fair' price lies a range of prices within which reasonable minds with access to all information might disagree."

Valid reasons for disagreement could include:
- differing expectations of the future
- differing degrees of risk averseness
- differing liquidity preferences

The negotiations resulted in both registration rights and co-sale rights. Nevertheless, plaintiff contends that the discount should be no less than 20%, supported by plaintiff's expert witness, Mr. Miller.

Miller testified, "the discount customarily employed is on the order of 20 to 30%, and I had no reason to go higher or lower, I guess. I chose a mid-range. I chose 25%."

Judge Allen noted, "while (the plaintiff) relies on typical price discounts, the evidence shows that price discounts vary greatly... specific discounts negotiated ranged from a price discount of 84% to a premium of 12.7%... (the) evidence ... does not reflect an evaluation of the specific circumstances of the transaction that might warrant a deviation from some average price discount."

Continental Partners performed "five standard methods of valuation analysis."

- Comparable company analysis (publicly traded companies). Because there were no "pure play" direct comparables, they used three groups of comparables with characteristics shared by NL:
  - commodity chemical companies
  - specialty chemical companies
  - cyclical chemical companies
- comparable transaction analysis
  - acquisitions
  - 10% to 20% block transactions
- Market value analysis (current and historical price and volume)
- Discounted cash flow analysis
- asset value/replacement cost analysis

Judge Allen concluded, "plaintiff has failed to show by a preponderance of the evidence that the price of the stock was not fair to Tremont....the evidence shows that the price was within a range that a reasonable, fully informed buyer might accept.

The price was not generous to Tremont; indeed the 7% discount from market on the day of contracting is about as small as could be accepted as fair in the circumstances. But generosity is not the standard.... circumstances indicate that the relatively small discount from market was not unfair to the buyer."

Shannon Pratt Comment: Independent professional advisors and a competent and thorough valuation analysis saved the day.

McCann Ranch, Inc. v. Sharon Quigley-McCann

Citation: 276 Mont. 205, 915 P.2d 239, 1996 Mont. LEXIS 63
Court: Supreme Court
State/Jurisdiction: Montana
Date of decision: April 18, 1996
Judge: Turnage

Sharon McCann divorced after a 37-year marriage, and her property settlement included 600 of the couple's 1200 shares of McCann Ranch, Inc. (MRI) out of 2400 shares outstanding.

Subsequently, the Board omitted its dividend and reincorporated the company, an action which gave rise to dissenter appraisal rights. However, Sharon was not notified of dissenter rights and did not file.

This lawsuit was filed pursuant to the Montana Declaration Judgment Act. Sharon and MRI stipulated to allow the District Court, sitting in equity, to determine the value of Sharon's shares.

The court determined the value of the shares to be $162,144, after applying a 25% minority discount.

Sharon claims she is entitled to "fair value," which she maintains is the value without a minority discount. She claims this because she was oppressed and also because she should have been entitled to it under dissenters' rights.

The Court concluded, "Sharon has not established to the satisfaction of this court that 'fair value' necessarily excludes an application of a minority discount.... While minority shareholders ... must be treated fairly ... the lack of control makes such shares less valuable. This is a known fact, which is reasonably contemplated by every person who holds a minority interest in a small corporation. We agree with the District Court's findings ..."

Ryan v. Tad's Enterprises, Inc.

Citation: 709 A.2d 682, 1996 Del. Ch. LEXIS 54
Court: Court of Chancery
State/Jurisdiction: Delaware
Date of decision: April 24, 1996
Judge: Jacobs

This abstract summarizes certain key points in a dissent from a May 5, 1988, merger that squeezed out minority stockholders.

Before a series of transactions, Tad's owned three businesses:
- A chain of six New York restaurants
- An algae health food supplement production and marketing firm, *Cell Tech, Inc.* (Cell Tech), acquired in 1983
- A geothermal power production firm, *EPG*, started in 1984

Certain salient facts of the transactions were as follows:
- The Townsend brothers owned 72.6% of the stock.
- Prior to the merger, Tad's sold its chain of six restaurants. In conjunction with the restaurant sale, the two Townsend brothers received $1 million each for noncompete and consulting agreements.
- Bernard Bressler, an attorney and a defendant, acted in the capacity of a board member, represented the corporation in the transactions, and represented the Townsend brothers personally in negotiating the consulting and noncompete agreements.
- Tad's board did not retain any unaffiliated law firm, financial advisor or other independent representative to represent or negotiate the merger on behalf of the Tad's minority shareholders.

Ryan v. Tad's Enterprises, Inc.

- Tad's board did hire Muller and Company, an investment banking firm, to furnish an opinion that the $13.25 merger price was fair to the minority stockholders. However:
- It was not asked to, nor did it, opine on the fairness of the Townsend's noncompete and consulting agreements.
- At the board meeting when the merger was approved, Muller did not discuss its valuation analysis or provide any written materials.
- Muller's subsequent written opinion listed information considered, but no projections or forecasts were provided by the board.

The court noted that it normally would defer to a boards judgment, on the presumption of due care and good faith. "However, that presumption vanishes in cases where the minority shareholders are compelled to forfeit their shares in return for a value that is determined as a result of a bargaining process in which the controlling shareholder is in a position to influence both bargaining parties. In such cases, the Court will carefully scrutinize the board's actions to ascertain:
- whether the board instituted measures to ensure a fair process, and
- whether the board achieved a fair price for the disinterested stockholder minority ..."

> The business judgment review standard will not apply where the decision under challenge is made by a board a majority of whom have a material conflict of interest in the transaction.
>
> Because the Merger transaction is concededly one in which the Townsends stood on both sides, the defendants have the burden of demonstrating that the Merger was entirely fair.
>
> The board's decision not to provide independent representation or other structural protections for the minority shareholders interests fatally impaired the fairness of the negotiation and approval process ... neither Bressler, as legal counsel, nor Muller, as financial advisor, were shown to have independently or adequately represented the distinctive interests of the minority shareholders ...

The defendants say the reason they adopted no other measures to ensure adequate minority shareholder representation was to avoid "expenditures disproportionate to the business to be valued in the merger."

The Court said, "I find the defendants response wholly unpersuasive ... the absence of any adequate independent representative for the minority shareholders, and of any arm's length negotiation over the merger terms, precludes a finding that the merger was a product of fair dealing ... the defendants desire to minimize transaction costs ... can not relieve corporate fiduciaries from their duty to assure that the interests of minority shareholders in a self-dealing transaction are adequately protected."

The Court concluded, "Defendants are liable to the plaintiffs for breaching their fiduciary duty of loyalty. The question then becomes, what is the extent of that liability... *the measure of damages for breach of fiduciary duty is not limited to the corporations fair value as determined in an appraisal"* (emphasis supplied).

For the two years preceding the announcement of the merger, Tads stock traded at $.50 to $4.00 per share. The price paid in the May 5, 1988 merger was $13.25 per share, approved by the Board on November 4, 1987 and approved by stockholders February 11, 1988.

Plaintiffs argue that the consulting and noncompete agreements were a sham because:
- Townsends were never called upon to provide consulting services
- They were unlikely to pose a competitive threat
- They were ages 72 and 79
- One lived in California and the other intended to move to Nevada.

They were each entitled to receive $200,000 per year for five years whether or not they survived.

The Court said, "The defendants presented no testimony of ... any independent expert on (the noncompete) question. The circumstances make it apparent that at the time agreement was reached, the parties were aware that those provisions would likely never be invoked." The Court added the $2 million to the amount to be allocated among the shareholders.

The Board deducted $3,964,000 for anticipated taxes on the sale of the restaurants. That liability turned out to be $2,597,205, resulting in an over-reserve of $1,366,795 that benefited the Townsends. Defendants say that was unplanned and fortuitous, due to a delay in the asset sale closing, which moved that closing into the more advantageous 1989 fiscal year.

The Court concluded that the defendants failed to show that the deduction was fair, noting that "they made no effort to protect the minority stockholders interests if the reserve later proved to be excessive," and added the over-reserve to the amount to be allocated to shareholders.

The indemnity reserve was to remain in place for two years, at which point any unutilized funds would be returned to Tads. The funds were paid back.

Defendants claim the deduction was fair because it was compensation to the Townsends for assuming risk of possible contingent liabilities. The Court rejected the defendants reasoning, saying, "The claim that the $337,518 deduction was fair compensation to the Townsends for assuming unique risks created by the Asset Sale agreement is without evidentiary support."

Plaintiffs argue that the board valued Cell Tech solely on Tad's historical dollar investment in that business ($563,000), without taking into account Cell Tech's significant future earnings potential.

Plaintiffs advanced three, separate valuations of Cell Tech, of which the Court adopted the discounted cash flow methodology. The court noted, "The discounted cash flow valuation model is well-accepted and established in the financial community."

The Court adopted plaintiff's experts "total free cash flow projections." However, plaintiff's expert used a discount rate of 17.7%, while defendant's expert used a discount rate of 30%. The Court adopted the 30% discount rate, commenting, "Cell Tech, at the time of the merger, was an unusually risky investment ... I find it entirely plausible that a prudent investor in a venture of that kind would demand an annual return in the 30% order of magnitude."

Plaintiff's expert valued EPG at $2,390,000. Defendant's expert, using a similar cash flow methodology, concluded that EPG should be valued at $445,000.

The Court said, "I find the defendants' valuation of EPG to be the more credible .... However ... I cannot accept the defendants' lower valuation ... because it is significantly less than the value that Tad's board approved in the merger. ... Given the adjudicated disloyalty of the directors, I find the $1,136,000 value they fixed for purposes of the Merger to be the lowest acceptable valuation of EPG for damages calculation purposes."

The Court found the plaintiffs' other miscellaneous claims "too speculative." The final adjudicated value was $23.86 per share.

McDuffie v. O'Neal

Citation: 324 S.C. 297, 476 S.E.2d 702, 1996 S.C. App. LEXIS 123
Court: Court of Appeals
State/Jurisdiction: South Carolina
Date of decision: August 12, 1996
Judge: Stilwell

Respondent, Steven McDuffie, brought a stockholder oppression action against defendants, Thomas and Patricia O'Neal, Joseph Minshew and Blue Flame Gas Co. The three main valuation issues in this case are the relative ownership percentages between McDuffie and O'Neal, the amount of money Blue Flame MTP was entitled to receive from the O'Neals for misappropriation of corporate funds, and the price at which McDuffie's shares should be purchased by Thomas O'Neal and/or Blue Flame MTP, a distributor of propane gas.

The original action was heard by a Special Master, who found McDuffie and O'Neal to be equal owners of Blue Flame MTP, who found all of the transactions that McDuffie challenged to be corporate misappropriations and who required Blue Flame MTP and/or Thomas O'Neal to purchase McDuffie's shares for $467,317. Appellants Thomas and Patricia O'Neal, dispute all three findings.

After the appellate court upheld the Master's finding of a 50/50 ownership, it turned its attention to the valuation. The Master heard testimony from two expert witnesses. Joe M. Gasaway for McDuffie and Gregory Padgett, CPA for Blue Flame MTP.

Gasaway conducted an asset valuation of Blue Flame MTP based primarily upon information provided to him by McDuffie, which included estimates of Blue Flame MTP's profit margins, the number of gallons of fuel it owned and its total number of customers, including retail clients. He also looked at lists of vehicles, real estate, equipment and accounts receivable belonging to the corporation. According to the transcript, "Not considering the debts of the corporation or its cash on hand, Gasaway valued Blue Flame MTP at $889,609."

Padgett reviewed financial statements, capital costs and real estate. Then, utilizing the income approach, he valued Blue Flame MTP at $410,000.

Two ancillary issues were critical to the Master's valuation. First, McDuffie alleged a $270,000 misappropriation of funds. Second, the O'Neals argued that the lack of a covenant not to compete reduced the value of Blue Flame MTP and that reduction of value was not properly considered by the Master.

The Master determined funds in the amount of $270,000 were, indeed, misappropriated. He then averaged Padgett's and Gasaway's values, and added half of the misappropriated funds to the amount to be paid to McDuffie.

Regarding the issue of the covenant not to compete, the Master's order included language which, according to the transcript, "clearly prohibited McDuffie from utilizing any customer list, business manual, or other business procedure of the corporation for three years in competition with Blue Flame MTP."

The appellate court upheld the Master's calculations regarding damages and stated, "while we do not necessarily recommend this method (averaging), we find no error in the Master's decision in this case. Faced with conflicting opinions from two apparently qualified experts, both with seemingly reasonable opinions, and not having more reason to accept one than the other, the Master split the difference between the two."

The appellate court adjusted the Master's average by taking into account the corporate debts and cash on hand that Gasaway's valuation did not consider and it held the final valuation of Blue Flame MTP to be $633,993.80.

Adding $135,000 (half the misappropriated funds), the appellate court affirmed, "but modified it to require the defendant corporation and/or defendant, Thomas O'Neal, to purchase McDuffie's shares for $452,063.87."

Gonsalves v. Straight Arrow Publishers, Inc. (I)

Citation: 1996 Del. Ch. LEXIS 144
Court: Court of Chancery
State/Jurisdiction: Delaware
Date of decision: November 27, 1996
Judge: Allen

The case involves the appraised value of the common stock of Straight Arrow Publishing, whose primary product is *Rolling Stone* magazine. Indirect control of the stock existed through the founder and editor of the company, Jann and Jane Wenner. On January 8, 1986, Straight Arrow Publishers Holding Company was merged with and into Straight Arrow Publishing. The plaintiff, Laurel Gonsalves, owned 2,000 shares of Straight Arrow Publishing common stock, and dissented from the merger.

When the merger was initiated, it converted the remaining shares into the right to receive $100 cash. Martin Whitman, the defendant's expert, issued a fairness opinion with a 1985 tender offer, concluding that $100 was a fair price. When the fairness opinion was issued, the 1985 second-half financial results were not yet available, although the tender offer materials disclosed that management expected an increase in earnings. Because the 1985 financial results are now known, they have been incorporated in the valuation of Straight Arrow Publishing by the two experts.

Expert uses only Rolling Stone earnings

James Kobak, the plaintiff's expert, estimated Straight Arrow Publishing's fair market value by valuing only *Rolling Stone* magazine. His rationale was that the magazine was the sole operating asset of the company. He capitalized 1985 earnings and adjusted them by:
- Eliminating income tax expenses
- Eliminating other non-recurring expenses
- Adding an incremental yearly increase in deferred subscription income
- Adding back to net income the general and administrative expenses associated with the discontinued operations that caused the expenses.

After the above adjustments, Kobak concluded that *Rolling Stone*'s calendar year net income was $6,002,000. To capitalize the adjusted earnings base, Kobak selected what he considered to be a prudent Price/Earnings ratio, which was a multiple of 14. To arrive at 14, Kobak looked to sales of comparable magazines and companies from 1971 to 1988. According to his analysis, the range of median P/E rations of such transactions was nine to 14. Kobak picked the high end of the range based on his view that *Rolling Stone* was in a position to enjoy increasing profitability, as of the merger date. Using the 14 multiple, Kobak calculated *Rolling Stone*'s value to be $84 million as of the merger date. When he added a $6.5 million value for Straight Arrow's non-publishing assets, his total calculated value was $90,500,000, or $1,059.37 per share outstanding.

Whitman employed a similar analytical technique. He capitalized an adjusted historical earnings base by an appropriate multiple. In a /Delaware block form of analysis, Whitman included two other components, Straight Arrow Publishing's "asset value" and its stock's "market value," with each given a 10% weight. Mr. Whitman's methodology was:

- Calculating Straight Arrow Publishing's earnings for a five-year period ending December 31, 1985
- Using five-year averages of EBIT and EBITDA as proxies for earnings
- Analyzing the implied capitalization rates of comparable companies with publicly traded stocks
- Multiplying the five-year average EBIT and EBITDA numbers by the corresponding multiples.

Whitman justifies lower multiple

Based on this methodology, Mr. Whitman estimated that Straight Arrow Publishing's enterprise value was $13 million, or $131.60 per share. Whitman further explained his methodology by stating that the company's operating margins, profitability, and ration of capital expenditures to total revenue were lower than his selected comparable companies. Based on the comparison, Whitman chose EBIT and EBITDA multiples of 9.5 and 8.5, respectively. Mr. Whitman believed that the lower multiples were appropriate due to Straight Arrow Publishing's small size, dependence on a single-print publication, low EBIT and EBITDA margins, volatile operating profits, low level of capital reinvestment, speculative use of its excess cash, non-dividend-paying policy and contingent liabilities, along with *Rolling Stone*'s lower-than-median readership demographics.

Kobak's method questioned

Another expert witness brought in by Straight Arrow publishing was Daniel McNamee, President of the Publishing and Media Group. Although McNamee did not perform a valuation, he did comment on Kobak's methodology. McNamee was critical of Kobak's use of only 1985 earnings as opposed to using a five-year average, his selection of a high earnings multiple, and conclusions concerning *Rolling Stone*s market positioning as of the date of the merger.

Whitman's valuation found accurate

The court found that Whitman's valuation accurately estimated the value of Straight Arrow Publishing as of the date of the merger, while Kobak's valuation did not reflect an accurate value. Because Kobak did not present a compelling reason to depart from the standard use of a five-year earnings base, his decision to use only one year of earnings was not approved by the court. Furthermore, the court also found that, given the financial situation of the company, Whitman's choice of earnings multiples was more reasonable than Kobak's. The court concluded that the fair value of the stock as of the merger date was $131.60 per share.

Weigel Broadcasting Co. v. Smith

Citation: 289 Ill. App. 3d 602, 682 N.E.2d 745, 1997 Ill. App. LEXIS 941
Court: Appellate Court
State/Jurisdiction: Illinois
Date of decision: December 12, 1996
Judge: Wolfson

The issue in this case is the "fair value" to be assigned to the dissenting shareholders' common stock in Weigel, a company engaged in the business of commercial television broadcasting.

Company seeks S Corp status

Weigel sought to repurchase common stock in a 1 to 1,750 reverse stock split. Fractional shares would not be allowed and shareholders holding less than one share after the split would be required to turn in their shares for cash, allowing Weigel to become an S corporation.

Weigel and the minority shareholders could not come to an agreement regarding the price to be paid for the stock, so the company's Board of Directors hired Valtec to resolve this dispute. According to the opinion, "Based on Valtec's valuation, Weigel offered $115 per sold share of stock as the cash buy-out price." 16 of the 143 shareholders chose to exercise dissenter's rights.

Expert applies combined discount of 50%

John McCluskey, Weigel's expert witness, valued the stock by using discounted cash flow and the market approach. McCluskey applied a 50% total discount for minority and marketability. He also considered that dividends were never paid and were never expected to be paid, and opined that $115 was fair value for the stock.

Thomas Buono, the dissenting shareholders' expert, considered three different methods, determined that the fair value for the stock should be a simple pro-rata division of corporate assets without any discounts, and reached a value of $578.41.

The court went on to state that "the testimony of Mr. McCluskey has a more credible and relevant impact on these factors as compared to the testimony of Mr. Buono… and found the fair value of the stock to be $126 per share…" Both sides appeal.

Dissenters claim no discounts are warranted

The dissenters' position, as outlined in the opinion, stated that, "fair value does not equal fair market value. … Fair value is a proportional share of the corporation as a going concern … without any discount for marketability or minority." Furthermore, the dissenters opined that if any adjustment factor is to be considered, it should be a control premium since control of the company was reverting to the original owners.

First the appellate court stated, "There is no precise method for determining fair value." The appellate court went on to list the factors that the trial court specifically considered:
- Nature and history of the business
- Economic outlook of the industry
- Book value of the stock
- Weigel's financial condition and earning capacity
- Weigel's dividend paying capacity
- Goodwill
- Previous sales of stock
- Market price of similar corporations.

"If the court in determining fair value gave greater weight to the stocks market value, it does not mean that other factors were not taken into account." After citing case law which supports the consideration of a minority interest and a marketability factor, the appellate court decided that "Applying such discounts is left to the trial courts discretion."

Appellate court affirms fair value

In its final analysis, the appellate court stated, "The $578 per share figure reached by the dissenters' expert was based on projected models of the corporation that the trial court found not credible. ... [$126 per share] was close to the value set by Weigel's expert, whom the court found to be more credible. The record indicates that the figure was reached after a close examination of all of the evidence presented. ... [and] The trial court, we think, was justified in finding the marketability and minority factors had a significant bearing on the intrinsic value of the stock." Therefore, the appellate court affirmed the trial courts determination of the stocks "fair value."

Ansin et al. v. River Oaks Furniture, Inc., et al.

Citation: Nos. 96-1734, -1735
Court: US Court of Appeals
State/Jurisdiction: First Circuit
Date of decision: February 3, 1998
Judge: Cyr, Boudin, and Lynch

The following court case abstract was originally published in Valuation Case Digest®

In *Harold S. Ansin et al. v. River Oaks Furniture, Inc., et al.*, Nos. 96-1734, -1735, February 3, 1997, the U.S. Court of Appeals for the First District considered whether a trial court should have instructed the jury to assess securities law claim damages under Rule 10b-5 as of the time of a fraudulent transfer. River Oaks' executives convinced Ansin, a shareholder, to redeem his interest for $300,000 in November, 1992. They failed to let Ansin know of discussions with an investment bank regarding an IPO in early 1993, and they successfully completed an IPO in August, 1993. As part of the IPO, River Oaks stock made a 28.8:1 split and sold for $12 per share. At this price, the value of Ansin's stock would be approximately $1.2 million. River Oaks also distributed $2,465,000 of previous earnings to its pre-IPO shareholders from the proceeds of the offering. Ansin sued for securities law violations and fraud, and was awarded damages. River Oaks appealed claiming that the value of the stock at the time of transfer was significantly lower, evidenced by the immediate resale of Ansin's stock to a knowledgeable insider at no gain or loss.

Damages under Rule 10b-5 are held to be the difference between the fair value the seller received and fair value the seller would have received but for the fraudulent conduct. "The trier of fact may draw reasonable inferences in determining 'fair value,' and 'is not restricted to actual sale prices in a market so isolated and so thin' as one for a close corporation's stock." *Affiliated Ute Citizens v. United States*, 406 U.S. 128, 155 (1972).

"A variety of factors, including anticipated future appreciation, may affect the value of stock, so that an appraisal 'demand[s] a more sophisticated approach than the simple application of a price index to the shares.' *Holmes v. Bateson*, 583 F.2d 542, 558 (1st Cir. 1978)." A jury determined that a reasonable investor, fully informed of the IPO discussions, would not have sold his stock in November 1992 for less than his proportionate share of the IPO proceeds. The appellate court affirmed the award, noting that 'the analyses and projections [of a 1993 IPO] were, to some extent [in November, 1992], contingent does not mean that they are irrelevant to determining fair value."

Berens v. Ludwig (I)

Citation: 953 F. Supp. 249, 1997 U.S. Dist. LEXIS 1551
Court: United States District Court
State/Jurisdiction: Illinois
Date of decision: February 13, 1997
Judge: Alesia

A bank consolidation gave rise to minority stockholders' appraisal rights which Berens exercised. (In this situation the Comptroller of the Currency was responsible for the appraisal.)

The original offer was $12,071 per share. The Comptroller appraised the stock at $13,034 per share. Berens complained that the stock was worth $16,700 per share. The Comptroller brought this action for summary judgment to award Berens $13,034 per share.

Chapter 7: Court Case Abstracts

Case illustrates ambiguities of usage

This case demonstrates both ambiguities in the definitions of commonly used valuation terms and inconsistencies in the application of valuation methodologies from one jurisdiction to another.

The Comptroller stated that he used three measures of value (per the "Delaware Block Method"):
- Market value
- Investment value
- Adjusted book value.

"Market value" was based on actual prior transactions in the stock, an interpretation of market value found frequently in dissenting stockholder actions. Since the stock had been relatively inactive, the Comptroller decided to reject the market value for this case.

The Comptroller noted that "investment value" involved establishing a peer group of banking institutions with similar earnings potential and determining an appropriate P/E ratio.[1] He determined investment value per share was $12,018.50.

'Adjusted book value' defined as P/BV

The most unusual aspect was the Comptroller's treatment of "adjusted book value" as the market-price to book-value ratio of the group of peer bank stocks used in this investment. He determined that the peer group's price/book ratio of 1.29 times the bank's book value of $12,464 yielded an adjusted book value of $16,078.56 per share.

He then weighted the methods 75% to investment value because it is "most reflective of going concern value" and 25% to adjusted book value "because it is more reflective of value in a voluntary liquidation:"
- Investment value $12,018 x .75 = $9,014
- Adj. book value $16,079 x .25 = 4,020
- Weighted value 13,034

Berens alleged that the Comptroller erred by not reflecting the widely accepted DCF method (analysis of which was submitted by his appraiser) and by not adjusting for $4,900,000 excess capital relative to the peer group.

---

[1] This clearly differs from the conventional definition of investment value as the value to a particular investor. As noted in the discussion of the term "investment value" in Valuing a Business, 3rd edition, on page 26, "the term investment value often has a different meaning when used in the context of dissenting stockholder suits. In this context, it often means a value based on earning power ... except that the appropriate discount or capitalization rate is usually considered to be a consensus rate rather that a rate peculiar to any investor." –BVR Editor

Block method not necessarily capricious

The Court noted that "the mere use of the Delaware Block Method does not render the appraisal arbitrary and capricious." It also noted that the excess capital was reflected, at least indirectly, in the adjusted book value figure. Motion for summary judgment granted.

WCM Industries, Inc. v. Trustees of Wilson Trust

Citation: 948 P.2d 36, 1997 Colo. App. LEXIS 88
Court: Court of Appeals
State/Jurisdiction: Colorado
Date of decision: April 3, 1997
Judge: Casebolt

Plaintiff, WCM Industries, Inc., appeals the trial court's determination of the number of outstanding shares at the time of a merger, and also challenges the court's refusal to apply a discount for lack of marketability in the determination of the fair value of dissenter's shares. In a cross-appeal, defendants assert as error certain findings made by the court appointed appraiser as well as the court's award of only 6% post-judgment interest.

In 1992, WCM had 60,300 shares of common stock issued and outstanding, with the defendants owning 16,500 shares, certain employees owning 5,300 shares, and the remaining shares owned by WCM's president and his sister. In July 1992, WCM's Board determined that $192 was the appropriate price for those persons who would no longer be shareholders in WCM under the proposed merger. The president's sister accepted $192 and the dissenters rejected the offer. Prior to the merger, WCM exercised its rights under stock purchase agreements to redeem the 5,300 employee shares. While the merger agreement required WCM to pay 100% of the merger price, those stockholders waived such rights, and instead received $68.62 per share, along with an option to purchase an equal number of shares in the surviving company.

Defendants dispute fair value determination

Following the merger, the Board determined that the fair value of defendant's shares was $153.60 per share, as of one day before the merger. The defendants disputed the Board's determination and insisted that the per share value was at least $365.

The trial court accepted all findings and conclusions of the court appointed appraiser, who determined that:
- The enterprise value of WCM was $12,658,000
- There were 55,000 outstanding shares of stock, as opposed to 60,300
- A discount for lack of marketability was not appropriate
- Fair value of dissenter's shares was $230.15 per share.

Discount not a matter of law

With regard to WCM's claim that as a matter of law, a discount for lack of marketability must be applied to closely-held shares, the appeals court disagreed, stating, "…a marketability discount may, in appropriate circumstances, be applied, but that such a determination is a factual one that must be made on an ad hoc, case-by-case basis… [and] our review of the out-of-state cases cited by WCM reveals a majority rule that a marketability discount is not required as a matter of law but, rather, may be employed by a fact finder, depending upon the particular facts and circumstances."

However, the appeals court also stated that, "…We are unable to discern whether the appraiser realized that he could, in his discretion, consider application of a marketability discount under factual circumstances present here, or whether he concluded that no marketability discount could, as a matter of law, be applied… Indeed, there are no factual findings that would indicate what facts the appraiser considered, if any, that would support or negate the application of a marketability discount, or whether he in fact considered marketability in reaching his conclusion."

Inadequate records cause remand

Because the appeals court was unable to determine whether the appraiser correctly applied the law, and also because no factual discussion existed concerning the applicability of a marketability discount, the appeals court remanded the cause for further consideration. The court emphasized that the appraiser and the trial court may consider any relevant factor relative to the worth of the corporation and its stock that is reasonable under the circumstances and is justified by the evidence presented.

Regarding the other outstanding issues, the appeals court concluded that the appraiser could decline to count the 5,300 employee shares as outstanding, remand would be required to further clarify if and how the appraiser considered potential liability regarding those shares in establishing value, and that post judgment interest was incorrectly determined by reference to the wrong statute. Reversed and remanded.

Oakridge Energy, Inc. v. Clifton

Citation: 937 P.2d 130, 315 Utah Adv. Rep. 10, 1997 Utah LEXIS 40
Court: Supreme Court
State/Jurisdiction: Utah
Date of decision: April 18, 1997
Judge: Howe

This is the case of first impression under Utah's dissenting stockholder statute, Utah Code Ann. s 16-10a-1302 (1995), conferring on dissenting stockholders the right to receive "fair value."

Oakridge Energy, Inc. a publicly traded company, sold substantially all its assets to Cometra Oil and Gas, Inc., for $21.5 million. This action triggered dissenting stockholder rights, which certain stockholders exercised.

Oakridge sent payment of $2.75 per share to the dissenters, based on a market price for the stock of $2.50 per share immediately before the shareholder vote approving the sale plus a $.25 dividend declared in connection with the sale. The dissenters accepted the payment, but then exercised their appraisal rights, and Oakridge petitioned the trial court for a valuation of the stock.

Company presents asset value expert

At trial Oakridge presented expert testimony as to asset value by Aaron Cowley, a petroleum engineer, who had also performed annual valuations of Oakridge's oil and gas properties for several years. His valuation considered geological factors, production and operating cost history, and future production forecasts prior to the sale to Cometra. Using this valuation, Oakridge arrived at net asset value of $2.13 per share.

Oakridge also presented evidence that the stock's OTC market price had ranged from $1.37 to $2.56 per share.

Dissenters rely on pro forma data

The dissenters maintained that the fair value was $3.57 per share. This was based on pro forma financial statements sent to the stockholders with the notice of the meeting at which the sale was approved, showing an estimated net asset value per share after taking effect of the proceeds of the sale to Cometra.

The trial Court concluded that the "fair value" of the stock equaled the "market value," and approved the $2.75 that had been paid. Dissenters appealed.

Court looks to other states' cases

Since this was a case of first impression in Utah, the appellate Court reviewed and cited case law from other states which have similar statutes, including Iowa, Maryland, Maine, Delaware and Massachusetts. This Court noted that the statute specifies "the value of the shares immediately before the effectuation of the corporate action to which the dissenter objects, excluding any appreciation or depreciation in anticipation of the corporate action."

The court noted that the consensus of the cases cited is that the component elements to be relied on in determining 'fair value' are market value, net asset value, and investment value, and "the courts have traditionally favored investment value, rather than asset value, as the most important of the three elements."

Trial court erred

The court stated, "we conclude that the trial court erred in using the stock market price . . . as the sole criterion for determining the fair value."

The court stated, "we agree with the courts cited above that a dissenting shareholder disclaims both the burden and the benefit of the disfavored corporate action . . . under the plain language of the statute, any effect of the Cometra sale must be excluded. . . . No informed expert even ventured to suggest the Oakridge assets could be valued at $21.5 million prior to Cometra's offer . . . fair value is not measured by any unique benefits that will accrue to the acquiring corporation . . . the sale price here was not reinforced by several buyers bidding against each other . . . " Therefore, the court turned to Cowley's valuation of the properties as evidence of asset value.

The court concluded, "the stock market price and a reasonable approximation of the asset value were before the trial court, each supported by substantial evidence. Neither party submitted evidence of investment value. . . . Absent evidence of investment value, the trial court should at least have considered the asset value as well as the market price of the stock."

"However, since the per share value based on asset value ($2.13) is less that the stock market price ($2.50), no choice of weighting would have resulted in a per share value greater than $2.50 for the Oakridge stock. Thus the trial courts error is harmless, indeed beneficial to the dissenters since Oakridge has not sought an adjustment of the $2.75 already paid."

"We affirm the judgment of the trial court."

Prentiss et al. v. Wesspur, Inc. et al.

Citation: No. 36321-2-I
Court: Court of Appeals Division I
State/Jurisdiction: Washington
Date of decision: April 28, 1997

The following court case abstract was originally published in Valuation Case Digest®

In *Stewart Prentiss et al. v. Wesspur, Inc. et al.,* No. 36321-2-I (April 28, 1997), unpublished, the Court of Appeals Division I, State of Washington, considered applying a marketability discount when determining the fair value of a minority interest in a closely-held company in a minority freeze-out. The trial court determined that the minority shareholder was the equivalent of a dissenting shareholder; thus, was entitled to receive the fair value of his stock. Fair value is defined as "the shares' value at the moment just before the majority committed misconduct."

Both parties presented expert business valuation testimony, and the court accepted Wesspur's expert as to the company's value. Considering the circumstances, the court concluded that neither a minority nor a marketability discount were applicable because Prentiss was entitled to a pro rata share of the company valued as a going concern, his fair value. Wesspur appealed. It argued that a marketability discount must be applied to accommodate for the inherit difficulty in selling stock in a closely-held company.

The appellate court determined that when the minority is forced to sell to the majority, "the minority shareholder is not selling on the market. . . ." Therefore, the court concluded that the application of a marketability discount would compound the unfairness of the freeze-out by providing the majority with the benefit of a discount. This court affirmed the trial court's decision not to discount the stock because "the valuation appropriately reflects the then existing intention of the minority to continue as a participating shareholder."

Kahn v. Tremont Corporation (II)

Citation: 694 A.2d 422, 1997 Del. LEXIS 205
Court: Supreme Court
State/Jurisdiction: Delaware
Date of decision: June 10, 1997
Judge: Walsh

Plaintiff Alan Kahn appealed the decision handed down by the Court of Chancery which approved the purchase of 7.8 million shares of NL Industries by Tremont Corporation. The shares in question comprised 15% of NL's outstanding stock, and were purchased from defendant Valhi, Inc. Interestingly, all three companies were controlled by Harold Simmons. Kahn alleged that, resulting from Simmons control, the company structured the transaction in a manner beneficial to Simmons at the expense of Tremont Corporation.

Kahn challenges fairness of price

The Court of Chancery concluded that because Simmons was a controlling shareholder, the transaction must be evaluated under the entire fairness standard of review as opposed to the business judgment rule. However, the court found that Tremont's employment of a Special Committee of disinterested directors adequately shifted the burden to Kahn on the fairness issue. The Court of Chancery concluded that both the price and process were fair to Tremont. During the appeal, Kahn raised two issues:
- The court erred in applying the entire fairness standard
- The process was tainted and the price was unfair to Tremont

In addressing the issues of standard and burden of proof, the Supreme Court observed that the burden of proof may be shifted from the defendants to the plaintiffs through the use of a committee of independent directors.

Court finds committee not independent

However, the court noted that the special committee chose as its financial advisor a bank which had lucrative past dealings with Simmons related companies. Furthermore, the Special Committee's legal advisor was previously retained by Valhi in connection with a convertible debt offering and also by NL in connection with a proposed merger with Valhi.

The Court concluded that under the circumstances prevailing, the special committee did not act in an independent and informed manner, therefore the case was reversed and remanded for a new fairness determination with the burden of proof shifted the defendants.

Croxton v. MSC Holding, Inc.

Citation: 227 Ga. App. 179, 489 S.E.2d 77, 1997 Ga. App. LEXIS 865
Court: Court of Appeals
State/Jurisdiction: Georgia
Date of decision: July 9, 1997
Judge: Birdsong

The issue in this case is whether shareholder, Croxton, waived his right to receive an individual, independent contractual amount for his shares in Magnus Software Corporation (MSC) when he demanded fair value for his stock under Georgia's dissenter's rights statutes.

Grimes v. Vitalink Communications Corporation

Sale stipulated upon termination

The essence of the employment agreement stated that upon Croxton's termination without cause, "the company shall purchase and employee shall sell one-half of the shares owned by employee on April 30, 1995 and sell the remainder of the shares on April 30,1996. Furthermore, Croxton's employment agreement with MSC stated, that upon Croxton's termination, he must sell his shares to the corporation for either $400,000 or their "fair value," whichever is greater.

In the appellate court's final analysis, it reversed the trial courts dismissal of Croxton's contractual claim stating that, Croxton's actions "...did not constitute an 'exclusive election of remedies by a 'dissenting shareholder because his contract independently required him to sell and entitled him to a definite sum of $400,000 or more."

Minimum price already established

The appellate court further stated that "[Croxton's] minimum price is already established. It is pre-established by the parties' contract that Croxton is to be paid at least $400,000. The "value" of his shares must be established only so the parties can determine whether that value is greater than $400,000."

According to the corporation's valuation under the statutory procedure, the shares "value" is $0.00. If this is confirmed, this establishes Croxton's entitlement to $400,000 as promised him in his contract for the mandated sale of his shares.

Grimes v. Vitalink Communications Corporation

Citation: 1997 Del. Ch. LEXIS 124
Court: Court of Chancery
State/Jurisdiction: Delaware
Date of decision: August 26, 1997
Judge: Chandler

In a dissent to a typical statutory merger of a company called Vitalink, dissenters owning 201,900 shares claim a fair value of $13.32 per share versus respondent's $8.50 per share.

The parties agreed on several issues:
- Use of a DCF model ("increasingly the model of choice for valuations in this Court"- emphasis supplied)
- Use of comparable company multiples to estimate the terminal value at the end of a 5-year forecast period.
- A 20.83% discount rate to be applied to forecasted net cash flows.

The difference in the parties' values resulted from three areas of conflicts:
- Assumptions underlying the product and sales forecast (50% of difference)
- Selection of comparable companies by which to estimate terminal value multiples (40% of the difference) and
- Selection of the company's tax rate (10% of the difference).

In reaching its opinion, the court focused on:
- The credibility of the expert.
- Their methods.
- The data relied on.

Dissenter's expert was William Becklean of Tucker Anthony Incorporated, a long-time friend of petitioner. Becklean had never served as an expert witness in an appraisal action or any other litigation.

Defendant's expert was Kevin Dages of Chicago Partners, who had no knowledge of Vitalink until he was hire for this case. Dages had seven years of litigation consulting experience and several times served as a consulting and testifying expert.

Becklean relied on a forecast which contained assumptions the court considered unattainable without the merger or a relationship with the merger partner, while Dages prepared a forecast on a stand-alone basis. Because the value can not, by law, reflect potential of the action to which the party dissents, the court accepted Dages' forecast.

Becklean derived terminal value multiples from an "upper tier" of potential comparables, while Dages selected from a "lower tier." The court concluded that, by the merger date, "Vitalink clearly had become a lower tier company," and selected Dages' comparables. The court also accepted Dages' higher tax rate.

Having agreed with the defendant's expert on all three areas of disagreement, the court found the fair value to be $8.50 per share.

Sieg Co. v. Kelly

Citation: 568 N.W.2d 794, 1997 Iowa Sup. LEXIS 243
Court: Supreme Court
State/Jurisdiction: Iowa
Date of decision: September 17, 1997
Judge: Ternus

This action was brought to obtain a court appraisal of the fair value of stock owned by the Kelly's. The Kelly's objected to the price offered for their shares in Sieg-Fort Dodge Company, resulting from a merger between Sieg-Fort Dodge and Sieg Company. Sieg filed an appraisal action which resulted in a bench trial, and a valuation unsatisfactory to the Kelly's.

Merger stipulated by reorganization plan

Historically, Sieg-Fort was a successful company, with substantial net profits, and annual dividends. However, the company's position changed in the late 1980s when large losses on its non-auto parts business investments thrust the company on the verge of bankruptcy. After several mergers, Sieg began operating Sieg-Fort Dodge as a division of Sieg. Sieg also replaced the board members and officers of Sieg-Fort Dodge with individuals who were also board members and officers of Sieg. The company hired a new CEO, Katz, who developed a reorganization plan that raised additional capital, but conditionally required Sieg-Fort Dodge to merge into Sieg. To effectuate the merger, all Sieg-Fort Dodge shareholders were offered cash or Sieg stock for their shares, the cash price being $22.60 per share. The Kelly's rejected Sieg's offer and sought a per-share price of $184.59.

Expert relies on market approach

At the bench trial, Sieg presented testimony from Richard Maroney, Jr., who testified that the Kelly's stock was worth $40.74 per share. Maroney relied solely on the market approach, and used a price-to-book value multiple. Maroney rejected an asset-based approach because the inventory and fixed assets of Sieg-Fort Dodge had not been appraised. He also rejected the income approach because the company was not profitable for several years.

Experts restate inventory to FIFO

In determining his multiple, Maroney used financial information from December 1993, and incorporated several adjustments. He added back a portion of the LIFO reserve to restate inventory to a FIFO basis, but did not add back the entire LIFO reserve because, in his opinion, Sieg-Fort's LIFO reserve was too high as compared to his selected five guideline companies. Maroney also discounted the book value of Sieg-Fort's assets by 20% to adjust for the company's operating losses since 1990. Maroney noted that the five guideline companies were more profitable and in better financial condition than Sieg-Fort Dodge. As a result, Maroney started with the lowest multiple, and reduced it by an additional 32% to reflect Sieg-Fort's recent operating losses and reduced equity. Maroney arrived at a per-share value of $62.67. From that, he proceeded to take a 35% marketability discount, and testified his final opinion of fair market value was $40.74 per share.

The Kelly's presented testimony from Steve Givens, who also employed the market approach, using a price-to-book value multiple. Givens added back a larger portion of the LIFO reserve than Maroney, but used the same five guideline companies. Rather than using the lowest multiple however, Givens used an average of the multiples, and arrived at a per-share value of $220.39. Unlike Maroney, Givens did not apply a marketability discount.

Maroneys approach 'more convincing'

The trial court found Maroney's approach, "more convincing and supported by the evidence," with one exception. The court did not believe that a marketability discount was permitted under Iowa law. As a result, the trial court adopted Maroney's pre-marketability discount value of $62.67. Furthermore, the court rejected Givens opinion because he viewed Sieg-Fort's financial position as if selected related dealings had not occurred. Specifically, the court refused "to ignore the reality of the years preceding the merger." The court also found Given's use of an average multiple unrealistic because the comparable companies were all profitable, whereas, at the time of the merger, Sieg-Fort Dodge was not.

Upon reviewing the expert testimony and the trial courts decision, the Supreme Court stated that there was clearly substantial evidence supporting the trial courts determination of fair value. The court also noted that, "although Sieg undervalued the dissenters' shares by $40.70 per share, the dissenters' overvalued their shares by $121.92 per share. Consequently, we think the objective and subjective process by which a party arrives at its fair-value figure is more important than the accuracy of that party's valuation, as later determined by the trial court... [and] conclude there is substantial evidence to support a finding Sieg had a factual and legal basis for its fair-value determination, and made a good faith effort to honestly assess the fair value of the dissenters' shares."

Marketability discount a question of law

In turning its attention to the marketability discount, the Supreme Court stated, "the action of Sieg in discounting the dissenters stock for lack of marketability is more problematic. No one disputes there was a factual basis for such a discount... the question is whether such a discount is legally allowed... Although Iowa law was clear at the time Sieg made its valuation that a minority discount is not permitted, we have never decided whether a discount applicable to all shares of a closely-held corporation is permissible." The court further noted that some jurisdictions allow marketability discounts and others do not. Therefore, the court stated that "we cannot say Sieg had no legal basis for taking such a discount here."

In its final analysis, the Supreme Court found no error in the trial courts decision, stating again that substantial evidence supports the valuation of Kelly's stock. Affirmed.

Gilbert v. MPM Enterprises, Inc.

Citation: 709 A.2d 663, 1997 Del. Ch. LEXIS 141
Court: Court of Chancery
State/Jurisdiction: Delaware
Date of decision: October 9, 1997
Judge: Steele

Petitioner dissented from a merger agreement, and pursued his statutory right to an appraisal of his 8% interest in MPM Enterprises, Inc., a company that manufactures screen printers for the surface mount technology industry. In March 1995, MPM and Cookson Group, PLC signed a merger agreement that provided immediate cash payment of $62.698 million to MPM's stockholders, plus an additional $73.635 million of potential earn-out payments.

Vice Chancellor comments on appraisals

Vice Chancellor Steele prefaced his methodology in determining the fair value of the shares with some general observations of the statutory appraisal process. He noted that,

> Typically both sides in an appraisal proceeding present expert opinions on the fair value of the petitioner's shares. In theory, these opinions facilitate judicial fact finding and conclusions by wrapping the experts' factual assumptions in complicated financial models with which they, and not the court, are conversant. One might expect the experts' desire to convince the Court of the reasonableness and validity of their assumptions and financial models would produce a somewhat narrow range of values, clearly and concisely supported, despite the individual parties' obvious conflicting incentives. Unfortunately, as this case and other cases most decidedly illustrate, one should not put much faith in that expectation, at least when faced with appraisal experts in this Court.

'Dr. Pangloss v. Mr. Scrooge'

The Court, articulating its observations of experts providing extreme values favorable to clients, cited this as, "…perhaps the best reason for this Court to consider appointing an independent expert to sort through the clutter submitted." Regarding the facts and circumstances of this particular case, Vice Chancellor Steele noted, "Reading petitioner's submissions, one might easily conclude that MPM was poised to become the Microsoft of the SMT industry. By contrast, respondent's submissions give the impression that a more likely comparison, given MPM's myriad management, technical and legal problems, is Apple [Computer]. In sum, one report is submitted by Dr. Pangloss, and the other by Mr. Scrooge."

Petitioner submitted expert testimony from Patricof & Co. Capital Corp., who determined the fair value of petitioner's shares using a comparable company approach and a discounted cash flow (DCF) approach. Patricof relied equally on the two approaches, and averaged the two results. Based on that calculation, Patricof concluded that the fair value of MPM's equity was $357.1 million, and Petitioners interest was worth $26 million.

Court rejects 'buy side' DCF

Respondent retained Advest, Inc., who also relied on a comparable sales approach and a DCF approach. Advest constructed a DCF approach that represented the transaction from the sellers point of view (the sell-side DCF), and also constructed and additional model representing the transaction from a buyers point of view (buy-side DCF). The Court noted that it is unclear why Advest constructed the buy-side model, as the report recognized that under Delaware law, petitioner is entitled to his pro- rata share of the corporation valued as a going concern without consideration of "any element of value arising from the accomplishment or expectation of a merger."

Regarding the comparable company analysis, Advest concluded that the approach did not provide an accurate valuation of MPM because MPM was not in a position to go public. Based on the results of the sell-side analysis, Advest concluded that the value of MPM's equity was worth $81.7 million, and petitioners shares were worth $5.942 million.

Court reconciles differing value conclusions

Again, because of the disparities in values, Vice Chancellor Steele concluded "...that the only appropriate way to determine the fair value of petitioner's shares is to compare petitioners DCF model with respondents sell-side model." He further stated that when the experts cannot resolve the differences, the Court will. In analyzing the two DCF approaches, the Court:
- Concluded that management was in the best position to forecast MPM's future cash flows, and therefore accepted managements projections with minor changes to reflect MPM's actual financial results
- Accepted respondent's terminal value calculation using an EBITDA multiple, based on their choice of more appropriate comparable companies (both parties calculated terminal value by applying multiples of comparable companies)
- Accepted petitioner's approach in determining the appropriate discount rate for MPM.

Court accepts CAPM discount rate

Regarding the discount rate, respondent argued that the CAPM is used primarily for companies with publicly traded shares and is therefore inappropriate. However, the court noted that respondent does not object to the use of other data from comparable companies in its DCF, just the use of data required for CAPM. Again, Steele noted, "I find no convincing explanation of why respondent's survey provides a more accurate estimate of MPM's cost of capital than petitioner's CAPM approach. If anything, respondent's survey comes dangerously close to providing an estimate of the cost of equity for an acquiring company... a practice that is not acceptable when valuing a company as a stand-alone entity under our [Delaware] appraisal statute." The Court further concluded that MPM's discount rate should be determined via the CAPM, however, the comparable beta coefficient was based on the average beta of respondents comparable companies.

Gonsalves v. Straight Arrow Publishers, Inc. (II)

Citation: 701 A.2d 357, 1997 Del. LEXIS 369
Court: Supreme Court
State/Jurisdiction: Delaware
Date of decision: October 21, 1997
Judge: Walsh

Appellant-petitioner contends that the Court of Chancery erred in its acceptance of the appellee-respondent's valuation evidence, resulting in the exclusion of petitioner's valuation evidence. The underlying dispute involves the appraised value of the common stock of Straight Arrow Publishing, whose primary product is *Rolling Stone* magazine.

The Supreme Court noted that the Court of Chancery has traditionally been granted "a high level of deference," and reflects a recognition that appraisal cases tend to be factually intensive and often involve competing valuation methodologies. However, "the deference standard also assumes that the Court will employ its own expertise which is essential to the appraisal task."

Furthermore, the Supreme Court stated that the issue is not merely that the Chancellor made an uncritical acceptance of the evidence of Straight Arrow Publisher's appraiser, but that he *(Judge Allen)* disclosed in advance that he intended to choose between the two extreme values. However, the Supreme Court also noted that although the Chancellor did not indicate which side he would favor, the evidentiary construct he established for the subsequent trial created a standard for value determination "which is at odds with Section 262's command that the court 'shall appraise' fair value."

Finding that the approach chosen by the Chancellor was a question of law, the issue before the Supreme Court became, "whether the Court of Chancery may adopt an expert's valuation views under a previously announced 'hook, line and sinker' rationale in the face of significant arguable considerations advanced by both sides of the dispute."

Ultimately, the Supreme Court found that the Court of Chancery's pretrial decision to adhere to, and rely upon, the methodology and valuation factors of one expert, and excluding other evidence presented the other expert, and the implementation of that mind-set in the appraisal process was in error. Reversed and remanded for a new valuation hearing.

Berens v. Ludwig (II)

Citation: 160 F.3d 1144, 1998 U.S. App. LEXIS 28797
Court: United States Court of Appeals
State/Jurisdiction: 7th Circuit Federal
Date of decision: November 17, 1998
Judge: Posner

Marks Berens, minority shareholder in Marquette Bank Shakopee, was required to surrender his shares pursuant to a consolidation by the majority shareholder of the bank (a bank holding company). Under the terms of the consolidation, Berens was to be paid the cash value of the shares as determined by the company. Berens thought the value set by the company was too low, and requested valuation of the shares by the Comptroller of the Currency under 12 U.S.C. § 215(d). Berens was equally unhappy with the value set by the Comptroller, and filed suit against the Comptroller and Marquette Bank under 28 U.S.C. § 1331, on the grounds that the Comptroller's valuation was arbitrary and therefore violated the Administrative Procedures Act.

In calculating the value under each method, Berens' appraisers divided the capital of the bank into "productive capital" of $7 million, and "excess capital" of $5 million. This division was made on the theory that the Comptroller only required the bank to maintain capital in the amount of $7 million, and that the $5 million should have been paid out in dividends over prior years rather than being invested in low-risk, low-yield securities.

Plaintiff uses three methods

After making this division of capital, Berens' appraisers employed three separate methods of determining the value of the bank:

(1) Under the capital valuation method, the appraisers applied a multiple of 1.3 to 1.4, derived from the value of comparable banks, to the $7 million of productive capital. Then the appraisers added the $5 million of excess capital to the total without applying any multiplier to it.

(2) Under the price-earnings valuation method, the appraisers applied a multiple of 10.5, again derived from the comparable banks, to the bank's annual earnings. Then the appraisers "added the $5 million in excess capital on the theory that this entire amount could be paid out in the form of a dividend without impairing the bank's earnings."

(3) Under the discounted cash flow method the appraisers treated the $5 million in excess capital as earnings.

Berens v. Ludwig (II)

Comptroller uses two methods, different weights

The Comptroller employed two of the three methods employed by Berens' appraisers, and weighted the price-earnings method valuation 3 times heavier than the capital valuation method:

(1) Under the capital valuation method, the Comptroller applied the 1.3 to 1.4 multiplier to the total capital of $12 million.

(2) Under the price-earnings valuation method, the Comptroller did not add the $5 million in excess capital to the total calculated by applying the multiple to the earnings.

'Excess' capital not excessive

The Comptroller did not divide the banks capital into "productive" and "excess" capital before calculating his valuation. The court found that the Comptrollers failure to make adjustments for the so-called excess capital was not arbitrary. The court reasoned that the banks management style of keeping $5 million in low-yield, low-risk investments allowed it to make higher yield, higher risk investments with the $7 million of productive capital. Accordingly, the banks total return on assets was high, possibly higher than it would have been if the bank were more thinly capitalized.

Deference given to Comptroller's valuation

The issue before the court was whether the Comptrollers valuation was arbitrary. Pursuant to prior cases before the 4th, 7th, and 11th Circuits, the court gave deference to the to the Comptrollers valuation, and held that the Comptroller did not act arbitrarily.

PARTY	PRICE TO CAPITAL VALUATION	PRICE-EARNINGS VALUATION	DISCOUNTED CASH FLOW
Berens' appraisers	($7 million capital x 1.3 to 1.4) +$5 million excess capital weighted equally	(Annual earnings x 10.5) +$5 million weighted equally	Weighted equally
Comptroller	$12 million capital x 1.3 to 1.4 Given less weight	Annual earnings x 10.5 Given 3 times greater weight	Not used

Chapter 7: Court Case Abstracts

Hintmann v. Fred Weber, Inc.

Citation: 1998 Del. Ch. LEXIS 26
Court: Court of Chancery
State/Jurisdiction: Delaware
Date of decision: February 17, 1998
Judge: Steele

As of September 15, 1992 (the Valuation Date), Industries' principal asset was 100% of the Class A shares of Fred Weber, Inc. (FWI). Employees of FWI owned 100% of FMI's Class B shares. Industries had one class of common stock, of which the FWI Employee Stock Ownership Plan owned 95%. On the valuation date, Industries merged into the operating company, FWI. The ESOP participants who voted in favor of the merger received $127.50 in cash plus one share of newly-issued FWI nonvoting 10% convertible preferred stock for each share of Industries' common stock, for a total consideration of $260 per share. Four ESOP participants voted against the merger and sought appraisal, as did one Class B shareholder.

Both sides use DCF and market methods

Petitioner's expert, Ben Buettell of Houlihan, Lokey, Howard & Zukin, valued FWI's Class A common stock at $391 per share on the Valuation Date. Respondent's expert, Richard Braun of Willamette Management Associates, valued the Class A shares at $271. Both experts computed the value of FWI by calculating the simple average of the results of their respective discounted cash flow and market capitalization analysis. As the Court did not discuss the "market capitalization" (comparable company) analyses, it appears that there were not material differences in valuation using that approach.

Beuttell calculated the WACC at 15% for his DCF calculations. The Court commented, "Although Beuttell stated that the numbers he used to represent FWI's beta and cost of debt were in the comparative analysis summarized in the Market Capitalization section of the report, the actual numbers used do not appear to be listed in, or calculable from the information that is listed in Beuttell's valuation report. Neither were these numbers provided at trial. Although, for privately held companies, beta *must* [emphasis in original] be an estimate based on the betas of comparable, publicly traded companies, the same is not true for the cost of debt. Beuttell did not indicate why he felt it was more appropriate to estimate FWI's cost of debt based on the cost of comparable companies' debt than to use FWI's actual cost of debt. Similarly, I cannot discern exactly how Beuttell chose to weight FWI's cost of equity and debt, although this decision was also based on the capital structures of comparable companies."

Court prefers CAPM cost of equity

Braun used both the build up method and the CAPM in determining the WACC for FWI. Braun first calculated FWI's cost of equity using the CAPM, as did Beuttell. His CAPM results

Hintmann v. Fred Weber, Inc.

yielded a cost of equity of 16.8%. (The small stock premium used by Braun is not stated, but, at 16.8% either his beta or that premium was unusually low.) In his build up methodology, Braun calculated a WACC of 21%, which included a 3% company-specific risk premium. However, the court rejected Braun's build up approach, noting that "This method differed from the CAPM in only one respect: it did not employ beta... The CAPM would seem to be more useful than the build up method because it offers more complete information. Specifically, the CAPM includes a measure of a stocks systematic risk..."

Braun weighed FWI's cost of capital using 98% equity and 2% debt, based on FWIs capital structure prior to the merger. The Court accepted this, saying, "As with all other areas of business valuation, this Court prefers to use a company's actual information when possible, unless it is shown that the actual information would yield unreliable results."

Company-specific risk not supported

With respect to company-specific risk, the Vice Chancellor noted that it "remains largely a matter of the analysts judgment," citing Pratt, *Valuing A Business*. He rejected the 3% premium, as he felt that Braun's reasons for adding the extra premium did not translate into greater risk.

Braun considered FWI's financial data as of July 31, 1992, but Beuttell relied on April 30 data. The Court made the obvious determination that the date closer to the Valuation Date should be used.

FWI had $14 million of cash on its balance sheet. Beuttell treated $10 million as excess cash. Based on information he acquired from FWI's management, Braun concluded that all the cash was needed to meet future "working capital expenses." FWI management testified that it had accumulated cash to prepare itself for expected environmental legislation, the purchase of additional quarry locations and for future capital improvements. The Court concurred with Braun.

Both parties experts assumed that the value of the Class B stock was to be determined pursuant to FWI's by-laws, which provided that, upon death, termination of employment of retirement, all Class B Common shares must be offered to FWI for redemption at book value, with good will valued at $1.00. FWI's auditor had determined that book value of the Class B shares was $203.83 per share. The Vice Chancellor ruled, "The [by-law] provision expressly applies to redemptions and only to redemptions; it does not contemplate a merger and later appraisal." He concluded that the class B should be valued on a going concern basis, and said, "At present, there is not evidence in the record from which this Court can make such a determination. Furthermore, both parties' experts relied on the [book] value of FWI's Class B shares to determine the value of its Class A shares." He requested further briefing on this issue.

Control premium placed on subsidiaries

Industries was a holding company whose primary asset was 100% of FWI's Class A common stock, which represented approximately 90% of FWI's value. Based on *Rapid-American v.*

Harris, the Court decided that a control premium should be added to the value of FMI as a subsidiary of Industries. Based on control premia paid for publicly-held companies in the 12 months ended June 30, 1992, Beuttell found that the mean premium was approximately 45% and the median premium was about 55%. Because a portion of those premia reflected post-merger values expected form synergies, Beuttell arbitrarily adjusted the premium down to 20%, which the Court accepted.

Gonsalves v. Straight Arrow Publishers, Inc. (III)

Citation: 793 A.2d 312, 1998 Del. Ch. LEXIS 45
Court: Court of Chancery
State/Jurisdiction: Delaware
Date of decision: March 26, 1998
Judge: Chandler

This opinion is the latest in a string of decisions on a dissenting stockholder suit originally filed May 5, 1986.

Losing operations discontinued

Straight Arrow Publishers (SAP) main operating asset at the valuation date was *Rolling Stone Magazine*. However, they had also engaged in other publishing ventures, which generally lost money and were discontinued.

In the initial trial, former Chancellor Allen found that the valuation of SAP's expert, Martin J. Whitman provided a more acceptable valuation of SAP overall and rejected the valuation of petitioner's expert, James B. Kobak. The parties generally agreed that earnings capitalization was the most important methodology. According to Chancellor Chandler, "Most of the issues on remand concern the inputs to the earnings capitalization method, such as:

1. What of SAP's reported earnings should be adjusted,
2. what is the earnings period that should be capitalized, and
3. what multiple should be used"

Chancellor Chandler notes that "all of these decisions are intertwined, for each depends on which view of SAP one accepts: that of the phoenix soaring out the ashes or that of the Icarus rising dangerously toward the sun...Petitioner's valuation places too much weight on the recent success ... Respondents valuation, on the other hand, is based on an overly pessimistic view of the company's future."

On the subject of the multiple, the Courts at every level accepted Whitman's multiple. This was partly because Kobak's multiples were based on acquisitions and thus Kobak's method (improperly) includes a pro rata share of a control premium.

Post merger evidence may be admissible

Petitioner capitalized the latest year's earnings because most of the former year's operations had been discontinued. Plans in effect at the time of the merger, however, were ignored. The Chancellor noted that "post-merger evidence is not necessarily inadmissible to show that plans in effect at the time of the merger have born fruition."

Respondent capitalized SAP's five year average results. The Court ultimately chose to capitalize the company's five-year weighted average results. The Court rejected proposed adjustments to earnings, stating "nowhere in Kobak's report nor at trial does petitioner provide an explanation for the need for such adjustments." The Court also rejected Kobak's proposal to add deferred subscription revenue to the value.

Treatment of cash a major issue

A major issue in the case is the treatment of cash. The analysis contained in Whitman's report defined *enterprise value* as follows:

Market value of Common Equity
+ Total Interest Bearing Debt
+ Preferred Stock
+ Minority Interest
- Cash & Cash Equivalents

The above is a definition of enterprise value which is commonly used by investment bankers. The cash is taken out from the guideline companies because it can vary a great deal from one to another relative to their operating needs, and then the subject company's cash is added to the value indicated by the value indicated by the valuation multiple.

Court rejects cash add-back

However, the court rejected the cash add-back (which amounted to $5 million), on the grounds that the cash was not "excess cash," because the company needed it for working capital.

Hansen v. 75 Ranch Company (I)

Citation: 1998 MT 77, 288 Mont. 310, 957 P.2d 32, 1998 Mont. LEXIS 55
Court: Supreme Court
State/Jurisdiction: Montana
Date of decision: April 9, 1998
Judge: Leaphart

Minority shareholder family members appeal a decision denying them the ability to exercise dissenting shareholders' rights under the Montana Business Corporation Act.

Stockholders' agreement stipulates transfer provisions

In 1980, the Tully family incorporated the 75 Ranch Company as a closely-held corporation in hopes of avoiding estate and inheritance tax liability. The company also established a stockholders agreement, providing a method of transferring the shares of a deceased shareholder and restricting the transfer of shares by shareholders during their lifetime. The parents, Robert and Joan, together held a majority position (25,600 shares) in the stock. Each of the five Tully children held 2,880 shares.

During the period of 1986 and 1989, Robert and Joan Tully passed away. During probate of Robert's estate, the shares were assigned a value of $12.26 per share. Following the estate distribution, the son, Peter Tully, owned 51% of the outstanding shares, and each of Peter's four siblings owned 12.5% each. Peter took over as President and his wife Rhonda assumed the role of Secretary/Treasurer, both living on the ranch and tending to the daily operations of the company.

Son executes Contract and Exchange agreement

In December 1989, the shareholders discussed the possibility of selling the ranch, and Peter's sister Jennifer specified that if Peter were to relocate the ranch, she desired to sell her shares. In 1992, Peter executed a Contract and Exchange agreement which sold the Montana property for $875,000, and purchased a New Mexico property for $850,000. However, Peter did not provide the minority shareholders with notice of the proposed exchange, and did not submit copies of the exchange documents for shareholder approval.

In 1993, Peter received a letter from Jennifer reiterating her desire to sell her shares. In response, Peter contacted the corporate accountant to determine the value of the shares in compliance with the stockholders agreement. Peter made an initial offer of $14.63 per share, based on a balance sheet dated November 30, 1992.

Jennifer rejected Peter's initial offer, and upon receiving a copy of the balance sheet, discovered the per share valuation included a 30% minority discount. Jennifer presented a counteroffer of $20.90, the value of the shares excluding the discount. Peter's sister Frances also wished to sell her shares for that price. Not understanding the legal ramifications of dissenters' rights, Peter consulted an attorney and responded with a compromise offer of $15 per share.

Transaction gives rise to dissenter's rights

On appeal, the Supreme Court determined that the pertinent issues were legal in nature, and therefore were required to review whether or not District Courts conclusions of law were correct. With respect to the stockholders agreement, the Supreme Court found that the provisions of the agreement did not cover an exchange transaction, but instead gave rise to dissenters' rights, governed by the Montana Business Corporation Act. The Court further noted, "...recent versions of this remedy allow a dissenting shareholder to demand that the corporation buy back his shares at fair value if the corporation takes an action which fundamentally alters the character of the shareholders investment."

Because the minority shareholders were not given an opportunity to vote regarding the exchange, nor were they given notification of their right to dissent, the Supreme Court found that the minority shareholders were entitled to statutory notice of dissenters' rights.

Discounts disallowed under 'fair value' standard

Turning to the issue of the 30% minority discount, the Supreme Court stated, "Because we have determined that the Montana business Corporation Act controls, we further conclude that the minority shareholders are entitled to 'fair value' in accordance with the statutes, rather than 'fair market value' as provided in the stockholders agreement." As a result, the Supreme Court prohibited the consideration of a minority discount when establishing fair value.

Reversed, and remanded with instructions that, "...the District Court must determine 'fair value' as opposed to 'fair market value'. ...the court must bear in mind that 'fair value,' as explained above, means the value of the shares immediately before the effectuation of the corporate action to which the dissenter objects."

Steiner Corp. v. Benninghoff

Citation: 5 F. Supp. 2d 1117, 1998 U.S. Dist. LEXIS 8040
Court: United States District Court
State/Jurisdiction: Nevada
Date of decision: May 26, 1998
Judge: Reed

On July 26, 1994, Steiner Corporation merged with Steiner Holding Corp., and bought out all minority shareholders at a price of $1,200 per share, except for respondents who exercised dissenters' rights. Steiner contends that the fair value of the shares is no more than $840 per share, while respondents claim fair value is at least $1,950 per share.

Steiner is a linen supply and textile rental business, with domestic and foreign operations. Before the merger, there were 367,351 outstanding shares, with over 93% owned by the Steiner family. Respondents are descendants of George Benninghoff, who acquired his shares around the year 1900, and worked for Steiner for over 50 years.

Merger avoids accumulated earnings taxes

In 1993, facing potential accumulated earnings taxes, Steiner decided to pursue the cash-out merger transaction. In determining what price to offer, Steiner retained Houlihan, Lokey, Howard and Zukin, which determined the per share price of Steiner stock to be $1,418. However, the HLHZ report was never released to the board. Instead, the board appointed a Special Committee who hired J.P. Morgan to perform a valuation, which resulted in a value range of $1,100 to $1,500 per share. After brief negotiations, the Steiners and the Special Committee agreed on the $1,200 per share price.

Fair value is legal standard

The court heard testimony from Steiners' experts, J.P. Morgan and Dr. Allan Kleidon, and from dissenter's expert, David Nolte with Arthur Andersen. Before trying to determine the fair value of the dissenter's shares, the court set forth a four-pronged methodology and addressed several key issues affecting the case. The court stated that the proper standard of value is fair value, a specified by the Nevada dissenter's rights statute, determined by considering:

1.) The pre-merger market value of the shares, discounted for illiquidity
2.) The pre-merger enterprise value of the company as a whole
3.) The pre-merger net asset value of the company
4.) Any other factor bearing on value

The Court further stated that, "...it became evident at trial that the parties have misconstrued and consistently mischaracterized parts of this order. We do not necessarily blame the parties for this, however, for while our order was consistent with the established case law, the sad fact is that the established case law is not entirely consistent with economic theory. Of course, it is the law we must follow, which the various experts in valuation theory and economics who testified at trial may not have completely realized."

Prong I: Pre-merger market value of shares

Steiner relied on the limited prior trading history of its stock. However, the court stated that because the repurchases were on an intermittent basis with prices determined by Steiner, the court would not put any significant weight on prior stock purchases. The court turned its attention to the comparable sales method. Both Nolte and J.P. Morgan used the following companies as comparable to Steiner's linen business: Angelica, Cintas, G&K Services, Health Care Services Group, National Services Industries, Unifirst and Unitog. The court also noted evidence presented at trial that other valuation studies of Steiner over the years have shown a remarkable consistency in their choice of comparable companies. For its 1993 study, HLHZ used all of the same linen companies.

Steiner presented Dr. Kleidon, who although he considered the method, ultimately decided that it deserved little weight. Nolte calculated P/E and Total Invested Capital to EBITDA, and derived an unadjusted value of $515,534,000. The court ruled that since Nolte's value fell within the ranges suggested by both of Steiners' experts, it was a reasonable figure to accept as the market value of Steiner. The court took Nolte's value and added excess cash, applied a 25% discount for lack of marketability, and determined that the value of Steiner under the first prong was $1,191.98 per share.

Prong II: Pre-merger enterprise value of Steiner as a whole

To determine the pre-merger enterprise value, the court examined both the discounted cash flow method and the acquisitions method. With respect to the discounted cash flow approach, the court examined both Nolte's and Kleidon's valuations, and used a 15% EBITDA margin and determined projections of after tax debt free net cash flows for the years 1995-1999. The court applied a perpetual growth rate of 5% to determine the terminal value.

Noting that the discount rate is probably the most hotly contested issue in the case, the court turned its attention to calculating the WACC for Steiner. The court determined that a 5% market risk premium was appropriate, and that the proper beta was .75, giving Steiner a cost of equity capital of 10.65%. The court further determined that Steiners' cost of debt was 8.57%, and determined that the WACC was 9.78%. The court concluded that the DCF approach yielded a value of $1,273.64 per share.

Despite Steiners' contention that the acquisitions method is forbidden by previous court order, the court deemed the method appropriate, and used Nolte's deal value to last twelve month earnings multiple of 1.3, which gave a per share value of $1,958.95. The court weighted the acquisitions method at 30% and the DCF method at 70%, to determine a final per share enterprise value of $1,479.22.

Third and fourth prongs not considered

The court stated that given the facts and circumstances of the case, the pre-merger net asset value of Steiner should be given no weight at all. Additionally, the court stated that since no other factor for which an actual money figure could be calculated was suggested, no weight would be given to the fourth prong either.

Finally, the court concluded by weighting the market value figure by 25% and the enterprise value figure by 75%, and determined that the per share fair value of dissenters shares was $1,407.42. Therefore Steiners' owed dissenters an additional $2,435,366.64, plus interest.

Balsamides v. Perle (I)

Citation: 313 N.J. Super. 7, 712 A.2d 673, 1998 N.J. Super. LEXIS 281
Court: Superior Court, Appellate Division
State/Jurisdiction: New Jersey
Date of decision: June 17, 1998
Judge: Dreier

The main issues in this case were the valuation techniques used to value Perle's (the defendant's) half interest in the business that he was ordered to sell to Balsamides (the plaintiff).

Two 50% owners disagree

Balsamides and Perle built a successful chemical business together. Balsamides handled the sales and marketing aspects of the business while Perle used his technical talents and administrative skills. The two men were both exceptional at their respective positions. However, problems arose between these erstwhile friends, leading to litigation to resolve their irreconcilable disputes. The trial court ordered Perle to sell his half interest to Balsamides for $1,960,000. Perle appeals, claiming that the valuation is too low.

At trial, Balsamides presented expert testimony by Thomas Hoberman, a C.P.A. Perle presented testimony by Robert Ott, a Chartered Financial Analyst.

Ott used an income approach, reaching a value for the company of $8,285,000, which he corroborated with a market approach using four publicly traded guideline companies.

Hoberman uses excess income method

Hoberman said that no comparable companies could be found and that he could not use the income approach because he could not speak with Perle to get the necessary expense and capital expenditure information to make a credible estimate of cash flow. He, therefore, used the excess earnings method.

Hoberman used an 11% return on net tangible assets ($306,000) and capitalized the "excess earnings" at 30%, citing six negative factors to justify the rate. He then applied a discount for lack of marketability of 35%.

Ott criticizes both method and rates

Ott objected to the use of the excess earnings method for this type of a company, to the 11% rate on tangible assets, to the 30% cap rate on excess earnings, and to the use of any marketability discount except for a possible brokerage fee.

The use of the excess income approach was noted by the trial judge not to be the preferred method of valuation. He nevertheless found it appropriate in this case, and accepted Hoberman's valuation.

Appeals court rejects marketability discount

The appellate court, noting that the statutory standard of value was "fair value," vacated the 35% discount for lack of marketability. On remand for review, the appellate ruling stated that the court may consider a brokerage discount.

On the other issues, the appellate court raised questions about the valuation, including the justification for using the excess earnings method and the rationale for the capitalization rates. It did not specifically make any adjustments, but directed that the issues be reexamined by the trial judge on remand.

Zatz, et al. v. U.S.A., et al

Citation: No. 97-4287
Court: U.S. Court of Appeals
State/Jurisdiction: Second Circuit
Date of decision: July 9, 1998
Judge: Meskill, Cabranes, and Nickerson

The following court case abstract was originally published in Valuation Case Digest®

In *Donald Zatz, et al. v. U.S.A., et al.*, No. 97-4287, July 9, 1998, The U.S. Court of Appeals for the Second Circuit considered whether the Surface Transportation Board could determine the fair value of minority shares. Zatz held a minority interest in St. Louis Southwestern Railway Corporation (SSW). The corporation was acquired in a two tier merger by Southern Pacific Railway. The Surface Transportation Board determined the fair value of the shares subject to the first tier of the merger. The Board concluded that the fair value of each share was $6,800. Zatz appealed. He argued that the Board did not have jurisdiction to determine the fair value of the shares, and if it did have jurisdiction, then the Board's valuation was not supported by the evidence.

The Second Circuit concluded that the Surface Transportation Board "has exclusive authority to approve and authorize a proposed railroad merger or control transaction. . . ." including

"... the authority and obligation to determine 'just and reasonable' rates of compensation to minority shareholders." The court further affirmed the Board's determination value. The Board received detailed valuation analyses from two expert witnesses. The Board did not accept the minority shareholders' expert because his valuation was based on an offer to buy that "... was not firm and that included substantial non-SSW assets." Thus, the Second Circuit affirmed the Board's valuation.

Lawson Mardon Wheaton, Inc. v. Smith (I)

Citation: 315 N.J. Super. 32, 716 A.2d 550, 1998 N.J. Super. LEXIS 375
Court: Superior Court, Appellate Division
State/Jurisdiction: New Jersey
Date of decision: August 26, 1998
Judge: Cuff

Twenty-six shareholders of Wheaton, Inc., a closely held family corporation, invoked their right to an appraisal and purchase of their shares pursuant to New Jersey statute. They had dissented from a corporate restructuring. Their appeal of the valuation of their shares primarily raises the issue of whether a discount for lack of marketability should be applied.

At the request of many of the Wheaton shareholders that the company play a greater role in estate tax management, company management initiated a series of events to make the stocks more liquid. Wheaton decided that a limited initial public offering (IPO) was the best way to provide that liquidity.

26 shareholders dissent

As part of the process for the IPO, the company planned to restructure the company and recapitalize the shares. It was at this point that the 26 shareholders, holding approximately 15% of the company's five million shares, formally dissented from the plan pursuant to the appraisal statute and demanded fair value payment for their shares.

George Weiksner, a managing director and chairman of First Boston's investment banking committee, was the expert for the company. Weiksner used a two-step process. In the first step he used the comparable company method, discounted cash flow analysis, and a comparable acquisition analysis. The second step then involved applying a 25% marketability discount and a 5% discount due to the restrictions on stock transfers contained in the shareholders' and liquidity agreements. He concluded that the shares were worth between $36.86 and $39.69 per share.

Mark Lee, managing director in the investment banking department of Bear Sterns & Company, was the expert for the shareholders. Lee used the pro rata equity value, minority interest value, and discounted minority interest value. He determined the marketability discount to be between 10% and 17% and found the restricted value of each share to be between $51.00 and $59.00.

Trial judge: 25% marketability discount

The trial judge determined their shares to be worth $41.05 per share and was predicated on two primary factors: application of a 25% lack of marketability discount and fixing the embedded minority discount at zero. All defendants appealed the application of the marketability discount. Two defendants claim the judge erred in fixing the embedded minority discount at zero.

The court applied the 25% marketability discount to the shares, relying on the American Law Institute's Principles of Corporate Governance section 7.22 (1992). The trial court arrived at the $41.05 figure by multiplying the company's own estimate of its 1992 earnings ($20.5 million) by 13.5 (the average of the price/earnings multiples used by the experts), adding that figure to the amount of Wheaton shares outstanding on the date in question, and then subtracting the 25% marketability discount.

Marketability discount usual rule

The trial court concluded that the circumstances of this case dictated application of the "extraordinary circumstances" exception to the general rule against application of a marketability discount announced by the American Law Institute. Section 7.22(a) recommends that a marketability discount should be applied only in "extraordinary circumstances."

The court believed that, "The dissenters could have maintained both their private equity interest and their voting rights in Wheaton after the asset transfer and recapitalization.... [T]he restructuring was a harmless action and done in order to prepare for a limited IPO to give the dissenters as well as some other shareholders the liquidity they sought. To allow it to bestow upon the dissenters a price significantly higher than any shareholder could have obtained in a market transaction under such circumstances would bring about an unfair wealth transfer from the remaining shareholders to them unless a marketability discount was applied. Put bluntly, the dissenters exploited a change they themselves championed and possibly prevented an IPO to the detriment of other shareholders."

Corporate restructuring 'non-material'

While the Superior Court found that, as a general rule, no marketability discount should be utilized in a fair value determination in a fair value appraisal proceeding, the "trial court was well-founded in classifying this case as 'extraordinary circumstances.' The record clearly supports the trial judges ultimate conclusion that the dissenters seized upon a non-material corporate restructuring to trigger an appraisal remedy."

Carter Crookham v. Peter Riley, et al.

Citation: No. 161/96-1930
Court: Supreme Court
State/Jurisdiction: Iowa
Date of decision: September 23, 1998

The following court case abstract was originally published in Valuation Case Digest®

In *Carter Crookham v. Peter Riley, et al.*, No. 161/96-1930, September 23, 1998, the Supreme Court of Iowa considered whether a damage award for legal malpractice was appropriate. Crookham was employed by and a minority shareholder in various Musco companies. He was dismissed and the companies offered to repurchase his stock for $390,000. Thereafter, Crookham hired Riley to bring suit against the Musco companies and its owners for damages under various theories including breach of fiduciary duty. During that time the Musco companies consolidated into one new corporation. Riley, acting on Crookham's behalf, filed a demand for dissenting shareholders' rights. However, the demand was filed after the statutory period. Therefore, Crookham's right to an appraisal was not protected. He later settled on a related matter for less than $350,000. Thereafter, he brought this attorney malpractice claim against Riley.

The measure of damages in an attorney malpractice action is the difference between what the client received and what he might have received had the claim not been negligently handled. In this case, the appropriate measure of damages was the fair value of Crookham's shares less the amount of his settlement. At trial, expert witness testimony established that the value of Crookham's stock in the Musco companies at the time of the merger was between $500,000 and $600,000. The jury concluded that Crookham was damaged in the amount of $230,000 by Riley's failure to protect Crookham's shareholders' rights. Riley appealed.

On appeal, Riley argued that he did not commit malpractice because Crookham had an "equally satisfactory alternative remedy" which was the damages suit. However, the appellate court affirmed the jury's finding that Riley was liable for failing to properly perfect and preserve Crookham's appraisal remedy. It also affirmed the jury's damage award because the award was supported by substantial evidence including expert testimony.

Grace v. Rosenstock

Citation: 23 F. Supp. 2d 326, 1998 U.S. Dist. LEXIS 17386
Court: United States District Court
State/Jurisdiction: New York
Date of decision: October 29, 1998
Judge: Levy

Defendants Robert Genser and Robert Rosenstock owned approximately 72% of Briggs Leasing Corporation. On Jan. 19, 1985, Genser and Rosenstock contributed all of their shares in Briggs (29,961 and 384,350 shares, respectively) to Briggs Acquisition Company (BAC), a shell corporation, and received a share for share exchange for the stock.

Proxy statement includes dissenter rights

Shortly thereafter, the defendants issued a proxy statement to inform the minority shareholders of their intentions to merge BAC and Briggs. The proxy statement included a fairness opinion rendered by Prudential-Bache Securities stating that $1.50 per share was a fair price for the minority shareholders. The proxy statement further provided that any dissenting shareholders "had the right, pursuant to section 623 of New York's Business Corporation Law, to seek an appraisal by filing a written objection with the company prior to the vote." It is unclear whether plaintiffs filed a written objection with the company.

On Feb. 26, 1985 the issue was voted on and approved. Briggs became wholly owned by the defendants. The plaintiffs voted against the merger.

Plaintiffs file Section 10(b) suit

Plaintiffs filed suit for money damages, rescission and other appropriate relief under Section 10(b) of the Securities Exchange Act of 1934 and under state law. Plaintiffs alleged a breach of fiduciary duty by defendants. They claimed that the defendants effectuated the merger through the use of a materially false proxy statement, thereby freezing out the minority shareholders at the allegedly inadequate price of $1.50 per share.

Among several arguments, the plaintiffs' primary contention relates to Briggs' interest in real estate. They claim that the share price was based on a valuation of Briggs' real estate at $479,000, when in fact it had a fair market value of $2,530,000. According to the plaintiffs, the fair value of Briggs, based on the true value of its real estate holdings at the time, was in excess of $5.00 per share.

Plaintiffs have no federal claim

Under New York law, the remedy of appraisal is a dissenting stockholder's exclusive remedy. To state a federal claim under Section 10(b), the plaintiffs must show that the alleged misrepresentation in the proxy statement resulted in the loss of that state court remedy. Since plaintiffs did not allege or prove the loss of their appraisal remedy, the court dismissed their federal claims.

Appraisal right is exclusive remedy

Although plaintiffs' federal claims were dismissed, the court retained supplemental jurisdiction over the state law claims because of the substantial investment of court resources that had already been made in the case. In ruling on the merits of plaintiffs claim, the court held that it must be dismissed under New York Business Corporation Law § 623(k), which provides that an appraisal action is shareholders exclusive remedy, except under certain circumstances. Plaintiffs' state law claim did not fall under the exception because they were not (at the time of this opinion) seeking equitable relief and their breach of fiduciary duty claim was derivative in nature.

Connector Service Corp. v. Briggs

Citation: 1998 U.S. Dist. LEXIS 18864
Court: United States District Court
State/Jurisdiction: Illinois
Date of decision: October 30, 1998
Judge: Leinenweber

CSC effectuated a reverse stock split, intended to result in the corporation redeeming Briggs' 25% stock interest at its book value of $769,814. Briggs claims that he is entitled to fair value, and the parties agreed that Delaware law governs.

Battle of experts

Briggs called one expert, Gilbert Matthews, who estimated the value of Briggs' stock at $10,000,000 or more. CSC called Robert Stillman to rebut Matthews and David Fischel, who estimated the value of Briggs' stock between $666,000 and $1,345,000.

Matthews used a multiple of EBITDA and a DCF analysis. Fischel used a multiple of EBITDA and a "roll-forward" analysis, based on tracking public companies alleged to be comparable. The court found the multiple of EBITDA to be the better analytical procedure in the particular case.

Multiple from prior acquisitions

After much discussion by experts, the court settled on a projected EBITDA figure of $8,800,000. It decided on a multiple of 3.375, based on multiples paid by CSC in two prior acquisitions, which accounted for essentially all of the company's operations at the valuation date.

This resulted in an invested capital value of $29,700,000. After subtracting debt, the value was $25,000,000, or $6,250,000 for a 25% interest on a pro rata basis before considering discounts. The amount was corroborated by an alleged offer for the company of between $30 and $35 million, less debt.

Minority discount a big issue

The final issue was a minority discount. The court recognized that "There is no question that a minority interest in a corporation is worth less than a majority interest.... A 25% to 30% discount is a common figure. Briggs does not dispute this economic fact of life. His position is that Delaware law forbids a minority discount in situations such as this."

The laws governing reverse split cash-outs is found at 8 Del. C.5 155. There are no cases directly on point under this statute. The law governing cash-out mergers is found at 8 Del. C.5 262, and case law under that section has not allowed minority discounts.

Reverse split and merger laws similar

The court concluded that the language under the two statutes is similar and that "Delaware laws does not allow for a minority discount for reverse stock split cash-outs.... The court therefore evaluates Briggs' 25% interest in CSC to be $6,250,000."

Settles v. Leslie

Citation: 701 N.E.2d 849, 1998 Ind. App. LEXIS 1959
Court: Court of Appeals
State/Jurisdiction: Indiana
Date of decision: November 6, 1998
Judge: Sullivan

Plaintiffs were minority shareholders of Mi-Tech Metals, Inc., an Indiana corporation. In 1994, the board of directors of Mi-Tech negotiated a merger with Birco, Incorporated. After receiving notice of a Special Meeting of Shareholders to vote on the proposed merger, the plaintiffs filed a Complaint for Accounting and sought a temporary restraining order preventing the directors from voting on the merger. The complaint alleged that the majority shareholders breached their fiduciary duty owed to the minority shareholders by misappropriating corporate funds. Plaintiffs' temporary restraining order was denied.

Notice of Dissent filed

At the shareholders' meeting, plaintiffs gave the directors a written Notice of Dissent stating that they opposed the merger and they estimated the value of their stock in Mi-Tech to be

$19,018.40 per share. The merger was approved and the corporation mailed each plaintiff a Notice of Dissenter's Rights. The notice required plaintiffs to tender their stock to Mi-Tech in exchange for $14,000 per share. Plaintiffs didn't tender their stock or demand payment at that time. Rather, they chose to pursue their Complaint for Accounting.

Judicial appraisal remedy exclusive

Defendants claimed in their Answer that plaintiffs were not entitled to an accounting and that their exclusive remedy was a judicial appraisal under Indiana Code 23-1-44-1 to -20. Thereafter, defendants moved for summary judgment on the same grounds, which was granted.

The court held that the Indiana dissenters' rights statutes provided that the dissenting shareholders were entitled to receive fair value for their stock. It further found that plaintiffs' exclusive remedy for obtaining fair value was a judicial appraisal.

Appraisal accounts for fraud

This remedy is exclusive even where the plaintiffs allege breach of fiduciary duty and fraud because the appraisers can take those claims into account in determining the value of the stock.

Summary judgment granted

The plaintiffs failed to exercise this remedy and the court refused to allow them to "circumvent the legislature's chosen mechanism for evaluating the value of stock held by dissenting shareholders." Because plaintiffs' failure was dispositive of the issue before the court, it concluded that there was no genuine issue of material fact and the trial court properly granted summary judgment for defendants.

G & N Aircraft, Inc. and Paul Goldsmith v. Erich Boehm

Citation: 703 N.E.2d 665 (Ind. Ct. App. 1998)
Court: Court of Appeals
State/Jurisdiction: Indiana
Date of decision: November 30, 1998
Judge: Baker

The following court case abstract was originally published in Valuation Case Digest®

In *G & N Aircraft, Inc. and Paul Goldsmith v. Erich Boehm*, 703 N.E.2d 665 (Ind. Ct. App. 1998), the Indiana Court of Appeals considered whether a minority shareholder could recover

G & N Aircraft, Inc. and Paul Goldsmith v. Erich Boehm

the fair value of his interest when the majority shareholder destroyed the value of the minority's interest. Goldsmith, Boehm and two others were members of a consortium who owned and operated G & N Aircraft. Prior to these events, Boehm held 34%, the largest interest in the business. Besides G & N, Goldsmith, a 26% shareholder, held interests or controlled entities which supplied G & N and rented it space. These other businesses suffered losses in the 1990's while G & N profited. The losses made Goldsmith personally liable for his companies' outstanding loans. In order to avoid being personally liable, Goldsmith sought professional advice. His accountant suggested that he merge his corporations, including G & N, into one entity in order to set off the losses with G & N's profits. To that end, Goldsmith formed a plan to gain control of the corporation which included raising G & N's rent by $13,500 per month as well as threatening liquidation of his other related companies. The remaining shareholders, except Boehm, sold their interest in G & N to Goldsmith, who then held over 59% of G & N. As a result of Boehm's refusal to sell, Goldsmith changed the locks, refused Boehm admittance to the premises, and transferred the accounting records to another of his companies. Boehm then brought a minority shareholder and derivative action suit against Goldsmith and G & N for breach of fiduciary duty among other claims.

The trial court found both Goldsmith and G & N liable for breach of fiduciary duty. It ordered Goldsmith and G & N to repurchase Boehm's shares. The court received testimony from both parties' expert witnesses regarding the value of the interest. The court determined that Boehm should receive the fair value of his interest or his pro rata interest in business' total value. It awarded him $521,319. It rejected both the application of a minority interest discount to G & N's fair value or a fair market valuation of Boehm's interest. The trial court additionally awarded Boehm 34% of G & N's corporate income until Boehm's stock had been repurchased as damages for G & N's breach of fiduciary duty. The court further awarded Boehm $175,000 in punitive damages against Goldsmith for his oppressive conduct. Goldsmith and G & N appealed all the damage awards.

Goldsmith first argued that the trial court erred in ordering the buyout of Boehm's interest in G & N because the dissenter's rights statute precludes recovery when a merger or sale did not occur. The appellate court agreed, but found that "[I]nasmuch as no merger occurred here, the statutory dissenter's remedy could not properly be invoked. Moreover, there is nothing contained in the dissenter's right statute which would foreclose a buyout remedy for activities which effectively force one into a minority position and then destroy the value of an individual's stock." Thus, the appellate court affirmed the court-ordered buyout of Boehm's interest at fair value. It defined fair value as "the value of the stock of a closely held corporation valued as if 100% of the stock is being sold and where oppression of a minority shareholder exists." It further affirmed the court's denial of any discount for minority interest. The appellate court also affirmed the award of punitive damages against Goldsmith for his oppressive conduct as the majority shareholder.

G & N appealed the order requiring it to pay Boehm 34% of the corporate income since the freezeout. It claimed that it did not distribute dividends because it could not afford to pay them. The appellate court disagreed. It concluded that G & N stated that dividends could not be paid because the corporation was repaying its bank debt and purchasing new equipment. However, Boehm showed that neither of those reasons had been acted upon. The court affirmed the trial court's order, noting that "it is apparent that such an award was for the ongoing injury sustained by Boehm which simply served as a mechanism to enforce the court's order that G & N and Goldsmith purchase Boehm's stock."

Demoulas v. Demoulas

Citation: 428 Mass. 555, 703 N.E.2d 1149, 1998 Mass. LEXIS 712
Court: Supreme Judicial Court
State/Jurisdiction: Massachusetts
Date of decision: December 22, 1998
Judge: Greaney

Stock sold at inadequate price by coexecutor of estate

Plaintiffs filed this shareholder derivative action seeking damages against defendant Telemachus Demoulas for fraud, conversion, and breach of fiduciary duty arising out of his conduct as coexecutor of the estate of George Demoulas. Telemachus allegedly sold stock owned by the estate to himself and family members at an inadequate price, to the detriment of plaintiffs who were beneficiaries of the estate.

The valuation issue presented in this case was whether the trial judge properly admitted and considered evidence of the "fair value" of the stock sold in determining liability of the defendant for fraud, conversion and breach of fiduciary duty. Telemachus argued that "fair value" evidence should not be considered "because that valuation technique does not discount for a minority interest or poor marketability of closely held interests." Rather, he argued, the court should only have considered the "fair market value" of the stock for purposes of determining whether the price he sold the stock for was inadequate. "Fair market value" does include minority interest and marketability discounts.

'Fair value' prevails over 'fair market value'

The appellate court held that the trial court properly considered "fair value" rather than "fair market value" in the circumstances of this case. The court said:

> There is no reason in this case ... that evidence of the undiscounted value would not have relevance. ... Evidence of undiscounted value thus has probative force, because the minority interests might not have chosen to sell to Telemachus and his family at discounted values if full disclosure had been made. Therefore, evidence of fair value tended to show a violation of the obligations on Telemachus' part, and tended to show

that he was self-dealing in a way which failed to obtain the "best possible price" for the assets transferred from George's estate.

Ely, Inc. v. Wiley

Citation: 587 N.W.2d 465, 1998 Iowa Sup. LEXIS 293
Court: Supreme Court
State/Jurisdiction: Iowa
Date of decision: December 23, 1998
Judge: Carter

Ely, Inc. was formed by Wiley and others to develop and sell a process for grinding coal and other substances into fine powder for power plants. After four years in the development stage, the company experienced operating cash reserve problems and substantial net losses. After considering its options, the board of directors opted to accept an offer made by Fuller Corporation to purchase substantially all of the assets of the corporation. Wiley was the only shareholder to vote against acceptance of the offer to purchase, and perfected a dissent from the transaction with respect to his 12% minority interest in the corporation.

The corporation offered Wiley $24,200 (12% of cash reserves) plus an assignment of 12% of future royalties to be received from Fuller Corporation. Wiley rejected this offer and sought judicial determination of the fair value of his stock under Iowa Code § 490.1302 (1993).

Experts testify on fair value

Ely's expert witness, Paul Much of Houlihan, Lokey, Howard & Zukin, testified that the sale transaction with Fuller Corporation was an accurate reflection of the fair value of Wiley's stock. He opined that Wiley's stock was worth what the corporation had offered for it.

Wiley's expert witness, Yale Kramer of McGladrey & Pullen, CPAs, testified that the sale transaction was not an accurate reflection of fair value. He opined that Wiley's stock was worth 40 cents per share, or $378,714 for his interest. He based his opinion on a combination of factors, "many of which included affirmations of the value of the company and its stock by the corporation's own financial analysts or analysts employed by the controlling shareholder."

Compulsion sale not evidence of fair value

The trial court accepted the valuation opined by Kramer and held that the fair value of Wiley's stock was 40 cents per share. It rejected the opinion of Much on the grounds that the sale transaction with Fuller Corporation was made under compulsion and was therefore not an arms-length transaction, or an accurate reflection of fair value.

Trial court not bound by formula

The Iowa Court of Appeals reversed on the grounds that the trial court had not adequately considered the testimony of Much or assigned it any weight in the fair value determination. The Iowa Supreme Court reversed the Court of Appeals ruling, and upheld the trial courts determination of fair value. The Supreme Court rejected the reasoning of the Court of Appeals:

> The second opinion of the court of appeals appears to require the district court to assign some weighted value to the Much valuation testimony, however imperfect the trier of fact finds it to be, and to apply that weighted value in some formula that the court derives to determine the fair value from all of the evidence. That is precisely what this court has decided triers of fact in fair value cases do not have to do.

Value based on pre-litigation projections more reliable

The Supreme Court further found that the trial courts determination that Kramer's testimony was more reliable and more credible was supported by substantial evidence in the record. Further, his valuation was based upon projections made by the corporation "at a time when there was no threat of litigation."

Pacific Telecom, Inc. v. Gabelli Funds, Inc.

Citation: 1998 U.S. App. LEXIS 33130
Court: Court of Appeals
State/Jurisdiction: 9th Circuit Federal
Date of decision: December 30, 1998
Judge: Canby

In this unpublished memorandum opinion, the Ninth Circuit reversed the district court's appraisal of the fair value of Gabelli's shares of Pacific Telecom, Inc.

The district court adopted a per-share value advanced by PTI's experts, who did not incorporate third party sale value into their calculations. This was error.

Where, as here, there is evidence of third party sale value in the record it must be considered if relevant. The district court did not consider this evidence for the erroneous reason that it believed that it was prohibited from considering third party sale value by Washington and Delaware law.

The court reversed and remanded with instructions to reappraise the shares.

# In re 75,629 Shares of Common Stock of Trapp Family Lodge, Inc.

Citation: 169 Vt. 82, 725 A.2d 927, 1999 Vt. LEXIS 5
Court: Supreme Court
State/Jurisdiction: Vermont
Date of decision: January 15, 1999
Judge: Johnson

Trapp Family Lodge, Inc. (TFL) gave notice of a special meeting of shareholders to vote on a proposed merger. Several shareholders filed a notice stating their opposition to the merger and demanding fair value for their shares. The merger was approved, and the dissenters tendered their shares along with a demand for payment. TFL paid the dissenters $33.84 per share based upon the expert valuation of Arthur Haut, CPA. The dissenters demanded $61.00 per share, and TFL, unwilling to pay that price, filed this dissenters' rights action seeking judicial determination of the fair value of the stock.

CPA and CFA testify to value, methods used

At trial, Haut testified that the dissenters' stock was worth $33.84 per share. In reaching this value, Haut divided TFL's assets into three groups. He used the capitalized cash flow method to value the lodge operations, relied upon an outside real estate appraisal to value the excess land, and discounted the option price to present value to value the guest house options.

The dissenters' expert witness, Howard Gordon, CFA, of Gordon Associates, Inc., testified that the stock was worth $63.44 per share, which he reached by averaging the results of two different valuation approaches. To reach this value:

> Gordon... conducted his appraisal using a net asset value approach; he used different methods to arrive at the values for individual assets, which were the lodge, the guest house option, the other guest house subsidiary assets, the royalties, and the excess land. Gordon used two methods to determine the value of the lodge. First, he used a discounted cash flow method; the value of the lodge added to the value of TFL's other assets resulted in a share value of $64.00. Second, Gordon recalculated the net asset value using a prior real estate appraisal by Frank Bredice for the lodge; the Bredice value of the lodge added to the other TFL assets resulted in a share value of $62.67.

TFL argues improper methodology adopted

The court determined the fair value of the stock to be $63.44 per share. TFL appealed, citing four errors by the trial court:
- Rejecting the valuation of Haut and adopting the valuation of Gordon;

- Failing to consider the tax consequences of a hypothetical sale of all TFL's assets;
- Refusing to give weight to the "agreed values" stated in a shareholders agreement; and
- Applying a 30% control premium.

The court thoroughly reviewed TFL's four main objections to Gordon's valuation, which were based on elements of his methodology, and held that they were without merit. The court rejected Haut's valuation because it "lacked the thoroughness and credibility of Gordon's valuation." The Supreme Court held that the trial courts reliance on Gordon and rejection of Haut were supported by the evidence and not clearly erroneous.

Tax consequences of sale not relevant for going concern value

The Vermont Supreme Court held that trial court was correct in not considering tax consequences.

Under the dissenter's rights statute, the court is required to value the corporation as a "going concern." *Weinberger*, 457 A.2d at 713. Accordingly, courts have generally rejected any tax discount "unless the corporation is undergoing an actual liquidation." *Hansen*, 957 P.2d at 42.

Shareholder agreement values not evidence of fair value

The Vermont Supreme Court held that trial court correctly disregarded the "agreed values" of the stock as stated in a shareholders agreement because they "were based upon the fair market value for minority interest shares and were not timely representations of fair value of the shares in January 1995."

Control premium appropriate to adjust for use of minority values

The trial court applied a 30% control premium in determining the fair value of the stock.

Because Gordon's valuation was based on publicly-traded minority interest values, he applied a control premium to account for the value of owning the lodge as a whole. For the same reason, Haut also applied a control premium in his valuation.

The Supreme Court upheld the use of the control premium because it was supported by the testimony of both experts.

Hansen v. 75 Ranch Company (II)

Citation: Musselshell County No. DV-95-23
Court: District Court
State/Jurisdiction: Montana
Date of decision: February 1, 1999
Judge: McKeon

The controlling shareholder of 75 Ranch Company sold the company's major asset, a Montana ranch, and bought an Arizona ranch. The controlling stockholder did not provide the minority shareholders with notice of the proposed exchange, "a failure to substantially comply with the applicable statute," and did not submit copies of the exchange documents for shareholder approval.

The control owner offered $14.63 per share, based on book value less a 30% minority discount. The minority shareholders counter offered at $20.90 per share, excluding the discount. The control owner countered at $15.

Stockholders' agreement or dissent statute?

A major issue on appeal to the Montana Supreme Court was whether the stockholder agreement applied or the exchange transaction gave rise to dissenters' rights governed by the Montana Business Corporation Act. The Supreme Court found that the minority shareholders were entitled to statutory notice of their dissenters' rights.

The court also prohibited the consideration of a minority discount when establishing fair value.

Because we have determined that the Montana Business Corporation Act controls, we further conclude that the Minority Shareholders are entitled to "fair value" in accordance with the statutes, rather than "fair market value" as provided in the Stockholder Agreement.

Supreme Court overruled previous decision

In reaching this conclusion, the Montana Supreme Court overruled its own decision in a 1996 shareholder oppression suit:

> In McCann Ranch, we held that nothing in § 35-1-826(4), MCA, prohibits consideration of a minority shareholder's lack of control and lack of marketability for minority shares when establishing "fair value." McCann Ranch, 915 P.2d at 242-43. We further reasoned that "[a] discount for a minority interest is appropriate when the minority shareholder has no ability to control salaries, dividends, profit distributions and day-to-day corporate operations." McCann Ranch, 915 P.2d at 243 (citations omitted). However, the majority of courts addressing the issue of minority discounts has held

that discounts should not be taken when determining fair value of minority shares sold to another shareholder or to the corporation. See John J. Oitzinger, Fair Price and Fair Play Under the Montana Business Corporation Act, 58 Mont. L.Rev. 407, 420 n. 82 (1997). These courts clarify that discounts at the shareholder level are inherently unfair to the minority shareholder who did not pick the timing of the transaction and is not in the position of a willing seller. Thus, these courts hold that a dissenting shareholder's position should be the equivalent of what it would have been had the fundamental change not occurred. Moreover, they reason that valuing the shares at less than their proportionate share of the corporation's fair value produces a transfer of wealth from the minority shareholder to the shareholders in control. Oitzinger, 58 Mont. L.Rev. 420-21 (citing In re McLoon Oil Co. (Me.1989), 565 A.2d 997, 1005). We find the policies expressed by these courts compelling and therefore overrule our decision in McCann Ranch to the extent that it holds that a minority discount is appropriate when calculating "fair value" for the sale of a minority shareholders shares in a closely-held corporation to a majority shareholder or to the corporation (emphasis supplied).

Supplemental testimony heard on remand

On remand, the district court heard supplemental testimony by expert valuation witnesses on the issue of "fair value." It rejected the income approach in favor of the asset value approach:

> In this case, the most appropriate and equitable valuation method for determining "fair value" is the asset value approach. An income or earnings approach is too speculative and subject to manipulation... In valuing shares for other purposes, the Stockholders Agreement contemplated an asset value approach.

No capital gains tax deduction

Even though the asset approach reflected substantial appreciation in land and buildings, the district court disallowed any tax discount. This position seemed clearly pursuant to language in the Supreme Court opinion:

> On remand, the District Court must determine "fair value" as opposed to "fair market value." In deciding whether to assess costs of the exchange or apply a tax discount in the "fair value" analysis, the court must bear in mind that "fair value," as explained above, means the value of the shares immediately before the effectuation of the corporate action to which the dissenter objects. Thus, if costs are incurred after effectuation of the exchange, those costs should not be assessed against the dissenting shareholders. Likewise, as to applying a tax discount, in cases arising under appraisal statutes, courts have recognized that "ordinarily when dissenting stock is accorded net asset value, that value is to be determined by considering the corporation as a going concern and not as if it is undergoing liquidation." Tinio, 48 A.L.R.3d at 465.

Plaintiffs awarded experts fees

The district court concluded, "Based on the asset value approach, the value of Plaintiff's dissenting shares in 75 Ranch is $28.09 per share," compared with $20.90 that plaintiff's had earlier offered to accept. The court awarded plaintiffs 7% interest (the company's bank borrowing rate) from Jan. 29, 1993 until the date of payment.

75 Ranch was assessed $11,220 for the plaintiff's reasonable expert appraisal fees for the failure to provide notice of the proposed exchange. They required 50% of the award to each of the two minority shareholder plaintiffs (50% of $195,495.16 each) to be paid within 90 days, with the option of amortizing the balance over four years.

Tifft v. Stevens

Citation: 162 Or. App. 62, 987 P.2d 1, 1999 Ore. App. LEXIS 1373
Court: Court of Appeals
State/Jurisdiction: Oregon
Date of decision: March 11, 1999
Judge: De Muniz

VPI, a custom manufacturing corporation, was formed by three shareholders. Stevens initially held 51%, and the other two 24.5% each. A Buy-Sell Agreement provided that each would be a director and an officer, and that no director or officer could be removed or reduced in compensation without 70% agreement. The Buy-Sell also provided that no shareholder would engage in similar business or deal with VPI customers.

Soon after formation, Tifft proposed that the company engage in product design, and not just custom manufacture, but was told by the two others that the liability risk was too high and that if he wanted to do design work he should do so on his own. Thereafter Tifft formed a design company. For five years he subbed out the parts manufacture to VPI, and sold the finished parts to a VPI customer, all with knowledge of both of the other shareholders.

Tensions rise among parties

Stevens formed his own company and imposed an onerous build-to-suit lease on VPI, which Tifft protested, but he did not take legal action. Stevens personally purchased, and rented to VPI on an hourly basis, a large press, which competed for VPI parts business with VPI-owned presses. Tifft objected, but acquiesced.

Serious tension developed when Stevens wanted changes in the Buy-Sell Agreement to accommodate his personal estate planning objectives, but did not want to make other changes desired by the minority in exchange. Stevens, who controlled VPI's finances, threatened to discontinue sub-S distributions if the minority did not agree. Stevens then unilaterally terminated one of the minority shareholders as an officer and employee, asserting that he had misused a company charge account.

When the two minority directors voted to reinstate the dischargee, to require a sub-S reserve, and to form a special committee to review VPI's business with Stevens' separately owned company, Stevens refused to comply, and called a shareholders' meeting where he voted his shares to overrule each of the Board's actions. Stevens unilaterally caused VPI to sue the discharged employee for breach of the non-competition portion of their agreement, and then negotiated a settlement under which Stevens personally purchased his stock (giving Stevens over 70%). As part of the settlement, Stevens obtained agreement by the other shareholder to breach Tifft's first refusal right to his pro rata portion of the shares. Thereafter Stevens refused to pay Tifft any bonuses as had been the prior years' practice, and excluded him from decision-making.

Minority claims oppressive conduct

When Tifft sued Stevens for oppressive conduct under ORS 60.661, Stevens and VPI (controlled by Stevens) countered by suing Tifft under the non-compete agreement and non-solicitation clauses in the Buy-Sell Agreement because of Tifft's design business, even though Stevens had known of the business for six years, and VPI had benefited from it.

Trial court finds non-compete unenforceable, pattern of oppression

The non-compete provisions of the buy-sell agreement are no longer enforceable by either party because of both parties' mutual and long-standing acceptance of actions in apparent violation.

Stevens engaged in oppressive conduct under ORS 60.661 based on his sustained course of conduct. The court emphasized the withholding of subchapter S distributions to force amendments to the Buy-Sell, and Stevens' agreement with the other shareholder to violate provisions of the Buy-Sell beneficial to plaintiff. *Iwasaki v. Iwasaki Bros.*, 58 Or App 543, 649 P2d 598 (1982), was distinguished because here there was no evidence of a legitimate corporate purpose for withholding the sub-S payments, and the parties clearly had agreed VPI would fund them. In addition, decision on sub-S should have been made by the Board of Directors, not Stevens unilaterally.

Other breaches included Stevens' actions precluding VPI from redeeming stock at a beneficial price, pursuit of litigation on behalf of VPI without Board approval or co-shareholder consent, and settlement on a basis personally advantageous to himself. The court found that the onerous building lease and Stevens' unfair profits on press rental were oppressive, but, based apparently on Tifft's prior acquiescence, relied on these facts only as indicating a pattern of conduct sufficiently serious to require a remedy.

The trial court's order compelling the majority to buy out Tifft's stock at appraised fair value, excluding any minority or marketability discounts, was affirmed. The court treated Tifft's claims for additional damages for individual breaches of fiduciary duty as subsumed under the buy-out remedy.

Minority discount issue not contested on appeal

Stevens did not contest on appeal the valuation methodology applied by the trial court (Greg Gilbert of Corporate Valuations for plaintiff and Ralph Arnold, III, of Arnold & Olds for defendant), although that was a strongly contested issue at trial. Under *Chiles v. Robertson*, 94 Or App 604, 767 P2d 903 (1989), a court-ordered buy-out for oppression is to be valued without either minority or marketability discounts. By contrast, a valuation under the dissenter's appraisal statute, while excluding a minority discount, will include a marketability discount. See *Columbia Management Co. v. Wyss*, 94 Or App 195, 765 P2d 207 (1989).

Pink v. Cambridge Acquisition, Inc.

Citation: 126 Md. App. 61, 727 A.2d 414, 1999 Md. App. LEXIS 60
Court: Court of Appeals
State/Jurisdiction: Maryland
Date of decision: April 9, 1999
Judge: Smith

Minority shareholders were forced to give up their shares of Cambridge, Inc. stock in a management buyout. Cambridge Acquisition, Inc. was formed to effectuate the buyout. The minority shareholders were to receive $40 per share for their stock.

In this appeal, the shareholders challenge a trial court ruling that terminated their efforts to exercise their judicial appraisal rights.

The shareholders mailed a demand for payment of fair value for their shares to Cambridge Acquisition, Inc. and named Cambridge Acquisition, Inc. as defendant in the Petition for Appraisal to Determine Fair Value of Stock. However, Cambridge Acquisition, Inc. was not the proper defendant. Rather, Cambridge, Inc. was the "successor" corporation that should have been named in the demand and Petition. The shareholders subsequently sent an amended demand to Cambridge, Inc. and filed an Amended Petition correctly naming Cambridge, Inc.

Cambridge Acquisition, Inc. filed a Motion to Dismiss, or alternatively, for Summary Judgment. Cambridge Acquisition, Inc. and Cambridge, Inc. also filed a joint Motion to Dismiss or to Strike Amended Petition. The trial court granted the first motion and ruled that the second motion was unnecessary.

The Court of Appeals held that trial court did not properly resolve the rights of Cambridge, Inc. because it was not a party to the first motion. The trial court order was vacated and the case was remanded for a ruling in compliance with the Court of Appeals opinion.

The main issue, according to the Court of Appeals, was that the statute granting appraisal rights are in derogation of common law and therefore must be strictly construed. The shareholders' second demand and Petition were not filed within the time allowed in the statute and therefore the shareholders' action was time barred. To address this issue, the trial court should have granted the second Motion to Dismiss filed by both Cambridge Acquisition, Inc. and Cambridge, Inc.

Le Beau v. M.G. Bancorporation

Citation: 737 A.2d 513, 1999 Del. LEXIS 143
Court: Supreme Court
State/Jurisdiction: Delaware
Date of decision: April 30, 1999
Judge: Holland

Delaware court relies on comparable acquisition method[1]

Vice Chancellor Jacobs issued an opinion with respect to the appraisal of a bank holding company. MGB had squeezed out its public shareholders at $41 per share in 1993 and had received a fairness opinion from Alex Shesunoff & Co. Investment Bankers. No weight was given to that opinion in the appraisal, as Shesunoff had determined only the "fair market value" of MGB's minority shares rather than their pro rata share of enterprise value [fair value]. Respondent's expert, David Clarke, valued MGB at not less than $85 per share, while petitioner's expert, Robert Reilly of Willamette Management, valued it at $41.90 per share.

The Vice Chancellor stated:

> The fact that Reilly's fair value determination serendipitously turned out to be only 90 cents more than Shesunoff's legally flawed $41 valuation cannot help but render Respondent's valuation position highly suspect and meriting the most careful judicial scrutiny. As a matter of plain common sense, it would appear a proper fair value determination, based on a going concern valuation of the entire company, would significantly exceed a $41 per share fair market valuation of only a minority block of its shares [emphasis in original].

---

1 This abstract of *Le Beau v. M. G. Bancorporation, Inc.* has comments by Gil Matthews, Senior Managing Director and Chairman of the Board, Sutter Securities Incorporated.

Le Beau v. M.G. Bancorporation

Public price may exceed control value

GM Comment: Although this "common sense" assumption may be true some of the time, there certainly are many occasions when the market for publicly-traded shares may exceed their pro rata share of fair value for the entire company, and this criticism of Reilly appears be questionable.

The Court observed, "Neither side contests the validity per se of either the comparative publicly-traded company or the DCF valuation approaches. Both sides claim that the other improperly applied these methodologies to MGB." In contrast to most Delaware appraisal cases, the Court rejected both discounted cash flow and comparable company analysis because of perceived errors, and chose not to adjust the valuations for such alleged errors. It relied on a comparable acquisition analysis, a methodology used only by Clarke. The Vice Chancellor concluded that, "because the Court has rejected the parties valuations based on their other methodologies, by process of elimination the only evidence of MGBs fair value is the $85 per share Clarke arrived at by the comparative acquisition method."

Court rejects both discount rates

Clarke used a 12% equity discount rate for his DCF computation, while Reilly used 18%. Clarke's small stock premium was 1%, based on a 1996 Ibbotson study which was specific to banks; the Court rejected Clarke's DCF because the study on which he relied was prepared after the 1993 merger date.

Reilly's small stock premium of 5.2% came from a 1992 Ibbotson study which was not specific to banks, and he increased his discount rate slightly for certain unspecified material risks. The Court noted that Shesunoff had used 10%, and described Reilly's discount rate as "inappropriately high" and not specifically related to banks.

The Court did not reach its own conclusion as to discount rate and, unlike some other cases, neither attempted to do its own DCF calculation nor requested the parties to calculate DCF value based on Court-determined assumptions.

Court rejects MVIC multiples

Reilly used a comparable company method which the Court described as a capital market approach. Reilly derived multiples from selected publicly-traded companies, and applied those multiples to MGB's EBIT, EBIDT and other financial measures. Respondents challenged this method as impermissible because it included a built-in minority discount, and also claimed that multiples of net income and book value, rather than MVIC multiples, are generally accepted by the financial community for purposes of valuing bank holding companies. The Court concurred with both objections, although it noted that MVIC multiples are commonly used in valuing companies in other industries.

Chapter 7: Court Case Abstracts

Court prefers local comparables

The Court preferred Clarke's comparables, which were banks having geographic locations and demographic factors similar to those of MGB's two bank subsidiaries. Reilly included some companies outside MGB's geographic location, in different economic environments. The Vice Chancellor wrote, "Clarke used historical financial data going back five years before the Merger, whereas Reilly used historical financial data going back 2.75 years [because of changes in the banking environment]. In performing bank valuations, five year historical information is typically used."

GM Comment: Based on security analysts' reports and on investment banking valuations published in recent years, it appears that the use of five years data for bank valuations is rare rather than typical.

Must use prices at time of merger

Clarke used market prices for his comparables from six weeks before the merger, while Reilly utilized prices on the day before the merger. Because Reilly's approach was correct, "the Court cannot accept Clarke's comparative company analysis, despite the validity of the technique itself."

The Court stated the "merger date (more specifically, the date before the public announcement of a merger) is normally the time that is relevant" to an appraisal.

GM Comment: The Courts parenthetical phrase appears to be in error. The valuation date for an appraisal is unrelated to the announcement date, which is normally weeks or months before the merger date. It also seems to be extreme to disregard totally the comparable company analysis because of a six-week difference, rather than adjusting for changes in the market; however, the record may have been inadequate to make such adjustment. Moreover, the Court in this case accepted the comparable acquisition method, even though most such transactions are much more than six weeks prior to the merger date.

Control premium misapplied

The Court, in summarizing Clarke's testimony, said that he "determined that during the period January 1989 through June 1993, acquirers of controlling interests in publicly-traded companies paid an average premium of at least 35%. On that basis, Clarke concluded that a 35% premium was appropriate, and applied that premium to the values he had determined for Greenwood and WBC [MGB's subsidiaries] ..."

GM Comment: This approach is flawed in several ways. First, the historical premiums over market are a biased sample; the universe includes situations in which a buyer was willing to pay a premium over market for acquiring a company, but obviously cannot include situations in which a company is considered by prospective acquirers to be fully priced in the market, and therefore no bid is made. Secondly, the survey is necessarily based only on publicly traded companies, as no market data is available for private companies or wholly owned subsidiaries (such as

Greenwood and WBC). Thirdly, the premiums are calculated in relation to market price (which often includes a minority discount), not fair value. Fourth, the premium which a buyer would pay in an acquisition results from the buyers' valuation; the premium is not the cause which determines the amount of his bid.

Clarke also added a 35% premium to his DCF calculation.

GM Comment: As the DCF methodology calculates the entire value of future cash flows, it is clearly improper to apply a control premium to a DCF calculation.

As the Vice Chancellor rejected Clarke's comparable company and DCF valuations, he did not directly address Clarke's arbitrary addition of 35% premium in those valuations.

Court accepts acquisition method

Based on Clarke's adjustments to Shesunoff's 1993 valuation (i.e. excluding Shesunoff's minority discount and updating data to the merger date), the Court pointed out, "if (for purposes of illustration) a 20% control premium were added, the resulting value would be…$82.57 per share; and if the premium were 35%, the resulting value would be … $91.66 per share."

GM Comment: This statement disregards the double-counting resulting from elimination of a minority discount and addition of an arbitrary premium. The comment appears to be a rationalization of the $85 conclusion, rather than a factor considered in the Courts analysis.

The comparable acquisition method has often been rejected in Delaware appraisals as impermissibly including a control premium. However, the Vice Chancellor noted that, in *Harris v. Rapid American*, "the Supreme Court ruled that a holding company's ownership of a controlling interest in its subsidiaries is an independent element of value that must be taken into account in determining a fair value for the parent company."

Although the respondents argued that this decision should apply only to subsidiaries operating in different businesses, the Vice Chancellor disagreed.

GM Comment: This reasoning leads to the absurd conclusion that a business conducted through a subsidiary is entitled to a control premium, but an identical business conducted through a division is not! The application of a control premium at a subsidiary level, when such premium is not permitted at the parent level, is an anomaly that is difficult to justify.

Chapter 7: Court Case Abstracts

Le Beau v. M.G. Bancorporation/Nebel v. Southwest Bancorp, Inc.

Citation: 737 A.2d 513, 1999 Del. LEXIS 143
1999 Del. Ch. LEXIS 30
Court: Supreme Court and Court of Chancery
State/Jurisdiction: Delaware
Date of decision: April 30, 1999
March 9, 1999
Judge: Holland Jacobs

M.G. Bancorporation (MGB) was merged into its 91.68% stockholder parent Southwest Bancorp, Inc. (SWB) in a short form cash-out merger on November 17, 1993. SWB hired Alex Sheshunoff & Co. Investment Bankers to determine the "fair market value" of the MGB shares to be cashed out. Based on the Sheshunoff appraisal, the merger consideration offered to the minority shareholders was $41 per share. This corporate action spawned two separate cases: a judicial appraisal suit (*M.G. Bancorporation v. Le Beau*) and a breach of fiduciary duty class action suit (*Nebel v. Southwest Bancorp, Inc.*).

Breach of fiduciary duty class action suit not dismissed

The plaintiff in this class action, on behalf of all the minority shareholders of MGB, attacked the merger with SWB on three grounds:

1. Substantive unfairness,
2. Disclosure violations, and
3. A "wrong page" claim, based upon the inclusion of another state's appraisal statute in the notice of merger.

Defendants filed a Motion to Dismiss for failure to state a claim upon which relief could be granted. In a memorandum opinion dated July 5, 1995, the Chancery Court granted the motion with respect to the substantive unfairness and disclosure violation claims, but not the "wrong page" claim. Plaintiff subsequently filed two Amended Complaints. The Second Amended Complaint is at issue in the present memorandum opinion of the Chancery Court following defendants' most recent Motion to Dismiss.

No independent committee

Based upon the law of the case doctrine, the Chancery Court granted defendants' motion with respect to the claims that had been dismissed by the July 5, 1995 memorandum opinion. However, the court held that the substantive unfairness allegations now stated a claim upon which relief could be granted. The court concluded that, the new allegations in the Second Amended Complaint are now sufficient to state cognizable claims of 'unfair dealing' and 'unfair price.'

In assessing the validity of the substantive unfairness claims, at least two factors are pivotal. The first is the defendants' failure to establish an independent committee of directors to represent the minority stockholders' interests. . . . [I]n the s 253 context the absence of a negotiating committee of independent directors, without more, does not constitute unfair dealing as a matter of law. Nonetheless, that circumstance is evidence of unfair dealing that, when combined with other pleaded facts, may state a cognizable unfair dealing claim that the fiduciaries will ultimately have the duty to negate.

The second critical factor, of which the Court takes judicial notice, is that the fair value of the plaintiffs' shares has now been adjudicated at $85 per share [in the judicial appraisal action]. The significant gap between the $41 merger price and the $85 appraisal value, combined with the other substantive unfairness allegations (including the improper manner in which the $41 merger price was arrived at), create an inference that the Merger was the product of unfair dealing.

Opinions of value in the judicial appraisal suit

The minority shareholders initiated appraisal proceedings pursuant to 8 Del. C. § 262. At trial both sides presented expert testimony regarding the value of the stock.

The shareholders' expert, David Clarke, of The Griffing Group, Inc., used three methods to value the stock:
- The comparative publicly-traded company approach,
- The discounted cash flow method, and
- The comparative acquisitions approach.

Clarke also applied a control premium to reflect the fact that MGB held a controlling interest in its two subsidiaries. He testified, based on his analysis, that the fair value of the MGB stock was $85 per share.

The shareholders also introduced evidence regarding the Sheshunoff appraisal revised to exclude the minority discount so that it reflected "fair value" instead of "fair market value."

The corporations' expert, Robert F. Reilly, of Willamette Management Associates, used two methods to value the stock:
- The discounted cash flow method, and
- A "capital market" analysis.

Reilly did not apply a control premium, as Clarke did, because he viewed MGB as only a holding company and therefore he opined that a control premium was not appropriate. Based upon his analysis, Reilly testified that the fair value of the MGB stock was $41.90 per share.

Chancery Court value upheld

Based upon the evidence before it, the Court of Chancery held that the fair value of the MGB stock was $85 per share. The corporation appealed, and the Delaware Supreme Court upheld the Chancery Court's findings and valuation of the stock.

The primary basis of the court's holding was the doctrine of collateral estoppel.

> In the context of this Merger, the breach of fiduciary duty damage action was adjudicated first. In writing the decision in the statutory appraisal action that is now before this Court, the Court of Chancery specifically noted that it had previously "issued an opinion in the companion class action holding that Sheshunoff had performed its appraisal in a legally improper manner."
>
> ...Respondents were collaterally estopped from arguing in the statutory appraisal action that Sheshunoff's $41 determination represented MGB's fair value per share, given the entry of the Court of Chancery's prior final judgment in the breach of fiduciary duty damage action involving the same Merger.

Delaware adopts Daubert, Kumho

The Supreme Court also upheld the Chancery Court's finding that Reilly's capital market approach was not generally accepted in the financial community and not proper in a statutory appraisal action because it had a built-in minority discount. In upholding this finding, the Supreme Court held that the Chancery Court properly acted as a "gatekeeper" with regard to the admissibility of expert testimony.

"Although this Court is not bound by the United States Supreme Court's interpretation of comparable federal rules of procedure and evidence, we hereby adopt the holdings of Daubert and [Kumho v.] Carmichael as the correct interpretation of Delaware Rule of Evidence 702."

Paskill Corp. v. Alcoma Corp. (I)

Citation: 1999 Del. Ch. LEXIS 129
Court: Court of Chancery
State/Jurisdiction: Delaware
Date of decision: June 16, 1999
Judge: Steele

This judicial appraisal action arose out of the cash-out merger of Okeechobee Inc. with its majority shareholder, Alcoma Corp. Okeechobee was a non-public, closely held closed-end investment fund that held marketable securities, mortgage-backed notes, and real estate. The minority investor accepted the corporation's current market values for its investment portfolio. The primary issue was whether adjustments for future capital gains taxes and sales expenses were appropriate in determining the fair value of the minority shareholder's interest in the corporation.

AICPA principles play a part

The court noted that the minority shareholder is entitled to his proportionate interest in the fair value of those investments, and to value investment assets, a net asset valuation incorporating current market value estimates is appropriate. The court also noted that taxes triggered by sale of an asset are not caused by the sale, but are incurred as the asset's value rises above its purchase price. The court decided that tax liability encumbers the appreciated asset at the time of the merger and should be shared proportionately with the minority shareholder. This decision was based in part on the American Institute of Certified Public Accountants' (AICPA) principles governing accounting for capital gains tax on unrealized asset appreciation.

The reduction for future sales expense, however, was a different matter. The company argues that giving the minority shareholder fair value involves estimating the liquidation value of the stock, and this liquidation involves sales expenses. The court disagreed for two reasons. First, the sales expense only occurs when there is a sale. Those expenses are not an accrued, deferred liability like the tax. Sales expenses represent transaction costs in only one of the many uses for the investment.

Second, there is no AICPA principle governing accounting for future sales expenses. The court presumed that none existed, which indicated to the court that sales expenses were not suited to the same treatment as taxes. Investment assets should be valued as held assets, not including any allowance for future sales expenses.

Chapter 7: Court Case Abstracts

HMO-W, Inc. v. SSM Health Care System (I)

Citation: 228 Wis. 2d 815, 598 N.W.2d 577, 1999 Wisc. App. LEXIS 722
Court: Court of Appeals
State/Jurisdiction: Wisconsin
Date of decision: June 17, 1999
Judge: Dykman

SSM Health Care System (SSM), a minority shareholder of HMO-Wisconsin Inc. (HMO-W), appealed the circuit court decision to apply a minority discount when it valued the fair value of SSM's HMO-W's shares prior to HMO-W's merger with United Wisconsin Services.

At trial, HMO-W's expert, James Pizzo, testified that immediately prior to the merger, the corporation's value was $10,544,000. While SSM's expert, Patrick Hurst, testified that the value was $19,250,000. The lower court agreed with Pizzo and applied a minority discount of 30%, and SSM appealed the decision to apply a minority discount.

Statutory language ambiguous

The appeals court looked to the definition of "fair value" in its dissenters right statute, § 180.1301(4).

The appeals court stated that the statutory language, as well as legislative history, related statutory provisions, and case law were ambiguous as to whether minority discounts should be applied when determining the fair value of dissenter shares. Then the court turned to other jurisdictions for guidance.

Unfair enrichment of majority shareholders

The court reviewed cases from several states, including Delaware, New York, and Oklahoma and concluded that minority discounts should not be applied. The court agreed with the rationale that was stated in *Cavalier Oil Corp. V. Harnett*, 564 A.2d 1137 (Del. 1989):

> Discounting individual share holdings injects into the appraisal process speculation on the various factors which may dictate the marketability of minority shareholdings. More important, to fail to accord to a minority shareholder the full proportionate value of his shares imposes a penalty for lack of control, and unfairly enriches the majority shareholders who may reap a windfall [emphasis added] from the appraisal process by cashing out a dissenting shareholder, a clearly undesirable result.

Because of this "clearly undesirable result," the Wisconsin Court of Appeals held that minority discounts are inappropriate in dissenters rights cases as a matter of law, and it remanded to the lower court to award SSM the pro rata share of HMO-Ws net assets without a minority discount.

Swope v. Siegel-Robert, Inc. (I)

Citation: 74 F. Supp. 2d 876, 1999 U.S. Dist. LEXIS 15973
Court: United States District Court
State/Jurisdiction: Missouri
Date of decision: June 23, 1999
Judge: Webber

Shareholders were offered $20 per share in a squeeze-out merger, effective July 31, 1997. Shareholders owning 426,900 shares dissented. The Court determined a fair value of $63.36 per share, and awarded that judgment plus 5.115% simple interest from July 30, 1997.

Discounts on case-by-case basis

Perhaps the most important aspect of this opinion is that the U.S. District Court reached its decision consistent with the Missouri Court of Appeals case of *King v. F.I.J., Inc.*, 765 S.W.2d 301 (Mo.App., 1989). That case said that the question of whether minority and marketability discounts are applicable in Missouri dissenting stockholder cases is to be determined depending on the facts and circumstances, on a case-by-case basis.

In this case, the court determined that the shares should be valued on a minority basis, but that there should be no discount for lack of marketability.

CEO recommends merger price

The CEO (who had been in charge of the acquisitions) recommended the $20-per-share price. In conjunction with the transaction, he did not consult the Board of Directors, any appraiser (although one of the dissenters had suggested that he hire an appraiser), any accountant, or any member of senior management.

The CEO based his $20 price on "intrinsic factors" and partly on the fact that the company had a history of making small purchases and sales of stock at a 35% discount from book value. There was no explanation offered as to why the $20 price actually represented closer to a 45% discount from the book value of $34 to $35 per share. The Court stated that it was not convinced that the CEO conducted an in-depth financial analysis.

Parties vilify opposing appraisers

The Court stated:

> During the course of the hearing, each party attempted to substantiate their respective conclusions or to vilify opposing appraisers, based upon conclusions reached in other

reported cases. Some testimony was helpful, while some was distracting to the Court's ultimate responsibility in arriving at the fair value of the subject shares.

The Court offered the following commentary on the respective experts' views:

> If defendant's witnesses' testimony is accepted literally, this Company is headed for certain collapse. While this apocalyptic view is exaggerated in the Court's view, the evidence in this case suggests that the very impressive growth the Company has experienced in the last five years is unlikely to continue.

The Court's view was that, while defendant's views were too pessimistic, plaintiff's views were overly optimistic.

Experts use 'three levels of value'

The opposing experts agreed on the traditional "three levels of value" framework:
- Control or enterprise value
- Marketable minority value
- Nonmarketable minority value

Plaintiff's primary expert, Robert Reilly of Willamette Management Associates[1], valued the shares at $72.90 on a marketable minority basis. He applied a 35% control premium to arrive at a value estimate of $98.40 per share.

Defendant's primary expert, Kenneth Patton of Mercer Capital[2], valued the shares at $46.20 on a marketable minority basis. He applied a 35% discount for lack of marketability to arrive at a value estimate of $30.00 per share (rounded).

Prior purchases not at fair value

Reilly examined the treasury share transactions and concluded that the price paid did not represent fair value transactions. The company suggested a price to shareholders who wanted to sell, and no negotiation process was involved. The price was set by the company as a "take it or leave it" proposition.

Reliability of guideline companies

Both appraisers utilized a guideline public company method. The Court observed the following:

> [T]he conclusions of any analysis by use of this method are only as reliable as the selection of the guideline companies used.

Swope v. Siegel-Robert, Inc. (I)

At the valuation date, a little over half the company's revenues were from automotive parts, where competition was increasingly intense. In recent years the company had diversified by making several acquisitions in other industrial product lines.

Reilly selected a separate set of guideline companies for each of the parent company's operating units, and aggregated the values. Patton used only automotive parts companies. The Court criticized this aspect of Patton's methodology:

> His election to value the Company as a 100% automotive parts manufacturing company seriously disables his analysis. . . . In reality, the Company is seven different business units.

Both experts use income approach

Reilly used both the "build-up" and the capital asset pricing model (CAPM) to develop discount rates for the discounted cash flow method and capitalization rates for the capitalization method. The Court describes the methods and the numbers utilized in developing the discount and capitalization rates in detail. Patton also used an income approach, although the Court accords it only limited discussion.

It was the Court's view that Reilly's discount and capitalization rates were too low (resulting in overvaluation by the income approach), and that Patton's were too high (resulting in undervaluation by the income approach).

Fair value a 'malleable term'

The Court explained the following:

> 'The central concern of the Courts legal analysis is fair value. The Court must discern Missouri courts interpretation of this malleable term, focusing particularly on the appropriateness of application of minority and marketability discounts . . . [A]scertaining the legal mind of Missouri on the issue of discounts is not a simple task, in large part because of the dearth of cases.'

Application of discounts discretionary

The case contains a lengthy and informative discussion of dissenter's appraisal case law from several states. However, it ultimately relies most heavily on *King, supra*. The Court discussed *King* as follows:

> 'The most important guidance of this case, relied on heavily by Defendant, is its holding that the application of both marketability and minority discounts "in determining fair value pursuant to § 351.455, when a shareholder of a corporation objects

to a merger or consolidation, rests within the sound discretion of the trier of facts after every relevant fact and circumstance is considered." 765 S.W.2d at 305, 306. Although both parties in their thorough briefs argue at various junctures that this case or that policy mandates that the Court apply or decline to apply discounts, the principle which emerges most strongly and clearly from King is that such a decision is discretionary. The Court's discussion of Missouri case law, as well as that of other states, must, therefore, proceed with the understanding that no law or policy requiring or forbidding the application of discounts may hold sway with the Court, which is required by its interpretation of Missouri law to rest its decision on its own discretion, after considering every relevant fact and circumstance.'

1. Michelle Matava of A.G. Edwards was plaintiff's rebuttal expert.

2. Chris Mercer of Mercer Capital was defendant's rebuttal expert.

SIEGEL-ROBERT, INC.- FAIR VALUE PER SHARE			
	Robert Reilly for Plaintiffs	Ken Patton for Defendants	Courts Conclusion
Control Value	$98.40*		
Marketable Minority value	$72.90	$46.20	$63.36
Nonmarketable Minority value		$30.02**	
* After adding 35% control premium ** After subtracting 35% marketability discount			

M.P.M. Enterprises, Inc. v. Gilbert

Citation: 731 A.2d 790, 1999 Del. LEXIS 205
Court: Supreme Court
State/Jurisdiction: Delaware
Date of decision: June 25, 1999
Judge: Veasey

This case came before the Delaware Supreme Court on appeal from the Court of Chancery opinion in this statutory appraisal action. The two issues before the Supreme Court were:
- Whether the Court of Chancery committed legal error or, alternatively, abused its discretion by applying an appraisal analysis that accorded no weight to the terms of the merger giving rise to the appraisal action or to the terms of two prior offers for equity stakes in the subject corporation; and
- Whether the Court of Chancery erred in refusing to consider the dilutive effect of alleged obligations incurred by the company to non-stockholder employees.

Prior remand to clarify reasoning

In reviewing the record and opinion of the Court of Chancery to determine why it accorded the terms of the merger and prior offers no weight, the Supreme Court found that there was insufficient information to determine whether the Court of Chancery erred on this issue. Accordingly, it remanded the matter by Order dated Nov. 23, 1998, "for clarification so that it could provide a better explanation of its analysis with respect to both the merger and the prior offers." The Court of Chancery issued its supplemental opinion on Feb. 4, 1999, after which this appeal proceeded.

No nexus between prior offer values and going concern value

The Supreme Court noted that the standard of review on this issue depended upon the Court of Chancery's reasoning. If it had found, as a matter of fact, that the merger and prior offers should be accorded no weight, then the standard of review would be abuse of discretion. If, on the other hand, the Court of Chancery had found, as a matter of law, that the merger and prior offers could not be considered in determining the fair value of Gilbert's shares, then the standard of review would be de novo. In summarizing the Court of Chancery's reasoning, the Supreme Court said:

> In its remand opinion, the Court of Chancery clarified its position with respect to the merger and the prior offers. The Court stated that it did not mean to imply that § 262 barred consideration of specific offers for a company, and that it did, in fact, consider the relevance of each of these offers to the fair value of MPM at the date of the merger. It explained that, while potentially relevant, the evidence with respect to both the merger and the prior offers was of only marginal utility and therefore received no weight in the final analysis. The Court further explained that, rather than relying on specific evidence supporting its decision to accord zero weight to these offers, it relied on the absence of any credible evidence provided by MPM that established a nexus between the values derived from the offers at issue and the going concern value of MPM at the date of the merger.

Since the Court of Chancery admitted the evidence of the merger and prior offers into evidence, and its decision to accord them no weight was a factual one, the Supreme Court's review was for abuse of discretion.

MPM argues that the merger and prior offers were "relevant factors" that the trial court was required to consider and compare to its DCF analysis value. The Supreme Court noted that MPM's argument was based upon language in the appraisal statute "requiring the trial court to 'take into account all relevant factors' when determining the fair value of a petitioner's shares."

Supreme Court finds no abuse of discretion

The Supreme Court ultimately upheld the Court of Chancery's decision on this issue.

Values derived in the open market through arms-length negotiations offer better indicia of reliability than the interested party transactions that are often the subject of appraisals under § 262. But the trial court, in its discretion, need not accord any weight to such values when unsupported by evidence that they represent the going concern value of the company at the effective date of the merger or consolidation.

In this case, MPM proffered evidence of the merger and the prior offers only as part of Lundquist's buy-side DCF. . . In this case, MPM failed to present this additional evidence with respect to either the merger or the prior offers.

The Supreme Court also noted in a footnote that the prior offers were only marginally useful because they "were remote in time from the date of the merger and neither was actually consummated."

Insufficient evidence of obligations to non-stockholder employees

MPM's second claim of error is based upon the Court of Chancery's finding that there was insufficient evidence of MPM's obligation to give an equity interest in the corporation to non-stockholder employees. MPM argued that this obligation diluted the percentage of Gilbert's ownership share in the corporation.

At trial, MPM admitted into evidence three written employment agreements that gave three employees a potential right to acquire stock in the company, subject to rules, regulations, restrictions, and the discretion of the Board of Directors. MPM also presented the testimony of Thomas Bagley, its president and CEO, that the company had made oral commitments to these employees.

The trial court was not convinced by this testimony and found that MPM had failed to provide sufficient evidence to prove that these payments of equity actually were legal obligations of MPM rather than merely costs of the merger.

Because the Court of Chancery's finding on this issue turned on issues of credibility of a live witness, the Supreme Court upheld the Court of Chancery's finding.

The Supreme Court affirmed the Court of Chancery's opinion in all respects.

Lawson Mardon Wheaton, Inc. v. Smith (II)

Citation: 160 N.J. 383, 734 A.2d 738, 1999 N.J. LEXIS 835
Court: Supreme Court
State/Jurisdiction: New Jersey
Date of decision: July 14, 1999
Judge: Garibaldi

The primary issue before the New Jersey Supreme Court in this dissenters' appraisal rights case, decided the same day as *Balsamides v. Protameen Chemicals, Inc.*, is whether a marketability discount should be applied in determining the fair value of the dissenters' shares of Lawson Mardon Wheaton, Inc. (Wheaton).

The dissenter's appraisal rights were triggered by a corporate restructure. The corporation offered the dissenters $41.50 per share. The dissenters rejected this sum and filed this judicial appraisal action.

Before trial of this matter was concluded, the corporation voted to rescind the restructure, and entered into a merger with Alusuisse. Under the merger, dissenting shareholders were offered $63.00 per share.

Expert valuation methods identical except for discount

At trial, both sides offered the testimony of a valuation expert. Wheaton's expert, George Weiksner, of First Boston, Inc., testified that the fair value of the shares was in the range of $39.49 to $42.53 per share. The dissenter's expert, Mark Lee, of Bear Stearns and Co., Inc., testified that the fair value of the shares was in the range of $67.00 to $75.00 per share.

> As the courts below recognized, both experts used essentially the same methodology in determining the liquid or free trading value of Wheaton's stock. [FN5] Both experts analyzed and compared Wheaton's financial data with that of five comparable public companies to impute a multiple or price/earnings ratio for Wheaton. Both arrived at a price earnings ratio of about 13.5 times earnings. Both then multiplied that ratio by their estimate of Wheaton's 1992 earnings per share to determine the price per share. Both experts selected the same five companies for analysis and comparison, although the dissenter's expert used an additional two. Both agreed that The West Company, Inc. was most similar to Wheaton.

At this point in the valuation analysis, however, Weiksner applied a 25% marketability discount, followed by a 5% discount "due to the Company's share ownership, restrictions on stock transfers, and control issues." Lee applied no discounts in reaching his fair value opinion.

Chapter 7: Court Case Abstracts

Trial court applied marketability discount

Based in part upon Weiksner's valuation, the trial court applied a 25% marketability discount and concluded that the fair value of the dissenters' shares was $41.05 per share. Relying on 2 ALI, Principles of Corporate Governance: Analysis and Recommendations, 7.22(a), the trial court concluded that the application of a marketability discount was appropriate in this case because of "extraordinary circumstances" that were present.

The New Jersey Superior Court, Appellate Division, upheld the trial courts fair value determination.

Supreme Court grants certification, rejects marketability discount

The dissenters filed a Petition for Certification in the New Jersey Supreme Court, which was granted.

The Supreme Court thoroughly discussed:
- the history and purpose of dissenters rights statutes,
- the distinction between minority and marketability discounts,
- the application of a marketability discount in determining fair value in various suits in other states, particularly dissenters rights suits, and
- the approach recommended by the ALI.

Following this discussion, the Supreme Court stated:

> The history and policy behind dissenters' right and appraisal statutes lead us to conclude that marketability discounts generally should not be applied when determining the fair value of dissenters shares in a statutory appraisal action. Of course, there may be situations where equity compels another result. Those situations are best resolved by resort to the extraordinary circumstances exception in 2 ALI Principles, 7.22(a).

'Extraordinary circumstances' defined by Supreme Court

In applying this principle to the case before it, the Supreme Court held that the trial courts finding of "extraordinary circumstances" that warranted application of a marketability discount was not supported by evidence in the record. The Court held that:

> Such circumstances require more than the absence of a trading market in shares; rather, the court should apply this exception only when it finds that the dissenting shareholder has held out in order to exploit the transaction giving rise to appraisal so as to divert value to itself that could not be made available proportionately to other shareholders.

Subsequent merger price relevant as comparison

Another issue arose in response to Wheaton's merger with Alusuisse. The dissenters moved to reopen the record to admit evidence of the $63.00 merger price, but the trial court denied the motion.

The New Jersey Supreme Court ordered that the record be reopened on remand to admit this evidence. The Court stated:

> Given Wheaton's financial history, the record should be reopened for the limited purpose of enabling the trial court to consider the $63.00 per share Alusuisse acquisition price in its determination of the fair value of the dissenters stock on December 5, 1991. Even though the Company's fortunes waned during the 1991 to 1996 period, the stock, in an arms-length transaction, was worth $63.00 per share in 1996. We question the Company's assertion that the fair value of the dissenters stock on December 5, 1991, was only $41.50 per share.

Balsamides v. Protameen Chemicals, Inc. (II)

Citation: 160 N.J. 352, 734 A.2d 721, 1999 N.J. LEXIS 836
Court: Supreme Court
State/Jurisdiction: New Jersey
Date of decision: July 14, 1999
Judge: Garibaldi

The primary issue in this case, decided the same day as *Lawson Mardon Wheaton, Inc. v. Smith*, was whether a marketability discount should be applied in determining the fair value to be paid in a court-ordered buyout in a shareholder oppression suit.

Plaintiffs' expert, Thomas J. Hoberman, CPA, testified that the value of the company was $4,176,000, after applying a 35% marketability discount. Defendants' expert, Robert E. Ott, CFA, testified that the value of the company was $8,285,000. Ott did not apply a marketability discount.

The trial court adopted Hoberman's valuation, including the marketability discount. The New Jersey Superior Court, Appellate Division, reversed and remanded to the trial court for reconsideration of the valuation issue, stating that the application of the marketability discount was error. Plaintiff petitioned the New Jersey Supreme Court for certification on this issue, which was granted.

Excess earnings method best approach

Hoberman's valuation was based primarily on the excess earnings method. Defendants argued that this method was not the best method and should not have been relied upon by the trial court. The Supreme Court upheld the use of this method in this case.

"The court noted that although not preferred, 'excess earnings' is an acceptable method, and Hoberman chose it, in part, because defendants would not provide the information needed to employ any other method."

Marketability discount applied in oppression valuation

Following a thorough discussion of the methods used by the two expert witnesses, as well as the purposes behind the minority oppression statutes, the Supreme Court held that a marketability discount should be applied in this case.

"The position of the Appellate Division ignores the reality that Balsamides is buying a company that will remain illiquid because it is not publicly traded and public information about it is not widely disseminated. Protameen will continue to have a small base of available purchasers. If it is resold in the future, Balsamides will receive a lower purchase price because of the company's closely-held nature.

"If Perle and Balsamides sold Protameen together, the price they received would reflect Protameen's illiquidity. They would split the price and also share that detriment. Similarly, if Balsamides pays Perle a discounted price, Perle suffers half of the lack-of-marketability markdown now; and Balsamides suffers the other half when he eventually sells his closely-held business. Conversely, if Perle is not required to sell his shares at a price that reflects Protameen's lack of marketability, Balsamides will suffer the full effect of Protameen's lack of marketability at the time he sells. Accordingly, we find that Balsamides should not bear the brunt of Protameen's illiquidity merely because he is the designated buyer."

"To secure 'fair value' for Perle's stock, a marketability discount should be applied. To do otherwise would be unfair, particularly since Perle was the oppressor and Balsamides was the oppressed shareholder."

Punitive damages also awarded

In addition to the court-ordered buy-out, the trial court awarded Balsamides punitive damages against Perle in the amount of $75,000, which was affirmed by the Appellate Division. Perle cross-petitioned for review of this issue. The Supreme Court denied his cross-petition, effectively upholding the award.

Borruso v. Communications Telesystems International

Citation: 753 A.2d 451, 1999 Del. Ch. LEXIS 197
Court: Court of Chancery
State/Jurisdiction: Delaware
Date of decision: September 24, 1999
Judge: Lamb

The issue in this judicial appraisal action was the fair value of petitioners' 500,000 shares of WXL International, Inc. Petitioners' shares constituted 5% of the total common stock of WXL. On December 16, 1997, Communications Telesystems International (CTI), the holder of the other 95% of the WXL common stock, unilaterally effected a short-form merger of WXL and CTI. The price offered the petitioners for their 5% interest was $.02 per share. The petitioners rejected this offer and filed this judicial appraisal action.

At trial, both parties presented expert valuation reports and testimony. Peter S. Huck of the Milwaukee Financial Valuation Group of American Appraisal Associates represented petitioners, and Anthony P. Kern of PriceWaterhouseCoopers represented respondent.

Both experts used only the comparable company method, because there was insufficient financial history data of WXL to use a discounted cash flow analysis. Although they differed greatly in the ultimate value they placed on the petitioners' shares,

> [T]he experts' analyses differed materially in only a few respects: (i) whether, in deriving a multiplier for WXL from the data generated as to comparable companies, a premium should be added to reflect WXL's better than average rate of growth over the 12-month period leading up to the merger, (ii) at what point in the analysis the information derived should be adjusted to eliminate the minority discount inherent in the comparable company method, and (iii) whether the value derived from that analysis should, in this case, be reduced to account for any observed "private company" discount.

Choosing comparables

Both experts used data from eight comparable companies. The court chose five comparable companies that were common to both groups, plus one other comparable company from Huck's group. The court discussed why the other five comparable companies were rejected.

> I agree that Colt and IDT are not useful comparables and should be eliminated from the analysis. Colt is a local exchange carrier in the UK. It is not a long-distance company, but rather the company that owns the wires that connect homes or offices to the local switch. Thus, it does not compete with WXL or the other comparable companies. Its lack of comparability is also apparent from the great variation of its derived revenue multiplier (10.5x) from those of the other guideline companies utilized by Huck (ranging from 1.2x

to 4.5x). I also agree that IDT should be disregarded in the analysis due to the fact that a substantial portion of its revenues is derived from its operations of an Internet network. The growth of that segment of IDT's business is very strong and, as is commonly known, current valuations of all Internet related businesses are unusually high. While Petitioners are correct that IDT also competes in the European long-distance market and might otherwise be a good comparable, its participation in the Internet market offers too great a chance of distortion to allow its inclusion.

Petitioners continue to object to the inclusion of any of Kern's distinct comparables: ACC, Startec and Telegroup. I agree with Petitioners that the inclusion of any one of these three companies presents substantial issues. ACC was, at the relevant time, subject to an announced agreement for its acquisition by another company. Thus, reliable information about its stock trading activity during the pertinent period of time could not be directly observed. Because there is otherwise a sufficiently large group of other companies to use, this is a sufficient reason to reject ACC as a comparable. Startec derives most of its revenue from non-European markets and only 2.2% from Western Europe and, thus, was not significantly involved in the same market as WXL. Telegroup has a highly concentrated share ownership, with 85% of its stock held by founders or otherwise in private hands. On the record before me, I am not able to discern whether there is a sufficiently active market for its shares from which to derive reliable information for valuation purposes. For these reasons, I will exclude Startec and Telegroup from the basket of companies used for purposes of comparison.

Calculating the derived multiple

In calculating the multiple to be used in the valuation calculation, each expert adjusted the multiple derived from the comparable companies to account for differences in size, profitability and growth. However, Huck applied his adjustments to the median multiple of all the comparable companies. Kern, on the other hand, applied his adjustments to each individual comparable company, also taking into account revenue and operating markets/product, and then calculated the median multiple. The court adopted Kerns company-specific method because it "more reliably correlates WXL to the guideline companies."

Huck made one other adjustment to the median multiple. He adjusted the multiple upward to account for "WXLs superior" fiscal year (FY) 1997 revenue growth. The court rejected this adjustment because there was no evidence in the record that this growth rate was sustainable or accurate. The evidence before it left the court "unable to conclude that anyone would pay a premium to acquire WXL on account of its higher than median growth rate in FY97."

Control premium should be applied to result

Both experts agreed that a control premium should be applied to adjust for the recognized fact that a comparable company analysis includes an inherent minority discount. However, they disagreed as to when the premium should be applied. Huck applied the premium early in his calculations, by adding "a 30% equity control premium to the median multiple used to determine" the market value of invested capital for WXL. Kern, on the other hand, applied a control premium to the comparable company analysis result. The court adopted Kerns methodology and rejected Hucks.

> I am persuaded that Petitioners approach to the control premium is wrong. The observation that the comparable company method of analysis produces a minority equity value does not require that I change the methodology of that analysis. Rather, it requires only that I adjust the result derived from it to eliminate the implicit minority discount. Instead of adjusting the result, Huck undertook to alter, in a significant way, the methodology itself. Doing so, in my view, introduced an analytical distortion that, in this case, significantly overstates the value of the WXL equity. Neither Petitioners nor Huck has supplied authority in the valuation literature justifying this change in the accepted methodology.

Private company discount rejected

Kern applied a final 20% discount, which he called a "discount for lack of liquidity." The court rejected this discount because it was essentially a discount for lack of marketability, which is inappropriate in a Delaware fair value determination.

> To the extent Respondent is arguing for the application of a "corporate level" discount to reflect the fact that all shares of WXL shares were worth less because there was no public market in which to sell them, I read Cavalier Oil as prohibiting such a discount. This is simply a liquidity discount applied at the "corporate level." Even if taken "at the corporate level" (in circumstances in which the effect on the fair value of the shares is the same as a "shareholder level" discount) such a discount is, nevertheless, based on trading characteristics of the shares themselves, not any factor intrinsic to the corporation or its assets. It is therefore prohibited.

In support of its rejection of this discount, the court also discusses relevant financial literature, including *Valuing a Business* by Shannon Pratt, Robert Reilly, and Robert Schweihs and an article by Z. Christopher Mercer entitled *"Should Marketability Discounts Be Applied to Controlling Interests of Private Companies?"*

Compound interest awarded

The court awarded interest on the judgment from the date of the merger until the date of the judgment. In deciding whether to award simple or compound interest, the court cited *Onti, Inc. v. Integra Bank*, 1999 Del. Ch. LEXIS 130, in which Chancellor Chandler stated the following:

It is simply not credible in today's financial markets that a person sophisticated enough to perfect his or her appraisal rights would be unsophisticated enough to make an investment at simple interest.

The court concluded that the petitioners' shares were worth $0.6253 per share, as opposed to the $0.02 offered in the merger.

Advanced Communication Design, Inc. v. Follett (I)

Citation: 601 N.W.2d 707, 1999 Minn. App. LEXIS 1181
Court: Court of Appeals
State/Jurisdiction: Minnesota
Date of decision: November 2, 1999
Judge: Forsberg

The issues in this breach of fiduciary duty case were:
- Whether a discount for lack of marketability should be applied in valuing a minority shareholder's shares when the sale results in the buyer becoming the sole owner of the company;
- Whether a minority shareholder has a fiduciary duty to other shareholders; and
- Whether the trial court abused its discretion in making the payment to the minority shareholder payable over ten years.

In this case, Advanced Communication Design, Inc. (ACD) was formed by one man, Marco Scibora. Several years later, Brian Follett became vice president of ACD and purchased 1,500 shares of nonvoting stock, thus acquiring a one-third equity interest. At that time, the parties executed a buy-sell agreement giving ACD the right of first refusal on any departing shareholder's stock.

Six years later, Scibora brought his wife onboard as chief operating officer and paid her 1,500 shares of nonvoting stock. Later that year, Scibora demoted Follett to manager of special projects and reduced his salary. Follett resigned, and Scibora offered to purchase Follett's stock for $24,646.

Litigation ensued, and following trial of Follett's breach of fiduciary duty claims, the trial court awarded Follett $475,381 in exchange for his stock, as well as attorney fees of $87,137. Both parties appealed on different issues, listed above.

Marketability discount issue of first impression in Minnesota

The Court of Appeals noted that there was no Minnesota law regarding whether a marketability discount should be applied in this case. Accordingly, the Court turned to two recent New Jersey cases: *Balsamides v. Protameen Chemicals, Inc.* and *Lawson Mardon Wheaton, Inc. v. Smith.*

The Court restated the guiding principle from *Balsamides* and *Lawson*:

> [A] marketability discount cannot be used unfairly by controlling or oppressing shareholders to benefit themselves to the detriment of the minority or oppressed shareholders.

The Court concluded that, applying that principle to this case, a marketability discount should not be applied in this case because Follett was the minority shareholder and was oppressed by Scibora's conduct.

Minority shareholder owes no fiduciary duty

Scibora argued that Follett owed a fiduciary duty to ACD and the other shareholders. However, the Court found that he did not owe a fiduciary duty because he had no control or power within the company.

Follett was never a director, he ceased being an officer before the events complained of occurred, and he had no power of appointment. Follett had only nonvoting stock in ACD; he in no sense controlled the corporation. He had no fiduciary duty.

Payment over time appropriate

The trial court ordered that ACD purchase Follett's stock, but allowed ACD to purchase it in part with a ten-year promissory note. The trial court found, based on ACD's financial condition, that to pay the entire amount in a lump sum would "result in an unreasonable hardship." The Court of Appeals upheld this portion of the trial court's order because it was not clearly erroneous. In addition to the trial court's reasonable assessment of ACD's financial condition, the trial court had before it the buy-sell agreement, which allowed the corporation to exercise its right of first refusal through payment of a promissory note of up to ten years.

Arnaud v. Stockgrowers State Bank

Citation: 268 Kan. 163, 992 P.2d 216, 1999 Kan. LEXIS 645
Court: Supreme Court
State/Jurisdiction: Kansas
Date of decision: November 5, 1999
Judge: Abbott

The Supreme Court of Kansas heard an issue of first impression in this case:

> Is it proper for a corporation to determine the 'fair value' of a fractional share pursuant to K.S.A. § 17-6405 by applying minority and marketability discounts when the

fractional share resulted from a reverse stock split intended to eliminate the minority shareholder's interest in the corporation?

The majority shareholders of Stockgrowers State Bank of Ashland formed a holding company. The plaintiffs refused to transfer their minority shares to the holding company, and the bank initiated a reverse stock split, reducing 4000 outstanding shares to 10. Under Kansas statutory law (K.S.A. § 17-6405), the bank has a right to refuse to issue fractional shares and pay the fair value of those shares in cash. The bank hired Deloitte & Touche and Petty & Company to determine the fair value. It appeared that the bank averaged the two appraisals, which included minority (23.1%) and marketability (25%) discounts, and paid $1.50 more than the average of $1,372 per share.

Even though the Court stated that there was no Kansas case law that interprets the meaning of "fair value," the Court often looked to Delaware corporate law. The court looked to the Delaware case of *Cavalier Oil Corp. v. Harnett*, 564 A. 2d 1137 (1989), where the Court of Chancery disallowed a minority or marketability discount in a short form merger. The Court did recognize that some courts have allowed minority and marketability discounts in similar cases.

The Supreme Court of Kansas overruled a previous decision that allowed a minority discount in an action for appraisal, *Moore v. New Ammest, Inc.*, 630 P.2d 167 (Kan.1981). The Court held that:

> In answering the certified question before us, we hold that minority and marketability discounts should not be applied when the fractional share resulted from a reverse stock split intended to eliminate a minority shareholder's interest in the corporation.

Paskill Corp. v. Alcoma Corp. (II)

Citation: 747 A.2d 549, 2000 Del. LEXIS 117
Court: Supreme Court
State/Jurisdiction: Delaware
Date of decision: March 7, 2000
Judge: Holland

This appeal arose out of a cash-out merger of the minority stockholders of a closed-end investment fund known as Okeechobee, Inc. The merger consideration was established by Okeechobee's majority stockholder, Alcoma Corporation, by calculating Okeechobee's "net asset value" as of the date of the merger and deducting therefrom both (i) the accrued (but unrealized) tax liability on assets that had appreciated in value, and (ii) the expenses that would be incurred in connection with the ultimate disposition of the assets.

After the merger was approved, Paskill Corporation, a minority stockholder of Okeechobee eliminated in the merger, filed a statutory appraisal action in the Delaware Court of Chancery (*see* abstract in February 2000 *BVU*, p. 7). Notably, Paskill did not challenge Alcoma's use of

Paskill Corp. v. Alcoma Corp. (II)

"net asset value" as the measure of "fair value." Nor did Paskill challenge Alcoma's calculation of Okeechobee's "net asset value." Rather, Paskill limited its challenge to the reductions taken by Alcoma for accrued (but unrealized) tax liabilities and future sales expenses.

The Court of Chancery observed the following:

> Paskill accepts Okeechobee's use of a net asset valuation to calculate fair value for the cashed-out shares and is satisfied with the numbers actually calculated by Okeechobee's accountants. Paskill disputes, however, Okeechobee's right to deduct amounts representing the future tax liabilities and the future sales expenses of its investment assets.

Paskill and Alcoma filed cross motions for summary judgment limited to what they characterized as the purely legal issue of the propriety of Alcoma's two reductions from Okeechobee's net asset value. The Court of Chancery held that it was appropriate for Alcoma to reduce the net asset value by the amount of accrued (but unrealized) tax liabilities on appreciated assets, but that the potential transaction costs were too speculative to support a further reduction. Both sides appealed:

- *Paskill*-from the allowance of a deduction for the accrued, but unrealized, tax liability that would be due if Okeechobee's assets were sold.
- *Alcoma*-from the refusal to consider the potential transaction costs associated with the disposition of Okeechobee's assets (which would have caused recognition of the accrued tax liability.

On appeal, the Delaware Supreme Court agreed with Paskill and disagreed with Alcoma, holding that the Court of Chancery "should have excluded any deduction for the speculative future tax liabilities" associated with uncontemplated sales, and "properly denied any deduction from Okeechobee's net asset value for speculative expenses relating to future sales that were not contemplated on the date of the merger." Had the Delaware Supreme Court stopped there, it would have been a complete victory for Paskill. But the Supreme Court continued.

Net asset value not fair value

After reviewing the issues raised by the parties, the Delaware Supreme Court went on to consider and reverse the Court of Chancery's use of "net asset value" to determine the "fair value" of Okeechobee—even though none of the parties had taken issue with the use of net asset value as the measure of "fair value" in the appraisal proceeding. According to the Supreme Court, the "net asset value" approach is a form of "liquidation" analysis, which cannot be used as the exclusive measure of value in a statutory appraisal proceeding. As the Delaware Supreme Court explained:

> The Court of Chancery erred, as a matter of law, by relying upon the net asset value as the sole criterion for determining the fair value of Okeechobee's stock. It compounded that error when it discounted the speculative future tax liabilities from its net asset value calculation. That deduction was inconsistent with the theoretical nature of the

liquidating value that this Court ascribed to the term net asset value in Tri-Continental [Corp. v. Battye, 74 A.2d 71 (Del. 1950)] and converted Okeechobee's theoretical net asset value into an actual liquidation value. Since it is impermissible to appraise a corporation on the sole basis of its theoretical liquidation net asset value, a fortiori, a statutory appraisal can never be made solely on the basis of an actual liquidation net asset value.

The Delaware Supreme Court reiterated that the object of a statutory appraisal proceeding is to provide to a dissenting stockholder "a proportionate share of fair value in the *going concern* on the date of the merger, rather than value that is determined on a liquidated basis." To determine this value, the subject corporation "must first be valued as an operating entity." Moreover, in performing this valuation, one of the most important factors to consider is the "nature of the enterprise that is the subject of the appraisal proceeding."

Court rejects NAV as sole measure

Accepting Alcoma's contention that Okeechobee was a closed-end investment company, the Delaware Supreme Court agreed that it was appropriate to focus upon the corporations assets. Nonetheless, the Supreme Court rejected the notion that "net asset value" could be the sole measure of Okeechobee's value. Drawing upon the fifty-year-old decision in *Tri-Continental*, which is "one of Delaware's seminal appraisal cases," the Delaware Supreme Court instructed that the valuation determination must also take into account "leverage; discount; net asset value; market value; management; earnings and dividends; expenses of operation; particular holdings in the [corporations] portfolio; and a favorable tax situation."

That the foregoing factors all must be taken into account, however, is not to say that they all will have an influence upon the ultimate determination of fair value. As the Delaware Supreme Court acknowledged in *Paskill*, it was ultimately determined in *Tri-Continental* that "under the unique circumstances presented, the factors of management, earnings and dividends, expenses of operation, and the portfolio of the corporation did not merit being debited or credited in arriving at a value for the common stock."

Court of Chancery to determine 'exact nature'

On remand, the Court of Chancery is charged with the responsibility to "ascertain the exact nature of Okeechobee as an enterprise," and "determine Okeechobee's fair value as a going concern on the date of the merger by any admissible valuation technique that is based on reliable and relevant record evidence." After that value is determined, Paskill is entitled to receive "its proportionate interest in that operating entity at the time of the merger without any discount at the shareholder level."

Remand to consider discount at corporate level

Notably, however, the Supreme Court instructed in Paskill that it may be appropriate, on remand, for the Court of Chancery to consider whether the "fair value" of Okeechobee as a going concern includes any element of "discount" from its "net asset value" at the corporate level. The precise nature of any such discount, however, is unclear, and the parties are likely to dispute whether the "law of the case" doctrine precludes the Court of Chancery from admitting expert opinion testimony respecting the propriety of "discounting" Okeechobee's net asset value to account for accrued (but unrealized) tax liability associated with assets that have appreciated in value and/or the costs likely to be associated with selling the assets. If evidence of such "discounts" is permitted on remand, Alcoma may be able to achieve, indirectly, the reduction in value that it was unable to achieve directly. If so, Paskill's apparent victory on appeal would be a Pyrrhic victory, at best.

Smith v. North Carolina Motor Speedway

Citation: Mecklenberg County Case No. 98-CVS-3766
Court: Superior Court
State/Jurisdiction: North Carolina
Date of decision: April 26, 2000
Judge: Doughton

A jury verdict in a dissenters' rights appraisal case awarded $23.47 per share, as opposed to the company's offer of $19.61 per share, in the acquisition of North Carolina Motor Speedway by a subsidiary of Penske Motorsports, Inc.

In April 1997, Carrie DeWitt gave Penske the right to buy her shares, representing about 65% of those outstanding, at $18.61 per share. Based on 2,236,731 shares outstanding, this reflected a total value of just under $42,000,000, plus just under $5 million debt assumed by Penske. On Dec. 2, 1997, Penske Motorsports merged with North Carolina Motor Speedway. The stockholders were offered $19.61 in stock or cash.

Bruton Smith, chairman of Speedway Motorsports (then the largest auto racing company) and owner of just over 530,000 shares, dissented along with other stockholders totaling about 7,000 shares. Penske offered the dissenters $16.77 per share, based on a fairness opinion by investment bankers Interstate/Johnson Lane Corporation. The dissenters claimed a value of $55 per share.

Price Origin	Per Share
Merger Price	$19.61
Dissenters' Claim	$55.00
Jury Verdict	$23.47

Chapter 7: Court Case Abstracts

Experts testifying for the plaintiffs during the two-week trial were T. Randolph Whitt, CPA, ABV, of Hitchner Whitt & Co., P.A., and Mark W. Montgomery of Rocker Partners, a private investment fund. Experts testifying for the defendants were Brent Kulman of Wachovia Securities, Inc. (formerly Interstate/Johnson Lane), Adam Simmonds -formerly of Merrill Lynch and currently with Houlihan Lokey Howard & Zukin, and Shannon Pratt, CFA, FASA, MCBA, CM&AA of Willamette Management Associates.

At the time of the merger, there were three publicly-traded Motorsports companies featuring NASCAR races, which all of the experts used in one way or another: International Speedway (headed by Bill France, also chairman of NASCAR), Penske Motorsports, and Speedway Motorsports. Since then, International acquired Penske, making International the largest motorsports company. Experts for the plaintiffs tended to focus on values per seat, while experts for the defense tended to focus on multiples of EBITDA and EBIT. Both Bruton Smith and Bill Frances testified as fact witnesses at the trial.

In addition to the guideline public companies, there were also several acquisitions that the experts referenced.

Tim Frost, of Frost Motorsports, LLC, an economic and financial consultant to the motorsports industry, noted that jurors might have had a hard time isolating conditions at the acquisition date because several subsequent events occurred. For one thing, NASCAR rode the boom in equity markets. Both International and Speedway used public offering proceeds and "made acquisitions at prices and multiples that exceeded the value of the North Carolina Motor Speedway transaction." In addition, he noted, television contracts for the premier races have been renegotiated at significantly higher prices.

HMO-W v. SSM Health Care System (II)

Citation: 2000 WI 46, 234 Wis. 2d 707, 611 N.W. 2d 250, 2000 Wisc. LEXIS 313
Court: Supreme Court
State/Jurisdiction: Wisconsin
Date of decision: June 7, 2000
Judge: Bradley

The Wisconsin Supreme Court affirmed the ruling of the Court of Appeals in this dissenting shareholder action.

HMO-W Incorporated contemplated a merger with another health care system. SSM Health Care System, one of its minority shareholders, recommended DeanCare Health Plan. HMO-W rejected this recommendation, and ultimately entered into a merger agreement with United Wisconsin Services.

Before submitting the merger to the shareholders for approval, HMO-W obtained a net asset valuation from Valuation Research Corporation, which stated that the net value of HMO-W was between $16.5 and $18 million. Upon vote by the shareholders, SSM and another minority shareholder dissented, but the merger passed.

SSM demanded fair value for its shares, and HMO-W hired a new appraiser to value SSM's stock. This appraiser valued HMO-W at $7.4 million, and therefore HMO-W tendered $1.5 million to SSM for its stock. SSM objected and asserted that its stock was worth $4.7 million.

Under Wisconsin dissenters' rights statutes, a corporation is entitled in this situation to bring an action to determine the fair value of a dissenter's shares, and HMO-W did so. In response, SSM asserted that HMO-W was bound by the appraisal by Valuation Research Corporation that was provided to the shareholders in the proxy materials in connection with the merger.

Trial court rejects proxy valuation

At trial, the court rejected the Valuation Research Corporation (VR) appraisal due to various flaws that were not discussed in detail by the Supreme Court. Both parties presented valuation experts at trial. HMO-W's expert, James Pizzo, testified that the corporation was worth $10.5 million and SSM's expert, Patrick Hurst, testified that it was worth $19.25 million.

Minority discount applied

The trial court accepted the valuation proffered by HMO-W's expert, and applied a 30% minority discount is reaching its valuation conclusion. The Supreme Court noted, "The circuit court concluded that it was required to apply a minority discount as a matter of law."

SSM objected that the trial court had not adequately considered its argument that HMO-W was bound by the VR report, but the trial court stated that it had specifically considered SSM's unfair dealing claim based upon that report.

Court of Appeals rejects minority discount

The Court of Appeals reversed the trial court's ruling regarding the application of a minority discount, and remanded the case for a new determination of fair value without applying the discount. The Court of Appeals held that, as a matter of law, no minority discount could be applied in determining fair value under the dissenters' rights statute because to apply the discount would "frustrate the purpose of dissenters' rights statutes."

The Court of Appeals upheld the trial court, however, on the issue of the VR report, stating that SSM had failed to prove that it had relied on the report in making its decision whether to vote for or against the merger.

Chapter 7: Court Case Abstracts

Supreme Court frames two issues

The Supreme Court framed the two issues on appeal as follows:

1. Whether a minority discount may apply in determining the fair value of a dissenter's shares, which is a question of law requiring statutory interpretation, and
2. Whether a court in making its fair value determination may consider evidence of unfair dealing relating to the value of the dissenter's shares.

In discussing the first issue, the Supreme Court first looked to the statute itself, and the definition of fair value. Both parties argued that this statutory definition is unambiguous, but differed in their interpretation.

HMO-W argued that the statute clearly gave the trial court broad discretion to determine whether to apply a minority discount.

SSM argued that the juxtaposition of "fair value" with "market value" in the statute depending upon the type of corporation involved is clear evidence of the legislature's intent to exclude the application of a minority discount in determining fair value as opposed to market value.

Fair value ambiguous

The Supreme Court held that the term "fair value" as used in the statute is ambiguous and does not directly address the question of whether a minority discount should be applied. Accordingly, the Court looked for legislative history on the issue, but found none. Finally, the Court resorted to case law from other jurisdictions to assist in interpreting the legislative purpose of the dissenters' rights statute.

The Court turned to the seminal case of *Cavalier Oil Corp. v. Harnett*, in which the Delaware Supreme Court held that a minority discount was not appropriate in determining fair value, because to apply such a discount would not be consistent with the statutory purpose of the dissenters' rights statutes. The Court quoted *Cavalier* for the following proposition:

> [T]he appraisal process is not intended to reconstruct a pro forma sale but to assume that the shareholder was willing to maintain his investment position, however slight, had the merger not occurred. . . . To fail to accord to a minority shareholder the full proportionate value of his shares imposes a penalty for lack of control, and unfairly enriches the majority shareholders who may reap a windfall from the appraisal process by cashing out a dissenting shareholder, clearly an undesirable result.

The Wisconsin Supreme Court concluded that a minority discount could not be applied in determining fair value, and that the focus of a fair value determination should not be on the value of the stock as a commodity, but on the minority's proportionate share of the enterprise as a whole.

HMO-W v. SSM Health Care System (II)

Other cases rejected

The Supreme Court rejected the cases cited by HMO-W for the proposition that a minority discount should be applied because they were not dissenting shareholder cases. The Court noted:

> [T]he principles governing valuation of stock for tax or property division purposes may not be imported into the appraisal process. That is because the standard of valuation in any given context should reflect the purpose served by the law in that context.

Marketability discount not addressed

In a footnote, the Supreme Court defined both minority and marketability discounts and discussed their respective purposes. The Court then stated that it was not addressing the issue of whether a marketability discount should be applied because that was not at issue in this case.

Unfair dealing adequately considered

With respect to the second issue, the Supreme Court held that, as a matter of law, where the claim of unfair dealing concerns the value of the shares it is properly considered in the appraisal proceeding. In this case, however, the trial court did adequately consider SSM's claim of unfair dealing in reaching its fair value determination.

Wis. Stat. § 180.1301(4) states:

"Fair value", with respect to a dissenter's shares other than in a business combination, means the value of the shares immediately before the effectuation of the corporate action to which the dissenter objects, excluding any appreciation or depreciation in anticipation of the corporate action unless exclusion would be inequitable. "Fair value", with respect to a dissenter's shares in a business combination, means market value, as defined in s. 180.1130(9)(a)1. to 4.

Wis. Stat. § 180.1130 (9)(a)1. to 4. states:

(9) "Market value" means the following:
  (a) In the case of shares:
    1. If the shares are listed on a national securities exchange registered under the securities exchange act of 1934 or are quoted on any national market system, the highest closing sales price per share reported on the exchange or quoted on the system during the valuation period.
    2. If bids for the shares are quoted on the National Association of Securities Dealers automated quotations system, or any successor system operated by the association, the highest closing bid per share quoted on the system during the valuation period.

3. If the shares are listed on an exchange or are quoted on a system under subd. 1. but no transactions are reported during the valuation period or if the shares are neither listed on an exchange or system under subd. 1. nor quoted on a system under subd. 2., and if at least 3 members of the National Association of Securities Dealers are market makers for the securities, the highest closing bid per share obtained from the association during the valuation period.

4. If no report or quote is available under subd. 1., 2. or 3., the fair market value as determined in good faith by the board of directors of the resident domestic corporation.

DiLuglio v. Providence Auto Body

Type of case: Corporate Dissolution
Citation: 755 A. 2d 757, 2000 R.I. LEXIS 159
Court: Supreme Court
State/Jurisdiction: Rhode Island
Date of decision: June 30, 2000
Judge: Flanders

One of the issues in the corporate dissolution action was whether the trial court erred in refusing to apply a minority discount and a discount for lack of marketability when it valued plaintiff's 20% interest in the defendant corporation.

Plaintiff Thomas DiLuglio received weekly payments from defendant Providence Auto Body, Inc. that were designated as his distribution of profits for his 20% interest in the corporation. Upon learning that defendant John Petrarca, owner of the other 80% interest in the corporation, was receiving a salary of $200,000 per year, DiLuglio demanded to receive a larger share of the profits. Petrarca not only denied this request, he then claimed that DiLuglio did not own any interest in the corporation.

In response, DiLuglio filed an action for dissolution of the corporation. Three years later, and before any trial or hearing on the plaintiff's complaint had been held, Petrarca filed an election to purchase DiLuglio's shares, contingent upon DiLuglio proving that he was, in fact, owner of a 20% interest.

Upon trial of the matter, DiLuglio proved that he was owner of 20% of the corporation, and the trial court appointed a special master to determine the value of that interest. The special master determined that the corporation as a whole was worth $874,000, and that DiLuglio's 20% was therefore worth $174,800.

Petrarca argued that the trial court should apply minority and marketability discounts totaling $150,000 to the special master's valuation. The court concluded that the discounts should not be applied and awarded DiLuglio a judgment in the amount of $174,800 plus interest from the date of the election to purchase. Petrarca appealed.

The Supreme Court upheld the trial court's determination of value because it was supported by the evidence. It further upheld the trial courts decision not to apply minority and marketability discounts.

As the trial justice correctly noted, the sale of this block of minority stock was assured because a known and qualified buyer (Petrarca) existed to purchase DiLuglio's PAB shares. Hence, the court properly refused to consider that these shares lacked a controlling value or a readily available market for their sale.

The Supreme Court also cited its prior holding, in *Charland v. Country View Golf Club, Inc.*, 588 A.2d 609 (R.I. 1991), that such discounts should not be applied in dissolution proceedings.

Cooke v. Fresh Express Foods

Citation: 169 Or. App. 101, 7 P.3d 717, 2000 Ore. App. LEXIS 1128
Court: Court of Appeals
State/Jurisdiction: Oregon
Date of decision: July 12, 2000
Judge: Armstrong

One of the issues in this shareholder oppression action was the valuation of plaintiff Terry Cooke's 25% interest in Fresh Express Foods Corporation, a closely held Subchapter S corporation.

Defendants John Quicker and Joni Quicker are father and daughter, and plaintiff was Joni's husband at the time the business was started and later incorporated. Through a series of transaction and a pattern of conduct, defendants squeezed plaintiff out of the corporation and denied him any benefit of his shareholder interest. Plaintiff filed this action to recover the fair value of his stock.

Following a trial, defendants were ordered to buy out plaintiff at the amount the court determined to be fair value. The plaintiff did not seek to dissolve the corporation at trial. The Court of Appeals affirmed the trial court's decision.

S corps benefits of ownership important

Plaintiff presented the expert testimony of Lewis Olds of Lewis Olds & Associates regarding the fair value of plaintiff's stock. The expert testified to the value of the company as a profitable going concern, made several adjustments to account for excessive expenses, and calculated plaintiff's 25% share of that going concern value. Olds then added to that amount plaintiff's unpaid wages from the time defendant John Quicker had terminated his employment with the corporation.

Defendants, on the other hand, presented the testimony of the company accountant, Robert Johnson. The accountant calculated the liquidation value of the company, and testified that plaintiff was entitled to 25% of that value.

The trial court rejected the testimony of the defendant's expert as having limited relevance to the issue of fair value, and awarded plaintiff the sum recommended by his expert. The trial court allowed the inclusion of the lost wages:

> [The court] recognized that the owners of close subchapter S corporations generally receive their benefits in a variety of generally interchangeable ways, including salaries, 'loans, and distributions of profits.'

Since plaintiff was deprived of the benefits of ownership because of defendant's oppressive conduct, the trial court felt it was appropriate to include this sum in its buy-out award.

Liquidation value rejected

The Court of Appeals found that the trial courts valuation was not erroneous. The rejection of the liquidation value evidence was appropriate because the company was a going concern, and the plaintiff was entitled to his pro-rata share of that going concern. The Court also agreed with the trial courts rationale for including the lost wages.

The Court of Appeals also affirmed prior Oregon case law holding that no minority or marketability discount should be applied in determining fair value in a shareholder oppression action where the oppressors are ordered to buy out the oppressed shareholder.

BVR Editor Comment: Defendants in this matter would have been better served, it seems, if they had hired an independent appraiser to value the corporation as a going concern-based on a case law definition of "fair value." This would have given the trial court relevant valuation evidence to consider from both sides.

Advanced Communication Design, Inc. v. Follett (II)

Citation: 615 N.W. 2d 285, 2000 Minn. LEXIS 417
Court: Supreme Court
State/Jurisdiction: Minnesota
Date of decision: August 3, 2000
Judge: Stringer

In November 1999, the Minnesota Court of Appeals ruled, in a case of first impression in Minnesota, that a marketability discount should not be applied to determine the fair value of Brian Follett's one-third interest in Advanced Communication Design, Inc. (ACD). The corporation and its only voting shareholder, Marco Scibora, appealed to the Minnesota Supreme Court.

'Majority report' accepted

At trial of this matter, the parties agreed to an appraisal procedure in which each party appointed one appraiser and the court appointed a third appraiser. The court appointed appraiser and the appraiser appointed by Follett agreed upon a "majority report," and the appraiser appointed by ACD and Scibora presented a "minority report." The trial court accepted the majority report with respect to the enterprise value, but declined to apply a marketability discount.

The Court of Appeals affirmed the trial court ruling, and held that a marketability discount should not be applied in this case because Follett was an oppressed minority shareholder.

Bright-line rule rejected

On appeal, the Minnesota Supreme Court reviewed the Minnesota Business Corporation Act definition of fair value, as well as case law from other jurisdictions on the issue. The Court found that, as a starting point, fair value in a court-ordered buy-out "means the pro rata share of the value of the corporation as a going concern." Had the Court stopped here, it would have affirmed the Court of Appeals ruling.

However, the Court went on to say that, under the Minnesota statute, the value assigned by the trial court must be "fair and equitable to all parties." Accordingly, the Court rejected a "bright-line rule" rejecting the application of a marketability discount in all cases.

> [A] bright-line rule that would foreclose consideration of a marketability discount in all circumstances could lead to a valuation that is unfair to the remaining shareholders, a result also contrary to the purpose of section 302A.751.

The Court then turned to the American Law Institute (ALI) Principles of Corporate Governance for guidance. The ALI principles suggest that a marketability discount should be applied in a case where "extraordinary circumstances" exist, such as the possibility of an unfair wealth transfer.

> An example of an 'unfair wealth transfer' is where the exercise of a minority shareholder's appraisal rights in a financially strained corporation with illiquid assets would yield a price far greater than the price that would actually be paid for the shares in a market transaction.

Supreme Court finds extraordinary circumstances

In reviewing the trial court record, the Court found that extraordinary circumstances existed in this case that warranted the application of a marketability discount. In particular, in looking at the financial information in the majority report, it was clear that ACD's financial and cash-flow position was such that paying Follett $475,381 for his stock would result in an unfair wealth transfer and put "unrealistic financial demands on the corporation."

The Court pointed out that the "fair value" of Follett's shares determined by the trial court was five times ACD's net worth, seven times its average annual operating cash flow, and eight times its average net income.

The Court noted that such payment would also interfere with ACD's historical practice of reinvesting cash flows to promote growth of the company, leaving the corporation and the remaining shareholders with an "extremely doubtful potential for growth."

The Court remanded the case to the trial court for a determination of the appropriate marketability discount, but directed that the discount should be somewhere between 35% and 55%, the discounts opined in the majority and minority reports presented at trial.

No fiduciary duty

A second issue on appeal was whether the minority shareholder, Brian Follett, owed a fiduciary duty to the corporation and the other shareholders. The Supreme Court affirmed the Court of Appeals ruling that no fiduciary duty was owed because Follett held only nonvoting stock and was not a director. Therefore, he had no ability to control corporate decisions. The relationship of Follett to the other shareholders was not similar to that of partners.

BVR Editor Comment: The Minnesota Supreme Court seems to have eliminated the issue of oppression from its analysis. Although it focused on fairness to all the parties, it failed to address the fact that Scibora's oppressive conduct was unfair to Follett, and that he should not be rewarded for that conduct. The Court mentions the "guiding principle" from the New Jersey cases of Balsamides and Lawson Mardon Wheaton, that an oppressing shareholder should not benefit from a marketability discount, but does not apply that principle in this case.

English v. Artromick International, Inc.

Citation: 2000 Ohio App. LEXIS 3580
Court: Court of Appeals
State/Jurisdiction: Ohio
Date of decision: August 10, 2000
Judge: Kline

This is an appeal of the trial court's determination of the "fair cash value" of plaintiff Thomas J. English's 11.43% interest in Artromick International, Inc.

The majority shareholders of Artromick decided that they wanted to sell the corporate assets or merge with another business entity and began to explore their options. In preparation, Artromick hired The Harmon Group Corporate Finance to appraise the corporation and seek out potential buyers. Harmon determined that the value of Artromick was between $22.46

million and $30 million. Several potential investors submitted letters of interest, one of which the corporation elected to pursue.

Artromick offered English $1.16 million for his stock in preparation for a merger with Medicart Industries, Inc., but English refused the offer and filed suit under Ohio Revised Code Annotated §1701.85 for a judicial determination of the fair cash value of his stock.

At trial, English offered the expert testimony of Anthony Mollica of Anthony F. Mollica & Associates. Mollica determined the overall value of Artromick to be approximately $21 million, and the value of English's 11.43% interest to be $2.4 million. Mollica did not apply any discounts in reaching his valuation opinion.

Artromick offered the expert testimony of Dr. Stephen Buser. Buser determined that the overall value of Artromick was $14 million, that English's pro rata share was $1.2 million, and that the "fair cash value" of English's 11.43% interest was $361,532. To reach the fair cash value, Buser applied a 50% minority discount and a 40% marketability discount. The trial court accepted Buser's valuation, and awarded English $361,532 for his Artromick stock. The court rejected the testimony of Mollica as unhelpful, because he failed to apply a minority or marketability discount.

English appealed, asserting the following:

> (1) [T]he trial court should have relied on [Mollica's] stock valuation instead of Buser's opinion, (2) Artromick's offer to buy his shares [for $1.16 million] should serve as a minimum value for his shares, (3) minority discounts should not be applied to freeze-out mergers, and (4) marketability discounts should not be applied to freeze-out mergers.

The Court of Appeals of Ohio rejected each of English's arguments and upheld the trial court's ruling because it was supported by competent evidence in the record. The trial court acted within its discretion in accepting Buser's testimony and rejecting Mollica's.

Artromick's offer to purchase was not a binding admission of the fair cash value, and was not even good evidence of fair cash value, because it potentially included the value to Artromick of avoiding this litigation.

As for the application of minority and marketability discounts, the Court of Appeals turned to prior case law that defined the term "fair cash value" as used in the Ohio dissenter's rights statute. Pursuant to *Armstrong v. Marathon Oil Company*, 32 Ohio St. 3d 357, 513 N.E.2d 776 (1987), fair cash value is defined as the following:

> [T]he amount a willing seller, under no compulsion to sell, would be willing to accept, and a willing buyer, under no compulsion to purchase, would be willing to pay for a share of stock of the corporation to be merged.

Under this standard, the trial court could consider any factor that a willing buyer or willing seller would consider, including the fact that the stock represented a minority interest or that it was relatively unmarketable. The Court of Appeals rejected the foreign case law cited by English in support of his argument that the discounts should not be applied. Those cases, the Court noted, were interpreting "fair value," and "[t]he concept of 'fair value' is far different from the 'fair cash value' concept."

BVR Editor Comment: This is yet another case illustrating the importance of reviewing the case law in the jurisdiction in which a case is heard to determine the proper standard of value. A simple reading of the Ohio statute, which uses the term "fair cash value," could easily lead one to the conclusion that fair cash value is akin to fair value, as used in the dissenter's rights statutes of other jurisdictions. In fact, fair cash value is more akin to "fair market value" as used in federal tax matters.

Blitch v. The Peoples Bank

Citation: 246 Ga. App. 453, 540 S.E.2d 667, 2000 Ga. App. LEXIS 1265
Court: Court of Appeals
State/Jurisdiction: Georgia
Date of decision: October 23, 2000
Judge: Johnson

Minority shareholder J. Dan Blitch, III, owned 763.5 shares of The Peoples Bank (Bank), which composed 5.5% of the outstanding stock of the corporation. The Peoples Holding Company (Holding Company) owned the remaining shares.

The Bank was merged with another corporation that was owned by the Holding Company, and Blitch dissented. The Bank filed this appraisal action seeking a determination of the fair value of Blitch's stock.

Trial court rejects Blitch's expert testimony

In a non-jury trial, the court heard expert appraisal testimony from both sides. The expert for the Bank testified that Blitch's stock was worth $1,214 per share. He applied both minority and marketability discounts in his calculations. The expert for Blitch testified that the stock was worth $2,342 per share, which was based upon Blitch's proportionate share of the corporation as a whole.

The trial court rejected the valuation of Blitch's expert because, among other things, he failed to use minority and marketability discounts. The court found the valuation of the Bank's expert to be generally sound, applied minority and marketability discounts, and concluded that the fair value of each share was $1,418.

Applying discounts was error

Blitch appealed, citing the court's application of discounts in determining the fair value of his stock as error. The Court of Appeals reversed the trial court, holding that minority and marketability discounts should not be applied in determining the fair value of a dissenting stockholder's shares, and remanded the case for a new fair value determination.

Only one prior appellate case in Georgia had addressed this issue. In *Atlantic States Const. v. Beavers,* the Georgia Court of Appeals had determined that minority and marketability discounts could be considered in the fair value calculation, but should not be overemphasized. The Court did not follow this case because it was not binding precedent due to at least one dissent, and because it found authority to the contrary to be more persuasive.

Model Act comments relevant

The Court noted that the Georgia dissenting shareholder statute is based upon the Model Business Corporation Act, and that the Georgia legislature specifically stated in comments to the statute that the official comments to the Model Act (*see* below) were relevant to any interpretation of the Georgia statute. In looking at the official comments, the 1999 amendments to the Model Act, and case law from other jurisdictions holding that minority and marketability discounts should not be applied, the Court of Appeals concluded that they were more persuasive than *Atlantic States* and adopted that rule.

Crismon v. Crismon

Citation: 72 Ark. App. 116, 34 S.W.3d 763, 2000 Ark. App. LEXIS 795
Court: Court of Appeals
State/Jurisdiction: Arkansas
Date of decision: December 13, 2000
Judge: Koonce

Suzanne Crismon, appellant, and John Crismon, appellee, divorced in September 1996, and entered into a property settlement agreement. The agreement allowed Mrs. Crismon to take over Mr. Crismon's partnership interest in two convenience stores and certain commercial property, in which Mr. Crismon had a 50% partnership interest with Larry Garland. Garland refused to allow Wife to take over Husband's interest, and she brought this action seeking one-half of Husband's partnership interest and one-half of his pension plan. Garland testified that the fair market value of the entire partnership was $350,000. Wife's expert, Cheryl Shuffield of Moore Stephens Frost, valued the partnership using the fair value standard at over $1 million, with Husband's interest worth $555,000. Shuffield then applied a marketability discount of 10%, lowering Husband's interest to $500,000. Husband's expert, Bruce Engstrum, valued Husbands interest at $286,000, using a cash flow discount rate of 15% and a marketability discount of 12%. The trial court held that the fair market value of the entire partnership was $365,000 and rewarded Wife $182,500. Wife appealed the trial courts application of a marketability discount rate.

Marketability discount turns on selling

Wife argued that there was controlling case law that supports her contention that the court should not have applied a marketability discount. She cited *Jones v. Jones*, where the Arkansas Court of Appeals disallowed a 32% marketability discount on the value of an accounting firm. The Court rejected Wife's contention that *Jones* was controlling, because the proposed discount in *Jones* reflected the costs associated with selling the partnership interest when there was not evidence that the interest would have been sold:

> In the Jones decision our court did not specifically reject applying a 'marketability discount to marital property divisions of businesses, but found that the justification for the discount (based on a buy-sell agreement among the partners and the anticipated loss of business if a partner left) was not appropriate under the facts of that case. In the present case, the discount(s) in dispute do not purport to represent future lost business, as in Jones, but reflect expenses that would be incurred in marketing and selling the partnership interest.

The Court held that the trial courts valuation was not erroneous and affirmed its decision.

Trial court should consider "low-balling" motivation

The dissent, on the other hand, agreed with Wife that the trial court should not have included a marketability discount. The dissent stated that the trial court did not take into account "the obvious joint interest shared by Garland and Husband in setting the value low," and "low-balling" the value of Husbands interest. The dissent pointed out that nowhere in the property settlement agreement did it provide for the partnership to be sold if Garland refused Wife as a partner. If the agreement had provided for that, only then should the fair market value standard be applied.

Fair value more appropriate

The dissent argued that the Court should have applied the fair value standard, because "the concept of fair value in the context of a dissenting stockholder facing a corporate merger seems more applicable to the situation in this case. Under that standard, fair value is determined by ascertaining all assets and liabilities of the business and the intrinsic value of its stock rather than merely appraising its market value." Therefore, the dissent concluded that the fair market value standard should not have been applied, because it "assumes that the partnership would be sold."

First Western Bank Wall v. Olsen

Citation: 2001 SD 16, 621 N.W.2d 611, 2001 S.D. LEXIS 16
Court: Supreme Court
State/Jurisdiction: South Dakota
Date of decision: January 31, 2001
Judge: Gilbertson

This shareholder dispute appeal raised issues of expert testimony admissibility and the trial court's interpretation of fair value. The First Western Bank Wall (Bank) was controlled by the holding company First Western Bancorp (Bancorp), which was, in turn, controlled by Paul Christen. Bancorp owned 13,000 shares of Bank's 15,000 outstanding shares. The defendants, collectively referred to as the Olsens, owned 1,100 Bank shares.

Majority shareholder Bancorp amended the Bank's Articles of Incorporation to provide a reverse stock split that reduced the Olsens' shares to .88 shares. The Olsens submitted their shares for redemption following Bank's fair value estimate of the shares, received $601,263, and then filed a written demand for a deficiency payment. After failing to reach a settlement, Bank petitioned the circuit court for a fair value determination of the Olsens' shares.

Bank appealed the trial courts admission of the testimony of the Olsens expert appraiser, Paul Thorstenson, CPA/ABV, CVA, of Ketel Thorstenson, LLP, and the courts interpretation of "fair value" under the South Dakota code.

Expert testimony admissible based on professional credentials and experience

Bank challenged the expert's qualifications because he had not valued banks prior to this valuation.

Bank argued that Thorstenson's testimony was irrelevant and unreliable because it "was speculative, not based on reliable foundations, and contradictory within its own definitions, and thus would be of no aid to the finder of fact in determining just compensation in this case."

Relying on SDCL 19-15-2 (which is identical to FRE 702) as well as *Daubert* and *Kumho* (which had been previously adopted by the South Dakota Supreme Court), the appellate court upheld the trial courts admission of this testimony. The court noted that the expert had the following qualifications:
- Business valuation involvement since 1983
- NACVA certification
- Preparation or supervision of more than 75 business valuation reports
- Knowledge of economic climate in Banks branch location through client contact

The court also noted that Thorstenson used the same valuation methods as Bank's expert and that the difference in their valuations was attributable to the emphasis they put on the various methods.

Fair value does not require minority or marketability discount

The appellate court upheld the trial court's refusal to apply a minority discount. To encourage investment in minority corporate interests and to prevent penalizing one for lack of control, the court prevented a windfall for the "insider" majority holder. This would unfairly enrich the majority by not providing "full proportionate value" when "cashing out" the minority shareholder.

Bank also asserted that the court should apply a 15% discount to the Olsens' shares for lack of a "ready and available market." Noting that the ready market in a dissenters' rights context is the majority shareholder or the corporation, this court sought to value the business as a whole and divide up the proportionate share.

The court noted that the precedents relied upon by Bank in support of the argument that "fair value" is equivalent to "fair market value" involved a property value dispute, a marital dissolution, and a deficiency judgment statute. These cases were not controlling here "because the purposes and policies expressed in those cases are inconsistent with the purpose and policies behind our dissenters rights statutes." Instead, the court relied upon precedent from other jurisdictions in support of its decision that fair value is the minority shareholders proportionate share of the corporation as a whole.

M Life Ins. Co. v. Sapers & Wallack Ins. Agency, Inc.

Citation: 40 P.3d 6, 2001 Colo. App. LEXIS 166
Court: Court of Appeals
State/Jurisdiction: Colorado
Date of decision: February 1, 2001
Judge: Nieto

Respondent was a Class A shareholder of petitioner. In 1996, petitioner merged with another corporation, resulting in its issued and outstanding shares being converted into shares of the new entity. Respondent dissented to the merger, triggering the provisions of the Colorado dissenters' rights statute. Petitioner asked the trial court to determine the fair value of respondent's shares, and this appeal followed.

Respondent's unique corporate structure and bylaws

Petitioner assigned as error the trial court's determination of the fair value of respondent's shares. More specifically, petitioner argued that its unique corporate structure and bylaws precluded consideration of going concern value in the determination of fair value.

M Life Ins. Co. v. Sapers & Wallack Ins. Agency, Inc.

The court then described petitioner's corporate structure as follows: Petitioner was an agent-owned reinsurance company. Its Class A shareholders were all life insurance agents. Petitioner only issued reinsurance policies on life insurance policies sold by its agent/shareholders through other life insurance companies. Petitioner divided its reinsurance policies into groups referred to as "generations." Petitioner's bylaws allocated profit and loss created by each new generation of reinsurance policies only to that generation.

Respondent wrote policies in earlier generations but did not write any policies that were reinsured with petitioner after December 1987. Nevertheless, the policies that respondent wrote continued in force to the date of the valuation and thus continued to generate income to petitioner.

Evidence supported consideration of fair value on going concern basis

The court of appeals noted that the determination of fair value for a dissenting shareholder is controlled by the dissenters' rights statute and not by a company's bylaws. A fair value determination also depends, however, on the particular circumstances of the corporation involved—in this case, petitioner's unusual corporate structure.

The term "going concern" refers to "an existing solvent business, which is being conducted in the usual and ordinary way for which it was organized." "Going concern value," the court said, means "the value of a firm, assuming that the firm's organization and assets remain intact and are used to generate future income and cash flows."

The court stated:

> It is undisputed that [petitioner] continued doing business after the merger and that the reinsurance policies attributable to [respondent] continued to generate income to [petitioner]....[Respondent's] shares constituted a share of ownership in the entire corporation and not just a share of ownership in the assets constituting a specific generation of reinsurance policies.

Weighing the evidence, including expert testimony from both sides, the trial court concluded that fair value of respondent's shares included a consideration of petitioner on a going concern basis. Because there was support in the record for the trial court's findings of fact, the appellate court found no error.

No minority discount

Petitioner next argued that the trial court erred in failing to consider a minority discount. Citing *Lawson Mardon Wheaton*, 160 N.J. 383, 398-99, 734 A.2d 738, 747 (1999), the court of appeals approved the distinction discussed in that opinion between minority and marketability discounts.

According to the appeals court, the application of a minority discount in a dissenters' rights action involving a corporation that continues to do business is a case of first impression in Colorado. The court in *Walter S. Cheesman Realty Co. v. Moore*, 770 P.2d 1308 (Colo. App. 1988) held that a minority discount was not appropriate if the corporation was being dissolved and all assets were being liquidated, a different situation from that presented in this case.

The court then concluded that, in a dissenters' rights action, where the corporation continues as a going concern, a minority discount does not apply to the valuation of the dissenters' shares of stock as a matter of law. It found the analysis in *Friedman v. Beway Realty Corp.*, 87 N.Y.2d 161, 661 N.E.2d 972, 638 N.Y.S.2d 399 (1995), to be compelling. There the court rejected a minority discount under the same circumstances because it would:

(1) Deprive minority shareholders of their proportionate interest in a going concern;
(2) Value minority shares below majority shares and result in unequal treatment of the same class of shares;
(3) Undermine one goal of the dissenters' rights statute, i.e., preventing minority shareholders from being forced to sell at unfairly low values while allowing the majority to proceed as it desires; and
(4) Encourage oppressive majority conduct.

Marketability discount depends on facts of case

Petitioner also argued that the trial court failed to consider a marketability discount. Here the court of appeals agreed. A prior Colorado case, *WCM Indus. v. Trustees of Wilson Trust*, 948 P.2d 36 (Colo. App. 1997), held that a marketability discount may, in certain circumstances, be applicable, but that such a determination is a factual one and must be made on a case-by-case basis. The case set forth a non-exclusive list of factors that may be considered in determining whether a marketability discount is appropriate.

Thus, the court found that the trial court erred in rejecting the discount as a matter of law and remanded the case back to the trial court to make findings of fact on this issue and, if necessary, revalue the shares to include such discount.

Swope v. Siegel-Robert, Inc. (II)

Citation: 243 F.3d 486, 2001 U.S. App. LEXIS 2760
Court: United States Court of Appeals
State/Jurisdiction: 8th Circuit Federal
Date of decision: February 26, 2001
Judge: McMillian

The Eighth Circuit reviewed *de novo Swope v. Siegel-Robert*, 74 F. Supp. 876 (E.D. Mo. June 23, 1999). Siegel-Robert, Inc. contested the district court's holding that fair value of the company's shares did not require a marketability discount, and argued that the court erred in not providing adequate reasons for its valuation determination.

One of the issues raised on cross-appeal by the minority shareholder argued that the district court erred in its fair value calculation by applying a minority discount.

No discount for lack of marketability

In valuing the shares at $63.36 per share, the district court held that a minority discount was appropriate but a lack of marketability discount was not appropriate. Siegel-Robert argued for including a lack of marketability discount because "the lack of control over minority shares and the absence of a liquid market are relevant circumstances [that] reduce the value of the stock."

The Eighth Circuit refused to apply a discount for lack of marketability in determining the fair value of the dissenting shareholders' stock. The court sought to equitably compensate the minority shareholders for lack of control.

The court held that minority stock valuation considers the value of the corporation as a whole and awards a pro-rata share of the value to the minority shareholders. This ensures that the dissenters "retain the same proportionate value of their stock regardless of undesired changes dictated by majority vote." Fair value maintains equality between the value of minority and majority shares by reflecting actual interest prior to corporate change, independent from the influence of market variables.

In dissenting shareholder stock appraisals fair value is not the same as fair market value because dissenters are not the same as "willing and ready buyers of the open market. Rather, they are unwilling sellers with no bargaining power." The court followed the ALI's "fair value" interpretation, which does not include any discount "absent extraordinary circumstances for lack of marketability." These circumstances must include more than an absence of a trading market for the shares.

Furthermore, majority shareholders would benefit at the expense of the minority shareholders if a court imposed a marketability discount. The majority would "reap a windfall" in a buyout or corporate squeeze-out.

The Eighth Circuit noted that the purpose of the Missouri appraisal statute is to protect minority stockholders in closely held corporations. The statute seeks to compensate dissenting shareholders for full proportionate value of the stock.

Minority discount inappropriate in dissenting shareholder valuation

The court noted that dissenting shareholders are unwilling to sell their stock. "[A minority] discount injects a market factor into the determination of fair value." Therefore, the dissenting minority shareholders' position is not reflected by the market because they are entitled to "the full value of their shares as if they were able to retain the stock."

The Eighth Circuit noted that applying a minority discount would defeat the appraisal statute's purpose "by penalizing shareholders for their lack of control and encouraging majority shareholders to take advantage of their power."

Trend toward disallowing discounts

Siegel-Robert argued that, under the Erie doctrine, the Eighth Circuit had no authority to disallow minority or marketability discounts. They argued that only Missouri state courts could interpret Missouri statutes. The Eighth Circuit noted, however, that under Erie it is only bound by state case law from the highest state court. Since the Missouri Supreme Court has never ruled on whether minority and marketability discounts are applicable as a matter of law in a fair value determination, the federal court was free to determine what it believed the Missouri Supreme Court would rule in such a case.

The Eighth Circuit looked to Delaware corporate law and their expertise in the subject matter as persuasive. The court noted the "compelling logic of the current trend toward disallowing" minority and marketability discounts in dissenting shareholders fair value appraisals, and found that the Missouri Supreme Court would follow this trend.

Specific valuation calculations not required from trial court

Siegel-Robert also argued that the district court erred by not providing "precise mathematical calculations" for its fair value determination. The Eighth Circuit refused to find clear error because the courts valuation fell within the range submitted by the experts.

Revaluation on remand

The Eighth Circuit remanded the case to the district court to redetermine the fair value of the Siegel-Robert stock consistent with this opinion, that is, without applying any discounts.

Shannon Pratt Comment: In reading this case, I wondered what the district court will determine is the fair value on remand? Will the district court simply adopt the control value opined by Robert Reilly at the original trial of this matter (see table below)? Or will the district court hold a new hearing and receive new evidence of fair value?

BVR Editor Comment: Because of the sweeping rejection of discounts in this case, it is important to consider whether and when it is binding on other courts. This is a federal court case, in which the Eighth Circuit decided what it thought the Missouri Supreme Court would do in this situation. Accordingly, it is not binding on the Missouri Supreme Court, should that court hear a case on this issue. It is also not binding on other Missouri state courts, but is very persuasive. However, given the existence of King v. F.I.J., Inc., 765 S.W.2d 301 (Mo.App., 1989), a Missouri Court of Appeals case which held that the application of discounts should be determined on a case-by-case basis, a Missouri state trial court could still apply such discounts.

However, a federal district court trying a case is bound by the Eighth Circuit decision in this case, at least until the Missouri Supreme Court creates some precedent to the contrary.

Siegel-Robert, Inc. Fair Value per Share			
	Robert Reilly for Plaintiffs	Ken Patton for Defendants	Court's Conclusion
Control Value	$98.40*		
Marketable minority value	$72.90	$46.20	$63.36
Nonmarketable Minority value		$30.02**	
* After adding 35% control premium ** After subtracting 35% marketability discount			

Hayes v. Olmsted & Assoc.

Citation: 173 Or. App. 259, 21 P.3d 178, 2001 Ore. App. LEXIS 404
Court: Court of Appeals
State/Jurisdiction: Oregon
Date of decision: March 28, 2001
Judge: Brewer

Plaintiff brought this action under the Oregon dissenters' rights statute, claiming oppressive conduct of the majority shareholders and requesting judicial dissolution of the subject company. Plaintiff was a former employee, officer, director, and shareholder of the company, a food brokerage firm.

The parties settled most of the issues in the case, agreeing that the company would purchase plaintiff's shares and providing for payment terms. The settlement agreement did not stipulate, however, the value of the shares or the method for determining that value, explicitly reserving those issues for judicial resolution.

Although it reviewed the case *de novo*, the court of appeals agreed with the trial court's finding that the majority shareholders had acted oppressively toward plaintiff in excluding him from management decisions and information.

'Fair and reasonable price' for minority buyout

The court of appeals next considered the appropriate measure of value for plaintiff's stock under the settlement agreement. As part of the agreement, plaintiff had abandoned his claim for judicial dissolution of the company. The appeals court quoted *Baker v. Commercial Body Builders,*

264 Or. 614, 633, 507 P.2d 387 (1973), for judicial authority to provide alternate remedies for oppressive conduct, including:

> The ordering of affirmative relief by the entry of an order requiring the corporation or a majority of its stockholders to purchase the stock of the minority stockholders at a price to be determined according to a specified formula or at a price determined by the court to be a fair and reasonable price. (emphasis added by court of appeals)

The appeals court noted that, following *Baker*, the Supreme Court had not had further opportunity to explain the meaning of the term "fair and reasonable price." The court stated, however, that this determination is inherently dependent on the evidence presented by the parties.

Rule of thumb formula used to value going concern

Plaintiff's expert witness, Michael Bathurst, CPA, CVA, used a rule of thumb formula in valuing the company's stock. He explained that it was the most reliable method because of the company's history of using the formula in arms-length negotiations and transactions with other food brokerages. Bathurst arrived at $171.35 per share as plaintiff's proportionate share of the corporations going concern value.

Prior redemptions under stock purchase agreement

The defendants submitted no expert opinion evidence regarding the company's value. They relied exclusively on testimony of the Executive Committee members, who testified that there was no industry rule of thumb formula applicable to food brokerage transactions. They claimed that the actual price would simply depend on the market and the particular brokerage. Defendants asserted that the Stock Purchase Agreement (SPA) provided the most reliable value of the shares, because the company had redeemed other minority shareholders stock based on this price. The SPA value had been set at $64 per share and had not been increased since 1994.

Plaintiff's experts evidence deemed most persuasive

The trial court had rejected plaintiff's argument that the stock should be valued as a pro rata share of the corporations going concern value. The court of appeals held that the evidence did not support the trial courts conclusions.

Unlike the trial court, the court of appeals gave no weight to the previous redemptions because there was no evidence that those situations involved oppression. It also rejected the SPA price because it had not been updated since 1994, was the result of a contractual balancing of shareholder and corporate interests, and did not reflect the fair value of the company in the context of shareholder oppression.

The best evidence, the court said, came from plaintiff's expert. Moreover, the undisputed evidence that the company had previously relied on the rule of thumb formula completely discredited defendant's position that the formula was inapplicable in its industry.

No discounts in case of oppression

The court summarily dismissed minority and marketability discounts, stating that Oregon courts had previously determined that these discounts were not appropriate in determining the fair value of the stock of a victim of oppressive conduct.

The court also rejected defendant's argument that awarding plaintiff a pro rata share of the company would impose an undue burden on the company, as there was no evidence to support this assertion.

The court remanded for entry of judgment reflecting a value of $171.35 per share for plaintiffs stock.

In re Penepent Corp.

Citation: 96 N.Y.2d 186, 726 N.Y.S.2d 345, 750 N.E.2d 47, 2001 N.Y. LEXIS 978
Court: Court of Appeals
State/Jurisdiction: New York
Date of decision: May 1, 2001
Judge: Rosenblatt

In 1979 New York enacted legislation authorizing judicial dissolution proceedings by oppressed minority shareholders of closely held corporations. The statute, Business Corporation Law (BCL) §1104-a, is counterbalanced by BCL §1118, which gives the corporation and the other shareholders the right to avoid dissolution by electing to purchase the petitioner's(s') shares for "fair value," to be determined by the court absent agreement among the litigants.

Over the past 22 years the state's highest court, known as the New York Court of Appeals, has decided only a handful of cases construing these two statutes.1 With its recent decision in *In re Penepent Corporation*, the court of appeals has weighed in on two important aspects of the statutory scheme: the election to purchase and valuation discounts.

Sibling rivalry

In one respect *Penepent* presents a typical (you might even say biblical) dissolution fact pattern: ownership and control of a long-established, prosperous, family-owned business, which passes from the founding parent to a set of siblings who later divide into bitterly opposed factions. In this case, four brothers each holding 25% interests split into two 50% camps, setting the stage for an unusual turn of events.

In May 1990, brother Philip petitioned for dissolution under BCL §1104-a. Allied brothers Richard and Angelo promptly elected to purchase Philip's shares at fair value. Within the next month, in the following order, Angelo died and Philip's ally, Francis, filed his own §1104-a petition. The trial court permitted Angelo's estate to revoke his election, putting Richard in line to become sole shareholder after he also elected to purchase Francis's interest.

Then things got really strange. In December 1991, before completion of a valuation hearing, Francis died. Richard, acting as corporate secretary, promptly notified Francis's estate that upon his death the estate was obligated to surrender his shares to the corporation at the $200-per-share price specified in the shareholder agreement which, not surprisingly, was far below fair value. In 1992, Philip obtained a fair value award of approximately $350,000, which was affirmed on appeal. This decision is reported at 198 A.D.2d 782, 605 N.Y.S.2d 691 (N.Y. App. Div. 1993).

Richard thereafter moved unsuccessfully to enforce the stock surrender clause against Francis's estate or, alternatively, to revoke his election. At a second valuation hearing, Richard's expert asserted that, due to the pendency of Philip's dissolution proceeding at the time Francis filed his dissolution petition, Francis's shares should reflect a greater discount than Philip's for lack of marketability. The trial court rejected the expert's argument and the appellate division affirmed the valuation award.

Election trumps buyout provision

In the court of appeals, Richard argued that Francis was still a shareholder when he died and thus, at any time before a consummated transfer of shares to Richard in the valuation proceeding, the corporation was entitled to acquire Francis's shares at the fixed price and retire them. Francis's estate countered that Francis was a shareholder in name only when he died and that Richard was legally bound by his irrevocable election to purchase.

The court of appeals agreed with the estate, holding that "upon Richard's election, Francis had a vested right to recover fair value for his corporate stock and that right survived his death." The general rule in favor of enforcing shareholder agreements gave way to enforcement of Richard's election which preceded Francis's death by a year and a half.

The result, the court observed, follows the evolution of BCL §1118 which, as originally enacted, permitted electing shareholders to revoke their elections at any time. Due to legislative concern for illusory and frivolous elections used for delay purposes, the statute was amended in 1986 to make elections irrevocable unless the court in its discretion permits revocation for "just and equitable considerations."

Dissolution discount denied

Richard also argued that, because Philip's prior dissolution proceeding was pending when Francis commenced his dissolution proceeding, Francis's shares were less marketable than Philip's and therefore subject to a greater discount. Richard also appears to have argued that a hypothetical purchaser would demand a greater discount because, when Francis filed his petition, allied brothers Richard and Angelo together stood to control 75% of the company, that is, their own 25% shares each plus Philip's 25% which they had elected to purchase.

The court of appeals rejected both arguments. "To be sure," said the court, "any litigation pending against the corporation could be considered in assessing the fair value of the corporation's shares." Because of Richard's and Angelo's joint election to purchase Philip's shares, however, "the corporation itself was in no danger of dissolution" and, indeed, it "had no financial interest in the litigation."

Richard's second argument resembled a minority or lack-of-control discount, which New York courts consistently have rejected in the context of both §1118 valuations and dissenting shareholder appraisals. A minority discount would "deprive minority shareholders of their proportionate interest in the corporation as a going concern" and "would result in shares of the same class being treated unequally."

Conclusion

The highly unusual facts in *Penepent* likely will limit the decision's precedential utility. Nonetheless, like each of the high court's previous forays into this terrain, the tenor of the *Penepent* decision undoubtedly will influence a broad array of future cases. Certainly, *Penepent* suggests that the courts appropriately will continue to frown upon efforts by majority shareholders to convert the very existence of §1104-a and 1118 proceedings into tactical or financial leverage against petitioning minority shareholders.

Devivo v. Devivo

Citation: 2001 Conn. Super. LEXIS 1285
Court: Superior Court
State/Jurisdiction: Connecticut
Date of decision: May 7, 2001
Judge: Satter

This trial court matter arose from the plaintiff shareholder's action to dissolve defendant corporation. The corporation elected to purchase the plaintiff's stock, and a hearing to determine fair value was held.

Chapter 7: Court Case Abstracts

Facts

Two brothers, Edward and Louis Devivo, started a motor transportation corporation called Dattco, Inc. Each brother owned 50% of the stock. Edward was the secretary treasurer and Louis was the president. Both brothers worked in the corporation and both received the same salary.

Later, Edward's son Tom and Louis' son Donald came to work for the company. Tom did not stay, but Donald did. Over time, he assumed more and more responsibilities and eventually began to run the entire corporation, effectively freezing Edward out. Louis, without consulting Edward, increased Donald's salary and gave him annual bonuses. Edward brought an action under the state statute alleging oppressive conduct and corporate deadlock.

Edward sought dissolution of the corporation, which elected to purchase Edward's share at fair value. In the event that the corporation's election was ineffective, Louis elected to purchase Edward's share.

Trial court findings

This was a case of first impression because it was the first time that a Connecticut court had been asked to define "fair value" as used in the dissolution statute in a case involving two 50% shareholders.

There were two legal issues the court had to resolve:

> (1) Whether to determine the value of the shares directly without regard for the value of the corporation as a whole, or whether to determine the value of the corporation as a whole and allocate value to the shares in proportion to the percentage interest they represent in the corporation; and (2) whether or not to discount the value of shares of a closely held corporation by reason of their lack of marketability, lack of control or for any other reason.

Because there was no direct Connecticut precedent defining fair value in this context, the bulk of the opinion was spent analyzing the meaning given to the term "fair value" by various courts, legislatures, and scholars. The court looked at the way that "fair value" is defined in tax assessment cases, condemnation cases, and other court cases. It analyzed the legislative intent and history behind the Connecticut statute. The court looked to the plain meaning of the words "fair value." After exhaustive research and long discussion, the trial court determined that the proper method to ascertain "fair value" was "to ascertain the value of the corporation as a whole and allocate value to the shares of the petitioning shareholder in proportion to the percentage interest they represent in the corporation."

As for minority and marketability discounts, the court provided extensive research and documentation of the way various courts treat these discounts. It analyzed the underlying rationale for allowing or disallowing them. It discussed the difference between applying a marketability discount at the shareholder level (which was almost never allowed) and applying it at the entity level (which may be appropriate in certain cases). The court concluded that "discounts for lack of control or of marketability should not be allowed in determining fair value within the meaning of §33-900."

An additional issue was whether the court should consider the shareholders' agreement definition of value to be used upon voluntary or involuntary sale of stock. In this case, the agreement defined "fair market value" as not including any discounts. The court concluded that it would give the agreement some weight, but that it did not control the method to be used by the court.

The final issue, which the court did not discuss until after it had discussed the valuation evidence, was whether "extraordinary circumstances" warranted the application of a marketability discount in spite of the general rule that such a discount should not be applied. Citing the Minnesota case of *Advanced Communication Design v. Follett,* 615 N.W.2d 285 (Minn. 2000), the court found that similar extraordinary circumstances existed in this case.

Valuation evidence

The court discussed the expert testimony on the value of Edward's share. Joseph Floyd provided an appraisal for the defense. He estimated that Edward's share was worth $3,965,000. The court found Floyd's appraisal methods flawed because his analysis was premised on his statement that fair value had the same meaning as fair market value. In addition, Floyd attempted to value Edward's interest independently rather than evaluate the corporation as a whole, and he discounted Edward's share for lack of control, lack of marketability, and key man status of Louis and Donald.

Plaintiff presented the expert testimony of Stanley Matuszewski, who determined the value of the corporation using the market and transactional approaches. Under the market approach, he analyzed the corporation's operating performances and financial matters and compared them to a selected group of guideline public companies. Matuszewski took into consideration total capitalization of revenues, total capitalization to EBITDA, total capitalization to EBIT, price to earnings, and price to book equity. After assigning weights to these factors, he concluded that the corporation was worth $30,153,368.

In applying the transaction approach, Matuszewski researched sales of various bus companies on the open market. He determined the transaction price as a multiple of revenues and applied that multiple to the corporation's revenues for 12 months. From this, Matuszewski came to a value of $32,963,420. He weighted the market approach at 40% and the transaction approach at 60%, and concluded the corporation was worth $31,800,000 and Edward's 50% interest was worth $15,900,000.

The second expert witness for the plaintiff was Peter L. Becket. Becket approached the valuation by first determining the value of the corporation as a going concern. He attempted to ascertain its fair market value by researching the sales of other bus companies and determining the proper multiple to apply to factors such as EBITDA, annual revenues, and net tangible assets. Becket then applied the multiples to Dattco's factors and concluded that the price for sale on the open market would be $41,477,591. From this, he deducted long-term liabilities in the amount of

$9,556,392 and concluded the final equity value in the corporation was $31,921,199. Based on this, the fair value of Edward's 50% interest was rounded to $16,000,000.

The trial court agreed with Becket's analysis, but it modified his calculations to reflect the company's entire debt of $14,240,000 instead of just long-term. This brought the value of Dattco to $27,237,591 and Edward's share to $13,618,781.

It was at this point that the court considered the issue of extraordinary circumstances. Recognizing that its fair value determination was 1.6 times Dattco's net worth, more than 2.7 times Dattco's operating cash flow, and more than seven times its net income that year, the court determined that this constituted "extraordinary circumstances." Accordingly, the court applied a 35% marketability discount, concluding that the fair value of Edward's share was $9,852,208.

Offenbecher v. Baron Services, Inc. (I)

Citation: 2001 Ala. Civ. App. LEXIS 219
Court: Court of Appeals
State/Jurisdiction: Alabama
Date of decision: May 18, 2001
Judge: Thompson

Minority shareholder James Offenbecher, owned 130 shares of Baron Services, Inc., an Alabama corporation. On March 31, 1998, the Board of Directors approved a merger plan with Baron Services Delaware. Each shareholder was offered $562.47 per share, the value determined by Gary Saliba of Saliba Financial Group. A second valuation accounted for lagging sales, and the value was revised to $547.77 per share. Offenbecher disagreed with this amount and Baron Services proceeded to file suit against him to determine the fair value of his stock.

The circuit court ruled in favor of Baron Services and ordered Offenbecher to exchange his shares at the value determined by Saliba. Offenbecher appealed, arguing, among other things, that the court erred in determining the fair value of the stock and applying a marketability discount.

Fair Market Value

In calculating the fair market value of Baron's stock, Saliba first determined the "value per share on a freely traded basis" to be $1,124.94. Saliba based his valuation on the company's financial records, future operations, management, the financial information of similar businesses, and the relevant market conditions. He then applied a 50% marketability discount to adjust for the fact that Baron's stock was not publicly traded. The expert for Offenbecher, James "Butch" Williams, valued his shares at $1,653.85. In calculating this value, he assumed higher profits, lower costs, and outstanding shares of 3,190. The trial court agreed with Saliba's appraisal, regarding it as fairer and more reasonable.

Offenbecher v. Baron Services, Inc. (I)

Marketability discount applied

One of the issues discussed by the trial court was the difference between a discount applied for lack of marketability and a discount applied to minority shares. The court stated the following:

> In determining the "fair value" of the shares of a closely held corporation, discounts for lack of marketability of such shares are appropriate and do not provide a windfall to the majority shareholders merely because the shares to be purchased by the majority pursuant to their election under Business Corporation Law § 1118 constitute a minority interest in the corporation (see Matter of Blake, [sic] supra).

In this case, Saliba applied a 50% discount for marketability to all shares and not just minority shareholders. Saliba testified that if he had not applied this discount, he would have made other adjustments in his calculations due to the closely held status of the corporation. These calculations would have resulted in a similar valuation of the stock.

Offenbecher rejected the application of a marketability discount, citing *Balsamides v. Protameen Chems., Inc. and Lawson Mardon Wheaton, Inc. v. Smith*. In both cases, the court agreed that absent "extraordinary circumstances," marketability discounts should not be applied in valuing a dissenting shareholder's stock.

The trial court, however, did not find sufficient evidence in these cases to reject the use of a marketability discount. Instead they referred to *Onti, Inc. v. Integra Bank*, in which it was found that a marketability discount that affects the whole company is allowable, but one that only affects some shareholders is not. The court also cited *Cavalier Oil Corp. v. Harnett*, in which the Delaware Supreme Court allowed corporate-level discounting and not shareholder level discounting. The court stated that a shareholder level discount:

> [F]ails to accord to a minority shareholder the full proportionate value of his shares [which] imposes a penalty for lack of control, and unfairly enriches the majority shareholders.

The appeals court confirmed the trial court's decision.

Dissenting opinion

Judge Murdock disagreed with the courts ruling, stating that most rulings have agreed that discounting should not be allowed in the calculation of "fair value." Murdock cites *"Measuring Stock Value in Appraisals Under the Illinois Business Corporation Act,"* stating:

> Any rule of law that gave shareholders less than their proportionate shares of the whole firms fair value would produce a transfer of wealth from the minority shareholders to the shareholders in control. Such a rule would inevitably encourage corporate squeeze-outs.

Murdock regarded the decision by the court as "the sort of squeeze-out oppression that the appraisal remedy based on fair value was designed to frustrate."

Advanced Communication Design, Inc. v. Follett (III)

Citation: 2001 Minn. App. LEXIS 589
Court: Court of Appeals
State/Jurisdiction: Minnesota
Date of decision: May 29, 2001
Judge: Shumaker

In *Advanced Communication Design v. Follet*, 601 N.W.2d 707 (Minn. Ct. App. 1999), the court ruled that a marketability discount should not apply because a majority shareholder's conduct had oppressed a minority shareholder.

This appeal arose from a partial reversal and remand from the Minnesota Supreme Court for the district court to determine, among other issues, the marketability discount for the minority's shares. On remand, the district court adopted the majority's valuation but applied the minority's 35% marketability discount.

Advanced Communication Design (ACD) argued in this appeal that the district court erred by mixing the majority appraisal with the minority discount.

District Court's fair value not abuse of discretion

The appellate court determined that the district court did not abuse its broad discretion, which arose from the remand that contained no specific valuation directions. The district court applied a 35% marketability discount, which followed the state supreme court's direction to "apply a marketability discount of between 35% and 55%."

The majority shareholders' valuation raised their "discount rate" to 55% even though their empirical studies reflected an average marketability discount of between 30% and 40%. However, they did not envision a discount significantly larger than the average discount. The evaluator noted that:

> [M]anagement had not established a pattern of excessive bonuses or other behavior suggestive of taking out money against the benefit of the Company shareholders. On the other hand, the absence of dividend distributions to shareholders argues that there should likewise be no reduction in the average discount.

The minority shareholders' valuation applied a 35% marketability discount under the average of the studies concerning:

- marketability discounts
- dividend payment
- potential buyers
- restrictive transfer provisions
- voting versus non-voting stock
- the size of the company
- the level and trend of earnings

'Mix and match' rule does not apply

ACD argued that *Genge v. City of Baraboo*, 72 Wis.2d 431, 241 N.W.2d 183 (Wis. 1976), prevents the fact finder from "mixing and matching" the results of separate appraisal reports. The court distinguished the two cases by noting that in a land condemnation action the jury accepted two valuations for different time periods:

> The jury took the difference of the before-value from one witness and the after-value from another witness. The Wisconsin Supreme Court found that the jury's award was higher than the testimony of either witness could support.

Allenson v. Midway Airlines Corp.

Citation: 789 A.2d 572, 2001 Del. Ch. LEXIS 89
Court: Court of Chancery
State/Jurisdiction: Delaware
Date of decision: July 6, 2001
Judge: Jacobs

The sole issue in this dissenting shareholder suit under the Delaware appraisal statute was whether certain concessions made under a cash-out merger agreement were "elements of value" to be considered in determining the corporation's statutory fair value.

Concessions in exchange for capital

Midway Airlines Corporation was in such severe financial trouble that it could not avoid bankruptcy without a significant capital infusion. An investor was found, but it extracted several concessions.

The majority shareholder, the key creditors, and the outside investor reached an agreement. Both parties agree that the concessions would not have been granted absent the merger, and the merger would not have been consummated without the concessions.

The public shareholders were cashed out for nominal consideration-$0.01 per share. Certain preferred and common shareholders of Midway brought this appraisal proceeding, asserting that the merger consideration was inadequate because it failed to include relevant elements of value, specifically, the concessions.

The Cede case

The resolution of this issue turned on the application of a Delaware Supreme Court case, *Cede & Co. v. Technicolor, Inc.*, 684 A.2d 289 (Del. 1996), to the facts of this case. The cash-out merger in that case was the second step of a two-step acquisition of Technicolor, the first being an all-cash tender offer.

The dissenting shareholders in *Cede* argued that the acquirer's business plan for Technicolor should have been included as an element of fair value, because it had been implemented by the date of the merger and added significant value to the company. The Supreme Court agreed, reversing the lower court. It held that the business plan, though an element of future value, was not impermissibly speculative, but was "operative reality," clearly known, susceptible of proof, and being implemented.

The parties' contentions

The plaintiffs in this case argued that the concessions here were known, fixed (i.e., contractually agreed upon), and therefore susceptible of proof and not speculative. They likened them to the business plan in *Cede* and claimed that the two cases were indistinguishable.

Midway admitted that the concessions were known and foreseeable, but argued that as of the merger date neither the company nor its controlling shareholder had the unilateral power to implement them. Therefore, unlike in *Cede*, Midway's "operative reality" on the merger date did not include the concessions.

The court's conclusion

The court rejected both parties' arguments and arrived at its conclusion by independent analysis of the *Cede* case and its application to what it termed "unique facts." It distinguished *Cede* primarily because of its two-step nature. There the implementation of the business plan added value to Technicolor during the interim period that accrued to the benefit of all the shareholders.

The court phrased the appropriate inquiry in this case as whether, on the date of the merger, the acquirer had "added value" to Midway as a going concern by reason of the concessions.

> To that question the answer must clearly be no, because the [Cede Court] recognized that the value of the [business plan] as of the merger date consisted of its actual implementation, not simply its existence on paper. Here, as of the merger date, the Concessions existed only on paper and were not being implemented. Nor could they

be, because the parties to the merger agreement had contracted that the Concessions would not become legally operative until after the merger closed.

[Cede] also exposes the incomplete character of [Midway's] argument that the company or the persons controlling it must have the power to implement the plan as of the merger date. To be sure, those persons must have the "power to implement" the plan, but that alone is not enough. What is also legally essential is that as of the merger date that power has been exercised. Because Midway and its controlling stockholder neither possessed nor exercised the legal power to implement the Concessions on or before the merger date, the inescapable conclusion is that any value attributable to the Concessions cannot be considered as part of Midway's going concern value for [statutory] appraisal purposes.

Torres v. Schripps, Inc.

Citation: 342 N.J. Super. 419, 776 A.2d 915, 2001 N.J. Super. LEXIS 294
Court: Superior Court, Appellate Division
State/Jurisdiction: New Jersey
Date of decision: July 9, 2001
Judge: Wallace

In this dispute over the valuation of closely held corporation stock, the appellate court reversed and remanded the trial court's valuation of the corporation. Dan Marcus incorporated Schripps, Inc., a wholesale gourmet bakery business, and Danilo Torres handled the day-to-day operations. Marcus initially owned all of the stock in Schripps, but Torres eventually acquired a 25% interest.

Parties unable to agree on buyout

After Schripps became "marginally profitable," Torres demanded more money from the corporation by seeking, among other things, a 50-50 profit split. Torres's demands upset Marcus and the parties agreed it would be best for Marcus to buy out Torres's shares. Marcus obtained an independent appraisal, which listed the net equity of the corporation at $98,764. Torres believed the appraisal undervalued the corporate assets and wholly excluded other assets. A series of offers and counteroffers between the parties in the range of $200,000 to $300,000 did not lead to an agreement.

Torres then left Schripps and formed Alpine Bakery, Inc., which directly competed with Schripps. The master baker left Schripps and started working for Alpine Bakery.

Torres sued Schripps and Marcus alleging that Marcus depleted Schripps' profits and cash reserves. He claimed these actions constituted fraud, illegality, mismanagement, and oppression. After defendants' concessions, the only issue left for trial concerned the value of the corporation.

Chapter 7: Court Case Abstracts

Trial court rejects only expert evidence

Schripps' expert, Stephen C. Chait, CPA, used the capitalization of net income method to arrive at a value of $222,400. He testified that he could not use the capitalization method for the Sept. 29, 1997 valuation date because the company was in much worse financial condition and had lost $114,000 by that time. For this date, he used the cost approach and derived a value of $64,000.

He also testified that he was unable to use a market approach because he could not find comparable sales of similar corporations within the industry.

Chait did not compute a separate figure for goodwill but included it in the income stream he capitalized; he did not compute goodwill at all in the cost approach for the Sept. 29, 1997 date.

The trial court rejected Chait's valuation, citing (1) his failure to include financial figures for the last quarter of 1997; (2) his value was considerably less than the negotiations between the parties themselves; and (3) his failure to consider goodwill.

The superior court, appellate division, rejected Schripps's claim that the trial court erred by not accepting Chait's valuation, even though he was the only expert who testified. The court found that the trial judge was not bound to accept Chait's valuation and it was within its discretion to reject his valuation on the grounds cited.

Reliance on loan application

The trial court reached an independent valuation based upon an amount listed by Marcus in a November 1997 loan application, on which he listed Schripps as an asset valued at $850,000. Although Marcus denied this figure represented the real value and claimed that it was "made up," the trial court disagreed. It valued the corporation at $1,133,000, Marcus's share at $850,000, and Torres's share at $283,333.

Fair value determination remanded

The superior court held that there was no evidence in the record that the $850,000 listed on the loan application bore any relation to the fair value of Marcus's shares. Although the trial court was entitled to reject the expert's opinion, it was still required to determine fair value. Torres's failure to present expert valuation evidence "enhanced the problem."

The appellate court remanded the case to determine the fair value of Schripps. The parties failed to present sufficient expert testimony, which requires the trial court to "seek assistance from other sources to aid [its] decision of fair value." The court thus required the trial judge on remand to appoint an independent appraiser to report on the fair value of the corporation.

Gagliano v. Brenna (I)

Citation: 344 N.J. Super. 83, 780 A.2d 553, 2001 N.J. Super. LEXIS 331
Court: Superior Court, Appellate Division
State/Jurisdiction: New Jersey
Date of decision: August 1, 2001
Judge: Steinberg

Plaintiff minority dissenting shareholders appealed, and defendant corporation cross-appealed, the trial court valuation of corporate stock.

Bank squeezes out minority

Amboy Bancorporation, a bank holding company, had one class of stock and one subsidiary, Amboy National Bank (collectively, Amboy). Amboy decided to reorganize to qualify for taxation as a Subchapter S corporation. It sent a proposed plan of the merger and a proxy to shareholders, providing for a cash-out of minority shareholders. After passage of the plan, certain shareholders sued, either individually or in class actions, alleging misrepresentation and failure to offer a fair price.

Experts give diverging valuations

Bank Advisory Group, Inc. (BAG) gave Amboy a financial fairness opinion in which it concluded that the price of $73 per share was "fair, from a financial standpoint, to all shareholders of the Company, including those shareholders receiving the Cash Consideration."

Robert Walters testified for defendants, stating that BAG used several different valuation approaches. BAG concluded that the fair cash value per share, for a minority interest of about 20% of Amboy's stock, was $69.50.

Certain individual plaintiffs obtained a fairness opinion and fair value report from FinPro, Inc. President and owner Donald Musso testified that he performed an acquisition valuation and agreed with BAG's acquisition-value result of $110 per share but disagreed with the 25% minority discount BAG used to reduce that result to $82.50 per share.

Another individual plaintiff retained David Budd of McConnell Budd & Downs. Budd criticized BAG's use of a minority discount and opined that the "appropriate value" of Amboy's stock was $120 per share. He testified to a number of different approaches, each indicating a value in excess of $73 per share.

The class action plaintiffs used The Griffing Group as their expert. Griffing's founder, David Clarke, testified that he also used different approaches. Under the guideline company approach, he valued the stock at $121.08 per share. He also considered the discounted cash flow method, under which he used Amboy's projections for asset growth and profitability to project Amboy's "available or free cash flow" for 10 years and discounted it to a present value. Using that approach, he valued the stock at $117.40 per share. However, Clarke gave more weight to the guideline approach because it reflected "actual trading values" of the five guideline banks' stock and ultimately concluded that Amboy's adjusted fair market value was $120 per share.

The trial judge appointed an expert, Christopher Hargrove, to assist in determining fair value. He valued Amboy as a going concern, without marketability or minority discounts, and without a control premium. He also used a number of different approaches and derived a figure of $92.50 per share.

Trial court finds shareholders not offered fair value

The trial court concluded that the proxy contained misleading statements of material facts and failed to disclose all material facts about the true value and future prospects of Amboy and the true value of Amboy's stock. Specifically, it found that the proxy was deficient for reciting the offered price without mentioning that it was derived by applying minority and marketability discounts, and also for failing to explain that the offered price was "fair market value" rather than "fair value."

The judge further determined that the representation that the price of $73 per share was fair to minority shareholders was misleading, erroneous, and incomplete, and that the vote of the consenting shareholders who approved the transaction was not a fully informed shareholder vote. The judge set a value of $90 per share.

Directors breached duty of fair dealing

The superior court, appellate division, stated that the record clearly supported the trial courts conclusion that the proxy statement was materially deficient and misleading regarding statements of value. Thus, it held that the directors breached their duty of fair dealing with the minority shareholders and therefore had the burden of proving that the price offered for the shares was fair.

Fair value does not include discounts

The trial court ruled that Amboy was to be valued as a going concern and that minority and marketability discounts and control premiums were prohibited as a matter of law. After reviewing New Jersey Supreme Court rulings, as well as looking to Delaware law for guidance, the superior court concluded that the trial court correctly declined to apply minority or marketability discounts to the shares.

Control premium permissible in appraisals

Delaware law does allow consideration of control premiums. However, the Delaware Supreme Court has cautioned that it may not be used as a vehicle to capture value of anticipated future effects of the merger. This would, in effect, allow an element of value representing expected synergies, which is prohibited by the Delaware statute.

Because New Jersey has a similar statute, the superior court concluded that in a valuation proceeding, a control premium should be considered in order to reflect market realities, provided it is not used to include the value of anticipated effects of the merger.

Because the trial court determined a control premium was prohibited as a matter of law, the superior court reversed and remanded with instructions to consider what, if any, control premium should be added to the value of the stock and what, if any, adjustments are necessary to exclude synergies.

Trial court erred in automatically rejecting valuations

The trial court rejected acquisition valuations because (1) they might include an element for anticipated synergies and (2) they would yield a corporations "sale value" rather than its value as a continuing business. Delaware law, however, permits any means of stock valuation as long as the technique is generally acceptable in the financial communities. Thus, courts may not exclude any valuation automatically. Of course, in the case of an acquisition valuation, there must be a correction for synergies.

The superior court also found that the trial court erred in automatically excluding from consideration several of the expert's methods that contained an inherent control premium.

Consequently, the superior court reversed with instructions that the trial court must consider valuations that determine the acquisition value of Amboy as a going concern and that it may not automatically reject methods of valuation involving a control premium: "On remand, the parties shall be given the opportunity to explore and seek to develop a methodology to correct for the inherent minority discount, and exclude the element of synergies and future benefits before applying a control premium."

Johnson v. Johnson

Citation: 2001 Conn. Super. LEXIS 2430
Court: Superior Court
State/Jurisdiction: Connecticut
Date of decision: August 15, 2001
Judge: Bishop

This case is a trial court matter and we review the trial court's memorandum of decision. Two minority shareholders, brother and sister, Cindy Johnson and James Johnson, brought an action against their brother Randy Johnson, who was the majority shareholder, the corporation, and two

Chapter 7: Court Case Abstracts

members of the board of directors. The minority shareholders sought the dissolution of the corporation. In response, the corporation gave notice of intent to purchase the stock owned by the plaintiffs. This case was bifurcated so that the court could determine the fair value of the stock.

Facts

Johnson Corrugated Products Corporation was started by the Johnson's father, Melvin Johnson, in 1964, with two others.

Randy Johnson owned 35 shares, which represented a 70% interest in the corporation. He was chairman of the board and chief executive officer of the corporation.

Cindy and James Johnson each owned 7.8 shares of stock, which represented a 30.83% combined "equity interest in the corporation." Cindy and James both were employed by the corporation at one time, though neither was employed there at the time this litigation was commenced. However, both continued to receive wages from the corporation. Neither was a member of the board of directors, though both claimed they were entitled to be on the board due to their stock ownership.

Valuation evidence

The parties agreed that the stock should be valued as of March 31, 1999. To determine the fair value of the plaintiff's stock, the court first had to determine the equity value of the corporation. Once the equity value of the corporation is determined, the court must then consider whether to apply any discounts based on market conditions or based on their minority status. The court noted that it would also take issues of corporate waste and oppression into account in determining the value of the stock.

The court heard testimony from expert witnesses for both sides. Both experts, the court noted, were "experts on business valuation and both experts employed essentially the same valuation methodology." The method that was used was the income approach, capitalizing net free cash flow. Both experts attempted to determine the present value of the future net benefit and with that future stream discounted to present value at an appropriate discount rate. However, the experts came to two different conclusions. John H. Kramer, the plaintiffs' expert, determined the value of the corporation at $8,070,000, while Walter King, expert for the defendants, arrived at a value of $4,383,000.

The two experts could not agree on three issues: (1) the amount of savings that the corporation would receive as the result of having recently installed a new corrugator; (2) "the extent to which the corporate income should be normalized to account for arguably excessive compensation paid to management and others;" and (3) the correct amount of depreciation.

In attempting to clarify the first issue, the court heard evidence that Johnson Corrugated had recently purchased and put into operation a new corrugator. It was assumed that the new corrugator would save the company money by reducing labor costs and waste while increasing productivity. The parties disagreed on how much money this machine would save the company. Minutes from the board of directors meetings were introduced into evidence that the board anticipated an annual savings of almost $700,000. The plaintiffs' expert factored this into his calculations in valuing the company. The defendants' expert disagreed with this figure. He reviewed the operation of the new machine for a period of a few months prior to the valuation date to reach his figure of $60,000 in annual savings.

The second issue was compensation for management and the normalization of income. Plaintiffs alleged that Randy Johnson received excessive compensation for his work. In 1998, the court noted that Randy Johnson received $333,536 in compensation as chief executive officer. The court also noted that Randy Johnson was a high school graduate with "no special educational qualifications for his position."

In arguing this point, both experts used executive compensation surveys upon which to base their opinions, although the figures they presented were different.

On the third issue of depreciation, the court accepted the calculations of the plaintiff's expert, Kramer, and found them to be "reasonable."

Trial court findings

To normalize earnings, both experts analyzed the corporations reported earnings for an agreed-upon three-year period. The court found that neither extrinsic economic or market conditions nor company specific data indicated a need to give any of the three years more weight than the other. The yearly earnings before income taxes were averaged. The court found that the corporation's average annual normalized earnings before taxes were $1,720,087. From this amount, the court deducted $262,250 for reasonable management compensation for the chief executive officer and the financial officer. The court added $60,000 in anticipated savings from the new corrugator and arrived at the normalized annual earnings before taxes to the corporation of $1,517,837. Assuming income taxes at an aggregate rate of 40%, the company's average normalized net earnings for the three-year period were $910,702. The court accepted Kramers computations to convert normalized earnings to cash flow, involving the addition of claimed depreciation of $517,861, and subtraction of amounts for capital expenditures and a decrease in working capital, to arrive at a net free cash flow of $944,443.

Next, the court determined the capitalization rate so as to convert the anticipated future net cash flow to present value. To do this, the court had to determine an appropriate discount rate and the weighted average cost of capital. The court was persuaded by Kings analysis and accordingly applied a capitalization rate of 7.69% to arrive at the sum of $12,281,443 as the value of invested capital. From this, the court deducted interest-bearing debt of $5,235,122 to arrive at the sum of $7,046,321 as the value of equity from operations. After factoring in the liabilities and non-operating assets, the court determined that the equity value of the corporation was $6,973,725.

Chapter 7: Court Case Abstracts

Minority discount and oppression factors

The court noted that fair value of plaintiffs shares could not be determined by simply apportioning 30.83% of the corporation's equity value to the plaintiffs. The statutes allowed the court to consider whether issues such as fraud, waste, and oppressive conduct occurred as well as the minority status of the shares being valued. Fair value is not explicitly defined by the statutes, so the court was guided by the Model Business Corporation Acts Official Comment to C.G.S. § 33-900, which states:

> In cases where there is dissension but no evidence of wrongful conduct, "fair value" should be determined with reference to what the petitioner would likely receive in a voluntary sale of shares with a third party, taking into account his minority status.

With respect to the amount of discount in minority oppression cases, the Model Business Corporation Act states,

> If the court finds that the value of a corporation has been diminished by the wrongful conduct of controlling shareholders, it would be appropriate to include as an element of fair value the petitioners proportional claim for any corporate injury.

The court found that the conduct in this case did not rise to the level of oppression. The fact that the corporation did not declare dividends was not oppressive because historically dividends had never been declared. Although Randy Johnson's compensation was somewhat excessive, it was not oppressive. The fact that the minority shareholders were not employed by the corporation was not oppressive because they nonetheless received wages for which they did not have to work.

Accordingly, the court found that fair value for the plaintiff's shares should not include a premium over their pro rata share because there was no oppression. The court further found that a 20% minority discount was appropriate. The trial court concluded that the aggregate fair value of the plaintiffs stock was $1,720,000.

The expert speaks...

Walter King, one of the experts in this case, submitted the following comment regarding this case that we thought our readers would find of interest:

> There is an instructive point that I would like to make. I was flattered by the reference that the Judge "was persuaded by King's analysis and accordingly applied a capitalization rate of 7.69%"—however, I had used a Weighted Average Cost of Capital (WACC). As we know, this methodology weights the valuation of equity and value of debt in determining the cost of capital. The Judge had made certain adjustments that were different from ours. These differences increased income and thus increased the value of equity in relation to the value of debt. Equity, of course, has a much higher

cost of capital than does debt. Accordingly, using our standard model for WACC and inputting the courts numbers, the capitalization rate should have been 8.90%, rather than 7.69%, which results in a value of equity of $5,304,000 rather than $6,974,000. The instructive point is that a small change in WACC (say 16%) results in large change in equity value (say 24%). This is due principally to debt being a constant deduction.

Pueblo Bancorporation v. Lindoe, Inc. (I)

Citation: 37 P.3d 492, 2001 Colo. App. LEXIS 1330
Court: Court of Appeals
State/Jurisdiction: Colorado
Date of decision: August 16, 2001
Judge: Roy

In this corporate dissenter's rights action, Lindoe, Inc. appealed the trial court's valuation of its stock in Pueblo Bancorporation, a bank holding company. Lindoe, also a bank holding company, held 6,525 of the 114,217 outstanding shares of Pueblo. To obtain more favorable tax treatment, Pueblo formed a Subchapter S corporation into which it would merge, with Pueblo being the surviving entity. The experts in this case were Leslie A. Patten, CPA, CVA, Patten MacPhee & Associates, Inc. (for Pueblo); Z. Christopher Mercer, ASA, CFA, Mercer Capital (for Lindoe); Gerald A. Feil, Alex Sheshunoff & Co. (for Lindoe); and Charles W. Murdock, Loyola School of Law (for Lindoe).

C corporation 'squeezed out' as shareholder of S corporation

Because an S corporation may not have a C corporation as a shareholder, Lindoe could not remain a shareholder in the merged company. The merger was approved by Pueblo's shareholders, with only Lindoe dissenting. Pueblo determined the fair value of its stock to be $341 per share and sent payment to Lindoe. Lindoe estimated fair value to be $775 per share and sent demand for payment.

Pueblo instituted action under Colorado's dissenters' rights statute to obtain judicial appraisal of the fair value of its shares. The trial court concluded the pro rata value was $666.16 per share. It then applied minority and marketability discounts of 30% each and found the fair value to be $362.03 per share.

Trial court correctly determined enterprise value

Lindoe first argued that the trial court erred in determining the enterprise value of Pueblo as a going concern. Colorado law requires the court to consider all relevant value factors when determining fair value, most importantly market value, investment or earnings value, and net asset value. Because fair value cannot be determined with precise mathematical analysis, how the court weighs each value factor depends on the facts and circumstances of each case. The determination is a factual one and the trial court's findings will not be disturbed unless clearly erroneous.

At trial, each appraiser used acceptable techniques to value Pueblo but gave differing weights to the value factors. Pueblo's appraiser weighted net asset value at 20% of total value, while Lindoe's appraisers placed no weight on that value. Pueblo's appraiser found the enterprise value was $70,700,000. Lindoe's first appraiser found the enterprise value to be $82,768,000 and its second appraiser found the enterprise value was between $82,800,000 and $88,500,000.

The trial court determined the enterprise value of Pueblo was $76,087,723, or $666.16 per share. Although it found Pueblo's appraiser most credible, it did not rely solely on that appraisal. Apparently, the trial court considered all three appraisals, as well as other factors like stock sales and book value. The court of appeals found there was adequate support in the record for the trial courts determination.

No minority discount as a matter of law

Lindoe argued that the trial court erred by applying 30% minority and marketability discounts to the pro rata value of the shares. The court of appeals agreed. Previous Colorado cases have held that, in appraising a going concern, a minority discount should not be applied as a matter of law. At the time of the merger, Pueblo was profitable, financially stable, and growing; neither dissolution nor liquidation was being considered. Thus, the trial court should not have applied a minority discount as a matter of law.

No marketability discount except under 'extraordinary circumstances'

Regarding a marketability discount, the appellate court conducted an extensive analysis of the law in other jurisdictions. The court was persuaded by and adopted the American Law Institutes position that the discount should not be applied in dissenter's rights actions except in "extraordinary circumstances." It further concluded, as a matter of law, that Pueblo's conversion to an S corporation by merger was not an extraordinary circumstance triggering an appropriate application of a marketability discount. It reversed and remanded with instructions to enter judgment that the fair value of Pueblo's shares was $666.16 per share.

Conti v. Christoff

Citation: 2001 Ohio 3421, 2001 Ohio App. LEXIS 4534
Court: Court of Appeals
State/Jurisdiction: Ohio
Date of decision: October 2, 2001
Judge: Waite

This case was on appeal from a magistrate's findings and the trial court's rulings regarding valuation of a 25% limited partnership interest. The primary issue on appeal was the correct definition of value.

Facts

Crestwood Center Co. was a real estate partnership with two general partners, Alex Christoff and George Guerrieri, and two limited partners, James Conti and John Conti. Each partner owned a 25% interest in the partnership.

The primary asset of Crestwood was a commercial office building, valued in 1996 at $1.7 million. At the time this complaint was filed, the building had approximately $300,000 in mortgage debt against it.

On May 16, 1997, John Conti sent a letter to Guerrieri notifying him that he was withdrawing from the limited partnership. Approximately seven months later, Conti filed a complaint requesting the cash value of his 25% partnership interest upon his withdrawal.

The trial court referred the case to a magistrate, who decided that Conti was entitled to 25% of the net partnership assets and that he was entitled to receive this value in cash. The magistrate ordered the parties to submit evidence related to the valuation of the partnership's assets.

Valuation evidence

The remaining partners provided evidence of the fair market value of a 25% interest in the partnership. They presented expert evidence, using three methods to determine value, which were unspecified in the opinion. The partners argued that the value of the 25% partnership interest was diminished due to a lack of marketability and minority status.

For his evidence, Conti submitted a 1996 appraisal of the value of the real estate, subtracted the mortgage still due on the property, and divided that amount by four to come up with his 25% share.

Magistrate and trial court findings

The magistrate agreed with Conti's valuation method, determining that the real estate plus on-hand cash of the partnership was worth $1.718 million and that the partnership had $312,146.56 in liabilities (which included the mortgage on the property). Subtracting liabilities from assets, the magistrate came to a total of $1.405 million in net assets owned by the partnership. The $1.405 million in net assets was divided by four and Conti was awarded his 25%, which equaled $351,492.58.

The other partners objected to the magistrate's decision. The trial court found the magistrate's award too high and referred the case back to the magistrate for a further hearing on the "fair value" of the partnership interest, with the order that the magistrate use the definition of "fair cash value" found in another part of the state partnership statute. The definition basically encompassed the willing seller/willing buyer standard of value. Conti appealed the trial court's order.

Holding on appeal and rationale

The court of appeals noted that, because there was no provision in the partnership agreement providing for withdrawal of a limited partner, Conti was therefore entitled to receive "fair value" for his interest in accordance with the state partnership statute.

Conti argued that the trial court, in reviewing the magistrate's decision, was not permitted to use the definition of "fair cash value" because that section referred only to a dissenting partner's rights after a merger or consolidation of a partnership, and not to the rights of a partner withdrawing from a limited partnership.

The court of appeals found this argument unpersuasive. Because of the similarities of the two statutory schemes, the court of appeals found that the trial court did not abuse its discretion in looking to fair cash value for guidance in defining fair value.

In support of the trial court's order, the remaining partners asserted that the market value of a partnership interest that is a going concern is not calculated merely by adding up the assets and subtracting the liabilities. The court of appeals agreed, noting that "partnership interest" was not synonymous with "partnership assets," and that intangibles such as goodwill are a factor in value. The court also observed that fair value is often discounted for lack of marketability and minority status, although it noted that such discounts were not mandated by the authorities presented by the parties.

The court of appeals found no abuse of discretion by the trial court in remanding the case to the magistrate for further findings and in directing the magistrate to use the definition of fair cash value.

Richton Bank & Trust Co. v. Bowen

Citation: 798 So. 2d 1268, 2001 Miss. LEXIS 294
Court: Supreme Court
State/Jurisdiction: Mississippi
Date of decision: October 31, 2001
Judge: Diaz

This case came to the Mississippi Supreme Court on appeal from the court of chancery. The issue was whether the chancellor erred in eliminating discounts for lack of marketability and minority status from his determination of fair value.

Facts

Richton Bank and Trust Company proposed a plan of share exchange with the holding company Centon Bancorp, Inc., under which the bank shareholders would receive one share of holding company stock for each share of bank stock. Elizabeth and Evelyn Bowen dissented under the Mississippi dissenters' rights statute, thereby requiring the corporation to purchase their interests at fair value. The Bowens owned about 13% of the outstanding stock in Richton Bank.

Valuation evidence

The bank hired Southard Financial to determine the fair value of the Bowens' shares. Southard found that the Bowen's stock was worth $1,357 per share on a non-marketable, minority interest basis. The Bowens accepted this amount as partial payment for their stock, but made a demand for $2,800.00 per share in total. The bank filed an action asking the court to resolve this dispute.

At trial, the bank submitted an appraisal conducted by David A. Harris, ASA, CFA concluding a fair value of $1,809 per share on a marketable, minority interest basis and $1,357 per share on a non-marketable, minority interest basis.

The Bowens' expert, Richard A. Place, ASA, submitted an appraisal in which he concluded that the fair value of the Bowen's shares was $2,700 per share. Place valued a controlling interest in the bank without any minority or marketability discounts.

Trial court findings

The chancellor ruled that marketability and minority discounts were not allowed under Mississippi law in determining the fair value of a dissenting shareholder's stock. He noted that the Bowens were compelled to sell their shares because the holding company was "a significantly different entity" than the bank. The chancellor rejected Place's appraisal as "somewhat imprecise" and used the bank's appraisal but eliminated the discounts, calling them "arbitrary and unwarranted." He determined the fair value of the Bowens stock to be $2,726.55 per share.

Chapter 7: Court Case Abstracts

Holding on appeal and rationale

The Supreme Court began by noting that the original purpose of dissenter's rights statutes was to provide a remedy for shareholders so they are not forced to invest in a business that no longer mirrors the original investment.

The court referred to the case of *Cal-Maine Foods, Inc. v. Duvic*[1] as the only other case to come before the Supreme Court on the issue of fair value in a dissenter's rights action. In that case, the court held that the determination of fair value is within the trial courts discretion and that the chancellor is in the best position to evaluate the evidence. Fair value is a question of fact to be reversed only upon a finding of manifest error.

The court also looked to *Hernando Bank v. Huff*,[2] the only other Mississippi case addressing the application of minority discounts in a fair value setting. In *Hernando*, a minority discount was granted, but the Bowens argued that it was discretionary. The Supreme Court agreed.

The Bowens also cited cases from other jurisdictions indicating that the current trend in the law is to disallow minority and marketability discounts. Mississippi followed suit in 2000 by statutorily eliminating minority and marketability discounts from the definition of "fair value" in a dissenters' rights case. Although the amendment was not in place at the time of the chancellor's determination, he used his discretion under the then-existing statute. The court found no manifest error and affirmed the chancellor's fair value determination.

Interesting dicta

The court concluded its opinion by summing up reasons why minority discounts are increasingly treated with disfavor by the courts, quoting from *Pueblo Bancorporation v. Lindoe, Inc.*[3] It noted that these reasons were "merely academic," since the current Mississippi statute eliminates minority discounts. The reasons did serve, however, to lend additional support to the chancellor's findings.

---

1 264 So. 2d 383 (Miss. 1972).
2 609 F. Supp. 1124 (N.D. Miss. 1985), *affirmed*, 796 F.2d 803 (5th Cir. 1986).
3 2001 Colo. App. LEXIS 1330 (Colo. Ct. App. 2001).

Garlock, et al. v. Southeastern Gas & Power, Inc. and Hilliard

Citation: No. 00-CVS-01018
Court: Court of Appeals
State/Jurisdiction: Florida
Date of decision: February 11, 2004
Judge: Tennille

The following court case abstract was originally published in Valuation Case Digest®

In *Tammy L. Garlock, et al. v. Southeastern Gas & Power, Inc. and Aubrey L. Hilliard*, No. 00-CVS-01018 (N.C. Supr. Ct. Mecklenburg County November 14, 2001), the North Carolina Superior Court for Mecklenburg County determined the fair value of stock in a natural gas marketing company. The plaintiffs and Hilliard formed Southeastern in 1997 and began operations at the start of 1998. Southeastern was formed as a corporation. Hilliard held 61% of the stock, was CEO, and the sole director of the company. The plaintiffs each held 13% of Southeastern. None of the shareholders executed non-compete or employment agreements with Southeastern. While the business was formed as a corporation, by the agreement of the shareholders, it operated more like a partnership in light of the fact that Hilliard, Southeastern's salesman and rainmaker, had to do eight months prison time on a tax fraud conviction. The business was successful in Hilliard's absence, but really took off after his release from prison. In 1999, Hilliard sought to expand the business, but realized that under the current profit-sharing agreement, established during his prison sentence and favorable to the plaintiffs, he could not. He then sought to change the agreement through the use of employment agreements and other devices, but was unsuccessful. Leveraging his voting power and position as sole director, he then fired two of the plaintiffs and the third resigned. The plaintiffs then brought suit for dissolution of the business. Through Hilliard, the business elected to purchase the plaintiffs' 39% interest.

The Mecklenburg Superior Court considered the matter. It determined that Hilliard, by exercising control over the company, frustrated the plaintiffs' reasonable expectations that were negotiated prior to and during Hilliard's incarceration. The reasonable expectations included (1) employment with the company and autonomy over their respective departments, (2) meaningful participation in the company's management, (3) access to company financial information, (4) profit-sharing as agreed to by the parties in 1997 and 1998, and (5) pro rata participation in the proceeds of a sale of the business. The court then determined that Hilliard was guilty of oppression and appointed an appraiser to determine the fair value of the stock on the date Hilliard terminated the plaintiffs.

The appraiser valued the business using an income approach. In valuing the business, he applied a high equity risk premium. The premium was large, in part to account for Hilliard's key man position in Southeastern. Hilliard's key man position was also considered in the expert's use of a high salary for Hilliard. The expert also considered a 1999 offer to purchase the business for $5.5 million, which was rejected by Hilliard and the plaintiffs. The expert lastly applied a discount for lack of marketability to the whole company in his valuation. He determined that the fair market value of the company was greater than $2.4 million.

In considering the court-appointed expert's valuation, the court noted that "[a]s a general proposition, the Court considered market value, equitable considerations, practical considerations and changes in condition of the company from the market valuation date" when determining the fair value of a company. It found that minority and lack of marketability discounts were inappropriate under the facts of this case. It also considered the importance of Hilliard to the company, the lack of non-compete agreements, and the volatility of the natural gas market. It concluded that the company had a fair value of $2.4 million, and the plaintiffs were collectively entitled to $936,000.

The court then considered Southeastern's ability to pay the fair value of the plaintiffs' stock. Since Southeastern had few tangible assets to offer as security, the court found that it would be difficult for Southeastern to obtain a loan to pay the plain tiffs. Therefore, the fair value would come from Southeastern's operating income. To that end it, the court structured the sale of the minority interest to be 25% due at closing and the balance paid over 36 months with interest secured by all of the company's assets.

Trifad Entertainment, Inc. v. Brad Anderson, et al.

Citation: 2001 MT 227
Court: Supreme Court
State/Jurisdiction: Montana
Date of decision: November 15, 2001
Judge: Leaphart

The following court case abstract was originally published in Valuation Case Digest®

In *Trifad Entertainment, Inc. v. Brad Anderson, et al.*, 2001 MT 227 (November 15, 2001), the Montana Supreme Court determined that a minority shareholder had squeezed out the majority shareholder and was liable for damages therefrom. In 1993, Trifad was formed by Anderson, who held onethird of the stock, and Phil Furtney, through his wholly owned corporation, Joe Lee, Inc., held the rest of the stock. Trifad was formed to own and service fifteen pool tables, which were leased to Anderson's wholly owned tavern. In 1996, Furtney was arrested on RICO charges and extradited to Florida. Anderson was advised by the State of Montana to distance himself from Furtney if he wished the sale of another tavern, Dr. Feelgoods, to his wife to proceed.

In order to comply with the advice, Anderson contacted a pool table supplier and learned that each table had a value of between $900 and $1000. He obtained a $15,000 loan, and effected a sale of the tables from Trifad to himself for that amount. Anderson then paid any taxes Trifad owed and withdrew his one-third from the Trifad's bank account.

He did not contact Furtney, or Furtney's attorney prior to or after the sale of Trifad's assets. Furtney discovered the sale and effective dissolution of the company after inquiring as to Trifad's year-end dividends. On behalf of Trifad and Joe Lee, Inc, Furtney then brought suit against Anderson for breach of fiduciary duty and conversion among other claims. The district court found that Trifad and Joe Lee, Inc. were not harmed in the transaction because the sale occurred at fair market value. Furtney appealed.

The Montana Supreme Court determined that Anderson violated the Montana Business Corporation Act § 35-1-823. This section requires that shareholders must be notified of sales in other than the normal course of business, a shareholder meeting must be held on the sale, and the sale must be approved by 2/3rds of the voting shareholders. The court further concluded that since Anderson failed to comply with the business corporation act when he sold Trifad's assets to his tavern, he exercised unauthorized dominion over Trifad's assets. Thus, it found that Anderson was liable for violation of the business corporation act as well as conversion of Trifad's assets. The court then remanded the matter for consideration of damages. On remand, the Supreme Court noted that Trifad may be entitled to recover lost future income and profits. It further noted that since the facts of this case are analogous to those in shareholder oppression cases, Joe Lee, Inc. may be entitled to recover the fair value of its Trifad shares as of the day prior to Anderson's conversion of Trifad's assets.

Billigmeier v. Concorde Marketing, Inc.

Citation: 2001 Minn. App. LEXIS 1273
Court: Court of Appeals
State/Jurisdiction: Minnesota
Date of decision: December 4, 2001
Judge: Peterson

This case involved a claim for unpaid commissions and stock buyout valuation by Jon Billigmeier, the minority owner of Concorde Marketing, Inc., against the corporation and Glenn Willing, the majority owner. In May 1998, Concorde terminated Billigmeier's employment. There were unpaid commissions still owed to him and the corporation continued to receive commissions on the work that Billigmeier had done.

Valuation evidence

Larry Plowman, CPA, was the only expert to testify; his testimony was not rebutted. Plowman valued Concorde at approximately $600,000, based on gross revenues for a three- to five-year period around the date of Billigmeier's termination. He also testified that the value of a business like Concorde would range from 80-120% of gross revenues, depending upon the financial strength of the company and the overall strength of its markets. Plowman testified that the 80% multiplier was compatible with Concorde having $170,000 and $250,000 lines of credit.

Plowman also applied discounts of:
- 20% to reflect the company's uncertain financial strength and the difficulties it faced in the marketplace,
- 40% because revenues that the corporation generated were primarily based on its relationship with a small group of vendors, and
- 5-10% for key person discount because the company did not have a long established relationship with its vendors or a reasonable succession plan.

Plowman opined that the reasonable value of Billigmeier's 36% interest in Concorde as of May 4, 1998 was $93,312 ($600,000 X 80% multiplier = $480,000 X 60% sole vendor discount = $288,000 X 90% key person discount = $259,200 X 36% interest = $93,312).

Trial court findings

The trial court found that Billigmeier was entitled to $93,312. It also found that he was also entitled to $280,099 for unpaid commissions and frustration of reasonable expectations of continued employment. The trial court accepted Plowman's unrebutted testimony in full, and applied all his discounts. The court did not apply a minority discount because Billigmeier's departure was involuntarily imposed by the majority shareholder.

Holdings and rationale on appeal

Willing argued that the trial court erred by not applying an additional discount to account for the $288,099 judgment of unpaid commissions. The court of appeals noted that when a buyout is ordered under the Minnesota Business Corporations Act, fair value means "the pro rata share of the value of the corporation as a going concern."

Willing argued that Concorde had a value of negative $170,000 after subtracting a $170,000 bank loan and the judgment for unpaid commissions from the trial courts $288,000 valuation. He argued that Concorde therefore had no going concern value.

The appellate court rejected this argument, stating that Willing's analysis would only apply if the trial courts valuation was based on book value. However, Plowman testified "that book value of the assets and liabilities of the company are unrelated to the value that will be the result of the [revenue-based] analysis" that he used.

The appellate court noted that even though the trial court did not expressly account for the corporate debt owed to Billigmeier and the bank, it did consider the corporations financial situation by applying a low-end multiplier of 80% that reflected Concorde's "questionable financial strength." The court of appeals was unable to conclude that the trial courts valuation was clearly erroneous.

Boyd v. Boyd

Citation: 67 S.W.3d 398, 2002 Tex. App. LEXIS 16
Court: Court of Appeals
State/Jurisdiction: Texas
Date of decision: January 3, 2002
Judge: Livingston

In this marital dissolution, husband complained, among other things, that:
- the trial court improperly characterized his stock options as 100% community property,
- the trial court erred in selecting the date of valuation of the stock options, and
- the trial court erred in its valuation of the stock options.

The trial court findings

The trial court found that the stock options were 100% community property because they were acquired during the marriage. The trial court determined what it called the "contingent value" of the stock options, assuming that husband could either exercise the options if the company went public, or could sell the options if his employment was terminated before they vested.

> The trial court determined that [husband's] fair value stock options had a contingent value at divorce of $5,628,776. This value was determined by using a formula that did not take into account [husband's] post-divorce work for his company or the company's future productivity. The formula was fixed at the time of the divorce.

The trial court awarded wife one half of the contingent value of the stock options as her 50% share of the community estate.

The appellate court affirmed, holding that the trial court did not abuse its discretion on any of the issues. The appellate court noted that no Texas court has considered how to determine the community property value of stock options at divorce, and that the trial court's method was reasonable under the circumstances.

Mart v. Severson

Citation: 95 Cal. App. 4th 521, 115 Cal. Rptr. 2d 717, 2002 Cal. App. LEXIS 791
Court: Court of Appeals
State/Jurisdiction: California
Date of decision: January 23, 2002
Judge: Haerle

Facts

This was a voluntary corporate dissolution proceeding. Bradley Mart and Leland Severson were each directors and 50% shareholders of Bay World Trading Ltd, a California corporation engaged in the sale and export of meat and meat by-products.

Mart delivered to Severson a written consent of shareholders to dissolve Bay World. Mart then filed a petition requesting court supervision of the winding up of the company. Severson exercised his right under California Corporations Code section 2000 to purchase Mart's shares at their fair value to avoid dissolution.

Valuation evidence

The court appointed three appraisers who submitted a joint report valuing Bay World. They defined fair value the same as in section 2000: "the liquidation value as of the valuation date but taking into account the possibility, if any, of sale of the entire business as a going concern in a liquidation."

The appraisers stated that Bay World would be sold as a going concern. They determined that the cost approach was not applicable. Instead, the appraisers employed the income and market approaches because they provided "a more realistic indication" of what the company would sell for as a going concern. They unanimously concluded that fair value was $5.6 million.

Severson filed a motion arguing that the appraisal was erroneous because it calculated fair market sale value rather than liquidation value. The trial court requested a clarification, instructing the appraisers to explain whether they had calculated liquidation value or sale value as a going concern in litigation. The order also asked whether the appraisers' valuation reflected a forced sale under court supervision, and whether they had assumed a covenant not to compete by the shareholders and directors.

Supplemental appraisal letter

In their supplemental letter to the court, the appraisers stated that they equated liquidation value with the cost approach, which is used to value companies that are insolvent or incapable of earning a return adequate to support the value of the assets. Each of the appraisers considered "piecemeal liquidation value," and all three independently concluded that value was irrelevant "in light of Bay World's historical earnings record and future earnings capacity."

They repeated their unanimous opinion that Bay World would be sold as a going concern in liquidation, explaining that a seller would not accept liquidation value because it "would not reflect the value of the intangible assets of the business, such as the brand name and client relationships, which is best reflected through going concern, earnings-based approaches." They clarified that they interpreted fair value to mean the price that would be received in a forced liquidation sale under court supervision.

The appraisers also explained that they assumed that "hypothetical covenants not to compete would be executed by both shareholders and key employees." Although they did not attempt to estimate the impact on value if such agreements were not signed, it was their opinion that a sale of the company as a going concern without such agreements would be difficult, if not impossible.

Trial court findings

At the hearing, the court ruled that Bay World could be valued as a going concern only if Mart executed a valid covenant not to compete, and it rejected a noncompete signed by Mart as too narrow. The court then instructed the appraisers to calculate Bay World's piecemeal liquidation value.

The appraisers concluded that liquidation value was $1,480,000, which the trial court accepted as fair value. The court also found that the revised noncompete submitted by Mart was inadequate because it did not give an "absolute guarantee" that Mart would not compete with Bay World. Even if such a guarantee were given now, the court said it was too late because it did not exist as of the valuation date.

The court rejected the $5.6 million value because it was "premised upon the execution of an effective covenant not to compete by the parties" and no such covenant had been or could be executed in this case. Mart appealed.

Holdings on appeal and rationale

The court of appeals found that the trial court's conclusion was not supported by substantial evidence. It stated that the "overwhelming evidence" in the record indicated that the fair value of Bay World was $5.6 million, the unanimous conclusion of three disinterested appraisers.

Contrary to the trial court's findings, the appraisers did *not* condition their conclusions on Marts execution of a noncompete. In fact, they did not even consider Mart. The question they answered was whether the entire corporation would sell as a going concern in liquidation, *not* whether Mart would sell his share of the corporation to Severson.

The court found that the appraisers properly applied section 2000 by assuming that a hypothetical willing seller of Bay World would execute a noncompete with the corporation. In fact, the court held that *section 2000 necessarily requires that the appraisers assume a noncompete within a hypothetical sale scenario.* The court reversed and instructed the trial court to set the value as determined in the appraisers' original report.

Brown v. Brown

Citation: 348 N.J. Super. 466, 792 A.2d 463, 2002 N.J. Super. LEXIS 105
Court: Superior Court, Appellate Division
State/Jurisdiction: New Jersey
Date of decision: February 28, 2002
Judge: Wecker

The issues raised in this marital dissolution case were (1) whether the trial court erred in valuing husband's interest in Union County Florist Supplies, Inc. (Florist), the family florist business, (2) whether the trial court erred in refusing to discount the value of the stock for minority interest status or lack of marketability, and (3) whether the trial erred in not treating the stock as a gift.

Facts

The parties were married on August 21, 1975 and separated in October 1997. The divorce was filed in November 1997 and the judgment entered on September 7, 2000. The husband worked in his family's wholesale florist business, and acquired a 47 1/2 % interest in the firm.

Valuation evidence

The trial court received valuation evidence from two expert witnesses. Stephan C. Chait, CPA testified for the wife, and Kalman A. Barson, CPA testified for the husband.

Chait valued the entire business of Florist at $1,183,000, and the husband's 47 1/2 % interest at $561,925. Chait did not apply discounts for marketability or lack of control.

Barson, on the other hand, applied discounts of 25% for lack of marketability and 15% for lack of control. He initially valued the husband's 47 1/2 % interest in the business at $339,000. Barson also valued the shares at the time the husband acquired them from his parents between 1980 and 1996, on the assumption that the shares were acquired by gift. Barson then subtracted the $121,000 acquisition value from the value at the time of the complaint for dissolution, and concluded that the value of the marital interest in the husband's shares was $238,000.

Both experts used both the market approach and the income approach in valuing the business, and both gave the income approach substantially more weight than the market approach. Chait used a four-to-one ratio, allocating relative weights of 80% for the income approach and 20% for the market approach. Barson used a three-to-one ratio, allocating 75% for the income approach and 25% for the market approach.

The experts used different capitalization rates in their income approach valuations. Chait used 20%, whereas Barson used 25%. "Chait's 20% capitalization rate translates to a multiple of five times annual income, whereas Barson's 25% capitalization rate translates to a multiple of four."

Neither expert offered an opinion with respect to whether the shares were gifts. Instead each operated based upon the assumption provided by the party they testified for.

Trial court findings

Although the trial judge acknowledged and discussed the valuations of both of the experts, it adopted Chait's valuation, reasoning that Chait's conclusions were more credible than Barson's.

Accordingly, the trial court held that the value of the husbands interest in Florist was $561,925, which excluded discounts for lack of marketability and lack of control and assumed that that the stock was not acquired as a gift. The trial judge awarded to the wife 40% of this value, $225,000, in equitable distribution.

No discounts absent extraordinary circumstances

The appellate court noted that, although there were minor differences between the two experts general methodology, the primary difference in their resulting values centered on two issues: (1) the application of discounts, and (2) whether the stock was considered a gift. Using the following formulas, the appellate court determined that Barson's valuation without the discounts would have been $500,000, very close to Chait's $561,925:

[T]o add back both discounts to Barson's income approach (25% for marketability and then 15% for a minority interest), the formula is:

$$0.85I \,(.75)\, I = 266,000$$
$$0.6375\, I = 266,000$$
$$I = 417,000$$

where "I" equals the undiscounted income approach value.

To add back the minority (15%) discount to Barson's market approach, the formula is:

$$.85\, M = 637,000$$
$$M = 749,000$$

where "M" equals the undiscounted market approach value.

Finally, the three-to-one weighted average of Barson's undiscounted approaches to valuation is:

> Income approach value   I x 3 = 1,251,000
> Market approach value   M x 1 = 749,000
> M + I = 2,000,000
> 2,000,000 divided by 4 = 500,000

The appellate court discussed the trial courts refusal to discount the shares value for minority interest status or lack of marketability. The appellate court included a thorough discussion of its reasoning on this issue, citing to the prior New Jersey shareholder cases of *Balsamides v. Protameen Chemicals, Inc.,* 160 N.J. 352, 368, 734 A.2d 721 (N.J 1999), and *Lawson Mardon Wheaton, Inc. v. Smith,* 160 N.J. 383, 397, 734 A.2d 738 (N.J. 1999), and the fair value standard. The appellate court adopted, for marital dissolution purposes, *2 ALI Principles of Corporate Governance §7.22,* which states that minority and marketability discounts should not be applied absent extraordinary circumstances to warrant their application. This is the same principle that was previously adopted in *Balsamides* and *Lawson.*

Finding that there were no such extraordinary circumstances in this case, the appellate court held that the trial court did not err in refusing to apply discounts to the value of Florist.

Evidence supports stock was a gift

The appellate court also addressed the issue of whether the stock was a gift, so that the value at the time the husband received the stock should be deducted from the value at the time of dissolution. The appellate court agreed with the husband that there was no credible evidence in the record to support the trial courts finding that the stock was not a gift, and that, on the contrary, all the evidence supported a conclusion that the stock was gifted to the husband by his parents. Accordingly, the appellate court held:

> The value of [the husbands] shares as of the dates they were received as gifts must be deducted from the complaint-date value to calculate that portion of [the husbands] interest in Florist that is subject to equitable distribution. We stress that the valuation of Florist, and thus of the shares when received by [the husband], must be determined in accordance with our holding that neither marketability nor minority discounts are appropriate. In other words, the valuation approaches for each date must be consistent with the approaches taken for the complaint-date valuation.

Since the trial court valued the stock under the assumption that it was not a gift, the appellate court reversed the trial courts judgment and remanded the case for a new determination of the value of the husband's interest in Florist consistent with its opinion.

In re Vetco, Inc.; Wolk v. Kornberg

Citation: 292 A.D.2d 391, 738 N.Y.S.2d 599, 2002 N.Y. App. Div. LEXIS 2244
Court: Supreme Court, Appellate Division
State/Jurisdiction: New York
Date of decision: March 4, 2002
Judge: Per Curiam

Vetco, Inc. is a private, closely held corporation. Kenneth Wolk is Vetco's minority shareholder. Wolk commenced this proceeding to dissolve Vetco and Vetco opted to purchase Wolk's shares in lieu of dissolution. A valuation hearing was held before a referee to determine the fair value of the shares.

Wolk appealed the court's order directing Vetco to pay him only $819,561 as the fair value of his shares in the corporation.

Valuation evidence and trial court findings

The referee rejected a "comparative appraisal" approach utilized by Wolk's expert, Douglas Land, because Land compared Vetco to other corporations that were not "in similar financial situations."

In computing a capitalization rate, the referee accepted Land's use of a 15% long-term growth rate. The referee also applied a 40% illiquidity or marketability discount, to the value that Land calculated under the investment value approach.

Holding on appeal and rationale

The appellate court held that the evidence, which showed that Vetco had an "appreciable growth rate," supported the referee's decision to accept Lands use of the 15% long-term growth rate in computing a capitalization rate.

The court further held that the referee abused his discretion by applying a 40% illiquidity discount. The court concluded that the appropriate percentage for the illiquidity discount was 25%. Accordingly, the court found that $1,023,735.60 was the fair value of Wolk's 47.76% interest in Vetco.

Chapter 7: Court Case Abstracts

Offenbecher v. Baron Services, Inc. (II)

Citation: 2002 Ala. Civ. App. LEXIS 365
Court: Court of Appeals
State/Jurisdiction: Alabama
Date of decision: May 10, 2002
Judge: Murdock

This opinion is the result of an application for rehearing in the Alabama Court of Appeals, and replaces the court's earlier opinion of May 18, 2001.

A minority shareholder challenged the trial court's application of a 50% marketability discount in calculating the fair value of Baron Services (Baron) stock.

Facts

Baron was incorporated in 1990. Baron sold weather-radar systems and related software. Offenbecher, who was employed by Baron, designed some software for Baron. Offenbecher received 130 Baron's shares.

On March 31, 1998, Baron's board of directors approved a plan to merge Baron into a separate Delaware corporation. That plan included a "cash-out" provision providing for a cash payment to any shareholder owning fewer than 150 Baron's shares. The plan also denied such shareholder any ownership stake in the Delaware corporation after the merger. In response, Offenbecher, a minority shareholder, demanded payment from Baron for the fair value of his 130 shares of stock. The parties could not agree on the value of the stock.

Valuation evidence

Baron's expert, Gary Saliba, determined that the value of the Baron stock as of December 31, 1997 was $562.47 per share. In calculating this "marketable value" of the Baron Services stock, Saliba used a "discounted annual rate of return" of 19.82%. Saliba considered the following factors in calculating this discount rate: an equity risk premium of 7.5%, a micro-capitalization premium of 3.5%, and a company-size premium of 4.35%. At the request of Baron Services, Saliba later reevaluated the value of the stock, based on management's revised sales and income projections. Saliba's revised valuation indicated a stock value of $547.77 per share.

Offenbecher's expert, Butch Williams, valued Offenbecher's 130 shares of Baron stock as of April 19, 1998, at $215,000, or $1,653.85 per share. Williams did not apply a marketability discount because he felt it was inappropriate in this case.

Offenbecher v. Baron Services, Inc. (II)

Trial court findings

In reaching its conclusion, the trial court relied heavily upon the testimony of Barons expert, Saliba. The trial courts reasoning was that Saliba could have employed other acceptable appraisal methods that would have decreased the value of Baron stock below $547.77 per share, but he did not do it.

The trial court concluded that Baron offered Offenbecher the fair value of his shares, $547.77 per share which represented a fair appraisal. It reasoned that Saliba's decision to apply a marketability discount 'at the corporate level was reasonable and necessary to the determination of the fair value of Baron stock. The trial court also concluded that a marketability discount was appropriate as a matter of law.

Holding on appeal and rationale

In an interesting reversal of roles, Judge Murdock, who previously dissented, now writes the majority opinion, and Judge Thompson issues a dissent. The earlier opinion upheld the trial courts application of a 50% marketability discount on the grounds that it was applied at the entity level. In this new opinion, the court of appeals reversed the trial court, finding that the application of the discount was error as a matter of law.

Quoting from case law and a learned treatise on the subject, the appellate court stated:

> We conclude that the application of a facially neutral marketability discount has made possible a squeeze-out merger. In 1998, the business generated pre-tax income of over $1,150,000. During the first five months of 1999, the post-merger corporation generated almost $2 million in profit. Had the majority shareholders not pursued their squeeze-out merger, Offenbecher would have received a proportionate share of over $1 million that the merged corporation distributed in the 18 months immediately following the merger, while still maintaining ownership of his stock.
>
> The controlling shareholders are the owners of the new corporation they formed for the purpose of merging Baron Services, and Offenbecher's ownership therein, out of existence. They have achieved that purpose. They will continue to reap the benefit of future earnings of the parties' business enterprise, while Offenbecher has been squeezed out. Such a result, if allowed, will enable the controlling shareholders to accomplish indirectly what Alabama decisions regarding oppression of minority shareholders will not allow them to accomplish directly. See, e.g., Brooks v. Hill, 717 So. 2d 759 (Ala. 1998).
>
> While ... [a marketability] discount can claim more theoretical support than the minority discount, and ostensibly could apply to all shares, majority as well as minority, there is the likelihood for this to be a refuge for practitioners and courts that do not recognize the changed role of appraisal. 1 F. Hodge ONeal & Robert B. Thompson, ONeal's Oppression of Minority Shareholders, § 5.32 (2d ed. 1999). In crediting

Saliba's testimony regarding the appropriateness of a 50% marketability discount, the trial court not only failed to recognize the role of the modern appraisal remedy, it made possible in this case precisely the sort of squeeze-out oppression that the appraisal remedy based on fair value was designed to prevent.

Collision Depot Inc. v. Zigman

Citation: 294 A.D.2d 497, 742 N.Y.S.2d 856, 2002 N.Y. App. Div. LEXIS 5236
Court: Supreme Court, Appellate Division
State/Jurisdiction: New York
Date of decision: May 20, 2002
Judge: Santucci

In *In the Matter of Collision Depot, Inc., et al., v. Robert Zigman, et al.*, 2002 N.Y. Slip Op. 04186 (N.Y.A.D. 2 Dept. April 9, 2002), the New York Supreme Court, Appellate Division, Second Department affirmed the lower court's valuation of three closely held companies in this business dissolution case. The defendants elected to purchase the plaintiffs' stock in order to avoid dissolution. Valuation testimony was received by the Supreme Court, Nassau County, who valued the plaintiffs' stock, in aggregate, at $48,040. The plaintiffs appealed the valuation of their interests.

The Second Appellate Department rejected the plaintiffs' contrary views regarding the lower court's valuation of the businesses and the credibility of the witnesses. The court noted, "The determination of a fact-finder as to the value of a business, if it is within the range of testimony presented, will not be disturbed on appeal where the valuation rests primarily on the credibility of the expert witnesses and their valuation techniques." It further noted, "The petitioner's contrary interpretation of the facts and credibility of the witnesses does not warrant disturbing the Supreme Court's determination." Thus, it affirmed the lower court's valuation.

Trahan v. Trahan

Citation: 99 Cal. App. 4th 62, 120 Cal. Rptr. 2d 814, 2002 Cal. App. LEXIS 4216
Court: Court of Appeals
State/Jurisdiction: California
Date of decision: June 7, 2002
Judge: Kline

The issue in this case was whether the trial court erred as a matter of law in confirming the award of the appraiser, where the appraiser did not include the estimated value of construction contracts that had not been completed as of the valuation date.

Trahan v. Trahan

Facts

Appellants and respondents were the sole shareholders of Trahan Bros., Inc., each owning 50% of the shares. Appellants filed this action to dissolve the corporation. Respondents sought to avoid dissolution by electing to purchase appellants' shares for fair value. The parties could not agree on the fair value of appellants' shares, and the matter proceeded to a fair value hearing. The court appointed only one appraiser, Teresa Arrighi-Campbell.

Definition of value and valuation date

The term "fair value" is defined by section 2000 of the California Corporation Code as follows:

> The fair value shall be determined on the basis of the liquidation value as of the valuation date but taking into account the possibility, if any, of sale of the entire business as a going concern in a liquidation.

Section 2000 further stated that the valuation date was to be "the date upon which that proceeding was initiated."

Valuation evidence

Arrighi-Campbell filed with the court a summary valuation report stating that she had determined the fair value of Trahan Bros. to be negative $164,487. Therefore, "appellants' shares correspondingly had a combined fair value' of negative $82,243 (negative $57,570 for Jeffrey Trahan's 35% ownership and negative $24,673 for David Trahan's 15% ownership)."

In response to the appraisers' valuation, respondents tendered $35 to Jeffrey Trahan and $15 to David Trahan in exchange for their shares, but the appellants refused to relinquish their shares. They believed the appraisers fair value determination was incorrect because she did not include the value of uncompleted construction contracts. Respondents argued that the appraisers should have used all five methods of valuation listed in Revenue Ruling 59-60 (i.e., adjusted net worth, capitalization of income, capitalization of EBIT, discounted cash flow, and market approach) in valuing Trahan Bros.

After respondents filed a motion to confirm the appraisers' award, the trial court received additional information from Arrighi-Campbell.

First, in a declaration filed with the court, Arrighi-Campbell stated:

> The valuation of the shares filed with the court did not include the value of the construction contracts or the maintenance contracts of the corporation as of the valuation date, or the profits or losses to be derived there from as the court documents called for liquidation value.

Chapter 7: Court Case Abstracts

Second, in response to interrogatories issued by the court, Arrighi-Campbell sent a letter to the court in which she stated that:

> The liquidation value as of the May 30, 2000 valuation date for the unperformed portion of Trahan Bros., Inc.'s construction contracts amounts to approximately $271,745, or the profit recognized to date." She stated that although the company had contract backlogs of approximately $3.3 million with a total estimated gross profit of $924,767 as of the valuation date, "assignability or lack thereof is the key factor which drives the value down. The main reason for this devaluation is that the Company would generally not have been able to sell these contracts as there is 1) little or no market for partially completed contracts and 2) on the public works and or bonded work, assignability is generally not allowed. Please note that the anticipated gross profit upon completion of the public works or bonded projects would have amounted to approximately $650,000 of the $924,767 of total estimated gross profit.

The letter [further] stated:

> ...there are two important items one must consider 1) the courts [sic] originally asked for and received the liquidation value as of May 30, 2000 which by its terms implies the contracts would not be completed and therefore the above estimate of $653,022 would not come to fruition and 2) if the contracts were performed through completion by the parties or someone else there would be incidental and overhead costs incurred which are not considered in the $653,022.

Trial court findings

The trial court stated that it was satisfied that Arrighi-Campbell had considered the impact of the uncompleted contracts on the liquidation value and confirmed the award of the appraiser. This appeal followed.

Holding on appeal and rationale

The court of appeals upheld the trial court decision. The court of appeals rejected the appellants' argument that all five of the Revenue Ruling 59-60 methods of valuation should have been used because those methods were relevant to a determination of investment value. The court of appeals held that "calculation of investment value is a pointless exercise where there is no possibility the enterprise could be sold as a going concern in liquidation." That option was ruled out in this case, and the decision that the company could not be sold in liquidation as a going concern was not challenged.

Because the standard of value in this case was liquidation value, the appraiser's method of valuation was correct. The statutory definition of fair value "necessarily anticipates the piecemeal valuation of the corporations existing assets and liabilities as of the valuation date, without consideration of any winding up period." Accordingly, the appraiser's failure to consider what profit might have been gained from the contracts during a winding-up period was appropriate.

Gagliano v. Brenna (II)

Citation: 173 N.J. 177, 801 A.2d 245, 2002 N.J. LEXIS 1071
Court: Supreme Court
State/Jurisdiction: New Jersey
Date of decision: July 16, 2002
Judge: Per Curiam

This case is on appeal from the New Jersey Court of Appeals case, 2001 N.J. Super. LEXIS 331, that was abstracted in the October 2001 issue of the *BVU*. The appellate division determined that the price offered in a cash-out merger was not fair value, but also ruled that the minority shareholders that were to receive only cash in the cash-out merger were not statutory dissenters and not entitled to recover fees and costs.

The petition for review challenging that ruling was granted.

Holding on appeal and rationale

The supreme court issues a one-sentence per curiam opinion affirming the appellate division holding. However, two judges joined in a dissenting opinion arguing that, although under a literal reading of the statute the minority shareholders that were to receive cash for their shares were not statutory dissenters, this ruling was against the public policy purpose of ensuring fair treatment of all shareholders.

G.I. Joe's, Inc. v. Nizam

Citation: 183 Or. App. 116, 50 P.3d 1282, 2002 Ore. App. LEXIS 1191
Court: Court of Appeals
State/Jurisdiction: Oregon
Date of decision: July 31, 2002
Judge: Linder

The issue in this case was the existence of certain stock options in favor of the company's president, which would affect the value of a dissenting shareholder's shares.

Chapter 7: Court Case Abstracts

Facts

Plaintiff, G.I. Joe's, Inc., brought this judicial appraisal action to determine the fair value of defendant's stock after defendant exercised his right to dissent from a proposed merger. The purpose of the merger was to allow the president of the G.I. Joe's to acquire majority control by buying out the previous majority shareholder.

All shareholders were given the opportunity to redeem their shares. Defendant and another shareholder did not redeem their shares. The president of G.I. Joe's owned a majority of the outstanding shares, with defendant and another shareholder being the only remaining shareholders. After acquiring majority ownership, the president of the G.I. Joes formed N.D. Holdings.

For N.D. Holdings and G.I. Joes to merge into one company, shareholder approval was required. Defendant voted against the merger. As a result, plaintiff determined that the fair value of defendants 18,720 shares plus accrued interest was $153,757. Plaintiff tendered that amount, but defendant asserted that the fair value of his shares was $203.95 per share, for a total of $3,818,000.

Trial court findings

Relying on plaintiff's witnesses, the trial court held that, although the merger documents did not mention the stock options, they did indeed exist. The court thus took the options into account when valuing defendant's shares, concluding that they were worth $160,618, and so entered judgment for defendant in the amount of $6,861, the difference between the fair value and the amount already tendered to him.

Holding on appeal and rationale

The court of appeals affirmed the trial court's decision regarding the stock options. The court of appeals reasoned that the only inquiry it was allowed to conduct was whether there was a record to support the trial court findings that the options existed. The court concluded that witnesses' testimony did support the trial court's decision and therefore affirmed its valuation decision.

Matthew G. Norton Co v. Smyth

Citation: 112 Wn. App. 865, 51 P.3d 159, 2002 Wash. App. LEXIS 1841
Court: Court of Appeals
State/Jurisdiction: Washington
Date of decision: August 5, 2002
Judge: Kennedy

The issue, in this case of first impression in Washington, was the propriety of discounts for lack of marketability and built-in capital gains in a dissenters' rights proceeding.

Facts

Matthew G. Norton Company (MGN) was formed in 1979 as a privately held company to consolidate the real estate and securities investments of the Norton Clapp family. Northwest Building Corporation (NWBC) was founded in 1936. In 1979 the real estate assets of the Norton Clapp family were transferred to a subsidiary that was merged into the preexisting NWBC. In 1999 the boards of directors of MGN and NWBC proposed a corporate reorganization. Under the proposed reorganization:
   a) MGN would merge into NWBC;
   b) the corporate status would change from a "C" corporation to an "S" corporation;
   c) each MGN shareholder would exchange his or her MGN shares of stock for the same number of NWBC shares of stock; and
   d) the name of the reorganized company would be Matthew G. Norton Company.

MGN had 43 individual shareholders. Stephen G. Clapp was the only MGN shareholder who dissented from the proposal. Clapp held 25,016 MGN shares, which constituted 3.1% of the outstanding shares. NWBC had only two shareholders, MGN owning 99.65% and Theodore H. Smyth owning the remaining 142 shares. Smyth also dissented.

Valuation evidence

To determine the fair value of the MGN and NWBC dissenters' shares, Matthew G. Norton Company hired the accounting firm of Arthur Andersen to conduct valuations of MGN and NWBC as of the date of the merger.

Arthur Andersen concluded that the value of one share in MGN was $138 and that the value of one share of NWBC was $1,451, as of March 31, 1999.

Arthur Andersen used a "net asset" valuation method, which involved "the adjustment of each company's balance sheet to reflect current market values of assets and liabilities as of the valuation date."

Chapter 7: Court Case Abstracts

Arthur Andersen used the market approach and the cost approach through a review of prices paid for limited partnership interests in determining the market value of certain corporate assets for purposes of such balance sheet adjustment.

Arthur Andersen did not directly use the income approach, but utilized corporate management's valuation of certain assets that were calculated using a discounted cash flow model. Where the corporation owned less than a controlling share of a particular corporate asset, Arthur Andersen applied a minority discount factor to reflect lack of controlling interest and marketability of the corporation's interest in that particular asset.

In adjusting liabilities, Arthur Andersen raised MGN's deferred taxes from a book value of $9.008 million to $44.258 million, and raised NWBC's deferred taxes from a book value of $5.744 million to $36.983 million, "to recognize the net appreciation of asset values to fair market value." All of this indicated a net asset value of $170.246 million for MGN and $99.446 million for NWBC.

In its valuation report for MGN, Arthur Andersen noted that the shareholders were severely restricted in their ability to transfer or sell their shares because shareholders wishing to sell their stock must first offer the shares to the lineal descendants of Matthew G. Norton at a price to be determined by the board of directors. Any unsold shares must next be offered to MGN for redemption at the price set by the board. No such restrictions existed in NWBC, but there was no public market for the stock in either corporation. Because of that and some other factors, Arthur Andersen opined that it was appropriate to discount the net adjusted value for MGN by 35% and for NWBC by 40%.

Matthew G. Norton Company paid Clapp $3,509,146 (including accrued interest) for his shares in MGN, and paid Smyth $208,050 (including accrued interest) for the shares of NWBC. Both Clapp and Smyth were dissatisfied with these amounts. Clapp demanded a total amount of $6,858,928 for his shares, while Smyth demanded a total amount of $458,864.

Robert Duffy was an expert retained by Clapp and Smyth. He did not offer a legal opinion on the issue of applying discounts for lack of marketability and built-in capital gains in dissenter's rights valuations. However, he concluded that if such discounts were appropriate:
   (1) Arthur Andersen did not utilize methodology for computing lack of marketability discounts that is generally accepted in the financial community for purposes of determining "fair value" and
   (2) discovery had not progressed sufficiently to allow a determination of present value of future tax impacts as of the valuation date.

Trial court findings

The trial court held that, as a matter of law, the company could not apply a lack of marketability discount or a discount for future taxation of imbedded capital gains in determining "fair value" of the dissenter's shares.

Holding on appeal and rationale

The court of appeals spent a considerable part of the opinion reviewing the case law from other jurisdictions on the applicability of discounts in a dissenters rights proceeding. Washington adopted its version of the Model Business Corporation Act in 1989, 10 years before the Act was amended to exclude marketability and minority discounts from the definition of "fair value." In light of the Washington statutes silence on this issue, the court looked to other states for guidance.

Discount for lack of marketability

The court of appeals held that discounts for lack of controlling interest or lack of marketability are appropriate on a corporate level, and if the trial court order intended to preclude these discounts on a corporate level, the decision was reversed. The court of appeals concluded, however, that Arthur Anderson improperly equated "fair value" of the shares with "fair market value."

The court of appeals further held that if the trial court intended to preclude the possibility of any lack of marketability discount at the shareholder level, even in the face of extraordinary circumstances (i.e., a "bright line rule"), the decision was also reversed. However, the court of appeals also held that the trials court decision would be affirmed to the extent that the trial courts order was intended to declare that, absent extraordinary circumstances, no such discount can be applied at the shareholder level.

Discount for built-in capital gains taxes

The court of appeals also held that the trial courts "bright line ruling" with respect to the tax discount issue was too broad as well, or at least premature in this case in light of the state of discovery. The court of appeals affirmed the trial court holding that a "wholesale discount for built-in capital gains on all the appreciated assets of the companies based on hypothetical liquidation at some indefinite time in the future is not appropriate."

However, the court further held:

> [F]acts that were known or could be ascertained as of the date of the merger that relate to disposition of a particular appreciated asset such as contemplation of sale of the asset in accord with pre-existing planning in the normal course of business are properly considered in determining net asset value in a dissenting shareholders case, provided, however, that the shareholder will not effectively be paying his or her proportionate share of the tax on this same appreciation, upon taxation of the proceeds of sale of his or her appreciated stock back to the corporation. To the extent that the trial courts ruling was intended to preclude any such considerations, we reverse.

Finally, the court stated that the company needed to provide the trial court with a reasonable explanation of why such built-in gains should be considered.

Gonsalves v. Straight Arrow Publishers, Inc. (IV)

Citation: 2002 Del. Ch. LEXIS 105
Court: Court of Chancery
State/Jurisdiction: Delaware
Date of decision: September 10, 2002
Judge: Chandler

This is the latest installment in the ongoing saga of the *Gonsalves v. Straight Arrow Publishers, Inc.* dissenting stockholder suit. This is the court of chancery's response to a remand with instructions from the Delaware Supreme Court.

Four issues to resolve

The Supreme Court specifically noted four issues to be determined on remand:
1. The appropriate capitalization multiple
2. Treatment of deferred subscription income
3. Treatment of excess cash
4. An explanation for the form of interest awarded

The Supreme Court affirmed that a five-year weighted average EBIT was the financial performance variable to be capitalized. The experts disagreed on the valuation multiple to be applied.

Expert values wrong property

Plaintiff's expert, James Kobak, based his selection of comparables on Straight Arrow's primary operating asset, *Rolling Stone* magazine. Straight Arrow's expert, Marty Whitman, based his valuation on Straight Arrow as the operating entity, rather than limiting his focus to *Rolling Stone* as the operating entity.

The court-appointed expert, Donald Puglisi, viewed Kobak's methodology as flawed and used Whitman's comparables.

> As [Puglisi] correctly pointed out, Gonsalves owned stock in [Straight Arrow], not Rolling Stone magazine. Also, [Straight Arrow] had additional operating activities beyond Rolling Stone not accounted for by Kobak. Use of this flawed methodology resulted in Kobak failing to "identify[y] a sample of comparable companies whose valuations and financial attributes can be used in the process of determining the fair value of the common stock of [Straight Arrow] on the [Merger] Date."

Puglisi capitalized Straight Arrows weighted five-year average EBIT at 11 times. Whitman used a lower capitalization figure and Kobak used a higher multiple. The court accepted Puglisi's number.

Gonsalves v. Straight Arrow Publishers, Inc. (IV)

Deferred subscription revenue addback denied

Kobak argued that EBIT for each year should be adjusted for changes in deferred subscription income. Puglisi rejected this adjustment and the court also denied it.

Treatment of cash

In calculating the market value of invested capital (which the court referred to as "enterprise value"), Puglisi and Whitman used the formula:

Value of common stock
+ Interest-bearing debt
- Cash
= Enterprise value

Therefore, since cash was subtracted at the beginning for the comparable companies, arguments about "excess" cash were irrelevant. To be consistent, the methodology required that *all* of Straight Arrows cash be added back to the indicated value of the enterprise based on the comparables.

Two questions unanswered

The court left two questions unanswered and invited the parties to submit additional evidence:
1. Whether a piece of land was an operating or a non-operating asset (if determined to be a non-operating asset, the value would be added back).
2. Whether an adjustment should be made to account for any minority ownership discount inherent in the use of public stocks as comparables.

On the latter point, Chancellor Chandler said:

> I believe that a more thorough examination of this issue is required before I can make a final determination of what, if any, adjustment should be made to eliminate a possible minority ownership discount here.

Interest rate explanation inadequate

On the interest rate issue, the court said:

> Kobak did not provide sufficient explanation for the calculations upon which he ultimately based petitioners proposed prudent investor rate, while Whitman thoroughly explained and supported the calculations used to determine [Straight Arrow's] proposed rate.

Chancellor Chandler concluded:

If the parties are content to accept my valuation without further adjustment, I conclude that the fair value of Gonsalves' [Straight Arrow] stock at the time of the merger was $262.96 per share.

Baltrusis v. Baltrusis

Citation: 2002 Wash. App. LEXIS 2241
Court: Court of Appeal
State/Jurisdiction: Washington
Date of decision: September 16, 2002
Judge: Ellington

A major issue in this trial was whether a marketability discount was appropriate.

Facts

The parties were married in 1982. Each party owned shares of Anchor Bancorp, Inc., which was a five-bank holding company owned by wife's family. Wife owned 43,560 shares while husband owned 16,800 shares.

Anchor's sole asset was Gentwo, L.L.P., a limited liability partnership consisting of wife and her family members. Gentwo started as a limited liability partnership called Harbourside, in which both wife and husband were limited partners. After the separation, Harbourside was dissolved and Gentwo was formed by having wife's entire family recontribute the same Anchor shares.

Swansea, L.L.P. was a limited liability partnership that held securities. Wife held a 10% interest in Swansea.

Valuation evidence

Husband did not use an expert witness. Wife used Steven Kessler, CPA. In valuing Anchor's stock, Kessler relied heavily on an appraisal done in 1998 by Alex Sheshunoff & Company Investment Banking for "estate planning purposes." Sheshunoff "arrived at a range of estimated fair market value between $14.80 and $23.30 per share, depending upon methodology, and selected $19.40 as the most accurate figure." Sheshunoff also applied a 33% discount for lack of marketability and came up with $13.00 per share.

Kessler also testified that, after discounts to the Anchor stock for lack of marketability, wife's interest in Gentwo must be further discounted by 25% for lack of marketability and an additional 35% for minority status. He therefore valued her interest in the partnership at $6.34 per share. Sheshunoff had opined that the additional discount for family limited partnership units was only 15%. He therefore concluded that the value of Harbourside was $11.00 per unit.

Kessler testified that, including discounts for lack of marketability and wife's minority stake, her interest in Swansea had a value of $191,588.

Trial court findings

The trial court valued husband's Anchor stock at $19.40 per share, declining to adopt either Kessler's or Sheshunoff's values, because both applied discounts for lack of marketability.

The trial court held that wife's separate interest in Gentwo had a value between $11.00 and $23.50 per unit.

Finally, the trial court valued wife's interest in Swansea between $191,580 and $393,002.

Holding on appeal and rationale

The court of appeals held that the trial court did not abuse its discretion in declining to apply a marketability discount in valuing the Anchor stock:

First, the transaction was court ordered and the parties were acting under compulsion. The only "market" for [husbands] Anchor Bancorp shares is his ex-wife's family. Second, as a member of the Jones family, [wife] is in a position to enjoy the full value of the shares, while [husband] is not. In this regard, [husband] is in a situation somewhat similar to dissenting shareholders, who are "unwilling sellers with no bargaining power." When appraising a dissenting shareholders stock, courts determine fair value, not fair market value. Absent extraordinary circumstances, marketability is not a relevant consideration.

Applebaum v. Avaya, Inc., et al.

Citation: No. 375, 2002
Court: Supreme Court
State/Jurisdiction: Delaware
Date of decision: November 20, 2002
Judge: Veasey, Holland, and Steele

The following court case abstract was originally published in Valuation Case Digest®

In *Milton Applebaum v. Avaya, Inc., et al.* No. 375, 2002 (Del. November 20, 2002), the Delaware Supreme Court considered the definition and calculation of fair value for the purposes of a reverse/forward stock split under 8 Del. Sec. 155. In order to reduce its costs associated with maintaining a large number of small shareholders, Avaya decided to affect a reverse stock split of at least 30-1 followed by a forward stock split in the same amount. In the reverse stock split, shareholders holding a fractional share would be cashed out either through a sale of the fractional shares on the market or by an amount representing the average 10-day trading price of the stock. Avaya's stock is actively traded over the New York Stock Exchange (NYSE). Applebaum held 27 shares, and sought to enjoin the transaction. He argued that the amount offered in that transaction was too low and did not comply with the definition of fair value used in other sections of 8 Del.

The Supreme Court noted that a shareholder is entitled to receive the fair value of his interest in the corporation when cashed out in a Sec. 155 transaction. It then found that the fair value of stock for the purposes of this section is best determined by reference to the trading price of the stock in "a well informed, liquid trading market." It noted that since Avaya is actively traded over the NYSE, the trading price is the best evidence of its value. It further recognized that stock price is volatile, but the use of a 10-day average trading price "has been recognized as a fair compromise that will hedge against the risk of [price] fluctuation."

It rejected the notion that fair value as used in Sec. 155 and as used in Sec. 262 (the appraisal statute) have the same meaning. It stated, "[A] Section 155(2) inquiry may resemble a Section 262 valuation if the controlling stockholder will benefit from presenting a suspect measure of value, such as an out-dated trading price, or a wrongfully imposed private company discount." However, neither situation has arisen in this case. Moreover, Avaya will not capture its full going-concern value in the transaction at issue as opposed to a merger or consolidation transaction. Here, it found "the cashed-out stockholders could capture the full proportionate value of the fractional interest, return to the market and buy the reissued stock at the market price, and realize the going concern value a second time should Avaya ever merger or otherwise become subject to a change of control transaction." Thus, it affirmed the lower court's definition of fair value as market value for Sec. 155 purposes.

Wenzel v. Hopper & Galliher, P.C.

Citation: 779 N.E.2d 30, 2002 Ind. App. LEXIS 1937
Court: Court of Appeals
State/Jurisdiction: Indiana
Date of decision: November 22, 2002
Judge: Hoffman

The primary issue in this withdrawing shareholder action was the fair value of the withdrawing shareholder's interest in the law firm, Hopper & Galliher, P.C. (H&G). As an issue of first impression in Indiana, the court of appeals addressed whether minority and marketability discounts should be applied in determining fair value.

Other issues before the court included whether prejudgment interest should have been awarded, whether the withdrawing shareholder was entitled to costs and attorney fees, and whether either party had prevailed on their claim for breach of fiduciary duty.

Wenzel v. Hopper & Galliher, P.C.

Facts

Mark Wenzel, George Hopper, and Mark Galliher practiced law as the professional corporation of Hopper, Wenzel, & Galliher, P.C., (now H&G). After several years, Wenzel decided he did not like working with Hopper and believed that Hopper was not being completely forthright with respect to compensation due to Wenzel. At the annual shareholders' meeting, it was agreed that Wenzel would seek employment elsewhere and that Hopper and Galliher would buy out his share of the firm upon his departure.

During negotiations regarding the fair value of Wenzel's shares, Wenzel requested $400,000 for his stock and his a share of the firm's outstanding contingency fees. H&G counter offered $27,000 for the stock, plus an undisclosed amount for his interest in the contingency fees. Because the parties could not agree, H&G filed a petition for the determination of the fair value of Wenzel's stock. After the petition was filed, H&G offered to pay Wenzel $77,500 for his stock, plus a share in the contingency fees.

Both parties also filed claims for breach of fiduciary duty, and Wenzel also claimed that Hopper & Galliher had sought to freeze him out.

Valuation evidence

Both parties presented the testimony of an appraisal expert. Both experts agreed that the net asset approach was appropriate, but disagreed regarding the inclusion of several liabilities in the net asset value calculations. H&G's expert deducted $179,000 for H&G's obligation on its sublease and $9,497 for H&G's obligation on a telephone service contract. In addition, H&G's expert reduced the value of Wenzel's shares by 15% for a minority discount and 10% for a marketability discount. The court did not provide any details of Wenzel's expert's valuation opinion.

Trial court findings

The trial court determined that the fair value of Wenzel's shares was $48,265.62. The trial court specifically adopted the testimony of H&G's expert and deducted the sublease and telephone service contract liabilities.

The trial court also applied the minority and marketability discounts opined by H&G's expert, and found that the application of these discounts was "based on generally accepted principles." The trial court cited and relied upon *Perlman v. Permonite Manufacturing Co.*, 568 F. Supp. 222 (N.D. Ind. 1983).

In addition, the trial court found that H&G had not breached its fiduciary duty to Wenzel, that Wenzel was not entitled to prejudgment interest or costs and fees, and that Wenzel had breached his fiduciary duty to the firm. Wenzel appealed.

Chapter 7: Court Case Abstracts

Holdings on appeal and rationale

The court of appeals found that whether the sublease and telephone service contract liabilities should be included in the net asset value calculations was a question of fact, to be reversed only if clearly erroneous. Because the inclusion of these liabilities was based upon the testimony of an expert witness, the court of appeals found that the trial court did not clearly err.

Application of discounts

The court of appeals found that whether minority and marketability discounts were applicable in a fair value determination was a matter of law. Noting that there was no prior case law on this issue in Indiana, the court turned to case law from other jurisdictions.

First, the court noted that "fair value" is not the same thing as "fair market value." Accordingly, it held that the trial courts reliance on *Perlman v. Permonite, supra*, was misplaced because that case dealt with fair market value.

Quoting from several cases and law review articles, the court determined that the majority position was to not apply discounts in determining fair value, and adopted this rule for Indiana as a matter of law.

The court noted, however, that there may be "extraordinary circumstances" that might constitute issues of fact and warrant the application of a marketability discount. However, because H&G's expert did not present any "extraordinary circumstances" in his testimony, such a factual determination was unnecessary in this case.

Interest, costs and fees

The court of appeals refused to reverse the trial courts denial of prejudgment interest because Wenzel was as much at fault for litigation delays as H&G. Therefore, the trial court did not abuse its discretion in refusing to award fees.

The court of appeals also upheld the trial courts failure to award costs and fees because the fair value determination of $48,265.62 was less than the last written offer of $77,500. However, the court noted that if fair value as recalculated with discounts on remand exceeds $77,500, then Wenzel should be awarded costs and fees. The court of appeals upheld the trial courts finding that H&G did not breach its fiduciary duty to Wenzel because Hopper and Galliher refuted every allegation of fraud in their testimony at trial. Although the trial court erred in not shifting the burden of proof to H&G after Wenzel had raised the presumption of fraud, the evidence presented by H&G was sufficient to meet the burden of proof if it had been officially shifted.

The court of appeals reversed the trial courts finding that Wenzel breached his fiduciary duty to H&G by surreptitiously soliciting clients of H&G while still employed by the firm. H&G

presented no evidence to support this claim, and the testimony of Wenzel indicated that he did not breach his fiduciary duty in this manner. The court of appeals criticized the trial court for adopting H&G's finding of fact on this issue without its own considered judgment.

The case was affirmed in part, reversed in part, and remanded for a new determination of the fair value of Wenzel's stock.

Hogle v. Zinetics Med., Inc.

Citation: 2002 UT 121, 63 P.3d 80, 2002 Utah LEXIS 185
Court: Supreme Court
State/Jurisdiction: Utah
Date of decision: December 13, 2002
Judge: Howe

The issue in this dissenting shareholder action was whether the trial court erred in its valuation of the minority shareholders' Zinetics Medical, Inc. stock pursuant to a forced sale of the stock to Zinetics' parent corporation, Medtronic, Inc.

Facts

Zinetics began in 1983 as a stand-alone corporation that developed and manufactured a specialized catheter for use in diagnostic equipment. The company was not financially successful, and in 1991 81% of the company was sold to Synetics for $255,000. Due to the worldwide distribution network and customer base of Synetics, Zinetics experienced steady increases in revenue and profitability.

Synetics was later acquired by Medtronic. Soon disagreements arose between Medtronic and the minority shareholders of Zinetics over the management and future goals of Zinetics. To settle their differences, Medtronic offered to purchase the minority shareholders' stock. Negotiations ensued during which each side made counteroffers to purchase the Zinetics' stock owned by the other. The minority shareholders' final offer to Medtronic was for 10 cents per share, which Medtronic rejected. Medtronic then initiated a forced merger of Metronic and Zinetics. The minority shareholders dissented, and Medtronic filed a petition under the dissenter's rights statutes for a judicial determination of the fair value of the minority stock.

Valuation evidence

Both parties presented expert testimony concerning the fair value of the minority shareholders' interest in Zinetics. The minority also argued that their offer to purchase 80% of the Zinetics' stock held by Medtronic at 10 cents per share was evidence of the fair value of the stock.

Chapter 7: Court Case Abstracts

Both experts used the market approach and the "investment valuation method" or income approach. No evidence of asset value was presented, and so the trial court did not consider asset value.

Medtronic's expert, Merrill R. Norman, opined that the minority's stock was worth 1.97 cents per share. The minority's expert, Robert F. Reilly, opined that the minority's stock was worth 18 cents per share.

Market approach

In assessing the market approach, Norman rejected prior trades of Zinetics on the NASDAQ exchange. Norman then selected a number of comparable publicly traded companies for his market approach calculations.

> [He] chose a mixture of companies in the medical device field, including several extremely large organizations very dissimilar to Zinetics, notably Abbott Laboratories, Baxter International, and United States Surgical. Using standard appraisal techniques, Norman calculated a multiplier based on the ratio of price to earnings for the guideline companies. Under his methodology, such a multiplier applied to actual earnings yields market value. However, Norman then applied a 42.76% downward adjustment in value to compensate for the differences between Zinetics and the guideline companies.

In his market approach, Reilly also rejected prior trades of Zinetics on NASDAQ because the stock was too thinly traded to be a reliable indicator of value. Reilly also selected a number of comparable publicly traded companies for his market approach.

> [He] identified guideline companies through a computer search screening for catheter manufacturers similar to Zinetics in size and revenues that had brought a product to the production stage. Eleven companies met the criteria. None of these companies, however, had ever shown a net profit. Therefore, Reilly could not use the usual per share price over earnings ratio as the multiplier applied to earnings. Instead he resorted to market value of invested capital (MVIC) divided by revenues of each of the guideline companies (MVIC/revenue).

The trial court rejected both experts' market approach values. It rejected Norman's selection of comparable companies as "seriously flawed" because the need for a 42.76% adjustment suggested that these companies were not really similar to Zinetics. The court rejected Reilly's use of MVIC/revenue as a multiplier because this approach "yielded values which fluctuated inexplicably over time in a manner unrelated to the fundamental financial performance of the companies."

Income approach

In his income approach calculations, Norman determined a weighted average of values derived from discounted cash flow, capitalized cash flow, discounted earnings, and capitalized earnings methods. He used future earnings projections that were 15% lower than Zinetic's 1997 adjusted earnings.

Hogle v. Zinetics Med., Inc.

In his income approach, Reilly used only the discounted cash flow method. He consulted Zinetic's management for earnings projections, and used those projections as the basis for his discount and capitalization rates.

> Reilly relied on two sets of projections supplied by Zinetic's president, Steve Davis. Reilly also prepared a third set of projections based on Davis deposition and on information from the previous projections. Respectively, these projections predicted total revenues of $4,153,000, $3,918,000, and $3,190,000 for the 1998 fiscal year.

The trial court criticized Norman's reduction of his future earnings projections from actual 1997 earnings. It also criticized Reilly's use of only the discounted cash flow method. The trial court adopted Norman's valuation model, but stated that it used Reilly's projections, discount rate, and capitalization rate. Based on these calculations, the trial court found that the value of the minority's Zinetics stock did not exceed 4.528 cents per share, which is what Medtronic's originally offered.

The minority shareholders appealed.

Holdings on appeal and rationale

The Supreme Court agreed with the trial court that both experts' market approach valuations were unreliable. Therefore, it was not error for the trial court to disregard this approach.

The Supreme Court also upheld the trial courts selection of Norman's valuation model and Reilly's projections, discount rate, and capitalization rate. However, the Supreme Court found that the trial court did not adequately explain its calculations:

> [T]he courts memorandum decision refers to inserting the Minority's projections for "revenue" rather than cash flow into Norman's model. Furthermore, Reilly's exhibit XI (Discounted Cash Flow Synthesis) sets forth three "scenarios" valuing Zinetics, respectively, at $11,263,000, $3,811,000, and $12,096,000. Each is based on a separate set of five yearly projections and a terminal value. The court did not indicate which of these sets, or what combination, it inserted into Normans model. Finally, the court did not indicate whether it restricted its calculations to substituting Reilly's numbers in Normans discounted cash flow model only, or whether it included other models.

> These omissions are troubling because when the direct capitalization multiple and the projected cash flows set forth in Reilly's exhibit XI for years one through five and the terminal values for each of the three scenarios are inserted into Normans Schedule J (Zinetics Medical Inc. Discounted Cash Flows as Part of Synetics) and the final results are averaged and then divided by the number of shares outstanding, the result is substantially more than 4.528 cents per share. This is also the case using the values from either scenario one or three. Only scenario two yields a value per share of less than the amount offered. The choice among the three options, or the average of all three or any

two, is a factual determination within the discretion of the district court. Yet the court has not explicitly made this determination.

Accordingly, the Supreme Court remanded the case to the trial court to recalculate the fair value of the minority's stock.

Stand-alone v. subsidiary

The Supreme Court also addressed the issue of what was being valued. The arguments of the minority tended to focus on what Zinetics would be worth as a stand-alone company. The argument regarding the 10-cent offer to purchase was based on this assumption. The Supreme Court stated, however, that the minority clearly owned a minority interest in a subsidiary—not a stand-alone company—and that this is the interest that was to be valued. The Supreme Court pointed out that Zinetics was not profitable and did not experience significant growth until it became a subsidiary of Synetics. Therefore, there was no basis for valuing it on a stand-alone basis.

Application of discounts

The Supreme Court also addressed the issue of discounts, because Norman had applied a 31.9% marketability discount to his income approach value determination. Reilly did not apply a marketability discount in his calculations.

The trial court, in adopting Norman's income approach model, appears to have also applied his marketability discount, but the Supreme Court did not specifically state that it did so. Nonetheless, because this issue could affect the outcome on remand, the Supreme Court specifically found that a marketability discount is inappropriate in determining fair value in a dissenting shareholder action. The trial court was directed not to apply a discount on remand.

Pueblo Bancorporation v. Lindoe, Inc. (II)

Citation: 63 P.3d 353, 2003 Colo. LEXIS 53
Court: Supreme Court
State/Jurisdiction: Colorado
Date of decision: January 21, 2003
Judge: Rice

In this case, Pueblo Bancorporation appealed the court of appeals' reversal of the trial court's determination of the shares owned by Lindoe, Inc., a minority shareholder of Pueblo.

The facts, valuation evidence, trial court findings, and holding by the court of appeals are set out in detail in the discussion of *Pueblo Bancorporation v. Lindoe, Inc.*, 37 P.3d 492, 2001 Colo. App. LEXIS 1330 (Colo. Ct. App. 2001).

The parties did not disagree over the value of Pueblo as a company. The sole issue before the Supreme Court was whether Lindoe's minority shares should be discounted for lack of marketability. The trial court applied a marketability discount, but the court of appeals reversed, holding that such a discount could not be applied as a matter of law. The Supreme Court granted certiorari to resolve the conflict in the court of appeals over the meaning of "fair value."

The court first determined that the term "fair value" was ambiguous and did not have "a commonly accepted meaning in ordinary usage, much less in the business community." Thus, the court was required to look to other sources to interpret the statutory term.

Prior Colorado case law

The court first discussed previous Colorado cases interpreting the term, three cases in particular: *WCM Indus., Inc. v. Trustees of the Harold G. Wilson 1985 Revocable Trust*, 948 P.2d 36 (Colo. Ct. App. 1997); *M Life Ins. Co. v. Sapers & Wallack Ins. Agency, Inc.*, 40 P.3d 6 (Colo. Ct. App. 2001); and the proceedings below in the case at hand, *Pueblo Bancorporation v. Lindoe, Inc., supra*.

The court stated that the court of appeals had not provided a consistent interpretation of "fair value," particularly on the issue of discounts. Because the court was unable to resolve the meaning of "fair value" by reference to the plain language of the statute, and because of the conflicting interpretations of the term in prior Colorado case law, the Supreme Court said that the role of this court was to determine the meaning of this phrase.

Possible interpretations of fair value

The court listed three possible interpretations of the term. First, fair value could be determined on a case-by-case approach, in which the trial court has discretion to apply whichever fair value definition the court thinks appropriate.

Second, fair value could be the value of the dissenter's specific allotment of shares, just as one would value a commodity. This interpretation effectively equates fair value with fair market value and minority and marketability discounts would normally apply.

Third, fair value possible interpretation fair value could be the dissenting shareholder's proportionate interest in the value of the entity. Under this interpretation, shareholder-level discounts are inappropriate.

Court rejects case-by-case approach

The court first held that the meaning of "fair value" was a question of law, "not an issue of fact to be opined on by appraisers and decided by the trial court on a case-by-case basis." The court rejected an approach that would leave the decision of whether to apply a marketability discount to the discretion of the trial court.

A case-by-case interpretation of "fair value" results in a definition that is too imprecise to be useful to the business community. Under a case-by-case approach, the parties proceed to trial without knowing what interest the trial court is valuing. Although the difference between the two measures [of a pro rata interest and a specific allotment of shares] is the single largest variable in the appraisal process, the court's choice of which interpretation to adopt is largely determined by whichever expert the court finds more persuasive. Both the corporation and the dissenting shareholder are disadvantaged because of the subjective and unpredictable nature of the case-by-case approach. A case-by-case interpretation encourages unnecessary litigation. A definition of "fair value" that varies from one courtroom to another is no definition at all.

The court then held that, to the extent that *M Life Ins. Co.* and *WCM Indus., Inc.* adopted a case-by-case approach, they are overruled.

Fair value is not fair market value

Next, the court held that fair value must have a "definitive meaning." Either it is the proportionate interest in the company or it is the specific allotment of shares. The court concluded that the legislature chose "fair value" for a reason and that it must therefore mean something different than "fair market value." If the legislature had wanted to provide for dissenting shareholders to receive "fair market value" for their shares, "it knew how to provide it; the phrase has been used many times in a wide variety of statutes."

Fair value is proportionate ownership interest

Finally, the court held that the proper interpretation of fair value is the shareholders proportionate ownership interest in the value of the corporation, without discounting for lack of marketability. It stated that this view was consistent with the underlying purpose of the dissenter's rights statute and the strong national trend against applying discounts.

> The purpose of the dissenter's rights statute would best be fulfilled through an interpretation of "fair value" which ensures minority shareholders are compensated for what they have lost, that is, their proportionate ownership interest in a going concern. A marketability discount is inconsistent with this interpretation; it injects unnecessary speculation into the appraisal process and substantially increases the possibility that a dissenting shareholder will be under-compensated for his ownership interest. An interpretation of "fair value" that gives minority shareholders "less than their proportionate share of the whole firms fair value would produce a transfer of wealth from the minority shareholders to the shareholders in control. Such a rule would inevitably encourage corporate squeeze-outs."

The court noted that this interpretation of fair value is the clear majority view, adopted by most courts that have considered the issue, the Model Business Corporation Act (MBCA) (on which the Colorado dissenters rights statute is based), and the American Law Institutes Principles of Corporate Governance.

> The clear majority trend is to interpret fair value as the shareholders proportionate ownership of a going concern and not to apply discounts at the shareholder level. The interpretation urged by [Pueblo's expert] would position Colorado among a shrinking minority of jurisdictions in the country. We decline to do so.

The Supreme Court also found persuasive the recent amendments to the MBCA, amending the definition of fair value to reflect the national trend against discounts in fair value appraisals. The court affirmed the court of appeals.

Extraordinary circumstances

The court of appeals had found, as a matter of law, that no extraordinary circumstances existed in this case. Therefore, no marketability discount should be applied under the ALI exception. The Supreme Court found that the court of appeals should not have addressed this issue on the facts of this case. This ruling effectively left open the issue of whether an extraordinary circumstances exception is available under Colorado law.

Dissenting opinion

Judge Kourlis filed a dissenting opinion, joined by two other justices. He based his opinion on several factors. First, he argued that Colorado case law requires a consideration of "all relevant factors," one of which is market value. Second, he inferred, from the Colorado legislatures failure to adopt the MBCA amendments eliminating discounts, that it intended to leave the existing statute in place. Finally, he argued that without "a marketability discount, the amount the dissenting shareholder will receive for his shares will exceed that which he would have received had he sold his stock for some unrelated reason prior to the corporate action." Because any investor would not buy minority shares in a close corporation without accounting for the relative illiquidity of the stock, not discounting for that illiquidity allows the shareholder to collect a windfall.

Pro Finish USA, Ltd. v. Johnson

Citation: 63 P.3d 288, 2003 Ariz. App. LEXIS 16
Court: Court of Appeals
State/Jurisdiction: Arizona
Date of decision: February 6, 2003
Judge: Lankford

In this case of first impression under the Arizona dissenters' rights statute, the corporation appealed a trial court ruling accepting the dissenting shareholders' expert's conclusion of fair value over that of the corporation's expert. The Supreme Court affirmed the trial court and held that fair value was the pro rata share of the sales price in an arm's-length sale of substantially all of the corporation's assets. It also upheld the trial courts ruling that no discounts should be applied in determining fair value.

Facts

In 1998 a buyer agreed to pay $5 million for substantially all of the assets of Pro Finish USA, Ltd., a seller of nail care polishes, finishes, and other personal care products. The buyer also agreed to assume almost all of the company's $1 million in liabilities. The dissenters voted against the sale and the corporation paid them each $1,200 per share. The shareholders objected to the $1,200 price and the corporation filed suit for a determination of fair value under the state dissenter's rights statute.

Valuation evidence and trial court findings

The shareholders expert, Stephen Clarke, based his calculations on the asset sale price and determined that the fair value was $2,504.64 per share. Clarke did not apply either minority or marketability discounts.

The corporation's expert, James Larson, discounted the payment stream to present value and compared that figure to the price per share in a previous minority shareholder stock sale. Larson applied both minority and marketability discounts. He concluded that fair value was $977 per share.

The trial court accepted Clarke's fair value conclusion and Pro Finish appealed.

Holding on appeal and rationale

The court of appeals first considered whether Arizona law required fair value to be determined without regard to the asset sale. Pro Finish first argued that fair value could not be based on the asset sale because it would take into account "appreciation in anticipation of the corporate action." However, the court noted that the Arizona statute permitted such consideration if exclusion would be inequitable.

Even if appreciation could not be considered, the court stated that the asset sale did not cause an *appreciation* in the stock value, but merely provided the best evidence of the *existing* value.

> The common-sense answer to the question of an assets value is what a third-party is willing to pay for it. Methods of valuation short of third-party sales value are "guesswork" and "merely a second best substitute for valuing the property in an actual third party sale." Thus, "the best evidence of value, if available, is third-party sales value," and reliable evidence of third-party sales should be considered in determining fair value.

The court further said that the risk of appreciated value was greater in a merger than in an asset sale, and it saw no reason why the shareholders should not "share in the fruit of an advantageous price for the corporate assets."

No discount for fair value

Finally, the court agreed with the trial court's refusal to apply minority and marketability discounts to the dissenting shareholders pro rata share of the sale price. Noting the trend in this direction among other jurisdictions, it held that the focus should be upon the value of the firm as a whole, which should be "prorated equally."

Offenbecher v. Baron Services, Inc. (III)

Citation: 2003 Ala. LEXIS 103
Court: Supreme Court
State/Jurisdiction: Alabama
Date of decision: April 4, 2003
Judge: See

The issue of first impression in this dissenting shareholder action was whether the trial courts application of a marketability discount in determining the fair value of the dissenters shares in a cash-out merger was appropriate.

The original court of civil appeals opinion in this case held that an entity-level marketability discount was appropriate in determining fair value. Upon rehearing, the court of civil appeals' revised opinion reversed its former opinion and held that a marketability discount was not appropriate.

In this opinion, the Alabama Supreme Court affirmed the revised opinion of the court of civil appeals, holding the application of a marketability discount to be inappropriate.

Additional facts revealed on appeal

Although the facts of this case were generally set forth in the prior opinions of the court of civil appeals, the Supreme Court revealed two additional interesting facts. First, the Supreme Court quoted expert Gary Saliba's report:

> Saliba Financial Economics Group was retained to render an opinion as to the fair market value of certain common shares in Baron Services, Inc. The purpose of the valuation was to assist the Company's Board of Directors in determining the fair market value, at the Shareholder level, regarding an ownership position in the Company's common stock." (emphasis added).

Chapter 7: Court Case Abstracts

The Supreme Court also quoted the definition of fair value from Saliba's report:

> [F]air value represents a proportionate share of the value of the whole, with entity value based on such factors as individual assets values, ongoing concern values, and/or a combination of approaches. A material factor with respect to fair value is that the lack of marketability is not considered, in that the interest would be considered marketable." (emphasis in original).

In spite of these statements in Saliba's report, the trial court found that his application of an entity-level marketability discount was "reasonable and necessary to the determination of the 'fair value' of Baron Services' stock."

Holding and rationale of Supreme Court

The Supreme Court held that the application of a marketability discount was inappropriate in this case, addressing four points and arguments of Baron Services.

First, the court reviewed case law and literature on this issue, finding that fair value and fair market value are not the same. The court rejected Baron Services definition of fair value because it was basically fair market value. Fair market value is the willing buyer and willing seller standard. However, "[i]n the context of a cash-out merger, a minority shareholder is not a willing seller; instead, the minority shareholder is selling his or her share under the compulsion of the majority shareholders who approved the merger."

Second, the court adopted the Delaware fair value standard, which prohibits the application of a marketability discount at the shareholder level. Quoting from *Cavalier Oil Corp. v. Harnett*, 564 A.2d 1137 (Del. 1989), the court stated:

> The application of a discount to a minority shareholder is contrary to the requirement that the company be viewed as a going concern. ... Where there is no objective market data available, the appraisal process is not intended to construct a pro forma sale but to assume that the shareholder was willing to maintain his investment position, however slight, had the merger not occurred. Discounting individual share holdings injects into the appraisal process speculation on the various factors which may dictate the marketability of minority shareholdings. More important, to fail to accord to a minority shareholder the full proportionate value of his shares imposes a penalty for lack of control, and unfairly enriches the majority shareholders who may reap a windfall from the appraisal process by cashing out a dissenting shareholder, a clearly undesirable result.

Third, the court addressed the issue of applying a marketability discount at the entity level rather than the shareholder level. Baron Services argued that this is what Saliba and the trial court did, and that it was appropriate based on the reasoning of *Onti, Inc. v. Integra Bank*, 751 A.2d 904 (Del. Ch. 1999). The court distinguished *Onti* on the grounds that the marketability discount was applied to a value determined under the comparable companies approach, using comparables that were traded on the stock market, where the subject company was closely held. Because Saliba did not use a market approach with publicly traded comparables, the court held that the reasoning of *Onti* did not support his application of a marketability discount.

Fourth, the court addressed Baron Services argument that the marketability discount accounted for "cost of capital differences between it and public companies." However, the court found that Saliba accounted for these differences in his discount and capitalization rates:

> In deriving appropriate discount and capitalization rates for use in his valuation models, Saliba did account for the fact that Baron Services was a small closely held company that presented a higher degree of investment risk than a larger publicly traded company. Saliba included in the discount rate a "micro-capitalization risk premium" of 3.5% and a "company size premium" of 4.35%...

> ...By including the above premiums in the discount rate, Saliba directly accounted for the market differences between Baron Services and larger public companies. Based on the justifications given by Saliba for including in his valuation the "micro-capitalization risk premium" and the "company size premium," permitting a marketability discount would amount to double counting the market premiums included in the discount rate.

The judgment of the court of civil appeals, which had reversed the trial court, was upheld.

Lawton v. Nyman

Citation: 2003 U.S. App. LEXIS 8069
Court: Court of Appeal
State/Jurisdiction: 1st Circuit Federal
Date of decision: April 29, 2003
Judge: Lynch

One of the issues in this shareholder dispute was the proper measure of damages owed to minority shareholders who were bought out at substantially less than subsequent sale price to a strategic buyer.

The directors and officers (D&O) with voting control of Nyman Manufacturing Co. redeemed the minority shareholders' stock at $200 per share to increase their own ownership interests in anticipation of a possible sale of the company. Sixteen months later, the company sold to a strategic buyer for a total of $1,667.38 per share.

At trial, the minority shareholders argued that the D&O breached their fiduciary duties in failing to disclose material facts about the potential sale of the company and the value of the stock. They claimed that the redemption price they were paid was less than the stock's value.

Valuation evidence and trial court findings

The district court found a breach of fiduciary duty. On the damages issue, the court rejected the testimony of the minority shareholders' expert, Steven Carlson, for a number of reasons. The court accepted the testimony of the D&O's expert, William Piccerelli, who opined that the fair market value of the Nyman stock on the redemption date was $303 per share. Yet the court concluded that the correct measure of fair value was the per-share difference between the redemption price ($200) and the sale price to the strategic buyer ($1,667.38).

Holding on appeal and rationale

Both parties appealed. The court of appeals affirmed liability but remanded for further findings on damages.

The court found a number of problems with the district court's reasoning. Primarily, it rejected the assumption that the sale price 16 months later was a "reasonable proxy" for the market value of the shares on the redemption date, which is the appropriate date to measure fair value. Because the eventual sale was only a mere possibility on the redemption date, not even the D&O could have known of the huge strategic premium they would receive.

The court reiterated that the damages must be tied to the information withheld or misrepresented. Unfortunately, however, the record was replete with "a great many unanswered" questions about the disclosures to the shareholders and "perhaps unanswerable questions" about whether they would have demanded a premium; indeed, whether the D&O would have offered one.

The appellate court's solution was to remand with instructions for the district court to consider whether a strategic premium was appropriate and, if so, whether the fair market value of $303 already included a premium for a possible sale. The court made no recommendations, except to say that the difference between $200 and $303 per share was "the floor of the damages plaintiffs will receive."

Fierro v. Templeton

Citation: 2003 Fla. App. LEXIS 14375
Court: Court of Appeals
State/Jurisdiction: Florida
Date of decision: September 24, 2003
Judge: Shahood

The issue in this corporate dissolution action is whether the shareholder who elects to purchase the shares of the shareholder who filed the dissolution action can, after a buy-out value has been determined, elect to have the corporation dissolved instead.

Templeton and Fierro were each a 50% shareholder of The Omega Consulting Group, Inc., Omegacal Consulting, Inc., and Omega Data Solutions, Inc. Disagreement arose between the parties, and Templeton filed a suit to dissolve the corporations. Fierro filed an election to purchase Templeton's stock at fair value.

Valuation evidence

The trial court heard expert testimony offered by both parties. Templeton's expert opined that the fair value of a 50% interest in Omega was $1,789,000, and that Omegacal and Omega Data were worth nothing. In reaching this conclusion, the expert considered income statements, statements of gross income, and operating expenses.

Fierro's expert opined that the fair value of all three corporations was $200,000, and that Templeton's 50% interest was worth $70,000 after application of a 30% discount for lack of marketability. In reaching this conclusion, the expert considered gross profit, operating expenses, and net income or loss as indicated on the corporation's tax returns.

Trial court findings

The trial court determined that the fair value of Omegacal and Omega Data was zero, and that the fair value of Omega was $2,563,108. Therefore, the trial court entered its final judgment ordering Fierro to purchase Templeton's 50% interest for $1,281,108.

After judgment was entered, Fierro filed a notice of intent to dissolve the corporation and claimed this notice nullified the previous election to purchase and the resulting judgment. Templeton objected and the trial court agreed with Templeton's objection. Fierro appealed.

Holding on appeal and rationale

The court of appeals found that the trial court committed error. The statute clearly gives the corporation the right, within a specified period of time, to file a notice of intent to dissolve after the trial court has determined the fair value pursuant to an election to purchase. The case was remanded for further proceedings to dissolve the corporation.

Thompson, et al. v. Miller Jr., et al

Citation: No. C037787
Court: Court of Appeals, Third District
State/Jurisdiction: California
Date of decision: September 30, 2003

The following court case abstract was originally published in Valuation Case Digest®

In *Gary Thompson, et al. v. Allen B. Miller, Jr., et al*, No. C037787 (Cal. App. 3 Dist. September 30, 2003), the California Court of Appeals, Third District considered a jury's determination that a majority shareholder did not breach his fiduciary duty to the minority shareholders when he purchased their stock. In 1984, Miller established a closely held company that placed information technology workers in temporary positions. At all times, Miller held at least 50% of the stock in this company. Shortly after the business was formed, the plaintiffs purchased stock in the company for $0.25 per share at Miller's urging. In 1992, the company was experiencing financial hardships and the plaintiffs began looking to recoup their investment. In 1994, Miller, in his individual capacity, offered to purchase the stock from anyone wishing to sell it for $0.16 per share. Miller's offer included the company's financial statements. Between late 1994 and early 1995, the plaintiffs sold their stock in the company to Miller. Miller then offered the same stock to a consultant at $0.24 per share to induce the consultant to the company. This consultant was also provided an option on other shares. This option had a strike price of $0.21 per share. In 1997, the company was sold for $7 million. The plaintiffs brought suit against Miller under a variety of theories. They claimed that Miller breached his fiduciary duty to them by purchasing the stock at less than it was worth.

At trial, both parties presented expert testimony regarding the value of the stock on the date of the sales. The plaintiffs' expert valued the stock under the fair value premise, which excludes discounts for minority interest and lack of marketability. This expert's valuation far exceeded the actual selling price. Miller's expert valued the stock under the fair market value standard, which includes discounts for lack of marketability and minority interest. His expert concluded that the stock's fair market value was less than $0.16 per share. The jury returned a verdict in favor of Miller. The plaintiffs appealed.

On appeal, the plaintiffs reargued their claim that the stock was worth more than the $0.16 per share that Miller paid. They particularly claimed that the value of the stock should not, as a matter of law, have been discounted for lack of marketability. The appellate court disagreed. It first noted that the plaintiffs did not submit a jury instruction to that effect. Therefore, it reasoned, "Since there was evidence that the shares were worth less than $.16 per share, applying the lack of marketability discount, the jury was justified in concluding that Miller did not pay less than their value to the plaintiffs." Thus, the court concluded, "The plaintiffs withheld from the jury this theory rejecting the lack of marketability discount but now argue it to this court to invalidate the verdict. Fairness and judicial economy are served by preventing them from doing so."

The plaintiffs alternatively argued that a discount for lack of marketability should not be applied when determining the value of stock transferred from minority shareholders to the majority shareholder in a voluntary sale. They cited *Brown v. Allied Corrugated Box Co.*, (1979) 91 Cal. App. 33d 477, for this position. The appellate court differentiated *Brown* from the facts of the case at hand. It noted that *Brown* involved an involuntary sale of corporate stock from the minority shareholders to the controlling shareholder to avoid dissolution of the business. Since this case involved a voluntary sale, the appellate court stated, "the public policy reasons for not using a discount to value the stock do not apply here." The court further noted, "Also, the *Brown* court dealt with the lack of control discount placed on shares held by minority shareholders, not the lack of marketability discount for which there was expert evidence here." Thus, it affirmed the application of the discount for lack of marketability when determining whether a majority shareholder breached his fiduciary duty to the minority shareholders to pay them a fair price for their stock in a voluntary sale context.

Anjoorian v. Kilberg

Citation: 2003 R.I. LEXIS 215
Court: Supreme Court
State/Jurisdiction: Rhode Island
Date of decision: December 4, 2003
Judge: Per curiam

The issue in this corporate dissolution was the fair value of a 50% interest in Fairway Capital Corporation. Paul Anjoorian was a 50% shareholder of Fairway, a small business investment corporation engaged in making and servicing small business equity loans. Arnold Kilberg was Fairway's investment advisor, responsible for day-to-day management. Kilberg himself didn't own stock in Fairway, but his two children owned the other 50%.

Anjoorian disapproved of Kilberg's management and filed an action against him and the other shareholders for dissolution of Fairway. The shareholders filed an election to purchase Anjoorian's shares in lieu of dissolution.

Valuation evidence and trial court findings

The trial court appointed Girard Visconti as the appraiser to determine the fair market value of the shares. After numerous hearings, Visconti determined that the value of Anjoorian's stock was $809,382.85, and the trial court apparently accepted his valuation, although the record on appeal was incomplete.

Holding on appeal and rationale

Kilberg appealed, arguing that the trial court overvalued Anjoorian's Fairway stock. Specifically, he claimed that the court improperly considered evidence not available before the date the petition for dissolution was filed, resulting in the court's failure to consider a potential liability.

The Supreme Court expressed its frustration at the incomplete appellate record, which did not even include the transcript of the trial court's decision itself. Without the benefit of the lower court's findings, the court's hands were tied. "Without a transcript of the trial justice's bench decision, we simply are unable to ascertain upon what evidence he relied....Moreover, we find nothing in the available record to indicate that the trial justice overlooked or misconceived evidence, erroneously relied upon improper evidence, or failed to give due deference to the appraiser's report." The Supreme Court was therefore compelled to affirm the trial court's decision.

BVR Editor Note: Although the opinion refers to fair market value, the Rhode Island dissolution statute says that the shareholder's shares will be purchased at fair value. Further, the Rhode Island Supreme Court has, on more than one occasion, held that no discounts apply to a determination of the fair value of a shareholder's shares.

The Union Illinois 1995 Investment Ltd. Partnership v. Union Financial Group Ltd.

Citation: 2003 Del. Ch. LEXIS 136
Court: Court of Chancery
State/Jurisdiction: Delaware
Date of decision: December 19, 2003
Judge: Strine

The issue in this case was the fair value of the shares of a bank holding company for purposes of appraisal rights following a merger. The court concluded that the price of the shares determined by the merger most closely approximated fair value and set the appraisal right recovery amount at $8.74 a share, the merger price less synergies.

Facts

Union Financial Group (UFG) was a bank holding company with two subsidiaries, Union Bank of Illinois and the State Bank of Jerseyville. Because of failed ventures and mismanagement the

The Union Illinois 1995 Investment Ltd. Partnership v. Union Financial Group Ltd.

board of directors ousted CEO Denis O'Brien. UFG was then labeled, by the Federal Reserve, as a troubled financial institution because it was undercapitalized and heavily leveraged.

Litigation began when O'Brien, the ousted CEO, filed a suit challenging change of control severance agreements among other things. The O'Brien family, owning 38% of UFG's stock, was unhappy with the ousting of Denis O'Brien. Their suits, in combination with the classification by the Federal Reserve and the heavy debt, made the company a high capital risk. The company was unable to secure other financing and was forced to seek a purchaser.

After a competitive auction, a merger agreement was reached with First Banks at $9.40 a share with two additional payments of 80 cents a share to be paid if certain contingencies were met over the next two years.

Valuation evidence

The O'Brien family's expert, Michael Mayer, testified that the fair value of the UFG shares were more than $16.00 per share. To support this conclusion, Mayer relied upon the discounted cash flow (DCF) method. Mayer used the management's projections as a beginning but made adjustments based on his prediction of a more optimistic future for UFG. In addition, Mayer ignored the management's assumption and used a net interest margin of 4.29 instead of 3.62. The court noted that, "Mayer's optimistic choice of a 4.29 NIM is one of the most important elements of his analysis."

Mayer also testified that the growth rate of non-fixed expenses would be held to 3.44%, contrary to management projections. In addition he assumed that the $12 million outstanding debt could be carried at face value with no reduction in principle.

Mayer, using a SIC code for commercial banks, applied the median results of all banks in that category to derive a cost of capital of 10.43% using the capital asset pricing model (CAPM) plus a size premium. Because UFG was not publicly traded, the beta was derived from comparisons to other companies. The beta Mayer used suggested that a rational investor would face less systematic risk by investing in UFG than in a large, publicly traded bank operating free of Federal Reserve supervision.

UFG's expert, David Clarke, testified that he believed the merger price was the best indication of the fair value price. He gave a synergy discount of 13% and arrived at a net present value of $8.74 per share. Clarke relied upon the management's projections believing there was no basis for the assumption that the company would perform any differently in the future.

For comparison purposes, Clarke also conducted a DCF analysis. Clarke discounted the company's cost of equity using the management projections and arrived at 16% plus a company-specific discount of 2%. Clarke also noted that the rocky history and high debt of UFG made it atypical of other publicly traded bank holding companies. Clarke's conclusions led to a DCF value of $5.06 per share.

Chancery Court findings and ruling

The court was extremely critical of Mayer's DCF analysis and optimistic assumptions, which the court found were not supported by the evidence. The court conducted it's own DCF analyses substituting more realistic assumptions for Mayer's assumptions. The court used both CAPM and the Fama-French three factor model to calculate the cost of capital. Depending on combination of NIM, cost of capital, and other assumptions used, the court's conclusions ranged from $1.35 to $5.44 per share.

Ultimately, the court rejected use of the DCF model in this case altogether, stating that:

> More generally, our case law recognizes that when there is an open opportunity to buy a company, the resulting market price is reliable evidence of fair value. Or, as then-Vice Chancellor, now Justice Jacobs, aptly put it: "The fact that a transaction price was forged in the crucible of objective market reality (as distinguished from the unavoidably subject thought process of a valuation expert) is viewed as strong evidence that the price is fair."

The court concluded that the fair value of the shares was the merger prices minus synergies, which was $8.74 per share. In its holding the court stated that the exclusion of synergies was in accordance with Delaware law that the appraised company be valued as a going concern.

G&G Fashion Design, Inc. v. Enrique Garcia

Citation: 2004 Fla. App. LEXIS 1349
Court: Superior Court for Mecklenburg County
State/Jurisdiction: North Carolina
Date of decision: November 14, 2001
Judge: Wells

The issue in this corporate dissolution was the value of Enrique Garcia's 50% interest in a closely held corporation, G&G Fashion Design, Inc., which operated two clothing stores in an up-scale mall. Garcia filed suit to dissolve the corporation and the remaining shareholders elected to purchase his stock.

The court of appeals upheld the trial court's valuation, stating that calculating "fair value" was a fact-specific determination that must take into account market value, net asset value, investment value, and other factors.

G&G Fashion Design, Inc. v. Enrique Garcia

Valuation evidence

Both parties presented evidence in support of their valuation claim. G&G Fashion relied on the valuation of Leslie Avener who used the "investment value method" and determined that the shares had a fair value of zero. The court of appeals noted that Avener did not perform a true valuation, but rather estimated fair value based on information provided by one of the other shareholders and "on assumptions that did not reflect the realities of this business."

Garcia presented the testimony of Julia Rodriguez, a clothing store owner in the same mall, who had made an offer to purchase Garcia's shares prior to dissolution. Rodriguez testified that she had offered $150,000 after reviewing the financial records of G&G and with full knowledge of the $300,000 debt that she would have to personally guarantee.

Trial court findings

The trial court adopted the market approach supported by Garcia's testimony of her arm's-length offer to purchase, and determined that the fair value of the stock was $150,000.

Holding on appeal and rationale

The court of appeals upheld the trial court stating, "we cannot say that the trial court erred in considering or in relying upon either the market value approach or on Rodriguez's good faith, bona fide, arm's-length offer in valuing Garcia's shares."

In support of its holding, the court of appeals noted that the Florida statute does not define "fair value," and that Florida case law has not provided "criteria by which 'fair value' could be measured." The court instead relied on New York case law interpreting a similar statutory provision. The court noted that "'fair value' rests on determining what a willing purchaser in an arm's-length transaction would offer for an interest in the subject business."

BVR Editor note: The court stated that "The value of the corporation should be determined on the basis of what a willing purchaser, in an arm's-length transaction, would offer for the corporation *as an operating business" (emphasis added). But then it accepted evidence of an offer to purchase a 50% interest in this closely-held corporation as the equivalent of an offer to purchase the corporation as a whole. In this case, fair value and fair market value have been rendered indistinguishable! The New York case law relied upon by the court involved the consideration of the illiquidity of a corporation as a whole, not of a 50% interest, and does not support the court's opinion in this case.*

Chapter 7: Court Case Abstracts

Spivey v. Page

Citation: 2004 Tenn. App. LEXIS 132
Court: Court of Appeals
State/Jurisdiction: Tennessee
Date of decision: February 24, 2004
Judge: Cottrell

The issue in this case was whether the trial court erred in determining the value of a 50% shareholder interest in a professional corporation on the date the shareholder withdrew from the corporation.

Facts

Spivey and Page, both accountants, agreed in 1996 that Spivey would join Page in his professional corporation. They agreed Spivey would get a 50% interest in the corporation and its profits in exchange for contributing his entire practice, which would be combined with Page's continuing practice, and $67,000. The resulting corporation was Terry Page & Associates, P.C.

On November 3, 1998, Spivey told Page that he wanted to withdraw from the corporation. On November 19, 1998, Page gave Spivey a written offer to purchase his 50% interest in the corporation for $30,626. Spivey refused the offer.

On November 30, 1998, Page loaned the corporation $34,000 by way of a note secured by all the assets of the corporation. Page foreclosed on the note two days later, then created a limited liability company (LLC), transferred all the assets from the professional corporation to the LLC, and continued to operate in the same location with the same staff.

Spivey filed suit for an accounting and to recover the value of his 50% share in the professional corporation. Spivey also sought to pierce the corporation veil of Terry Page & Associates, P.C. so that he could recover directly from Page.

Valuation evidence

Only Page and Spivey testified at the trial. Spivey argue that the corporation should be valued on November 3, 1998, and that the proper method would be the same method the parties used when Spivey entered the corporation. Under that method, the billings, or book of business, of both Page and Spivey were added together with the other assets of the corporation, and the outstanding debts subtracted. This method resulted in a total value of $173,310, and a value for Spivey's 50% interest of $86,655.

Page presented the December 31, 1998, balance sheet showing the corporation to be insolvent and argued that Spivey was not entitled to anything. The balance sheet included the $34,000 debt owed to Page, but did not include either party's book of business.

Trial court findings

The trial court found that both parties had withdrawn from the corporation on November 3, 1998. The court concluded that the balance sheet was persuasive and held that Spivey was not entitled to recover anything because the company was insolvent. The court specifically found that Spivey's formula was in error. The court also denied Spivey's request to pierce the corporate veil so he could recover directly from Page.

Holding on appeal and rationale

The court of appeals reversed the trial court and held that the proper valuation date was November 3, 1998. The court found that the evidence clearly showed that Page had not also withdrawn on that date because he offered to purchase Spivey's shares at a later date.

The court also held that the proper valuation method was not necessarily the one suggested by Spivey, but that it should be a method that would result in the fair value of Spivey's shares.

The court of appeals remanded the case for a new determination of the fair value of Spivey's 50% interest as of November 3, 1998. The court also held that the corporate veil should be pierced for all transactions that occurred after that date so Spivey could recover his 50% share of the corporation's value from Page.

BVR Editor Comment: The statutory language as quoted by the court in this case is confusing and apparently contradictory. One statute states that a professional corporation must offer to purchase the withdrawing shareholder's interest at "fair value." Another statute states that in an action by the withdrawing shareholder, the court shall determine the "fair market value" of the shares. The apparent contradiction is cleared up, however, when one realizes that the court misquoted the second statute, which actually uses the term fair value as well.

Detter v. Miracle Hills Animal Hospital, P.C.

Citation: No. A-02-688
Court: Superior Court
State/Jurisdiction: Nebraska
Date of decision: April 6, 2004

The following court case abstract was originally published in Valuation Case Digest®

In *Jere D. Detter v. Miracle Hills Animal Hospital, P.C.*, No. A-02-688 (Neb. April 6, 2004), the Nebraska Supreme Court considered whether goodwill should be included in the valuation of a professional corporation when one party elects to purchase the interest of the other party to avoid dissolution of the business. In 1991, Detter and Schreiber combined their veterinarian practices and opened Miracle Hills Animal Hospital. After a dispute over management fees, Detter moved to dissolve the business and Schreiber, through the business, elected to purchase his interest at fair value. Both parties presented expert testimony from certified public accountants regarding the valuation of the practice.

Detter's expert had substantial experience valuing veterinary practices. She indicated that it was very difficult for departing veterinarians to retain their clients, and cited an example. She concluded that the practice had a value of $182,082 inclusive of goodwill.

Schreiber's expert valued the practice at $35,912, exclusive of goodwill. He held the opinion that "in a professional practice of this nature, goodwill primarily rests with the provider and not the practice."

The trial court accepted Schreiber's valuation. In doing so, it found that Detter's expert utilized an incorrect valuation method. It cited the divorce case of *Taylor v. Taylor*, 222 Neb. 721 (1986), for the position that "goodwill was not to be added to the valuation of a professional corporation." It stated, "'good will for members of a professional corporation does not have a value when one or the other part[y] leave[s]" and that 'any good will that might have been present with ... Detter's participation in [MHAH] left with ... Detter." Detter appealed.

On appeal, Detter argued that the lower court erred when it excluded goodwill from the valuation of the business. The Supreme Court noted that the lower court relied on a divorce case whose "logic ...remains sound", but could find no Nebraska case law directly on point. Thus, it looked to case law from other jurisdictions including Texas and Wyoming. Based on its analysis of that case law, it ruled, "goodwill is not an asset with an assignable value in a professional corporation; it is not a marketable asset that stays with corporation, but, rather, a nonmarketable one that leaves with a professional." Therefore, it concluded that since Detter's expert included goodwill in her valuation of the practice, the trial court appropriately rejected that valuation. Thus, it affirmed the lower court's valuation.

Rainforest Cafe, Inc. v. State of Wisconsin Investment Board, et al.

Citation: 2004 Minn. App. LEXIS 330
Court: Court of Appeals
State/Jurisdiction: Minnesota
Date of decision: April 13, 2004
Judge: Peterson

The issue in this dissenters' rights action was the fair value of the shares of Rainforest Cafe Inc. The court of appeals affirmed the district court's decision to ignore the expert testimony and value the shares at the bargained for tendered price.

Facts

On December 1, 2000, the shareholders of Rainforest voted to merge with Landry's Seafood Restaurants. Eighty percent of the shareholders either voted for the merger or did not invoke their dissenters' rights. The remaining shareholders, including the State of Wisconsin Investment Board (SWIB), asserted and perfected their dissenters' rights and an appraisal proceeding followed.

Valuation evidence

Both parties presented expert testimony and rebuttal expert testimony. Christopher Mercer testified for Rainforest Cafe. He used three methods of valuation. Mercer determined that the net asset value of the company was $3.81 per a share, excluding excess assets valued at $22,130,000. Mercer gave this valuation no weight. Mercer then used the guideline-company method and arrived at a value range of $4.80-4.91 per share, excluding the excess assets. He weighted these valuations 37.5% and 25%, respectively.

Mercer's third valuation method was the discounted cash flow (DCF) method. In his use of DCF, Mercer used Landry's projections and determined the value of the shares to be $5.23. Mercer weighted the third valuation method at 37.5%. The weighted value of the share was $4.98 as of the valuation date.

Mercer then took into account the excess assets, which included cash and a federal tax receivable, and arrived at $5.95. He then increased the value of the shares to $6.10 by taking into account the value of severance payments included in the merger and the tax benefits that Landry would receive as a result of the merger.

Don Nicholson testified as the rebuttal expert for the SWIB. Nicholson criticized Mercer because he, "(1) did not interview Rainforest I's or Landry's management; (2) failed to consider Rainforest I financial information for October and November 2000; (3) used guideline companies that bore little resemblance to Rainforest I; (4) failed to consider the public stock price of Rainforest I as an indicator of the market's valuation; and (5) used financial projections prepared by Landry's for its lenders and did not take into account changes Landry's made based on later information."

Donald Erickson testified as SWIB's expert. Erickson used DCF to determine the value of the shares. He applied the DCF to four different scenarios. "Two of the scenarios assumed that Rainforest I reorganized under bankruptcy protection and two did not. The other variables were: (a) variations in the number of store closings; (b) variations in the outlook for Rainforest's Fisherman's Wharf store; (c) variations in the outlook of Rainforest's foreign operations; and (d) variations in the discount rate."

Erickson declined to use the market-based comparative approach because Rainforest was unique. "Erickson also rejected book value as an indication of fair value … because it does not take into consideration contingent liabilities … that others in the marketplace consider when evaluating the company." Erickson determined that the book value was approximately $5 per share.

Richard May testified as the rebuttal expert witness for Rainforest Cafe. May criticized Erickson's valuation because, "[I]t projected future sales out 12 years rather than the standard five years; used an inappropriate discount rate for the level of risk associated with Rainforest or the entertainment industry as a whole; assumed an unreasonably low long-term growth rate; and erroneously assumed the closure of too many stores." May also stated that by correcting Erickson's errors, the value was between $4.69 and $5.06 per share. May then applied the guideline-company method to Erickson's "corrected" figures and arrived at $7.23 per share.

Trial court findings

The district court determined the fair value of the shares to be $3.25, the amount that was tendered during the merger. The court determined that, "[T]he experts' conflicting testimony provided no aid in determining the fair value of the stock, finding that appellants' experts were overly optimistic and respondent's experts were overly pessimistic." The court also concluded that book value was not a good indicator of fair value.

Holding on appeal and rationale

The court of appeals held that the district court was not in error to reject the experts' testimony. "The weight that the district court attributed to the experts' testimony, which was admitted at trial, might reasonably have changed the result of the trial, but that does not mean that attributing no weight to the testimony was prejudicial error."

The court also noted that book value is, "[O]nly [a] minor element to be considered in arriving at true value of stock and that book value is entitled to little, if any, weight in determining true value of stock." The court of appeals affirmed the district court's opinion.

Boettcher, et al. v. IMC Mortgage Company

Citation: No. 2D03-3101
Court: Court of Appeals, Second District
State/Jurisdiction: Florida
Date of decision: May 12, 2004
Judge: Wallace

The following court case abstract was originally published in Valuation Case Digest®

In *Dwayne R. Boettcher, et al. v. IMC Mortgage Company*, No. 2D03-3101 (Fla. 2 DCA May 12, 2004), the Florida Court of Appeals, Second District considered whether the market price of stock on the date prior to the dissented to event could be the fair value of the subject company in a dissenting shareholders' appraisal action. IMC was a publicly traded company trading on the Over the Counter Bulletin Board. By late 1999, it was in financial straits and considered filing for bankruptcy protection. To avoid a bankruptcy, IMC's board recommended a sale of a substantial amount of IMC's assets to Citigroup, Inc. in September 1999. The shareholders approved the sale on November 12, 1999.

Boettcher dissented to the sales and sought the fair value of his shares under the appraisal statute.

IMC determined its fair value by reference to its market price. It showed that over the month prior to the vote, its stock traded between $0.054 and $0.0271 per share on a volume between 756,100 to 25,100 shares. On the day prior to the shareholder vote, the stock closed at $0.035 per share on a volume of 756,100 shares. IMC argued that the market price of the stock on the day prior to the shareholder vote was the fair value of IMC stock, and presented the trial court with a motion of summary judgment to that effect. Boettcher did not provide the trial court with an alternative estimate of IMC's fair value on November 11, 1999. Rather, he presented the court with a legal expert who testified that the market price considered appreciation or depreciation in anticipation of the merger with Citigroup and therefore was an inappropriate measure of the fair value of the stock on the valuation date. The trial court granted IMC's motion and ruled that the fair value of the stock was $0.035 on the valuation date. Boettcher appealed.

On appeal, he argued that the trial court erred in granting IMC's motion for summary judgment because the methodology used by IMC to establish fair value was insufficient within the statutory meaning of fair value. The appellate court first considered the definition of fair value—"the value of the shares as of the close of business on the day prior to the shareholders' authorization date, excluding any appreciation or depreciation in anticipation of the corporate action unless exclusion would be inequitable." The Second District found no guidance in Florida case law and looked to other jurisdictions including Ohio, Wisconsin, Colorado, Indiana and Washington. It concluded, "[A]bsent factors making exclusion inequitable, the determination of the 'fair value' of IMC's shares in the circuit court required the exclusion of any appreciation or depreciation in

IMC's shares based upon anticipation of the consummation of the proposed asset sale." It then determined that IMC's motion did not address the exclusion of any appreciation or depreciation in anticipation of the dissented to action or present any reasons why it would be equitable to include such appreciation or depreciation. Thus, the court ruled, "Since the closing price of IMC shares on the relevant date did not exclude appreciation or depreciation in anticipation of the proposed transaction and IMC did not contend that exclusion was inequitable, IMC's submission of evidence of the closing price of its shares on the relevant date was insufficient to establish a prima facie case on the issue of fair value." Thus, it reversed the lower court's grant of summary judgment in favor of IMC.

In re Emerging Communications

Citation: 2004 Del. Ch. LEXIS 70
Court: Court of Chancery
State/Jurisdiction: Delaware
Date of decision: May 3, 2004

A recent decision of the Delaware Chancery Court, *In re Emerging Communications, Inc.*, placed an amazing fair value of $38.05 per share on the stock of Emerging Communications, Inc. (ECM), which was acquired in a two-step going private transaction at $10.25 per share based on a fairness opinion by Houlihan Lokey Howard & Zukin.

Company is small telephone utility

The primary business of ECM was as the exclusive provider of local wired telephone service in the U.S. Virgin Islands. A few months prior to the merger with Innovative Communications Corp., LLC (Innovative), ECM had acquired SMB Holdings, which provided cellular service to the island of St. Maarten/St. Martin.

As in past cases, the standard under which the court reviewed the transaction was "entire fairness," which includes both "fair dealing" and "fair price." The court ruled against the defendants on the "fair dealing" issue as well as the "fair price."

Both dissent and fiduciary breach

The case is a consolidated statutory appraisal under dissenters' stockholder rights and a class action for breach of fiduciary duty. In the appraisal action, the court found Innovative liable to Greenlight Capital, LP in the amount of $38.05 per share for the 750,300 shares subject to the appraisal action ($28,548,915) plus 6.27% interest, compounded monthly, from the date of the merger (October 19, 1998) to the date of the judgment (May 3, 2004).

Company, CEO and directors liable

In the fiduciary duty action, the court found Innovative, Prosser and two other directors of ECM jointly and severally liable to the plaintiff class and to Greenlight (in its capacity as the holder of 2,026,685 shares of ECM to which it had been assigned litigation rights) in the amount of the difference between $38.05 per share and the amount the original holders had been paid of $10.25 per share.

Jeffrey J. Prosser (Prosser) owned 52% of the stock of ECM at the time of the privatization and 100% of the stock of Innovative, the surviving company into which ECM was merged.

Directors found 'not independent'

While it is clear that a person who stands on both sides of a transaction is conflicted, most of the directors were also considered not independent because of their ties to Prosser. For example, one director was Prosser's long-time lawyer, for whom virtually 100% of the fees generated by him for the most recent three years were attributed to Prosser and Prosser-owned entities, and had recently negotiated a $2.4 million payout arrangement which was not disclosed to other board members. Another director was a consultant to Prosser on an annual $200,000 retainer. Most of the board had similar ties to Prosser.

Another aspect of unfair dealing was other nondisclosures. The most controversial of these was that the Special Committee and Houlihan (its advisor) were working with projections prepared in March. Later projections were prepared in June and provided to the Rural Telephone Financing Company (RTFC) for the purpose of providing financing and to Prudential (Prosser's financial advisor), but not to the Special Committee or their financial advisor.

Houlihan not called at trial

The opinion states that:

> Whatever evidentiary force Houlihan's opinion might have had was totally undermined by the fact that (i) Houlihan never had the benefit of the June projections, and (ii) the defendants never called Houlihan, upon whose valuation the Special Committee and the board relied, to testify at trial in support of its valuation conclusion.

Plaintiffs' valuation expert was Mark Zmijewski, an accounting professor at the University of Chicago Business School. The lead expert for the defendants was Daniel Bayston of Duff and Phelps. The defense also called Gilbert Matthews, an investment banker with Sutter Securities and former senior managing director of Bear Stearns & Co., and Burton Malkiel, a professor at Princeton University.

Several differences in valuation assumptions between the experts accounted for the very wide gap between values. Although the defendants also used a guideline company method, the court focused entirely on the DCF method.

Discount rates differ substantially

A critical difference was the discount rate used by the respective experts (8.8%/8.5% for Zmijewski vs. 11.5% for Bayston). The court presented a succinct explanation of a company's cost of capital:

WACC is the sum of: (1) the percentage of the company's capital structure that is financed with equity, multiplied by the company's cost of equity capital, plus (2) the percentage of the company's capital structure that is financed with debt, multiplied by its after-tax cost of debt.

One element of the WACC formula—the "cost of equity capital"—is determined by the CAPM model. Under CAPM, the cost of equity capital is the risk-free rate of return plus the subject company's risk. The subject company's risk is determined by multiplying the equity risk premium for the market by the company's beta. "Beta" is the measure of a given company's non-diversifiable risk relative to the market, specifically, the tendency of the returns on a company's security to correlate with swings in the broad market. A beta of 1, for example, means that the security's price will rise and fall with the market; a beta greater than 1 signifies that the security's price will be more volatile than the market; and a beta less than 1 indicates that it will be less volatile than the market.

Court accepts small stock premium

The primary argument between the appraisers was over 1.7% small stock premiums that Bayston applied to the cost of equity and Zmijewski did not; the 2.4% "supersmall" risk premium that Bayston applied and Zmijewski did not; and the 1-1.5% specific risk premium (because of hurricane risk) that Bayston applied and Zmijewski did not. The court accepted the small stock premium, but did not accept the incremental super-small premium or the hurricane risk premium.

Other differences in the cost of capital were in the cost of debt and the assumed capital structure.

Regulator sets cost of capital at 11.5%

According to the defendants' consolidated post trial brief, the Public Service Commission (PSC) set the local telephone company's cost of capital at 11.5%. Since the PSC's mission is to use this for rate making on behalf of the consumer, I have suggested this rate "can be viewed as a reasonable benchmark for a minimum boundary of the overall cost of capital."[1]

---

[1] Pratt, Shannon, Reilly, Robert, and Schweihs, Robert, *Valuing a Business* (4th ed.. McGraw-Hill 2000). p. 182.

Depreciation exceeds CapX in perpetuity

According to the defendants' consolidated post trial brief, the net cash flow in Zmijewski's terminal value included $22,458,000 in depreciation but only $9,363,000 of annual capital expenditures, both growing at 2.9% in perpetuity, "which is impossible."

In light of what I regard as the Delaware Chancery Court's general sophistication in valuation matters, coupled with its succinct explanation of the cost of capital in this case, I find it curious that so wide a discrepancy between CapX and depreciation was accepted without comment.

Another major difference according to the defendants' brief was the plaintiffs' assumption that the St. Maarten's cellular revenues would remain at the January/February (peak tourist month) annualized rates throughout the year.

Court dismisses market price

The ECM stock had traded on the American Stock Exchange. The most recent price before the buyout was $7.00 per share, and the stock's trading history indicated a trading range consistently below the buyout price at all times prior to the merger. The opinion says that:

> Delaware law recognizes that, although market price should be considered in an appraisal, the market price of shares is not always indicative of fair value...the record undermines any assertion that ECM's common stock was traded in an efficient market.

While I don't totally agree with professor Malkiel's assertion (quoted in the opinion) that the AMEX is an "efficient market," I don't believe that it is so inefficient as to have a discrepancy in value as wide as a range of $7.00 per share to $38.00 per share.

Importance of fair dealing

I think that this is a case that dramatically demonstrates the importance of fair dealing in a transaction involving minority shareholders, and especially a transaction in which the CEO is conflicted.

Jahn v. Kinderman

Citation: 2004 Ill. App. LEXIS 628
Court: Court of Appeals
State/Jurisdiction: Illinois
Date of decision: June 7, 2004
Judge: McNulty

The issue in this minority oppression case concerning Chicago Metallic Corporation was the application of a marketability discount in determining fair value. In addition, the court discussed prejudgment and postjudgment interest. At trial, the minority shareholders were awarded $55,485,000 for the fair value of their shares.

Defendants appealed, arguing that although the valuation may have otherwise been correct, a marketability discount was required. The court of appeals dismissed that claim stating, "These citations ignore the more prevalent current trend toward rejection of such discounts because they fail to fully credit the minority owner's percentage stake in the value of the enterprise in its entirety."

The court of appeals reversed the trial court's ruling denying the minority shareholders of postjudgment interest but upheld the court's denial of prejudgment interest.

Finkelstein, et al. v. Liberty Digital, Inc.

Citation: No. 19598
Court: Court of Chancery
State/Jurisdiction: Delaware
Date of decision: April 25, 2005
Judge: Strine

The following court case abstract was originally published in Valuation Case Digest®

In *Harold Finkelstein, et al. v. Liberty Digital, Inc.*, No. 19598 (Del. Chan. April 25, 2005), the Delaware Court of Chancery determined the value of a contract associated with emerging technology in this dissenting shareholder action. Liberty Digital was a public company. It held a variety of assets, but its most attractive asset was an access agreement it had with AT&T. At this time AT&T was still involved with cable television. Under the agreement, AT&T agreed to agree to terms that would give Liberty Digital preferential access to 6MHz of bandwidth for interactive television programming when and if AT&T decided to deploy such technology. It further provided for an initial term of five years with an option on another four years. The interactive television programming model was a marriage of cable television programming with internet-based marketing and sales controlled through the television remote control device.

Finkelstein, et al. v. Liberty Digital, Inc.

Between 1999 and 2001, Liberty Digital attempted to pressure AT&T into moving forward on this agreement. Also during this period, market analysts had a favorable position toward this technology and viewed Liberty Digital's access agreement as a competitive advantage; therefore, in their discounted cash flow analyses, the market analysts highly valued Liberty Mutual. In September 2001, Liberty Digital received a letter from AT&T that indicated that it did not have any plans to deploy the required technology. Additionally, AT&T was actively looking to divest itself of its cable television business. Moreover at this time, Liberty Digital was in financial trouble. Its long-term debt of $100 million was coming due and it had no growth products. After receiving the AT&T letter, Liberty Mutual, which owned 90% of Liberty Digital, determined that it was financially best to effect a short-form merger and take Liberty Digital private. On March 14, 2002, it affected a stock for stock reverse merger and provided Liberty Digital's shareholders a 0.25 share of Liberty Mutual for each share of Liberty Digital. This transaction had an implied value of $3.31 per share. The Finkelsteins dissented to the transaction.

Prior to trial on judicial determination of the fair value of the Liberty Digital stock, the parties stipulated to the value of most of the underlying assets except for the access agreement. Both parties presented testimony from financial experts as to the value of this agreement.

The Finkelsteins engaged a finance professor to value the access agreement. The court initially noted, "... [this expert] is an experienced academic but has no real experience in the telecommunications or cable industries." The professor employed a discounted cash flow method. Because there were no management projections, the professor formulated his own revenue and expense projections. He valued the access agreement by reference to the revenues generated by television programming channels launched during the nine-year contractual period. He initially determined the 6MHz of bandwidth represented approximately 12 digital channels and Liberty Digital would launch two channels each year beginning in 2004. He determined the annual revenues as a function of profit per subscriber, which was computed by reference to comparable home shopping analog channels, and AT&T's digital subscriber base. The per-subscriber profit would be $0.75 which would increase by 2% per year for inflation. The annual subscriber base would grow at a rate of 20% per year until it reached 80% of AT&T's overall customer base at which point it would grow at 3% per year thereafter. He computed the annual revenues associated with the channels over the nine-year contract, but did not compute a terminal value for the channels at the end of the contract. He then reduced the revenue streams to present value using a weighted average cost of capital. He concluded that the access agreement had a value of $2.2 billion.

The Chancery Court rejected this expert's analysis. In doing so, it reiterated the maxim: "If wishes were horses ..." It found that this expert's analysis failed to take the economic realities of Liberty Digital's circumstances and the contract's terms into effect. It first noted that the technology required to make the interactive television business model work was not in place and AT&T had firmly stated that it did not intend to pursue the technology at that time. The court concluded "Put simply, that interactive television might be commercially valuable in the future does not logically translate into a large present value for the Access Agreement as of the merger date." Moreover, the court noted that without a firm commitment from AT&T, Liberty Digital did not have the ability to get commitments from product or programming partners. Additionally, both the potential partners and AT&T were interested in obtaining an ownership interest in the channels. Thus, the professor's channel launch analysis was speculative and even if it was not, attribution of the entire revenue stream from each channel to Liberty Digital was speculative. Moreover, it noted that the professor assumed that each and every channel Liberty Digital launched would be profitable. It noted that this ignored the economic evidence that most channels did not turn a profit within their first three years of operation and that many channels are not successful. In summary, the court stated, "... rather than addressing the operative reality of Liberty Digital, as required by law, [the professor] ... imagines an ideal world for Liberty Digital and values the Access Agreement on that basis." Thus, it rejected this valuation as fanciful.

The Finkelsteins attempted to salvage their expert's analysis by pointing to the market price leading up to the merger as well as the market analysts' projections. The court rejected both indicators. It noted that the market price assumed an imminent release of the necessary technology that, like the professor's analysis, failed to reflect the reality of the situation. Thus it rejected the market price as overstated. It similarly found fault with the market analysts' projections. It stated, "Put summarily, the petitioners have done nothing to demonstrate the reliability of these analyst 'valuations' and there is nothing about the recent history of analyst projections of issuer worth that would inspire judicial confidence in using them as an important determinant of appraisal value."

The court next considered the testimony of Liberty Digital's expert, an investment banker specializing in the telecommunications industry. The petitioners attempted to exclude this expert on the basis of bias because his firm was engaged by Liberty Mutual in connection with its investment banking needs as well as the fact that the firm dealt in Liberty Digital and Liberty Mutual securities. Moreover, the expert admitted that he would not have served as an expert for the petitioners. Despite his full disclosure of bias, the court permitted this expert to testify. It found that the bias went to the weight of the expert's testimony rather than his admissibility.

As opposed to Finkelstein's expert, Liberty Digital's expert did not use a discounted cash flow method to value the business that the access agreement may have produced. Rather he found that the lack of detail in the access agreement made such a valuation "untenable." Thus, he valued the agreement by reference to potential cost savings implied by the contract. Since the only material benefit of the contract was a guaranteed 6MHz of bandwidth and the parties had specifically deleted a provision for access charges when negotiating the contract, this expert used cost savings as proxy for value. He assumed that Liberty Digital would not have to pay launch or carriage fees in connection with the channels.

He then determined the average range of carriage fees by reference to 16 precedent transactions occurring in a six-year period. The transactions involved digital, analog, and satellite channels. He concluded that the digital transactions were most appropriate even though there were only three of them. They indicated a range of carriage fees between $1 and $3 per subscriber, with a mean of $2.58 per subscriber. He then identified the potential benefits and drawbacks to this agreement. He did not assign any weight to a particular benefit or drawback, but determined the appropriate per-subscriber fee in light of those factors using a "gut" analysis. He concluded that the appropriate per-subscriber fee was $2 per subscriber. He multiplied this figure by the number of AT&T digital subscribers on the date of the merger. He then multiplied that sum by the number of stations (12) implied by the 6MHz bandwidth guarantee. He concluded that the value of the agreement was $83.4 million.

The Chancery Court adopted this method of calculating value. It concluded that while the contract guaranteed nothing more than an indefinite promise to agree to terms later involving 6MHz of bandwidth and undefined "preferential status," the parties behavior in negotiating the contract made launch and carriage fees a reasonable proxy for value. However, the court disagreed with the calculation made by this expert. It found that the expert's deviation from the mean per-subscriber carriage fee was not supported by any rational analysis. Thus, the court adopted the $2.58 mean per-subscriber carriage fee as appropriate. It further rejected the determination that 6MHz equated to 12 digital channels. It noted that the evidence showed that the 6MHz bandwidth could support between 12 and 18 channels. It considered that the changing state of bandwidth compression made the likelihood of more channels reasonable. Therefore, it concluded that 15 channels could be created out of 6MHz of bandwidth. It then applied those adjusted figures in Liberty Digital's calculation and concluded that the access agreement had a value of $134.55 million.

The Chancery Court then determined the fair value of Liberty Digital. It added the value of the access agreement to the stipulated value of the remaining assets, and concluded that Liberty Digital had a fair value of $2.74 per share, an amount less than the $3.31 merger consideration.

Cede & Co. v. Technicolor, Inc.

Citation: 2005 Del. LEXIS 177
Court: Supreme Court
State/Jurisdiction: Delaware
Date of decision: May 4, 2005
Judge: Ridgely

This dissenting stockholder appraisal action, arising out of a cash-out merger of the minority shareholders of Technicolor, Inc., has been in litigation for over two decades, and has generated numerous Delaware Chancery Court and Supreme Court decisions (see the December 1996, May 1999 and October 2000 issues of *BVU* for treatment of some of the earlier cases). This is the latest Supreme Court decision on the Chancery Court's appraisal of the fair value of Technicolor stock.

Correct review standard is abuse of discretion

Before reaching the Court of Chancery's decisions, the Supreme Court ruled that the determination of fair value in an appraisal proceeding at the Court of Chancery level "is accorded a high level of deference on appeal," and is to be reviewed pursuant to the abuse of discretion standard, so long as the Court of Chancery has committed no legal error.

Because often in statutory appraisal proceedings a valuation dispute becomes a battle of experts, the Supreme Court will accept the Court of Chancery's factual determinations if they turn on a question of credibility and the acceptance or rejection of particular pieces of testimony.

Record supports inputs used to arrive at value

In reviewing the record, the Supreme Court found that the Chancery Court's findings as to various financial inputs, such as depreciation, revenue and material cost income spread, margins, and fixed capital expense forecasts resulted from an orderly and logical deductive process and were supported by the record. Accordingly, the Supreme Court held that the Chancery Court did not abuse its discretion regarding these inputs.

Chancery Court erred by not using a law-of-the-case discount rate

The law of the case doctrine posits that "findings of fact and conclusions of law by an appellate court are generally binding in all subsequent proceedings in the trial court or latter on appeal." When the Court of Chancery originally calculated the cost of capital, or discount rate—at 15.28%—both parties accepted this calculation as reasonable and neither party challenged the calculation on appeal to the Supreme Court. However, on retrial, the Chancery Court disregarded its prior determination of 15.28% and calculated a 19.89% cost of capital.

The Supreme Court ruled that the 15.28% discount rate was the law of the case, that there was no exception that would permit applying a 19.89% discount rate, and that the Chancery Court erred by not applying the previously determined rate.

Applying the smaller rate resulted in a judgment of $5,653,720, versus $4,345,920 using the larger, 19.89% rate.

Finally, the Supreme Court said, "We remand this case with instructions to enter judgment consistent with this opinion so that this litigation, at long last, is brought to an end."

Note: The term "law of the case" as generally used designates the principle that if an appellate court has passed on a legal question and remanded the cause to the court below for further proceedings, the legal question thus determined by the appellate court will not be differently determined on a subsequent appeal in the same case where the facts remain the same. –Black's Law Dictionary, 6th ed.

Montgomery Cellular Holding Co., Inc., et al. v. Dobler, et al.

Citation: No. 496,2004
Court: Supreme Court
State/Jurisdiction: Delaware
Date of decision: August 1, 2005
Judge: Holland, Berger, and Jacobs

The following court case abstract was originally published in Valuation Case Digest®

In *Montgomery Cellular Holding Co., Inc., et al. v. Gerhard Frank Dobler, et al.*, No. 496,2004 (DE August 1, 2005), the Delaware Supreme Court reviewed the Chancery Court's fair value determination. Dobler and the other defendants were minority shareholders in Montgomery Cellular Holdings Co., Inc. (MCHC), and their aggregate holdings comprised 4.96% of its stock. The remaining stock was held by Palmer Communications. Palmer Communications also held 15 other cellular companies, which together with MCHC comprised a contiguous coverage area of Florida, Georgia and Alabama. MCHC was its most valuable company because it wholly owned a company, Montgomery, that held the cellular rights to the Montgomery metropolitan statistical area (MSA). Palmer was in turn owned by Price.

In 2000, Price and Verizon entered negotiations. They agreed that Verizon would acquire Palmer for $2.05 billion. However, the deal was conditional upon the successful initial public offering of Verizon. Additionally, Verizon did not want to separately deal with the minority shareholders associated with Palmer's subsidiaries. Therefore, it proposed to reduce the purchase price by an amount equal to the pro rata minority interest based on a multiple of 13.5 EBITDA. Thereafter, Price set about cashing out the minority shareholders in its subsidiaries. MCHC shareholders were cashed out in a short form merger for $8,102.23 per share. The cash out price was not established by an independent valuation, but was based on the settlement of another dissenting shareholder action involving Price and the minority shareholder of a subsidiary. The settlement involved the stock in a rural statistical area (RSA) cellular company and the agreed cash out price was based on $470 per POP. Dobler dissented.

The Chancery Court was faced with the task of determining the fair value of MCHC. Both parties presented the Chancery Court with valuation experts. The Chancery Court rejected MCHC's expert, which relied upon the comparable companies and discounted cash flow methods. The court found that this expert improperly valued MCHC as a stand-alone company, which deprived the minority shareholders of the value associated with MCHC's contractual affiliation with the other cellular companies under the Palmer umbrella that it enjoyed before the Verizon transaction. Additionally, the Chancery Court found fault with the application of his methods. With respect to the discounted cash flow model, the court took issue with the expert's use of a constant growth rate during the entire projection period, the growth rate selected was generic (based on long-term growth in gross national product) and bore no relation to the growth rate experienced in the industry, and the expert manufactured his own projections, since MCHC had no in-house projections, without reference to any available sources of relevant information.

The court also faulted MCHC's expert's comparable companies analysis. It found that the expert considered both cellular companies operating in MSAs and RSAs, but gave more weight to the multiples derived from RSAs. The court found this contrasted with the fact that MCHC was a MSA cellular provider in the largest Alabama MSA. Furthermore, the court found that the expert inconsistently utilized the mean or median data without adequate reason for doing so. Lastly, the expert utilized data from the C-Block auctions, which the court found outdated, considered different technology, and involved emerging markets with inexperienced bidders. Therefore, the Chancery Court gave no weight to this expert's valuation.

The Chancery Court adopted the valuation put forward by the dissenters' expert. This expert valued MCHC using three methods: A comparable transactions method, a discounted cash flow method, and a comparable companies method. In performing his comparable transactions method he identified three classes of transactions: five transactions occurring between 2000 and 2001, the Verizon transaction, and the settlement transaction. He analyzed these transactions and the comparable companies used in his comparable companies method by four metrics: POP, per subscriber, operating cash flow, and revenue. He weighted the results of this approach 80%. He then valued MCHC using a discounted cash flow approach. Since MCHC did not have contemporaneous projections, the expert utilized data from an industry expert, Paul Kagan, to create projections. He further utilized the weighted average cost of capital in computing the valuation. He determined that the results of this method should be weighted 15%. He lastly valued the company using a comparable companies approach. Under this method, he identified two comparable companies. He weighted the results of this method 5%.

The Chancery Court adopted the valuation of the dissenters' expert with modifications. With respect to the weighting of the methods, it reweighted them 65-30-5 because it found the expert's weighting gave too much weight to the Verizon transaction, which was weighted 50% in the comparable transaction method. It further increased the value of the settlement comparable by 15%. This premium accounted for the fact that the value was produced by settlement, which took into account the costs avoided and risks of litigation. Lastly, the court declined to adopt the 31% control premium the expert applied in his discounted cash flow valuation. Based on its analysis, the court determined that the stock had a value of $21,000 per share. MCHC appealed.

On appeal, MCHC challenged the Chancery Court's comparable transaction method on several fronts. It made several arguments regarding the inclusion of the Verizon-Price transaction. It argued that the value of the Verizon-Price transaction included synergy value that was not removed. Additionally it argued that the Verizon-Price transaction did not reflect the going concern value of MCHC. The Supreme Court disagreed. It noted that the Verizon-Price transaction was indicative of the going concern value of MCHC on the date of the merger transaction. The court found that the Verizon-Price transaction was announced in early 2001 and was conditional upon the successful IPO of Verizon. Verizon had an obligation of good faith and fair dealing to work toward the completion of the IPO. It was not until one month after the date of the MCHC cash out merger that the Verizon IPO would not be launched as scheduled. Therefore, the Supreme Court concluded that on the date of the cash out merger, the Verizon IPO was an operative reality for the Palmer companies.

The Supreme Court next considered whether the Chancery Court erred when it did not adequately account for the synergies generated by the Verizon-Price transaction. The court noted that MCHC was the most valuable, strategically located, and largest MSA included in the Verizon transaction. Moreover, it found the only synergies derived from the transaction were deal-making synergies – those synergies relating to purchasing the Palmer subsidiaries as a group as opposed to individually. Furthermore, MCHC failed to present any evidence as to the impact any deal making or business collateral synergies may have had on the purchase price. Therefore, the Chancery Court, which recognized the deal making synergy, accounted for its presence by reducing the weight attributable to the comparable transaction method. The Supreme Court noted, "Although in a perfect world that may not have been the ideal solution, in this world it was the only one permitted by the record evidence, given MCHC's failure to obtain a pre-merger valuation to present legally reliable expert valuation testimony during the trial." Moreover, "Given the paucity of synergy-related evidence for which MCHC was responsible, the Vice Chancellor coped admirably with the evidence that was presented, and reached a reasonable valuation using the analytical tools and evidence that were available to him."

MCHC next challenged the chancellor's decision to increase the settlement value by 15%. The Supreme Court again affirmed the chancellor's decision. It found that the communications between the dissenters' attorney and Price/Palmer as to the fair value of the stock in that company expressed a reduction from the fair value of the stock to account for the costs and risks associated with litigation of the dissenters' claim. The Supreme Court stated, "That percentage was based on the evidence that the … minority shareholders had accepted a price lower than … fair value, as well as the Court of Chancery's extensive expertise in the appraisal of corporate enterprises—an expertise that this Court has recognized on several occasions. To reiterate, where, as here, one side of the litigation presents no competent evidence to aid the Court in discharging its duty to make an independent valuation, we will defer to the Vice Chancellor's valuation approach unless it is manifestly unreasonable."

Lastly, MCHC challenged the Chancery Court's acceptance of the dissenters' expert's decision to ignore the management fees MCHC paid to Palmer in performing his discounted cash flow method. The Supreme Court agreed with that decision. It found that the management fees were a pretext for upstreaming funds to Palmer. It noted that management fees were only paid by Palmer subsidiaries that had minority shareholders, the management fees ceased being paid after the cash out merger, and Price's CEO referred to the fees as "accounting bulls**t." Therefore, the Supreme Court agreed that the management fees were properly eliminated from the earnings projections used by the expert in his discounted cash flow valuation.

The Supreme Court next turned to the dissenters' appeal. The dissenters argued that the Chancery Court erred when it declined to award them attorney and expert fees. The Supreme Court agreed. It noted that generally the parties are required to pay their own way under the American Rule, but that rule may be ignored where one party has exhibited bad faith. Here, the Supreme Court found ample evidence of MCHC's bad faith. It noted that the merger price was set unilaterally by Price's CEO without having an independent appraisal performed. Additionally it noted that Price's CEO committed perjury and Price violated discovery rules. The Supreme Court also heavily weighed the fact that MCHC put forward a valuation expert at trial whose valuation was designed to deprive the minority shareholders of existing value and this opinion was duly rejected

by the chancellor. The Supreme Court stated, "Ultimately, the problems in ... [MCHC's expert's] analysis led the Court to conclude that ... [he] had 'established a pre-determined valuation figure,' and developed his expert testimony to fit into that figure." Therefore, the court heavily factored MCHC's expert's perceived bias in the equation when it reversed the chancellor and remanded for a fee-shifting determination.

Andaloro v. PFPC Worldwide, Inc.

Citation: 2005 Del. Ch. LEXIS 125
Court: Court of Chancery
State/Jurisdiction: Delaware
Date of decision: August 19, 2005
Judge: Strine

PNC Financial Services Group, Inc. (PNC), the parent of PFPC Holding Corp. (Holding), had planned to take Holding's subsidiary, PFPC Worldwide, Inc. (PFPC), public via an initial public offering (IPO), but the opportunity did not arise. To create liquidity for minority shareholders, most of whom were employee-managers, Holding, which held over 98% of PFPC's stock itself, acquired PFPC through a merger.

Holding did not actually offer appraisal rights to the minority stockholders but originally conditioned its willingness to effect the merger on the agreement by all the minority stockholders to waive any appraisal rights or other claims as a condition of receiving the merger consideration. The minority stockholders' position in PFPC was eliminated for $34.26 per share.

Two minority stockholders did not accept these conditions, but Holding nonetheless completed the merger, and the dissenters brought an appraisal action. Five days of trial, and voluminous submissions of the parties, focused exclusively on the question of PFPC's fair value on the merger date. PFPC's expert, Dr. Donald Puglisi, came up with $19.86 per share, and the minority shareholders' expert, Dr. Brett Margolin, came up with $60.76 per share.

Andaloro v. PFPC Worldwide, Inc.

Court uses management projections

The Delaware Chancery Court, finding itself between two extremes, conducted an independent valuation and determined that the fair value PFPC on the merger date was $32.81 per share.

The court used optimistic management assumptions to estimate the acquired corporation's cash flows for the period from the merger (2003) until 2007. With regard to these assumptions, the court said, "[t]he typically dismaying chasm in the experts' DCF outcomes is a real achievement given a happier aspect of the record: both experts relied on the same management projections in building their DCF models."

The court also assumed—giving the benefit of doubt to the plaintiffs—an additional three years of high growth at 8% annually for 2008 through 2010. In light of that second stage aggressive growth, the court relied on a generously high terminal growth factor of 5%, used a target capital structure of 100% equity and applied a 13.5% discount rate.

Chancery Court prefers DCF

In arriving at his valuation, Judge Strine said, "The DCF method is frequently used in this court and, I, like many others, prefer to give it great, and sometimes even exclusive, weight when it may be used responsibly." He also said, "a DCF valuation is the best technique for valuing an entity when the necessary information regarding the required inputs is available."

Accordingly, the court gave two-thirds weight to its determination of PFPC's valuation under the discounted cash flow (DCF) method of valuation ($32.08 per share), and one-third weight to its determination of PFPC's valuation under the comparable companies method of valuation ($34.99).

BVR Editor Comment: Unfortunately, the court viewed the experts as "finance professionals paid to achieve diametrically opposite objectives." The court's perception underscores that valuation professionals need to be as independent and objective as possible, regardless of their clients' positions, so that courts come to trust them as advisors, rather than seeing them as adversarial advocates wedded to their clients' goals.

Henke v. Trilithic, Inc.

Citation: 2005 Del. Ch. LEXIS 170
Court: Court of Chancery
State/Jurisdiction: Delaware
Date of decision: October 28, 2005
Judge: Parsons

The principal issue in this appraisal action was the fair value of dissenters' stock in Trilithic, Inc. (Trilithic), a close corporation that had merged with and into another corporation of the same name.

Trilithic had serious financial difficulties during most of its operating history, had breached covenants in its loans, and had not paid on certain loans. Before the merger date, June 1, 1993, Trilithic's independent auditor, Deloitte & Touche, would not even issue an unqualified opinion that Trilithic was a going concern. The merger effected no changes in Trilithic's management or its business plan.

Disparate expert results

James Henke, a 25% shareholder, dissented. Henke's expert, R. Victor Haas, performed a discounted cash flow (DCF) analysis based on Trilithic's audited financials for the four months ended May 1993 and arrived at an equity value of $6,494,526. Haas therefore appraised Henke's 25% interest to be worth $1,623,631.50.

Trilithic's expert, Brett A. Margolin, neither believed that reliable management projections made contemporaneously with the merger existed, nor did he consider it appropriate to use the 1993 stub period financials in his DCF analysis. Margolin thus developed and used his own financial projections for Trilithic. Ultimately, using DCF, he arrived at a negative value for Trilithic's common equity. Margolin also performed a comparable company analysis (which he did not include in his weighting, because he did not believe he could compensate for the differences in size between Trilithic and the comparable companies), and a transaction analysis that yielded a value of $55, 606 for Henke's interest.

Court conducts independent DCF analysis

The Delaware Chancery Court found that neither party fully satisfied its burden of persuasion regarding its valuation. Therefore, the court undertook its own independent valuation. As the Chancery Court has frequently done in appraisal actions, the court looked to the DCF method. The court indicated that, "[t]his method is widely accepted in the financial community and has frequently been relied upon by this Court in appraisal actions."

The court found that Haas' revenue growth rate (10%) was not supported by the record, and also concluded that Haas failed to account for the seasonality of Trilithic's sales. Finding no such flaws in Margolin's DCF methodology, the court used his analysis as its starting point.

While acknowledging that ordinarily, "contemporary pre-merger management projections are particularly useful in the appraisal context because management projections, by definition, are not tainted by post-merger hindsight and are usually created by an impartial body," the court nonetheless determined that Trilithic's projections for "annual sales" were not useful because "there is no way of knowing what went into the numbers or, for example, to what lines of business the sales are attributable and what profit margins were assumed for those lines of business."

Nonetheless, the court was reluctant to disregard these projections in their entirety, as annual sales numbers with real consequences for the company were one-half of the projected amounts. Accordingly, the court incorporated these midpoint amounts into its analysis, which used a five-year valuation horizon.

Performing a DCF analysis using these and other parameters, the court arrived at a debt-free value of Trilithic's common equity of $1,858,134. Although Trilithic was neither insolvent nor on the verge of bankruptcy as of the merger date, it could not refinance its line of credit and thus could not take advantage of the spread between its face value and its market value. Accordingly, the court subtracted the line of credit at its full face value. Deducting this and other debt, the court arrived at an enterprise value of $298,525. After adding the value of certain non-operating assets, the court concluded that Trilithic's total value was $651,062, or $217.02 per share. Henke's interest, therefore, was worth $162,765.

East Park Ltd. Partnership v. Larkin, et al.

Citation: 2006 Md. App. LEXIS 32
Court: Court of Appeals
State/Jurisdiction: Maryland
Date of decision: March 6, 2006

There's rarely any question that discounts apply to a fair market value analysis of a business interest, as the "willingness" of most arms-length buyers is likely to depend on such factors as minority control and/or lack of marketability. But are discounts for lack of control and marketability appropriate in a "fair value" analysis; i.e., in the context of withdrawing limited partners (and, by analogy, dissenting shareholders)?

On a case of first impression in Maryland, the Court of Special Appeals said that—absent unusual circumstances, they are not. "Because no open market transaction takes place when a partner withdraws from a limited partnership, we hold that, ordinarily, discounts should not be applied."

'Fair value' open to interpretation

Unlike fair market value, for which "countless cases" and statutory provisions establish a clear definition, the term "fair value" in the Maryland uniform partnership and limited partnership laws appears without clarification or guidance. Ditto for the dissenting shareholder provisions of the state's Corporations and Associations Act, which use "fair value" without explanation. There was no local case on point, although the Court noted that the majority of states to consider the issue in the dissenting shareholder context have concluded that discounts do not apply to a fair value analysis. These opinions plus the legislative purpose behind the relevant statutes helped sway the Court—along with the "competent and material" evidence from expert valuators.

Appearing for the withdrawing limited partners, M. Ronald Lipman CRE, MAI (Lipman Frizzell & Mitchell LLC, Columbia, MD) testified that the fair market value of the limited partnership's only asset, a shopping center, was $19.5 million. A second expert for the limited partners, William Bavis, CPA/ABV, CVA (Clifton Gunderson LLP, Baltimore) accounted for the property's liabilities to reach a going concern value of approximately $14.64 million.

To prove its version of value, the partnership provided a state tax assessment of the property at $13.9 million. More importantly, it also proffered Joel Charkatz, CPA, CVAS, CFE (Katz Abosch Windesheim Gershman & Freedman P.A., Baltimore), who testified that the "fair value" of the limited partners' interests necessitated applying a 25% discount for lack of control and a 31.27% discount for lack of marketability.

At trial, the court agreed with the limited partners' experts, finding that the fair market value of the shopping center was $19.5 million, and its "net" or going concern value was $14.64 million. As for what constituted "fair value," the court also determined:

It is not the same as fair market value, for if that had been the intent, the state legislature would have used the FMV term in the uniform partnership laws. Also, in the context of "cashing out" a limited partnership interest, it would be incorrect to apply a fair market analysis where third parties are not involved, but only withdrawing partners surrendering their interests.

In the shareholder dissent statutes, "fair value" requires reimbursement for a withdrawing shareholder's proportionate interest in a going concern, or "the intrinsic value of the shareholder's economic interest in the corporate enterprise."

By analogy to shareholder cases, the objective is to ascertain the actual worth of what the withdrawing limited partner loses because he/she is not willing to "go along with" a controlling partner's decision; this includes the appraisal of all material factors that affect going concern value, such as nature of the partnership operations, its assets and liabilities, future prospects, etc.

Although fair value does not necessarily equal liquidation value, in this case the two are indistinguishable, as the sole asset at stake (real property) had no goodwill or other intangibles.

In conclusion, as the withdrawing limited partners would not be selling their interests in the open market, discounts would not apply; or as the trial court put it, "the remaining partners would end up acquiring the...interests for less than they were worth if those interests had remained in the hands of the withdrawing partners."

On appeal, the Court confirmed the ruling and its reasoning, noting in particular that testimony by the limited partners' expert was supported by case law and statutes, whereas the partnership's expert had admitted that he was unfamiliar with the partnership laws, and had simply equated fair value with fair market value. The Court also confirmed that "the application of discounts is appropriate only under a fair market value analysis; that is, in determining what price a willing buyer would offer, and a willing seller would accept, on the open market."

An interesting aside on the value of hindsight

To discredit the limited partners' experts, the general partner had also wanted to introduce evidence regarding events that took place after the valuation date—such as the anchor tenant "going dark," declining rents, etc. The trial court had allowed the testimony only for impeachment purposes, but even then, had limited it to facts that the experts could have "reasonably" known on the valuation date, which was the day the limited partners withdrew.

"Expert opinions as to valuation are not always correct; they are merely reasonable predictions based on certain assumptions," the Court confirmed. "That those predictions may one day be proved wrong does not mean that they were unreasonable at the time there were made."

Delaware Open MRI Radiology Associates, P.A. v. Kessler

Citation: No. 275-N
Court: Court of Chancery
State/Jurisdiction: Delaware
Date of decision: April 26, 2006
Judge: Strine

The following court case abstract was originally published in Valuation Case Digest®

In *Delaware Open MRI Radiology Associates, P.A. v. Howard B. Kessler*, No. 275-N (Del. Chan. April 26, 2006), the Delaware Court of Chancery determined the fair value of stock in this statutory appraisal action. Kessler and the other defendants (Kessler Group) held 37.5% of Delaware Open MRI Radiology Associates, PA (Delaware MRI), which was formed to own MRI centers in Delaware and pass the MRI reading activities on to its owner-radiologists.

When Delaware MRI, an S corporation, was formed, all its shareholders practiced together in a Philadelphia radiology practice. Eventually, the defendants separated from the initial group

Chapter 7: Court Case Abstracts

(Broder Group) and started a competing radiology practice. This split did not initially disrupt Delaware MRI's activities. However, as competition between the Kessler and Broder Groups increased, the Broder Group, which held the remaining interest in Delaware MRI, began to divert more MRI reading activities to itself, eventually cutting the Kessler Group out all together. Contemporaneously, the Broder Group commenced a freeze-out merger to remove the Kessler Group from participation in Delaware MRI. The Broder Group obtained a valuation of Delaware MRI, which indicated a value of $16,000 per share.

At the time of the freeze-out merger, Delaware MRI owned interests in two MRI centers located in Delaware and had plans to expand throughout Delaware. It signed a lease and formed an operating company for a third location days after the merger. Plans for the fourth location were formed shortly thereafter, but these plans were accomplished through an entirely separate business that did not involve the Kessler Group. A fifth location was under consideration, but no material steps were taken toward opening a fifth location on the date of the merger. The three post-merger locations were operated in a substantially similar fashion to the first two. Each location's revenue was split: 15% to radiologists-owners for services (which was increased to 17.5% shortly before the merger); 1% to management fees, which was increased to 2% shortly after the merger; and 5 to 7.5% to marketing, which was increased to 7.5% for all facilities after the merger.

The Kessler Group dissented from the freeze-out merger. Delaware MRI brought this action to establish the fair value of the dissenters' interests. The Kessler Group counter-sued, claiming breach of fiduciary duty, which required the Broder Group to establish the entire fairness of the transaction. The Chancery Court initially concluded that the transaction did not satisfy the entire fairness test. In reaching this decision, it noted that the Broder Group's appraisal was based entirely on the two established MRI centers and did not consider any value attributable to the three centers that would be opened shortly after the merger. Moreover, the appraiser did not consider whether the amount paid to the radiologist owners for reading services was reasonable (e.g., occurred at the market rate or was effectively a diversion of corporate profits) or whether the amount paid as management fees was reasonable. The court determined that since the fair value of the dissenters' interests in Delaware MRI was the heart of both the fiduciary duty and appraisal claims and since it concluded that the Broder Group breached its fiduciary duty to the Kessler Group in connection with the transaction, "principles of equity infuse my valuation analysis, because I have endeavored to resolve doubts, at the margins, in favor of the Kessler Group, the minority stockholders who were involuntarily squeezed out."

The court then determined the fair value of the stock. Both parties presented expert valuation testimony regarding the value of the stock, and both experts utilized the discounted cash flow method, including the buildup method to compute the discount rate. Moreover, since the business had contemporaneous pre-litigation projections for most of the MRI centers that were used to secure financing, the court and the experts relied upon those projections. In doing so, the court stated: Traditionally, this court has given great weight to projections of this kind because they usually reflect the best judgment of management, unbiased by litigation incentives. This is especially so when management provides estimates to a financing source and is expected by that source (and sometimes by positive law) to provide a reasonable best estimate of future results. However, the experts disagreed regarding other aspects of the valuation, which included the amount to be reconciled for excess management and MRI reading fees, whether to tax effect the stock because of its S corporation status, and whether the expansion plans should be taken into account as part of the operative reality of the business on the valuation date.

First, the court considered whether the MRI reading fees paid by Delaware MRI to the radiologists and management fees were appropriate. The court noted that when all the radiologist-owners were at the same firm and shared equally in the MRI reading revenues there was no unfairness in the amount paid by Delaware MRI to the doctors. However, after the Kessler Group split from the Broder Group, unfairness arose when the Broder Group transferred all the MRI reading fees to itself without making an adjustment for the prior above market rate of 15% of revenues. The Kessler Group argued that the amount improperly received by the Broder Group due to the transfer of all the fees should be the difference between the lowest bidder price (the bargain basement) and the amount received by the Broder Group. The Chancery Court rejected this position. It reasoned that the proper offset should be the market rate of fees charged by comparable radiology groups. However, it noted that neither party presented it with this information. Since there was evidence of the Medicare reimbursement rate, which equated to a 13.7% fee, the court utilized that figure because of the uncertainty created by the Broder Group's wrongful conduct. Thus, it added the difference between the Medicare rate and the actual rate charged by the Broder Group back to the revenue projections used to compute the fair value of the business.

The Chancery Court was next presented with two views of the operative reality of the company. The Broder Group's expert failed to take the plans for future expansion into account and accord them any value because the three later centers were not open for business on the merger date. The Kessler Group's expert included the value of the third and fourth centers in making his appraisal of Delaware MRI because the plans for one had been finalized but not formally executed and negotiations were well underway for the other. The court agreed with the position taken by the Kessler Group's expert, stating, "Obviously, when a business has opened a couple of facilities and has plans to replicate those facilities as of the merger date, the value of its expansion plans must be considered in determining the fair value" because those plans are the companies' operative reality. It explicitly rejected the position of the Broder Group's expert as inconsistent with established theories of corporate finance. It stated that he "has a jarringly novel view of corporate finance, in which the value of McDonald's does not include the revenues it expects to make from the new franchises it will open." Thus, the Chancery Court included the full value of the third and fourth MRI centers, which were opened shortly after the merger date, based on the projected earnings of those centers. Moreover, it included the value of the fifth center, which did not open until a year after the merger date, at one-third the value of the fourth center to compensate the Kessler Group for the "Broder Group's decision to usurp for itself the exclusive right to control the statewide network for itself."

The court then turned to the issue of whether the earnings of Delaware MRI should be tax affected due to its S corporation status. The Broder Group's valuation expert treated Delaware

MRI as a C Corporation and tax affected its earnings at a 40% tax rate. Conversely, the Kessler Group's expert made no adjustment for taxes because the operative reality was that Delaware MRI incurred no corporate-level taxes. The Chancery Court found neither expert's position persuasive, but acknowledged that there was some case law supporting the Kessler Group's position. However, the Chancery Court rejected the operative reality rationale of those cases because under an appraisal situation, failure to tax affect to some degree resulted in a windfall for the dissenting shareholder since they would inevitability pay tax, albeit at their personal level, on the earnings of the business, whether or not those earnings were received from the business. It stated, "To capture the precise advantage of the S corporation structure to the Kessler Group, it is necessary to use a method that considers the difference between the value that a stockholder of . . . [the company] would receive in . . . [the company] as a C corporation and the value that a stock- holder would receive in . . . [the company] as an S corporation." It then reasoned that the since the C corporation tax rate of 40% was roughly equal to the income tax rate experienced by the high-income earning members of the Kessler Group, the primary advantage of the S corporation status to the Kessler Group was the avoidance of dividend tax. It then applied the following formula to determine the appropriate amount by which to tax affect the S corporation in a fair value scenario:

> S Corp pre-tax earnings x personal tax rate of shareholder
>   = dividends available
> Dividends available / (1 – applicable dividend tax rate)
>   = available earnings
> (S Corp pre-tax income – available earnings) / S Corp pre-tax earnings = Assumed Corporate Tax rate.

Using this formula, the Chancery Court determined that the dissenters' interest should be tax affected by a rate of 29.4%. It reasoned, "This calculation allows me to treat the S corporation shareholder as receiving the full benefit of untaxed dividends, by equating its after-tax return to the after-dividend return to a C corporation shareholder." The court applied these adjustments to the discounted cash flow method. It generally adopted the application used by the Kessler Group's expert, noting that the expert's approach was conservative. It concluded that the fair value was $33,232.26 per share.

Tax-Affecting and Beyond: Dela. Radiology Experts Discuss 'Landmark' Case

By John Mitchell and Douglas Evan Ress[1]

Eighteen! That is the precise number of minutes the minority shareholders' forensic and valuation expert, John Mitchell, testified on direct in *Delaware Open MRI Radiology*,[2] a "landmark" case on tax-affecting, fair value pricing, and judicial appraisal. Twenty-seven is how long Mitchell's cross-examination took—for a total forty-five minutes of testimony. On what basis, then, did the Delaware Chancery Court double the challenged $2.4 million merger price for minority shareholders, to yield nearly $6 million, with interest?

The answer has far-reaching implications for forensic BV experts and attorneys. Contrary to the all-too-popular notion that appraisers should simply stake out a position opposite their counterparts', *Delaware Radiology* demonstrates that when a valuation is done the right way, success can be assured even with short, focused trial testimony.

Critical holding on tax-affecting

After their efforts to establish MRI centers in Pennsylvania and Delaware, a group of radiologists split up, forming two distinct blocks of majority and minority shareholders and filing lawsuits in both states.[3] In the Delaware litigation, the minority shareholders of the S Corporation alleged a "squeeze-out" merger by the majority, presenting the Delaware Chancery Court with an equitable entire fairness and a statutory appraisal claim, or what Vice Chancellor Leo E. Strine Jr. called "one of our law's hybrid varietals." At the crux was the financial fairness of the merger, determined by the fair value of Delaware Radiology's shares on the merger date; one of the key issues concerned tax-affecting.

The BV profession has debated tax-affecting for years. The central question: Should there be a difference in business value between two otherwise identical companies, where one is a publicly traded C corporation, which pays income taxes at the corporate level; and the other is a pass-through entity (PTE), which does not?

---

[1] Douglas Evan Ress, Esq. is a trial lawyer and president of Kaufman Coren & Ress, P.C. (Philadelphia), recently selected for The Best Lawyers in America (2007); dress@kcr-law.com. John Mitchell, CPA, CVA (Gocial Gerstein, LLC; Jenkintown, PA) has practiced for over twenty years in a variety of forensic accounting and valuation services; jmitchell@gocialgerstein.com.

[2] *Delaware Open MRI Radiology Associates, P.A. v. Kessler*, 898 A.2d 290 (Del. Ch. 2006) (Delaware Radiology). The abstract of this case is included in this Guide..

[3] Mr. Ress was co-counsel in the PA litigation with Marvin L. Wilenzik, Esq. (Elliott Greenleaf & Siedzikowski, P.C.); his co-counsel in Delaware was Cathy L. Reese, Esq. (Fish & Richardson, P.C.). Mr. Mitchell was assisted in both cases by Ann Marie Albert, CPA, of his firm.

Chapter 7: Court Case Abstracts

Many business appraisers agree that the earnings of a PTE should be tax-affected when valuing its underlying business interests, particularly when the applicable standard of value is fair market value. But the appraiser must consider the benefits of ownership in a PTE beyond that enjoyed by a shareholder of a publicly traded stock.

Why, then, did the minority shareholders' expert (Mitchell) decline to tax-affect in *Delaware Radiology*?

Delaware Chancery vs. U.S. Tax Court

Mitchell did not tax-affect for two reasons: prior Delaware case law, which dictates the fair value standard; and guidance from recent U.S. Tax Court memorandum decisions.

As defined by Delaware appraisal law, the fair value standard precludes application of marketability and/or minority discounts. By contrast, fair market value assumes a pool of hypothetical willing buyers and sellers with relatively equal access to information and the ability to negotiate on substantially even terms. In *Delaware Radiology*, no hypothetical pool was needed to determine fair value, as the seller was the minority group, the buyer was the majority group (or the S corporation itself); and the squeezed-out minority should receive fair value for their shares in the entity on a going-concern basis. Thus, in Mitchell's opinion, the traditional (and rightful) arguments for tax-affecting did not apply.[1]

Mitchell also considered the relevant quartet of Tax Court memorandum decisions that declined to tax-affect earnings.[2] The persistent theme: Tax-affecting turns on the facts of each case, as in many situations, continuing the business as a PTE creates additional value to a shareholder/member, above the value of the underlying business. The extent of this value became an issue in *Delaware Radiology*.

(Notably, after *Delaware Radiology*, the Tax Court decided *Dallas v. Comm'r*,[3] affirming its prior holdings; specifically, it distinguished the fair value standard in *Delaware Radiology*, a combined merger/appraisal case, from the fair market value standard applicable to its own facts, and concluded that there was insufficient evidence that a hypothetical buyer and seller would tax-affect the business. Whether that distinction is meaningful in applying an income approach no doubt will remain the subject of discussion in the legal and business valuation communities.)

---

1 See also, *In re Radiology Associates*, 611 A.2d 485 (Del. Ch. 1991), which coincidentally involved radiologists, in which earnings were not tax-affected.
2 *Gross v. Comm'r*, T.C. Memo. 1999-254, No. 4460-97, aff'd, 272 F.3d 333 (6th Cir. 2001); *Estate of Wall v. Comm'r*, T.C. Memo. 2001-75; *Estate of Heck v. Comm'r*, T.C. Memo. 2002-34; *Estate of Adams v. Comm'r*, T.C. Memo. 2002-80.
3 *Dallas v. Comm'r*, T.C. Memo. 2006-212.

Tax-Affecting and Beyond: Dela. Radiology Experts Discuss 'Landmark' Case

The Chancery's 'hybrid' solution

The expert for the majority in *Delaware Radiology* opined that income taxes should be applied at regular C corporation rates, thereby reducing income by 40%, with the minority shareholders also paying capital gains tax on the squeeze-out sale of their stock.

Vice Chancellor Strine rejected this approach, as it would deny the minority the value they would have received as continuing S Corp shareholders, which should include the favorable tax treatment. V. C. Strine also considered, but rejected, established Delaware and Tax Court cases, distinguishing these at the level of implementation rather than principle. To value the minority group's interest in a free market of willing buyers and sellers of S Corps, the Court felt it essential to quantify the actual benefit of the S Corp status to the shareholder. In essence, to tax-affect fully would penalize the minority shareholders of an S Corp, by double taxing at both the corporate and shareholder level; while not tax-affecting at all would overstate the value to the minority shareholders.

The Court considered it necessary to measure the difference between Delaware Radiology as a C Corp and an S Corp; consequently, V. C. Strine performed his own analysis, estimating "an equivalent, hypothetical 'pre-dividend' S corporation tax rate" of 29.4% to apply to earnings, thus treating "the S corporation shareholder as receiving the full benefit of untaxed dividends, by equating its after-tax return to the after-dividend return to a C corporation shareholder." By taxing corporate earnings at 29.4%, and then taxing dividends at 15%, the result approximates the estimated combined 40% federal and state income tax rate that S Corp shareholders (in that assumed bracket) would pay on their share of corporate earnings.

This was an excellent solution to create equity among minority and majority shareholders, taking into account the taxation on the S Corp shareholders' stream of earnings without double taxing them. But this "hybrid" solution still leaves the tax-affecting debate with unanswered questions.[1]

Benefit of increased tax basis

For example, is there any benefit of an increased tax basis accruing to the majority shareholders for the cost of acquiring the minority shareholders' stock? The increased basis arising from the purchase of the minority's stock will reduce the majority's tax burden when they ultimately sell their shares, while the minority group will face capital gains tax on their court-awarded share price, which has already been subject to the court-imposed 29.4% effective rate. The combination of these two taxes on the minority group approximates the estimated 40% tax the majority group will pay on corporate earnings; but at some future point, when the majority shareholders sell, they will pay only the capital gains tax on the sales price in excess of their increased basis. At

---

1 Despite lauding the decision by V. C. Strine, a brilliant jurist, well-versed in the nuances of business appraisal, both sides appealed, each challenging the tax-affecting determinations, among others. The parties would have continued to thrash out these questions, but ultimately, in settling the Pennsylvania litigation, they withdrew their appeals, leaving V.C. Strine's opinion as the "final word" on tax-affecting in the case.

the point when the majority shareholders sell their stock in the PTE, will the price also necessarily be subject to the same court-imposed 29.4% effective rate? If not, even under a "hybrid" tax-affecting scheme, the majority shareholders might later benefit from having earlier squeezed-out the minority. That is, depending upon how the majority's later sale is ultimately achieved, the minority perhaps might not have received full fair value for their shares, even though the valuation of the minority interests had fully accounted for the income stream to perpetuity.[1]

Another question is whether there could be an inherent benefit to the preservation of the PTE status, which allows the majority to receive favorable tax treatment (incurring taxes only on corporate income, not on distributions/dividends) for as long as they continue the business as a PTE. An underlying tenet of the Delaware fair value statute is to value the business as a going concern, thus perpetuating the favorable tax treatment. While a valuation on future cash flows discounted to present value certainly accounts for the full value of the future income stream to perpetuity, such a valuation does not reward the minority if there is any additional inherent benefit to the majority to owning that income stream in a PTE, let alone if there is any inherent benefit to owning the income stream in a PTE in which there are no longer minority shareholders to whom the majority would otherwise owe fiduciary duties.

Inevitably, another aspect of the debate will focus on whether one should tax-affect using the assumed model of a minority shareholder in a 40% combined federal and state tax bracket; or whether the particular facts and circumstances warrant inquiry into the actual tax rate applicable to the "squeezed out" shareholder.

Beyond tax-affecting: a fifth input to the BUM

In developing their discount rates, both *Delaware Radiology* experts used the build-up method (BUM) as a substitute for the Capital Asset Pricing Model (CAPM). The Court paid particular attention to Mitchell's use of Ibbotson's industry risk premium data, which he added to the traditional four inputs to the build-up method (risk free rate, equity risk premium, size premium, and company-specific risk premium). The majority's expert did not include an industry risk premium in his build-up model, and V.C. Strine, an avid student and teacher of corporate finance and advocate of CAPM, considered Mitchell's use of Ibbotson's industry risk premium data to be a fair proxy for beta under CAPM, recognizing that CAPM cannot be applied in its true form to small, non-publicly traded companies such as Delaware Radiology.

By adopting Mitchell's use of a fifth BUM variable (an industry risk premium), the Court took into account the Ibbotson's market return data that indicate investments in a healthcare business of a certain size present less market risk than average. The Court's recognition of the industry risk premium differs from that of the company-specific risk premium, which compares the risk

---

[1] Left for another day is whether empirical evidence demonstrates that fair value on a going-concern basis truly differs from fair market value. However, this certainly was not Vice Chancellor Strine's charge in *Delaware Radiology*, but is perhaps more the objective of the BV community.

of companies in the same business sector; thus, for certain sized companies, *Delaware Radiology* is instructive on the inclusion of an industry risk premium as part of the BUM, despite various treatises referring only to four variables.

How do Cornfields relate to opportunity?

The majority's expert valued the two MRI centers that were operating as of the merger date, but failed to place any value on three additional centers in various stages of development at the time of the merger. The Court criticized this approach as "a jarringly novel view of corporate finance, in which the value of McDonald's does not include the revenues it expects to make from the new franchises it will open."

By contrast, V.C. Strine noted Mitchell's citation of *Cornfields*, a "thoughtful academic paper" addressing the value of an asset with an additional investment opportunity component,[1] in concluding that two of the three developing centers were clearly part of Delaware Radiology's "operative reality" as of the merger date. Factors such as lease negotiations, management projections—and most importantly, the existence of a successful business model, also helped the Court characterize the fifth center as a natural culmination of the company's active, pre-merger business strategy. Like the others, it was "an opportunity: (1) in the line of the corporation's business and is of practical advantage to it; (2) within the corporation's financial ability to capture; and (3) one in which the corporation has an interest or a reasonable expectancy." Applying an appropriate discount to its value accounted for uncertainty surrounding its opening and operations.

More on management projections

So, too, the Court appreciated Mitchell's consideration of management projections prepared for financing purposes, in conformity with the great weight Delaware courts attribute to management projections submitted to potential lenders, especially those reasonably estimating future results. For example, pre-merger projections are "particularly helpful" because "by definition, [they] are not tainted by post-merger hindsight and are usually created by an impartial body."[2] In another Delaware case, where management suggested that its budget was highly inspirational—like a football coach's diagramming a Hail Mary pass, the Court found that to be a "gross exaggeration that undermines the credibility of [management's] entire presentation."[3]

---

[1] Lawrence A. Hamermesh and Michael A. Wachter, "The Fair Value of Cornfields in Delaware Appraisal Law" (U. Penn. Institute for Law and Economic Research, July 2005). The authors describe a corporation that owns a cornfield worth $50 million as a cornfield, but $60 million as an office building; in squeezing out the minority shareholders, a fair value standard "must include not only the present value of the firm's existing assets, but also the future opportunities to reinvest free cash flow, including reinvestment opportunities identified, even if not yet developed, before the merger." See http://papers.ssrn.com/sol3/papers.cfm?abstract_id=810908. Interestingly, the Delaware Chancery appears to be paying particular attention to research by Professors Hamermesh and Wachter; see V.C. Parsons' discussion of their work on the implied minority discount in the article entitled "The World According to Delaware Chancery: A Vice Chancellor Offers Ten Tips to Appraisers" in this Guide.

[2] *Cede & Co. v. Technicolor, Inc.*, 2003 WL 23700218 (Del. Ch. 2003).

[3] *Gholl v. eMachines, Inc.*, 2004 WL 2847865 (Del. Ch.), aff'd, 875 A.2d 632 (Del. 2005).

Chapter 7: Court Case Abstracts

In *Delaware Radiology*, management claimed the projections for bank financing were prepared in "minimal time," merely "throw-ins" after securing the financing; its expert disavowed these projections, especially those valuing centers not yet operational. But given the Delaware precedent, the Court "regarded with rightful suspicion" attempts by parties to disclaim projections they have previously produced, particularly "when that denial serves their litigation objective." In contrast, Mitchell had "used the extant projections as the beginning for his analysis and built off of them in a manner that I find to be reasonable and conservative," V.C. Strine wrote. "In fact, in projecting a reimbursement rate, Mitchell took a more conservative approach than [management did in its] projections…"

Valuation modeling

The final key to success may very well have been the painstaking detail with which Mitchell presented his financial models, providing electronic copies so the Court could "play with the numbers." The models worked; in addressing the applicable discount rate to reduce cash flows to present value, V.C. Strine noted:

> [The exhibits] to Mitchell's expert report suggest that Mitchell correctly weighed the debt of the MRI centers and the equity in the MRI centers as of [the valuation date]. He ran several iterations in order to achieve the correct WAAC value, so I will apply his values to determine present value.

The moral of the story: To succeed in any courtroom—especially one as sophisticated as the Delaware Chancery, the business appraiser must account for all relevant factors, including additional investment or expansion opportunities and management projections prepared in the ordinary course. The valuation report must demonstrate a conservative, restrained analysis that, while reflecting the client's objectives, reasonably includes all variables impacting the value of the company. To do otherwise will only serve to taint, and perhaps destroy, all credibility with the ultimate fact-finder.

Casey v. Amboy Bancorporation

Citation: No. A-0715-04T3
Court: Superior Court, Appellate Division
State/Jurisdiction: New Jersey
Date of decision: August 8, 2006
Judge: Fall, Parker, and Yannotti

The following court case abstract was originally published in Valuation Case Digest®

In *Kathryn Casey v. Amboy Bancorporation*, No. A-0715-04T3 (N.J. Supr. August 8, 2006), the New Jersey Superior Court, Appellate Division considered a lower court's calculation of

Casey v. Amboy Bancorporation

fair value and its treatment of synergies in this dissenters' rights action. In 1997, Amboy Bancorporation, a C corporation, sought to convert to an S corporation. Since an S corporation was limited to 75 shareholders and Amboy had in excess of 400 shareholders, it determined to execute a cash-out merger that eliminated shareholders having less than 15,000 shares. The cash-out price was determined to be $73 per share, which was supported by a fairness opinion. Several suits were spawned from this transaction. The fair value issues were consolidated into one action, which has been to the appellate division twice before.

The lower court determined the fair value of the stock in the second remand. Five experts, including one appointed by the court, testified to the fair value of the stock. The court noted that fair value was defined as the going concern value, exclusive of appreciation or depreciation resulting from the contested event and exclusive of discounts for minority interest or lack of marketability. However, the court found that a control premium may be warranted, but in considering a control premium care should be taken to exclude a synergistic value arising from the contested transaction.

The company's expert sought to value the bank on the basis of comparable stock for cash transactions because the operative reality of the transaction was stock-for-cash. In doing so, he removed excess capital from the valuation since minority shareholders could not access the capital. The trial court rejected reliance upon stock-for-cash transactions because the operative reality was that 90% of bank transactions were acquisition transactions involving stock-for-stock swaps.

It rejected one dissenter's appraiser, who valued the business based on the comparable public company method and the discounted cash flow (DCF) method. It found that this expert utilized too high a discount rate in his DCF method and dissimilar comparables. Additionally, it found that this expert took each opportunity to issue an updated report as an opportunity to increase the value of the subject company's stock.

The court preferred the approach of an expert that valued the business based on comparable acquisitions, which included embedded control premiums. His valuation resulted in $120 per share. While he acknowledged that synergy value was generally included in control premiums, there was no method to extract the synergistic premium from the overall control premium. Moreover, he tested his valuation using a proprietary feasibility analysis, which was fully explained at trial. Under this analysis, he identified seven potential acquirers and concluded that only two could undertake an acquisition of the subject company at $120 per share without diluting their own earnings, but six companies could undertake the acquisition at a price of $114 per share.

The court rejected the court appointed expert's public company guideline method. The court found it problematic to value the business on a marketable minority basis and apply a control premium. The expert reasoned that some synergistic value may be imbedded in the marketable minority per share price, thus double counting the synergistic value in the control premium, if the market believed that the subject company was to be imminently acquired. However, the court credited this expert's opinion that 90% of the transactions were consummated using stock-for-stock transactions. Moreover, he testified that synergistic value represented between 3 and 5% of a transaction price.

It rejected another expert because he utilized incomparable companies in his analysis, failed to make a feasibility analysis, and declined to address the issue of synergy.

The court adopted the $114 per share value. It determined that this was the highest feasible sale price of the stock. Several parties appealed.

The parties' appeals break down into two complaints: (1) the trial court erred when it valued the stock at fair value using the highest feasible sale price, and (2) the trial court improperly accounted for the effects of synergy. The appellate court disagreed on both counts.

On the first point, the appellate division noted that New Jersey's fair value statute is similar to Delaware's, and New Jersey courts appropriately look to both Delaware law and the American Law Institute for guidance on appraisal issues because they agree that the main objective of appraisal statues is the protection of the minority shareholder. In making this pronouncement the court stated, "That means a court may rely on the provision in 2 ALI Principles, supra, § 7.22(c), that courts 'generally should give substantial weight to the highest realistic price that a willing, able, and fully informed buyer would pay for the corporation as an entity.'" It further noted that the trial judge is limited in his selection of valuation methods to only those that are "legally acceptable" and "reasonable."

Amboy Corporation argued that the trial court erred when it utilized comparable stock-for-stock transactions rather than stock-for-cash transactions since the operative reality of the underlying transaction was stock-for-cash. The appellate court rejected this argument. It noted that the testimony showed that when valuing an acquisition target, the market reality was that 90% of transactions were stock-for-stock transactions. Moreover, it noted that Delaware case law supports the position that stock-for-stock transactions provide an adequate basis for computing going concern value. Therefore, it affirmed the lower court's decision to value the business as a going concern by reference to stock-for-stock transactions.

Amboy further argued that the trial court erred when it relied upon the expert's proprietary feasibility study in determining the fair value of the stock because that proprietary method was not generally accepted in the appraisal community. The appellate court rejected this argument. It reasoned that since the "feasibility analysis was a confirmatory test separate from the acquisition valuation itself, [the trial judge] ... did not err by finding it credible for its stated purpose without concern for whether its methodology was generally accepted as a primary valuation tool." It further stated, "Our courts have readily recognized that valuation, which relies on significant exercises of judgment, is accordingly more of an art than a science; that makes it only natural for experts to use different 'proprietary' approaches rather than a rigidly uniform methodology, and for the trial court to assess their credibility and decide for itself how much reliance they merit when determining fair value in the particular circumstances before it."

Amboy lastly argued that the trial court's use of stock-for-stock transactions as an indictor of fair value violated its federal right to reorganize itself as an S corporation. The appellate division rejected this position, finding that "Amboy seeks to elevate its desires to maintain Amboy's independence above its duty to pay fair value as defined by statute and case law." Since there was no authority presented for that position, the court concluded that Amboy had an obligation to pay its shareholders fair value, and if it could not do so, it needed to find an alternative.

The court then considered the second prong of the arguments: those relating to synergy.

One question presented to the court by the parties was whether the trial court erred when it reduced the going concern value of the business for inherent synergies arising from the conversion of the company from a C corporation to an S corporation. The experts agreed that control premiums were present in comparable stock-for-stock acquisitions, but that any value allocated to synergies could not be quantified. Nonetheless, the experts opined that synergies could make up as much as 5% of the value of the stock or $5 per share on $120 per share.

The trial court was required to adhere to the fair value statute and the remand instructions. They required that the subject company be valued without depreciation or appreciation arising from the contested action, but that a control premium should be applied so long as it did not include any synergistic value. Furthermore, the court could adjust the values in order to comply with this mandate. The trial court did just that. It valued the business based on comparable stock-for-stock transactions that included control premiums. It received evidence regarding the value allocated to synergies. While acknowledging that there was no reliable estimate of the embedded synergies in a control premium, it estimated a $6 dollar adjustment from the value computed by reference to comparable transactions. The parties appealed this adjustment.

On appeal, the parties argued that the trial court erroneously adjusted for the synergies by adjusting for synergies in the comparable transactions when the fair value statute required only exclusion of synergies arising from the contested transaction. The appellate court noted:

> [The trial judge] correctly observed that the synergies embedded in the prices at which comparable mergers occurred did not cease to exist simply because outsiders could not have as clear a view of them as the participants, and furthermore, that applying the financial multiples derived from those prices without a synergy adjustment necessarily carried the synergy element into the resulting valuation .... His determination that the acquisition valuations needed a synergy adjustment was logically unavoidable, and consistent with our categorical instruction to exclude synergies.

Moreover, in the absence of direct evidence of the quantum of synergistic value, the trial court did not err in estimating the effect of this transaction's synergistic value. The court noted that this approach is in accordance with Delaware law. In Delaware, the courts have adjusted for the synergistic element by (1) adjusting the prices of comparable transactions based on expert testimony as to the effect of synergy on value, or (2) they "consider the simple existence of a range of otherwise legally acceptable valuations as a demonstration that synergies are present." Since the trial court valued the business based on the highest feasible price, it was appropriate to apply a discount to back out the synergies.

The judge relied upon the testimony of three experts, which included a feasibility analysis, an opinion that the $5 of a $120 per share price was synergy, and an opinion that 5% was a reasonable general estimate for synergies. Since the trial judge's analysis was supported by the record and comparable to analyses applied in Delaware, the appellate court affirmed the synergy deduction.

In re PNB Holding Co.

Citation: 2006 Del. Ch. LEXIS 158
Court: Court of Chancery
State/Jurisdiction: Delaware
Date of decision: August 18, 2006
Judge: Strine

In yet another erudite, informed opinion, the Delaware Chancery Court (Vice Chancellor Leo Strine) examined the familiar but "depressingly" wide parentheses of expert values presented in a hybrid appraisal/unfair merger action, "within whose capacious bounds I am to identify a single estimate of...value."

The two case experts had presented three conclusions of value, two based on the comparable company and comparable acquisitions approaches—which the Court all but dismissed as unreliable "brush." As a result, the Court focused exclusively on the experts' discounted cash flow (DCF) analyses, providing additional precedent to support the valuation method many believe the Delaware Chancery to prefer.

Rural bank holding company converts to S Corp

To complement its strategic expansion plan, a rural bank holding company in Illinois (PNB) decided to convert to an S Corporation, which meant reducing its 300 shareholders to seventy-five, to meet eligibility requirements. In late 2002, the PNB Board retained Prairie Capital Advisors, Inc. (Oakbrook Terrace, IL) to appraise the company and determined the fair value of its common stock. Based on a DCF analysis (20% weight) and comparable company and acquisitions approaches (40% each), Prairie Capital arrived at a value of $40.74 for PNB stock.

Relying on this valuation as well as a fairness opinion by an investment bank, the Board voted to approve the conversion/merger price at $41 per share; the lawsuit arose from shareholders who voted against the conversion and perfected an appraisal action, as well as those who were cashed out in the merger and sought equitable relief (the difference between the merger price and the fair value of PNB shares).

Based on an exhaustive review of the facts, the Court concluded the merger was subject to an entire fairness review, which led it to the "confluence of two jurisprudential rivers," equity and the appraisal action, and the appropriate standard of value:

In re PNB Holding Co.

In other words, to measure whether the merger price was unfair, the court must conduct the same essential inquiry as in an appraisal, albeit with more leeway to consider fairness as a range and to consider the remedial objectives of equity.

Court cannot create new data

At trial, PNB retained a new expert, Chris Hargrove (Professional Bank Services, Chicago), while the plaintiffs offered David Clarke, ASA (Griffing Group. Inc.; Oakbrook, IL). Both conducted market approaches, as follows:

1. *Comparable company.* Hargrove relied on thirteen publicly traded bank holding companies located in the Midwest, focusing on the three most similar to PNB to calculate an ultimate value of $43.50 per share for PNB. Clarke took a more restrictive approach, focusing on comparables in PNB's locale with a rural presence; using the three companies that met these criteria, he calculated a $51.60 per share price. Applying a 20% premium to correct for a minority discount reflected in the data, he reached a $61.96 per share value for PNB.

2. *Comparable acquisition.* Hargrove examined only cash acquisitions, finding eleven comparables nationwide within the relevant time frame, to calculate a $49.14 per share value for PNB. Applying a 20% discount based on PNB's lower financial performance, he reached a $39.31 share value. Clarke decided to focus on either cash or stock acquisitions that met criteria of asset size, equity to asset ratios and returns on assets, and found seven comparables. Averaging the values, he found a $59 per share value for PNB, discounted by 20% to preclude synergies, resulting in $49.17 per share.

But the Court found none of the comparables "convincingly similar" to PNB; most were significantly larger, or had too wide a range of returns. As Clarke admitted, it was "hard to find good comps, because the comps that are supposed to be the same size are illiquid."

"In any case like this, the court necessarily relies on the record the parties shape regarding the company and its value, and is not in a position to conduct a new search for data." Given its lack of faith in the data and supporting detail (and the relative lack of weight each expert attributed to his market approaches), the Court swept away the brush of guideline companies to focus exclusively on the experts' DCFs.

Court sticks with the tried and true

The Court complimented Hargrove on his direct and helpful testimony, but found his valuation approach was "idiosyncratic and involved intuitive moves that might not be irrational, but which were not grounded in traditional…techniques." For example, in calculating a discount rate, Hargrove used a "unique 'in-house' method" that involved the core earnings-to-price ratio of the banking industry combined with the sustainable growth rate. But the Court "could not grasp the explanation of this method or find a basis for it in respected valuation literature," and so did not adopt this input—or Hargrove's general DCF framework.

By contrast, Clarke's DCF was "not without its own problems," but it was easier for the Court to follow, as it tracked the methodology found in leading texts and followed a more traditional, if not conservative, analysis. (As plaintiff's expert, Clarke also benefited from the burden of proof in the case, which proponents of the merger needed to carry.) Although Clarke made some moves the Court did not adopt—in particular, his "subjective" calculation of beta for use in the CAPM, the Court generally used his DCF model for its own detailed analysis, with particular emphasis on three components: the acceptable capital ratio at which to keep the bank; the resulting effect on free cash flows; and the discount rate.

After determining all the necessary inputs to its DCF analysis—and providing another "must read" Delaware Chancery appraisal opinion—the Court concluded a fair value price for PNB stock at $52.34.

Brown v. Arp and Hammond Hardware Co.

Citation: 2006 Wyo, LEXIS 115
Court: Supreme Court
State/Jurisdiction: Wyoming
Date of decision: August 29, 2006

On a case of first impression, the Wyoming Supreme Court considered whether the state's adoption of the Model Business Corporation Act (MBCA) precluded the application of discounts to the "fair value" appraisal of a minority interest in a closely-held company. Subsequent amendments to the MBCA have specifically precluded discounts in these "fair value" determinations—but Wyoming, among many states with the original MCBA on the books, has yet to adopt the amendments.

District court applied 35% combined discounts

After a reverse stock split that effectively cashed out their interest, the 21.86% shareholders in a long-time, family-owned Wyoming business exercised their statutory dissent rights and filed an appraisal proceeding. In applying Wyoming's version of the MCBA, the trial court found that the shares' "fair value" included a 30% discount for lack of control and a 5% embedded capital gains discount. The lack of control discount was appropriate, according to the court, because the majority and minority took "radically different positions" regarding the company's future; and the trapped-in tax discount anticipated the company selling some assets to satisfy any judgment.

On appeal, the Wyoming Supreme Court reviewed the meaning of "fair value" in the context of shareholder dissent for the first time in state history. The opinion contains a thorough overview of "fair value" case law from the original MCBA to the present. Among its key findings:

• *Purpose.* The statutory appraisal action protects minority interests from forced participation in majority-approved corporate actions that may involve oppression, self-dealing, and opportunism.

Brown v. Arp and Hammond Hardware Co.

- *Distinguished from other contexts.* A forced or oppressive transaction is "fundamentally different" from the minority's voluntary decision to abandon the enterprise because of a majority-driven change in the business.

- *Ambiguous standard.* The official comment to the original MCBA "leaves to the parties (and ultimately the courts) the details by which 'fair value' is to be determined." The ambiguity helped courts preserve existing case law as well as develop future decisions; it also recognized the then-split in judicial authority in certain areas of valuation, including application of discounts.

- *Post-MCBA decisions.* Shortly after Wyoming's adoption of the MCBA, the Delaware Supreme Court decided *Cavalier Oil Corp. v. Hammond* (1989), which held that minority discounts contradicted the requirement of valuing the enterprise as a "going concern" in shareholder dissent cases.

- *Majority followed Cavalier Oil.* The vast majority of courts have since held that minority discounts do not apply when determining fair value in this context.

- *Endorsement by American Law Institute (ALI).* The ALI's *Principles of Corporate Governance* (1994) provide that fair value in appraisal proceedings preclude minority and marketability discounts, except in "extraordinary" cases.

- *1999 MCBA revisions.* Amendments to MCBA's fair value definition included a specific prohibition against applying minority/marketability discounts.

- *Effect of failure to adopt amendments.* Courts in states without the revised MCBA have nevertheless considered them persuasive in rejecting discounts.

- *Question of law.* Although valuation is a fact-specific exercise, affording wide discretion to the district court, the question of minority discounts in shareholder oppression cases is one of law, subject to *de novo* review.

- *Fair value ≠ fair market value.* Courts have generally rejected the notion that the ambiguity in "fair value" can be resolved by resorting to "fair market value."

Discount for embedded capital gains, and a final word from the experts

Using this policy and legal analysis, the Wyoming Supreme Court rejected the application of minority discounts, and also those for tax consequences. Absent clear evidence that the company is undergoing liquidation, a discount for trapped-in capital gains would violate the purpose of the statute: to compensate dissenting shareholders for the "fair value" of their shares in a going concern.

Lastly, the Court added back into its final determination of value several assets that the district court had omitted from its calculations. The opinion doesn't explain why the lower court overlooked these assets—nor does it mention the experts involved in the underlying valuations.

Chapter 7: Court Case Abstracts

However, the *BVU* heard from Eric Six, CPA/ABV (CBIZ ATA-Colorado) and Melinda Harper, CPA/ABV, CFE (Harper Lutz Zuber Potenza & Associates, LLC; Denver), who appeared on behalf of the minority shareholders. (Chris Treharne, ASA, CBA, BVAL, MCBA [Gibraltar Appraisals, Inc., Longmont, CO] was the expert for the majority).

"This was a very interesting dispute," Harper says. "For a little background, Eric did a great job researching the then-current case law and putting together clear summaries for our report, which formed the basis for my testimony. The Judge was very interested and asked lots of questions, but made it clear that he didn't feel bound by the case law trends in other states."

"Obviously," Harper says, "the Supreme Court of Wyoming disagreed."

Anderson v. Anderson

Citation: 2006 Tenn. App. LEXIS 592
Court: Court of Appeals
State/Jurisdiction: Tennessee
Date of decision: September 5, 2006
Judge: Franks

In valuing the husband's minority interest in a mobile home company, its CPA (and also the parties' joint expert) first calculated its "fair value" as a going concern, which he estimated at just over $2.7 million. He then calculated 43.75% of that value, representing the husband's shares; and discounted this by 38.3% for lack of control.

Discount for marketability—or marketing?

But then the CPA applied a 10% "marketability discount," which he said accounted for the costs to market the husband's business—including advertising and broker's fees, etc. On review, the Tennessee Court of Appeals accepted the CPA's initial valuation, which had referred to Rev. Ruling 59-60 factors (nature of the business, book value, economic outlook, etc.). It also accepted the 38.3% discount for lack of control.

But the Court held the application of the "marketability" discount was "inappropriate because no sale was ordered and there is no indication on the record that the husband has any intention on selling his minority stock."

It seems clear that the Court denied any discount for contingency sale of the company, which the CPA had called a "marketability" discount. What's not clear from the record is whether a true discount for lack of "marketability" might have applied to the husband's minority interest in the privately-held corporation. The Court does recite case law imposing the burden on the parties to "produce competent evidence of value" at trial, and binding them to the evidence they do present—because like history, trial records cannot be rewritten.

Hall v. Glenn's Ferry Grazing Assoc.

Citation: 2006 U.S. Dist. LEXIS 68051
Court: District Court
State/Jurisdiction: Idaho
Date of decision: September 21, 2006
Judge: Winmill

There was a lot of wrangling going on over sales of stock in this Idaho association, whose purpose was to "engage in the business of providing...lands for grazing and recreational purposes." So although most of its assets lay in real property—pasture and meadow—plus related grazing rights, when a new minority shareholder sought judicial dissolution of the corporation, based on alleged oppression, statutory fair value came into play.

Expert uses adjusted net tangible asset method

To evaluate the fair value of the minority owner's shares, David Cooper, CPA, CVA (Cooper Norman & Co., Twin Falls) employed the adjusted net tangible asset method, subtracting tangible liabilities from tangible assets, then adjusting for market value. To determine the market value of the real property, Cooper relied on an appraisal by Scott Calhoun (H.S. Calhoun Appraisal & Consulting, Boise), which the Court found credible, based on thirteen comparable sales, aerial photos, BLM studies, and "on the ground analysis." Based on the real property valuation of $2 million, and grazing rights of $300,000—plus assorted personal property, farm credit stock, and minus liabilities—the net equity of the Association came to just over $2.1 million. As there were 77 outstanding shares at the time, Cooper concluded that the equity value per-share was $27,371.

The Court also applied an 8.74% minority discount, as calculated by the Association's expert, Dennis Reinstein, CPA/ABV, ASA, CBV (Hooper Cornell, PLLC, Boise), which brought the per-share value to $24,979. Accordingly, the Court found the 30-shares of the minority owner to be worth $749,370.

Minority discount appropriate

The minority shareholder objected to the application of a discount, relying on a comment to the controlling Idaho statute, which provides:

> In cases where there is dissension but no evidence of wrongful conduct, 'fair value' should be determined with reference to what [the minority shareholder] would likely

receive in a voluntary sale of shares to a third party, taking into account his minority status (emphasis added).

As evidence of wrongful conduct, the minority owner claimed the Association had made below-market sales of stock to consolidate voting power, and modified the by-laws without proper notice. He also cited his expert's opinion that "fair value" is a "term of art for business valuation appraisers meaning a shareholder's overall value in the corporation, excluding the application of any minority discount."

While a minority discount might be appropriate in calculating fair market value of the thirty shares, he argued, it's not contemplated in the "fair value" determination of the shareholder dissent statute.

But the Court found no basis for the allegations of wrongful conduct (which would have perhaps evidenced shareholder oppression). It also relied on the clear language of the Idaho statute as well as recent sales of the Association's stock, which had reflected a minority discount. "Under the circumstances of this particular case," the Court noted, the discount was appropriate.

Small v. Sussman and Day Surgicenters, Inc.

Citation: No. 1-98-1113
Court: Court of Appeals
State/Jurisdiction: Illinois
Date of decision: June 1, 1999
Judge: Preston

The following court case abstract was originally published in Valuation Case Digest®

In *Richard A. Small v. Paul Sussman and Day Surgicenters, Inc.,* No. 1-98-1113 (June 30, 1999), the Illinois Court of Appeals for the First District considered whether a former shareholder could bring a direct action against the majority shareholder for breach of fiduciary duty. Small was a 10% shareholder in Day Surgicenters (DSI). Sussman controlled that company. Sussman completed a reverse merger and eliminated the minority shareholders. Thereafter, Small dissented and brought an appraisal action which is still pending. He also filed this action, claiming that Sussman breached his fiduciary duty in diverting DSI's profits to other entities Sussman controlled. The trial court dismissed this action because "Illinois law is well settled that a shareholder seeking relief for an injury to the corporation, rather than a direct injury to the shareholder himself, must bring his suit derivatively on behalf of the corporation." Small appealed.

On appeal, he made the argument that Illinois should adopt the American Law Institute's recommendation that a "court in its discretion may treat an action raising derivative claims as a direct action." See *American Law Institute's Principals of Corporate Governance: Analysis and recommendations,* sec.

7.01(d)(1992). The appellate court rejected this argument on the same grounds as the trial court. In doing so, the court noted that the type of freeze-out merger that occurred here, a reverse stock split with the elimination of fractional shares, is authorized under Illinois' Business Corporation Act.

See 805 ILCS 5/11.05.

Lastly, Small argued that "the valuation process cannot remedy the wrongs done to the corporation because the proceedings will focus narrowly upon the value of the DSI shares at the precise time of the merger." The appellate court declined to fully address this issue. However, it did note that "the court is given the power to appoint appraisers to receive evidence and assess costs against either a dissenting shareholder or the corporation if either party has suggested a buyout price which 'materially exceeds' the fair value as determined by the court." It further stated that "where the value of ... [a derivative] cause of action was substantial, the court would necessarily need to assess the impact of the claim amidst all other relevant factors in setting the fair price on the dissenter's shares."

In re Marriage of Becker

Citation: 2007 Iowa App. LEXIS 1223
Court: Court of Appeals
State/Jurisdiction: Iowa
Date of decision: November 29, 2007
Judge: Vaitheswaran

The case abstract of In re Marriage of Becker first appeared in the Dec. 2007 Business Valuation Update™. At a subsequent rehearing, the husband requested the Iowa Court of Appeals to reconsider its decision based on a revised expert valuation report, originally presented (and rejected) at trial, which lowered the value of the husband's business from $3.07 million to $2.66 million. The reduced value was based on a court-authorized shareholder distribution of $800,000 prior to trial, which resulted in decreased cash flow and corporate equity. At all times the wife argued that this lower value failed to consider the value of buildings and its land, and her arguments had succeeded on appeal.

On rehearing, the Court of Appeals found the evidence from the husband's expert credible. It accepted the $2.66 million revised figure, adjusting it upward $588,000 to account for the value of buildings and land (including two operating quarries). On a more subtle note, the only major difference between the original Becker opinion and this substituted opinion, aside from the lower accepted value, is that the Court omitted citation to *Northwest Investment Corp. v. Wallace*. This 2007 Iowa Supreme Court opinion considered—and accepted—application of a control premium in the dissenting shareholder context, based on statutory fair value precedent that also precludes marketability discounts. (The Wallace abstract appears in this Guide) Whether the Iowa appeals court specifically intended to omit reference to Wallace—and if so, what the Court may be implying regarding the application of statutory fair value to divorce cases—is not clear simply from a reading of the substituted opinion.

Bernier v. Bernier

Citation: 2007 Mass. LEXIS 598
Court: Supreme Court
State/Jurisdiction: Massachusetts
Date of decision: September 14, 2007
Judge: Marshall

Debate over the valuation of S corporations has "bedeviled the professional appraisers' community for some time," the Massachusetts Supreme Court observed at the beginning of this divorce case. Here, the debate played out in the "vastly different" appraisals by the parties' experts—and their reliance on different precedent. A more subtle debate over the application of fair value versus fair market value in marital dissolutions also played out, making *Bernier* a "must-read" for its overview of the complex financial issues and related case law.

Discounts at issue, too

At trial, both experts agreed that the income approach was the most accurate approach to valuing the couple's two S corporations, which owned successful supermarkets in the upscale Martha's Vineyard market. The experts also agreed that any potential buyers of the S corporations would seek a required rate of return. But the experts took "diametrically opposed" approaches to tax-affecting the businesses.

The husband's expert treated the couple's S corporations as if they were C corporations, applying a 35% "average" tax rate to earnings. This was appropriate, he said, because a potential purchaser would factor these tax consequences into the expected rate of return. He also applied a 10% "key man" discount, because the husband was undisputedly important to the supermarkets' operation, and a 10% "marketability" discount to account for the costs of any sale. He used no growth rate in his valuation, because of declining revenues and uncertain future growth. Overall, the husband's expert reached a $7.85 million valuation for the S corporations.

The wife's expert declined to apply C corporation tax rates, because no sale of the business was contemplated and the S Corps did not pay taxes at an entity level. Because the husband intended to maintain full ownership and control after the divorce, no discounts applied, the expert said, and because revenues were just emerging from the downward growth trend, he applied only a 2.5% growth rate to account for inflation. Overall, the wife's expert valued the S Corps at a $16.4 million.

The trial judge adopted the husband's "tax-affected" value, citing the Tax Court's decision in *Gross v Commissioner* (affirmed by the 6th Circuit in 2001). It also faulted the wife's expert for "improperly" combining pre-tax and post-tax data in establishing a capitalization rate, applying an incorrect growth rate, and omitting discounts.

Tax Court vs. Delaware Chancery

On review, the Massachusetts Supreme Court first noted that shareholders in a Subchapter S corporation enjoy the "considerable benefit of avoiding the 'double taxation' of corporate dividends that is hallmark of the C corporation." But this distinction "does little in itself to clarify the issue of valuation" and begs the questions "whether, and how," to account for tax consequences.

Judges, appraisers, and academics have debated the questions, it added. The debate may have begun with an old Internal Revenue Service training manual, *Valuation Guide for Income, Estate and Gift Taxes: Valuation Training for Appeals Officers*, in which the IRS appeared "to have endorsed the practice of tax affecting an S corporation in the manner that [the husband's expert] followed." Since the *Gross* decision, however, "both case law and professional scholarship have cast serious doubt on the validity of this practice," the Court said, citing the Tax Court cases that followed *Gross*, from *Estate of Adams* and *Estate of Heck,* both decided in 2002, through *Dallas v. Commissioner* in 2006.

Looking to the other side of the debate, the Court cited *Del. Open MRI Radiology and Assoc. v. Kessler* (2006), in which the Delaware Chancery Court reviewed an S Corp merger for fair process and statutory fair value. In that case, treating the enterprise as a C corporation failed to account for the comparative tax benefits of S corporation ownership and therefore depressed the estimate of the business's fair value. But not tax affecting at all would lead to a windfall for the minority shareholders. As a result, the Chancery Court crafted a "hybrid" approach to capture the value of the tax benefit to the shareholders (and potential buyers of the shareholders' interests) by imputing a "pre-dividend" corporate tax rate of 29.4% to the S Corp. This left the S Corp shareholder "with the same amount of money in his or her pocket as the shareholder of a C corporation," assuming the latter were taxed at the hypothetical 29.4% rate.

Trial court misapplied Gross

The Delaware Chancery Court's "trenchant" analysis proved more persuasive. By applying the presumed 35% C corporation tax rate, the trial court in this case had understated the value of the S corporation supermarkets and failed to adequately compensate the wife for the loss of the attendant ownership and tax benefits. This was particularly true given the "uncontroverted" evidence that the husband would continue to own and operate the profitable supermarkets after the divorce, including the historic practice of making cash distributions. Even though *Del. Radiology* was decided after the trial, these facts should have prompted the judge to "look past the all-or-nothing approach" of the parties' experts.

Moreover, the trial court misapplied *Gross*, citing it for the proposition that "tax affecting Subchapter S income for valuation purposes should be reflected in determining the 'cost of capital.'" But then it ignored the Tax Court's application of a zero% corporate tax rate when it adopted the 35% rate proposed by the husband's expert. "The husband has cited no cases, nor have we found any, that apply the presumed [35%] rate of taxation of a C corporation to estimating the fair market value of an S corporation using the income approach," the Court held. The judge's reliance on the IRS training manual was also improper. "The IRS valuation guide cannot be cited as authority."

A finding for fair value in divorce?

Under these circumstances, the Court found that the metric employed by the Delaware Chancery Court "provides a fairer mechanism for accounting for the tax consequences" of transferring ownership of the S corporations from one spouse to the other. In particular, it likened the fiduciary considerations that constrain the equitable property division in divorce cases to those that constrained the minority/majority shareholders in *Del. Radiology* and statutory fair value cases. In the context of divorce, where one party will retain and the other be entirely divested of ownership in any marital asset, "the judge must take particular care to treat the parties *not* as arm's-length hypothetical buyers and sellers in a theoretical open market but as fiduciaries entitled to equitable distribution" (emphasis added).

The Court didn't clearly state "fair value" as the applicable premise of value. In fact, a few paragraphs after the quoted passage, above, the Court also observed that "[c]areful financial analysis tells us that applying the C corporation rate of taxation to an S corporation severely undervalues *the fair market value* of the S corporation" (emphasis added). But in its review of the "key man" and marketability discounts, the Court held that both discounts were inappropriate where the husband would remain in complete control, contemplated no sale, and intended to continue the businesses as "going concerns." A 2.5% growth rate was also appropriate where there was no evidence that future growth would fall short of inflation.

The Court remanded the case for a determination on the tax affecting, discount, and growth rate issues. It acknowledged the "complex" valuation issues and the trial court's prior efforts to render a decision without the benefit of the *Del. Radiology* analysis. As a final note, "We emphasize the judge's role in...[ensuring] that the final judgment reflects the statutory requirements of equitable distribution."

Erp v. Erp

Citation: 2007 Fla. App. LEXIS 18726
Court: Court of Appeals
State/Jurisdiction: Florida
Date of decision: November 28, 2007
Judge: Altenbernd

In this case, the Florida Court of Appeals considered whether, as a matter of law, a discount for lack of marketability (DLOM) should *not* be applied when valuing a business for divorce purposes.

Erp v. Erp

During the marriage the couple purchased an RV dealership, formed as an S corporation, which they grew to a business that earned more than $1 million annually. Each spouse owned a 40% interest while their two children held the remaining shares equally. Prior to trial, the parties agreed that one of them should be awarded the entire 80% interest with the other spouse receiving an equalizing payment of one-half the fair market value of that interest.

Demonstrative exhibit makes impact

At trial, both parties' experts generally used an income-based approach to value the business. The wife's expert valued the business at $12.5 million and $5 million for her 40% share. By contrast, the husband's expert valued the business at $4.56 million and the wife's one-half share at only $720,000. Although the appellate court notes that both experts testified in "great detail" about their calculated values, the opinion fails to specify further.

However, the husband's expert presented a "demonstrative exhibit" to the trial court, which presumed to detail the differences between the two appraisals. Specifically, the exhibit explained that the husband's expert had: 1) tax affected the income stream; 2) performed a regression analysis; 3) concluded a working capital adjustment was not appropriate; 4) measured income based on a "last in, first out" (LIFO) accounting method (as opposed to a "first in, first out" [FIFO] method); 5) applied a minority discount to each party's shares; and 6) applied a 25% discount for lack of marketability.

The trial court awarded the 80% interest in the business to the husband, with an equitable distribution to the wife. The court took a piecemeal approach, using parts of each expert's appraisal, and ultimately valued the business at $6.2 million. Further, it valued the wife's one-half interest at $2.48 million (or 40% of the total value of the corporation).

The trial court explained its determination by reference to the demonstrative exhibit, and: 1) rejected tax affecting the income stream; 2) applied the regression analysis; 3) included a working capital adjustment; 4) utilized a LIFO accounting method; 5) rejected the application of a minority ownership discount; and 6) applied the marketability discount, but at a reduced level of 10%. Among other issues, the wife appealed the application of a marketability discount.

Should DLOMs be precluded in divorce?

The wife argued that a marketability discount should be prohibited as a matter of law in a divorce valuation. She analogized the divorce context to that of an oppressed and/or dissenting shareholder case. Because a court orders judicial "buyout" in those cases (as it does in divorce), and because local (Florida) law does not permit DLOM in the oppression context, the wife argued that the court should not be permitted to apply a marketability discount in this case.

The appellate court found this argument unpersuasive. Dissenting shareholder cases arise in the context of an "involuntary change in the fundamental corporate structure." The appraisal remedy protects minority shareholders who are cashed out of their investment by precluding further reduction of their interests through marketability discounts. This situation is not present in the divorce context:

> The debate is sometimes led astray by the application of broad generalizations that do not differentiate between the types of proceedings within which valuations are required, nor acknowledge that the appropriate analysis for the valuation of a business may change depending upon the specific legal and factual context presented. What is appropriate in the oppressed shareholder or minority appraisal rights cases may not necessarily be desirable in a judicial dissolution of a corporation or in an action for dissolution of marriage involving equitable distribution.

In this case, the wife was not the victim of majority shareholder oppression. She and the husband agreed that they could not run the business together but disputed who should retain it. The closer and more proper analogy, the court reasoned, is to a judicial dissolution of the business based on shareholder deadlock. In these cases, a court has discretion to determine whether a marketability discount is appropriately applied to a closely held corporation.

Accordingly, the Florida Court of Appeals declined to prohibit a DLOM as a matter of law in divorce cases. Finding no abuse of discretion, it affirmed the trial court's application of a 10% marketability discount.

In the Matter of Overbey

Citation: 2007 Wash App. LEXIS 1651
Court: Court of Appeals
State/Jurisdiction: Washington
Date of decision: June 18, 2007
Judge: Dwyer

In this divorce case, the husband owned a one-third interest in a relatively small, closely held insurance benefits brokerage firm in Seattle. A buy-sell agreement provided that upon certain triggering events—including transfer of a member's interest occasioned by divorce, the company would buy back the interest at the greater value of 1) one-and-a-half times the annual commissions of the company, on an accrual basis, or 2) $1.25 million.

Buy-sell value is excessive

The couple jointly retained Neil Beaton (Grant Thornton LLP) to assess the company. He began with the buy-sell agreement, which priced the enterprise at just over $13.7 million. But "such a value, although potentially achievable through the sale of the whole Company," Beaton said, "is well in excess of what current cash flows generated by the Company can support."

In the Matter of Overbey

The market approach yielded a similarly inflated value for the firm of nearly $13.5 million. By contrast, the income approach established a fair value of the company of $3.4 million—which, according to Beaton, was more realistic given the smaller size and revenue streams of the firm. "The reason for the discrepancy lies in the genesis of the revenue multiples" used in determining the firm's value pursuant to the market approach, he said. Further:

Insurance brokerages tend to sell for a multiple of commission revenue between 1.25 and 2.0 times depending on the company. Larger insurance brokerages are willing to pay such multiples since they are able to take advantage of synergies created by their size.

But a smaller, standalone firm would not be able to achieve that magnitude of cost savings or generate the returns necessary to support a higher value.

A sliding value scale

Since there was no indication that the company would be sold, Beaton determined its fair value at $3,403,000 and the husband's 33.34% interest at $1,134,000. He also suggested a "sliding value scale:" If the husband was awarded his interest in the company and if it was sold in the next five years, then the wife would receive a certain percentage of any sales revenue greater than $3.4 million, ranging from 50% of the one-third interest in the first year to 7.5% in the fifth.

The trial court adopted Beaton's conclusions as well as his sliding value scale. The wife appealed, claiming that it should have adopted the opinion of her rebuttal expert, who used the buy-sell formula to value the firm at $22 million. Alternatively, she urged the adoption of Beaton's market approach value.

The Court of Appeals disagreed. The buy-sell agreement was not a binding separation contract. Its formula was relevant but not determinative—and it was never triggered, since there was no transfer of the husband's interest to the wife.

The record also indicated that Beaton was experienced in valuating closely held companies and buy-sell agreements, more so (in the trial court's opinion) than the wife's rebuttal expert. His in-depth analysis applied accepted valuation methodologies. Further, he "articulated reasonable grounds" for valuing the company using the income rather than the market approach and for rejecting the "artificially inflated" value of the buy-sell. Finally, the "reasonableness" of Beaton's conclusion was supported by his sliding value scale, which the trial court adopted to bridge the wide discrepancy in values.

Chapter 7: Court Case Abstracts

Crescent/Mach I Partnership v. Turner

Citation: 2007 Del. Ch. LEXIS 63
Court: Court of Chancery
State/Jurisdiction: Delaware
Date of decision: May 2, 2007
Judge: Noble

In this hybrid breach of fiduciary duty/appraisal action, the Delaware Chancery Court once again demonstrates its preference for the discounted cash flow method. The opinion (by Vice Chancellor Noble) also illustrates the Chancery Court's comfortable sophistication with the financial inputs and projections that frequently form the core of any DCF analysis—including the Court's own.

Merger in a 'stark market reality'

A soft drink packaging and distributing company (Holdings) in Texas held franchises for Dr. Pepper, Seven-Up, and Canada Dry; it also distributed "new age" beverages such as Evian, Perrier, and Snapple. In 1997, Holdings expanded into Southern California, acquiring distribution rights to all but Dr. Pepper. But sales in the soda market were slumping; prices in Texas, especially, were the lowest in the nation. While Coke and Pepsi bottlers benefited from the support of their national sponsors—and the consolidation of supermarket chains, which preferred buying from national distributors—Holdings did not have the same resources.

Meanwhile, a large Midwest franchisor for many of the same beverages (Cadbury) wanted to expand and develop distribution along the lines of Coke and Pepsi. It turned to Holdings for its significant market position in the southwest as well as the established experience and management skill of its CEO (Turner).

By this time, Turner was already concerned about increasing competition and succession plans. No family member was involved in Holdings, and buyers were limited. Coke and Pepsi faced "insurmountable" antitrust hurdles—and Cadbury had already provided greater support to Holdings and was restructuring their franchise relationship. At the same time, Cadbury indicated that it would not consent to an external private equity acquisition. Turner faced a "stark market reality," that Cadbury (and its investment partners) presented the only viable purchaser during "troubled" times in the industry.

Two sets of growth projections

After lengthy bargaining, Turner accepted Cadbury's price of $25 per share; he also agreed to invest $25 million of his own resources in the new enterprise and to stay on as CEO at his former salary, plus stock options. (As a majority shareholder in Holdings, Turner had "powerful" incentives to maximize the share price.) The Holdings board approved the merger in August 1999. A fairness opinion relied on Turner's projections of 3% annual growth over five years to calculate a discounted cash flow value between $19 and $31 per share, while comparable market analyses established values between $20 and $29 per share. Shareholders also received the 3% growth figures among the disclosures.

To raise money for the transaction, however, Holdings' CFO ran a set of projections for investors based on a 4% growth rate. The disparity between these two projections formed the core of the ensuing legal dispute. Several large shareholders dissented to the merger and claimed that Turner had breached his fiduciary duty by deliberately understating projections and "unreasonably denigrating" the company's prospects. Petitioners also perfected appraisal rights for approximately 1 million shares; their expert DCF analysis calculated a fair value of nearly $49 per share.

Turner contended that he sold the company only to realize its greatest value, and his disclosures to fellow shareholders represented his best understanding of the company's prospects, based on his lengthy experience with Holdings and the beverage industry. A DCF analysis by his expert posited fair value at slightly over $25 per share.

Which projections were more accurate?

To complicate this case, there was a third set of projections, prepared by Cadbury and its investment partners (the Acquisition Model.) This projected annual growth rates slightly less than the 4% model; the following summarizes EBITDA growth (in millions of dollars) resulting from each set of projections:

	1999	2000	2001	2002	2003	2004
3% volume growth	90.0	92.7	95.5	98.4	101.3	104.3
4% volume growth	90.0	94.9	100.1	105.7	111.4	117.5
Acquisition model	90.1	95.2	99.6	104.4	109.5	114.1

Typically, the Delaware Chancery Court gives "substantial weight" to projections prepared by management, "especially if the numbers have not been generated with a view toward the merger at issue." But several factors supported Petitioners' claims that Turner "did not believe" in the 3% growth projections.

First, with regard to the Acquisition Model, a footnote alluded to Turner as the source for one year's (1999) data. Second, a Cadbury executive testified that the acquisition projections were reasonable at the time and based on Holdings' (i.e., Turner's) numbers. Finally, the same executive transmitted a post-merger set of EBITDA projections similar to the three above, noting in reference to the second (4% or equity plan) that "JT [Turner]" had supplied the numbers as a basis for his compensation plans.

But a footnote to only one data point (the 1999 numbers) did not create a reasonable inference that all other projections in the Acquisition Model could "attach" to Turner, the Court said. Underlying income statements also showed volume as a series of percentages over the years, each less than 3%--which supported management's view that volume would not increase by more than 3% annually.

The post-merger transmittal was more troubling. Labeling the 4% equity plan as "JT's numbers" could support the argument that Turner believed in the 4% growth projections, adopting them to "sell the deal" to investors while disclosing a different rate to shareholders. His compensations incentives, which were tied to achieving stated levels of growth, could also support his making the 3% projections public.

By contrast, "highly credible" testimony from Cadbury's lead partner suggested that the management plan was not the same as the acquirer's plan, which incorporated the benefits of the merger. Further, according to this witness, Turner did not prepare the more optimistic numbers or solicit investors.

Credibility of the chief executive

Given the ambiguous record, the Court ultimately looked to Turner, who theoretically should have been "the best source of going-forward" projections for Holdings. In this case, however, the 3% growth model was not prepared on the "proverbial clear day," but when Turner was personally committed to the merger. Given these "unusual" circumstances, the case really came down to whether the Court believed the CEO (and to a lesser extent, the lead acquisition partner).

Turner testified that he did not prepare the 4% growth model, which was put together after the agreed-upon $25 merger price (though he admitted that Cadbury and its investor adopted them). On the other hand, his preparation of the 3% projections were based on the highly competitive soft drink market and the company's relatively disadvantaged position, especially compared to national bottlers (Coke and Pepsi), which enjoyed lower costs of capital and stronger ability to drive prices.

The Petitioners' more "robust" projections were not implausible, but in the context of their breach of fiduciary duty claims, the Court ultimately concluded that Turner believed the 3% projections. As he provided them for preparation of the fairness opinion and shareholder disclosures, he'd satisfied his fiduciary duty and these claims were dismissed. Further, as to the appraisal action, the Court found that 3% was a fair and reasonable projection of annual volume increases following the merger, along with an annual 0.4% pricing growth. The remaining assumptions for a DCF analysis, however, came under closer scrutiny.

Experts vary key inputs

Both sides submitted credible, comprehensive expert appraisals that focused primarily on the DCF method and also comparable market analyses. Petitioners' expert Robert Taylor IV, CPA/ABV (Taylor Consulting Group, Inc., Atlanta) had extensive experience in valuing soft drink entities. Respondents (Holdings' successor) retained Kevin Collins (Houlihan Lokey Howard

& Zukin, New York City), who had extensive valuation experience outside of the soft drink industry. Each premised his opinion on different variables, including:

	Petitioners	Respondents
EBITDA growth	5.5%	3%
Annual NOL carryover	$6.125 million	$4.5 million
Outstanding debt	$392.8 million	$402.2 million
Annual CapEx	3% net revenues	$25 million
Tax rate	38.11%	40%
Terminal value	3.5% perpetual annual growth (after projection period)	7.5x EBITDA
Discount rate	9.41%	10%
Depreciation/amortization	3% of revenues/$5.4M	drawn from proxy statement
Valuation conclusion	$48.69 per share	$25.10 per share

Court conducts its own analysis

In its fair value determination, the Chancery Court decided to 1) examine each variable, 2) weigh the facts regarding the company's past performance and future prospects, and 3) consider the methods of each expert in making its ultimate determination of fair value. It reviewed both expert reports by reference to ten critical inputs and assumptions:

1. *Discrete projection period.* The Court confirmed that it "frequently uses" a five-year projection period, which formed the basis for the management projections. Petitioners pointed to an [unnamed] "best practices guides" that recommended seven- to ten-year projection periods; they also offered that some of the DCF variables (CapEx, NOL, depreciation/amortization) would reach a steadier state over a longer period. However, they also admitted the effect would be minimal. More significantly, the Court trusted the company's defense of five-year projections as more reliable in the soft drink industry.

If the five-year period was accepted, then Petitioners wanted the Court to use a growth rate during the perpetuity period that gradually declines to the "steady state perpetual rate" (citing a 2004 Dela. Chancery case). But, "care must be taken to distinguish between the growth modeled rate during the projection period—EBITDA growth—and the growth considered during the perpetuity period—debt free cash flow." Further, unlike the growth rates (sales) projected in the prior case—which differed dramatically from projection period to perpetuity, the debt-free cash-flow growth rate during the projection period trended toward the perpetuity growth rate. Accordingly, the Court adopted a discrete projection period of five years.

2. *EBITDA growth.* The Court had already accepted annual volume growth of 3% and pricing growth of 0.4%.

3. *Tax rate.* Holdings' rapid expansion into California prior to the merger made an historical tax rate inapplicable. In addition, neither expert had properly accounted for unitary taxation in California. While Petitioners' model attempted an accommodation, Respondents' expert admitted lack of tax expertise and no basis to contest the California allocation. Based on reasonable inferences from the experts' range, the Court split the difference and adopted a 39% tax rate projection.

4. *Discount rate.* Both experts calculated the company's weighted average cost of capital (WACC) in a similar way, except Respondents' used a Decile-adjusted beta, while Petitioners' argued that this adjusted the WACC calculation twice for the same company-specific beta. "The selection of an appropriate discount rate has a profound effect on share price," the Court observed, adding that adjustments are "unavoidably subjective." While Respondents' expert concluded a 10% discount rate from a range of 9.5% to 10.5%, Petitioners' offered a discount rate, amended for errors, of 9.41%.

Given the market conditions and capital structure of the company, for which an adjustment of calculated WACC by 0.35 was appropriate, the Court found a range of 9.25% to 10.25% acceptable. It adopted the midpoint ("appropriate" but "not required") for a final discount rate of 9.75%.

5. *Capital expense.* While Petitioners' expert used a dynamic method (3% of net revenues) to measure CapEx, Respondents' used a static measure ($25 million annually). The Court found legal and factual support for both methods—and a rough equivalence between them. Given the "relative brevity of the projection period," it adopted the $25 million annual projection for CapEx.

6. *Net operating losses.* At the time of the merger, Holdings had accumulated NOLs totaling $49.3 million—significant, given their potential value to offset future taxes. Despite some debate, neither expert "had the accounting expertise or the stomach for vigorous engagement." Ultimately the Court adopted the pre-merger projections of the company's accountants, which applied the NOLs at a rate of $6.25 million annually.

7. *Debt.* The experts diverged by $9.4 million, explained by their consideration of three factors (the tax effect of cashed-out options, accrued interest prior to the merger, and rounding-up estimates). The Court accepted Petitioners' rounding estimates and interest rates, but applied its own tax rate (39%) to the cashed-out options for an debt estimate of $400.85 million in its own model.

8. *Depreciation/amortization.* Citing the recent *Delaware MRI Radiology v. Kessler* (2006), the Court restated its traditional emphasis on unbiased (and unchallenged) management estimates. Thus it rejected Petitioners' depreciation/amortization projections and accepted the Respondents'—which had been drawn from the proxy statement soliciting approval of the merger.

9. *Miscellaneous inputs/adjustments.* The Court accepted a $200,000 annual negative change in working capital from Petitioners' analysis and noted that two employee option plans would generate about $1.8 million upon exercise prompted by the merger.

10. *Terminal value.* This was a key factor, "unfortunately" comprising roughly three-fourths of the final valuation under both experts' models. Respondents proposed multiplying EBITDA by 7.5. Petitioners advocated the Gordon Growth model, assuming a 3.5% annual perpetual growth. Finding a lack of reliable industry comparables to establish the multiplier methodology, the Court adopted the Petitioners' model.

Reconciling the claims

After establishing the various inputs to the DCF analysis and the total number of outstanding shares (approximately 10.78 million), the Court established the fair value of the company on the merger date at $32.31 per share. (In an interesting footnote, the Court appears to "check" its conclusion against the market. Before the merger, Holdings stock was trading in the low $30s. "Although the result here is consistent with that market valuation, the Court has not considered the use of trading data" because the company was thinly traded with a sole market maker—who was also one of the Petitioners.)

The Court also defended its fair value conclusion against its finding that there had been no breach of fiduciary duty by the CEO. Turner could have agreed to sell the company for less than its fair value because there was only one buyer in the market (and "how often will the only buyer pay full price?").

The Court's fair value conclusion fell within the range established by the original fairness opinion. It also fell "within the range of reason," given the nature of the statutory appraisal process and the primacy (but also the variability) of a DCF analysis, which depends so much on thorough overview of the inputs and assumptions—and above all on credible, supportable, management projections.

Errors and Omissions in DCF Calculations: A Critique of Delaware's Dr Pepper Appraisal

By Gilbert Matthews, CFA[1]

The recent statutory appraisal of Dr Pepper Bottling Holdings, Inc. (Holdings) by the Delaware Chancery Court in *Crescent/Mach I Partnership v. Turner*[2] raises several conceptual and computational issues concerning discounted cash flow (DCF) valuations in an appraisal context. An analysis of the Court's calculations reveals the caution with which valuation practitioners should apply the DCF method, and the enduring benefit of using comparable market analyses as a reasonableness check.

---

1 Gil Matthews is Chairman of Sutter Securities Incorporated in San Francisco: gil@suttersf.com. He has been an investment banker for more than 40 years, and his practice centers on litigation support, fairness opinions and valuations. The author thanks Mark Lee for his helpful insights.

2 2007 Del. Ch. LEXIS 63 (Del Ch. May 2, 2007). The case abstract appears in this Guide.

Chapter 7: Court Case Abstracts

Unusual case arising from constraints on sale

The cash-out merger that led to this appraisal was unusual because it was arms' length; most statutory appraisal cases stem from freeze-outs of minority shareholders by controlling interests. In the *Crescent/Mach I* case, Jim L. Turner, Holding's controlling shareholder and chief executive, decided to sell the company because he feared "competitive challenges posed primarily by Coke and Pepsi," including "a price war in which Holdings would not have the same support and resources as its nationally-backed competition." In addition, "troubling" economic conditions and external constraints limited the prospects for sale. Cadbury Schweppes PLC (Cadbury), the franchisor for Holdings' primary soft drink brands, "made it clear to Turner that it would not likely consent to a private equity acquisition." Coca Cola and PepsiCo could not acquire Holdings for antitrust reasons. The only bidder was an entity owned by Cadbury and the Carlyle Group, which acquired Holdings in a cash merger at $25 per share on October 1999. Turner sold his shares at the same $25 price, subject to severe restrictions. "Turner obtained the best price that he could from Cadbury/Carlyle," the Vice Chancellor noted, "but how often will the only buyer pay full price?"

Dissenting shareholders sought appraisal[1] under the Delaware statute (8 Del. C. §262), and the Court undertook what it called "an independent valuation exercise."

In determining fair value, the Court may look to the opinions advanced by the parties' experts, select one party's expert opinion as a framework, fashion its own framework or adopt, piecemeal, some portion of an expert's model methodology or mathematical calculations. The Court, however, may not adopt an "either-or" approach and must use its judgment in an independent valuation exercise to reach its conclusion.

At trial, experts for both sides used a comparable company approach as well as a DCF; one expert also utilized comparable transactions. Similarly, the investment bank retained by Holdings to render a fairness opinion relied on all three approaches.

The Court rejected application of the market approach because of Holdings' unique market position and the lack of appropriate guideline comparables. Citing prior Delaware decisions, the Court reiterated its preference for the DCF method and its general opinion that "other methodologies—all based on comparables of one form or another—are of limited value." Adopting certain of the experts' inputs as to projections, discount rates, terminal value, taxes, and debt, the Court arrived at intermediate numbers for other inputs, and accepted the company's projections used by Holdings' expert. It determined a fair value of $32.31 per share, or 29% more than the transaction price (and far less than the dissenting shareholders' expert valuation at $48.69 per-share). The Court's conclusion was "within the range of reason," it said, in part because it fell within the ranges of the original fairness opinion: $19.32 and $31.05 for the DCF analysis, $22.29 and $34.84 for comparable transactions, and $19.75 and $28.53 for comparable

---

[1] Former shareholders also claimed that Turner breached his fiduciary duties, but the Court dismissed these claims.

Errors and Omissions in DCF Calculations: A Critique of Delaware's Dr Pepper Appraisal

companies. The Court further supported its $32.31 fair value determination by stating that Holdings "implicitly concedes that the merger consideration was less than fair value by sponsoring an expert who concluded that the fair value was in excess of the merger price."

However, in fact, the Court's $32.31 valuation is above the high end of two of the three very wide fairness opinion ranges. The Court's DCF-based conclusion was 4% above the high of the DCF range and 32% above its $25.19 midpoint. As to Holdings' implicit concession, its expert testified that the fair value of Holdings based on a DCF was $25.10 per share, only 0.4% above the $25.00 transaction price.

Errors in the Court's valuation

A review of the inputs selected by the Court and Holdings' expert reveals that the differences between them were not sizeable. In particular, the Court used a discount rate of 9.75% (vs. 10% by Holdings' expert), a tax rate of 39% (vs. 40%), and a faster use of operating loss carryforwards ($6.215 million per year vs. $4.5 million). Given these fairly close numbers, one would not expect the Court's valuation to be 29% higher than that of Holdings' expert.

The Court helpfully appended a summary of its calculations to the published decision. A close reading discovered two calculation errors, the first one minor. In calculating the after-tax debt-free cash flow for the 1999 stub period following the transaction date, the Court omitted the portion of pretax income sheltered by the loss carryforward. (It accurately totaled the projected data for years 2000-2004.) Correcting this small miscalculation lowers the Court's per-share value by $0.13

The second error was material. The Court included the post-2004 cash flow benefit of the tax loss carryforward as a line item in the calculation of equity value, reflecting the present value of the carryforwards after the end of the projection period. However, the numerator of the growth model (the 2004 free cash flow number) included the full amount of the pretax income being sheltered by the loss carryforward. Therefore, free cash flow for the perpetuity calculation was overstated by $2,424,850, *i.e.,* 39% (the assumed tax rate) of the annual sheltered income ($6,215,000). The present value of the second error caused the Court's valuation to be $2.40 per share too high.

After adjusting for these two errors, the fair value of the transaction is $30.04 per share, 7.4% below the Court's award of $32.31 per-share.

Conceptual questions left open

Based on a reading of the case, the experts failed to analyze and address certain conceptual issues. As a result, it appears that the Court may have adopted conceptually flawed inputs that may have increased its valuation. Analysts should review these factors for future valuations, where relevant, to aid the trier-of-fact in its independent determination of value under the DCF approach.

Chapter 7: Court Case Abstracts

1. *Effect on Discount rate of a weak competitive position.* The opinion acknowledged that Holdings was in a weak competitive position. Faced with the supermarket industry's consolidation and preference for national bottlers, the company "would encounter substantial market difficulties." Cadbury's support for Holdings was about to decline or end, further impairing Holdings' ability to compete.

In determining its discount rate, the Court looked in part to testimony regarding the volatility of national bottlers (Coca Cola and PepsiCo), which occupied a stronger market position than Holdings'. Given the stronger positions of the national bottlers, it would have been reasonable to adjust Holdings' discount rate upward.

Application of a 10% discount rate rather than 9.75% (and correcting for the two errors, discussed above) would have reduced the Court's calculated value of Holdings from $30.04 to $27.56 per share; a 10.25% discount rate would have further reduced it to $25.27 per share.

2. *Perpetual growth rate.* In calculating terminal value, the Court applied a perpetual growth rate of 3.5% to free cash flow, although it used a 3% EBITDA growth rate for the projection period. Based on the accepted management projections, the growth rate in projected free cash flow from 2000 to 2004 was 3.98%, but this resulted from using flat capital expenditures and increasing depreciation. If depreciation, capital expenditures, and changes in working capital in the projection had been increased by 3.0% annually, free cash flow would have increased at 2.7% per annum.[1] Applying a 3.0% (rather than 3.5%) perpetual growth rate and correcting for the two calculation errors, the Court's valuation of Holdings would have declined from $30.04 to $26.21 per share.

It is rare (except in turnaround situations) to find a long-term growth rate exceeding the anticipated growth rate for the medium-term projection period. Competitive factors, changes in consumer preferences, and obsolescence should normally cause the long-term growth rate to be lower than the medium-term rate.

3. *Capital expenditures and depreciation.* The Court adopted management's projection that capital expenditures would be $25 million each year of the projection period and that depreciation would increase each year. Although increasing revenues normally require increasing capital expenditures, the Court's (and management's) assumption that capital expenditures would not grow was not supported by a schedule of future capital expenditures. The assumption of flat capital expenditures is clearly inconsistent with management's projection that depreciation would increase each year, since it is almost impossible for depreciation to increase unless capital expenditures increase.[2]

In a perpetuity model (such as the Gordon Growth Model that the Court used), capital expenditures must be materially higher than depreciation because, in an inflationary economy, new capital expenditures must reflect increasing capital asset costs, while depreciation must reflect the amortization

---

[1] Free cash flow would increase at a slower rate than EBITDA because amortization and the loss carryforward were projected to be constant.
[2] Theoretically, depreciation might increase when capital expenditures are flat if a substantial portion of capital expenditures are for shorter-life assets than prior capital expenditures had been, *e.g.*, buying trucks instead of building plants.

Errors and Omissions in DCF Calculations: A Critique of Delaware's Dr Pepper Appraisal

of lower historical capital asset costs.[1] In a perpetuity model with a 3% growth rate and assuming a 10-year average life for fixed assets, capital expenditures would exceed depreciation by 15.5% using straight line depreciation and 11.6% using the double-declining method.[2] The Court's opinion gave no indication that the experts considered the appropriate relationship between capital expenditures and depreciation, which is a common error of omission in DCF analyses.

If capital expenditures and depreciation were both projected to increase at 3% per year after the first full year of the projection period (using the Court's 9.75% discount rate and correcting for the two errors), the calculated value of Holdings would drop from $30.04 to $27.20 per share. Combining this adjustment with a 3% perpetual growth, the calculated value of Holdings would have fallen to $23.56, less than the $25.00 transaction price.

In evaluating any projections, the practitioner should consider both the reasoning behind the projected capital expenditures and the relationship between capital expenditures and depreciation. When possible, management should explain its assumptions. It should always be able to calculate depreciation accurately based on historical and projected capital expenditures. When trial experts later examine management projections, they should consider making appropriate adjustments if the assumptions are questionable, and be prepared to support any revisions in court.

4. *Amortization has a limited life.* The Court's valuation model included $5.4 million of annual tax-deductible amortization as a non-cash charge. Amortization necessarily has a limited life, but the Court, by including it in the free cash flow in the growth model, effectively assumed that it was perpetual, thereby understating taxes and overstating value. (Without knowing how long the amortization was scheduled to continue, the overstatement cannot be quantified.) Moreover, applying a growth rate to free cash flow erroneously assumes that amortization will grow at the same growth rate, thereby further overstating terminal value.

In fact, amortization in a projection should normally be a constant or declining number.[3] The appropriate manner to value amortization subsequent to the projection period is to exclude it from the growth model calculation, and, instead, to determine the present value of the scheduled amortization over its life.

Since the Court did not explain the amortization's specific application or its scheduled life, it is not possible to quantify its impact on the valuation. However, assuming that the amortization continued for five years beyond the end of the projection periods, the calculated value of Holdings (corrected for the two errors discussed above) would be reduced from $30.04 to $28.44 per share.

---

1 *See* M. Mark Lee, "The Ratio of Depreciation and Capital Expenditures in DCF Terminal Values," *Financial Valuation and Litigation Expert*, August-September 2007, pp. 7-8. *See also*, Daniel L McConaughy and Lorena Bordi, "The Long Term Relationships between Capital Expenditures and Depreciation Across Industries: Important Data for Capitalized Income Based Valuations," *Business Valuation Review*, March 2004, pp. 14-24.

2 Gilbert E. Matthews, "Fairness Opinions: Common Errors and Omissions," in *The Handbook of Business Valuation and Intellectual Property Analysis*, R. Reilly and R. Schweihs, eds. (McGraw Hill, 2004), pp.223-4.

3 Amortization could increase during the projection period where the forecast assumed future events, such as acquisitions, that will lead to additional amortization.

Chapter 7: Court Case Abstracts

Caution when using DCF

This discussion demonstrates that practitioners must use caution in valuing a business based on discounted cash flow. A DCF analysis assumes the validity of the financial projections. However, any projection depends on the reasonableness of the underlying inputs, such as growth rate, profit margins, and capital expenditures. A DCF valuation is highly dependent on terminal value, which is a direct function of the final year of a projection; the final year is clearly more difficult to forecast than the near future. The selection of a discount rate is also subjective, particularly for smaller, less diversified companies.

Discounted cash flow is a valuable tool, but small changes in the inputs can materially affect the valuation conclusion. As this critique shows, with all other inputs in the case held constant, adjusting the perpetual growth rate assumption from 3.5% to 3.0% reduces the calculated value by 13%, and adjusting the discount rate from 9.75% to 10.25% reduces the calculated value by 16%. The subjectivity of many DCF inputs frequently makes the approach unreliable, producing a wide range of calculated results and rendering any mathematical precision illusory.

When analysts employ different approaches that lead to materially different conclusions, they should examine the inputs to determine the causes of the discrepancy. Alternative valuation methods serve as helpful "reality checks" to confirm whether a specific conclusion is reasonable. An examination of the implied multiples of data points in the final year of the underlying projection should help to establish whether a DCF valuation is reasonable. In valuing Holdings, it appears that the Vice Chancellor did not use the EBITDA multiple inherent in his DCF valuation as a reasonableness check. He called the dissenters' expert's valuation of Holdings at 8.9x EBITDA "somewhat high" because the comparable companies had "an implicit value premium stemming from the liquidity advantage of a closer relationship with their 'parent' companies." However, based on EBITDA in the final year of the projection, the EBITDA multiple was 8.6x, not far from the 8.9x that the Court rejected. If the Court's calculation is corrected for the two errors and if a 3% perpetual growth is applied, then the EBITDA multiple would be 7.6x.

In its seminal *Weinberger* decision, the Delaware Supreme Court held that "the methodology to be used for measuring fair value should be generally accepted techniques used in the financial community."[1] A review of the summaries of investment bankers' fairness opinions in proxy statements shows that an overwhelming majority of public company transactions rely on comparable companies and comparable transactions analyses. In recent years, several Delaware Chancery Court decisions have used DCF as the sole analytical measure of value. Sound practice, however, calls for using more than one method. Experts and courts should consider the widely used comparable company and comparable transaction methods whenever possible. Expert witnesses should be prepared to explain the basis for their selection of comparables and the adjustments that they consider appropriate and necessary in applying the comparables' multiples to the

---

1 Lawrence A. Hamermesh & Michael L. Wachter, *The Fair Value of Cornfields in Delaware Appraisal Law*, 31 Iowa J. Corp. L. 119, 123-4 (2005), citing *Weinberger v. UOP, Inc.*, 457 A.2d 701, 712 (Del. 1983).

subject company. A well-reasoned and appropriately adjusted comparables analysis should be helpful to a court both as a basic valuation approach and as a crosscheck on DCF calculations.

Highfields Capital, Ltd. v. AXA Financial, Inc.

Citation: 2007 Del. Ch. LEXIS 126
Court: Court of Chancery
State/Jurisdiction: Delaware
Date of decision: August 17, 2007
Judge: Lamb

This is yet another judicial appraisal action where the Delaware Chancery Court is less than satisfied with the widely disparate valuations offered by the litigants, and exercises its "independent business judgment" in crafting the final calculations, albeit relying on the more credible of the two expert reports. The Court also departs from its typical preference for the discounted cash flow (DCF) method where the merger price rose from an arm's-length transaction and industry standards favor a different analysis.

MONY ripe for merger

To remain competitive amidst the consolidation of the insurance industry in the 1990s, the Mutual of New York life insurance company "demutualized," and in 1998, its successor, the MONY Group, Inc. (MONY) completed a public offering at $23.50 per share. Despite substantial efforts to diversify, MONY's earnings and return on equity lagged significantly behind those of its peers. Considerable pressure from insurance ratings agencies further depressed its earnings, capital, and liquidity, eventually leading to a ratings downgrade in late 2002. MONY management instituted a long-range cost-cutting and restructuring plan and obtained a third-party actuarial appraisal to assist these efforts and help attract a merger partner or sale.

By this time, the industry and investment communities "all understood that MONY's days as a stand-alone were numbered," especially since New York insurance regulations requiring state approval for acquisitions in the company greater than 5% were due to expire. For the year 2002 to 2003, only one potential buyer, AXA Financial, Inc. (AXA) approached MONY. After lengthy negotiations, it offered $31.00 per share, a 7.3% premium over MONY's then-trading price. Several institutional investors criticized the price as too low, but others compared MONY's 2% return on equity to the industry average of 12% and found the price fair. Management feared the company faced a "meltdown" absent the transaction, and after consulting its legal and financial advisors, the Board approved and announced the merger in September 2003.

One of the institutional investors, Highfields Capital, Ltd. and its affiliates (Highfields)—which held 4.3% of MONY common stock—tried to enjoin the merger. It submitted a letter urging the Del. Chancery to abridge the vote of MONY stockholders who held "long" positions in the securities underwriting the transaction. What Highfields neglected to reveal was its own substantial "short" position on the securities, on which it stood to make $11 million should the merger fail.

The Court declined to grant the injunction, finding that MONY Board's acted in good faith. But the growing uncertainty caused MONY to suffer another ratings downgrade in February 2004. No other buyer came forward, and the stockholders finally approved the merger by 51%. After it closed in July 2004, Highfields was the only major stockholder to perfect its appraisal rights in the Delaware Chancery Court.

Highfields disputes merger price

The familiar "fair value" premise in judicial appraisal actions comprises a company's stand-alone value, excluding any shared synergies with a potential acquirer. If the subject transaction resulted from arm's-length bargaining between independent parties, "and if no structural impediments existed that might materially distort the crucible of objective market reality," the Court explained, then the merger price carries substantial weight as an indicator of fair value.

Under this standard, Highfields asserted that the $31 merger price was an unreliable indicator of MONY's fair value. It offered a financial expert who opined that factors such as management's financial incentives and its failure to open the auction to all bidders in the beginning "distorted the sale process in AXA's favor." But its case-in-chief consisted of valuation testimony from a finance professor who applied four different approaches to appraising MONY and the merger price:

1. *DCF.* In his DCF analysis, the expert relied on August 2003 management projections, believing these to better indicate standalone value than February 2004 projections, which followed the ratings downgrade. He used GAAP earnings to generate free cash flows; a 5% terminal growth rate, derived from an institutional investor database; and a 8.9% discount rate from CAPM to reach a $39.18 per-share value. He gave a 50% weight to this DCF value in his overall analysis.

2. *Comparable company analysis.* Thirteen comparable companies emerged from the expert's review of the S&P Life and Health Insurance (L&H) Index and also a list identified by MONY's investment advisor. Using a price-to-book multiple, which was more typical for the insurance industry than a price-to-earnings multiple, he derived a 0.89 multiple for MONY from the lower quartile of guideline companies. After applying a 30.1% minority discount, derived from transactions data, he arrived at a $46.69 value, weighted 30% overall.

3. *Comparable transactions analysis.* The expert found seven transactions in the life insurance industry from 1999 to 2004 where at least 51% of the target was acquired for more than $200 million. Based on price-to-book value, he assigned MONY a 1.37 multiple in the lower quartile of the data. After removing a 14.5% synergy premium from the MONY merger, he arrived at a $47.15 per-share value, weighted 20% overall.

4. *Market price analysis.* The Highfields' expert examined how the market would have priced MONY stock had the merger price not effectively acted as a cap. He took MONY's stock price a month prior to the merger ($28.20), adjusted for a minority discount, and multiplied by MONY's expected 15.1% return rate (derived from the L&H index's 21.7% appreciation during the same time and using a beta of 0.69). This resulted in a $42.22, control-basis, "expected unaffected price" as of the merger date. The expert also conducted an event study/volume analysis on MONY stock at the time of the merger announcement and found no statistically relevant fluctuations in price or volume.

Shared synergies and actuarial analysis

AXA enlisted expert testimony from the managing director of a boutique investment bank that focused exclusively on the financial services industry. He used five metrics to value MONY:

1. *Shared synergies.* The merger price ($31.00 per share) minus the synergies that AXA would develop from the transaction ($7.75 per share) was the best indicator of the company's going concern value, or $23.75 per share. No material impediments existed to a competing bid, the expert said, and materials from the Board's valuation process supported the analysis, including the February 2004 (post-downgrade) projections. The company was already at the bottom or the industry, and any further downgrade would significantly depress the only area in which MONY was still achieving sales. The expert ascribed an overall weight of 50% to this analysis.

2. *Sum of the parts.* Because MONY consisted of three segments (insurance, brokerage, and asset management), the next best method was an actuarial, sum-of-the-parts analysis. The insurance business also consisted of three components: i) net asset value, which the expert derived from MONY's statutory (as opposed to GAAP) earnings; and ii) in-force and iii) future business values, derived from projections that AXA used to develop its bid. For the brokerage business, the expert used a comparable companies analysis but not a DCF, due to lack of reliable projections; he did use a weighted average of both approaches to value the asset management business. Overall, he concluded a $17.68 per share value using the actuarial approach, weighted 35%.

3. *Comparable companies.* The expert selected publicly traded life insurance companies with market capitalization between $500 million and $5 billion, and then analyzed each firm's price-to-book, and price-to-estimated-earnings for both 2004 and 2005. Statistically, MONY was the "worst-performing and most troubled company" of its peer group, he found. After eliminating a 16.1% implied minority discount, he arrived at a $19.98 per-share value, weighting it only 7.5%.

4. *Comparable transactions.* After selecting six acquisitions of insurance companies between 2001 and mid-2004, the expert assigned a 10% weight to all but one—a sale of Safeco, a life insurance company that struggled with low returns, was operationally similar to MONY, and was sold three months before the AXA-MONY merger. Safeco's sale price was slightly less than MONY's, but after applying a 16.1% "synergies" discount, the expert weighted the transaction 50%. In his overall transactions analysis, he ultimately derived a $18.83 per-share value, giving it a 5% weight.

5. *DCF.* AXA's expert characterized his 10% discount rate as "aggressive," benchmarked against discount rates used in proxy statements for financial transactions between 1999 and 2004. He also criticized the use of GAAP earnings in Highfields' expert's DCF analysis, and used data that MONY prepared to meet statutory accounting requirements. His DCF value was $21.38 per-share, with a 2.5% weight overall.

Experts 'two ships passing in the night'

The parties' divergent valuations struck the Court as "two ships passing in the night," with each party showing equal "tedium in attacking (often with good cause) every assumption used or conclusion reached by the other party's expert." Generally, the Court found the metrics used by AXA's expert—in particular the shared synergies and actuarial analyses—to be more credible.

Strikingly, despite the industry standard of using a sum-of-the-parts appraisal methodology to value an insurance conglomerate as a going concern, and despite the reliance this court typically places on the merger price in an appraisal proceeding that arises from an arm's length transaction, [Highfields' expert] provided no testimony about MONY's value pursuant to these important models. [His] valuation not only suffers because of these analytical gaps, it is also markedly disparate from market price data for MONY's stock and other independent indicia of value.

For the same reasons, the Court also discredited the reliance Highfields' expert placed on his DCF analysis. For an insurance company, subject to statutory limits on distributions, GAAP earnings were not the appropriate basis by which to project free cash flows. The expert also used a constant growth rate beginning in 2005 without presenting any evidence that the company would be able to stabilize its future earnings. By relying on the August 2003 (pre-downgrade) projections, he "completely ignore[d] the fundamental nature" of MONY's situation. "Indeed, [his] DCF becomes nothing more than an extension of 2005 financial projections in which MONY's calculated terminal value represents almost 100% of [the expert's] total estimated value of the company."

By contrast, AXA's expert did not rely on outdated projections, and he used estimated statutory earnings as a cash flow proxy. More he importantly, as an analyst in the financial services sector, more importantly recognized that the insurance industry does not consider a DCF an important or useful framework, assigning it a mere 2.5% weight in his overall analysis. The Court agreed, noting that in this case, it would not use a pure DCF methodology in determining MONY's value.

Guideline public company methods suffer

Likewise, the Court did not give much weight to the guideline public companies analysis in this case. The companies selected by Highfields' expert were not sufficiently comparable to MONY. Further, the expert placed MONY at the median of the bottom quartile and assigned it a multiple of 0.89x using a price-to-book value metric. This represented a 27% discount from his comparable company medium and a 33% discount from the mean, more evidence that his analysis was "overly biased and subjective." Finally, his calculation of a 30.1% control premium was "questionable" because he relied on a pool of dissimilar transactions and ignored the synergies that financial buyers could enjoy from their acquisitions.

By contrast, AXA's expert conceded the lack of comparability between MONY and publicly traded life insurance companies, assigning this method a minor (7.5%) weight. But his analysis suffered similar flaws; i.e., using a price-to-book multiple that was a substantial discount (40%) from both the median and the mean. He also relied heavily on price-to-estimated earnings multiples when he testified that neither the market nor the insurance industry would typically value MONY on an earnings basis.

In light of the shortcomings of both experts, the Court rejected the comparable companies analysis, as it did the comparable transactions. The Highfields' expert used aged transactions, the majority five years removed from the AXA-MONY merger. He relied on non-comparable transactions while excluding the one real comparable—the Safeco sale. In post-trial briefing, Highfields tried belatedly to include Safeco in the expert's transaction analysis, but the Court found the effort "procedurally inappropriate," casting "great doubt" on the expert's objectivity.

AXA's expert didn't fare much better. In his transactions analysis, he relied on an implied price-to-earnings multiple of 12.5x, which resulted in a $4.50 per share value. The Court found "no conceivable basis" to assign any weight to such an "outlying value of MONY," yet the expert weighted it 30%. Further, he failed to adjust the price-to-book metric for each selected company's unrealized capital gains and losses, per SFAS 115.

The expert assigned a 0.53x price-to-book value multiple for the Safeco transaction, for example, but conceded that with SFAS 115 adjustments, the multiple would be 0.73x. The adjusted values were not publicly available for half of his selected transactions, and the expert's analysis could not recover from this "irreparable structural malady."

Market and merger price analyses

"Overwhelming evidence" showed that the market was well aware of MONY's merger prospects for a long time, including the date of the announcement (September 2003), when most likely the market price already reflected a merger speculation premium. Thus, the event and volume studies by Highfields' expert were not particularly meaningful when such an imbedded condition exists.

Moreover, his assumption that MONY's stock price would move in direct proportion to the L&H index was highly speculative, as MONY historically underperformed the index, and three of the seven companies on the list weren't comparable. AXA's expert criticized the indexing as "unprecedented" in the financial community, and the Court agreed, citing cases in which it had "considered, and rejected, the explanatory power of a similar model." Finally, the Highfields' expert incorrectly assumed that the merger price acted as a ceiling on MONY's stock value, when in reality, it served as a floor. "If the going-concern value of MONY was somehow depressed by AXA's bid during a time of highly favorite market conditions, the emergence of a topping bid would be all the more probable," including one by Highfields.

Further, the AXA-MONY merger negotiations were "clearly" arm's-length; no MONY officer or director participated in the buy-side, and none continued employment at the company after the merger closed. The three directors who would receive any change-in-control payments recused themselves from the merger vote. Given these facts, the reason why the merger proceeded was self-evident: No other strategic or financial buyer stood to gain the synergies that AXA anticipated in acquiring MONY at $31 per share.

To determine the amount of shared synergies imbedded in the price, the Court first looked to the evidence offered by AXA's expert. But contrary to his own testimony, he largely relied on a DCF analysis to conclude that shared synergies constituted 25%—or $7.75—of the merger price. The Court found the assumptions in his "sum of the parts" analysis more credible, which drew from the independent actuarial valuation performed at the merger announcement and viewed shared synergies at $9.54 per share. But AXA's actuarial analysis at the merger closing revealed a loss of $5.42 per share in synergies. The Court deducted the difference of $4.12 and found that $26.88 was the fair value merger price, according this analysis a 75% weight.

AXA's "sum of the parts" analysis also proved reliable, especially with respect to MONY's life insurance and asset-management businesses. Its expert erred by not placing forward-looking earnings metrics in his valuation of the broker-dealer business, and the Court removed these outliers. Overall, it concluded a $19.22 per-share value under the actuarial analysis, to which it assigned a 25% weight.

Given this comprehensive overview, the Court's conclusions and their respective weightings, it appraised the fair value of MONY at the time of the merger at $24.97 per share.

Kim v. The Grover C. Coors Trust

Citation: 2007 Colo. App. LEXIS 394
Court: Court of Appeals
State/Jurisdiction: Colorado
Date of decision: March 8, 2007

This Colorado Court of Appeals case is a good reminder that standard of value should be among the first, if not foremost, point of discussion between analysts and attorneys after initiating a valuation engagement.

Shareholder alleges unfair transaction

In 1999-2000, a packaging company owed $525 million for a prior acquisition of assets; it intended to fund the short-term debt through the sale of a paperboard mill—but the deal fell through, and the company needed a quick cash infusion. The company decided to sell 1 million shares of convertible preferred stock for $100 million to a trust for which at least two of the company's directors, members of the Coors family, served as trustees.

The company formed a special committee of independent directors to evaluate the transaction. The committee obtained a fairness opinion from an investment bank, indicating the stock sale was financially fair; and after several meetings, approved the sale. A minority shareholder sued the directors, among others, for breach of their fiduciary duty for approving and executing the deal.

Fairness has a broad, fact-based definition

The gist of the complaint alleged that members of the Coors family, sitting on both sides of the transaction, manipulated it sufficiently to dilute value and voting rights of the minority shareholders. According to local law and statute—Colorado's version of the Model Business Corporation Act (MBCA), the burden of proof was on the directors to show the "transaction is fair to the corporation." And because the Colorado MBCA is so close to the original (as is true in many states), the Court looked to the Act's official comments for further definition of "fair," finding these gave it a "special, flexible meaning and wide embrace."

Thus, as many state courts have also concluded, the Colorado court found that the fairness of the transaction turned on its facts and circumstances; in particular, whether there had been earmarks of an arms-length transaction, including the company receiving "full value." The Court also looked to the law of other state jurisdictions for guidance and support; the plaintiff/shareholder urged the adoption of Delaware's "entire fairness" test, which focuses on process and price, but the Court found no "functional difference" between that test and the local state law approach, which requires reviewing the transaction "as a whole."

Best price at best value includes discounts

The shareholder first argued the transaction price was unfair, but failed to provide evidence that a better price was available. By contrast, the company presented testimony that there was no public market for the convertible preferred stock and no third party buyer; and even if there were, that the purchaser wouldn't have offered any better terms. Likewise, the shareholder lost the arguments that the transaction lacked sufficient disclosure, independence, good faith, or price concessions.

As to the fairness of the transaction's value, the shareholder claimed the Coors expert incorrectly valued the company's controlling stock based on the non-controlling stock by applying a discount. The shareholder cited a Colorado case that minority discounts are improper in "dissenters' rights actions" except in extraordinary circumstances, because the MBCA's "fair value" provisions governing dissenters' right actions, as currently amended, preclude the application of marketability or minority discounts.

"However, this case is not a dissenters' rights action," the Court said. "It involves the question of whether a transaction was fair, not the 'fair value' of dissenters' shares." It was therefore proper, as a Coors expert testified, to discount the stock value by 15%-20% for lack of marketability, which made the $100 million price fair. The same expert "denied that he discounted the price for control because Coors already had control of the company," and this testimony was also accepted.

In further objections, the shareholder claimed the company's experts' value determinations used numerous faulty assumptions, including hindsight as opposed to historical data; an unsupported 19% cost of debt; a hypothetical cost of capital; and an inflated anticipated rate of return. But without additional explanation of the record or the underlying reports, the Court deferred to the determinations of the trial court, which had given greater weight and credibility to the company's valuation conclusions, including application of the marketability discount.

Marsh v. Billington Farms, LLC

Citation: 2007 R.I. Super. LEXIS 105
Court: Superior Court
State/Jurisdiction: Rhode Island
Date of decision: August 2, 2007

Two married couples were each in the real estate development business; one owned a company that built residential homes while the other was a contractor that built roads for subdivisions. Together, the couples purchased a large tract of land, subdivided it, and formed a limited liability company (LLC) to construct and sell homes on the unimproved lots, with each couple taking a 50% interest in the LLC. Each couple's business also contracted with the LLC to provide its respective services—one to construct the homes and the other to build the roads.

It sounds like a perfect match—but the contracts did not anticipate the problems. For example, the road-builder's contract fixed payment at $1.24 million, which failed to cover $655,000 in out-of-pocket costs and payment for additional site-preparation. The home-builder's contract provided a total price "to be agreed upon," but the parties couldn't agree, and the disputes eventually broke up the partnership. The home-builders sought judicial dissolution and then later agreed, pursuant to the applicable buyout statute, to sell their 50% interest to the road-builders at "fair value."

A viable project or a pipe dream?

To reach a fair value of the entire LLC, both parties relied on appraisals by qualified valuation experts. The home-builders' expert relied on an income approach, noting that by the time of dissolution proceedings (also the valuation date) the LLC had built and sold four high-end homes, had two more under contract, and four others under construction, leaving seventeen unimproved lots. The LLC was a "viable entity" for finishing the project and realizing the expected cash flows, the home-builder's expert said. The subdivision "wasn't just a pipe dream."

To analyze the expected cash flows, he projected sales prices less the LLC's historic building costs, increased by a fixed percentage over time. Using two different discount rates, the expert valued the LLC at either $5.8 million or $7.3 million, and the home-builders asked the Court to determine the more appropriate rate.

But the road-builders criticized the approach for relying on historic costs. Any future buyer would have to make alternate arrangements to finish the development at market rates, and deriving these market costs in an income approach would be a "very speculative enterprise."

Thus the road-builders argued for a net asset approach. The LLC's only assets were cash and real estate; there were no employees and no means for completing the project other than the owners' efforts. Their expert relied on a real estate appraisal of the remaining unsold and mostly unimproved lots at $2.6 million. After accounting for cash on hand, loans due, and unliquidated liabilities, he concluded the LLC was worth $1.765 million, a 50% share at $882,750.

Problems with both expert values

The Court agreed that an asset-based valuation was appropriate. The LLC was not a "mass assemblage" of assets—including intangibles such as employee and contractual relationships and goodwill—which usually characterize a going concern. Instead, a potential buyer would be purchasing primarily the real estate assets. "To replicate a market-based sale of the LLC, therefore, it is sensible to derive [its price] from the value of unimproved lots, even if the LLC had planned to develop them."

But while conceptually sound, the inputs that went into the road-builder's asset valuation were problematic, including: (1) using comparable sales too distant from the valuation date; (2) assuming three years for a buyer of the LLC to sell the unimproved lots; and (3) applying a 10% annual appreciation for the lots but discounting future cash flows by 12%. Plus, the expert deducted a 15% "entrepreneurial profit" expense to account for a buyer taking on the costs and risks of real estate development.

The home-builders offered a rebuttal expert, who countered with (1) comparable sales within months of the valuation date; (2) an assumption that the LLC could sell off groups of five to six lots within six months; and (3) a 10% "bulk" discount on the sales plus commissions. He included no "entrepreneurial profit" expense because the LLC had already incurred most of the costs and risks associated with the development. The rebuttal points were sound, the Court said. No seller would offer the real estate at the road-builder's heavily discounted value unless under some compulsion to sell. After substituting the rebuttal real estate appraisal ($4.865 million) into the "otherwise sound" asset valuation and subtracting unliquidated liabilities, the Court valued the LLC at $3.83 million and a 50% share at approximately $1.92 million—or approximately the midpoint between the lower income approach value and the net asset value.

Northwest Investment Corp. v. Wallace

Citation: 2007 Iowa Sup. LEXIS 87
Court: Supreme Court
State/Jurisdiction: Iowa
Date of decision: July 13, 2007

As of now, seven states have adopted the 1999 amendments to the Model Business Corporation Act (MCBA)—specifically, its provisions disallowing consideration of minority and marketability discounts in fair value assessments (Connecticut, Idaho, Iowa, Maine, Mississippi, Virginia and West Virginia; Florida has adopted a variation). But none of these state courts had considered whether the new fair value definition mandates appraising the corporate shares on a marketable, control basis—until this Iowa case.

'It's all about control'

In 2003 a bank holding company effectively "squeezed out" three minority shareholders in a reverse stock split. Based on an expert fair value appraisal, the bank's directors paid the minority owners $33.23 per share for their respective interests and provided notice of their statutory appraisal rights.

The minority shareholders rejected the payment and, based on their expert appraisal, demanded $64 per share. The bank refused, and filed an appraisal action in Iowa district court. This time, it submitted a second appraisal, which posited a fair value of $48 per share. The bank paid the difference to the minority owners, plus interest. The minority shareholders turned this down and went to trial.

A case of 'dueling appraisals'

In its second appraisal, the bank's expert relied primarily on an income approach, capitalization of earnings method, giving it a 90% weight. He also used the guideline-company method, deriving an estimated price-to-book multiple from public comparables, applying it to the bank's adjusted book value and adding a 15% control premium (necessary because the public stock prices reflected minority interests). Weighting this approach 10%, he then "rolled up" the combined values through the holding company and its various interests and assets, concluding a fair value of the bank's shares at $48.

The expert for the minority shareholders used a combination of discounted cash flow (DCF) and market approach. For the latter, he considered guideline sales of publicly traded stock and sales of controlling interests in financial companies, creating for each a price-to-tangible book value ratio and a price-to-earnings multiple, for a total of four values. He added a 40% control premium to the DCF value and the two valuations based on publicly traded stock transactions. (Sales of controlling interest in financial institutions already accounted for the premium.) Averaging the five values, which ranged from approximately $61 per share to $73, he determined the fair value of the bank's stock at $64 per share.

Prior inconsistent valuations

One serious evidentiary problem with the bank's appraisal: It was "significantly lower" than recent appraisals done for the bank's employee stock option plan and its own reverse stock split. The district court found these multiple inconsistent appraisals of substantially the same assets "difficult if not impossible to reconcile." Second, the court also could find no rational basis for the different weights accorded the valuation methods, and it simply disagreed with the bank's position that a "well-run, high-performing business....should either have no or very little control premium added to determine fair value."

The district court adopted the "more credible" fair value appraisal by the minority shareholders' expert, including his addition of a control premium. On appeal, in reviewing the applicability of a control premium, the Iowa Supreme Court looked to the official drafters' comments to the 1999 MCBA amendments; in particular, their explanation for precluding minority and marketability discounts from a fair value appraisal. Their intent:

> ...to adopt a more modern view that appraisal should generally award a shareholder his or her proportional interest in the corporation after valuing the corporation as a whole, rather than the value of the shareholder's shares when valued alone (Court's emphasis).

"If an appraiser is valuing the corporation as a whole," the Court added, "then a control premium is certainly proper" (citing *Valuing a Business: The Analysis and Appraisal of Closely Held Companies*, 4th ed., by "leading authority" Shannon Pratt). Further, by disallowing discounts for lack of marketability and control, the legislature "implicitly required shares to be valued on a marketable, control interest basis." A control premium, if supported by the evidence, is therefore appropriate.

A note on synergy

Lastly, the bank argued that the control premium was "inflated with synergistic value because the market data, upon which [it] is based, included corporate mergers." The bank's fair value should be determined on a standalone basis rather than in a possible merger.

The minority shareholders did not present evidence that a merger was in the bank's future or that its value should be based on anything but a going concern, standalone basis. "Nevertheless, there is nothing wrong with [the dissenters' expert] basing his opinion, in part, on the aggregations of actual sales data involving mergers and acquisitions," as this evidence reflected the market place. While the expert conceded that synergistic value was likely embedded in the data, comparable sales transactions are still "the best empirical evidence generally available to quantify a control premium," the Court said, once again citing Pratt for proposition—and the reminder that analysts should be simply be aware of synergies included in the underlying data and adjust accordingly.

Chapter 7: Court Case Abstracts

Based on the available data, the minority shareholders' expert determined control premiums ranging from 36% to 52% for companies comparable to the bank. His "conservative approach" also attempted to remove any marketplace distortions. "Although we cannot be certain what effect, if any, synergistic value had on [the expert's] calculations," the Court concluded, "it is more appropriate to accept [his] control premium in order to eliminate the [prohibited] minority discount ... than to make no adjustment at all."

Trietsch v. Circle Design Group

Citation: 2007 Ind. App. LEXIS 1306
Court: Court of Appeals
State/Jurisdiction: Indiana
Date of decision: June 19, 2007

The directors of a small, closely held company sent a notice to shareholders about meeting to discuss a proposed sale—but neglected to provide the statutorily required information regarding their dissenters' rights.

Prior to the meeting, the company offered to buy a minority owner's 21.2% interest for $118,000 over ten years. This represented the "fair value" of the shares based on a "limited valuation report" by the company's accountants and financial advisors. The shareholder rejected the offer. At the meeting, he also voted against the sale of the company, which the remaining shareholders approved. Payment was by a $346,000 note.

Attorneys wrangle but no counter-appraisal

The parties (and their attorneys) spent the next few months negotiating discovery issues; the company provided various documents, including profit and loss statements, balance sheets, and tax reports—but refused to turn over the directors' personal financial information. The company also sent another $118,000 note to the minority shareholder for his shares. This time it requested, pursuant to statute, that he send a written estimate of the fair value of the stock, should he refuse payment.

The shareholder rejected the offer and filed suit against the company and its directors for damages, failure to follow proper statutory procedure, and conversion. Apparently, he made no claim for a statutory appraisal action and did not submit (at any time during the proceeding) an alternate fair value appraisal of his interest.

A month later, the company called another shareholders meeting to ratify the prior sale, this time attaching appropriate notice of dissenters' rights. The plaintiff/shareholder voted against the sale and once again sent a written demand to the company for payment of his interest. The company responded with notice of his dissenters' rights, a copy of the statute, and a notice that his written demand for alternative fair value appraisal was due in thirty days. It also enclosed a check in the full amount of $118,000.

The plaintiff accepted the check but expressly reserved his rights to pursue the value of his shares, less the $118,000. He also wrote that it was "impossible" for him or his expert to arrive at an estimate of fair value without more detailed financial data from the company and its directors.

Dissenters' statute limits damages

Nearly a year after the original sale, the company moved for summary judgment, arguing that the plaintiff failed to provide his written estimate of fair value, as required by the dissenters' rights statute. The statute also limited his recovery to a judicial appraisal. Lastly, his conversion claims should fail, because the sale was not an exercise of unauthorized control over the plaintiff's assets.

The trial court agreed on all points and granted summary judgment. The minority shareholder appealed, drawing attention to the company's failure to provide dissenters' rights information with its notice of the shareholders' meeting and proposed sale.

The appellate court examined the statute's requirements and case law, and confirmed that a dissenting shareholder is limited to the statutory remedies. The company's initial failure to provide notice of dissenters' rights was harmless, as the plaintiff was aware of the impending sale and voted against it at the first meeting. The company also provided all statutorily required discovery.

Company's fair value included discounts

The company had provided its fair value appraisal—and paid for the shares. Once the company complied with its statutory duties, it was the plaintiff's burden to make a written demand of his fair value estimate—which he failed to do. Plaintiff was thus limited to the company's appraisal of his shares at $118,000.

The Court noted that this amount included minority and marketability discounts—and may have approximated fair market value. Indiana law generally precludes applicability of minority/marketability discounts in a statutory fair value appraisal. But in this case, the Court was not determining whether the company's valuation was the "best and/or only value that could be placed on those shares." It determined only the summary judgment motion issues of statutory compliance.

"This entire case and its outcome illustrate that, while the statutes are designed to achieve quick payment to a dissenting shareholder and minimize litigation," the Court concluded, "that purpose can only be attained by timely compliance by both the corporation and the shareholder."

Chapter 7: Court Case Abstracts

Winn v. Winn Enterprises, Ltd.

Citation: 2007 Ark. App. LEXIS 693
Court: Court of Appeals
State/Jurisdiction: Arkansas
Date of decision: October 10, 2007

The family limited partnership (FLP) in this case managed 880 acres of timberland, which had been in the Winn family for a century. The partnership agreement provided that upon withdrawal, a member was entitled to receive the interest's "fair value." When several minority members withdrew, a dispute arose over the appraised value of the partnership as well as the application of discounts to the minority interests.

At trial, the partners presented a forester and certified general real estate appraiser, who valued the land and timber at $1.9 million. He did not apply any discounts because they were not "part of the scope of his work." The partners also enlisted a certified business appraiser, who testified that the partnership's royalty interest was worth $29,000. He was also not asked to apply a discount, nor did he believe one was appropriate.

The partnership retained a certified public accountant, who adopted the valuation of the royalty interest. But he relied on a forester's appraisal of the timberland at just under $1.5 million to arrive at a total fair market value for the FLP of $1.63 million. Because it was "common" to apply discounts to minority partnership interests, he said, he also applied a 30% discount for lack of control and a 15% discount for lack of marketability. While he acknowledged that the partnership agreement called for applying "fair value," in this case, the expert believed that the standard was the same as "fair market value." On cross-examination, he conceded that there could be circumstances—as in dissenting shareholder cases—where "fair value" could be subject to a different interpretation and require a different method of valuation.

Trial court applies discounts

The trial court found the partners' appraisal of the FLP assets was more credible (perhaps because the opposing real estate expert admitted that his appraisal did not conform with state guidelines). It adopted the $1.9 million value as part of its overall valuation of the FLP, but then applied the discounts asserted by the partnership's expert—and the partners appealed.

Relying on federal and state law regarding "fair value" in the context of the dissenting shareholder cases, the partners argued that discounts were incompatible with their rights to recover their "complete investment" in the partnership. If discounts apply, they said, the partnership would obtain their interests at a windfall simply because the partners had chosen to exercise their withdrawal rights.

The Arkansas court of appeals agreed that the partners' situation was analogous to that of dissenting shareholders. Moreover, state partnership law characterized withdrawing partners in a similar manner—and both statutes used the "fair value" terminology to specify the applicable valuation method. But neither statute defined "fair value," and though the partnership's expert tried to equate this with "fair market value," the Court disagreed. "Fair value is determined by ascertaining all assets and liabilities of the business and the intrinsic value of its stock rather than merely appraising its market value." In the case of dissenting shareholders or withdrawing partners "there is no sale on the open market; their situation is more akin to a forced sale."

The Court concluded that "fair value" as provided for in the relevant sections of the state partnership code specifically does not include discounts for lack of marketability or lack of control. Notably, it distinguished this context from divorce cases, where the fair market value standard still applies to value stock in a divorce, as per state statute.

Edler v. Edler

Citation: 2007 Wisc. App. LEXIS 1130
Court: Court of Appeals
State/Jurisdiction: Wisconsin
Date of decision: December 27, 2007

Richard and Steven Edler were brothers and co-owners in a closely held trucking and excavating corporation, founded by their father. Steven was president and the majority shareholder with a 60% interest; Richard owned the remaining 40% and was vice-president. The corporation also owned two parcels of land on which the brothers lived separately.

In 2003 Steven began moderating Richard's role by: demoting him to an hourly, rather than a salaried, employee; taking away his corporate check-writing privilege; and finally, terminating his employment and replacing him with Steven's wife as vice-president. Steven also underpaid rent and retained revenue from the sale of corporate property.

Richard sought judicial dissolution of the corporation, claiming Steven's oppressive conduct. The parties retained a joint expert to calculate the fair market value of Richard's 40% interest. The expert used a net asset approach, appraising the company as a going concern and applying a combined 30% minority and marketability discount. Using this valuation as a starting point, the trial court ordered Steven to buy out Richard's interest, minus a 6% liquidation discount. But it declined to apply the minority/marketability discount, relying on precedent that rejected discounts in the dissenting shareholder context. The total buyout, including certain offsets and additional awards, amounted to approximately $334,000.

Steven appealed the trial court's determination of oppression as well as its rejection of minority and marketability discounts. Richard appealed the application of the liquidation discount.

Oppression analogous to dissent?

In reviewing the findings on oppression, the appellate court stressed the nature of the close family corporation. The stock purchase agreement urged "family members [to] continue their active association with the Corporation and to provide…rewards for efforts contributed." Steven's "squeeze out" tactics frustrated the agreement's purpose, the Court confirmed, and constituted a breach of fiduciary duty.

In determining the propriety of applying statutory remedy for shareholder dissent to shareholder oppression cases, the Court found a direct analogy. "The exclusion of Richard from the corporation created the same situation faced by a dissenter in a closely held corporation," it said. "The shareholder not only lacks control over corporate decision making, but also upon the application of a minority discount receives less than proportional value for loss of that control." The same rationale applied to the rejection of a marketability discounts. Any other ruling would "minimize the finding of oppression," the Court said, and confirmed the trial court's valuation.

As to the 6% liquidation discount, Richard conceded in his appellate brief that a "reasonable" remedy would be to put the parties in the same position as if the company were liquidated. He "cannot simultaneously complain that the liquidation discount was inequitable," the Court ruled, and affirmed the same.

Fisher v. Fisher

Citation: 1997 ND 176, 568 N.W.2d 728
Court: Supreme Court
State/Jurisdiction: North Dakota
Date of decision: September 8, 1997

In this case, the husband started the business but transferred ownership and control to the wife, to take advantage of minority-owned business contracts. Both parties owned stock in the business (the husband a minority interest), but shortly after filing for divorce the wife demoted the husband and removed him from the board of directors. The trial court valued the parties combined 88% interest at $9,094.74 per share and reallocated the interests 51% to the husband and 37% to the wife.

The wife appealed to the state Supreme Court. She argued that because of the husband's post-divorce oppression, she would have to sell her interest or petition for dissolution of the business. Further, if she sold her interest she would realize much less than the value that the trial court accorded to the stock, because it did not apply a minority interest discount.

The Supreme Court disagreed, finding that the trial court had properly valued the stock without reference to a marketability discount. Moreover, a minority business interest might be worth less to a potential purchaser, but this was not sufficient reason to discount her minority shares in the marital dissolution proceedings when the wife's corporate rights provided adequate remedies. For example, the wife could petition for dissolution of the business, the court noted, or enforce her dissenters' rights and obtain the stock's fair value. It further reasoned that in assessing fair value, other courts (including the Delaware Supreme Court in *Cavalier Oil Corp.*) have declined to discount minority stock interests because the discount was too speculative; it penalized the dissenter by denying the dissenter his or her pro rata share of the value; and it enriched the majority shareholders by allowing them to repurchase the dissenter's stock at a discounted price. By applying the fair value analogy from corporate cases, the *Fisher* court thus affirmed the denial of the minority interest discount in divorce.

MS Holdings, LLC v. Malone

Citation: 2008 WL 1700156
Court: Court of Appeals
State/Jurisdiction: Tennessee
Date of decision: April 14, 2008

Does Dissenting Shareholder Interest Include Value of Projected Future Income?

When a shareholder dissents from a corporate action—is he entitled to receive the projected benefits of that proposed action in a statutory fair value appraisal of his shares? One major factor, according to this Tennessee case, is how far along the company may be in its proposed new venture as of the date of dissent.

Company seeks celebrity brands

Up until June 2005, the plaintiff corporation was a distributor of several well-known meat brands. The defendant owned a part interest in the business (the record does not reveal his percentage share). When the company decided to explore licensing and selling products that bear celebrity likenesses, the defendant objected. After the company's members voted in favor of the new business plan (on June 6, 2005), the defendant demanded payment for his interest as a dissenting shareholder pursuant to local (Tenn.) statute.

The company paid the defendant $27,000 for his interest, even though its analysis indicated that the value of his interest was zero. The defendant demanded nearly $2.7 million—and the company sought judicial appraisal to determine the "fair value" of the defendant's interest, and to assess all costs and attorney fees against him.

Trial court rules on inclusion of future income

The court appointed an appraiser to determine the fair value of the defendant's interest. The appraiser found that the interest was nominal if the value excluded the future business prospects. If he considered future prospects, "the most optimistic estimate of value would be in the $100,000 to $150,000 range."

The appraiser asked the court to rule on whether the appraisal should include projected future performance. Citing a prior state Supreme Court decision, the trial court held that the defendant could not simultaneously dissent from the company's future business but also seek to benefit from any projected income that it might produce. The appraiser then submitted his report, excluding projected future income and finding the defendant's interest to be worth the "nominal" amount of $10,000 as of the date of the shareholder vote.

The trial court ordered the defendant to pay $17,000—the difference between the $27,000 he had already received and the $10,000 appraisal—as well over $63,000 in attorneys' fees and costs. The defendant appealed.

Future earnings too speculative?

The defendant challenged the trial court's exclusion of projected income by citing a Delaware Supreme Court case (*Weinberger v. UOP*, 1983), which permits a court, in a statutory fair value appraisal, to consider business plans that are in place but not yet executed as of the valuation date. The Tennessee Court of Appeals considered the case and found, even under *Weinberger*, that a judicial appraisal should not include future performance that is too speculative.

In this case, the new business venture "had not even been created on the valuation date," the court observed. The company had not yet finalized the contracts and licensing agreements upon which the venture's profitability would turn. Although the plaintiff hoped that the new business plan would be profitable, the court said, "as of the valuation date any future profits were just that, hope."

In its determination of attorneys' fees and costs, the court cited the defendant's failure to submit any proof or competing valuation to support his $2.7 million demand, despite the company's invitation. Nor did he file exceptions to the appraiser's completed report. Finding no justification for the defendant's demands, the court confirmed the assessment of fees.

Cox Enterprises, Inc. v. News-Journal Corp.

Citation: 2007 U.S. App. LEXIS 29533
Court: United States Court of Appeals
State/Jurisdiction: 11th Circuit
Date of decision: December 21, 2007

The News-Journal Corporation (NJC) is a closely held Florida company that publishes a daily newspaper *(The News-Journal)*, the 11th largest independently owned newspaper in the country, as well as several local shopping guides. Cox Enterprises owns seventeen daily newspapers throughout the Southeast and has owned a 47.5% interest in NJC since 1969.

Cox Enterprises, Inc. v. News-Journal Corp.

Beginning in the 1960s, NJC created several artistic and cultural non-profit endeavors. Not only did NJC provide substantial financial support to these cultural entities, management between the two was inextricably intertwined. Throughout the 1990s, NJC consistently contributed over $1 million to these entities, including paying $13 million for the naming rights to a new performing arts center. After discovering the naming rights agreement—and similar "business" expenses that exceeded allowable charitable contributions—Cox sued for fraud, waste, and mismanagement. Pursuant to Florida statute, NJC elected to purchase Cox's shares at fair value. The parties disputed this amount and sought judicial appraisal of the shares.

Expert valuations diverge by $200 million

Both sides presented expert valuation testimony at trial. Cox's expert was a partner at a firm that has appraised over $10 billion worth of newspaper transactions in its twenty-five year history, and more than 50% of U.S. newspaper sales in the past decade. Prior to joining the firm, the expert owned and managed a daily newspaper. The trial court found him "plainly qualified."

The expert began by establishing the fair market value (FMV) of NJC as a "going concern." He used a comparable sales analysis, measuring NJC in relation to the purchase prices of comparable newspapers. He also compared NJC's EBITDA margin to the average operating margin of eleven publicly traded newspapers. NJC's operating margin was 9.3%; the comparable companies operated at an average margin of 28.3%. Due to this data, the expert normalized NJC's margin to 28.3%.

Further, he selected seven transactions involving comparable newspapers based on fifty different measures—including growth, circulation, financial metrics, and market characteristics. After excluding two outliers, he calculated the average purchase price-to-revenue ratio (4.1:1) and purchase price-to-EBITDA ratio (14.4:1) of the comparables. In a "slight departure from his standard approach," he adjusted his multipliers downward to account for NJC's higher than average capital expenditures and a possible reduction in its growth rate. The expert performed a similar analysis for NJC's primary shopping guide, and arrived at a total fair market value for NJC holdings of $306 million. Cox's 47.5% interest totaled $145.35 million.

As a check on this approach, the expert conducted a discounted cash flow analysis, using a projected growth rate of 6% and the normalized operating margin of 28.3%. Under this method, he valued NJC at $289 million.

By contrast, NJC's expert was an experienced and accredited appraiser, albeit without a specific practice in valuing newspapers. The district court found him qualified, although "appreciably less so" than Cox's expert.

NJC's expert also valued the company as a "going concern," although he relied on a definition (by NJC's general counsel and board member) that assumes a company will operate in the future exactly as it has in the past, including maintaining its operating margins. NJC's expert also relied exclusively on a DCF analysis. His future cash flow estimates predicted that NJC would operate for roughly 2 ½ years at its present EBITDA margin of approximately 12%, and then increase to roughly 18.3% (based on the company's performance from 1998 to 2002). Using the Gordon Growth Model and applying a capitalization rate of 10%, the expert projected future cash flow of $82 million. After discounting this to present value, he added a $4.4 million tax shield related to depreciation and applied a 20% discount for lack of marketability. His final estimated value of NJC was $61.9 million, with Cox's share worth $29.4 million.

Focus on 'reasonably prudent' management

The trial court adopted the comparable sales analysis by Cox's expert, finding the method more accepted in the financial community and protective of minority shareholders. Notably, the court rejected NJC's definition of a going concern, explaining that it would "create an incentive for those with control over corporations to violate fiduciary duties...and drive down the value of minority shares." Instead, the court assumed that a company will be managed in a "reasonably prudent manner going forward," regardless of how it may have been run in the past.

The court also rejected the methodology—including application of discounts—that Cox's expert used, saying that it would "reward wrongdoing by permitting NJC to purchase Cox's shares at a bargain price." However, it adjusted Cox's expert's operating margin from 28.3% to 24.8% to reflect the average margin of comparable independent newspapers. It assessed NJC's total fair market value at $272 million, with the fair value of Cox's share equaling $129.2 million. NJC appealed the court's definition of "going concern;" its use of fair market value in its calculation of fair value; and its normalization adjustment. Cox also appealed, arguing that the court should have further adjusted its fair value to account for $31 million in mismanagement and corporate waste.

When is FMV a measure of fair value?

The 11th Circuit Court of Appeals acknowledged that "fair value" and "fair market value" are not synonymous; neither are they "mutually exclusive." While fair market value often accounts for the effects of an impending sale or merger, statutory fair value (under applicable Florida law) does not. When such "potentially distorting corporate actions are not at issue," the Court explained, then fair market value may serve as an estimate of fair value. In this case, NJC was a viable, marketable corporation that would command "an attractive price on the open market." In the absence of any imminent sale or other "distorting" corporate action, the fair market value/comparable sales analysis by Cox's expert was "most appropriate."

Similarly, the appropriate definition of "going concern" in valuation contexts requires an appraiser to exclude any consideration of a potential merger or liquidation. The Court also agreed that a valuation should assume the subject business will be managed according to the "reasonably prudent" definition. NJC claimed that it was incorrect to assume the company could perform at the same financial level as the comparable newspapers, but the Court disagreed. The trial court's normalization of its operating margins "better approximates the value of the corporation as a 'going concern,' or a reasonably prudently managed business."

Finally, the Court found that, while not specifically addressing waste in his valuation, Cox's expert did "effectively adjust for any impact [that] previous waste or mismanagement would have had on the value of the shares through normalizing the operating margin." To adjust further would have effectively double-counted the mismanagement, and the Court affirmed its exclusion.

Holiday Medical Center, Inc. v. Weisman

Citation: 2008 WL 2677504
Court: Superior Court
State/Jurisdiction: New Jersey
Date of decision: July 10, 2008

Should 'Highest and Best Use' Govern Fair Value Standard in Dissenting Shareholder Case?

The board of directors of a New Jersey nursing home wanted to sell the facility, its land and other assets, to a private, non-profit school for $8 million. After paying off an existing mortgage ($3,075,464) and other miscellaneous items—including a $3 million donation to the non-profit buyer—the nursing home would net about $2 million from the sale.

Liquidation value versus going concern

After the sale went through, a 5% minority shareholder dissented and sought a judicial appraisal of her shares. The judge appointed an independent appraiser, who found that the nursing home was "marginally financially feasible." Its value as a going concern was only $5,540,000, the appraiser concluded, compared to a liquidation value of $7 million, which lay primarily in the real property assets. Neither the shareholder nor the board of directors disputed the appraisal, its alternate valuations or its methodologies.

The shareholder tried to enjoin distribution of the sale proceeds, but by then the board had already distributed 80% to the remaining shareholders, holding 20% in escrow along with the dissenting shareholders 5% share ($100,000 of the net proceeds). The court ordered the board to pay the dissenting shareholder 80% of her share, or $80,000. But even after receiving this amount, the shareholder claimed she was due an additional payment of just over $116,000, based on her share of the appraised liquidation value ($7 million) minus the outstanding mortgage ($7M − 3,075,464) x 5% = $196,227 minus $80,000 already paid—but not including any charitable donation to the buyer, for which she had never received any benefit (in terms of a charitable deduction). In other words, she claimed that statutory fair value should be based on a 'highest and best use' analysis.

The board objected, claiming that the going concern appraisal ($5,540,000) represented the fair value of the nursing facility; and that at any rate, its $80,000 payment reimbursed the shareholder for the fair value of her interest.

Asset approach violates fair value standard?

The trial court agreed that the board did not owe any additional amounts to the shareholder, and it rejected her contention that the "highest and best use" standard should control the fair value accounting analysis. When the board went through with the proposed asset sale, the court explained, it stripped the dissenting shareholder of her ongoing interest in the nursing home. The independently appraised values established a range of value for the facility, anywhere from the best case scenario, $7 million liquidation value, to worst case $5,540,000 going concern value. Accordingly, given the acceptance of the appraisal methodologies by both parties, the shareholder's interest ranged from $40,000 to $80,000.

The trial court was also satisfied that—based on all the evidence, when the nursing home sold its business for $8 million, the arms-length sale established fair value for all the constituent shareholders, whether dissenting or not. But the shareholder appealed the decision, once again arguing that "as a matter of law" the fair value statute requires the "highest and best value" for the assets at issue.

The New Jersey Superior Court, in an unpublished decision, rejected this contention and confirmed the lower court's finding regarding the standard of value. Under local, as well as Delaware law (interpreted by Delaware Chancery Court cases), a corporation's going concern value is acceptable to determine the fair value share of a dissenting shareholder's interest. In this case, the trial court did not adopt the going concern value but merely used it to corroborate the arm's-length sales price, which—after deductions, including the charitable donation—resulted in a corporate value of $2 million.

However, the appellate court remanded the case for certain omissions in the record. In particular, the lower court needed to provide its basis for accepting the sale transaction price, which included the charitable donation, over the going concern value—which did not. It was also not clear whether the shareholder could have benefited from the charitable donation, the court held, and how this value would factor into the overall findings of fair value.

Kortum v. Johnson

Citation: 2008 WL 3931544 (N.D.)
Court: Supreme Court
State/Jurisdiction: North Dakota
Date of decision: August 28, 2008

Does Buy-Sell Agreement Trump Statutory Shareholder Remedies?

When the minority shareholder of a closely held, private professional practice is terminated as an employee, there is often a clash between the "at will" doctrine of employment law and the broad equitable remedies offered by a state's shareholder oppression statutes. Can a buy-sell agreement preempt the conflict by limiting the minority shareholder's rights upon termination to a nominal sum?

Doctors value practice at $5. In an attempt to escape a large corporate hospital practice, five physicians opened an independent clinic. Each doctor initially contributed $25,000 to the start-up corporation and received 5,000 shares in return, pursuant to their operating agreement. During the first five months, the doctors contributed another $50,000 apiece to cover expenses, after which they shared equally in profits, lab fees, and overhead contributions. The same agreement provided:

> If any Shareholder shall voluntarily or involuntarily terminate his employment with the Corporation, for any reason whatsoever, he shall sell his shares under the terms...hereof.
>
> ...The price of each share to be sold under this Agreement is hereby stipulated to be $0.04 per share ($1.00 for $25,000), subject, however, to the adjustments herein provided.

The agreement further provided that the shareholders "shall" review the stock price at each annual meeting, "including the worth of the company as a going concern." If they were unable to agree on a stock price, then the sale of any share would be at book value.

After three years in operation, the clinic terminated one of the doctor/shareholders, and offered her $1.00 in return for her stock. She refused, and sued the shareholders for breach of fiduciary duty and for the statutory fair value of her stock. The shareholders denied any wrongdoing and requested the court enforce the buy-sell provisions. At trial, the parties traded allegations of unprofessional and unfair conduct, but the court essentially ignored these, finding that in their agreement, the parties had anticipated termination of a physician/shareholder, "for any reason whatsoever." Thus, the doctor was an "at will" employee and had bargained away any rights to shareholder oppression remedies by signing the agreement. The court dismissed the doctor's complaint and ordered the corporation to pay her $1.00.

Owner/employee has different expectations. On appeal, the doctor argued that she'd been unfairly deprived of her entire investment in the practice, her continued earnings and employment, her patient base and accounts receivable—all in exchange for $1.00. She claimed entitlement to her pro-rata share of the medical corporation as a going concern. The shareholders reasserted their prior arguments; to wit: "a minority shareholder in a close corporation who contractually agrees to the repurchase of her shares upon termination of her employment acquires no right from the corporation or majority shareholder against an at-will discharge by virtue of her minority shareholder status."

The appellate court agreed that the doctor was an at-will employee. However, this doctrine is distinct from the "employment-based shareholder oppression" doctrine. "Increasingly, courts have come to recognize that within many closely held enterprises, it is not as easy to separate out the employment relationship from the ownership relationship." In these cases, courts have adopted the "reasonable expectations approach" of corporate law. That is:

> The threshold issue in a claim of shareholder oppression based on termination of employment is whether the minority shareholder had a reasonable expectation of continued employment.

Unlike the public corporation shareholder, who is merely an investor in the enterprise, or an employee who gains shares in the company by virtue of a compensation package, the minority shareholder in a close corporation is a co-owner of the business, who wants and expects "all the privileges and powers that go with ownership."

Failure was in the findings. Accordingly, the corporation's shareholders owed the doctor a fiduciary duty both in her capacity as a shareholder and a shareholder/employee. The trial court, in concluding that opposite, had relied on cases in which employees acquired a nominal ownership interest as part of their compensation packages. In this case, the doctor helped form and capitalize the corporation; she made the same contributions and received the same number of shares as the other members. The buy-sell agreement did not relieve the shareholders of their statutory duties, and the trial court should have determined whether their conduct toward the owner/employee was "unfairly prejudicial."

The court remanded the case for further findings. Among them, the trial court should consider whether the doctor had reasonable expectations of continued employment. Signing such a restrictive buy-sell agreement could be some evidence that she did not, especially if the agreement was negotiated at arms-length and for a legitimate business purpose; and all the other shareholders assumed the same risks. But the court should also consider other factors, such as whether a shareholder's salary and benefits constituted de facto dividends and whether procuring employment was a significant reason for investing in the business. If the shareholders acted unfairly, then she would be entitled to relief under the shareholder oppression statutes and the trial court would have broad discretion to fashion an equitable remedy.

If the trial court finds no unfair prejudice, then the buy-sell provisions would apply. While the shareholders claimed the total buy-out price was $1.00, the doctor argued that the agreement required the shareholders to revisit the share price annually; and if unable to agree, to price shares at book value. The appellate court disagreed with both interpretations. Under the terms of the agreement, which was never amended, a minority shareholder was entitled only to the $0.04 per-share price, or $200 for a total ownership of 5,000 shares.

In re Marriage of Thornhill

Citation: 2008 WL 3877223 (Colo. App.)
Court: Court of Appeals
State/Jurisdiction: Colorado
Date of decision: August 21, 2008

Colorado Court Considers Fair Value Standard in Divorce

Proponents of applying statutory fair value as the standard of value in divorce proceedings are meeting with mixed results. (For a recent recap of state courts that have decided this issue, see "The State of the Fair Value Standard in Divorce," by John S. Stockdale Jr. Esq. in the August *BVU*; the article is also available as a Free Download at BVResources.com). After considering conflicting precedent from other jurisdictions, the Colorado Court of Appeals becomes the latest court to rule on whether to extend the statutory fair value standard in dissenting shareholder cases—in particular, its preclusion of marketability discounts—to valuing a business in divorce.

Oil and gas interest worth $1.625 million

After a twenty-seven year marriage, the Thornhills executed a separation agreement, including the disposition of the husband's 70.5% interest in an oil and gas business. The husband's expert valued the husband's share at $1.625 million, after the application of a 33% marketability discount. The wife—who was not represented by counsel when she signed the separation agreement (and apparently did not retain her own valuation expert), disavowed the agreement at the hearing on final orders. The trial court ratified the agreement, despite her protest—and the wife appealed.

The appellate court voided the agreement, finding that its provisions were unconscionable. The wife was not legally or financially sophisticated, the court said, and had no access to counsel. More importantly, the agreement provided for the husband to pay the wife half of the marital assets—over $750,000—in equal monthly payments over ten years, without any provision of interest or security for the debt. The court remanded the matter to the trial division for new determination and disposition of the assets.

And "because it may arise on remand," the court considered the wife's contention that no marketability discounts should apply to the value of the husband's business. She offered a 2003 state Supreme Court case (*Pueblo Bancorporation v. Lindoe, Inc.*) that precluded marketability discounts when determining the fair value of a dissenting corporate shareholder's interest pursuant to the state dissenters' rights statutes. The court's conclusion in that case was based on an in-depth analysis of the relevant Colorado statutes as well as similar statutes in other jurisdictions and provisions of the Model Business Corporation Act.

Chapter 7: Court Case Abstracts

Statutory fair value discourages squeeze-outs

Critical to *Pueblo Bancorporation* was the court's finding that dissenting shareholder statutes are intended to protect minority owners from the vagaries and involuntary nature of most cash-out mergers. A rule that prevented minority shareholders from receiving "less than their proportionate share of the whole firm's value would produce a transfer of wealth from the minority . . . to the shareholders in control," the court said (quoting from *Pueblo Bancorporation*). "Such a rule would inevitably encourage corporate squeeze-outs."

But those same considerations do not apply in a divorce case, the court held. First, the applicable marital dissolution statutes do not contain the "fair value" language of the business corporation statutes. Second, in its comprehensive review of shareholder dissent statutes in other jurisdictions, the *Pueblo Bancorporation* court had found that the "fair value" standard did not equate to "fair market value" standard, "and as a result, the common practice of including a marketability discount in calculating fair market value is not permitted in dissenting shareholder valuations."

Further, the court declined to adopt *Brown v.* Brown (N.J. 2002), in which the New Jersey Superior Court of Appeals extended the reasoning of dissenting shareholder cases to hold that marketability discounts are not appropriate in dissolution proceedings. Instead, the court was persuaded by the decisions "of numerous other jurisdictions" that have applied marketability discounts when valuing interests in closely held companies for purposes of divorce. "Such a discount . . . [reflects] the fact that shares of stock in such corporations are less marketable than publicly traded stock, a factor that an ordinary buyer would take into consideration in deciding what to pay for the shares."

> Consistent with the reasoning of these cases, we conclude that a trial court's failure, in an appropriate case, to apply a marketability discount to an equitable division of marital property under [Colorado law] could unfairly penalize a party for ownership of shares that cannot be readily sold or liquidated.

Given its equitable mandates, trial courts should retain their discretion whether to apply marketability discounts in valuing closely held companies for purposes of divorce. In this case, the court expressed no opinion as to the appropriate amount of any discount (although it cited a range, from 10% to 35%, in other state law cases). It simply directed the trial court to make a clear record of its reasons for applying any discount, "to facilitate review on appeal."

Murphy v. U.S. Dredging Corp.

Citation: 2008 NY Slip Op 31535
Court: Supreme Court
State/Jurisdiction: New York
Date of decision: May 19, 2008

By Peter A. Mahler, Esq.*

New York Court's Fair Value Award in Shareholder Oppression Case Deducts Present Value of Built-In Gains Tax

The Eleventh Circuit's reversal last year of the tax court's decision in *Jelke v. Commissioner* (see the January 2008 *BVU*) represents a tipping point in the evolution of case law—beginning with the tax court's 1998 *Estate of Davis* decision—toward 100% discounts for built-in capital gains in valuing holding company assets. At least, that appears to be the case for estate and gift tax purposes in the appraisal of a C corporation under the fair market value (FMV) standard.

But what of shareholder oppression and dissenting shareholder cases involving application of a statutory fair value (FV) standard? Typically, the appraisal or buyout statute requires FV appraisal of the company on a going-concern basis as opposed to *Jelke*'s "arbitrary assumption" of liquidation on the date of death. Can the redeeming company or purchasing shareholder nonetheless seek a discount for built-in gains?

These questions were recently addressed in a post-trial valuation decision by Justice Warshawsky of the New York Supreme Court (the state's trial-level court) in *Murphy v. U.S. Dredging Corp.* The court's decision—to deduct the present value of built-in gains tax assuming a nineteen-year holding period—rejects the assumption of liquidation on the valuation date in favor of a reasonably foreseeable liquidation date based on evidence of the controlling shareholders' actual intent. In so ruling, the court reconciles the FV standard's stated purpose, to protect minority interests against majority overreaching, with economic market reality that would lead a hypothetical purchaser to demand—and the hypothetical seller to give—a tax discount based on non-speculative liquidation plans.

The Facts in *Murphy*

U.S. Dredging Corp. (USD) was formed in 1934 and owned by the families of its three founders. When USD ceased dredging operations in 1973, it owned valuable waterfront properties in Brooklyn, New York and Jersey City, New Jersey. USD sold the Jersey City property in 2001. In 2005, USD sold its Brooklyn property to the IKEA chain for $31.25 million. The bulk of the sale proceeds was invested in replacement commercial properties in tax exempt §1031 exchanges (under §1031, the exchange of certain types of "like-kind" property may defer the recognition of capital gains or losses due upon sale, and hence defer any capital gains taxes otherwise due), which deferred $11.6 million in capital gains taxes on the two sales. Major retailers under long-term triple net leases operated the replacement properties.

In 2006, a 36.77% shareholder faction petitioned for judicial dissolution of USD on the grounds of oppression, alleging that the controlling shareholders withheld distributions while enriching themselves and their children with excessive salary and pensions. USD elected to purchase the petitioners' shares. After the parties failed to agree on the buyout price, the matter went to trial to determine the fair value of the shares as of February 13, 2006.

Same approaches, much 'different values'

Both USD's expert, and the petitioners' expert used the adjusted book value (net asset) method and the discounted future cash flow (DCF) approach to value the shares. That's where the similarity ended, as the court noted, "each expert weighted the two approaches differently and reached different values as to each area."

The primary difference with respect to the net asset approach was treatment of built-in gains. USD's expert deducted 100% of the $11.6 million deferred capital gains tax on the 2001 and 2005 sales to arrive at a company value of approximately $15 million, to which he applied a 15% discount for lack of marketability (DLOM) to arrive at a value of $12.8 million.

The petitioners' expert deducted approximately $3.4 million in gains tax representing present value, assuming liquidation in the year 2024, to arrive at a company value of $24.8 million. He applied no DLOM.

The two experts' DCF values were even further apart, due primarily to their differing analyses of USD's working capital. The corporation's balance sheet on January 31, 2006, showed $16.2 million in current assets. The question for the court became whether any of this was excess working capital, and therefore a non-operating asset.

The petitioners' expert determined $14.1 million of this was a non-operating asset and included only $2.1 million in working capital into his calculations. He used the DCF Model to determine the present value of the future cash flows from 2006-2025 to be $6.0 million, to which he added $14.1 million in non-operating assets, resulting in a value for the corporation's equity of $20.1 million. In contrast, USD's expert claimed the $14.1 million to be working capital and determined the value of the corporation's equity to be $11.4 million.

After making adjustments for a DLOM and a January 2007 dividend payment, the petitioners' expert's fair value was $16 million, and USD's expert's fair value was $8.7 million.

The petitioners' expert weighted his net asset value 45%, and his DCF value 55%. He explained that the long-term nature of USD's real estate and mortgage financing transactions made giving more weight to its expected long-term cash flow, rather than its highly encumbered assets, more appropriate. USD's expert gave the two approaches equal weight; however he also testified that he would assign 85% weight to his DCF value if the court did not deduct 100% of the built-in gains tax in the net asset valuation. Based on these weightings, the petitioners' expert and USD's expert concluded that the value of the petitioners' 36.77% stock interest was approximately $8.14 million and $3.76 million, respectively.

Prior case law directs the court

The court began by noting that the New York statutes providing for appraisal rights and for elective purchase in dissolution proceedings use the term "fair value" without offering a definition, but that the case law has defined it generally as what a willing purchaser, in an arm's-length transaction, would offer for the corporation as an operating business. The court observed that, while case law recommends consideration of each of the three basic valuation approaches, net asset value (cost) is generally the approach most applicable in evaluating real estate and investment holding companies such as USD. Also, New York law generally supports application of a DLOM while prohibiting minority discounts.

Turning to the discount for built-in gains, the court, after referencing *Davis*, stated:

> Though we are not in Tax Court, and a Fair Value calculation...is not identical to the procedure of Tax Court...it is clear from the evidence that no liquidation was or is contemplated by [USD] in our case and thus a 'liquidation' or semi-liquidation scenario is not appropriate when dealing with the [built-in gains] tax.

The court agreed with the petitioners' expert's assumption of a nineteen-year holding period based, in part, on the following factors:

1. Historically, USD made long-term property acquisitions, i.e., it held the Jersey City and Brooklyn properties for thirty-six and twenty years, respectively, before selling;
2. The specific §1031 exchange properties acquired by USD were the "type of investments" which reflected long-term investment goals;
3. The possibility of converting to an S corporation gave the majority "tremendous incentive" to hold the property for at least ten years in order to avoid gains tax;
4. A willing buyer would not expect to deduct the entire gains tax.

Since the deduction of the entire tax would mean the payment of the tax at the time of sale, the court asked, "Why would such [a] buyer buy into this type of [REIC] if the corporation is going to sell [its] assets as soon as you buy?"

The court's opinion cites what appears to be the only previous New York decision on gains tax and fair value, in *Matter of LaSala* (Feb. 6, 2003), where that court rejected a deduction for built-in gains taxes. The court states that while the court "agrees with the logic" of *LaSala*:

> ...under these circumstances with the [built-in gains] representing such a large portion of corporate assets it appears that a willing purchaser would expect to deduct the present value of the [built-in gains] tax along with a percentage for lack of marketability.

The court deducted the $3.4 million present value of the gains tax liability and applied a 15% DLOM to arrive at a net asset valuation of the company of approximately $18 million; the petitioners' interest came to $6.7 million. Regarding the amount of working capital, the court found the petitioners' expert's working capital assumption to be "incorrect," and determined that a logical amount of working capital to be $6.45 million. Accordingly, the court directed both parties to recalculate their income approach calculations, and promised a final decision "giving appropriate weight to the two different methodologies" (i.e. reconciliation).

A new course for built-in gains deductions?

Murphy may well be the first decision permitting a deduction for built-in gains under a FV standard. While its precedential value may be limited by its unusual facts and circumstances, *Murphy* merits close study by appraisers and lawyers called upon to value C corporations with built-in gains, as it could be a harbinger of a new trend by the courts, particularly as the FV standard becomes more prevalent.

* Peter A. Mahler, Esq. is a litigation partner with Farrell Fritz, P.C. (New York City), and maintains the *New York Business Divorce* blog (www.nybusinessdivorce.com), which focuses on the dissolution and valuation of closely held business entities.

Khatkar v. Dhillon

Citation: 2009 WL 189846
Court: Court of Appeals
State/Jurisdiction: California
Date of decision: January 28, 2009

By John Stockdale Jr., Esq. *

In *Khatkar v. Dhillon*, 2009 WL 189846 (Cal. App. 5 Dist. Jan. 28, 2009), in an unpublished opinion, the California Court of Appeal, Fifth District, affirmed the lower court's valuation of stock in this judicial dissolution action, inclusive of deductions for capital gains tax, attorney's fees, accountant's fees, and brokerage fees. The appellate court determined that the statutorily defined standard for fair value in judicial dissolution was liquidation value, taking into account the possibility of any sale of the business as a going concern. Therefore, the court agreed that the deductions were proper.

* John Stockdale, Jr. is an associate with Schafer and Weiner, PLLC (Bloomfield Hills, MI). He has followed valuation case law since 1995, first as founder of Valuation Information, Inc. and currently as an Editor-at-Large with Business Valuation Resources, LLC.

Grelier v. Grelier

Citation: 2008 WL 5265056
Court: Civil Court of Appeals
State/Jurisdiction: Alabama
Date of decision: December 19, 2008

The Greliers spent the last two years of their twelve-year marriage in divorce proceedings. *Their primary dispute:* how to allocate the husband's 25% interest in a consolidation of closely held real estate development companies, which he owned with his father, his brother, and a family friend. In response to the wife's request—and an order drafted by her attorney—the trial court appointed a special master to audit and examine the books and records of the business, plus its physical assets, "for the purposes of identification and determination of the fair market value of all business entities in which the [husband] possesses any interest."

One expert turns to three. At trial, the husband testified that all of his various interests had suffered more than five years of financial difficulties, including poor sales, overdue construction loans, and forced debt. Because of these liabilities—and despite finding that the business owned real estate worth $59 million—the special master ultimately valued the husband's 25% interest at just over $1 million, and did not apply any minority or marketability discounts.

Each of the parties contested the valuation. The wife presented a financial expert who testified that the special master had "seriously" undervalued the interests by relying on outdated real estate appraisals, but he agreed that discounts were not applicable. By contrast, the husband's financial expert argued that by neglecting to apply discounts, the special master failed to comply with his court-ordered directive to determine fair market value. The husband had never owned a majority interest in any of the underlying businesses that formed the consolidated business; and he did not have the right to act independently from the majority-interest holders. Moreover, the husband could not convert his interest easily into cash, as all of the operating agreements required prior approval by the other owners before the husband could sell. Thus, his expert applied a 25% discount for lack of marketability and 25% minority interest discount, which, when combined, would have reduced the value of the husband's interest to just over $350,000.

After hearing the testimony from all three experts and soliciting legal briefs on the subject, the trial judge accepted the special master's $1 million valuation for the husband's 25% interest, but applied a combined discount of 40%.

Wife argues fair value. The wife appealed, arguing as a general matter that discounts were inappropriate when valuing business interests in the context of a divorce. The Alabama Civil Court of Appeals acknowledged that the question regarding which standard—fair market value or statutory fair value—applied in divorce cases would be a matter of first impression in the state. However, it did not need to reach the issue in this case, for several reasons:

1. Through her attorney, the wife drafted the order appointing the special master, specifically instructing him to determine "fair market value" of the husband's minority interests.
2. During the trial, both parties presented expert opinions and legal briefs regarding the application of discounts.
3. In her legal memorandum, the wife challenged only the application of discounts to a proper determination of fair market value; she did not challenge the use of the fair market value standard, but waited until the appeal to raise the issue for the first time.

"Having instructed the special master to determine the fair market value of the husband's business interest, the wife cannot now assert on appeal that the trial court should have applied a different standard," the appellate court held. "[A] party may not induce an error by the trial court and then attempt a reversal based on that error," it said, and upheld the trial court's valuation in all respects, including the 40% combined discounts.

Cannon v. Bertrand

Citation: 2009 WL 130341 (La.)
Court: Supreme Court
State/Jurisdiction: Louisiana
Date of decision: January 21, 2009

Three partners created a limited liability partnership a dozen years ago to develop Louisiana timberland. Per their agreement, each partner received an equal one-third share, but importantly, it did provide buy-out terms. When one of the partners withdrew in 2006, they were unable to agree upon payment and the withdrawing partner sought judicial determination of his interest.

At trial, the former partner presented an expert who valued the partnership at $1,324,203 and his one-third share at $457,401, without discounts. The expert for the remaining partners, however, appraised the partnership at $955,000 and then applied a 75% minority discount, valuing the withdrawing partner's interest at $80,000. The court found the underlying assets were worth just over $1 million and, after discounting the partner's interest by 35% (or nearly halfway between the parties' positions), arrived at a buy-out price of $228,000.

Fair market value applies in statutory appraisals. On review, the Louisiana Court of Appeals confirmed the trial court's valuation, citing a 1989 state Supreme Court case, *Schopf v. Marina Del Ray Partnership*, for the proposition that the higher court had "ratified" the use of minority discounts in statutory buy-outs. (See the June 2008 issue of *BVU* for an abstract of the appellate opinion.)

This time the withdrawing partner appealed to the Supreme Court, which began by discussing the Louisiana statute governing the rights of withdrawing partners. In particular, the buy-out provision entitles a former partner to "an amount equal to the value that the share of the former partner had at the time membership ceased." Importantly, the statute does not define "value," and so the court turned to its 1989 *Schopf* decision that valued a withdrawing partner's shares.

In *Schopf*, the trial court placed a zero value on a minority partner's shares in a real estate venture, because it posted a negative book value at the time of withdrawal. The state Supreme Court reversed, finding that:

> ...a proper value of a withdrawing partner's shares could be based on fair market value, or 'the price that a willing buyer would pay to a willing seller for a certain piece of property in an arm's length transaction, neither being under any compulsion to buy or sell and both having reasonable knowledge of the relevant facts.'

The *Schopf* court then looked for evidence of fair market value (FMV), including the amounts that the majority partner had paid to another withdrawing partner in an earlier deal and the amount that he had offered the withdrawing partner in this case. The court decided that the parties were willing but the transaction was not "arm's length" due to the forced buy-out. Thus, the fair market value for the shares "must be adjusted to account for other considerations," the *Schopf* court held, the "most significant" of which would recognize the withdrawing partner's minority interest. Although there was no testimony on the record regarding a discount, the court ultimately decided "some reduction" was warranted, and discounted the partner's shares by a third of their appraised value.

The *Cannon* court stretches to preserve precedent. After its discussion of *Schopf*, the Supreme Court went to great lengths to decide the discounts in the present case while at the same time preserving its own precedent and the trial court's broad discretion to determine fair market value in judicial appraisal cases. The rationale may have been a bit of a stretch.

First, the court confirmed that *Schopf* permits the fair market value standard in statutory appraisal cases. Next, it determined that because the *Schopf* court could not find evidence of fair market value on the record, it had to discount what evidence it had (the prior buy-out offers by the majority partner) to determine FMV of the withdrawing partner's shares. However, this discount "was not a 'minority discount,' ... which is applied to the pro rata share of the assets of a partnership due to lack of control in order to find fair market value," the *Cannon* court explained. "[R]ather, it might best be termed a kind of 'majority discount;' a discount applied to the 'unique' value placed on property by majority owners...to reach fair market value."

As such, because no minority discount was applied by the *Schopf* court, any mention of a minority discount by that court was merely dicta [non-binding], and cannot be relied upon as precedent.

Further, the *Cannon* court found that fair market value was not the "only means of establishing 'value'" per the Louisiana statute. Although it did not use the term "fair value," the court's ultimate determination more or less accords with the statutory fair value standard. In fact, although "[m] inority and other discounts, such as for lack of marketability, may have a place in our law," the court held, "such discounts must be used sparingly, and only when the facts support their use."

In this case, the buyers of the partnership were in fact the two remaining partners, who would not be subject to the same lack of control as a third party buyer. Moreover, because these partners decided to continue the partnership rather than liquidate, lack of marketability was not a factor. Finally, "discounting the market value of the partnership's property would be inequitable," the court said. "The withdrawing partner should not be penalized for doing something the law allows him to do, and the remaining partners should not thereby realize a windfall profit at his expense." In sum, the court declined to limit the term "value" in the Louisiana statute to any standard but the broader, more equitable FMV standard:

> [W]e hold that the 'value' of the partnership share of a withdrawing partner may be determined in any of several manners—book value, market value of the underlying partnership assets, fair market value of the partnership share, or other means-depending on the circumstances requiring the valuation. Because the circumstances surrounding a partnership withdrawal can vary so greatly, this court cannot fashion a 'one size fits all' method of valuation which would be fair in all cases.

When the remaining partners are the buyers of a withdrawing partner's share, the court concluded, the market value of the underlying partnership assets is the most equitable manner to value the shares at issue. Thus it adopted the trial court's valuation of the entire partnership (just over $1 million), and awarded the withdrawing partner one-third of that amount, without applying any discounts.

Drumheller v. Drumheller

Citation: 2009 WL 565020 (Vt.)
Court: Supreme Court
State/Jurisdiction: Vermont
Date of decision: March 6, 2009

The two major disputes in the Drumheller's divorce focused on valuation. The first related to the husband's 10% interest as CEO of a large printing company, which employed some 250 people. Also at issue was his one-third interest in the real estate partnership that owned the company's land and building.

At trial, each party presented "highly qualified and experienced" appraisers, both with extensive backgrounds in business valuation—one with particular experience with the husband's company. The appellate court opinion does not provide much detail concerning the technical aspects of the valuations, but it does excerpt some interesting comments from the trial court on the experts' general methodologies, their indicia of credibility, and their application of discounts.

Drumheller v. Drumheller

The experts were not too far apart. In valuing the printing company, both of the parties' experts applied the three traditional approaches (income, asset, and market). In fact, the experts agreed that under the income approach, the company was worth between $7 million and $7.5 million. Notably, they also agreed that this value was too low, given the company's before-tax profits in each of the five years preceding the valuation.

As a result, the wife's expert considered a net asset valuation, aggregating the company's cash and cash equivalents with the book value of its equipment and then subtracting liabilities. In his guideline public company (market) approach, the wife's expert calculated a straight average of the comparables, irrespective of size. The husband's expert used the same pool of comparables (five to six publicly traded companies) but put greater weight on the smaller ones.

Overall, the trial court did not find the net asset approach "helpful" in this case, explaining that "[t]he trouble with the net asset value is that it depends on tax depreciation schedules [that] have little relation to the market value of the equipment and other assets." In addition, measures that depend on book value are "inherently unreliable," it said, "unless the book values are shown to be equal to actual market value for the assets in question."

The court also did not find the market approach much help in this case. The pool of comparables was too small and the comparables too large. "By analogy, with enough adjustments for size and location, it is possible to compare a country cottage with Buckingham Palace," the court said, "but the integrity of the exercise suffers as the differences between the two properties widen."

The income capitalization approach appeared to be the "most accurate way to measure the value" of the husband's company. The court also found the husband's expert more credible, not only because he focused on the income approach but also because he had valued the printing company for twenty years, for purposes of its employee stock ownership plan (ESOP):

> It is unlikely that management selects [the husband's expert] every year…to maximize the value of the company for the benefit of retiring employees. To the extent there is an institutional bias, it is in favor of keeping ESOP values down to a manageable level.

The husband's expert brought an "outside professional perspective" to each year's valuation of the company, the court added. "The length of this experience adds credibility to [his] testimony."

Also bolstering the testimony from the husband's expert was his "minimal use" of minority and liquidity discounts. Once again, the appellate court opinion does not provide the precise percentage that each expert applied as discounts or their bottom-line conclusions. However, it notes the trial court's observation that in general, "the use of higher discount figures tends to push the appraisal values towards the realm of theory and away from actual life experience."

> In the real world, after all, these shares are not going to be sold. [Husband] has to hold onto them because he needs to control the company…to earn his income. Starting with

the higher figure and discounting it by 30% is inherently less persuasive than starting with a lower figure and discounting it by only 10%.

The wife appealed the valuation of the printing company. She essentially raised the same arguments that she made at trial advocating the credibility of her expert and his opinions over the husband's. The appellate court rejected her arguments as "out of place" on appeal and affirmed the trial court's valuation of the printing company.

Fair market valuation requires certain 'fictions.' At trial, both parties presented additional experts to value the husband's 33% interest in the real estate partnership that owned the land and the large building in which the printing company had leased space for many years. The husband's expert did not consider the rent that the printing company actually paid the partnership, because it was not negotiated in an arm's length transaction and was higher than market values. In contrast, the wife's expert relied on the actual lease terms in calculating income streams for the property, including the assumption that the printing company would rent for the next seven years (two years remaining on the lease plus a five-year renewal option).

This time, the trial court found the wife's expert more persuasive:

> In assigning values to the various assets, the court has to use the same standard of measurement—fair market value—consistently. The exercise requires a certain amount of fiction. As a practical matter, it is unlikely that within the foreseeable future, [the printing company] will move from its present location and that [the real estate partnership] will be faced with the task of refitting the structure to accommodate [new] tenants.

The court found no rule prohibiting it from relying on lease values not negotiated at arms' length. The only limitation was the Uniform Standards of Professional Appraisal Practice, which requires appraisers to "analyze such comparable rental data as are available and/or the potential earnings capacity of the property to estimate [its] gross income potential." The court adopted the $7.2 million value for the real estate partnership, as calculated by the wife's expert, and the husband appealed.

The husband argued that as a matter of law and under the fair market value standard, a court should have presumed a sale or transfer of the property *without* the presence of the printing company lease. The appellate court disagreed. "To refuse to consider the presence of the…lease would be to ignore the effect of prospective use on valuation." The lease represented a source of income for the partnership, "now and for some period in the future," it added, "whether or not it was negotiated at arm's length."

There was also evidence that the lease was fair to both parties, in particular because the ESOP trustee (and not the husband) had handled the negotiations on behalf of the printing company/tenant. "Whether the lease is above market rate is not determinative of its use in valuating the [real estate partnership], unless the rate somehow undermined the finding that the [printing company] would remain a tenant." The trial court found this prospect unlikely, as the building was one of the largest commercial properties in the county and was modified three times to suit the "unique needs" of the printing company.

The trial court also rejected the husband's proposed minority discounts to his one-third interest in the real estate partnership. There was no evidence that a sale of his interest was "in any way possible," especially given the husband's control of the only tenant (the printing company) as its CEO.

A nod to fair value standard. On review, the appellate court noted that the lower court considered expert evidence and gave credible reasons for rejecting discounts. Moreover, "[r]educing the value of the partnership interest, while husband received full income from the partnership based on full valuation, would be unfair to wife," the court held, citing *Brown v. Brown*, the 2002 New Jersey Supreme Court decision that is often cited for applying the fair value standard in divorce (an abstract of *Brown* is available in this section). "We conclude that the decision to disallow the minority discount in this case was within the family court's discretion."

Cotton v. Expo Power Systems, Inc.

Citation: 2009 WL 294935 (Cal. App. 2 Dist.)
Court: Court of Appeals
State/Jurisdiction: California
Date of decision: February 9, 2009

A minority shareholder in a California corporation sought two avenues of relief against the majority owners for their alleged breach of fiduciary duties. In one suit, the shareholder sought statutory dissolution of the company. In the other, he brought shareholder derivative claims, accusing the owners of diverting company assets for their own use. While the latter case was still pending, the majority shareholders invoked their rights to purchase the minority shareholder's 33% interest in the suit for dissolution.

The trial court appointed three appraisers. The applicable California business code defines fair value as liquidation value, but "taking into account the possibility, if any, of sale of the entire business as a going concern in liquidation."

If the parties dispute fair value, then the trial court appoints three independent appraisers. In this case, the appointed panel of three concluded that the "fair appraised value" of the entire company was $100,000, exclusive of the pending derivative claims. The appraisers did not believe they could extend their authority to a "quasi-judicial" evaluation of the shareholder suit, and they did not want to burden the parties with the cost of valuing claims that the court would eventually resolve. *In particular:*

> It is the judgment of the panel that no reasonable buyer would increase whatever amount he would otherwise pay for the business to obtain the benefits of the disputed claims. ...If anything, a reasonable buyer might place a relatively high valuation on the expense and burden of litigation as well as the risk of loss. ...Accordingly, in the real world, a potential buyer might reduce whatever amount he would otherwise pay.

The panel specifically did not try to quantify such an increase or reduction, but noted its concern that the majority shareholder's purchase of the minority's interest at the appraised value (exclusive of the litigated claims) "should not be a device to extinguish the claims and artificially eliminate whatever value they had." Thus, the panel recommended that in addition to an award of $33,333 for his one-third interest, the minority shareholder also received an assignment from the company to pursue his derivative claims, even though, technically, he would no longer be a shareholder.

The trial court adopted the panel's $100,000 appraised value, finding that it could not determine the impact, if any, of the pending shareholder suit. For this reason, it deferred the majority's purchase of the minority's shares until after the parties completed the shareholder litigation, and noted that if either disputed the fair value of the company at that time, they could file a motion for adjustment.

Appraised value incomplete. The defendants appealed from the order, contending that the corporate buyout statute requires the trial court either to: 1) obtain a complete appraisal of the fair value of the company, including the derivative claims; or 2) conduct a hearing to resolve the derivative suit.

The appellate court agreed. Deferring the majority shareholder's repurchase until after resolution of the derivative action did not comply with the statutory appraisal scheme, which "mandates" determination of the company's fair value as of the date a dissolution suit begins. In a notable aside, the court observed that five years had passed since that date, and the parties were entitled to a complete fair value appraisal of the company.

The court also noted that the appraisers' suggestion to condition the buyout on the company's assignment of the litigation was contrary to shareholder derivative law, which required that the plaintiff shareholder maintain continuous ownership throughout the proceedings. Should this ownership cease, the plaintiff lacks standing and any financial interest in a recovery that inures to the company's benefit.

"We conclude the order cannot be affirmed in any respect because the appraisal did not take into account the effect of the derivative action and was therefore incomplete as a matter of law," the court held. It remanded the case for a fair value appraisal of the company, including a proper accounting of the pending litigation.

Helfman v. Johnson

Citation: 2009 WL 437818(Minn. App.)(unpublished)
Court: Court of Appeals
State/Jurisdiction: California
Date of decision: February 9, 2009

In 1998, a title examiner came together with owners of a real estate closing company to form a new and profitable business. With the decline of the real estate market, however, the parties' relationship also soured. In 2003, the majority owners shut out a minority shareholder and took

Helfman v. Johnson

action that diluted his 24% interest by 5%. The minority shareholder sought a judicial buyout under the applicable (Minnesota) statute, which provides for purchase of the minority's interest at fair value, or "the pro rata share of the value of the corporation as a going concern."

The parties retained experts to value the corporation. The minority shareholder's expert used an income approach to determine a fair value of $1.85 million. Although the majority shareholders' expert declined to use an income approach, he testified that had he valued the company by this method, he would have concluded that it was worth $1,003,000. Instead, he used an adjusted assets method, explaining that:

> ...this approach is often used to value companies that do not have a consistent or predictable client base; when the company has little to no value from labor or intangible assets; when it is easy to enter the industry; and when there is significant chance of losing key personnel, which could negatively impact the company.

Under this approach, the expert for the majority shareholders valued the company at a mere eleven thousand dollars ($11,000.00).

The court used discount rate to bridge the gap. The trial court found that the valuation by the minority shareholder's expert was "overly optimistic," based largely on past performance. The valuation by the majority's expert was "unrealistically low," however, because it did not value the business as a going concern.

At the same time, the court found the majority shareholders' expert value of the company under an income approach was reasonable at $1,003,000. In an attempt to "balance the extremes" of the experts, it also applied a 24.60% discount rate. This rate was the same that the minority shareholder's expert used to discount future cash flows in his income valuations, the court explained. It was also based on three factors specific to this case: 1) the lack of a non-compete agreement; 2) the lack of employment contracts binding employees; and 3) a declining market at the valuation date.

The minority shareholder appealed, contending that the trial court impermissibly applied a minority and marketability discount to the valuation of the company, in contravention of the Minnesota statute. But in reviewing the record, the appellate court found that the trial court specifically stated that its discount was not related to minority or marketability discounts. Instead, the discount related to its consideration of the enumerated factors—i.e., that the company's employees were free to leave and the industry was in a serious downward cycle.

The appellate court found evidence that supported these facts, including the company suffering a 75% drop in business during the year prior to valuation. Further, the trial court expressly rejected the majority shareholders' request to apply a 40% discount rate, finding it too aggressive and the 24.60% rate more reasonable. Based on all the evidence—and the trial court's attempts to straddle a wide gulf created by expert opinions—the appellate court found no error in its valuation.

Chapter 7: Court Case Abstracts

Kaplan v. First Hartford Corp.

Citation: 2009 WL 737681 (D. Me.)
Court: District Court
State/Jurisdiction: Maine
Date of decision: March 20, 2009

An oppressed minority shareholder sought judicial appraisal of the First Hartford Corporation, a company that managed and developed real estate through several subsidiaries, with several attributes that made it unique. Although thinly traded on the Pink Sheets financial service, First Hartford acted more like a closely held company. It held investment properties for long-term income potential, but it differed from a real estate investment trust (REIT) in its structure, tax status, development strategy, and profit distribution. "In a word," the U.S. District Court (Maine) observed, "this is a difficult business to value."

Three very experienced experts differed by a factor of five. At a bench trial, the parties presented three qualified experts to value First Hartford. "Not surprisingly," the court noted, they disagreed with each others' opinions and methodologies. In fact, the court cited a wry observation from the Delaware Chancery that in shareholder oppression cases, "it is not unusual for the opinions of the experts to differ by a factor of ten." In this case, "perhaps I should consider myself fortunate, since the experts...vary by a factor of only about five."

1. *Plaintiff's expert.* The plaintiff retained the CEO of a private venture capital firm that invested in early stage companies. Although he had no credentials in business valuation or prior expert witness experience, "[h]is work requires him to utilize discounted cash flow methodology to value business entities and real estate," the court said. Earlier in the proceedings, the defendants challenged the expert's qualifications under *Daubert*, but the court admitted his testimony, finding that any mistakes or analytical weaknesses went to the weight of his conclusions.

To value First Hartford, this expert used an investment approach that relied on a discounted cash flow (DCF) model. He separated the company into its two component businesses: a portfolio of stable, income-producing properties; and a construction/development business. For the first, he adopted the conclusions of independent real estate appraisals that First Hartford obtained for its properties during the ordinary course of business (to secure financing), within one year of the valuation date. These appraisals, he said, "had already done DCF for him." Only one property (the "North Adams" parcel) was missing an appraisal, so he used three comparables to estimate its DCF value at just under $2 million.

For the second component, the plaintiff's expert collected income/expense data from First Hartford financials for three years prior to the valuation date, projected net income forward for ten years, and applied a 14% discount rate, which reflected the riskier nature of its development business, he said. He then took the two component values, added miscellaneous items (a pending contract for sale, excess cash, a "tax shield" from a net operating loss

Kaplan v. First Hartford Corp.

carry-forwards) reduced by the capitalized cost of its corporate center. He did not subtract income taxes, however, because the company had not paid federal income tax for the prior seven years and maintained the large loss carry-forward. Ultimately, he arrived at a fair value for the company of $48.3 million.

2. *Defendants' lead expert.* First Hartford retained a well-known, credentialed business valuation expert with over 20 years' experience. She used three traditional approaches (asset, market, income) to value the company:

(a) *Net asset value (NAV) approach.* The defendants' expert was given the same independent real estate appraisals that the plaintiff's expert used, but after a third party adjusted them to reflect circumstances as of the valuation date. (The court notes some concern that First Hartford declined to present this third party as a witness to offer direct evidence supporting the adjustments at trial.) Drawing on this "unintroduced evidence," the defendants' expert assessed the risks associated with each property (vacancies, cost of regulatory compliance, etc.) and adjusted for lack of cash flows from other risks (recession, interest rates, non-core investments). She subtracted capital gains taxes, transaction costs, and defeasances costs that a third party buyer would incur on selling the company, and concluded a NAV of $13.3 million.

(b) *Income approach.* Once again, the defendants' expert began with the adjusted real estate appraisals. Unlike the plaintiff's expert, she used their net operating income information rather than their bottom-line values, adjusted for entity-level expenses (such as debt) and eliminated non-recurring items (such as proceeds from a lawsuit). For the North Adams property, she relied on management statements and its outstanding debt to assign it a zero value. After, adjusting executive pay upward to reflect fair market value, she found that First Hartford was worth only $7.6 million under the income approach, largely due to its significant debt.

(c) *Market approach.* Using comparable REITs in her guideline company analysis, the defendant's expert concluded a $10 million dollar value, acknowledging that it depended in part on data from minority stock transfers of the publicly traded comps. She did not correct for any minority or marketability discount, however, citing BV authority (*Valuing a Business*, 5th edition, by Shannon Pratt and Alina Niculita) in support of this method.

She also noted that comparable sales "clearly [reflected] entire controlling interests" and "some exuberance" in the market at the time of the valuation, leading to a $9.6 million value under her guideline transactions analysis. Finally, she reviewed the sales of the company's stock (minority interests) on the Pink Sheets to reach a $10 million value, also without factoring out any implied minority or other discounts.

Overall, defendants' first expert accorded little weight to the net asset approach, but gave one-quarter weight to each of the remaining values (income-based and three market values) to reach a fair value for First Hartford of $9.3 million.

3. Defendant's second expert. The defendants also retained a professor of Real Estate and Urban Land Economics who taught real estate finance and investment. This expert also used a net asset approach, employing the same third-party adjusted real estate appraisals and then deducting taxes payable on liquidation to reach a value of $15.5 million. Notably, he then applied a 25% minority discount—because "he believed that to be his assignment"—to reach a $11.66 NAV. He did not apply any discounts for lack of marketability.

Under the investment approach, he relied on data from public REITs, adjusted for taxable gains and losses and other expenses, and found a value of $9.4 million—which included a built-in minority discount, he said, because it was based on data derived from comparable sales of minority interests. A review of Pink Sheets sales led to a $10 million stock market value, which also incorporated an implicit minority discount. He then accorded 10% weight to both the NAV and investment methods, and 80% weight to the market value, to reach an overall fair value for First Hartford of $9.8 million. Factoring out the 25% minority discount raised that value to $13.07 million.

The court found concerns with each expert. "My search here is for what a third party would pay for this entire company," the court began. Applicable case law required the court to determine the "best price" that a single buyer would pay, without minority or marketability discounts. With this standard in mind, it turned to the expert evidence:

1. Plaintiff's expert spent too little time. Although he had "abundant experience conducting business valuations in real-world settings," the plaintiff's expert presented the court with "many difficulties." In particular, he treated the real estate appraisals of First Hartford properties as full-blown DCF analyses, thus avoiding doing his own but ignoring their basis on a combination of income, comparable sales, and cost analysis. The court was also skeptical of the expert's $1.9 million appraisal for the North Adams property, noting the lack of "real" comparables. The plaintiff's expert also made several errors, including accounting for lawsuit proceeds as a recurring item, double counting the company's tax loss carry-forwards, and a $3 million error in cash distributions.

Finally, plaintiff's expert did not adequately consider the director's personal guarantees—which a prospective buyer might not be willing to match, and in his ultimate conclusion, he gave *no* weight to the NAV or stock market value (court's emphasis). "In sum, [plaintiff's expert] spent precious little time on valuing this complex corporation, his first time as an expert witness."

2. Defendant's lead expert was 'the most thorough.' Overall, the defendant's first expert "performed the most through valuation" among the three. Nevertheless, the court was troubled that her going concern value ($9.3 million) "was so much lower" than NAV ($13.3 million). "For a company like this, dependent heavily on real estate, the ability to liquidate some of it holdings could play an important part" in how much a third party would pay, even for the business as a going concern.

The court was also troubled that the expert's stock value ($10 million) was so much higher than her income-based value ($7.6 million), perhaps because the latter assumed no future sales of the properties. Although the plaintiff's expert may have overestimated future sales, they "cannot be ignored altogether," the court said. Defendants' expert also declined to adjust her Pink Sheets value for an implicit minority discount. Finally, the court had no way to assess "the reliability of her reliance" on the adjusted real estate appraisals, and questioned her "ready acceptance" of management statements that the North Adams property had no value when cross-examination revealed that leasing was ongoing and the mortgage debt was $3 million less than its financing.

3. Defendants' second expert gives the court pause. The defendants' second expert supported his heavy if not exclusive weight on Pink Sheets pricing with "substantial academic backing." However, he seemed to believe that his assignment was to value a minority interest, "which makes me question the rest of his instructions," the court said. (Apparently, these "instructions"—like the adjustments to the real estate appraisals—came from a third party whom First Hartford declined to present at trial.) First Hartford also informed its second expert about a $4 million error the morning of his deposition, but he did not disclose it, and only communicated the error to plaintiff's attorney on the eve of trial. Further, his report did not show any account for the company's tax loss carry forwards, although the expert insisted at trial that he included them.

Market value and minority/marketability discounts become the main focus. The plaintiff urged the court to discount any reliance on Pink Sheets pricing, because the stock was too thinly traded on an unreliable exchange, and it "hugely undervalue[d]" the oppressing control by the majority shareholder.

First Hartford was thinly traded, but its prices did not necessarily undervalue the business, the court found. Nor had any shareholder oppression led to thinner trading. To be sure, the stock suffered from "modest" lack of marketability, as evidenced by Lehman Brothers' inability to move a large block (35,000) of shares just one week after the valuation date. These factors did not make stock market value "irrelevant."

In fact, the court started with the stock market price as the guide to fair value, including a 100-share trade just three days before the valuation date at $3.25 per. That number was consistent with the weighted average monthly price of First Hartford stock for the year prior to the valuation date, which ranged from $2.00 to $3.95 per share. It also found, based on thin trading and Lehman Brothers' reverting the 10,000 shares back to the company for $2.50 per share, that a "marketability adjustment" was appropriate to the stock's pricing—though none of the experts suggested a number. Only the defendant's second expert applied an implicit minority discount of 25%, testifying that the relevant range for similar companies is up to 30%.

"[G]iven the need to recognize both discounts," the court applied the higher figure (30%) to the $3.25 per-share price, leading to the adjusted value of $4.64. As there were just over 3.08 million shares outstanding on the valuation date, the company was worth a total of approximately $14.3 million, which the court rounded up to $15 million "to ensure full recognition of the necessary marketability adjustment." That number "modestly" exceeded the NAV of defendants' lead expert ($13.3 million)—but her NAV reflected reductions for taxes and other transaction costs and also assigned a zero value to the North Adams property. The court's value was "modestly below" the NAV of the defendants' second expert ($15.5 million)—but that was before he reduced the figure on the "mistaken" belief that a minority discount was appropriate.

"I find net asset value to have significance for this company whose assets largely are real estate holdings," the court added, citing two law journal articles in support. ("[R]eal estate companies...are sometimes...undervalued by the stock market because they produce low reported earnings relative to their cash flow.") "Therefore, net asset value fortifies my confidence in the stock market value, the court said, "after adjustment for minority and marketability discounts."

The court also recognized that the market and asset values were much higher than the numbers that the two defense experts derived from their investment and income approaches. "But they are much lower than the number plaintiff's expert derived from his version of the same approach." The "wildly divergent" income approach values helped support the court's reliance on the NAV and market values. Further, applicable law (Maine) considers investment value a weak measure of fair value when the company's earnings are erratic and determination of the capitalization ratio is highly subjective. Defendants' lead expert repeatedly referred to First Hartford's volatile returns; and all of the experts had to make subjective adjustments to their cap rate, given the company's unique structure and two lines of real estate business.

After consideration of all the evidence and conducting its own extensive analysis, the court concluded a $15 million fair value for First Hartford, derived primarily from the stock trades, corrected for the minority and marketability discounts, and supported by the expert net asset valuations.

Hodas v. Spectrum Technology, Inc.

Citation: 1992 Del. Ch. LEXIS 252
Court: Court of Chancery
State/Jurisdiction: Delaware
Date of decision: December 7, 1992
Judge: Berger

Plaintiff and the other minority shareholder of Spectrum Technology, Inc. were offered $70.57 per share in a cash-out merger. Neither accepted the offer and plaintiff pursued his statutory appraisal remedy, arguing that the fair value of his shares was approximately $900 per share.

Spectrum's expert, Anne Danyluk, used both a market approach and a discounted cash flow analysis, and then applied a 40% lack of marketability discount. Her resulting fair value per share was $68. The plaintiff's expert, Jack Egan, CPA, did not independently analyze Spectrum; rather, he reviewed Danyluk's valuation report and identified adjustments he felt should be made. Among other things, he argued that the marketability discount must be rejected as inconsistent with Delaware law.

Hodas v. Spectrum Technology, Inc.

Although the court found Egan unpersuasive regarding his other arguments, it agreed with him on the elimination of the marketability discount. It noted, and Spectrum conceded, that the determination of fair value in an appraisal proceeding may not include any shareholder-level discount for lack of marketability. Despite Danyluk's protests, the court found that her discount was taken at the shareholder level:

Danyluk states...that the size of the holding being valued and the number of restrictions attached to the stock are factors in determining an appropriate lack of marketability discount. Both of these factors may affect the value of particular shares, but have no impact on the value of the company as a going concern.

The court found the fair value of the plaintiff's shares to be $134 per share.

Index for Chapter 7

A

Advanced Communication Design,
    Inc. v. Follett (I) 7-82
Advanced Communication Design,
    Inc. v. Follett (II) 7-94
Advanced Communication Design,
    Inc. v. Follett (III). 7-116
Allenson v. Midway Airlines Corp. . . 7-117
Andaloro v. PFPC Worldwide, Inc. . . 7-198
Anderson v. Anderson 7-220
Anjoorian v. Kilberg 7-175
Ansin et al. v. River Oaks Furniture,
    Inc., et al. 7-14
Applebaum v. Avaya, Inc., et al. . . . 7-157
Arnaud v. Stockgrowers State Bank . . 7-83

B

Balsamides v. Perle (I) 7-40
Balsamides v. Protameen
    Chemicals, Inc. (II). 7-77
Baltrusis v. Baltrusis 7-156
Becker, In re Marriage of. 7-223
Berens v. Ludwig (I) 7-15
Berens v. Ludwig (II) 7-30
Bernier v. Bernier. 7-224
Billigmeier v. Concorde Marketing, Inc. 7-135
Blitch v. The Peoples Bank. 7-98
Boettcher, et al. v. IMC Mortgage
    Company. 7-185
Borruso v. Communications
    Telesystems International 7-79
Boyd v. Boyd. 7-137
Brown v. Arp and Hammond
    Hardware Co. 7-218
Brown v. Brown 7-140

C

Cannon v. Bertrand 7-272
Carter Crookham v. Peter Riley, et al. . 7-44
Casey v. Amboy Bancorporation . . . 7-212

Cede & Co. v. Technicolor, Inc. . . . 7-193
Collision Depot Inc. v. Zigman 7-146
Connector Service Corp. v. Briggs . . . 7-46
Conti v. Christoff 7-129
Cooke v. Fresh Express Foods 7-93
Cotton v. Expo Power Systems, Inc. . . 7-277
Cox Enterprises, Inc. v. News-
    Journal Corp. 7-258
Crescent/Mach I Partnership v.
    Turner 7-230, 7-235
Crismon v. Crismon 7-99
Croxton v. MSC Holding, Inc. 7-22

D

Delaware Open MRI Radiology . . . 7-207
Delaware Open MRI Radiology
    Associates, P.A. v. Kessler. 7-203
Demoulas v. Demoulas 7-50
Detter v. Miracle Hills Animal
    Hospital, P.C. 7-181
Devivo v. Devivo 7-111
DiLuglio v. Providence Auto Body . . . 7-92
Drumheller v. Drumheller. 7-274

E

East Park Ltd. Partnership v. Larkin,
    et al. 7-201
Edler v. Edler. 7-255
Ely, Inc. v. Wiley 7-51
Emerging Communications, In re . . 7-186
English v. Artromick International, Inc. 7-96
Erp v. Erp. 7-226

F

Fierro v. Templeton. 7-173
Finkelstein, et al. v. Liberty Digital, Inc. 7-190
First Western Bank Wall v. Olsen . . 7-101
Fisher v. Fisher. 7-256

Index for Chapter 7

G

Garlock, et al. v. Southeastern
    Gas & Power, Inc. and Hilliard . . . 7-133
G&G Fashion Design, Inc. v.
    Enrique Garcia. 7-178
G & N Aircraft, Inc. and Paul
    Goldsmith v. Erich Boehm 7-48
G.I. Joe's, Inc. v. Nizam 7-149
Gagliano v. Brenna (I) 7-121
Gagliano v. Brenna (II) 7-149
Gilbert v. MPM Enterprises, Inc. 7-27
Gonsalves v. Straight Arrow
    Publishers, Inc. (I) 7-11
Gonsalves v. Straight Arrow
    Publishers, Inc. (II). 7-29
Gonsalves v. Straight Arrow
    Publishers, Inc. (III) 7-34
Gonsalves v. Straight Arrow
    Publishers, Inc. (IV) 7-154
Grace v. Rosenstock 7-45
Grelier v. Grelier 7-271
Grimes v. Vitalink Communications
    Corporation 7-23

H

Hall v. Glenn's Ferry Grazing Assoc. . 7-221
Hansen v. 75 Ranch Company (I) . . . 7-36
Hansen v. 75 Ranch Company (II) . . . 7-55
Hayes v. Olmsted & Assoc. 7-107
Helfman v. Johnson 7-278
Henke v. Trilithic, Inc. 7-200
Highfields Capital, Ltd. v. AXA
    Financial, Inc. 7-241
Hintmann v. Fred Weber, Inc. 7-32
HMO-W, Inc. v. SSM Health Care
    System (I) 7-68
HMO-W v. SSM Health Care
    System (II) 7-88
Hodas v. Spectrum Technology, Inc. . 7-284
Hogle v. Zinetics Med., Inc. 7-161
Holiday Medical Center, Inc. v. Weisman 7-261

J

Jahn v. Kinderman 7-190
Johnson v. Johnson 7-123

K

Kahn v. Tremont Corporation (I) 7-3
Kahn v. Tremont Corporation (II) 7-21
Kaplan v. First Hartford Corp. 7-280
Khatkar v. Dhillon 7-270
Kim v. The Grover C. Coors Trust . . 7-246
Kortum v. Johnson 7-263

L

Lawson Mardon Wheaton, Inc. v.
    Smith (I) 7-42
Lawson Mardon Wheaton, Inc. v.
    Smith (II). 7-75
Lawton v. Nyman. 7-171
Le Beau v. M.G. Bancorporation 7-60
Le Beau v. M.G. Bancorporation/
    Nebel v. Southwest Bancorp, Inc. . . 7-64

M

Marsh v. Billington Farms, LLC . . . 7-248
Montgomery Cellular Holding Co.,
    Inc., et al. v. Dobler, et al. 7-195
M.P.M. Enterprises, Inc. v. Gilbert . . . 7-72
Mart v. Severson 7-138
Matthew G. Norton Co v. Smyth . . . 7-151
McCann Ranch, Inc. v. Sharon
    Quigley-McCann. 7-5
McDuffie v. O'Neal 7-9
M Life Ins. Co. v. Sapers & Wallack
    Ins. Agency, Inc. 7-102
MS Holdings, LLC v. Malone 7-257
Murphy v. U.S. Dredging Corp. 7-267

N

Northwest Investment Corp. v. Wallace 7-250

O

Oakridge Energy, Inc. v. Clifton 7-19
Offenbecher v. Baron Services, Inc. (I) 7-114

Chapter 7: Court Case Abstracts

Offenbecher v. Baron Services, Inc. (II) 7-144
Offenbecher v. Baron Services, Inc. (III) 7-169
Overbey, In the Matter of. 7-228

P
Pacific Telecom, Inc. v. Gabelli
    Funds, Inc.. 7-52
Paskill Corp. v. Alcoma Corp. (I) 7-67
Paskill Corp. v. Alcoma Corp. (II). . . . 7-84
Penepent Corp., In re 7-109
Pink v. Cambridge Acquisition, Inc. . . 7-59
PNB Holding Co., In re. 7-216
Prentiss et al. v. Wesspur, Inc. et al. . . 7-21
Pro Finish USA, Ltd. v. Johnson . . . 7-167
Pueblo Bancorporation v. Lindoe, Inc. (I) 7-127
Pueblo Bancorporation v. Lindoe, Inc. (II) 7-164

R
Rainforest Cafe, Inc. v.
    State of Wisconsin Investment
    Board, et al. 7-183
Richton Bank & Trust Co. v. Bowen . 7-131
Ryan v. Tad's Enterprises, Inc.. 7-6

S
Settles v. Leslie 7-47
Sieg Co. v. Kelly 7-24
Slant/Fin. Corp. v. The Chicago Corp . .7-1
Small v. Sussman and Day
    Surgicenters, Inc. 7-222
Smith v. North Carolina Motor
    Speedway 7-87
Spivey v. Page 7-180
Steiner Corp. v. Benninghoff 7-37
Swope v. Siegel-Robert, Inc. (I) 7-69
Swope v. Siegel-Robert, Inc. (II) . . . 7-104

T
The Union Illinois 1995 Investment
    Ltd. Partnership v. Union Financial
    Group Ltd. 7-176
Thompson, et al. v. Miller Jr., et al . . 7-174
Thornhill, In re Marriage of. 7-265

Tifft v. Stevens 7-57
Torres v. Schripps, Inc.. 7-119
Trahan v. Trahan. 7-146
Trapp Family Lodge, Inc., In re
    75,629 Shares of Common Stock of 7-53
Trietsch v. Circle Design Group . . . 7-252
Trifad Entertainment, Inc. v. Brad
    Anderson, et al. 7-134

U
The Union Illinois 1995 Investment
    Ltd. Partnership v. Union
    Financial Group Ltd.. 7-176

V
Vetco, Inc.; Wolk v. Kornberg, In re . 7-143

W
WCM Industries, Inc. v. Trustees of
    Wilson Trust 7-17
Weigel Broadcasting Co. v. Smith . . . 7-13
Wenzel v. Hopper & Galliher, P.C. . . 7-158
Winn v. Winn Enterprises, Ltd.. . . . 7-254

Z
Zatz, et al. v. U.S.A., et al 7-41

In lieu of a complete index, we have provided supplementary files at BVLibrary.com that include the entire document of this Guide as a PDF, which will allow the user to search by any keyword.

BVR
What It's Worth

www.BVResources.com

Bulletproof your valuation conclusions with BVR's comprehensive line of product offerings.

Every top firm depends on BVR for authoritative market data, continuing professional education, and expert opinion. So, turn to BVR whenever you need unimpeachable business valuation conclusions for any purpose. BVR's market databases, publications, and analysis have won in the courtroom—and the boardroom—for over a dozen years. All BVR products include a subscription to the profession's leading weekly eNewsletter, BVWire™, absolutely FREE!

Our expansive line of products include:

- Pratt's Stats®
- Public Stats™
- BIZCOMPS®
- Mergerstat®/BVR Control Premium Study™
- The FMV Restricted Stock Study™
- Valuation Advisors' Discount for Lack of Marketability Study™
- Integra 5-Year Industry Data Reports
- **NEW!** Duff & Phelps Risk Premium Reports
- Business Valuation Update™
- Deluxe BVUpdate™
- Annual Guides and Books
- Business Reference Guide Online Database

- Economic Outlook Update™
- BVLaw™
- BVResearch™
- Special reports, guides, and books
- Continuing Professional Education (CPE)
- BVNewsletter™ service
- BVBasics™ Seminar Package
- Teleconferences and Webinars
- Live Conferences
- BV Firm Marketing Services
- Butler Pinkerton Model™ - Total Cost of Equity (TCOE) and Public company Specific Risk Calculator

Learn more at www.BVResources.com

Business Valuation Resources, LLC . 1000 SW Broadway, Suite 1200 . Portland OR 97205
Phone: (503) 291-7963 . Fax: (503) 291-7955 . Email: CustomerService@BVResources.com